"Sexual violence is a global crisis in institutioɪ UK is far from immune. While many survivors the weight of advocacy on their own, it has alv safer campuses must involve the entire universiʇ *in Higher Education* is a call to higher educatioɪ causes of violence, and encourage them to see ɪ an occupational responsibility. Towl and Hump of assembling a collection of thoughts from experts across the UK, and send an urgent message to educators: it's time to follow the lead of survivors, and join the fight to make our universities safer for all."

Andrea L. Pino-Silva, *co-author of* We Believe You: Survivors of Campus Sexual Assault Speak Out, *and co-founder of End Rape on Campus, USA*

"*Stopping Gender-based Violence in Higher Education* is an essential handbook that covers student–student, staff–student, and staff–staff violence. This collection will educate experts even as it provides direction for those new to handling complaints. Most importantly, the chapters centre in bold relief the experiences of victim-survivors."

Mara Keire, *University of Oxford, UK*

"This comprehensive exploration into the many facets, manifestations, and intersections of gender-based violence in higher education is long overdue. The insightful and well-researched contributions make this essential reading for all those who work in the sector."

Amatey Doku, *former Vice President Higher Education, National Union of Students (NUS) and Independent Board Member, Guildhall School of Music and Drama, UK*

"This volume is essential reading for anyone interested in tackling campus violence. Drawing on diverse perspectives from across fields, it paints a sophisticated tableau of the problems faced, root causes, and possible solutions. Achieving a diverse and inclusive higher education sector requires the ambition and inclusive approach that this volume reflects."

Georgina Calvert-Lee, *Senior Litigation Counsel, McAllister Olivarius, UK*

Stopping Gender-based Violence in Higher Education

Stopping Gender-based Violence in Higher Education provides a unique insight into how gender-based violence at universities is impacting students and staff and outlines the path towards tangible changes that can prevent it. Bringing together perspectives from academics, activists, practitioners, and university administrators, the book presents a diverse range of voices to constructively critique the field.

Structured in three parts, the book begins by addressing the context, theory, and law that stipulates how universities can effectively respond to reports of gender-based violence. It goes on to discuss the most pragmatic ways to address the issue while contributing to prevention and supporting victim-survivors. Finally, the book advocates for the development of beneficial working partnerships with key external services available to university communities and also working with students as partners in an ethical and safe way. Throughout the book, contributors are invited to demonstrate a comprehensive institution-wide and trauma-informed approach to centre the needs of the victim-survivor and prioritise resources to undertake this vital work. Each chapter ends with a brief summary of key points or recommendations and suggested further reading on the chapter topic. Although the authors draw on research and policy from the UK Higher Education sector, the insights will be a useful resource for those in universities around the world.

This book is an essential reference point and resource for professionals, academics, and students in Higher Education, as well as indispensable reading for activists, policymakers, police, rape crisis groups, and other organisations supporting these universities who want to make meaningful change in reducing, responding to, and preventing gender-based violence in Higher Education.

Clarissa J. Humphreys is a practitioner, trainer, and leading authority on addressing gender-based violence (GBV) in Higher Education. She is currently Sexual Misconduct Prevention and Response Manager at Durham University and has clinical experience working with survivors and perpetrators of GBV and with individuals with acute mental illnesses and co-occurring substance use issues.

Graham J. Towl is Professor of Forensic Psychology at Durham University and a former chief psychologist at the Ministry of Justice. He was peer (British Psychological Society) nominated as the most influential UK forensic psychologist. His publications on sexual violence at universities include two co-authored books and numerous blogs and articles in Higher Education outlets.

Stopping Gender-based Violence in Higher Education

Policy, Practice, and Partnerships

Edited by Clarissa J. Humphreys and Graham J. Towl

Routledge
Taylor & Francis Group
LONDON AND NEW YORK

Cover image: © Getty Images

First published 2023
by Routledge
4 Park Square, Milton Park, Abingdon, Oxon OX14 4RN

and by Routledge
605 Third Avenue, New York, NY 10158

Routledge is an imprint of the Taylor & Francis Group, an informa business

British Library Cataloguing-in-Publication Data
A catalogue record for this book is available from the British Library

Library of Congress Cataloging-in-Publication Data
A catalog record for this book has been requested

ISBN: 978-1-032-17249-1 (hbk)
ISBN: 978-1-032-17247-7 (pbk)
ISBN: 978-1-003-25247-4 (ebk)

DOI: 10.4324/9781003252474

Typeset in Bembo
by Apex CoVantage, LLC

Contents

All author royalties will be donated to Refuge

Home of the freephone, 24-hour National Domestic Abuse Helpline

0808 2000 247 or www.nationaldahelpline.org.uk

Contributors

Ngozi Anyadike-Danes (Northern Ireland) is a PhD researcher in psychology at Ulster University's School of Psychology and Institute of Mental Health Sciences. Currently, her research focuses on factors related to students' comprehension of sexual consent in the context of unwanted and non-consensual sexual experiences and any associated impact to their mental well-being.

Rosanna Bellini (USA) is Postdoctoral Associate in Information and Computer Science at Cornell University. She designs, develops, and deploys socio-technical systems for intimate partner violence with specialist charities and non-government organisations. She has been working on justice-orientated design principles, using data-in-place for combatting occupational bullying and harassment, and implementing trauma-informed computing.

Sunday Blake (England) is Associate Editor at Wonkhe. She started her career in student politics where she carried out policy change work locally and nationally in sexual misconduct, drug and alcohol use, and student sex work. She has also worked in university strategy with a specific focus on belonging and inclusion.

Emma Bond (England) is Pro Vice-Chancellor Research and Professor of Socio-Technical Research at the University of Suffolk. She has 20 years of experience of researching the interactions between people, society, and technology. She is internationally renowned for her work on sexual abuse, domestic violence, sexting, revenge pornography, and online harassment.

Anna Bull (England) is Lecturer in Education and Social Justice at the University of York, and co-director of The 1752 Group, a research and campaigning organisation working to address staff sexual misconduct in Higher Education.

Kathryn Dawson (Scotland) leads on sexual violence prevention for Rape Crisis Scotland, developing and coordinating prevention work with young people, schools, colleges, and universities across Scotland in partnership with local Rape Crisis centres. She also contributes to national-level strategic developments and collaborative efforts to prevent sexual violence.

Jim Dickinson (England) is Associate Editor at Wonkhe where he leads on student experience and students' unions (SU). His career background is in support for student leadership – he was a director at the NUS, a CEO of an SU, and has served on boards in both Higher Education and the voluntary sector.

Anni Donaldson (Scotland) is a feminist oral historian, academic, and writer. For over 30 years, Anni has specialised in preventing domestic abuse, violence against women, and campus sexual violence through her work in universities and local government in Scotland. She is Honorary Research Fellow at the University of Strathclyde.

Catherine Donovan (England) is Professor of Sociology and Head of the Sociology Department at Durham University. She has researched the intimate and family lives of LGBTQ+ individuals for over 20 years. For the last 15 years, her focus has been on their victimisation through and perpetration of domestic abuse and victimisation through sexual violence and hate incidents/crime. She has also conducted research on student victimisation by violence and abuse, student and community active bystander interventions, and Higher Education responses to students' victimisation.

Fiona Drouet (Scotland) is Founder and CEO of the charity, EmilyTest, which she founded after Emily Drouet took her own life after being subjected to physical, psychological, and sexual abuse while studying at university. Emily's tragic death was the result of a series of preventable failures. Since then, her mother Fiona has successfully campaigned to raise awareness of gender-based violence and stimulate change in policy, professional practice, intervention, and support in Further and Higher Education.

Rachel Fenton (England) is Associate Professor at the University of Exeter Law School. Her research includes gender and law, preventing GBV through bystander intervention, and regulating universities approaches to GBV. She has developed and evaluated evidence-based bystander prevention programmes for universities, sports settings, general communities, and workplaces.

Peta Franklin-Corben (England) is a social worker with a master's degree in global crime and justice and has amassed a decade's worth of experience addressing gender-based violence both in the UK and Australia working with adult and child survivors of domestic abuse and modern slavery. She is presently Senior Case Management Officer for sexual violence for Durham University.

Geetanjali Gangoli (England) is Associate Professor in the Department of Sociology at Durham University and a member of the Centre for Research in Violence and Abuse. She works in the field of gender-based abuse and is particularly interested in the intersecting roles of ethnicity, class, gender, sexuality, and disability in the perpetuation, the experience, and the prevention of gender-based abuse, including social and feminist responses, particularly in India and the UK.

Poppy Gerrard-Abbott (Scotland) is a PhD candidate in Sociology and Social Policy at the University of Edinburgh researching gender-based violence in UK Higher Education. She is Principal Researcher and Policy Manager for the charity EmilyTest, which created the Scottish Government–funded GBV Charter for Universities and Colleges, the first education charter for GBV in the world. Poppy teaches in the social sciences with a focus on research methods and feminist theory.

Samuel T. Hales (England) is a PhD researcher at the Centre of Research & Education in Forensic Psychology, University of Kent. Sam's research is funded by the Economic and Social Research Council and examines the causes of, and possible prevention strategies for, sexual violence perpetration amongst male students at UK universities.

Liz Hughes (Scotland) is Professor in the School of Health and Social Care at Edinburgh Napier University. She is a mental health nurse by background. Her research interests are focused on the intersection of sex, sexuality, and sexual violence and mental health (including trauma) and co-morbid physical health issues.

Clarissa J. Humphreys (England) is a practitioner, trainer, and leading authority on addressing gender-based violence (GBV) in Higher Education. She is Sexual Misconduct Prevention and Response Manager at Durham University and has experience working with survivors and perpetrators of GBV and with individuals with acute mental illness and co-occurring substance use issues.

Cassandra Jones (England) is an early career researcher and Lecturer in Criminology at the University of Winchester. Her research addresses gender-based violence in the general community, workplaces, and Higher Education. Her PhD explored male victims' experiences of domestic violence and the language they used to describe their relationships.

Janet Keliher (England) is Lecturer at the University of Exeter Law School. Her research includes considering the potential for regulation of universities when universities fail to prevent or respond to gender-based violence. She teaches Criminal Law, Gender Sexuality and Law, Contract Law, and the Law of Corporate Finance.

Niamh Kerr (Scotland) is Training and Education Coordinator for Universities and Colleges at Rape Crisis Scotland (RCS). Her role involves working with universities and colleges, Rape Crisis Centres, and other VAWG partners across Scotland as part of Equally Safe in Colleges and Universities work. Niamh is also Support Worker on the RCS Helpline where she provides crisis support to those affected by sexual violence.

Melanie McCarry (Scotland) has worked collaboratively in her research field of men's violence against women and children, including domestic abuse, GBV within Higher Education, forced marriage, and young people's relationships. Melanie teaches at the University of Strathclyde on the PG Social Policy programme and the UG programme which, as UG Programme Director, she established in 2015.

Carl Norcliffe (England) worked for 15 years as a detective in UK Policing. This included time specialising in the investigation of serious sexual offences, as well as developing investigation training for law enforcement and private industry. He entered the banking sector conducting financial crime investigations, before joining Durham University as Senior Investigating Officer for student misconduct.

Amy Norton (England) is Head of Equality, Diversity and Inclusion (EDI) at the Office for Students (OfS; Government regulator for Higher Education in England). She oversees the OfS's EDI strategy, leads OfS's work to tackle sexual harassment, violence, and hate crime affecting students, and policy and funding to support students experiencing mental health difficulties.

Kelsey Paske (Australia) is a recognised leader in gender-based violence prevention, having implemented innovative best-practice initiatives at La Trobe University in Australia, and Advance HE, University College London, and Culture Shift in the UK. She is currently working with Our Watch and the Tasmanian Government, and running a behavioural and cultural change consulting business, Kelsey Paske Consulting.

Andrea Pescod (England) is Senior Investigating Officer working within the Student Conduct Office at Durham University. Prior to this, she worked for 26 years within Law Enforcement. As a practitioner, she specialises within the Criminal Investigation Department and Safeguarding, investigating serious sexual crimes, high-risk domestic violence, and complex child and adult abuse.

Andy Phippen (England) is Professor of Digital Rights at Bournemouth University. He has researched online safeguarding issues across the education sector for over 20 years and is a frequent contributor to the media and parliamentary enquiries on these issues.

Kelly Prince (England) is Independent Researcher Consultant who has worked in the field of GBV for 20 years. Kelly worked in frontline domestic violence services before completing her PhD on human trafficking. From 2017 to 2021, she coordinated the response to sexual misconduct and violence at Keele University. Kelly co-authored the second edition of Epigeum's *Consent Matters*.

Nicola Roberts (England) is Senior Lecturer in Criminology at the University of Sunderland. Her research focuses on students' experiences of interpersonal violence, and their perceptions and strategies of safety, on and off campus. She has also evaluated university bystander training.

Graham J. Towl (England) is Professor of Forensic Psychology at Durham University where he was previously the Pro Vice-Chancellor Chair of the Sexual Violence Task Force in 2015–2016 and formerly Chief Psychologist at the Ministry of Justice for England and Wales. He has co-authored two books and numerous articles on addressing sexual violence in HE.

Tammi Walker (England) is Principal of St Cuthbert's Society and Professor of Forensic Psychology at Durham University. She is Chartered Psychologist and Fellow of the British Psychological Society, Registered Senior Fellow with Advance HE, and a mental health nurse by clinical background.

Abbreviations

ACAS	Advisory, Conciliation and Arbitration Service
ACPO	Association of Chief Police Officers
AHRC	Australian Human Rights Commission
ANROWS	Australia's National Research Organisation for Women's Safety
BAME/BME	Black Asian and Minority Ethnic
BLM	Black Lives Matter
CDC	Centers for Diseases Control and Prevention
CIPD	Chartered Institute of Personnel and Development
CJS	Criminal Justice System
COSLA	Convention of Scottish Local Authorities
CPS	Crown Prosecution Service
CSEW	Crime Survey for England and Wales
DVA	Domestic Violence and Abuse
ECR	Early Career Researcher
EHRC	Equality and Human Rights Commission
ESCU	Equally Safe in Colleges and Universities
ESHE	Equally Safe in Higher Education
ESRC	Economic and Social Research Council
EU	European Union
EVAW	End Violence Against Women coalition
FE	Further Education
FGM	Female Genital Mutilation
GBV	Gender-Based Violence
GCRC	Glasgow and Clyde Rape Crisis
GCU	Glasgow Caledonian University
HE	Higher Education
HEFCE	Higher Education Funding Council for England
HEI	Higher Education Institution
HERA	Higher Education and Research Act 2017
HR	Human Resources
LGBT/LGBTQ+	Lesbian, Gay, Bisexual, Questioning/Queer, Trans and Non-binary
MOU	Memorandum of Understanding

NDA	Non-Disclosure Agreement
NFS	Non-Fatal Strangulation
NUS	National Union of Students
NWCI	National Women's Council Ireland
OfS	Office for Students
OIA/OIAHE	Office of Independent Adjudicator for Higher Education (England and Wales)
ONS	Office of National Statistics
PTSD	Post-traumatic Stress Disorder
RASASH	Rape and Sexual Abuse Service Highland
RCS	Rape Crisis Scotland
RMA	Rape Myth Acceptance
RSHE	Relationships, Sex and Health Education
SA	Student Association at Glasgow Caledonian University
SARC	Sexual Assault Referral Centre
SRC	Student Representative Council at the University of Glasgow
SV	Sexual Violence
SVH	Sexual Violence and Harassment
SVLO	Sexual Violence Liaison Officer
TFGBV	Technology Facilitated Gender-Based Violence
TSII	The Scottish Intervention Initiative
UCL	University College London
UHI	University of the Highlands and Islands
UK	United Kingdom
UKHEI	United Kingdom Higher Education Institution
UoG	University of Glasgow
UUK	Universities UK
VAW	Violence Against Women
VAWG	Violence Against Women and Girls
VC	Vice-Chancellor
VLE	Virtual Learning Environment
WRASAC	Women's Rape and Sexual Abuse Centre Dundee and Angus

Tables

Figures

1 Introduction

We still have work to do

Clarissa J. Humphreys and Graham J. Towl

The first study that we are aware of that looked at men's perpetration of sexual violence towards women at universities was published in 1957 (Kirkpatrick & Kanin, 1957). That was 65 years ago. Yet for six and half decades as a sector, we have failed to keep women safe within Higher Education (HE) communities globally (UN Women, 2018; Towl & Walker, 2019). Towards the end of the twentieth century, two academics undertook a cross-cultural study of the United States and the United Kingdom about the problem of sexual exploitation at universities. They began their work by asking the rhetorical question: 'Should university staff enter into sexual relationships with their students?' (Carter & Jeffs, 1995). The researchers describe a murky world of academics sexually exploiting students in both the United States and the United Kingdom. They argued for urgent reform, especially in view of the power dynamics between students and staff. Most powerfully, they established that such relationships, in plain sight, are rarely challenged within the culture of academia where such perpetrators are heavily protected. It is difficult to be part of a sector that allows this and not feel a sense of shame in the academy.

What comes across very strongly from the 1995 study is that it is overwhelmingly male academics sexually exploiting young women students. In other words, there is a clear gendered pattern to such behaviours. In 2010, the National Union of Students (NUS) published their findings of women students' experiences of harassment, stalking, violence, and sexual assault within Higher Education Institutions (HEIs) in the UK. In 2021, the Office for Students (OfS)[1] issued a Statement of Expectations for addressing harassment and sexual misconduct with the most minimal of expectations for HEIs. Yet still some institutions have lacked the willingness within management to robustly address these issues.

Much of the leadership in the sector has come from student activists who have kept our problem with sexual violence in the spotlight. We have a high and positive regard for student activists who have kept these issues on the agenda; however, it surely should not fall to students to provide the leadership in this area. We, as in staff, managers, and leaders within HE, should be leading this work; we have a responsibility to our students and employees to do so (Humphreys & Towl, 2021). The burden of this work should not be on students.

DOI: 10.4324/9781003252474-1

Governing bodies too have the ability to hold executive teams to account for leadership in this area.

In 2022, we continue to write on this issue because of our concerns that we are simply not making enough progress as a sector. Hence, we continue to try and contribute to our understanding with a focus on making a positive difference. In this book, a broad cross section of authors offer context, explore the problem, and offer potential solutions to reducing, preventing, and responding to gender-based violence.

Gender-Based Violence (GBV)

The United Nations Declaration on the Elimination of Violence against Women (1993) defines violence against women as follows:

> [A]ny act of gender-based violence that results in, or is likely to result in, physical, sexual or psychological harm or suffering to women, including threats of such acts, coercion or arbitrary deprivation of liberty, whether occurring in public or in private life.
>
> (United Nations, Article 1, p. 3)

It is a human rights violation and a form of discrimination against women (Universities UK, 2016). The United Nations specifically highlights that this includes within the workplace and educational institutions. The term 'violence against women' is often used interchangeably with 'gender-based violence' (GBV). Women are not the only ones subjected to forms of GBV; however, women are overwhelmingly overrepresented amongst victim-survivors and men are overwhelmingly overrepresented in perpetrator roles, as will be demonstrated in later chapters in this volume. GBV includes a wide continuum of physical, sexual, and psychological violence, for example, rape, sexual assault, sexual harassment and intimidation, domestic abuse/intimate-partner violence, coercive and controlling behaviour, stalking, cyberstalking, technology-facilitated/online abuse, so-called 'honour-based abuse', forced marriage, and exploitation, to name but a few.

Universities UK began its focus looking at violence against women with a focus on sexual harassment and misconduct in 2016, and in 2018 the focus shifted to addressing gender-based violence in university settings (Donaldson et al., 2018). Gender-based violence, in many forms, is happening in HEIs impacting students and staff.

#MeTooOnCampus

We note that a large portion of activist work has been on sexual violence, particularly in England, since 2016. This work is not new. Anti-rape activism on university campuses began in the early 1970s in the United States. The first campus-based rape crisis centre was created in 1972 at the University of

Maryland (Gold & Villari, 2000). The first Take Back the Night march was held in 1978 in San Francisco (Jessup-Anger et al., 2018). In 1981, 'date rape' was identified as a university epidemic in mainstream media (Gold & Villari, 2000). And for every year after, activists continued and continue to ask and demand that universities do better.

Decades later, the #MeToo movement promotes breaking the silence, engaging in activism, and requiring organisations not to tolerate sexual violence. Despite all of this, we have to ask, 'When will academia/Higher Education have its #MeToo moment?' As a sector, we are yet to demonstrate convincingly that we do not tolerate sexual violence and other forms of GBV by taking robust actions and communicating with our wider communities the actions that we have taken, for example, dismissing perpetrators in positions of power (Towl & Paske, 2017). Indeed, the balance of evidence seems to indicate that we do tolerate comparatively high levels of sexual violence and GBV. One indicator of taking any area of activity in HE seriously be it research, teaching, or broader educational opportunities is the amount we financially invest in the area. It is still not unheard of to hear of institutional leaders making implausible claims that they cannot afford to invest in this area. In reality, such financial decisions reflect priorities. Perpetrators seem to us to continue to be protected, and resistance to substantive change is all too evident in academic communities. Those in the most senior leadership roles in HE overwhelmingly come from the academic community. The culture of academic communities is such that we seem to continue to tolerate GBV even when in plain sight. This amidst an invigorated emphasis on us addressing issues of equity, diversity, and inclusion.

Overview of this Volume

This volume gives a contemporary critique of the current state of the field in addressing GBV at universities in the UK and, although presented from a UK perspective, we present practical guidance that we hope may also be applied elsewhere, for example, in the United States and Australia, notwithstanding the different legal frameworks in each country. We purposely bring together the diverse perspectives and voices of leading academics, Early Career Researchers, activists, practitioners, and those working for some key partners (although they write in a personal capacity) to try to model that only when we work collectively can we create substantive progress. The unique voices and expertise are highlighted in this volume from academic perspectives to practitioner reflections on practice, policy, skills, and strategies. We can learn from each other with this range of perspectives.

As a collective of writers, we do not shy away from the severity of GBV or minimise the impact of this pervasive issue. This volume openly discusses different forms of GBV and the directly related impacts, including on mental health, suicidality, and homicide. We encourage you as a reader not only to reflect on how reading this volume impacts you and to practice self-care, but also to recognise the severity of this issue and the need to do this work well.

Although you will hear from us as editors and our individual contributors' voices, throughout this book, most importantly, you will hear victim-survivors' voices and stories. These will be noted in bolded italics. We thank the victim-survivors and their families represented in this book. Their stories, views, and the lessons they provide are presented here to help progress positive change in this sector. They are bolded because they are the most important voice we can hear when engaging in GBV prevention and response work. But we also recognise that not all survivors will be visible or necessarily wish to be so. We owe a debt of gratitude for their wisdom and willingness to contribute to our learning, and ultimately, we hope the prevention of future perpetration.

A Note on Language

As an edited book, there will be some variation in the style and language used which we welcome.

In the introduction and later in the conclusion of this book, we choose to discuss GBV in HE as our problem. We are part of HE and rather than push the problem away to an 'other' who is responsible for fixing it, we share ownership. GBV in HE is a problem for the sector, a problem for senior leaders, a problem for staff, a problem for students; it is our shared problem and we each have a role to play in fixing it, that is, reducing and preventing GBV in our communities.

As editors, we choose to use the term 'victim-survivor' to represent individuals subjected to GBV. We may, where appropriate or by choice of the individual, use a stand-alone label of 'survivor' or 'victim'. Our joint clinical experience working with those subjected to GBV has led us to acknowledge that the label of 'victim' or 'survivor' takes on different meanings and purposes at different points for that person. We respect their autonomy to choose a label that supports them at different points in their lives as we recognise the use of victim-survivor takes on the meaning of moving from victim to survivor and on to thriving in the recovery process highlighting an individual's resilience and strength. In addition, in our experience, excluding the use of the term 'victim' may leave a victim-survivor feeling as if their victimisation by the perpetrator was ignored or minimised, and that they were only asked to survive. Lastly and most disturbingly, not everyone who is subjected to GBV does survive; therefore, we choose not to hide this brutal reality. One in ten individuals subjected to sexual violence attempt suicide (Office for National Statistics, 2018), and every four days a woman is killed by her male partner or former partner in the UK (Long et al., 2020).

Structure

The book is organised into three parts, where the different voices can be amplified: Part I: Context, theory, and law; Part II: Practice; and Part III: Partnerships. In all three parts, we consider policy recommendations for HEIs. The range of chapters in this volume have some common underpinning themes, including a commitment to a comprehensive institution-wide approach, a trauma-informed approach, centring of the needs of victim-survivors in prevention and response initiatives, and prioritising resources to undertake this vital work. Each chapter ends with a brief summary of key points or recommendations and suggested further reading on the chapter topic.

In Part I beginning with Chapter 2, Melanie McCarry, Cassandra Jones, and Anni Donaldson argue that GBV within UK university communities stems from intersecting issues of sexism and other forms of discrimination in wider society. They demonstrate how Equally Safe in Higher Education – developed in Scotland – adopted a whole campus approach to GBV prevention and intervention grounded in feminist analysis, research, and practice.

In Chapter 3, Jim Dickinson and Sunday Blake trace interventions, campaigns, and initiatives by students and their groups and associations since the NUS's 2010 publication *Hidden Marks* and offer insights and lessons for working productively with activists, representatives, victim-survivors, and partners on GBV prevention.

In Chapter 4, Geetanjali Gangoli and Cassandra Jones draw on theories of intersectionalities to explore how women's experiences of GBV and HE are impacted by university interventions and women's social positioning. As an encouraging and unique finding, their study reveals the positive role that HEIs can play in tackling GBV and empowering women.

In Chapter 5, Catherine Donovan and Nicola Roberts argue that the public story about sexual violence constructs a perfect victim narrative which renders LGBTQ+ students invisible as potential and/or actual targets for victimisation despite data indicating they are likely subjected to higher rates of sexual violence and harassment than heterosexual counterparts.

In Chapter 6, Ngozi Anyadike-Danes explores definitions of sexual consent from a legal context and a sociocultural context considering factors that might contribute to students' sexual consent understanding and communication and examines UK HEI sexual misconduct policies and their responsibility to ensure the safety of their students.

In Chapter 7, Samuel T. Hales provides a comprehensive overview of university-based sexual violence perpetration presenting the prevalence of sexual offending on university campuses, the risk and protective factors associated with students' sexually aggressive behaviours, and staff sexual misconduct.

In Chapter 8, Rachel Fenton and Janet Keliher cover relevant legislation in connection with GBV. They helpfully highlight the limits to the legislation and how the onus currently remains with victim-survivors to take legal action to address GBV rather than with institutions.

In Part II: Practice, we focus on key areas of prevention and response within HE that university officials and practitioners can implement. We begin in Chapter 9 with the story of Emily Drouet told by Fiona Drouet, her mother and founder of the inspirational charity EmilyTest. Through Emily's story, we learn of the brutal reality of us failing to keep our students safe. Poppy Gerrard-Abbott discusses the EmilyTest Gender-Based Violence Charter launched in

Scotland in 2021 providing a model that promotes innovative solutions for universities and colleges.

In Chapter 10, we consider what it means to be 'comprehensive' when embedding a comprehensive institution-wide approach, highlighting potentially overlooked areas, including different forms of GBV, specific groups within an HEI, types of university business that is high risk, and the risks of inconsistent and unfair practice.

In Chapter 11, Anna Bull discusses staff sexual misconduct in its variety of forms, the life-altering impacts of staff sexual misconduct on victim-survivors, and the current practice of handling staff sexual misconduct complaints in HE and how HEIs often fail to offer a fair process to victim-survivors.

In Chapter 12, Kelly Prince and Peta Franklin-Corben present an innovative chapter on the role of case management in HE responses to GBV providing the rationale for including a dedicated case manager post, as well as offering a model for how such a post could function by supporting a GBV case from first disclosure and risk assessment, through to a disciplinary outcome.

In Chapter 13, Carl Norcliffe and Andrea Pescod provide a practitioners' perspective on investigating student sexual misconduct and present strategies and tools for conducting internal investigations in HE using the PEACE model.

In Chapter 14, Kelsey Paske explores what prevention is, what it looks like in practice, and why the language of prevention rather than 'zero tolerance' is preferred and argues the need to address gender inequality, concurrently with other forms of structural inequality: racism, ableism, classism, homophobia, and transphobia, to effectively address intersectional forms of GBV.

In Chapter 15, Rosanna Bellini presents a critical retrospective look at two research studies conducted in HE to identify lessons that may translate to hybrid-working cultures for the protection of women's well-being and considers the practical implications for the design of technologies and policy, with a focus on efforts aimed at disrupting and destabilising toxic workplace cultures which contribute to the subjugation of women in the workplace.

In Chapter 16, we, identify the different forms of resistance faced by those trying to implement change initiatives for GBV prevention. We consider ways to mitigate for resistance, work through, or even around resistance tactics and discuss ways to protect from practitioner and activist burnout.

In Part III: Partnerships, we look at ways to build partnerships with key stakeholders and organisations to progress this work and create safer and more supportive environments within our institutions. As editors, we feel it is important to note that we have one key partner missing from this volume; disappointingly, we were unable to secure a contributing author to discuss partnership working between universities and the police. Whether that speaks more to our own ability to engage contributors or is representative of the difficulty in building police partnerships themselves, we will let the reader decide. However, we have managed to secure two authors who are former police officers now working within the sector. Our excellent partners represented in Part III highlight how partnership working is crucial to the success of effective prevention and response initiatives for addressing GBV.

In Chapter 17, Sunday Blake and Jim Dickinson discuss student engagement in addressing GBV in HE by identifying the roles that students, student groups, and students' unions might play in the design and delivery of strategy and highlight the types of support and risk mitigation steps that should be considered to ensure that student and peer-led work is impactful and safe.

In Chapter 18, Liz Hughes and Tammi Walker outline the current GBV policy developments by UK universities, discuss how university leaders can create partnerships with the external organisations such as the NHS Sexual Assault Referral Centres (SARCs), and provide recommendations for optimising access to such support services for university students.

In Chapter 19, Niamh Kerr and Kathryn Dawson present how strong partnerships between universities, colleges, and their local specialist organisations, like Rape Crisis, should be a central focus of Further and Higher Education sectors' approaches and provide examples of partnerships through which Rape Crisis Scotland and local Rape Crisis Centres have worked with universities and colleges across Scotland to deliver gendered, intersectional, and survivor-centred approaches to addressing GBV.

In Chapter 20, Amy Norton and Graham J. Towl describe the development of the current regulatory landscape in English HE and how GBV is being tackled within that via sector-level and non-legislative means. They use the concept of mandatory reporting of GBV as a case study to exemplify the limits and possibilities of provider-level regulation.

In Chapter 21, Andy Phippen and Emma Bond present the importance of universities and schools working in partnership to support students of all ages by presenting the concern of online harms impacting school-aged and university students. They discuss challenges and barriers schools and universities face and argue that there is a need to refocus how we respond to disclosures to better support victim-survivors, rather than adopting a prohibitive position.

We conclude this volume in Chapter 22 with a frank appraisal of the work we still need to do as a sector offering both challenges and solutions. After 65 years from Kirkpatrick and Kanin's study and decades of activism and research, we hope this volume will be a useful reference point and resource for university leaders, governing bodies, practitioners, activists, university administrators, HE regulators, partner organisations, and students. We hope this will help make meaningful change to reducing, preventing, and responding to GBV to ultimately stop gender-based violence in Higher Education.

Note

1 The Office for Students is the independent regulator of Higher Education in England.

References

Carter, P., & Jeffs, T. (1995). *A very private affair: Sexual exploitation in higher education*. Education Now Books, Publishing Cooperative.

Donaldson, A., McCarry, M., & McGoldrick, R. (2018). *Equally safe in higher education tool-kit: Guidance and checklist for implementing a strategic approach to gender-based violence prevention in Scottish higher education institutions.* University of Strathclyde.

Gold, J., & Villari, S. (Eds.). (2000). *Just sex: Students rewrite the rules on sex, violence, activism and equality.* Rowman & Littlefield Publishers, Inc.

Humphreys, C. J., & Towl, G. J. (2021). What can university communities do to reduce sexual violence? Responsibility, prevention and response. In D. A. Crighton & G. J. Towl (Eds.), *Forensic psychology* (3rd ed.). Wiley, BPS Books.

Jessup-Anger, J., Lopez, E., & Koss, M. P. (2018). History of sexual violence in higher education. *Student Services*, 9–19. https://doi.org/10.1002/ss.20249

Kirkpatrick, C., & Kanin, E. (1957). Male sex aggression on a university campus. *American Sociological Review, 22*(1), 52–58.

Long, J., Wertans, E., Harper, K., Brennan, D., Harvey, H., Allen, R., & Elliott, K. (2020). *UK femicides 2009–2018: "If I'm not in Friday, I might be dead."* Femicide Census.

National Union of Students. (2010). *Hidden marks: A study of women students' experiences of harassment, stalking, violence and sexual assault.* Retrieved January 2022, from www.nusconnect.org.uk/resources/hidden-marks-a-study-of-women-students-experiences-of-harassment-stalking-violence-and-sexual-assault

Office for National Statistics. (2018). *Sexual offences in England and Wales: Year ending March 2017.* Retrieved January 2022, from www.ons.gov.uk/peoplepopulationandcommunity/crimeandjustice/articles/sexualoffencesinenglandandwales/yearendingmarch2017

Towl, G., & Paske, K. (2017, November 7). The Weinsteins of academia can no longer be tolerated. *Times Higher Education.* Retrieved January 2022, from www.timeshighereducation.com

Towl, G. J., & Walker, T. (2019). Tackling sexual violence at universities: An international perspective. In *New frontiers in forensic psychology.* Routledge.

UN Women. (2018). *Guidance note on campus violence prevention and response.* Retrieved January 2022, from www.unwomen.org/-/media/headquarters/attachments/sections/library/publications/2019/campusviolence%20note_guiding_principles.pdf?la5en&vs53710

United Nations. (1993). *Declaration on the elimination of violence against women.* Retrieved January 2022, from https://undocs.org/en/A/RES/48/104

Universities UK. (2016). *Changing the culture.* Retrieved January 2022, www.universitiesuk.ac.uk/policy-and-analysis/reports/Documents/2016/changing-the-culture.pdf

Part I

Context, theory, and law

2 The significance of culture in the prevention of gender-based violence in universities

Melanie McCarry, Cassandra Jones, and Anni Donaldson

In 2018, the authors (Donaldson et al., 2018b) discussed the different political framings of violence against women and gender-based violence taken by the four nations of the UK (England being synonymous with the UK Government approach). In this chapter, we demonstrate that the gendered analysis taken by the Scottish government has led to a radically different policy framework and a development of understanding strongly informed by the third sector feminist anti-male violence movements in Scotland.

Violence Against Women as a Policy Issue

During the 1970s and 1980s, preventing violence against women (VAW) became a progressive social policy issue in the UK, Europe, and the United States as a result of feminism and women's social activism (Htun & Weldon, 2012). This drew public and political attention to the physical and sexual abuse of women (Dobash et al., 1992) and deepened knowledge of women's lived and common experiences of violence, and offered directions for prevention strategies (Walby, 2011; Walby et al., 2014). Feminist research looked beyond individual pathology and scrutinised men's violence in its wider social and historical context. Definitions of violence derived directly from women's lived experience were developed whereby forms of violence against women were reconceptualised as gendered phenomena and reframed within a matrix of embedded public and private social controls which maintained women's historic social subordination (Hanmer, 1978, 1996; Littlejohn, 1978). In the twenty-first century, VAW has been described as a 'concrete manifestation of inequality between the sexes' (Garcia-Moreno et al., 2005, p. 1282), which presents a significant impediment to women's equality. There is also recognition that most women experience more than one form and that the negative and cumulative impact can reach beyond the home, across social space, and throughout the lifespan (Scottish Government, 2009).

Research on VAW policy development worldwide has shown that the most effective strategies are those which adopt an ecological perspective to instruct action across society at macro- and microlevels and which intersect with vertical and horizontal axes of power across public and private space (Heise, 1998;

DOI: 10.4324/9781003252474-3

Samarasekera & Horton, 2015; Stockdale & Nadler, 2012). Hearn and McKie (2008) suggest a three-point gender framework for examining VAW policy development, which includes a gendered definition and analysis of violence and abuse in all its forms; a recognition of the social norms and material conditions which facilitate the exercise of male power and privilege; and acknowledgement of the varied locations and contexts where such violence occurs (Hearn & McKie, 2008). The extent to which VAW policy developments in the UK since the late 1990s have adhered to this conceptualisation in current UK frameworks varies and can be contextualised within the constitutional changes which have taken place in the UK since 1998. Within the four UK home nations, only Wales and Scotland have adopted a gendered framework in their approach to VAW prevention (McCullough et al., 2017).

Whilst violence against women and girls is a global issue, it is conceptualised and responded to in a variety of ways dependent on the cultural and political context. Here, in Scotland, we pride ourselves on being a more radical nation than the UK as a whole, voting against Brexit, campaigning for independence from the tyranny of Westminster, conceptualising poverty as a social problem needing a societal response, and having a gendered, and feminist, understanding of violence against women and other forms of gender-based violence (GBV), including that happening on campus or directed towards or perpetrated by university staff and students. This has been the framework for our policy response to all forms of VAW.

For 2019–2020, Police Scotland recorded 62,907 reported incidents of domestic abuse with the majority (82%) having a male perpetrator and female victim (Scottish Government, 2021). In 2018–2019 alone, there were 13,547 recorded reports of sexual crimes, including sexual assault and rape/attempted rape (Scottish Government, 2019). In 2018, the Scottish Government (2018) estimated the annual financial cost of domestic abuse to be £1.6 billion with a further £4 billion spent annually on wider violence against women and girls each. Despite what is arguably a more progressive, feminist-informed conceptual understanding, and associated legal framework and policy response, levels of VAW are comparable to that of the wider UK. This, we would argue, is due to the wider framework of inequality in which gender norms and sex-based inequalities still persist and are manifest across all our social, cultural, economic, and political domains (Engender, 2020).

What makes Scotland stand out from its nation counterparts is our unequivocal stance on the causes of violence against women. In Scotland, the government understands that violence against women is both a cause and a consequence of inequality between women and men and that prevention work must involve tackling the underpinning social, political, and economic inequalities between women and men (Scottish Government, 2018). A snapshot of civic, economic, and political society demonstrates that men disproportionally hold leadership and management positions. On a global scale, it is estimated that women comprise a quarter of all senior positions (Grant Thornton, 2018) and at a local level, in Scotland, women hold less than a third

(27%) of all 'positions of power, authority and influence' (Engender, 2017). Where women do make seniority (across the UK, men comprise 73% of CEOs and senior officials and 70% of managers and directors), there remains a pay gap (ONS, 2018). Indeed, within the Scottish Higher Education sector in 2016–2017, only 23% of all Principals in Scottish Universities were women (Engender, 2017).

Patriarchal gender norms condition and encourage men to be leaders and financial breadwinners; so, in practice, men dominate senior positions at work and do less unpaid labouring at home; the uneven split in household responsibilities means men have greater long-term financial and career prospects (Arun et al., 2004). Gender norms foster male privilege and men may feel challenged by women who deviate from them, whether or not they actively seek to oppress women (Connell, 1995, 1998). 'Gender disruption' (Risman, 1998), where women have higher economic statuses than their male partners, does not necessarily disrupt the gender hierarchy: it may simply loosen the link between money and power, leaving men's dominant 'breadwinner' status intact (Tichenor, 2005). Women consistently face more challenges in their work lives than men (Gregory, 2003) and are paid less across all occupations in the UK (ONS, 2018). When women are in promoted posts, they may be respected to lesser degrees than comparable men and women may be penalised or receive less credit for work if they do not behave in accordance with prescribed gender norms (see Lup, 2018). Relatedly, despite it being in breach of legislation (see section 18 of the UK Equality Act 2010), employers may be reluctant to employ or promote women because of the perceived extent of their household responsibilities. For example, pregnant women still encounter discriminatory practice limiting both career prospects and progression (Masser et al., 2007; Petit, 2007). The result is a workplace hierarchy in which women occupy only a quarter of senior positions worldwide and are overrepresented at the bottom (Grant Thornton, 2018). Whilst this chapter focuses primarily on sex-based inequalities, it is important to recognise that these discriminations are exacerbated for particular groups of women, including women of colour and women with disabilities (Crenshaw, 1991).

The Scotland Act 1998 gave the new Scottish Parliament power to encourage equal opportunities and to ensure the observation of equal opportunity requirements and also the power to impose duties on Scottish public authorities and cross-border public bodies operating in Scotland. Devolution facilitated the development of political systems and structures in the new governments which supported the equal representation of women. This was seized upon by feminist and women's organisations, politicians, and trade unionists in Scotland. The introduction of quotas and other measures to support the increased participation of women in the new political structures resulted in what has been described as the 'feminisation' of politics, whereby women's increased participation also promoted the advancement of issues affecting women's lives in the political agenda (Lovenduski, 2012; Mackay & McAllister, 2012).

Violence Against Women Policy in Scotland

The changing gender landscape in the political life of Scotland and Wales has been credited with achieving a new emphasis on the mainstreaming of equality and in the development of national policies on domestic abuse and VAW in both countries (Ball & Charles, 2006; Breitenbach & Mackay, 2001; Mackay, 2010). The role of feminist campaigning and service providers such as the established national networks of Women's Aid and Rape Crisis centres have also had a significant impact on the development of VAW policy in Scotland through closer access to the policymakers and the development of successful lobbying strategies. Consistent and careful management of the tension between crime prevention–focused strategies, survivor-informed approaches, and clearly linked strategies to structural gender inequality has resulted in the gendered framework being adopted in Scotland (and Wales).

The Scottish Government's statutory obligations in relation to gender equality derive from the UK Human Rights Act 1998, the Equality Act 2010, the Public Sector Equality Duty 2011, and the more specific requirements of the Gender Equality Duty 2007 (Engender, 2014). Through its policy and funding frameworks, the Scottish Government aims to achieve gender equality in society and to address deep-rooted structural inequalities which prevent women and girls thriving as equal citizens. In *Equally Safe*, the Scottish Government and the Scottish Convention of Local Authorities (COSLA) provide a policy framework which incorporates the UN's gendered definition of VAW, supports the ratification of the Istanbul Convention, and utilises a human rights approach and a gendered analysis of abuse to emphasise the interplay between gendered power relations and inequalities (Scottish Government, 2020). By conceptualising VAW as 'gendered' and both a cause and consequence of gender inequality, the Scottish Government highlights the need to understand violence within the context of women's and girl's structural inequality and vulnerability to violence (Scottish Government, 2016, p. 10). *Equally Safe*'s gendered analysis thus institutionalises a national approach across the country which has been recognised as a progressive approach (Coy et al., 2008; Coy & Kelly, 2009). The approach stresses partnership working and outlines medium- and long-term goals for achieving gender equality through primary, secondary, and tertiary prevention emphasising trauma-informed support for victim-survivors and a robust criminal justice response to perpetrators. Since 2017, the Scottish Government has invested £19.5 million through its *Equally Safe* strategy in central funding for specialist domestic abuse and rape crisis services, national helplines, GBV prevention, research, and reforming the justice system. In 2016, funding was provided to a team (Melanie McCarry, Anni Donaldson, and Roisin McGoldrick) at the University of Strathclyde to create the national *Equally Safe in Higher Education* (ESHE) Toolkit to support a whole campus approach to GBV prevention in Scottish universities echoing the approach outlined in *Equally Safe*.

ESHE Toolkit

The ESHE Toolkit looked beyond individualist explanations for sexual violence and GBV and its prevention (Donaldson et al., 2018a; McCarry et al., 2018). It was grounded in feminist definitions derived from women's experiences, contextualised within feminist analyses of gender inequality and of the wider cultural context of male violence against women. The ESHE Toolkit provides guidance on addressing GBV responses, GBV prevention, GBV intervention, and curriculum and knowledge exchange. In terms of language, whilst the Scottish Government use 'violence against women', a decision was made to use 'gender-based violence (GBV)' in the Toolkit to assuage the institution that we were also concerned with abuse directed towards male staff and students, non-binary people, and abuse perpetrated by women and/or non-binary people. The development of the Toolkit was very much a collaborative enterprise and we established an advisory group of experts, including academics, practitioners, and policymakers. We involved, for example, Police Scotland, Glasgow City Council, Rape Crisis, and Glasgow Women's Support Project amongst others. This holistic approach ensured expertise on all aspects of work and including a wide range of university representatives – student well-being, campus security, disability services, student unions, staff unions, HR, and senior managers – and meant that our work was embedded in the institution (in structure at least). In addition to the ESHE Toolkit, there was a sister Research Toolkit that provided all the resources and guidance needed to collect data in an institution. Both Toolkits were freely available from the ESHE website and the team were available to help implement and support the data collection (Donaldson et al., 2018a; McCarry et al., 2018).

Following the publication of the Toolkit in 2018, the remit of the ESHE project was expanded to include the college sector, when the Scottish Government established the Equally Safe in Colleges and Universities Ministerial Working Group, of which the team are founder members and ESHE became *Equally Safe in Colleges and Universities* (ESCU). The Ministerial Working Group oversees the longer-term implementation of the ESHE Toolkit and ensures the sector's continued commitment to actions included in the Equally Safe Delivery Plan (Scottish Government, 2020). A further significant milestone was achieved in 2018 when the Scottish Government Minister for Higher Education and Further Education, Youth Employment and Training placed a requirement on Scottish universities and colleges to implement the ESHE Toolkit and to report their progress to the Scottish Funding Council in their annual Outcome Agreements (Donaldson, 2020; Donaldson & McCarry, 2018; Scottish Funding Council, 2020). ESHE/ESCU offered a unique opportunity to pioneer vital work which was fully informed by feminist approaches to VAW/GBV prevention and research in Scotland. The ESHE Toolkit project was also ambitious in its aim of drawing Scottish universities, for the first time, into the national GBV prevention strategy and to the Equally Safe Delivery Plan.

ESHE Research Toolkit

The Research Toolkit was developed to provide Scottish Higher Education Institutions with the means to build an evidence base of GBV on campus with the intention of using this to develop and tailor prevention strategies (McCarry et al., 2018). Included in the Toolkit was detailed guidance on research governance, participant recruitment, data collection tools, and data management and analysis. To develop a robust evidence base, a mixed method approach to data collection was suggested and the tools for interviews, focus groups, and surveys were provided.

The survey included in the Toolkit was the product of a rigorous three-year pilot process and informed by leading national and international academic experts and practitioners in gender-based violence (as discussed earlier). Using Kelly's (1987) continuum of violence framework, the survey aimed to capture different manifestations on GBV as well as the wider cultural context of the institution (Kelly, 1987). This was the first project in Scotland (and possibly the UK) to investigate this continuum in the Higher Education context. The survey comprised five sections: campus safety; attitudes to, and experiences of, emotional abuse, physical violence, stalking, sexual harassment, and sexual violence; impact of abuse; report and support pathways for victims-survivors; as well as broader issues regarding the gendered cultural context of the institution. The section on experiences of emotional abuse, physical violence, stalking, sexual harassment, and sexual violence contained 26 questions that were adapted from validated scales (McCarry et al., 2018). Building on international research (e.g., Fenton & Jones, 2017; Jones et al., 2020) highlighting the characteristic of university cultures that scaffold GBV, two sets of questions on lad culture and gender inequality were included in the cultural context section of the survey.

Analysis of this facilitated what Liz Kelly (2007, 2016) terms the 'conducive context' of abusive spaces, which in this case is the university campus. The conducive context refers to social messages and discourse that normalise harmful practices and are maintained by gendered power structures of universities (Connell, 2019). Queries on 'lad culture' were derived from the definition provided by Phipps and Young (2015): as 'a "pack" mentality that can be seen in activities such as sport and alcohol consumption, and "banter" that was frequently sexist, misogynist, and homophobic'. Gender inequality was described in the survey as 'where people are treated differently and unequally based on their gender. This might refer to a difference in pay between men and women or an unequal distribution of men and women in different roles or at different levels'.

Research Findings

The research team approached Universities across Scotland with an invitation to participate with full support and access to all materials. In total, only four universities participated with the condition that findings would be reported anonymously. This participation rate was disappointing, and the data cannot be regarded as representative of the sector, but does also indicate the reticence of the sector to expose its practice to scrutiny or invite change: reasons for not participating ranged from resource and timing issues to ethics committees refusing to give approval, despite evidence demonstrating research on this topic poses little to no risk of harm (e.g., Jaffe et al., 2015). Therefore, in the presentation of the data, none of the four participating universities are identified and all findings are aggregated. A total of 1,272 staff members and 2,268 students completed the survey and 18 staff and 73 students took part in an interview or focus group. For brevity's sake, only the main findings are presented. Survey participants reported the GBV they had been subjected to in their lifetime (since aged 16) and in the last 12 months. Most staff (93%) and student (93%) reported being subjected to at least one form of GBV during their lifetime and six in ten staff (60%) and eight in ten students (80%) reported being subjected to at least one form of GBV in the last 12 months. There were some key statistically significant differences between men and women. More female staff (61%) than male staff (57%) and significantly more female students (84%) than male students (70%) were subjected to GBV in the previous 12 months.[1] These gendered differences were reflected in interviews with female students and staff.

Female students described being subjected to a continuum of GBV behaviours. For instance, one female student described the emotional and physical violence she had been subjected to:

> *I had an emotionally and physically abusive boyfriend, he would strangle me. . . I was at University but my then boyfriend wasn't and this was ongoing behaviour from him for a while, at least two years and the behaviours were much worse towards the end.*

Another female student was subjected to stalking:

> *I've also got different exam rooms now for all of my exams because, although she [female student who is stalking her] won't be there, they can't explicitly stop her from coming on to campus. Because exam rooms and times, and locations and everything were all given out before any of this happened, obviously she has access to them.*

In interviews with staff, the impact of the cultural context, including the formal and informal hierarchy was explored when discussing GBV.[2] Interviewees referred to the ways in which the cultural context of the university (1) contributes towards the prevalence of GBV; (2) prevents reporting; and (3) 'protects' perpetrators. The following excerpt from a female administrative worker refers to a six-year period in which she was subject to systematic sexual assault, verbal abuse, and physical harassment from a male line manager:

> *In here, in this office, there was one particular person, a letch, leering – the number of times that he had an obvious erection, and stood too close behind me, shoving it in me, tickling and all the rest of it.*

The next quotation refers to an incident where a male professor used his seniority to intimidate and silence those he victimised:

> *I did have a personal situation quite a few years ago, probably about 10 years ago, maybe slightly more, where a professor in our department was very inappropriate with me, but again, I dealt with that myself. . . . Although I was taken very by surprise, it was just him and I in my office when it happened, and I was taken very by surprise and as you kind of do, and because as well I'm an admin person, he's a professor and you feel that kind of, I've got to be careful, kind of thing.*

This issue of seniority arose in a number of the interviews:

> *If I say that I'm not comfortable, what are the repercussions of that, because I have a senior member of staff in front of me. . . . You just question things in your head, you think – because my response to that in a different setting, like if I was out at a nightclub or a pub, I would bite back and put people in their place a little bit more in a social setting. I wouldn't put up with that kind of stuff. But in work you have this professional persona, you want to not cause any difficulty for yourself as much as possible.*

Interviewees discussed how hierarchy prevented them from responding to or reporting experiences due to concerns about negative career impact. For example, the following excerpt demonstrates how the cultural context can create an environment in which victims can come forward to disclose, or in this case, can prevent this from happening:

> *I feel my job is quite secure now, and yeah, I think that's basically – I've been here long enough that I know people, so I feel comfortable saying, and I know what tone I can use that will elicit a good response from them. . . . I'm comfortable enough that I know the people I interact with mostly on a daily basis. I know them well enough to be able to say, you know, I'll not get kick-back from it, but that's always a concern, and certainly was when I first started when I was just a PhD student, and then an early-career researcher. That was definitely something, you kind of had to stop yourself and be like, maybe not. I'll not say anything. I'll let that one slide.*

She referred to contract precarity as a barrier to female staff being able to challenge the behaviour of senior male staff:

> *I know other female colleagues who haven't called people out on it because they're like, 'actually, that's the person who's going to have to renew our contract in six months' time'.*

Interviewees also demonstrated ways in which hierarchy protects senior male perpetrators:

> *If it had been another member of staff or a researcher, I would have immediately gone to my immediate boss who's a professor, but because this was another professor, I felt very uncomfortable in doing so, so decided not to.*

These findings support a conclusion that gender inequality in academia creates a conducive context for the occurrence of a spectrum of GBV which is symptomatic of cultural resistance to gender equality and to prevention. Further supporting unequal gender relations of university campuses is 'lad culture' which is traditionally associated with certain male student populations, such as rugby group and their sexist 'banter' (Phipps, 2017), as described by a female student:

> *Just the sort of boys that think with the mentality of 'boys will be boys', that they can get away with doing what they like. Very misogynistic. Getting into the more sociology side, but a more hegemonic masculinity. Just being a lad's lad, and not having a lot of respect for women in general.*

The link between sexist 'banter' and increased tolerance for sexism and GBV perpetration is long evidenced (Angelone et al., 2005; Ford et al., 2015; Renzetti et al., 2018), which in turn makes the survey finding highly concerning. In the survey, 60% of student respondents and 45% of staff respondents reported that 'lad culture' exists in their institutions and 32% of staff and 44% of students reported that they had personally been subjected to 'lad culture'.

Challenges and Opportunities

Campaigns focused on preventing GBV on UK campuses in 2014–2015 emerged in the context of the #MeToo and #TimesUp movements. Research by NUS in 2011, previously cited, revealed what women students were subjected to, and protests against universities' poor response to campus sexual violence grew apace. Despite COVID-19 restrictions limiting university campus activity, GBV has not vanished from UK campuses and there has been a resurgence of impatience with the lack of progress in prevention and in effective responses. A report on a student survey about GBV on a Scottish campus argued that the institutional campaign was 'performative' (see also Phipps & McDonnell, 2021) and recommended an approach to GBV prevention 'with education in mind, to take on the toxic culture of coercive behaviour which is widespread in the University student community' (Reclaim Stirling 2021). The report also noted the need 'to stamp out toxic "lad culture" within male dominated sports teams' (Reclaim Stirling, 2021). The murders of Sarah Everard and Sabina Ness in 2021 created another upsurge in campaigning against male violence against women. Websites for survivors of sexual abuse such as *Everyone's Invited*[3] included, among the thousands of posts they received, claims of rape being perpetrated on Scottish university campuses (The Times, 2021).

Recent research carried out by the Scottish *#EmilyTest* Charity among staff and student groups at Scottish universities and colleges found there was 'a need to cover the spectrum of GBV, broadening focus from rape', and that 'GBV is also sometimes intertwined with institutionalised bullying cultures in education' (EmilyTest, 2021). These findings echo aspects of ESHE research showing that the harms of GBV continue to affect, (mainly) women students and staff on Scottish campuses and be carried out by (mainly) men within cultures which remain highly sexist in character. It is also clear that institutional approaches should address their prevention and response efforts to the full spectrum of GBV, to provide leadership which will ultimately eliminate those aspects of campus cultures which continue to sustain conducive contexts where discrimination, gender inequality, and GBV continue to thrive. That conducive cultures facilitate the perpetration of GBV is evident. Approaches to GBV prevention and intervention which sidestep this are likely to provide short-term solutions which fail to address the root of the problem. As Scotland's university and college sector look to the future however, there are signs for optimism.

Preventing GBV on Scottish campuses is now recognised as a priority within *Equally Safe*. The ESHE Toolkit's feminist analysis and theoretical framework provides institutions with a clear, consistent national framework for prevention, as they meet the Scottish Funding Council's requirements and report annually on progress. Implementation involves the development of partnership approaches, thus drawing institutions into local area VAW partnerships involving collaborations with the specialist VAW sector who bring the voices of victim-survivors to this work and with public sector bodies and the criminal justice system. Finally, building on the key principles, definitions, and aims of the ESHE Toolkit, the 'EmilyTest Charter' has been established. This will provide Scottish universities and colleges with a schema of internal and external markers and a national accountability framework which will gauge their progress in implementing whole campus approaches to preventing and responding to the full spectrum of GBV (EmilyTest, 2021).

Summary of Key Points

In this chapter, we argue that GBV within university communities across the UK stems from intersecting issues of sexism and other forms of discrimination in wider society. We argue that cultures of institutionalised sexism in our universities facilitate the persistence of GBV on our campuses.

- The different political framings of violence against women and GBV taken by the four nations of the UK is significant and impacts the various policy responses and frameworks.
- In Scotland, a gendered analysis is taken in which violence against women and GBV is regarded as both a cause and a consequence of gender inequality.
- Research on VAW policy development worldwide has shown that the most effective strategies are those which adopt an ecological perspective to

instruct action across society at macro- and microlevels and which intersect with vertical and horizontal axes of power across public and private space.

- The Scotland Act 1998 gave the new Scottish Parliament power to encourage equal opportunities and to ensure the observation of equal opportunity requirements and also the power to impose duties on Scottish public authorities and cross-border public bodies operating in Scotland. Devolution facilitated the development of political systems and structures in the new governments which supported the equal representation of women.
- Since 2017, the Scottish Government has invested £19.5 million through its *Equally Safe* strategy in central funding for specialist domestic abuse and rape crisis services, national helplines, GBV prevention, research, and reforming the justice system.
- In 2016, funding was provided to the Strathclyde team to create the national *Equally Safe in Higher Education* (ESHE) Toolkit to support a whole campus approach to GBV prevention in Scottish universities echoing the approach outlined in *Equally Safe*.
- The Toolkit provides guidance on addressing GBV responses, prevention, intervention, and curriculum and knowledge exchange.
- The conducive context refers to social messages and discourse that normalise harmful practices and are maintained by gendered power structures of universities.
- The research findings support the significance of the 'conducive context' in both perpetration and response and support a conclusion that gender inequality in academia creates a conducive context for the occurrence of a spectrum of GBV which is symptomatic of cultural resistance to gender equality and to prevention.

Further Reading

McCarry, M., Donaldson, A., McCullough, A., McGoldrick, R., & Stevenson, K. (2018). *Equally safe in higher education research toolkit: Guidance for conducting research into gender-based violence in Scottish higher education institutions.* University of Strathclyde. https://www.strath.ac.uk/media/1newwebsite/departmentsubject/social-work/documents/eshe/Equally_Safe_Doc_2_pgs_inc_ISBN.pdf

The Toolkit Guidance is predicated on the vision and aim of *Equally Safe* which provides a framework and reference point for preventing GBV in Scottish Higher Education Institutions. *Equally Safe* is endorsed by a wide range of statutory, public and third sector agencies all of whom play key roles in the oversight and delivery of the strategy at a national level through the Equally Safe National Delivery Plan (Scottish Government, 2018). This Guidance reflects Equally Safe's four priorities:

- Scottish society embraces equality and mutual respect, and rejects all forms of violence against women and girls.
- Women and girls thrive as equal citizens: socially, culturally, economically, and politically.
- Interventions are early and effective, preventing violence and maximising the safety and wellbeing of women and girls.
- Men desist from all forms of violence against women and girls and perpetrators of such violence receive a robust and effective response (Scottish Government 2016).

The *Equally Safe in Higher Education* (ESHE) Toolkit was developed to provide Scottish Higher Education Institutions (HEIs) with an approach to preventing GBV that will create a step change in how universities approach issues of inclusivity and equality. By acknowledging the need to address GBV at an institutional level, the ESHE Toolkit aligns itself with the Scottish Government and the United Nations in their recognition that GBV is both a cause and consequence of gender inequality.

The ESHE Toolkit and Guidance provides a framework informed by *Equally Safe* which can be used as a reference point for those Scottish HEIs developing their GBV prevention strategies and for those whose strategies are more advanced. This Guidance aims to:

- Introduce the ESHE Toolkit.
- Provide a framework for developing an effective, strategic and collaborative approach to preventing GBV on Scottish campuses based on the twin priorities of Prevention and Intervention.
- Support Scottish HEIs and their partners to integrate prevention activities into their strategic plans.
- Help build a consistent national approach across the Scottish sector based on a strategic evidence-based approach which incorporates four key work-streams:
  - GBV Response
  - GBV Prevention
  - GBV Intervention
  - Curriculum and Knowledge Exchange.
- Enable Scottish HEIs to contribute to local and national coordinated approaches to GBV prevention.

The Toolkit also incorporates a section on our theoretical framework and offers an opportunity for Scottish HEIs to reflect on current practice and procedures using the following framework:

- Key principles of a strategic, evidence-based approach to GBV prevention in Scottish HEIs;

- Key features of a strategic approach to GBV prevention in Scottish HEIs;
- Key work-streams for implementing a strategic approach to GBV prevention in Scottish HEIs
- A checklist to help identify gaps or areas for further/future development in GBV prevention in Scottish HEIs;
- Direction to relevant areas of the Toolkit containing further information, resources, templates and samples which can be adapted to individual campus settings.

Fenton, R., & Jones, C. (2017). An exploratory study on the beliefs about gender-based violence held by incoming undergraduates in England. *Journal of Gender-Based Violence*, 1 (2). https://doi.org/10.1332/239868017X15090095609822

There is a paucity of knowledge about beliefs regarding gender-based violence among UK university students and how receptive they are to help change university culture by participating in prevention programmes. Deeper understandings about university students are needed in order to ground effective prevention programmes such as bystander intervention. As the first study of its kind in the UK, this exploratory study expanded our understandings of the attitudes and beliefs about both sexual violence and domestic violence and abuse (DVA) held by students upon entry to university, which may underpin the cultural context in which gender-based violence occurs and is sustained in university settings.

This article used findings from the first cross-sectional study in the UK that measured beliefs, including rape and DVA myth acceptance, and readiness for change. A survey was given to 381 incoming undergraduate students attending a university. The findings suggest that men endorse rape and DVA myths more than women. Rape myths were associated with DVA myths and further analyses indicated that the subscales *He didn't mean to* and *It wasn't really rape* predicted DVA myths. Denial of the problem of sexual violence and DVA was predicted by myth endorsement but assuming responsibility for change was not.

These findings provided insight into the particular myths held by incoming undergraduates and how they operated together to scaffold gender-based violence in university settings. Rape and DVA myths need to be targeted in the development of effective prevention programmes in universities. Universities have reached a critical juncture in needing to tackle gender-based violence in their institutions effectively. This paper makes an important contribution to the growing research base about the current contextual culture in universities which tolerates gender-based violence thus maintaining and reproducing gender inequality, rendering women fearful of disclosure, and perpetrators free to act with impunity.

Notes

1 Female and male refers to participants' gender, as reported in the survey.
2 Whilst the following interview data are from the pilot, they are consistent with themes from the main study.
3 www.everyonesinvited.uk/.

References

Angelone, D. J., Hirschman, R., Suniga, S., Armey, M., & Armelie, A. (2005). The influence of peer interactions on sexually oriented joke telling. *Sex Roles, 52*(3–4), 187–199.

Arun, S. V., Arun, T. G., & Borooah, V. K. (2004). The effect of career breaks on the working lives of women. *Feminist Economics, 10*(1), 65–84. https://doi.org/10.1080/1354570042000198236

Ball, W., & Charles, N. (2006, March). Feminist social movements and policy change: Devolution, childcare and domestic violence policies in Wales. In *Women's Studies International Forum, 29*(2), 172–183. Pergamon.

Breitenbach, E., & Mackay, F. (2001). *Women and contemporary Scottish politics: An anthology.* Polygon at Edinburgh.

Connell, R. W. (1995). *Masculinities.* Polity Press.

Connell, R. W. (1998). Gender politics for men. In S. P. Schacht & D. W. Ewing (Eds.), *Feminism and men: Reconstructing gender relations* (pp. 225–236). New York University Press.

Connell, R. W. (2019). *The Good University: What universities actually do and why it's time for radical change.* Zed Books.

Coy, M., & Kelly, L. (2009). *Map of Gaps 2: The postcode lottery of violence against women support services in Britain.*

Coy, M., Lovett, J., & Kelly, L. (2008). *Realising rights, fulfilling obligations.* Violence Against Women.

Crenshaw, K. W. (1991). Mapping the margins: Intersectionality, identity politics, and violence against women of color. *Stanford Law Review, 43*(6), 1241–1299.

Dobash, R. P., Dobash, R. E., Wilson, M., & Daly, M. (1992). The myth of sexual symmetry in marital violence. *Social Problems, 39*(1), 71–91.

Donaldson, A. (2020). *Rapid review III: Report on a review of the Scottish colleges' ESHE toolkit pilot.* Equally Safe in Colleges and Universities, University of Strathclyde. www.strath.ac.uk/humanities/schoolofsocialworksocialpolicy/equallysafeinhighereducation/rapidresponsereviewofscottishhighereducationresponsestogbv-partiii/

Donaldson, A., & McCarry, M. (2018). *Rapid review II – Scottish higher education responses to gender based violence on campus.* Equally Safe in Higher Education Project Report, University of Strathclyde. https://strathprints.strath.ac.uk/66106/1/Donaldson_McCarry_UoS2018_Scottish_Higher_Education_Institution_Responses_to_Gender_based_Violence.pdf

Donaldson, A., McCarry, M., McCullough, A., McGoldrick, R., & Stevenson, K. (2018a). *Equally safe in higher education toolkit for implementing a strategic approach to gender-based violence prevention in Scottish higher education institutions.* University of Strathclyde. www.strath.ac.uk/humanities/schoolofsocialworksocialpolicy/equallysafeinhighereducation/eshetoolkit

Donaldson, A., McCarry, M., & McCullough, A. (2018b). Preventing gender-based violence in UK universities. In A. Sundari & R. Lewis (Eds.), *Gender based violence in university communities: Policy, prevention and educational intervention.* Policy Press. ISBN 9781447336594.

EmilyTest. (2021). *Emily test research report.* http://emilytest.co.uk/

Engender. (2014). *Gender equality and Scotland's constitutional futures.* www.engender.org.uk/news/blog/engender-launches-a-report-on-gender-equality-and-the-independence-debate/

Engender. (2017). *Sex and power in Scotland 2017.* www.engender.org.uk/content/publications/SEX-AND-POWER-IN-SCOTLAND-2017.pdf

Engender. (2020). *Sex and power in Scotland 2020.* www.engender.org.uk/content/publications/Engenders-Sex-and-Power-2020.pdf

Fenton, R., & Jones, C. (2017). An exploratory study on the beliefs about gender-based violence held by incoming undergraduates in England. *Journal of Gender-Based Violence, 1*(2). https://doi.org/10.1332/239868017X15090095609822

Ford, T. E., Woodzicka, J. A., Petit, W. E., Richardson, K., & Lappi, S. K. (2015). Sexist humor as a trigger of state self-objectification in women. *Humor, 28*(2), 253–269.

Garcia-Moreno, C., Heise, L., Jansen, H. A., Ellsberg, M., & Watts, C. (2005). Violence against women. *Science, 310*(5752), 1282–1283.

Grant Thornton. (2018). Women in business: Beyond policy to progress. *Grant Thornton.* www.grantthornton.co.uk/globalassets/1.-member-firms/global/insights/women-in-business/grant-thornton-women-in-business-2018-report.pdf

Gregory, R. F. (2003). *Women and workplace discrimination: Overcoming barriers to gender equality.* Rutgers University Press.

Hanmer, J. (1978). Violence and the social control of women. In G. Littlejohn, B. Smart, J. Wakeford, & N. Yuval-Davis (Eds.), *Power and the state.* Croom Helm.

Hanmer, J. (1996). *Women and violence: Commonalities and diversities (from violence and gender relations: Theories and interventions* (Brid Featherstone et al., Eds., pp. 7–21). Barbara Fawcett – See NCJ-162754).

Hearn, J., & McKie, L. (2008). Gendered policy and policy on gender: The case of 'domestic violence'. *Policy & Politics, 36*(1), 75–91.

Heise, L. (1998). Violence against women: An integrated, ecological framework. *Violence Against Women, 4*(3), 262–290.

Htun, M., & Weldon, S. L. (2012). The civic origins of progressive policy change: Combating violence against women in global perspective, 1975–2005. *American Political Science Review, 106*(3), 548–569.

Jaffe, A. E., DiLillo, D., Hoffman, L., Haikalis, M., & Dykstra, R. E. (2015). Does it hurt to ask? A meta-analysis of participant reactions to trauma research. *Clinical Psychology Review, 40,* 40–56.

Jones, C., Skinner, T. S., Gangoli, G., Smith, O., & Fenton, R. (2020). *Gender-based violence among UK university students and staff: A socio-ecological framework.* https://doi.org/10.5281/zenodo.4572506

Kelly, L. (1987). The continuum of sexual violence. In M. Maynard & J. Hanmer (Eds.), *Women, violence and social control.* Springer.

Kelly, L. (2007). A conducive context: Trafficking of persons in Central Asia. In M. Lee (Ed.), *Human trafficking* (pp. 73–91). Willan Publishing.

Kelly, L. (2016, March 1). The conducive context of violence against women and girls. *Discover Society, 30.* https://discoversociety.org/2016/03/01/theorising-violence-against-women-and-girls/

Littlejohn, G. (Ed.). (1978). *Power and the state* (Vol. 11). Taylor & Francis.

Lovenduski, J. (2012). Feminising British politics. *The Political Quarterly, 83*(4), 697–702.

Lup, D. (2018). Something to celebrate (or not): The differing impact of promotion to manager on the job satisfaction of women and men. *Work, Employment and Society, 32*(2), 407–425. https://doi.org/10.1177/0950017017713932

Mackay, F. (2010). Gendering constitutional change and policy outcomes: Substantive representation and domestic violence policy in Scotland. *Policy & Politics, 38*(3), 369–388.

Mackay, F., & McAllister, L. (2012). Feminising British politics: Six lessons from devolution in Scotland and Wales. *The Political Quarterly, 83*(4), 730–734.

Masser, B., Grass, K., & Nesic, M. (2007). "We like you, but we don't want you" – The impact of pregnancy in the workplace. *Sex Roles, 57*(9–10), 703–712. http://dx.doi.org/10.1007/s11199-007-9305-2

McCarry, M., Donaldson, A., McCullough, A., McGoldrick, R., & Stevenson, K. (2018). *Equally safe in higher education research toolkit: Guidance for conducting research into gender-based violence in Scottish higher education institutions* (p. 56). University of Strathclyde. www.strath.ac.uk/media/1newwebsite/departmentsubject/socialwork/documents/eshe/Equally_Safe_Doc_2_pgs_inc_ISBN.pdf

McCullough, A., McCarry, M., & Donaldson, A. (2017). *Rapid review of Scottish higher education responses to gender based violence, equally safe in higher education project report.* University of Strathclyde. https://pure.strath.ac.uk/portal/files/66736175/McCullough_etal_2017_Rapid_review_of_scottish_higher_education_responses_to_gender_based_violence.pdf

ONS. (2018). *Gender pay gap in the UK: 2018.* Office of National Statistics. www.ons.gov.uk/employmentandlabourmarket/peopleinwork/earningsandworkinghours/bulletins/genderpaygapintheuk/2018#glossary

Petit, P. (2007). The effects of age and family constraints on gender hiring discrimination: A field experiment in the French financial sector. *Labour Economics, 14*(3), 371–391.

Phipps, A. (2017). Speaking up for what's right: Politics, markets and violence in higher education. *Feminist Theory, 18*(3), 357–361.

Phipps, A., & McDonnell, L. (2021). On (not) being the master's tools: Five years of 'changing university cultures.' *Gender and Education.* Ahead-of-Print, 1–17. https://doi.org/10.1080/09540253.2021.1963420

Phipps, A., & Young, L. (2015). Lad culture in higher education: Agency in the sexualisation debates. *Sexualities, 18*(4), 459–479.

Reclaim Stirling. (2021). *An evaluation of the university of Stirling's efforts to tackle sexual violence, and of the perception of the #IsThisOkay campaign.* https://reclaimstirling.wordpress.com/reclaim-stirling-report/

Renzetti, C. M., Lynch, K. R., & DeWall, C. N. (2018). Ambivalent sexism, alcohol use, and intimate partner violence perpetration. *Journal of Interpersonal Violence, 33*(2), 183–210.

Risman, B. (1998). *Gender vertigo: American families in transition.* Yale University Press.

Samarasekera, U., & Horton, R. (2015). Prevention of violence against women and girls: A new chapter. *The Lancet, 385*(9977), 1480–1482.

Scottish Funding Council. (2020). *Gender based violence in Outcome Agreements 2019–20.* Edinburgh, Scottish Funding Council. www.sfc.ac.uk/web/FILES/Access/Gender_Based_Violence_in_Outcome_Agreements_2019-20.pdf

Scottish Government. (2009). *Safer lives: Changed lives – a shared approach to tackling violence against women in Scotland.* Scottish Government. www.webarchive.org.uk/wayback/archive/20180517125819/www.gov.scot/Publications/2009/06/02153519/0

Scottish Government. (2016). *Equally safe – Scotland's strategy for preventing and eradicating violence against women.* Scottish Government. www.gov.scot/Publications/2014/06/7483

Scottish Government. (2018). *Equally safe: Scotland's strategy for preventing and eradicating violence against women and girls.* Scottish Government. www.gov.scot/publications/equally-safe-scotlands-strategy-prevent-eradicate-violence-against-women-girls/

Scottish Government. (2019). *Recorded crime in Scotland 2018–2019.* Scottish Government. www.gov.scot/publications/recorded-crime- scotland-2018-19/

Scottish Government. (2020). *Equally safe: Year three update report.* Final Report. Scottish Government. www.gov.scot/publications/equally-safe-final-report/

Scottish Government. (2021). *Domestic abuse: Statistics recorded by the police in Scotland 2019/2020.* Scottish Government.

Stockdale, M. S., & Nadler, J. T. (2012). Situating sexual harassment in the broader context of interpersonal violence: Research, theory, and policy implications. *Social Issues and Policy Review, 6*, 148–176.

Tichenor, V. (2005). Maintaining men's dominance: Negotiating identity and power when she earns more. *Sex Roles, 53*(3–4), 191–205.

The Times. (2021). *Scottish students add rape claims to website.* www.thetimes.co.uk/article/scottish-students-add-rape-claims-to-website-lwt95jgnz

Walby, S. (2011). The impact of feminism on sociology. *Sociological Research Online, 16*(3), 158–168.

Walby, S., Towers, J., & Francis, B. (2014). Mainstreaming domestic and gender-based violence into sociology and the criminology of violence. *The Sociological Review, 62*, 187–214.

3 Hidden Marks

The contribution of student leaders to tackling gender-based violence on campus

Jim Dickinson and Sunday Blake

Introduction: Liv Bailey (2009–2011), "Hidden Marks", and student leadership

It seems hard to believe now, but in the autumn of her first term as NUS National Women's Officer, Liv Bailey was asked by the *Evening Standard* to comment on a story surrounding a university vice-chancellor (VC) who had said that attractive young women students were a "perk" to be enjoyed "at a safe distance" by older male academics. Terence Kealey of the University of Buckingham had taken to the Times Higher Education supplement in the autumn of 2009 to argue that some women students fantasised about male lecturers and "flaunted" their bodies, which he advised academics to "admire daily to spice up your sex, nightly, with your wife". This is an area where Bailey said the comments showed a lack of respect:

> Regardless of whether this is an attempt at humour, it is completely unacceptable for someone in Terence Kealey's position to compare a lecture theatre to a lap-dancing club . . . he does a disservice not only to the many female scholars who have struggled to get a foothold in academia, but also the many bright female students who have got their good grades through nothing more exciting than hard work.
>
> (Bailey, L in Kirby, 2009, 3rd paragraph from the end)

This is perhaps a dynamic that has played out on the HE landscape subsequently with the leadership in this area from student activists, while university VCs appear to have demonstrated largely defensive or otherwise inadequate or inappropriate responses to the problem of sexual violence at universities. But that rejection of the treatment of sexual harassment as a joke did not mean that Bailey was prepared to eschew all of the tactics of the traditional student representative. Mainstream student leader training at the time stressed the need for evidence to demonstrate a case, where previously NUS' "Liberation Campaigns" had tended to focus on raw activism as the means to achieve social change.

That summer Bailey had resolved to progress a manifesto promise from her election in the spring by commissioning staff at NUS to undertake research

DOI: 10.4324/9781003252474-4

into the prevalence of student sexual harassment, misconduct, and violence – including a review of existing research and statistics about violence against women in the UK, public policy approaches in the field, studies of gendered violence in student communities in other countries such as the United States, and surveys of attitudes towards victims of crime. But the centrepiece was a national online survey of 2,058 women students' experiences of harassment, financial control, control over their course and institution choices, stalking, violence, and sexual assault. The results were alarming:

- More than one-third of respondents reported that they sometimes felt unsafe when visiting their university or college buildings in the evening;
- Women were most likely to feel unsafe in the evening at their institution because of concerns that they were likely to be harassed or intimidated;
- Women students reported experiences of a range of unwanted behaviour during their time as a student, ranging from "everyday" verbal and non-verbal harassment to serious episodes of stalking, physical, and sexual assault;
- One in seven survey respondents had experienced a serious physical or sexual assault during their time as a student;
- Over two-thirds of respondents had experienced some kind of verbal or non-verbal harassment in and around their institution. This kind of behaviour – which includes groping, flashing, and unwanted sexual comments – had become almost "everyday" for some women students;
- Twelve percent of respondents reported being subject to stalking, and more than one in ten had been a victim of serious physical violence;
- Sixteen percent had experienced unwanted kissing, touching, or molesting during their time as a student, the majority of which had taken place in public;
- Seven percent had been subject to a serious sexual assault, the majority of which occurred in somebody's home;
- One in ten victims of serious sexual assault was given alcohol or drugs against their will before the attack;
- The majority of perpetrators of stalking, sexual assault, and physical violence were already known to the victim;
- Men were the majority of perpetrators of stalking (89%) and physical violence (73%);
- Students were the majority of perpetrators in most categories, the majority of whom were studying at the same institution as the respondent.

(National Union of Students (NUS), 2010)

In the foreword to the report, Bailey was keen to point out the lack of support on offer – noting that nearly a third of students did not even discuss the issue of violence against women with their friends. Very few students reported their experiences, either to their institution or to the police, in the category of serious sexual assault only 10% reported it to the police, and more than four in ten told no one about the attack:

> At the moment, women students are too often being forced to pick themselves up and carry on, without any help or support from their institution. Many women students are left feeling alone, and feeling like they are to blame for the violence committed against them. This report is a wake-up call. We must act now to break the silence: violence against women students is widespread, serious, and is hampering women's ability to learn.
>
> (Bailey, in NUS, 2010, Foreword)

Bailey's decision to take on the topic through the tactics of research findings attracted considerable press coverage – yet it was to take five more years before the government or the umbrella body for universities, Universities UK, was to formally acknowledge the scale of the issue through a taskforce whose recommendations are still not requirements on universities. In this chapter we describe what happened next.

Estelle Hart (2011–2012): shifting the narrative and broadening support

As the research for Hidden Marks was being carried out and the report was being prepared for launch, the Welsh Assembly Government was busy working on a six-year integrated strategy for tackling violence against women. Yet Estelle Hart, the NUS Wales Women's officer who would go on to succeed Liv Bailey in 2011, encountered disbelief amongst policymakers that university campuses was where there might be a problem:

> Well the attitude was very much that sexual assault is something that happens when a stranger randomly attacks you, and university campuses were assumed to be this safe place, this bubble where that wasn't happening. We talk a lot about the dangers of social media now, but at the time it was social media that was very slowly allowing women to start to share stories of what had happened to them – and those stories were almost always about other students.

It is notable that the Welsh Assembly Government's "The Right to be Safe" (2010) mentions students just twice – once with a generic line on encouraging universities in Wales to develop violence against women policies (and to "examine the need" for training of professionals in these education settings), and another on producing materials on personal safety in campus settings:

> Well when the data for Hidden Marks came through, and about 10% of the responses were from Wales, most of the findings were similar – and I just knew both unis and the government would get very defensive or slip into

denial. But I remember there was one big difference from the rest of the UK – this fear of walking home from university. And if you think about where some of the major HEIs are in Wales, I went to Swansea, which is in the middle of a park. Bangor is similarly in the middle of nowhere. And so what that data allowed me to do was get communication channels open, get in the door and get on the working groups, because if you instinctively want to think that the real problem is stranger danger, that's a finding that fits.

This tactical choice – to select from a breadth of evidence findings that complemented rather than challenged policymakers' perceptions of the issue in order to gain access to settings where a more difficult decision might be attempted – then became central to Hart's work when she moved to NUS UK.

Her first job was to build on Bailey's work in an attempt to shift concern surrounding student sexual harassment, misconduct, and violence out of seminar rooms hosting feminist society talks and into wider conversation on campus.

> When I first got involved it was all dominated by people from quite elite universities, a lot of people were studying gender – the cliché would be a bunch of us sat around theorising about the patriarchy with language that no one else understands, and occasionally shouting at passers-by in power.

That led to two major concerns. The first was to try to build a broader base of interest in the issues that would engage students studying science and business studies as much as it would those engaged in extracurricular feminist discourse. The second was to start to take the conversation out beyond activism and into males' spaces and leadership.

Hence Hart's initial period in office was very much marked by attempting to identify "with the grain" messages of "stranger danger" that student activists and universities were comfortable with, and to then use the findings in Hidden Marks to spark debates which could cause activists to question that framing:

> Universities and students' unions all did it, you know the personal defence class sort of thing. But for me it was about what we'd all been taught, like a constant background noise. Strangers in the dark is the thing you're taught to be afraid of, and you become more politicised by the things you're told to be scared of. But actually, you're not told you might know a man who does this or a friend or somebody in your family or a manager might do it.
>
> I remember I was at a students' union event in London and I went into the bathroom, and there was a classic victim blaming TfL poster up that said "don't get into unlicensed cabs", and I walked out onto the stage and held it up and just pointed out that we're telling women it was their fault for getting into the wrong sort of car. You went with the energy that was there. Reclaim the night events were popular too.

What the data in Hidden Marks did was allow me to open up a new conversation among those activists – because the more you talked about the findings and the more you shared the figures the more they realised that something that had happened to them or their friends was actually widespread, and that it was somehow their fault. It gave them confidence to pivot away from strangers and to start talking about the harassment and violence they faced in their own spaces.

Hidden from much of the narrative that surrounds student sexual harassment, misconduct, and violence is the role that student leaders have played in political education – fusing both data and narrative that is resonating with the nascent activism around to reframe perceptions of an issue.

As this work developed, and Hart became party to student activists that were turning private stories into a more empowering political narrative, she noticed that a common feature was the environments which they said had led to the harassment or assaults that students faced:

> Plenty of people said I was stupid for doing it. If you've got evidence of serious sexual assaults why would you start banging on about lad mags and lad culture? But the women we were talking to knew that a led to b. So you sort of hoped that if you took it on, you'd have a silent majority behind you who might not be confident enough yet to take a stand. And it was also something that was easier for men to talk about. If you say "look at all these rapes and sexual assaults" it's too easy to say "not all men, not me or my mates". But if you talk about misogyny in the media, they can see it.
>
> The Women's campaign had tended to talk to itself, but we ran a fringe meeting at the main NUS Conference on lad culture that year and we couldn't believe how many people turned up. I think the entire Loughborough delegation came to try to stare me out, I think they were all in matching tracksuits, a sort of very angry kind of sports type. But you could feel it in the room, they walked in thinking they were the majority and afterwards they were all a bit embarrassed, and women were coming up to me thanking us for doing the fringe, wanting to know more.

Hart describes endless, lengthy conversations with male student leaders – often sparked by men feeling angry or slighted – that almost always ended with a desire to know more or a request to help campaigns on campus.

> Yeah you'd go from some red faced President saying not all men to them going back to see if there was anyone that would support them taking Nuts or Zoo off their shelves of their SU shop. There's something about men and leadership I think that makes them think they have to defend. I couldn't magic up 200 more women in SU President roles, so I just thought it would be better if they decided it was more important to protect women on campus than the odd hurt feelings of someone that wanted to stare at the front page of Nuts.

Amongst students, then, the role of leadership in highlighting issues and "speaking the unspeakable" becomes an important factor in building support outside of traditional activist structures – as does, at least temporarily, playing into the desire of leaders to protect their "people". But support was still missing from universities themselves:

> It wasn't really on the cards for the sector, I think. We tried. I think there's something probably about people at a certain age, the idea of protecting the institution, a need to project a vision of safety and a squeamishness about punishing their own students. Even when they started understanding who the victims were, they were still all but who are the perpetrators? And the idea that the perpetrators might be people in that room with you, or your students who are good boys from good families – they just got angry and wanted names and evidence.

And this is perhaps a still common response, for example, from university governing bodies.

Kelley Temple (2012–14): causes, culture, and commitment

Just as Estelle Hart had cut her teeth in national student leadership in Wales, her successor had spent two years as NUS Scotland's Women's Officer, where a tour around the democratic structures of students' associations had taught Temple how to tackle attitudes that were acceptable and prevalent at the time:

> You'd get a lonely women's officer who would ask you to go to the student council, talk about Hidden Marks and what that it would mean if that institution took issues seriously. And it was always men Presidents at the time. I'd do the presentation and I'd say let's have a conversation about what leads to this, and then I'd open up to questions. Every time I'd get "well I think actually what you're doing is really irresponsible, because you don't know if bad things are happening here and it's not all men, you're blaming men for things which is very mean and unfair". Those I was ready for. But one of the narratives that kept coming up was, well, if you have zero tolerance policies, then what's going to happen is you're going to increase the level of rapes. Because if men can touch women in nightclubs, and they're less likely to go into rape, right? It seems astonishing now but it really brought home to me how normalised harassment was. It wasn't even something people were embarrassed or ashamed about.

Temple's story is remarkable – partly because attitudes of that sort are clearly no longer socially acceptable, at least in the culture of students generally and students' unions specifically. But is it that things have changed, or that such views are still there, lurking in "incel" internet forums?[1]

Either way, early on in her period of office as the NUS UK Women's Officer, Temple recalls a conversation where she identified that one of the major things holding back support and action on the part of both SU presidents and vice-chancellors was "reputation":

> I'd never really thought about reputation, but Higher Education seems to be historically built around it, and when you add in a version of that being used to sell universities, it was obvious that a lot of the resistance was about reputational risk. So internally we said look, what we need to do is shift the reputational risk away from admitting that this happens here, too. It happens everywhere. So as well as being clear about the impact of what we were calling lad culture, we needed to demonstrate that this harassment was happening everywhere and for the risk to become not doing something about it, not taking steps to prevent it, because it happens everywhere.

This mission – to tackle self-denial on the part of (largely male) leaders over the prevalence and impact of a culture of harassment on campus – led Temple to commission her own research.

In March 2012, NUS had invited interested staff and officers from across the sector to participate in a workshop about how to make campuses and students' unions more positive spaces for women. At the event, it had become clear that cultures in Higher Education were operating to make women students feel unsafe and to legitimise harassment.

But as Temple took office, there were still suggestions that a focus on "banter" or "lad mags" would alienate those the work needed to have on board:

> The problem was that even if we'd wanted to avoid it, we couldn't. Hidden Marks had opened it all up. You'd have a woman coming to you and saying she'd been raped but that she had been taking part in drinking games or a sports initiation, so really, she was told she was partly responsible. That link of the justification of the behaviour – victim blaming – because of the cultural expectations was so tied into the end result of the crime. So yes it was daunting but we knew we had to help people understand that lots of this "lower level" stuff was also a crime, led to more serious crimes, and stopped people coming forward.

"That's what she said: Women students' experiences of 'lad culture' in Higher Education" emerged in April 2013 to considerable press interest – but Higher Education was not necessarily ready to accept that it had a problem it could take responsibility for. Nicola Dandridge, then chief executive of Universities UK, argued at the time that the issue was not unique to the sector:

> It is important to remember that this is an issue for society generally, not just one confined to university students.
>
> (Dandridge, N in Williams, 2013, last paragraph)

A few months later in the summer of 2013, a song called "Blurred Lines" by American singer Robin Thicke (featuring fellow singer Pharrell Williams and rapper T.I.) had become the fastest selling single of 2013. Its lyrics and video had attracted commentary suggesting that it embodied the sort of culture that Temple et al. had been trying to describe – and by the autumn, Edinburgh University Students' Association (EUSA) had become the first student body to remove the song from being played in its own venues. Kirsty Haigh, the vice-president of services, explained:

> It promotes a very worrying attitude towards sex and consent. . . . This is about ensuring that everyone is fully aware that you need enthusiastic consent before sex. The song says: 'You know you want it.' Well, you can't know they want it unless they tell you they want it.
>
> (Haigh, K in Lynskey, 2013, paragraph 4)

For much of the media, the issue was about censorious students – but for Temple the wave of support for SUs removing the song from playlists that ensued was about putting a commitment into practice:

> By then the NUS Women's Campaign had taken zero tolerance to sexual harassment thing that Liv had started and for a couple of years had been making it something you could get accredited for – an SU would want the badge, the certificate that it took this seriously – the reputation thing. So a lot of SUs were actually talking about their own venues and listening to women who were saying look, when that song comes on, we're getting groped. So yes it was symbolic and political but it was also really practical. If you wanted less unwanted groping, you could choose not to play the song.

There are fascinating lessons here. On the one hand, the commodification of a "zero tolerance" statement into a quality model with a badge to be obtained helped turn the reputation objective into reality as SU officers instructed staff that they wanted the logo on the bottom of their email signatures too. On the other hand, while there were concerns about box ticking, assessment, and the sustainability of such a scheme, it was changing the way that venue operators were thinking about the culture they were enabling on (or adjacent to) campus.

Yet for all the public debate over the influence of popular culture over campus culture, there was still significant resistance to tackling the issue locally:

> There were usually two reactions, sometimes in the same sentence, from the men. One was well this happens everywhere don't blame us, and the other was well you've no evidence that this happens here. We sort of thought we'd done what we could on turning that around and decided that it might be better in the long term if we just had more women leading SUs. So when we started arguing for gender quotas at NUS' Annual Conference, that was partly about that event and its culture. But it was also about getting

a proper debate going about why it was that every year a tiny minority of SU Presidents and CEOs were women.

For Temple, central to the effort to win what had become a debate about "fair representation" wasn't so much the arguments or the evidence – but the visible championing of the agenda by the NUS National President, Toni Pearce:

> You just can't underestimate how important it is to have the ultimate leader, the MD or the CEO or the VC or in our case the National President, backing you up all the time. When people aren't sure they look to the leader for a signal, and every single time she stood there and said yes, this really is important, it's who we are. Tackling misogyny and the underrepresentation of women had always been something that was done somewhere, tolerated really. But in places like universities or SUs where you're not doing command and control all the time, you want the leader to say "we're all doing this". Toni helped make it mainstream and something people were really proud to get involved with.

It has become a cliché to suggest that tackling student sexual harassment, misconduct, and violence on campus requires visible and ongoing commitment from senior leaders. That may be because warm words lose their resonance if issues persist, if insufficient resource is allocated to strategic responses, or if specific incidents are not perceived to be handled by those leaders properly. But in any event, many clichés are nevertheless true.

Susuana Amoah (2014–2016): detective work, policy activism, and problem-solving

When Temple's successor had started to raise questions about culture on her own campus as a student, she recalls being pulled into a meeting where she was challenged on her assertions:

> Nobody likes being told it's them or their campus or their venue do they. So I remember being pulled into the SU office and they were saying like, we have got accreditation, and we got this pack of stickers and stuff. And I was like, that doesn't make sense, because we literally haven't changed anything. Like not one thing has changed, on the streets, in the union in or in this university at all. I was meeting with a senior manager in the SU and they said well what do you suggest? I was all well why are you asking me, I'm a second year student. So from day one, I knew there was something wrong with the zero tolerance thing. We had to try something else.

Even if the work on lad culture had helped trigger public conversations about cause, there was still the question of what universities were doing over incidents of rape and sexual assault on campus. On taking office, Amoah had decided to attempt to find the best practice that was out there, and on the promise of being able to supply top tips to SUs on what to lobby for, invited the submission of sexual misconduct policies from across the sector. Two things became apparent:

> Well the first was that a lot of the stuff was so similar that it looked less like people were sharing best practice and more like universities had been plagiarising each other's work, and the more I spoke to students on the ground the more I got this sense that in SUs and universities it was too easy to tick the box rather than do the work, that's the danger with these schemes. But the bigger issue for me was that almost every university policy said that if a student reported a sexual assault, it won't do anything until a police report is filed. And it had to go to trial, and the trial had to finish. I was like, What is this? Where's this coming from? Personally and politically I was aware of how awful the Police were and how low the rape conviction rate was, so I was like why is this thing in everyone's policy?

What Amoah had come to discover was something called the Zellick report – the product of a 1994 taskforce made up of members of the Committee of Vice Chancellors and Principals (CVCP, now Universities UK) headed by Graham Zellick, the then president of Queen Mary and Westfield College. The report had been created principally as a response to a high-profile case where a student had been suspended from university following an accusation of rape by another student in the early 1990s.

The student had successfully brought a legal challenge against Kings College London for its decision to suspend him, and resulted in the university having to pay significant damages. As a result, Zellick provided guidance on student disciplinary procedures, including in cases where a breach may also constitute a criminal offence, which effectively warned universities off from processing allegations themselves at all. The proposals and advice still applied in most universities 20 years on, causing Amoah to embark on a kind of programme of policy activism:

> It was being used as the sort of guidance that helped universities do nothing. Of course we don't have any policies, we don't need to because it's not our responsibility. I didn't think that stacked up morally, and I was wondering whether that was even compatible with stuff like duty or care or the Equality Act. But every submission showed me that universities were avoiding this stuff. So we produced a briefing and got legal advice and started supporting SU officers to try to fight the Zellick stuff locally (NUS, 2015). That was really hard going – you had women's officers who could barely meet their registrar or whatever and when they did they were told that legally nothing could be done. But then Sajid Javid appeared.

What took Amoah and many others by surprise early on in her second year in office was the announcement of a taskforce to help reduce violence against women and girls on university campuses by Business Secretary Sajid Javid (UK Government Department for Business, Innovation & Skills, 2015). The taskforce was to work with the sector to develop a code of practice to bring about cultural change, leverage existing complaints mechanisms more effectively, and improve engagement with Crime Prevention Officers. Amoah saw an opportunity:

> It was all there in the press release. A code of practice and a kitemark scheme was all well and good but they'd also mentioned better complaints mechanisms and the Equalities Act 2010 and its Public Sector Equality Duty. That was it then. We had to use that taskforce to get Zellick abolished.

What then ensued was a frantic period of attempting to persuade members of the taskforce that a central plank of their work had to include revising advice for universities on the practice of automatically referring cases to the police. Amoah had been prevented from joining the taskforce itself – that role went to the NUS President at the time, Megan Dunn – but that allowed Amoah to get to work on persuading the members of the committee of her case:

> I just worked around, one by one, trying to get to every member to a point where it had to happen. Where a VC or a registrar was on there I spent hours with the SU's President or whatever to get them to pile the pressure on. There were all these other campaigns springing up but I knew that without this all the toolkits and the shiny report at the end would be meaningless.

The eventual decision of the taskforce to commission law firm Pinsent Masons to revise guidance (see Pinsent Masons and Universities UK, 2016) was a significant moment – but there was also the content of the wider guidance to attend to. If universities were to process and tackle incidents of sexual violence and misconduct on campus, they needed to support survivors properly too. And part of the problem was that much of the development of the work was being done without their voices in the mix:

> It was like all these taskforces – lots of people running universities and the odd stakeholder. But I remember us saying we need to get in, in the rooms where they're deciding what the guidance is. So we did a really quick consultation with activists and groups and officers on campus and said, what's your dream system for dealing with sexual violence, what, what would that look like? It poured out of them. They had ideas for training, investigation systems that are survivor-centred, what a fair process would feel like. Of course they had all the answers. It's just that no-one had ever asked them.

Amoah gives the impression that this kind of survivor/trauma-informed approach had never dawned on those she had been deadline with nationally or locally – which she puts down to deeply ingrained ideas of authority and power that prevent Higher Education leaders from believing that they might have something to learn from students. And there seems little evidence that this has gone away. But attitudes were not the only issue – as Amoah was working to build momentum, she also came to see the role of Universities UK, NUS, and even the central administrations of Oxford and Cambridge as a major barrier to both this and wider change:

> They are all there to defend their own members and to protect the reputa-
> tion of their sector. I remember someone senior in Universities UK saying
> that they would back a lot of our recommendations but that they would stop
> short of agreeing that there should be regulation, like we'll say universities
> should do this but you can't make them do it! Why? People in NUS would
> tell me that we have to take SUs with us. And the Oxbridge people were like
> mafia bosses protecting the colleges from external influences like fairness.

What is clear from Amoah's commendable period in office is the extent to which student leadership is able and capable of providing legitimate challenge, policy and legal analysis, and survivor- and student-centred solutions to problems when others will not or cannot. What is less clear is why student leaders of her calibre both then and now faced such opposition and hostility for doing so. Maybe that was old-fashioned, everyday, and deeply embedded racism in HE?

Hareem Ghani (2016–2018): interventions, staff, and students as experts

The report of the Universities UK taskforce examining violence against women, harassment, and hate crime affecting university students finally published in October 2016, alongside new guidelines offering advice to universities on handling alleged student misconduct which may also constitute a criminal offence. One of the recommendations in the report that had caught the eye of the press had been the idea that universities should roll out "consent" education – partly because controversy over the tactic had landed on the desk of Amoah's successor just days before:

> Well the report came out in the October, and a few weeks before there had
> been a case at York University where a guy was saying there was a walkout
> from a sexual consent workshop and the story was taken up by all these
> media outlets (Sandhu, 2016). Of course it turned out that that hadn't hap-
> pened, in fact just a tiny handful of people had left, but obviously, it kind
> of garnered a lot of attention. And it kind of fed into this idea of what if
> people don't consent to taking part in consent education. And so I had to
> put together a piece for the Independent in which corrected the story. But
> I knew that if people weren't convinced by consent education it wasn't
> going to work, and that the battles over it would end up being a distraction.

Where Ghani got to was a two-pronged approach. First, she was convinced that it was student–student, "train the trainer" peer-delivered workshops and training that would have the most impact – partly on the assumption that sex and relationship education delivered by authority figures in schools plainly wasn't working, so any suggestion that that type of approach would work in universities was probably faulty. Second, Ghani reasoned that on their own, consent workshops weren't going to have the desired effect because while some of the issue was about the education and awareness of perpetrators, some of it was that other people didn't step in to stop it from happening:

> The problem was this idea that knowledge alone was power. Once they did know and you listened to them, what they would say is OK, but how would we stop it? They wanted to know what to do if their friends were going too far, or if they were at an event and saw something inappropriate. They wanted to know how to intervene.

Ghani had ended up being a member of the body charged with distributing grant funding to seed practice projects across universities arising from the Changing the Culture report, and found herself encouraging the adoption of several bystander intervention initiatives that she worried might not be scalable in the long term. But she also found herself worrying that good work on awareness might build confidence in reporting, only for internal practice to fail victims at a later hurdle. Fundamentally, she found a lack of depth in commitments to work with students:

> A lot of it felt very superficial. So it felt like a lot of universities were applying for this funding, because they knew that they needed to be seen to be doing something. A lot of them would say we've partnered up with our students union to do this. But when you asked the students union, they would say they weren't really involved, they were just asked for a nice quote for the form. And my other concern was just because you've got the SU on board, doesn't mean you've got student involvement. Hardly any of the projects thought about how you'd get actual student experiences into design or delivery, and some then complained afterwards that the SU officer had been flaky or whatever! As if it was their fault.

What Ghani had noted is that where student officers began to discuss sexual violence on campus as part of the projects, they became lightning rods for disclosure in ways that many found difficult to cope with:

> There's this idea I think that as long as the policy is clear on a website or whatever that students will come forward. Well maybe that's true but what I kept getting was that student leaders who were promoting projects kept getting disclosures. I think it's too easy to say "well they should have just referred them on" – there's something really important about students needing to talk

to and be supported by other students with this kind of thing. You have to be really careful about burdening amateurs but you also have to recognise how important it is that students are helped to support each other.

The recommendations from the Changing the Culture report and the projects that flowed from it were broadly well received by student activists and campaigners – but there was one significant problem. While the work had shone a spotlight on student–student misconduct, the documents were almost completely silent on the issues surrounding staff–student misconduct – a situation that Amoah's successor was keen to change:

> I remember at the time, there was a lot of criticism because it didn't focus on staff sexual harassment, and that was a problem because although there had been various bursts of "Me Too" activity around various sectors, nothing had happened in HE, which was weird because everyone we knew had stories of some lecturer or tutor that students avoided. So as well as work on consent and bystanders, it sort of became my priority campaign for the two years.

Like her predecessors, Ghani realised quickly that research was likely to be a key weapon, and worked with the 1752 Group to conduct the first-ever national survey in the UK examining staff sexual misconduct in Higher Education. "Power in the Academy" collated responses from 1839 current and former students, and found:

- Women respondents were around three times more likely than men to experience negative impacts because of misconduct;
- Four in ten respondents who were current students had experienced at least one experience of sexualised behaviour from staff (585 out of 1,535)
- Fewer than one in ten respondents who experienced staff sexual misconduct reported this to their institution.

(NUS and the 1752 Group, 2018)

Yet unlike the work surrounding students which had eventually found widespread support, Ghani found that work involving staff circled back to barriers surrounding reputation and power:

> So much of it was geared towards protecting the reputation of the institution, which meant that sometimes even if a staff member had all these allegations against them, well, they're a well known staff member. So it's better to keep them at the institution or just basically ask them to take leave for a few months and then return than to actually get rid of them completely.
>
> I remember a particular case at a university where I was approached by two people, because their lecturer had been inappropriate with them. And he was never suspended – at the time, he was just told, I think, to go on

leave or something along those lines, he just wasn't going to be teaching for that term. The signal that sends to victims is clear – you might say "Zero Tolerance" but in reality there's no repercussions – even if you tell them to go on leave, they're probably gonna be paid for that leave. So who are these actions serving because they're sure as hell not serving the survivor, the victim, they're serving, actually interests of the professor and the university.

Ultimately, for Ghani, the issue was about power – and the lack of understanding that universities had of the power that students felt was wielded over them by staff:

One of the conversations I kept having to have was people taking issue with rules around student staff relationships. They'd say well these people are adults, and they should be able to dictate for themselves who they want to have relationships with, these students are over 18. So the idea that you're going to tell them who they can and can't, you know, have relationships with or whatever is patronising. So part of what we were trying to do was shift that to say actually, yes, they may be adults, but there is this issue of the balance of power here. That lecturer has massively more power than the student, and so we need to think of it in that light as well.

Was that lack of understanding about naivety, a lack of listening, or a deeper unwillingness to be challenged? For Ghani, too much of it felt like a deep unwillingness to learn from or at least to be seen as learning from, those that universities are supposed to be teaching:

A lot of these students are coming in with a lot more knowledge and they know stuff that these senior academics who have all these accolades don't necessarily know, and the idea of learning from students is seen as embarrassing, but I don't understand it because surely the whole point of working in Higher Education is the idea that you dedicated your life to the pursuit of knowledge. And it doesn't matter where that knowledge comes from, whether it's a student, or whether that's an academic or whether I don't know, a book. But I also just think it also ultimately also comes down to the fact that a lot of senior leadership don't take students seriously. They assume it's dramatising and dismiss it instead of being curious about it.

In the end, Ghani's message for universities is similar to the message for all authorities when it comes to sexual violence. Start by believing women.

People don't just do things just for the sake of causing noise. It's only when they become frustrated that the change isn't happening or is taking too long to happen. So instead of being proud that they've trained the activism out of the student officers in the SU, they should be more proactive in terms of making links with student activists that have something to say about the university, taking their concerns on board and being receptive to what it is that their students are saying.

Conclusion: student leadership as the solution to problems

Since Ghani's time in office, student leadership on the issues has continued to flourish. Sarah Lasoye (2018–2019) was able to extend work into the Further Education sector by launching a study of students' experiences and perceptions of sexual harassment, violence, and domestic abuse in colleges. Rachel Watters (2019–2020) extended work on consent and launched a project in collaboration with AVA (Against Violence and Abuse) and UUK (Universities UK) on a "whole university approach" to misconduct on campus. Following a period of financial difficulty, NUS abolished the role of National Womens' Officer in 2020.

When stories of institutional and social change are published, there is a tendency to talk either of the leadership on offer from victims or "on the ground" activists, or alternatively to describe the travails of pushing through change faced by politicians and policymakers. Yet in Higher Education in the UK, these sorts of approaches tend to sideline the significant contribution from student leaders, who exist in a kind of third space. Bols (2015) describes "Chameleonic" as an important characteristic of the student representative – the idea that they need to be able to engage in the "management speak" so that they will be listened to more by the institution, but also be able to switch back and be able to relate to ordinary or activist students, and speak about education and the student experience in an engaging way.

That is difficult enough when discussing assessment feedback or the priorities for a new building, but what of the issues surrounding sexual violence in Higher Education? When "Hidden Marks" was published, Liv Bailey may have refused to "speak the management speak" on offer from Buckingham's vice-chancellor, but the adoption of a "research findings" approach gave her, successors, and the activists she represented the ability to get into rooms, spark debate, and engender change in attitudes and practice that had not been seen previously.

The twists and turns of the story since "Hidden Marks" offer insights and lessons for anyone wishing to engender social change. Treading the tightrope of advancing arguments within the understanding frames of decision-makers while being careful to use the opportunities that generates to shift the narrative is one thing; being prepared to channel anger about injustice in ways that play to concerns about reputation is another. Being concerned with matters of institutional policy rather than project funding is a mistake made by many a student leader; writing off the concerns of activists and students as passing political fad rather than a canary in the coalmine of student harms is a mistake made by many a policymaker and institutional leader.

What is obvious is that more often than not, the work of student representatives is vital to the success of change within the Higher Education sector. Both "ordinary students" and activists, and policymakers and university leaders, benefit from their tenacity, commitment, bravery, and leadership. We should do all we can to support them, remove barriers to their effectiveness, and above all listen and always be willing to learn.

Further Reading

National Union of Students. (2010). *Hidden Marks: a study of women students' experiences of harassment, stalking, violence and sexual assault.* **www.nusconnect.org.uk/resources/hidden-marks-a-study-of-women-students-experiences-of-harassment-stalking-violence-and-sexual-assault**

NUS' ground-breaking Hidden Marks report showed that two-thirds of women students had experienced a form of harassment, and one in seven had experienced serious physical or sexual assault. While critiques of claims to accuracy over prevalence prevail to this day given the self-selection of respondents to the survey component, the survey results and associated policy recommendations were arguably the first time that a national body managed to demonstrate and highlight that the perpetrators of student sexual misconduct were more likely to be drawn from within a university than outside of it.

National Union of Students. (2012). *That's what she said: women students' experiences of 'lad culture' in Higher Education.* **http://sro.sussex.ac.uk/id/eprint/49011/**

NUS' follow up report sought to identify some of the contributory causes to a campus culture that had normalised some of the findings in Hidden Marks. *That's what she said* interviewed students who described a "prevailing sexism, laddism and a culture of harassment" at their universities and kicked off a national debate surrounding "lad culture" on campus.

Note

1 An incel (an abbreviation of "involuntary celibate") is a member of an online subculture of people who define themselves as unable to get a romantic or sexual partner despite desiring one. Discussions in incel forums are often characterised by resentment and hatred, misogyny, misanthropy, self-pity and self-loathing, racism, a sense of entitlement to sex, and the endorsement of violence against women and sexually active people.

References

Bols, A. (2015, 24 November). Enhancing student representation systems. *Wonkhe.* https://wonkhe.com/blogs/enhancing-studtation-systems/

Ghani, H. (2016, 1 October). Sexual consent classes at universities are not 'patronising' – this is not a simple 'yes' or 'no' issue. *The Independent.* www.independent.co.uk/voices/sexual-consent-classes-universities-are-not-patronising-a7341031.html

Kirby, T. (2009, 23 September). *Academic: Why I said that pretty women students are a perk.* Evening Standard. www.standard.co.uk/hp/front/academic-why-i-said-that-pretty-women-students-are-a-perk-6749948.html

Lynskey, D. (2013, November 13). Blurred lines: The most controversial song of the decade. *The Guardian*. www.theguardian.com/music/2013/nov/13/blurred-lines-most-controversial-song-decade

National Union of Students. (2010). *Hidden marks: A study of women students' experiences of harassment, stalking, violence and sexual assault*. www.nusconnect.org.uk/resources/hidden-marks-a-study-of-women-students-experiences-of-harassment-stalking-violence-and-sexual-assault

National Union of Students. (2012). *That's what she said: Women students' experiences of 'lad culture' in Higher Education*. http://sro.sussex.ac.uk/id/eprint/49011/

National Union of Students. (2015). *How to respond to complaints of sexual violence: The Zellick report*. www.nusconnect.org.uk/resources/how-to-respond-to-complaints-of-sexual-violence-the-zellick-report

National Union of Students and the 1752 Group. (2018). *Power in the academy*. www.nusconnect.org.uk/resources/nus-staff-student-sexual-misconduct-report

Pinsent Masons and Universities UK. (2016). *Guidance for higher education institutions: How to handle alleged student misconduct*. www.universitiesuk.ac.uk/topics/equality-diversity-and-inclusion/guidance-higher-education-institutions

Sandhu, S. (2016, October 2). York Uni sexual consent row: Ben Froughi explains why he thinks students should boycott classes. *I News*. https://inews.co.uk/news/uk/york-student-encouraged-boycott-rape-consent-classes-explains-23872

UK Government Department for Business, Innovation & Skills. (2015). *Business secretary calls on universities to tackle violence against women on campus*. www.gov.uk/government/news/business-secretary-calls-on-universities-to-tackle-violence-against-women-on-campus

Welsh Assembly Government. (2010). *The right to be safe, a six year integrated strategy for tackling violence against women*. www.thewi.org.uk/__data/assets/pdf_file/0007/49885/100325besafefinalenv1.pdf

Williams, M. (2013, April 5). Student 'lad culture': The hidden victims of sexual abuse. *The Guardian*. www.theguardian.com/education/2013/apr/05/lad-culture-hidden-victims-of-sexual-abuse.

4 Intersectional approaches to gender-based violence in universities

Experiences and interventions

Geetanjali Gangoli and Cassandra Jones

Gender-based violence (GBV) is understood to be any act of violence and abuse that disproportionately affects women, and is rooted in systematic power differences and inequalities between women and men (Hester & Lilley, 2014). For the purposes of this chapter, GBV includes domestic violence and abuse, including coercive control, abuse mediated through the internet or mobile phones; stalking and harassment; 'honour-based' violence and abuse, including forced marriage; and sexual violence and abuse (cf. Gangoli et al., 2020). There is an international body of evidence indicating that one-third to one-half of university students are subjected to GBV during their time at university (e.g., Australian Human Rights Commission, 2017; Fedina et al., 2018), and nearly 16% of students have been subjected to GBV before joining university (Fisher et al., 2000). These diverse experiences have a profound impact on the lives of the victims and survivors, and their experience of Higher Education (e.g., Australian Human Rights Commission, 2017; Stenning et al., 2012).

While there is a wide body of work on GBV in the UK and internationally, there is a paucity of material that highlights the voices of victim-survivors in general (see Mulvihill et al., 2018); and in particular with victim-survivors of GBV in UK universities settings. This chapter draws on the conceptual framework of intersectionality (Crenshaw, 1991) to explore this in the context of GBV in university settings in the UK. We use the concepts of intersectionality to explore unique and original empirical interview data that address diverse women's experiences of GBV while at university, including university responses. We will explore women's positioning in terms of gender, student identity, ethnicity, and social class.

The research question guiding this study is: How do the intersections between GBV, universities, and women's societal positioning manifest to enable students to achieve their potential or disable women from achieving their potential within Higher Education, and what role can universities play in terms of interventions? We understand interventions as being both individualized, that is, instinctual/organic interventions, for example, steps taken by students and university staff to ensure their own safety, or those of their friends or students deliberate/planned interventions, such as counselling programmes and feminist societies.

DOI: 10.4324/9781003252474-5

The chapter will start by explaining the conceptual frameworks we use, and then explore key issues emerging from literature on GBV in university settings. Next, there will be a brief description of research methods for the interview data, moving on looking at key themes emerging from the sample. Finally, we will discuss the findings and the implications of the research.

Conceptual frameworks

We draw on the conceptual framework on intersectionality, which we understand as 'the notion that subjectivity is constituted by mutually reinforcing vectors of race, gender, class and sexuality' (Nash, 2008, p. 2). Kimberlé Crenshaw (1991) is credited with introducing the term 'intersectionality' to the feminist lexicon in the late 1980s as part of antiracist struggles that interrogated law's penchant in fixing identities, and therefore not paying enough attention to how Black women may suffer from both race and gender inequalities. Nash has argued that the notion of intersectionality is under-theorised, suggesting that it has focused so far on how marginalised people are (adversely) affected by their identities, rather than how those in power are able to use intersectional identities to their advantage. Victims have multiple identities and while some combinations disempower them, others might privilege them in some ways (for example, being a wealthy woman with disabilities).

Linked to this is Nils Christie's notion of the 'ideal victim' (1986) wherein some victims are deemed more readily deserving of the status than others, because they are weak (very old or young), they are performing a 'respectable project', and they cannot be blamed for being where they were. This construction has rightly been challenged as not recognising women's agency (Roberts et al., 2019), but is useful in this context in recognising how universities may respond.

Groups that may be most vulnerable to GBV in universities include young women and girls (Jones et al., 2020), those with disabilities (both mental and physical), or those from ethnic minority, working-class, or LGBTQ+ communities (Healthy Poverty Action, 2021). We believe that it is impossible to discuss the complexities of GBV without due attention to multiple sites of oppression, and privilege, and this is what we aim to explore further in this chapter by looking at how intersecting identities may impact on women's experiences of navigating Higher Education and GBV.

Setting the scene

Studies on GBV experienced by UK university students are relatively new in comparison to studies on US universities, but this body of literature is growing rapidly and thus far provides findings consistent with previous research in the United States (e.g., Krebs et al., 2017) and Australia (Australian Human Rights Commission, 2017). Most UK studies focused on sexual violence (SV) and used a range of operational definitions, research designs, and recruitment strategies to assess prevalence (Jones et al., 2020). Inconsistent methods led to findings varying from 31% to 77% of all students being subjected to SV (Cambridge University Students' Union, 2014; Edinburgh University Student Association, 2014) and from 37% to 68% of women being subjected to SV (Neville et al., 2014; Phipps & Smith, 2012). Despite these variations, the findings indicate that at best a substantial minority are subjected to SV, and at worst a majority of students are subjected to SV. Some university responses to disclosures have further compounded the trauma. Half of students who reported to their university described the university's response as denying what they had been subjected to, and 30.9% described the university's response as suggesting that their report could negatively impact the university's reputation (NUS, 2018). This is not to say that all university responses have been negative. One-quarter of students thought their university supported them after they made a report (NUS, 2018). These radically different responses have been attributed to wider institutional cultures (Bull & Rye, 2018) but they may also be influenced by preconceptions of which students are 'ideal victims'. Students deemed to be performing a 'respectable project' and not threatening the university's reputation may be the ones to receive a supportive response from universities. However, it is difficult to untangle how these preconceptions may influence university responses until more studies investigate other forms of inequality associated with and intersecting with GBV in universities, and universities' responses.

There are some excellent studies that address the intersectional role of racism, class, disability, and gender/sexuality in university students' experiences (Vaccaro, 2010; Vaccaro et al., 2020; Willis et al., 2019), but these do not always address intersections with GBV (Jones et al., 2020). Findings from these studies were consistent with previous research on GBV (e.g., Coulter et al., 2017) in that they indicated that occupying positions of less social power (e.g., women, Black, and Minority Ethnic) had an increased chance of experiencing SV and/or domestic violence (EUSA, 2014; Young et al., 2018), but there was less discussion on the experiences of these women in Higher Education.

There are a few studies using quantitative methods that look at the role of Higher Education as a protective factor for GBV (Aramsky et al., 2011). Campbell's study (2004) shows that women who had the lowest education levels were more likely to be killed by their male partners in comparison to women who were emotionally abused. There are also recent studies that look at the ways in which control over education or 'educational sabotage' by perpetrators can be a form of emotional abuse in cases of domestic violence (Voth Schrag et al., 2019) and forced marriage (Gangoli et al., 2011). This is often exercised as a part of financial abuse and can have severe consequences in terms of women's ability to escape the abuse.

There is a body of important work addressing how schools could respond to domestic violence and intimate partner violence witnessed or experienced by students (Dunne et al., 2006; Ollis, 2017; Lloyd, 2018, Barter et al., 2015), but there is very little on how universities may address the issue with students who may have been subjected to interpersonal violence or other forms of GBV in their parental home, or in relationships outside the university. Indeed, no UK study could be located which provided baseline data on student experiences of sexual and domestic violence, sexual harassment, and other related harm that students come with when they start university. As far as we are aware, there is very little UK-based research on the role that Higher Education can play in protecting victims of GBV where the perpetrators may not be part of the university communities, but are family members, friends, or acquaintances of the victim.

An important recent exception is the work by Phipps (2020) and more recently by Ahmed (2021) that situates sexual harassment and violence and institutional inaction in the neoliberal university. Phipps (2020) and Ahmed (2021) address this in the context of universities being subjected to increasing tuition fees, and a transformation from liberal universities as a space for critical thought, slow contemplation, and transformative becoming for both student and university worker. The neoliberal university aims to continuously increase performance – measurable in ultimately economic terms, imposing a new auditable disciplining, and quickening pace of learning, thinking, and working. When students complain of sexual harassment in this context, their complaints are articulated – and also dismissed – in the language of consumer rights.

Further, while there is research on young South Asian people's experiences of forced marriage and 'honour based' violence and abuse (cf. Gangoli et al., 2020), and some of these point to how some young women in particular use Higher Education as a way to postpone or escape forced marriage (see, for example, Gangoli et al., 2011). However, the specific experiences of and university responses to young people in universities being subjected to these forms of GBV are not addressed.

Methods

The Justice, Inequality, and GBV project team[1] consisted of ten experienced researchers. We conducted interviews with 251 victim-survivors of GBV. Most participants were interviewed individually (*n* = 227; 87%), with the remaining participants (*n* = 24; 9%) taking part in group interviews. The project sought and gained research ethics approval from the University of Bristol ethics board. The research design was phenomenological, as the intention of the research was to understand the meanings of justice from the perspectives of victim-survivors of GBV (Williamson et al., 2020). Following this design, participants were recruited by asking partner agencies, and other agencies working in the field of gender-based violence prevention to send information about the project to their service users. We offered language interpretation, or other support for the interviews. In total, we recruited participants through more than 80 different organisations, and these organisations supported the victim-survivors. The interviews were conducted in person, over the phone, or using online telecommunication software, and included some specific demographic and experience-related questions, including age, income, employment, and education. We asked questions about GBV they had been subjected to and tried to explore what justice meant to them both abstractly, and in the context of their own experience. Interviews lasted between an hour and two hours, with the average interview just over an hour. All the interviews were recorded, and transcribed verbatim either by a team member, or a professional transcriber, and pseudonyms were allotted to each participant.

Sample

While the aim of the interviews was not to look at university-based experiences of, or responses to gender-based violence, during analysis, we found that a subsect of respondents (*n* =10) had been in university during some of their experiences of gender-based violence. All were university students, and one was also a university lecturer who was studying for her PhD at the time of interview.

One of these had been at university over 20 years before the interview, and this respondent was removed from the sample. The majority of respondents (7/9) had decided to enter Higher Education as a response to GBV. Closer analysis of the material for this chapter revealed that some of the respondents had found that university services and structures had influenced their experiences. These interviews have been analysed at greater depth to analyse the intersections between education and victim-survivors' experiences of GBV.

This chapter will draw from the nine interviews, as explained earlier. We found that all but one participant were under the age of 30 at the time of the abuse; six of nine were white British women, one was Indian, and two were British Pakistani. The three Black and Minority Ethnic women in our sample had experienced GBV linked with forced marriage and 'honour based' violence. Eight women in our sample had experienced sexual violence and abuse, most commonly in the context of intimate partner abuse, and one had experienced sexual abuse as a child. Half of the women interviewed experienced domestic violence and coercive control. The three BME women in our sample identified as middle class. Of the white sample, two clearly identified as middle class, one as working class, one as mixed (middle-class father, but brought up with working-class mother), and two did not disclose their class status. See Table 4.1 for demographic information on each case, as well as the form(s) of GBV experienced, and help sought.

Findings

Our findings indicate that all our respondents came with previous or ongoing experiences of GBV both within and outside universities structures. We also found that the intersections between GBV, university structures, and women's identities, for example, class, sexuality/ethnicity/nationality, impacted on their experiences of higher education, and that university responses were mediated by these intersecting identities.

Table 4.1 Participant demographics, forms of gender-based violence experienced, and sources of support

Name*	Social class	Ethnicity/ nationality	Age at time of abuse	Nature of abuse	Help sought
Asha	Middle class	Indian	17–25	Forced marriage/ honour-based violence	University well-being services, police, immigration services
Gemma	Missing information	White British	21–25	Coercive control, physical abuse, unwanted sexual contact	Police, friend at university, family
Rachel	Missing information	White British	15–24	Three separate incidents of rape	Counsellor, friend at university
Melody	Working class	White British	15–19, 25	Physical confinement, sexual, coercive control, emotional, financial control, online harassment. Rape post-separation	Police, family
Sameera	Middle class	British Pakistani	20–30	Forced marriage, honour-based violence, rape, physical violence, confinement	Police, natal and marital family, college/ university and workplace
Amani	Middle class	British Pakistani	23–28	Forced marriage, honour-based violence, rape, physical violence, coercive control, financial control	Police, natal family, friends
Maria	Working-class mother and middle-class father	White British	20–40	Multiple experiences of intimate partner violence by three different perpetrators; sexual abuse, acid throwing	Police, bystander (university classmate)
Anna	Middle class	White British	25	Domestic violence	Police, solicitor, counsellor, line manager at university,
Alena	Middle class	White Other	10, 18–25	Historic sexual abuse, domestic abuse	University sexual abuse services/activist group, police

*Names changed

Ethnicity

The negative impact of ethnicity was experienced particularly by the BME respondents. Two BME respondents reflected on the ways in which parents or partners used the financing of Higher Education to control women. Asha described her experience of her father constricting her ability to obtain higher education because he refused initially to pay for the education.

> *I had to come to university. I was meant to stay in the house for 6 months because my father was not sure whether I should go to uni or not go to uni. I had to go through a lot and finally (father) decided I could come to UK.*
>
> (Asha)

In another case, choosing higher education was one of the triggers for forced marriage, as the community and family saw this as a sign of the woman exercising their agency.

> *I got a job in (redacted) which was the trigger for the community saying I should get married. Also the trigger that I actually went to [name of university].*
>
> (Amani)

Lack of understanding of minority women's cultural and familial situations meant that, at times, university responses were perceived by students as minimising, or unhelpful. Sameera recounted that when her father threatened her with forced marriage; an academic, she confided in minimised her experience.

> *[B]ut nobody really knew what to do, and (name of college lecturer) was the worst in the sense. . . . I said look I know they're going to marry me off, my dad's going to marry me off, you've got to help me. And she basically said 'That's a nice jumper you're wearing'. . . . [I]t was very much 'Do you really want to go [to a refuge]?' . . . Go home, you've got a nice jumper, you're not going to get that in a [refuge]' you know 'If you've got it bad now, you wait till you get in a [refuge]'*
>
> (Sameera)

Our findings indicate that international students are less likely to be able to access support and welfare systems than British students. Asha spoke of her experience when she was being threatened by her father and coerced into leaving the country to return to her family home.

> *But the harder bit is if you're not a British Citizen I don't know how they can help you, to be really honest, because . . . they can't really do much.*

There is . . . because there is no . . . legal laws in place for someone who is not a British Citizen, on how to help them out with their protection and everything. Yes, they'll help them in this country, but there's nothing that anyone else can do once you go away.

(Asha)

Social class, gender, and ethnicity

Our sample demonstrate a correlation between social class, race/ethnicity, and access to education. All the three BME women in our sample were middle class, while the white women were more diverse in terms of their class composition. The woman who seemed to have the best outcome in terms of university response to her abuse was a middle-class, white woman.

I come from a very lucky middle class white affluent background, very lucky upbringing, very happy, never had to worry about anything .

(Anna)

Anna also enjoyed social capital, in terms of family links with the police:

Some friends were involved in helping get me out of the situation. One of them's a retired police officer, and also my uncle and aunt are both retired police officers. So I was very lucky, I had a lot of help from family and friends.

Anna was both a university lecturer and a student at the time of the abuse, and found her line manager at work extremely supportive:

Um . . . it was a very new job, I think it was a week into a new job as a part time lecturer, and I told my boss as soon as it happened. And he . . . has been fantastic. . . . They've let me have days off to go to the lawyer, they've understood if my work hasn't been great . . . yeah I have been really well supported.

Anna was able to access counselling through her work, when she found that the NHS waiting lists were too long:

So I went to the doctor's too and they gave me a prescription to help me sleep. And I asked them about counselling and they told me that the waiting list was over 6 months. So it wasn't worth trying to get counselling through them. . . . I've just had some counselling now through my job. . . . I've had 9 or 10 sessions with a counsellor, and it's made massive. . . . I feel absolutely fine now, it's made a massive difference to me.

In contrast, Maria, a working-class student doing a professional postgraduate degree, who was undergoing domestic abuse at the hands of her partner, who was also her colleague at a professional internship she was working on towards her degree, found that her practice manager was not supportive, and chose to support her partner when she filed a complaint against him of domestic violence in a public space. The respondent at the time filed a counter-claim that Maria had sexually harassed him, and his violence was in response to this:

> *[I]nitially I was banned from our office, I couldn't go there, he could stay. Yeah yeah, that was my [practice manager's] decision, that I cannot come back to the office. So I was just put somewhere in exile when I was reinstated back to work.*

Gemma, a working-class white woman commented on how her class made her an outsider in the university:

> *So I was the one with a [regional] accent, tattoos and piercings, and everyone else was posh. I think the professors took them more seriously.*

Social class did not always protect BME women. Sameera reflected on the reality that immigrant women often did not enjoy the same class privileges as they would have in their country of origin:

> *[T]his isn't about what class or how educated you are. . . . [B]asically educated women . . . and it surprises me because the educated women I was talking to . . . .and they were like . . . oh I didn't realise that my degree here it isn't internationally recognised . . . they didn't realise the power of their own degree is missing.*

Empowerment through university

For three respondents, GBV was either a stimulus for entering Higher Education, or gave them the skills to escape it. Engaging in Higher Education in itself was a form of individualised intervention for these women. Maria explained that her ability to survive domestic abuse in a previous relationship gave her the confidence to enter Higher Education:

> *For me, it (abuse) was a bit of a catalyst to change then. . . . It changed my life, yes, because it was that terrifying at the time. I genuinely don't know how I got through it. So when you go through something like that, you do think, 'Actually, I can cope with anything.' So I went into terrifying education.*

Gemma, who was experiencing domestic abuse from her partner at the time of studying, found that university was a safe space for her:

> *I mean I was at university through three years of this relationship, so I would find that probably . . . and I was at placements and things . . . and so yeah I suppose I would find it a bit of an escape sometimes.*

Two respondents believed that they were able to process and understand their experiences of gender-based violence better because of the nature of their education. Gemma explained that she was able to explain what was happening to her better to her friends, because she was studying domestic violence at university, and was also able to understand it herself better.

> *When I read up on it (domestic violence) you know I can tell them [the class] things. . . . [I]t makes a lot more sense to them, and it makes more sense to me now as well.*

(Gemma)

Bystander interventions

Four of our respondents testified to the important role that bystander intervention can play in cases of GBV. Maria, a working-class woman, describes her experience when her abusive partner entered her classroom during a lecture, and no one in authority intervened to stop him:

Respondent: **The security guards didn't bother to come in.**
Interviewer: Really?
Respondent: **No, they didn't bother at all. The teacher picked the camera up and ran off, because they were videoing us that day. So she picked the camera up and ran off.**

(Maria)

Another respondent described her experience of sexual assault on public transport, while she was travelling to her university. No one on the train platform intervened, including some students from her university who were present at the time.

> *While I was saying, 'Can someone, please, go and get help?' I was yelling, and they could see very clearly an attack. Like stereotypical attack situation . . . I can't understand why people wouldn't want to intervene . . . I don't really understand why somebody wouldn't run out and get the police, who were already in the station.*

(Melody)

While lack of, or negative responses from bystanders was upsetting, our respondents spoke of the responses from friends being even more important in terms of their self-esteem. Rachel, who was raped on a night out talks about how her friend stonewalled her experience:

> *[M]aybe about 5, 6 months afterwards, I said to one of my friends . . . I told her that I'd been raped, and this was when I was like . . . And I said to her that I'd been raped, and . . . he was there at an event that was happening*

where I was with her . . . [we both] saw him, and I said to her 'Oh he did that to me'. And um . . . yeah so she knew but never asked me anything else about it. . . . No, she never mentioned it again.

(Rachel)

Rachel believes that the lack of response from her friend led her to 'clam up for years' about her experience.

In contrast, supportive responses from friends felt enabling for survivors, and gave them courage to deal with their experiences. Gemma, who was subjected to domestic violence from her partner, spoke about how she was able to share her experience with a friend who was also a victim of domestic violence at the time:

I had one friend who knew what was going on throughout the whole relationship, because she was going through something similar as well, so I felt I could speak to her.

(Gemma)

Other than listening, friends can sometimes offer support in other, more direct ways, particularly in validating women's experiences of abuse:

Yeah like a lot of my friends would say God help him if he ever runs into me. He actually . . . on court day he actually . . . I was with one of my friends came to support me, and he tried to speak to her on that day, and she just told him like fuck off basically. She ended up getting warned off [by] the security at the court because she was getting high pitched and stuff, but she was just so angry, she couldn't believe that he was actually approaching her. But yeah she's like 'God, I wanted to hit him'.

(Gemma)

Positive response from university services

Clear and efficient organisational response can increase the capabilities of women in situations of gender-based violence. This is clear when we look at Asha's experience. When she was at university in the UK, she converted to Christianity as an act of rebellion against her Hindu family and her father found out:

I don't exactly know how, if it was via my Facebook, or what really went on. But he found out and he threatened that, if I don't come back home, he's going to kill me, and he's not going to pay my fees any further. So that was . . . obviously I got really, really depressed and in fear of my life. At that time I was in contact with the University of xx Wellbeing Centre. They advised that this needs to be phoned to the police, because they were obviously worried, and I thought yeah maybe that's a good idea.

Asha also contacted the police at the behest of the Wellbeing services when she was threatened with death by her family, due to her relationship with a student in her university:

> *It was the Wellbeing [at the uni] which encouraged me to do that, because I otherwise wouldn't be . . . I would be really scared, I wouldn't know what to do, because of this situation where you don't know who you can trust, or what anyone can do. So I was told by them, if I contact them (police), they might be able to help me out, because my father's threatening me, and all of that, hence the reason I made contact.*

University peer groups and forums supported by the university also played an important role in enabling women to take action against gender-based violence. Three of our respondents were active in feminist debates and activism at university, and all of them attribute their involvement to their experience of abuse. For instance, Alena felt able to report her historical experience of sexual abuse to the police due to the support of the peer group in her university:

> *I was on the University [] Sexual Violence Forum for about five years the year after I went to uni. The police officer that came and was talking to us said, 'Basically, you can report it any time.' I was like, 'Oh, right.' So now, I was so much stronger, 20 years afterwards, I rang and reported it. I had a patrol officer come round to go through it with her. She was brilliant.*

Discussion

The findings indicate that the intersection of neoliberal educational systems, unequal immigration laws and policies, and lack of societal and peer empathy can exacerbate women's experience of gender-based violence in university settings. However, enabling factors – where they exist – can help survivors to escape and even transcend their abuse in an educational setting.

Our findings indicated that women entering Higher Education have a range of experiences of GBV. Many of these are experienced before they join colleges, and universities, but they continue to experience the long-term impacts of many of these incidents and experiences. Women also experience GBV during their time at universities, perpetrated by fellow students or staff, or by family members. University responses to these cases vary, but it is apparent that students are more likely to experience their time in Higher Education positively, and arguably gain more from their education where the response has been consistent, and experienced as helpful.

GBV and abuse is manifested in parental control over education. Current discourses on the neoliberalisation of Higher Education (Mahony & Weiner, 2019) in the UK and elsewhere (Saunders, 2007) address the impacts of tuition fees on student experience, and the growing consumerisation of Higher Education. Parental control over education through financing it, particularly in the case of international students who are not eligible to UK student loans, links directly to the idea of 'educational sabotage' (Voth Schrag, 2019). Educational sabotage can include financial and emotional abuse, and can further restrict women's choices to escape parental control. In the case of Asha, her father's refusal to pay her tuition fees can be understood within this prism, where she was unable to leave her home to join university until her father agreed. We can also see other forms of educational sabotage in the case of Maria's experience, where her abusive partner came to her university during a lecture to disrupt her education, and invade her safe space.

As evident from Asha's experience, the intersection of gender, ethnicity, and discriminatory immigration laws further complicates the experience of gender-based violence for international women students (cf. Gangoli et al., 2020). Higher Education can sometimes be used as a way to postpone or avoid forced marriage (Gangoli et al. 2020), but at other times it can be a trigger for forced marriage. Recent research on sexual violence and abuse among refugee and asylum-seeking communities (Bates et al., 2018) highlighted issues of immigration, familiarity with support systems, and lack of community support as key barriers in reporting 'honour based' and sexual abuse; and some of these may apply to international students on student visas.

Intersectional disadvantage can also be a product of what has been described in social work literature as 'race anxiety' (cf. Burman et al., 2004), and may be more accurately be understood as 'race related timidity'. Failure of those in power to intervene, due to lack of knowledge, or fear of appearing racist, can potentially cause harm. As implicit in Sameera's case, her lecturer was reluctant to intervene when she shared her experience of living in fear of forced marriage, and encouraged her to 'work with her family'. The response was experienced by Sameera as both insensitive and unhelpful. In contrast, positive intervention and advice by relevant university staff, which Asha received in the form of advice to approach the police, can empower victims in challenging the abuse.

University support can sometimes be indirect, for example, through university student groups, such as feminist support groups that may provide a safe space for students to reflect on, and process on past abuse and violence. This is apparent in Alena's experience, where she was able to articulate her abuse and seek help and redress for the historical abuse she had experienced.

Our research also indicated the importance of bystander intervention, which has been well-documented in literature (Fenton et al., 2016; Holland, 2019; Jones et al., 2015). Survivors of GBV can feel supported and empowered where bystanders respond positively to incidents of abuse. However, the reverse can happen where bystanders do not respond, and this can heighten when perpetrators enter university settings, previously experienced as safe spaces.

Victim-survivors of sexual and domestic violence sometimes choose to disclose their experiences to close friends or family members, in the hope of achieving an empathetic experience (Rodino-Colocino, 2018, Gregory et al., 2019). Research has demonstrated that friends and peers can act as buffers against effects of abuse and may also act as preventative factors for future abuse.

This is apparent in Gemma's experience, where her friends supported her during her traumatic experiencing of domestic abuse, and court hearings where she was confronting her abusive partner. Gemma's friend supported her throughout the journey, both by acting as an emphatic listener and by confronting her abusive partner during a court hearing.

However, negative or non-responses from friends and family can have a negative impact on victim-survivors, who can feel further silenced and isolated. Gregory's research (2019) reveals that family and friends often lack the knowledge and training to respond in empowering ways, and sometimes may find the experience of being confided in traumatic in itself. As is apparent in Rachel's experience, her friend's lack of engagement with the abuse contributed to her feeling silenced for a number of years.

Much literature focuses on the negative impact of GBV on the ability of women to access higher education, or to fully partake in it (e.g., Loots & Walker, 2015). Earlier research by the authors (Gangoli et al., 2011) has found that young women at risk of forced marriage can often 'use' higher education as a way to escape family pressure, but this appears an instrumental use of education. In our research, we found that in some cases, abuse is a catalyst for change and education; and that some survivors experience higher education both as empowerment and as a route for escaping some forms of gender-based violence.

The findings also indicate that universities respond best when the victim is seen as the ideal victim (Christie, 1986). In this context, an ideal victim is a middle-class, white, and young woman. Anna, as a young, white British, middle-class woman, who was both university student and staff, enjoyed the best outcomes and interventions of all our respondents, including counselling provided by the university, and sympathy from her line manager. Class alone does not protect women from ethnic minority backgrounds, as is evident in Asha's and Sameera's examples. Asha did get some support, but due to her status as an international student, did not have access to all the resources that a British woman would have.

There has been some literature on the impact of conducting research on GBV by victim-survivors, and some of these suggest that most victim-survivors found the experience as beneficial, or even transformational (Aroussi, 2020). Aroussi points out that many survivors of rape and sexual abuse feel alone, and isolated, and the process of researching GBV can both validate their experience and reclaim their voice. Two of our respondents chose to study gender-based violence, and found that their experiences of abuse gave them both an insight into their own abuse, and some of the academic learning. This enabled them to process their abuse. In our view, this is an important finding, as it considers how higher education may enable some victims to make the journey to being survivors.

Conclusions

The unique contribution of this chapter is that it highlights the positive role that universities and Higher Education Institutions can play in tackling and empowering women experiencing gender-based violence and abuse. This sample testifies to the importance of the role of higher education for women with current or historic experiences of gender-based violence and abuse. It enables women to have a sense of agency and control over their own lives, and possibly to escape an abusive relationship. We also found that perpetrators are aware of the empowering role of education, and through 'educational sabotage' (Von Schrag, 2019) can try and control women's agency.

This study also builds on earlier work on the importance of intersectional inequalities for victim-survivors of gender-based abuse, particularly, but not exclusively, in the context of ethnicity, immigration status (Gangoli et al., 2020), and social class This is exacerbated by the neoliberal nature of the higher educational sector in the UK, where rising tuition fees and commodification of higher education makes it more difficult for women of working-class backgrounds to access higher education, and this access was further controlled by abusive partners or family members. Interestingly, some middle-class ethnic minority women used higher education as a way to escape forced marriage. The importance of higher education for survivors of gender-based abuse and violence is further evident in the experiences of women who were able to process and understand their abusive experiences better after entering university. This could be due to the nature of their educational programmes, the role of university support services, friends and bystanders, or feminist activism within university settings.

These finding have important implications for policy and practice in Higher Education. Higher Education Institutions have the potential to play a significant role to reduce the power of perpetrators by effective and timely interventions, including bystander programmes (Taylor & Paule-Koba, 2020) for students, training for staff and resources for student networking groups, particularly for women and other marginalised groups. We recognise that this study is based in the UK, but the findings and recommendations may have resonance in wider international contexts.

Summary of key points

- Victim-survivors have multiple identities and while some combinations further disempower them, others might privilege them in some ways (for example, a first-generation immigrant woman may be wealthy, and that can empower her as compared to a white British working-class student, but she would lack the benefits that the latter would have with regard to immigration rights).
- Linked to this is Nils Christie's notion of the 'ideal victim' (1986) wherein some victim-survivors are deemed more readily deserving of the status than others, they are performing a 'respectable project', and they cannot be blamed for being where they were.
- The methods used in data collection and the analysis was victim-survivor led.
- Some women begin university having already been subjected to some form of gender-based violence, while others were subjected to gender-based violence while attending university.

- The intersection of neoliberal educational systems, unequal immigration laws and policies, and lack of societal and peer empathy can exacerbate women's experience of gender-based violence in university settings.
- Gender-based violence can be a catalyst for change and education; and that some victim-survivors experience higher education both as empowerment and as a route for escape.
- The findings also indicate that universities respond best when the victim is seen as the ideal victim (Christie, 1986). In this context, an ideal victim is a middle class, white, and young woman.
- Class alone does not protect women from ethnic minority backgrounds, as is evident in Asha's and Sameera's examples. Asha did get some support, but due to her status as an international student, she did not have access to all the resources that a British woman would have.
- Higher Education Institutions have the potential to play a significant role to reduce the power of perpetrators by effective and timely interventions, including bystander programmes for students, training for staff, and resources for student networking groups, particularly for women and other marginalised groups.

Further Reading

Jones, C., Skinner, T. S., Gangoli, G., Smith, O., & Fenton, R. (2020). *Gender-based violence among UK university students and staff: A socio-ecological framework* . https://doi.org/10.5281/zenodo.4572506

Theories have been used to explain GBV in U.S. universities (e.g., Gervais et al., 2014; Tewksbury & Mustaine's, 2001) but they have limited utility in UK universities, as the history, composition, geography, and culture of UK universities differs (Phipps & Smith, 2012; Stenning et al., 2012). Due to these differences, a theoretical framework relevant to UK universities is needed that can guide studies and contextualise findings. As a starting point, this working paper adapted Hagemann-White et al.'s (2010) framework, which was developed for the European Union (EU). To date, this framework is the most researched, demonstrated and wholistic model for the EU. The framework used an ecological model to identify and categorise factors facilitating and scaffolding GBV, including policies, sanctions, redress and implementation of laws, to provide nation states with a framework to guide developing and implementing policies that would more effectively prevent and combat GBV. This working paper tailored Hagemann-White et al.'s model to UK universities, using a more sophisticated understanding of intersectional disadvantage (such as ethnicity, gender, sexuality, disability, class, age), men and masculinities, peer-group support for GBV, environmental time-space and power relations, and legal duties in prevention and response. The resulting model included six social systems: ontogenetic (intrapersonal), micro (interpersonal), meso (university), exo (wider community), macro (societal and national) and chrono (change and consistency over time). For each social system, a critical evaluation of research on factors facilitating perpetration in universities was presented, as well as recommendations for prevention and response.

Gangoli, G., Bates, L., & Hester, M. (2020). What does justice mean to black and minority ethnic (BME) victims/survivors of gender-based violence? *Journal of Ethnic and Migration Studies*. **doi: 10.1080/1369183X.2019.1650010**

This paper addresses how 'justice' is understood, sought, and experienced by BME victim-survivors of GBV within the UK. The key aims of this paper are to explore (a) experiences of GBV for BME victim-survivors, (b) their experiences and perceptions of justice, and (c) factors enabling, or posing barriers to justice, including immigration status. We situate BME women's experiences and conceptualisations of justice within an ecological approach (Hagemann-White et al., 2010) and within Bourdieu's conceptualisation of 'social capital' (1986). We found that migrant women lack access to vital aspects of social capital, that make access to justice particularly challenging, and that immigration status in particular poses key barriers in migrant women's experiences of accessing justice. Women and girls with insecure immigration status lack structural and state support to escape GBV. We also found that while there is a focus on 'cultural' factors in particular forms of GBV that BME women and girls may be subjected to (for example: 'honour based' violence, forced marriage and female genital mutilation), women reported structural factors as equally, if not more important in accessing justice.

Note

1 Justice, Inequality and GBV project (ESRC grant number ES/M010090/1) https:// research-information.bristol.ac.uk/en/projects/justice-inequality-and-gender-based-violence(49bc49cc-1db3-4675-b2ed-94a46555a0e9).html

References

Ahmed, S. (2021). *Complaint!* Duke University Press.

Aramsky, T., Watts, C. H., Garcia-Moreno, C., Devries, K., Kiss, L., Ellsberg, M., Jansen, H. A. F. M., & Heise, L. (2011). What factors are associated with recent intimate partner violence? Findings from the WHO multi-country study on women's health and domestic violence. *BMC Public Health*, *11*(109). doi:10.1186/1471-2458-11-109

Aroussi, S. (2020). Researching wartime rape in Eastern Congo: Why we should continue to talk to survivors? *Qualitative Research*, *20*(5), 582–597.

Australian Human Rights Commission. (2017). *Change the course: National report on sexual harassment and sexual assault at Australian universities.* https://humanrights.gov.au/our-work/sex-discrimination/publications/change-course-national-report-sexual-assault-and-sexual

Barter, C., Aghtaie, N., Larkins, C., Wood, M., & Stanley, N. (2015). *Safeguarding teenage intimate relationships (STIR), connecting online and offline contexts and risks.* University of Bristol.

Bates, L., Gangoli, G., Hester, M., & Justice Project Team. (2018). *Policy evidence summary 1: Migrant women.* University of Bristol.

Bourdieu, P. (1986). The forms of capital. In J. Richardson (Ed.), *Handbook of theory and research for the sociology of education* (pp. 241–258). Greenwood.

Bull, A., & Rye, R. (2018). *Silencing students: Institutional responses to staff sexual misconduct in higher education.* The 1752 Group. https://pure.port.ac.uk/admin/files/11631036/Silencing_Students_The_1752_Group.pdf

Burman, E., Smailes, S. L., & Chantler, K. (2004). 'Culture' as a barrier to service provision and delivery: Domestic violence services for minoritized women. *Critical Social Policy, 24*(3), 332–357. doi:10.1177/0261018304044363

Cambridge University Students' Union. (2014). *Cambridge speaks out report.* www.womens.cusu.cam.ac.uk/Cambridge Speaks Out Report 2014.pdf

Campbell, J. C. (2004). Helping women understand their risk in situations of intimate partner violence. *Journal of Interpersonal Violence, 19*(12), 1464–1477.

Christie, N. (1986). The ideal victim. In E. A. Fattah (Ed.), *From crime policy to victim policy* (pp. 17–30). Palgrave Macmillan.

Coulter, R. W., Mair, C., Miller, E., Blosnich, J. R., Matthews, D. D., & McCauley, H. L. (2017). Prevalence of past-year sexual assault victimization among undergraduate students: Exploring differences by and intersections of gender identity, sexual identity, and race/ethnicity. *Prevention Science, 18*(6), 726–736.

Crenshaw, K. (1991). Mapping the margins: Intersectionality, identity politics and violence against women of color. *Stanford Law Review, 43*(6), 1241–1299.

Dunne, M., Humphreys, S., & Leach, F. (2006). Gender violence in schools in the developing world. *Gender and Education, 18*(1), 75–98. doi:10.1080/09540250500195143

Edinburgh University Student Association. (2014). *Student experiences of sexual harassment in Edinburgh.* A Report. Author.

Fedina, L., Holmes, J. L., & Backes, B. L. (2018). Campus sexual assault: A systematic review of prevalence research from 2000 to 2015. *Trauma, Violence, & Abuse, 19*(1), 76–93. https://doi.org/10.1177/1524838016631129

Fenton, R. A., Mott, H. L., McCartan, K., & Rumney, P. (2016). *A review of evidence for bystander intervention to prevent sexual and domestic violence in universities.* www.gov.uk/government/publications/sexual-and-domestic-violence-prevention-in-universities-evidence-review

Fisher, B. S., Cullen, F. T., & Turner, M. G. (2000). *The sexual victimization of college women. Research report.* Report number: NCJ 182369. ERIC. www.ncjrs.gov/pdffiles1/nij/182369.pdf

Gangoli, G., Bates, L., & Hester, M. (2020). What does justice mean to black and minority ethnic (BME) victims/survivors of gender-based violence? *Journal of Ethnic and Migration Studies.* doi:10.1080/1369183X.2019.1650010

Gangoli, G., Chantler, K., Hester, M., & Singleton, A. (2011). Understanding forced marriage: Definitions and realities. In A. Gill & A. Sunhari (Eds.), *Forced marriage: Introducing a social justice and human rights perspective.* Zed Books.

Gervais, S. J., DiLillo, D., & McChargue, D. (2014). Understanding the link between men's alcohol use and sexual violence perpetration: The mediating role of sexual objectification. *Psychology of Violence, 4*(2), 156–169.

Gregory, A. C., Taylor, A. K., Pitt, K. S., Feder, G. S., & Williamson, E. (2019). ". . . the forgotten heroes": A qualitative study exploring how friends and family members of DV survivors use domestic violence helplines. *Journal of Interpersonal Violence.* https://doi.org/10.1177/0886260519888199

Hagemann-White, C., Kavemann, B., Kindler, H., Meysen, T., Puchert, R., Busche, M., Gabler, S., Grafe, B., Kungl, M., Schindler, G., & Schuck, H. (2010). *Review of research on factors at play in perpetration.* European Commission. www.humanconsultancy.com/assets/understanding-perpetration/understanding-perpetration.html

Healthy Poverty Action. (2021). *Gender-based violence.* www.healthpovertyaction.org/how-poverty-is-created/women-girls/sexual-and-gender-based-violence/

Hester, M., & Lilley, S. J. (2014). *Domestic and sexual violence perpetrator programmes: Article 16 of the Istanbul Convention: A collection of papers on the Council of Europe Convention on preventing and combating violence against women and domestic violence.* Council of Europe. https://rm.coe.int/168046e1f2.v

Holland, C. (2019). Bystander responses to sexual assault disclosures in the U.S. military: Encouraging survivors to use formal resources. *American Journal of Community Psychology, 64*(1–2), 203–218. doi:10/1002/ajcp.12333

Jones, C., Smith, O., Skinner, T., Gangoli, G., & Fenton, R. (2020). *Overview and analysis of research studies on gender-based violence among UK university students and staff.* https://doi.org/10.5281/zenodo.4569042

Jones, L. M., Mitchell, K. J., & Turner, H. A. (2015). Victim reports of bystander reactions to in-person and online peer harassment: A national survey of adolescents. *Journal of Youth Adolescence, 44*(12), 2308–2320. doi:10.1007/s10964-015-0342-9

Krebs, C., Lindquist, C., Berzofsky, M., Shook-Sa, B., & Peterson, K. (2017). *Campus climate survey validation study. Final technical report.* Bureau of Justice Statistics.

Lloyd, K. (2018). Domestic violence and education: Examining the impact of domestic violence on young children, children, and young people and the potential role of schools. *Frontiers in Psychology, 9,* 2094. doi:10.3389/fpsyg.2018.02094

Loots, S., & Walker, M. (2015). Shaping a gender equality policy in higher education: Which human capabilities matter? *Gender and Education, 27*(4), 361–375. doi:10.1080/09540253.2015.1045458, doi.org/10.1080/19452829.2015.1076777

Mahony, P., & Weiner, G. (2019). Neo-liberalism and the state of higher education in the UK. *Journal of Further and Higher Education, 43*(4), 560–572. doi:10.1080/0309877X.2017.1378314

Mulvihill, N., Gangoli, G., Gill, A., & Hester, M. (2018). The experience of interactional justice for victims of 'honour'-based violence and abuse reporting to the police in England and Wales. *Policing and Society, 29*(6), 640–656. doi:10.1080/10439463.2018.1427745

Nash, J. C. (2008). Re-thinking intersectionality. *Feminist Review, 89*(1), 1–15. doi:10.1057/fr.2008.4

Neville, F. G., Goodall, C. A., Williams, D. J., & Donnelly, P. D. (2014). Sexual assault and harassment, perceived vulnerability, and association with alcohol use in a student population: A cross-sectional survey. *The Lancet, 384,* S56.

NUS (National Union of Students). (2018). *Power in the academy: Staff sexual misconduct in UK higher education.* www.nusconnect.org.uk/resources/nus-staff-student-sexual-misconduct-report

Ollis, D. (2017). The power of feminist pedagogy in Australia: Vagina shorts and the primary prevention of violence against women. *Gender and Education, 29*(4), 461–475. doi:10.1080/09540253.2017.1321737

Phipps, A. (2020). Reckoning up: Sexual harassment and violence in the neoliberal university. *Gender and Education, 32*(2), 227–243. doi:10.1080/09540253.2018.1482413

Phipps, A., & Smith, G. (2012). Violence against women students in the UK: Time to take action. *Gender and Education, 24*(4), 357–373.

Roberts, N., Donovan, C., & Durey, M. (2019). Agency, resistance and the non-'ideal' victim: How women deal with sexual violence. *Journal of Gender Based Violence*, *3*(3), 323–338.

Rodino-Colocino, M. (2018). Me too, #MeToo: Countering cruelty with empathy. *Communication and Critical/Cultural Studies*, *15*(1), 96–100. doi:10.1080/14791420.2018.1435083

Saunders, D. (2007). The impact of neoliberalism on college students. *Journal of College and Character*, *8*(5). doi:10.2202/1940-1639.1620

Stenning, P., Mitra-Kahn, T., & Gunby, C. (2012). *Gender-based violence, stalking and fear of crime: Country report United Kingdom (EU-Project 2009–2011 No. JLS/ 2007/ISEC/415)*. Ruhr-University Bochum, Keele University.

Taylor, E. A., & Paule-Koba, A. (2020). "It's our responsibility": Examining the integration of sexual harassment and assault education in sport management programs. *Sport Management Education Journal*, *14*(1), 1–11.

Tewksbury, R., & Mustaine, E. E. (2001). Lifestyle factors associated with the sexual assault of men: A routine activity theory analysis. *The Journal of Men's Studies*, *9*(2), 153–182.

Vaccaro, A. (2010). What lies beneath seemingly positive campus climate results: Institutional sexism, racism, and male hostility toward equity initiatives and liberal bias. *Equity & Excellence in Education*, *43*(2), 202–215.

Vaccaro, A., Lee, M. N., Tissi-Gassoway, N., Kimball, E. W., & Newman, B. N. (2020). Gender and ability oppressions shaping the lives of college students: An intracategorical, intersectional analysis. *Journal of Women and Gender in Higher Education*, *13*(2), 119–137.

Voth Schrag, R. J. (2019). Experiences of economic abuse in the community: Listening to survivor voices. *Affilia*, *34*(3), 313–324. doi:10.1177/0886109919851142

Voth Schrag, R. J., Edmond, T., & Nordberg, A. (2019). Understanding school sabotage among survivors of intimate partner violence from diverse populations. *Violence Against Women*. doi:10.1177/1077801219862626

Williamson, E., Gregory, A., Abrahams, H., Aghtaie, N., Walker, S-J., & Hester, M. (2020). Secondary trauma: Emotional safety in sensitive research. *Journal of Academic Ethics*, *18*, 55–70. https://doi.org/10.1007/s10805-019-09348-y

Willis, T. Y., Mattheis, A., Dotson, B., Brannon, L. J., Hunter, M., Moore, A., Ahmed, L., & Williams-Vallarta, L. (2019). "I find myself isolated and alone": Black women's experiences of microaggressions at an Hispanic- serving institution. *Journal of Women and Gender in Higher Education*, *12*(2), 186–204.

Young, H., Turney, C., White, J., Bonell, C., Lewis, R., & Fletcher, A. (2018). Dating and relationship violence among 16–19 year olds in England and Wales: A cross-sectional study of victimization. *Journal of Public Health*, *40*(4), 738–746.

5 Violence and abuse, universities, and LGBTQ+ students

Catherine Donovan and Nicola Roberts

Increasing attention is being paid to Higher Education in the United Kingdom where reported rates of sexual violence and harassment (SVH) are causing concern (UUK, 2016, 2019). Whilst most of those negatively impacted by SVH are women, the presentation of the category 'women' without any qualification can result in assumptions about who can be victimised, who the perpetrators are, what women are being subjected to, and what help might be available and/or drawn on. By adopting the categories 'women' and 'men' without recognition of people's multiple, intersecting identities, particularly, in the context of this chapter, including sexuality, but also of a broader, non-binary understanding of gender, the experiences of lesbians, gay men, bisexual, questioning, and/or trans women and men, and non-binary folk (LGBTQ+) are at worst left out of the narratives of concern and, at best, added on as an afterthought. By narratives of concern, we mean not only the public, policy, and media accounts about SVH in Higher Education but also in universities' campaigning and awareness-raising activities, and signposting (webpages, flyers) about university student services. We argue that the lack of visibility of LGBTQ+ students as potential targets for (and perpetrators) of SVH has consequences for their sense-making of the violence and abuse they are subjected to as well as their practices of help-seeking.

In this chapter, the experiences of LGBTQ+ students are at the centre of discussion. We use the term LGBTQ+ except where we use the term adopted in others' research. We acknowledge from the outset the paucity of data on the SVH LGBTQ+ students are subjected to in the context of the UK. This is part of the problem and also why this is necessarily an exploratory chapter. We use the concept of public stories to explain why LGBTQ+ students victimised by SVH are not as visible as they could be by considering the key University UK policy documents: *Changing the Culture: Report of the Universities UK Taskforce Examining Violence Against Women, Harassment and Hate Crime Affecting University Students* (2016); *Changing the Culture. Tackling Gender-based Violence, Harassment and Hate Crime: Two Years On* (2019). We also consider the findings from Project Emerald, a survey of SVH reported by LGBTQ+ and heterosexual students at a North Facing University during 2016.

DOI: 10.4324/9781003252474-6

In this chapter, there are four sections. The first section discusses the ways in which both methodology and policy (re)produce a public story of SVH that renders LGBTQ+ students invisible. Next, we explain our methodological approach, and in the third section we provide relevant findings. In conclusion, we provide suggestions about how the SVH LGBTQ+ students are subjected to might be better defined and included in universities' policies and provision of services.

Constructing and researching the problem of SVH and implications for LGBTQ+ students' experiences

Whilst research and development of policy and practice in relation to SVH experienced by Higher Education students is well-established in the United States, in the United Kingdom, concerted work in this area has only really taken off in the last 15 years (Phipps & Smith, 2012). As with research on interpersonal violence and abuse more broadly, feminists/feminist-informed researchers have been pioneers in this field (Donovan et al., 2020) because of concerns about the experiences and needs of women students who are victimised and their predominance in research and practice reporting SVH. Research designs adopt different definitions of the topic being explored, in this case SVH, use different measures of victimisation and impacts, and ask different questions – or none at all – about help-seeking. This makes it difficult to compare findings from different studies within a country or cross-nationally. Yet, even with these caveats, there is consistent evidence that women students are most likely to report higher rates of SVH than men whether that is in relation to physical, verbal, and/or emotional SVH (see Anitha and Lewis's collection for an overview, 2018).

Thus, SVH has been analysed theoretically through feminist frameworks. Typically, feminist approaches are less interested in understanding and explaining any individual (male) perpetrator's decision to be violent/abusive, but are instead interested in the social conditions that create opportunities for such behaviour. This implicates patriarchal, social structural, and hierarchical inequalities that position women and men unequally and create opportunities for those men who would do so to use SVH within a context that culturally, if not legally, condones their behaviour and tends to blame those victimised for the violence they have experienced (Stern, 2010). The work pioneered by Crenshaw (1991) enriches feminist theory with intersectionality both methodologically, in terms of whose accounts are counted and how, and theoretically. Intersectional approaches can challenge us to include in our analysis not only the impacts of a heteronormative, cisnormative patriarchy but also the intersecting impacts of colonialism and imperialism, capitalism, and eugenics. Only considering the social categories of 'women' and 'men' therefore provides a partial, albeit important, understanding. An intersectional approach allows us to consider which women and men, in what contexts, having what experiences with what impacts, and how their identities of sexuality, gender, race, faith, social class, age, capacity (mental, cognitive, and physical), and citizenship status might shape their understanding of victimisation, whether they seek help and from whom, as well as the responses they receive if they do seek help.

A methodological approach that only invites women students to take part in studies about SVH (e.g., NUS, 2011), whilst reflecting the statistics, immediately reinforces and constructs the problem as being of men for women. Survey questions should ask about perpetrators, their gender identity, and their sexuality as well as the gender identity of the women survey participants – and ideally include male students as well, otherwise the sexual victimisation of LGBTQ+ people are left out or not analysed. In addition to survey questions about demographics, decisions about sampling (Brubaker et al., 2017) are important. Donovan and Barnes (2019) also point to the problems arising from how gender and sexuality are understood and operationalised in surveys. They are focused on Walby and Towers' (2018) argument that the Crime Survey for England and Wales (CSEW) should only measure and count domestically abusive behaviours that would reach the threshold of a crime as domestic abuse (what they call domestic violence crime). Whilst this is beyond the remit of this chapter, this illustrates the point that how 'the problem' is defined shapes what counts as knowledge and from whom.

The CSEW also asks about sexual violence victimisation within and/or outside intimate relationships and Walby and Towers argue that four questions about 'gender dimensions' should be asked of CSEW participants. Included in these 'gender dimensions' are 'the relationship between perpetrator and victim (intimate partner or other family member; acquaintance; or stranger)', and whether or not 'there is a sexual aspect' (Walby et al., 2017, p. 13). Donovan and Barnes (2019) argue that this approach subsumes what should be questions about sexuality under 'gender dimensions' and results in sexuality being invisible in the collection of data and thus in its analysis.

In the same article, Donovan and Barnes (2019) also raise the problem of how analysis of minoritised groups' data can be set aside in studies that ask demographic questions about sexuality and transgender identity. Often the reason for not using the data is the small numbers recruited from those categories which make any statistical analysis impossible. Other times even when descriptive statistics are used and show worrying trends, they are not interpreted or commented on (Donovan & Barnes, 2019). Rarely in conclusions, Donovan and Barnes (2019) point out, do authors reflect on the necessity of developing better recruitment techniques to ensure increased participation of LGBTQ+ or other minoritised groups – so that their data can be counted. This apparent lack of attention to issues of recruitment and research design results in a lack of attention to LGBTQ+ people.

However, research has started to emerge from the United States that includes SVH victimisation of LGBTQ+ students – again described and defined in different ways across studies. For example, in Edward et al. (2015), the authors use the terms 'sexual minorities, SM' and 'non sexual minorities, NSM' to compare students' sexual violence reporting. In the study by Potter et al. (2020), the authors refer to 'lesbian, gay, bisexual and queer, LGBQ, students'. In neither study are transgender students visibly included because the focus of analysis is on the sexuality of participants. The results show worrying trends that SVH is reported at least as often (Walters et al., 2013), if not more than heterosexual participants, by LGBTQ+ students (Walters et al., 2013; Edwards et al., 2015; Brubaker et al., 2017, Potter et al., 2020).

In the UK context, there is very little that explores the experiences of LGBTQ+ students' SVH victimisation. The NUS (2011) Hidden Marks research reported on a survey of women students and included questions about gender identity and sexuality. However, there is no focused analysis of the data from those identifying as lesbian, bisexual, and/or transgender. The report states that there will be future publications focusing on these women and on disabled women, but these have not yet materialised. The CSEW data on interpersonal violence has recently been analysed to consider how the sexuality of participants is correlated with reporting (ONS, 2018). With respect to sexual violence, bisexual women are five times more likely to report sexual assault than heterosexual women (1.9% and 0.4%, respectively) with lesbian/gay women also more likely to report than heterosexual women (0.5%) (gay/bisexual men were not included in this analysis and the CSEW does not ask about transgender identity). More generally, the data consistently shows that young people, 16–24 years of age, are the age group most likely to report experiences of SVH and because most students are from this age group, it is clear that there is a problem.

The NUS (2018) has since conducted a survey including 1,839 students about sexual misconduct from university staff, in which 384 (21%, rounded to the nearest whole number) identified as gay, bisexual, or queer (GBQ). Women and GBQ students reported more sexual misconduct than men and heterosexual students. Using descriptive statistics, GBQ women were twice as likely to report staff making sexualised jokes or remarks, compared to heterosexual men. Of the GBQ women students, 23% had experienced touching that made them feel uncomfortable and 5% ($n = 10$) of GBQ women reported experiencing sexual contact without consent from staff once or more times. GBQ women were more likely to report suffering the most impacts from their experiences of sexual misconduct, compared to heterosexual women. In a similar vein, GBQ men were four times as likely to be sexually exploited, through reward or threat by staff, compared to heterosexual men. Regardless of sexual identity, women were twice more likely to report being touched by staff in ways that made them feel uncomfortable, compared to men. So women and non-heterosexual students were more likely to be victimised at university.

There is a fear that by removing the focus on the category 'women', there will be a 'weakened feminist analysis' (Brubaker et al., 2017, p. 2). By pointing out that women can be perpetrators of SVH, that men can be victimised by SVH, and that non-binary or gender queer folk can also be victimised and perpetrate SVH, a feminist understanding of patriarchal, structural power has to give way to an individualised model of understanding and addressing sexual violence and abuse. We would argue that this is not the case. Far from it. Our approach is an intersectional feminist one in which we consider how societies' material, economic, cultural, social, and political resources and entitlements, are unequally distributed in ways shaped by people's identities. And that the social positioning of social groups and the individuals within them will necessarily shape not only their chances of being victimised but also their chances of seeking and receiving redress. Christie's (1986) 'ideal victim' powerfully describes the social resources and entitlements that shape our willingness to blame those victimised by crime. In discussions of SVH, victim-blaming is central to understanding both who might be victimised and their help-seeking practices.

We argue therefore that to effect change, the public story about SVH needs to be changed to allow other stories of SVH to be told and heard. In their work, Donovan and Hester (2014) draw on Jamieson's notion of 'public stories' to explore the invisibility of domestic abuse in, as they called it 'same-sex relationships'. Public stories about everyday life (Jamieson, 1998) circulate in society and yet are distinctive and separate from actual lived lives. They provide templates about a lifestyle, a social role, a set of social relationships. Necessarily they are simplified, drawing on 'obvious' tropes to aid recognition in those listening or watching. However, whilst they might be simplified, they are rarely objective or neutral but 'invariably have an interest in telling a particular version of events' (Jamieson, 1998, pp. 10–11). They are not necessarily, or ever, 'the truth', but instead necessary, purposeful, fictions providing templates for living that are not static yet nevertheless achieve purchase in society – typically in ways that shore up the status quo and dominant power relationships.

Donovan and Hester (2014) argue that an unintended consequence of feminist scholarship and activism around violence against women and girls has led to a public story of domestic abuse in which the problem is constructed as one of cisgender heterosexual men for cisgender heterosexual women, a problem of physical violence, and a problem of a particular gender binary – the big 'strong' man being violent towards a small 'weak' woman (see also Donovan, 2017). Donovan and Barnes (2020, p. 6) develop this analysis to suggest that overlaying the heteronormative gendered binaries in the public story of domestic abuse is the binary of an ideal victim/perpetrator, in which, as they state, 'If there is any scope for victim-blaming, evidence of provocation or agency, it is difficult to establish a credible "ideal victim" identity, especially for those inhabiting minoritised identities' (see also Donovan & Barnes, 2018). The ideal victim can be read as stereotypically (heteronormatively) feminised, that is, weak, passive – another example of a public story.

Policy documents can illustrate how public stories can be constructed and/or reinforced. The title of the first report (UUK, 2016) maps out who this report speaks about and what the problems are – violence against women, harassment, and hate crime affecting university students. A word count of key terms (in footnotes as well as the main text) in this report (UUK, 2016) – women/female, men/male, LGBT – is insightful. In the first chapter, 'Setting the Scene and the Nature and Scale of the Problem' (UUK, 2016, p. 15), 'women' and 'girls' are referred to 39 times, men are referred to 5 times, and 'LGBT' students are referred to 10 times. Some of this is explained by the fact that the chapter situates its focus on SVH within the broader context of government policies across three countries in the UK – Wales, Scotland, and England – all of which locate SVH as one form of violence against women.

It is this conjoining of violence against women with SVH that acts to delineate the problem of SVH as a problem solely for women (see also Carrigan Wooten, 2015). For example, at the beginning of the first chapter, which is about the 'UK Policy Context', it states: 'Violence against women and sexual harassment. Much of the recent policy context of relevance to the Taskforce's remit has focused around sexual violence and sexual harassment' (UUK, 2016, p. 15). Immediately the association is made that when SVH are talked about, it is the victimisation of women that is being talked about. The ten references to 'LGBT' (the term used in the report) in this first chapter are in relation to hate incidents/crime and homo/bi/transphobic harassment. The definition of hate crime given in the glossary does refer to the fact that a sexual offence could be motivated by hate (UUK, 2016, p. 11) but LGBTQ+ people are never referenced in relation to SVH in the report.

In a later part of the report considering what might need to change in order to facilitate LGBT people reporting hate incidents/crime and homo/bi/transphobic harassment, suggestions are listed from Stonewall and Galop.[1] In the commentary about these, the report states: 'It is also clear that the above considerations are in line with the factors that have been raised in the evidence for responding to reports of violence against women and sexual harassment, suggesting that there are commonalities in the approach' (UUK, 2016, p. 84). There is no recognition that LGBTQ+ students could also be victimised by SVH and the two sets of problems are set alongside each other as similar yet distinct in nature and pertaining to two different groups of students.

Even where the report acknowledges that men can be victimised by SVH, sexuality is not included, neither is any mention given of who the perpetrators might be. In paragraph 25, it states: 'Men can also be victims of rape, sexual assault and sexual harassment. The institution-wide approach advocated by this report (chapter 5) will enable universities to take the necessary steps to respond irrespective of the gender of the victim/survivor'. The latter sentence illustrates the lack of understanding there is about how powerfully public stories shape not only how people make sense of their experiences, whether they name them as sexual violence, rape, hate crime, etc., but also how help providers understand the problem and how they should respond. We might ask whether services set up in line with the public story of SVH with heterosexual cisgender women students as core clients would be perceived to be inclusive of them by a gay (or heterosexual cisgender) male student. The dominant public story about SVH makes it difficult for other stories of SVH to be told and heard and has profound impacts for help-seeking (Donovan & Hester, 2014; Donovan & Barnes, 2020).

The later report (UUK, 2019) is based on a survey of universities' progress in implementing the original report's recommendations. Although the title refers to gender-based violence, hate, and harassment, suggesting a reconceptualisation of the problems, a search for terms 'women', 'men', and 'LGBT' (the term used in the report) continues to reinforce how the problems are being understood and presented. Women (and girls) are referred to 38 times, men 3 times, and LGBT 5 times. LGBT groups are only referred to in relation to hate incidents/crime and homo/bi/transphobic harassment.

The separation of LGBTQ+ students from discussion of them as potential/actual victims of SVH continues. In providing an overview of the survey findings, the authors conclude that most of the changes in universities since the UUK (2016) recommendations have been in relation to SVH, where they say 'good progress' has been made (UUK, 2019, p. 25). They explain this with reference to both the Minister of State for Universities and Science at the time and the Scottish government actively encouraging universities to pursue and prioritise activities 'for preventing and eradicating violence against women and girls' (UUK, 2019, p. 25). Again LGBTQ+ students are not included here as potential or actual targets of SVH but, separately, in the report as potential and actual victims of homo/bi/transphobic harassment and hate incidents/crime. The latter is reinforced with a discussion of the Government Equalities Office publication of an 'LGBT action plan to help improve the lives of LGBT and transgender people [sic]' (UUK, 2019, p. 66). To achieve this, the Office for Students is expected to ask universities to become 'places of tolerance for all students' and to ensure that those victimised by homo/bi/transphobic incidents have appropriate support (UUK, 2019, p. 66). It is yet to be explored whether and how LGBT students make sense of this and whether the ways in which the UUK 2016 recommendations are being implemented is impacting on their sense-making and help-seeking when they experience SVH. However, research suggests LGBTQ+ people do not turn to mainstream/specialist domestic abuse services (Donovan et al., 2021), so the prospects are not good. Further research is needed to explore these issues. We now consider the data from Project Emerald.

Methods

Project Emerald was a survey of violence and abuse reported by students at a North Facing University during 2016. Students from across the university's two city campuses took part in an online survey using both open and closed questions to ask about their perceptions of safety across the university estate and the city, and their experiences of four overarching types of violence and abuse: verbal abuse and bullying, physical violence, sexual violence, and stalking. Within these four types of violence and abuse, students were asked about their experiences of specific acts of violence and abuse. Questions were also asked about the worst example of each overarching type of violence and abuse, including where and when this took place, who the perpetrator(s) was, and what help-seeking they engaged with.

Analysing the data

As the survey asked closed questions, the data was analysed statistically in SPSS. To find statistically significant relationships in the data between two socio-demographic variables, such as sexuality and disability, cross-tabulations were used. If the results were significant ($p < .05$), binary logistic regression was used to assess the odds of one variable, sexuality, predicting the other variable, such as disability. This data analysis strategy was similarly applied to the relationship between variables, such as sexuality, gender, disability, and experiences of violence. If cross-tabulations were significant for the overarching type of violence and abuse (verbal abuse and bullying, sexual violence, physical violence, stalking), then further cross-tabulations were carried out on the specific acts of violence and abuse, with the variables sexuality, gender, and disability. If these results were significant, then binary logistic regression was used to test if sexuality, gender, and disability predicted specific acts of violence and abuse. The enter method was used where all variables were entered into the regression simultaneously and non-significant variables subsequently removed, and the regression re-ran. Only significant results are presented. As the survey also asked open questions, the data was also analysed qualitatively in a thematic manner. More about this qualitative data analysis and methods of research, including ethics, can be found in Roberts et al. (2019, 2020).

Describing the sample

The survey was completed by 1,034 students (10% response rate). They had a mean age of 25 and a modal age of 21: 70% were in the age range 18–24. Of the students, 67% were women and 32.5% were men (n = 691 and 333, respectively). Less than 1% (n = 5) of students identified as 'other' gender and 1% (n = 11) of students had ever identified as transgender. Most students described themselves as heterosexual/straight (89%, n = 910), and 11% (n = 116 including 'other' category) described themselves as LGBTQ+. Over half of the students, 64% (n = 657) were white British; 36% (n = 374) were broken down as follows: 11% (n = 116) other white background, 1% (n = 10) white Irish, 12% (n = 127) Asian or Chinese backgrounds, 7% (n = 66) Black backgrounds, 3% (n = 31) Arab backgrounds, 1% (n = 12) mixed/multiple ethnic group, and 1% (n = 12) other ethnic groups. Most students, 79% (n = 817), did not have a known disability; 21% (n = 208) said they had disability.

Of the 11% of the sample who described themselves as LGBTQ+ students, 33% (n = 38) were gay/lesbian, 49% (n = 57) bisexual, 6% (n = 7) queer, and 12% (n = 14) other sexuality (e.g., pansexual, asexual, questioning). Of these LGBTQ+ students, 68% (n = 79) were women and 29% (n = 34) were men. Three per cent (n = 3) of students identified as 'other' gender. Slightly less of the LGBTQ+ students, 4% (n = 4), compared to the total survey students had identified as transgender. More of the LGBTQ+ students, 80% (n = 92), compared to the survey students, were white British; 20% (n = 23) and other groups were 6% (n = 7) other White background, 2% (n = 3) white Irish, 8% (n = 9) Asian or Chinese backgrounds, 2% Black backgrounds (n = 2), 1% (n = 1) Arab backgrounds, and 1% (n = 1) mixed/multiple ethnic group. There was a statistically significant difference between the proportion of LGBTQ+ students, 50% (n = 57) reporting a disability, and the proportion of heterosexual students, 17% (n = 150) (p < .001). The LGBTQ+ students were 5.2 times more likely to report a mental health condition than the heterosexual students (Wald = 50.302, p < .001, OR = 5.214, 95% CI = 3.304–8.230). This is important because the LGBTQ+ students' experiences and responses are significantly more likely to be understood through the lens of their intersecting identities of sexuality and disability. The mean and modal age of the LGBTQ+ students were 26 and 21, respectively, with 68% in the age range 18–24. Table 5.1 details the socio-demographics of students.

Table 5.1 Socio-demographics of the students

		Survey students		LGBTQ+ students	
		n★	%	n★	%
Age	Mean	25	n/a	26	n/a
	Mode	21	n/a	21	n/a
	18–24	n/a	70	n/a	68
Gender	Women	691	67	79	68
	Men	333	33	34	29
	Other	5	1	3	3
Transgender	Yes	11	1	4	4
	No	1018	99	111	96
Sexuality	Heterosexual/ straight	910	89	n/a	n/a
	Gay/lesbian	38	4	38	33
	Bisexual	57	5	57	49
	Queer	7	1	7	6
	Other	14	1	14	12
Ethnicity	White British	657	64	92	80
	Other	374★★	36	23	20
Disability	Yes	208★	21	57	50
	No	817	79	58	50

★Difference in figures are non-responses.
★★Includes 'other ethnic group' responses.

Findings

Verbal harassment of LGBTQ+ students: statistical results

LGBTQ+ students were more likely to be verbally abused compared to heterosexual students. Eighty-three per cent ($n = 68$) of the LGBTQ+ students reported this compared to 52% ($n = 308$) of the heterosexual students ($p < .001$) (per cents have been rounded to the nearest whole number). Thus, the LGBTQ+ students were 4.2 times more likely to report experiencing any verbal abuse than heterosexual students (Wald = 21.700, $p < .001$, OR = 4.190, 95% CI = 2.293–7.657). In this model of analysis, gender was also significant. Sixty per cent ($n = 288$) of women students reported experiencing any verbal abuse compared to 43% ($n = 87$) of men students ($p < .001$). Thus, women were 1.9 times more likely to report experiencing any verbal abuse than men (Wald = 14.551, $p < .001$, OR = 1.938, 95% CI = 1.379–2.723). Sexuality and gender explain 9% (Nagelkerke R^2) of the variance in students experiencing any verbal abuse. The model correctly predicted 37% of cases of never experiencing any verbal abuse and 80% of cases of experiencing any verbal abuse, giving an overall percentage of correct prediction rate of 61%. The model was a good fit (Hosmer and Lemeshow chi-square = 0.044, df = 1, and $p = .834$, $p > .05$) (see Warner, 2013 for what makes a model a good fit). Of the eight questions asked about specific acts of verbal abuse, LGBTQ+ students were more likely to experience five of these acts of verbal abuse than heterosexual students, four of which are directly linked to sexual harassment. It is these behaviours that we concentrate on in this chapter. Table 5.2 shows

Table 5.2 Student experiences of verbal abuse by sexuality and gender

		Sexuality		Gender	
		LGBTQ+ *% (n)*	*Heterosexual* *% (n)*	*Women* *% (n)*	*Men* *% (n)*
Experience any verbal abuse	% (n)	83 (68)★	52 (308)★	60 (288)★	43 (87)★
	Odds ratio (OR)	4.190★		1.938*	
• Asked questions about your sexuality	% (n)	57 (45)★	12 (71)★	X	X
	OR	9.619★			
• Asked questions about your sex or romantic life	% (n)	51 (41)★	25 (148)★	32 (150)★★	19 (38)★★
	OR	2.959★		1.893★★	
• Sexual comments that made you feel uncomfortable	% (n)	48 (38)★	23 (133)★	33 (152)★	9 (18)★
	OR	2.881★		4.640*	
• Hurtful or abusive comments towards you	% (n)	52 (42)★	27 (163)★	X	X
	OR	2.867★			
• Wolf whistling, catcalling, or sexual noises at you	% (n)	40 (32)★★★	27 (159)★★★	X	X
	OR	1.807★★★			

★$p < .001$, ★★$p < .01$, ★★★$p < .05$.
X: not significant in the model.

the specific acts of verbal abuse that LGBTQ+ students are more likely to experience.

Of the LGBTQ+ students who reported being asked questions about their sexuality when it was none of their business, 57% ($n = 45$) said they had experienced this compared to 12% ($n = 71$) of heterosexual students ($p < .001$). Thus, the LGBTQ+ students were 9.6 times more likely to report this behaviour than heterosexual students (Wald = 75.742, $p < .001$, OR = 9.619, 95% CI = 5.777–16.015).

Of those who answered the question about someone asking them questions about their sex or romantic life when it was none of their business, 51% ($n = 41$) of LGBTQ+ students said they had experienced this compared to 25% ($n = 148$) of heterosexual students ($p < .001$). Thus, the LGBTQ+ students were three times more likely to report this behaviour than heterosexual students (Wald = 19.155, $p < .001$, OR = 2.959, 95% CI = 1.820–4.809). In this model of analysis, gender was also significant. Thirty-two per cent ($n = 150$) of women students were more likely to report being asked questions about their sex or romantic life when it was none of their business compared to 19% ($n = 38$) men students ($p = .001$). Thus, women students were 1.9 times more likely to this behaviour than men students (Wald = 9.366, $p = .002$, OR = 1.893, 95% CI = 1.258–2.848). Sexuality and gender explain 7% (Nagelkerke R^2) of the variance in someone asking students questions about their sex or romantic life when it was none of their business. The model correctly predicted 94% of cases of never being asked questions about sex or romantic life and 17% of cases being asked questions about sex or romantic life, giving an overall percentage of correct prediction rate of 72%. The model was a good fit (Hosmer and Lemeshow chi-square = 0.244, df = 1, and $p = .621$, $p > .05$).

To the question asking about someone making sexual comments that had made you feel uncomfortable, 48% ($n = 38$) of LGBTQ+ students said they had experienced this compared to 23% ($n = 133$) of heterosexual students ($p < .001$). Thus, the LGBTQ+ students were 2.9 times more likely to report this behaviour than heterosexual students (Wald = 16.849, $p < .001$, OR = 2.881, 95% CI = 1.738–4.774). In this model of analysis, gender was also significant. Thirty-three per cent ($n = 152$) of women students reported someone making sexual comments that made them feel uncomfortable compared to 9% ($n = 18$) of men students ($p < .001$). Thus, women students were 4.6 times more likely to report this than men students (Wald = 32.648, $p < .001$, OR = 4.640, 95% CI = 2.741–7.856). Sexuality and gender explain 13% (Nagelkerke R^2) of the variance in someone making sexual comments that made students feel uncomfortable. The model correctly predicted 94% of cases of never experiencing sexual comments that made them feel uncomfortable and 19% of cases of experiencing sexual comments that made them feel uncomfortable, giving an overall percentage of correct prediction rate of 75%. The model was a good fit (Hosmer and Lemeshow chi-square = 0.456, df = 2, and $p = .796$, $p > .05$).

Of the students who answered the question about someone had wolf-whistled, catcalled, or made sexual noises at them, 40% ($n = 32$) of LGBTQ+ students said they had experienced this compared to 27% ($n = 159$) of heterosexual students (p = .015). Thus, the LGBTQ+ students were 1.8 times more likely to report this behaviour than heterosexual students (Wald = 5.769, p = .016, OR = 1.807, 95% CI = 1.115–2.929).

The statistical analysis provides evidence that LGBTQ+ students were verbally sexually harassed because of their sexuality and as a woman. The next section of the findings presents the qualitative accounts to support the statistical data. Although no significant statistical data was presented about the relationship between verbal abuse and disability, and verbal abuse and ethnicity, some of the students' accounts reflect this relationship. Accounts are presented as students have written them and they are typical responses of the themes shown.

Verbal harassment of LGBTQ+ students: qualitative accounts

Whilst LGBTQ+ students were most likely to report sexual harassment through verbal abuse, they also reported other kinds of verbal abuse that might be more obviously identifiable as a hate incident/crime and/or homo/bi/transphobic harassment. For example, as the following woman student reports:

General harassment about personal details of my sexuality.

(woman, pansexual)

Some LGBTQ+ students were harassed because of a disability:

Due to having dyslexia i have had a comment made that i [sic] would be better suited to reading a beano magazine.

(woman, bisexual, specific learning disability)

Also because of their ethnicity:

When I was walking back from the library, two women on their balcony assumed that I was looking at them. Then they started to scream at me and said racial slurs.

(agender, other Asian background, pansexual)

However, LGBTQ+ students also experienced sexually verbal abusive behaviours:

Male shouting crude sexual words (not going to repeat them) from his car as he drove past. This happened once to me but i have seen it happen multiple times to other females and a male on one occasion.

(woman, gay/lesbian) [sic]

Sometimes verbal sexual harassment was a response to a student who had objected to physical sexual harassment. The verbal sexual harassment makes assumptions about the student's sexuality as a presumed rationale for their resisting being touched:

> **Being called 'dyke' & other abusive language for asking someone to stop touching me.**
>
> (woman, bisexual)

SVH is not uncommon in verbal but also in physical forms:

> **A man used force to 'grope' me under my skirt at a pub in [the city] which I would class as physical abuse.**
>
> (woman, bisexual)

Sometimes, however, it is not clear whether what LGBTQ+ students report would be understood (by them or by help providers) as verbal sexual harassment or a hate incident/crime. For example:

> **Being locked out on the balcony at midnight in the freezing cold because I refused to explain how 'lesbian sex' worked, a common question always directed towards me, usually with lewd comments and assumptions.**
>
> (woman, bisexual)

It is possible to read this behaviour both as SVH and as a hate incident/hate crime and, depending on how the student views it, this will shape how and whether they might report it, seek support in relation to it, and the response they receive.

Impact of the violence and abuse

The harassment impacted upon LGBTQ+ students in several ways: emotional, attitudinal, and behavioural. Emotional impacts, such as anger and annoyance, were particularly reported:

> **It has made me annoyed with myself for not standing up for myself and also annoyed that someone can get away with that sort of behaviour because they are cajoled by others and encouraged.**
>
> (woman, bisexual)

However, impacts on LGBTQ+ students' confidence was also reported which, as in this example, often led to behavioural impacts:

> **Definitely affected my confidence, I dont [sic] have any self confidence anyway, I find [sic] it hard to wear tight clothing or slightly low cut outfits because of unwanted attention.**
>
> (woman, bisexual)

Prior experience of verbal abuse/harassment led some LGBTQ+ students to adopt pre-emptive protective behaviours, altering their behaviours, and/or how they dressed:

> *At first I was scared to go to the cafe I [sic] case the same thing happened again or I saw him again. I also started covering my scars again [from self-harm].*
>
> (woman, bisexual, mental health condition)

While this 'safety work' of women (Vera-Gray & Kelly, 2020, p. 265) has been documented in existing research, the behaviour changes noted by some LGBQT+ students in this research appear extreme but necessary:

> *Though I know I can get out of a situation at the halls I don't like as I can lock myself in my room.*
>
> (woman, bisexual)

> *I had to hide behind a car to avoid them [a group of lads].*
>
> (woman, bisexual)

Half of LGBTQ+ students reported a disability, with almost one-third of these reporting a mental health condition. Such disability can shape the lens through which students view the world, as the following student begins her account:

> *I'm a naturally very anxious person so I'm often imagining the worst case scenario.*
>
> (woman, bisexual, mental health condition)

Similarly, other students write their accounts from a disabled person's viewpoint and how this leads to a perceived sense of heightened risk when assessing their safety:

> *I am a disabled student and therefore cannot drive. The transport links do not allow . . . people to get to other parts of the North . . . safely very far outside of the 9–5 work day . . . It is not a safe place to be on a platform waiting for a train or realising you've missed the last bus home. It is one of the biggest issues with me being a mature disabled student studying here.*
>
> (woman, bisexual, physical impairment or mobility)

Given LGBTQ+ students' reported levels of disability together with the emotional impacts of the violence they have also reported, it is important to pay attention to the help-seeking practices of students.

Help-seeking practices

Like heterosexual students, LGBTQ+ students are unlikely to report the violence and abuse committed against them. Reasons for this ranged from normalising the violence, believing nothing will be done, the student dealt with the violence and abuse themselves, and/or it had little impact, as the following student states:

> *Did not report the incident as i [sic] was not awfully affected by it and even if it were reported, nothing would be done as it was a stranger that could not be identified.*
>
> (woman, gay/lesbian)

Other common responses for not reporting were because they thought their experiences were normal and having little faith in what can be done:

> *In a club the bouncers do there best but cant handle everything [sic]. Often the middle aged men disappear after you shout at them anyway. Or they run off before u can even see their face. It happens so often, what can the club owners do?*
>
> (woman, bisexual)

Bouncers were often thought of as doing their best:

> **[T]he bouncers were informed and cctv was checked and the two men were kicked out. i was asked if i [sic] wanted to inform the police however did not.**
>
> (woman, bisexual)

Others whom LGBTQ+ students reported their experiences too included friends, support worker, counsellor, lecturer/tutor, campus police, security, and family. The reasons why students reported their experiences of violence and abuse were the same as heterosexual students (Roberts et al., 2019, p. 333): 'to get help, to stop it, to warn others, and because of the emotional impact'. As this student, victimised by domestic abuse, says:

> *Because the situation was difficult enough as it was as he was abusive and stole a lot of money, I was trying to move forward with my life and he kept popping up as a reminder and trying to persuade me to get back with him. I was so on edge, to the extent that I would not leave the flat and had to be persuaded to leave with other people. It affected my confidence, my motivation and has caused me to apply for extenuating circumstances to be able to re-sit the second semester.*
>
> (woman, bisexual)

LGBTQ+ students' responses to what the university could do to improve their safety and responses were largely about education:

> *Identify If [sic] there are any particular degrees or other educational opportunities where inequality, bullying or difference is heightened negatively. Due*

to myself being on a sociology degree I feel these issues are dealt with as part of my studies and improves my understanding in everyday life to overlook negative stereotypes [sic] and increased understanding of individuals who identify socially or biologically or even psychologically different from myself. However, I wonder if this is the case for other degrees that focus less on this particular line of academic materials/knowledge.

(woman, queer)

Lad culture was also mentioned:

Sex ed for consent Tackling lad culture How to discuss and identify sexuality and/or gender identity How to respectfully discuss sexuality and/or gender identity [sic].

(woman, queer)

LGBTQ+ students mostly did not mention in qualitative feedback individual services they might need to respond to their needs but instead suggest wider structural and cultural changes that might better prevent SVH for everybody. It is not clear whether this is because they do not envisage that their university might be able to appropriately respond to their individual needs as LGBTQ+ students and further research is required to explore this further.

Discussion

Existing evidence, though scarce and mostly from the United States, suggests that LGBTQ+ students experience SVH and do so at least at the same, and in most studies, at higher, rates than heterosexual students. Yet in the UK, key policy documents addressing SVH firmly both construct and reinforce a public story about SVH that renders it heteronormatively as a problem for cisgender women students. LGBTQ+ students, though named and discussed in these documents, are positioned within a public story of being victimised by hate incidents/crime and homo/bi/transphobic harassment.

The public story is reinforced and (re)constructed with research method-ologies that, we argue, make it difficult if not impossible for the accounts of LGBTQ+ students' experiences of SVH to be, literally, counted. Research designs often do not include questions about gender identity and sexuality and, where they do, data from these groups is rarely analysed and discussed or interpreted. Partly this is because their numbers are too small to allow for statistical analysis, however this does not lead to calls for research recruitment methods to be addressed in order to improve LGBTQ+ student participation. In other examples, as we have shown, LGBTQ+ students are included in the general descriptive analysis of the general data base using gender as the primary variable for analysis.

In Project Emerald, approximately 11% of the responding students identified as LGBTQ+ and their rates of reporting verbal sexual harassment are significantly higher than their heterosexual counterparts. The qualitative data also provides us with evidence of the range of verbally and physically abusive behaviour they experience and points to the importance of taking account of students' intersecting identities in making sense of their victimisation: in our data, there are disabled LGBTQ+ students reporting disabled hate speech and Asian LGBTQ+ students reporting racist hate speech. We argue that as a consequence of a dominant public story about SVH, unless their sexuality and/or gender identity is asked about, analysed, and interpreted in surveys of violence and abuse, students will be assumed to be part of the majority groups: white, able bodied, heterosexual (see also Brubaker et al., 2017) around whom the public story is built.

Whilst in this study impacts on LGBTQ+ students and their help-seeking practices appear similar to heterosexual students, these were not a major focus of the research, and these aspects of interpersonal violence and abuse are arguably better explored with qualitative research. Research from elsewhere (NUS, 2015) suggests gay (27.7%), lesbian (26.6%), and bisexual (30%) students are more likely to seriously consider dropping out of university than heterosexual students (25%) with the biggest reason given by LGB+ students being 'the feeling of not fitting in' (NUS, 2015, p. 2); and LGBT students who had experienced 'homophobic or transphobic harassment' were between two and three times more likely to withdraw from their studies. Their structural position as minoritised groups also positions them such that perpetrators of abuse can perceive them as easy targets to victimise because an assumption can be made that they are unlikely to report and/or seek help. The available evidence also supports this evidence suggesting that LGBQ students do not know what services are available to them if they are victimised by SVH (Schulzea & Perkins, 2017). Not being visible in university policy and practice settings as potential/actual targets of SVH can exacerbate this (Duenas et al., 2021).

Undoubtedly, LGBTQ+ students would feel better able to report and seek help for experiences of SVH if they felt better included more generally in university communities. Our research has drawn attention to the ways in which disability and sexuality intersect in the LGBTQ+ students in our sample and the prevalence of mental ill-health is significantly higher than in their heterosexual counterparts which can be both precursor to and result of being victimised. The Government Equalities Action Plan referred to in the follow-up report (UUK, 2019) if implemented fully would transform the culture in universities for them and help prevent hate incidents/crime and homo/bi/transphobic harassment as well as provide appropriate sources of help when it does occur. Research has shown the importance of academic tutors having positive attitudes towards LGBTQ+ students and intervening where homo/bi/transphobic attitudes and language behaviours are witnessed (Gallardo-Nieto et al., 2021). The actions of those in structurally powerful positions give strong messages to LGBTQ+ students about whether they will perceive their university as hostile or inclusive and open to meeting their needs (Gallardo-Nieto et al., 2021).

Finally, different public stories about SVH need to be told that include the possibility that LGBTQ+ students can be victimised (and can be perpetrators). This can be accommodated within a feminist structural approach to understanding SVH if an intersectional feminist approach is taken that understands gender in less rigidly binaried ways as well as being self-aware about how easy it is to make heteronormative and cisnormative assumptions about gender. The broader social context in which SVH takes place is of structural inequalities that position social groups hierarchically in ways that make them more easily targeted for SVH, that informs victim-blaming tropes, and that makes LGBTQ+ students less likely to approach mainstream help-providers or specialist women's services. Universities should raise awareness and provide training across their institutions to effect the construction of inclusive public stories about SVH. Whole institution-wide approaches have a better chance of achieving the change in culture required because then 'all university members [become] agents of change' (Gallardo-Nieto et al., 2021, p. 8). However, the size and complexity of universities can present serious challenges to achieving such changes. The role of senior management in championing the telling of different, inclusive public stories of SVH will be key (Chantler et al., 2019), although the individual feminist champion and their allies in universities are often the transformative agents of change needed (Donovan et al., 2020). Active bystander initiatives (Fenton & Mott, 2018) can be instrumental in engaging students as active members of their university communities and care should be taken to ensure that the public stories about SVH being told in these programmes are inclusive of the needs and experiences of LGBTQ+ students (see Duenas et al., 2021 for design and evaluation of educational programs that allow for identifying the most subtle types of violence).

Key steps in changing the public story of SVH are the realisation and acceptance that it needs to change and the confidence to change it whilst retaining an intersectional feminist understanding of structural inequalities in explanations of why these behaviours occur and what needs to be done to address them. This chapter's intention is to contribute to the discussions already taking place across universities in the UK, about how we support this process of making more visible the SVH that LGBTQ+ students experience, improve understanding of those experiences, promote help-seeking, and ensure help provision.

Summary of key points

In this chapter, we make the following points:

- Currently, there exists a public story about sexual violence and harassment (SVH) that constructs heterosexual, cisgender women students as the only students likely to be targeted by perpetrators.
- This public story of SVH renders LGBTQ+ students invisible as potential/actual targets for victimisation.
- The public story of SVH is constructed and reinforced in many ways, including those we consider in this chapter:

- Methodologically, in decisions made about the design of research tools, sampling strategies, and analysis/interpretation in research considering SVH and university students.
- In policy documents that provide a rationale, evidence recommendations for change to improve and 'change the culture' in Higher Education (HE) with regard to SVH.

- Existing evidence of SVH that LGBTQ+ students are subjected to is rare in the UK context however, both in Project Emerald that we discuss in this chapter and in the United States point to findings that LGBTQ+ are at least as likely to report SVH and most likely to report higher rates of SVH than heterosexual counterparts.
- Recommendations aim to change the public story about SVH to include the possibility of other stories of LGBTQ+ victim-survivors (and perpetrators). Suggestions include inclusive research methodologies and analysis: whole HE institution approaches to training and awareness-raising about LGBTQ+ students victimisation by SVH; the role of senior leaders in HE institutions in communicating a more inclusive public story of SVH; the role of active bystander programmes in presenting an inclusive public story about SVH.

Further Reading

Gallardo-Nieto, E. M., Gomez, A., Gairal-Casado, R., & del Mar Ramis-Salas, M. (2021). Sexual orientation, gender identity and gender expression-based violence in Catalan universities: Qualitative findings from university students and staff. *Archives of Public Health, 79 (16), 1–13.*

This article is based on 30 interviews with staff and students at Spanish universities. It explores discrimination and violence against LGBTQI+ (Lesbian, Gay, Bisexual, Transgender, Queer, Intersex) students. The authors found that the constant discriminatory comments, such as 'faggot' and 'butch' (p. 6) against the LGBTQI+ community were normalised in everyday discourses – used inside and outside the classroom, as one student says: 'Many times, I think they overlook these comments because we are used to them.' (p. 6).

Consequently, the underreporting of violence against LGBTQI+ students at the universities was viewed as an interrelated problem of a lack of awareness of violence based on sexual orientation, gender expression or gender identity *and* consequently, a lack of, and/or ignorance of, policies and practices in place to address such violence.

However, the authors found that universities are safe spaces for LGBTQI+ students. Firstly, academic staff's intervention can positively impact upon students' well-being. Secondly, the connection that academic staff have with Equality Units at their institution can enable the implementation of appropriate policies and practices to address violence against LGBTQI+ students. Thirdly, academic staff can raise awareness of violence against LGBTQI+ students and enable students to become active bystanders, by challenging such violence in their teaching practices in the classroom.

Schulzea, C., & Perkins, W. (2017). Awareness of sexual violence services among LGBQ-identified college students. *Journal of School Violence, 16* (2), 148–159.

This is a study of 140 college students in the United States who responded to an invitation to take part in research exploring their awareness of services that they could refer to if they experienced sexual violence victimisation. Most (*n* = 123) identified as LGBQ and most identified as white (*n* = 105). Questions included their experiences of sexual violence victimisation. Fifty-five students said they had been raped (39%). Those identifying as queer, lesbian or gay were most likely to report rape, 42% (*n* = 59) had disclosed an incident of sexual violence to somebody. Queer and other students were most likely to have disclosed. Most (72%, *n* = 101) had received a disclosure of a sexual violence incident and lesbian and queer students were most likely to have done so.

Students were provided with a list of 8 on-campus services they might approach if they were victimised by sexual violence. A significant minority of students (42%) were not able to identify any on-campus services for those victimised by sexual violence. LGBQ students were most likely to identify LGBQ friendly organisations in their top four on-campus services they would turn to. Campus safety and local police were the two least likely to be turned to. Non-white students were less likely than white students to name any of the campus services as somewhere they would turn to.

The study authors speculate about their findings and consider that LGBQ students might be less willing to approach services they perceive as heteronormative in their understanding of sexual violence victimisation. They also point to the non-white students' lower levels of awareness of what services might be available on campus as indicative of their perceptions of what universities have to offer them and their perceptions that campus services are set up to provide for white students. The authors recommend changing the 'script' about sexual violence; building on active bystander programmes to ensure that when friends are disclosed to they know how to respond appropriately; and climate surveys that better include sexual minorities.

Note

1 Stonewall and Galop are London-based organisations with national remits to represent the interests of LGBT people; Galop focuses specifically on services for LGBT+ people who are victimised by domestic and sexual violence and hate incidents/crime.

References

Anitha, S., & Lewis, R. (Eds.). (2018). *Gender based violence in university communities: Policy, prevention and educational initiatives*. Policy Press.

Baroness Stern for the Government Equalities Office and the Home Office. (2010). *The stern review*. www.equalities.gov.uk/PDF/Stern_Review_acc_FINAL.pdf

Brubaker, S. J., Keegan, B., Guadalupe-Diaz, X. L., & Beasley, B. (2017). Measuring and reporting campus sexual assault: Privilege and exclusion in what we know and what we do. *Sociology Compass*, 1–19, e12543. https://doi.org/10.1111/soc4.12543

Carrigan Wooten, S. (2015). Heterosexist discourses how feminist theory shaped campus sexual violence policy. In S. Carrigan Wooten & R. W. Mitchell (Eds.), *The crisis of campus sexual violence critical perspectives on prevention and response*. Routledge.

Chantler, K., Donovan, C., Fenton, R., & Bracewell, K. (2019). *Findings from a national study to investigate how British universities are challenging sexual violence and harassment on campus and sexual violence self-assessment checklist for universities*. University of Central Lancashire.

Christie, N. (1986). The ideal victim. In E. Fattah (Ed.), *From crime policy to victim policy: Reorienting the justice system*. Macmillan.

Crenshaw, K. (1991). Mapping the margins: Intersectionality, identity politics, and violence against women of color. *Stanford Law Review*, *43*(6), 1241–1299.

Donovan, C. (2017). An exploration of Spare Rib's treatment of violence between women in same sex relationships. In A. Smith (Ed.), *Re-reading Spare Rib*. Palgrave Macmillan

Donovan, C., & Barnes, R. (2018). Eligibility and ideal LGB&T victims. In M. Duggan (Ed.), *Revisiting the ideal victim concept*. Policy Press.

Donovan, C., & Barnes, R. (2019). Re-tangling the concept of coercive control: A view from the margins and a response to Walby and Towers (2018). *Criminology and Criminal Justice*. https://doi.org/10.1177/1748895819864622 First Published July 26, 2019.

Donovan, C., & Barnes, R. (2020). *Queering the narratives of domestic violence and abuse*. Palgrave.

Donovan, C., Chantler, K., Fenton, R., & Bracewell, K. (2020). Feminist activism among academic staff in the movement to address gender- based violence on campus. In S. Marine & R. Lewis (Eds.), *Collaborating for change transforming cultures to end gender-based violence in higher education*. Oxford University Press.

Donovan, C., & Hester, M. (2014). *Domestic violence and sexuality: What's love got to do with it?* Policy Press.

Donovan, C., Magić, J., & West, S. (2021). *LGBT+ domestic abuse needs assessment for central Bedfordshire council*. Galop.

Duenas, J. M., Racionero-Plaza, S., Melgar, P., & Sanvicen-Torne, P. (2021). Identifying violence against the LGTBI+ community in Catalan universities. *Life Sciences, Society and Policy*, *17*(3), 1–10.

Edwards, K. M., Sylaska, K. M., Barry, J. E., Moynihan, M. M., Banyard, V. L., Cohn, E. S., Walsh, W. A., & Ward, S. K. (2015). Physical dating violence, sexual violence, and unwanted pursuit victimization: A comparison of incidence rates among sexual-minority and heterosexual college students. *Journal of Interpersonal Violence*, *30*(4), 580–600.

Fenton, R., & Mott, H. (2018). Evaluation of the intervention initiative: A bystander intervention program to prevent violence against women in universities. *Violence and Victims*, *33*(4), 645–662.

Gallardo-Nieto, E. M., Gomez, A., Gairal-Casado, R., & del Mar Ramis-Salas, M. (2021). Sexual orientation, gender identity and gender expression-based violence in Catalan universities: Qualitative findings from university students and staff. *Archives of Public Health*, *79*(16), 1–13.

Jamieson, L. (1998). *Intimacy and personal relationships in modern society.* Polity Press.

NUS. (2011). *Hidden marks: A study of women students' experiences of harassment, stalking, violence and sexual assault.* Retrieved June 4, 2020, from www.nusconnect.org.uk/resources/hiddenmarks-a-study-of-women-students-experiences-of-harassment-stalking-violence-and-sexualassault

NUS. (2015). *Education beyond the straight and narrow. LGBT students' experience in higher education.* National Union of Students.

NUS. (2018). *Power in the academy: Staff sexual misconduct in UK higher education.* Retrieved November 30, 2021, from www.nusconnect.org.uk/resources/nus-staff-student-sexual-misconduct-report

Office for National Statistics (ONS). (2018). *Women most at risk of experiencing partner abuse in England and Wales: Years ending March 2015 to 2017.* ONS.

Phipps, A., & Smith, G. (2012). Violence against women students in the UK: Time to take action, *Gender and Education, 24*(4), 357–373.

Potter, S., Moschella, E., Moynihan, M. M., & Smith, D. (2020). Sexual violence among LGBQ community college students: A comparison with their heterosexual peers. *Community College Journal of Research and Practice, 44,* 10–12, 787–803.

Roberts, N., Donovan, C., & Durey, M. (2019). Agency, resistance and the non-'ideal' victim: How women deal with sexual violence. *Journal of Gender-Based Violence, 3*(3), 323–338.

Roberts, N., Donovan, C., & Durey, M. (2020). Gendered landscapes of safety: How women construct and navigate the urban landscape to avoid sexual violence. *Criminology and Criminal Justice,* OnlineFirst. https://doi.org/10.1177/1748895820963208.

Schulzea, C., & Perkins, W. (2017). Awareness of sexual violence services among LGBQ-identified college students. *Journal of School Violence, 16*(2), 148–159.

Universities UK. (2016). *CHANGING THE CULTURE. Report of the universities UK taskforce examining violence against women, harassment, and hate crime affecting university students.* www.universitiesuk.ac.uk/policy-and-analysis/reports/Documents/2016/changing-the-culture.pdf

Universities UK. (2019). *Changing the culture. Tackling gender-based violence, harassment and hate crime: Two years on.* www.universitiesuk.ac.uk/sites/default/files/field/downloads/2021-07/uuk-changing-the-culture-two-years-on.pdf

Vera-Gray, F., & Kelly, L. (2020). Contested gendered space: Public sexual harassment and women's safety work. *International Journal of Comparative and Applied Criminal Justice, 44*(4), 265–275.

Walby, S., & Towers, J. (2018). Untangling the concept of coercive control: Theorizing domestic violent crime. *Criminology and Criminal Justice.* Epub ahead of print 7 January 2018. doi:10.1177/1748895817743541

Walby, S., Towers, J., Balderston, S., Corradi, C., Francis, B., Heiskanen, M., Helweg-Larsen, K., Mergaert, L., Olive, P., Palmer, E., Stöckl, H., & Strid, S. (2017). *The concept and measurement of violence against women and men.* Policy Press.

Walters, M. L., Chen, J., & Breiding, M. J. (2013). *The national intimate partner and sexual violence survey (NISVS): 2010 findings on victimization by sexual orientation.* National Center for Injury Prevention and Control, Centers for Disease Control and Prevention.

Warner, R. M. (2013). *Applied statistics: From bivariate through multivariate techniques.* Sage.

6 Perceptions of consent in UK Higher Education

Implications for policy and training

Ngozi Anyadike-Danes

Much of the research discussed in this chapter focuses on sexual consent in the context of unwanted and non-consensual sexual experiences occurring at university as that has been a primary driving force within this research area. More specifically, I examine sexual consent definitions and understanding in reference to university students and from the perspective of UK Higher Education Institutions (HEIs).[1] An understanding of sexual consent does not suddenly occur when students arrive at university; thus, it is necessary to understand how students might define sexual consent prior to attending university. Similarly, as will be discussed, HEIs' sexual consent definitions (within their policies) may overlap with, or run parallel to, the law; thus, it is important to understand sexual consent from a legal perspective too. While the intent of this chapter is not to extensively review the law on sexual consent or non-consensual sexual activity, this chapter begins with a broader discussion of sexual consent in UK law and society. It is likely that some of students' sexual consent knowledge may be sourced from the law, but from elsewhere too.

Conceptualizing sexual consent

Sexual consent can be understood as a form of agreement between two people (or more) concerning sexual activity they wish to engage in together; each person involved should be informed about the proposed sexual activity, have the ability to agree and agree freely (or, voluntarily). Though some research seems to indicate that university students possess a basic grasp of sexual consent as an agreement to engage in sexual activity (King et al., 2020; Marg, 2020; Wignall et al., 2020), the conditions of when someone can give consent appear to be less understood.

The topic of sexual consent, from a legal standpoint, focuses exclusively on determining whether sexual activity was consensual. In the UK, sexual consent is attached to three conditions: capacity, agreement, and free choice (Sexual Offences Act, 2003; Sexual Offences Order, 2008; Sexual Offences [Scotland] Act, 2009). Outside of these conditions, an individual cannot or has not consented.

DOI: 10.4324/9781003252474-7

Capacity

An individual's capacity to consent can also be understood as their ability to agree. A person who has the ability to agree is determined to be of legal consenting age (16 years old in the UK)[2] and possessing the cognitive capacity to understand and make informed decisions without impairment (Crown Prosecution Service (CPS), 2021b). There are a number of related considerations regarding whether an individual has the cognitive capacity to agree, but the focus of this section will be on sobriety and substance-induced incapacity.

A rather contentious element relating to the ability to consent, particularly within a Higher Education (HE) student population, is the relationship between sexual consent and intoxication or incapacitation (lacking capacity; Jozkowski & Wiersma, 2015; Shumlich & Fisher, 2018). Unlike driving a car, for example, there is no legally quantified limit set for intoxication in sexual situations; in this context, a person must not be so intoxicated that they are unconscious, unable to recall and/or make decisions to engage in sexual activity (Clough, 2019; CPS, 2021b). Overconsumption of alcohol is a common practice at university, but it is difficult to quantify how much alcohol, or of a substance, results in a person's incapacitation because this can vary from person to person depending on, for example, their body type, gender, and tolerance level and also between types of alcoholic drinks and substances. Research suggests that some students lack understanding about sexual consent and inebriation (Hirsch et al., 2019; Marg, 2020).

To further complicate matters, the consumption of alcohol (or other substances) may be used as a confidence booster when new students attempt to assimilate into the university culture or impress their new peers (Banister & Piacentini, 2006). Up until this point, students may have sourced their consent understanding from a variety sources – official sources such as relationship and sexual health classes received whilst at school and unofficial sources such as peers, pornography, and social media (Dawson et al., 2019; MacDougall et al., 2020). For example, 54% ($n = 688$) of Irish university students reported using pornography as a source of sexual information (Dawson et al., 2019). If much of their knowledge is sourced from school, alcohol may not have been addressed at all given the likely age of students at the time. Sources outside of school may have normalized alcohol consumption in the context of sexual activity. Subsequent knowledge may have been provided by their university, but students receive competing messages – campus student culture encourages inebriation. Students may not have had the opportunity to discuss consensual sexual activity when under the influence of alcohol. Through consent workshops and other prevention initiatives (Salazar et al., 2014, 2019; Thompson et al., 2021), students can be educated about alcohol and substance use in the context of sexual activity, particularly regarding the signs of incapacitation (e.g., slurred, or incomprehensible speech, stumbling, or unable to stand).

Expressed agreement

Expressed agreement refers to the communication of consent – the law presumes that people actively communicate consent to one another in a manner that is understandable to both individuals. So, consent cannot be presumed by inaction;

silence does not mean yes and the lack of no does not mean yes. It is also implied that communication is constant throughout the activity and that individuals equally possess the confidence and self-awareness to communicate refusal or sudden loss of interest in participating. Consent, therefore, can be withdrawn before or during a sexual act. Communication may be non-verbal (e.g., gestures, body language) but explicit verbal communication is often considered the "gold-standard" (Beres, 2014). It is presumed that there could be no miscommunication if an individual has clearly, verbally, stated their consent and it also aligns the closest with the law (Munro, 2010). There is mixed research to suggest how students express consent – sometimes the research covers hypothetical sexual activity, specific sexual acts, genders, or people in committed relationships, less research has examined multiple conditions at once (see Muehlenhard et al., 2016 for review; Wood et al., 2019). Further discussion of university students' consent communication practices will be explored in the following section.

Free choice

Individuals must feel free to make their choice to participate without fear of coercion, force, intimidation, or threat. If an individual "consents" under any of these conditions, consent is negated as they were not free to give consent. So, if someone verbally said yes to a sexual act, but felt threatened into doing so, this is not consensual. Within this chapter, coercion is understood as "a continuum of tactics used to elicit sexual activity from unwilling partners" (Pugh & Becker, 2018, p. 3). Threatening, forceful, or coercive tactics may take many forms; for example, an individual may use threatening or intimidating language, physical force, or manipulate another individual into participating in a sexual activity. There are many reasons that an individual may feel that they are not freely able to consent to a sexual situation yet acquiesce because they judge it to be the safer option. It is necessary to educate students on appropriate ways to communicate sexual interest with a (potential) partner, as sexual scripts and behavioural double standards (as will be discussed later) may mean that one person's persuasion technique is actually considered manipulative or coercive by the other person. Additionally, "choice" suggests there are options – consenting or refusal; this presumes that, again, each individual feels free to adopt either option. For some, consent may be the default and they are unaware that it is possible to refuse (Muehlenhard et al., 2016).

The legal conceptualization of sexual consent provides the foundation for understanding consent. There is some research to suggest that students' conceptualizations of sexual consent are often inconsistent with the law (Beres et al., 2004; King et al., 2020; Thomson, 2004).

As with the legal construction of sexual consent, there are additional factors for consideration that may impact sexual consent understanding. This chapter considers the role of setting, sexual precedence, tacit knowledge, gender, and sexual scripts in sexual consent conceptualization. It should be highlighted that, unlike the law, there are likely to be differences amongst sexual and gender minorities – much of the research in this area concerns heterosexual relationships and/or cisgender[3] male and females.

Setting

Sexual consent is a highly nuanced construct, particularly when it is examined separately from a legal framework (Beres, 2007; Levand & Zapien, 2019). For some, they may perceive that the transition from a public setting to a private setting replaces the need for explicit verbal consent because an individual can infer willingness to engage in sexual activity from another individual's willingness to be alone with them (Beres, 2010; Jozkowski & Willis, 2020; Jozkowski et al., 2018; Wignall et al., 2020; Willis & Jozkowski, 2019). Interestingly, it is possible that men and women interpret this transition slightly differently; for men, the transition may be akin to explicit verbal consent communication, whilst women may associate the transition as part of the consent process and it may represent an indication of likelihood of sexual activity (Jozkowski et al., 2018). However, it must be noted that this is a rape myth identified by the CPS (2021a) and can be debunked or challenged in student training.

Sexual precedence

Research seems to suggest that sexual consent is understood and negotiated differently between people in a relationship rather than engaging in casual sex (Humphreys, 2007; Marcantonio et al., 2018; Marg, 2020; Wignall et al., 2020). Consent is regarded as important earlier in the relationship, but once the sexual relationship has been established, it appears a shift occurs where individuals may believe that consent can be assumed. It is theorized that these beliefs relate to sexual precedence theory (Shotland & Goodstein, 1992; Humphreys, 2007). Sexual precedence theory dates back to historic marital rape laws[4] where men were provided a claim upon women with whom they had previously had sex. Sexual precedence, therefore, can be understood as a blanket consent agreement between people who have had sex at least once with each other, which is contrary to the law. Research by Willis and Jozkowski (2019) suggested that participants engaged in less consent communication as sexual precedence increased up until a certain point where participants began to report more consent communication as sexual precedence increased. They stress that prior sexual history does not negate the need for sexual consent, but it might explain a reduction in consent communication. These beliefs, that a previous sexual history or relationship with someone (irrespective of the type of relationship) is tantamount to automatic consent to future sexual acts, are considered rape myths (CPS, 2021a) and can be dispelled through consent workshops.

Tacit knowledge

Beres' (2010) identified tacit knowledge as when two people know that both are interested in having sex. This knowledge is informed and supplemented by everything mentioned earlier and all adds up to indications of willingness to engage in sex. Tacit knowledge in reference to sexual consent and communication has been consistently reiterated by participants as "just knowing" (Beres, 2010; Hardesty et al., 2021; Holmström et al., 2020; Jozkowski & Hunt, 2013;

Schobert et al., 2021; Wignall et al., 2020; Willis & Jozkowski, 2019). Tacit knowledge directly opposes clear verbal communication of sexual consent as it relies on each individual to be highly literate in each other's body language. By implementing consent initiatives, participants may become more confident and knowledgeable about communicating consent and interpreting their partner's consent language.

Gender

There is a paucity of research focusing on sexual consent definitions, generally and in reference to university students (Beres, 2007; Fenner, 2017; Muehlenhard et al., 2016). There is some indication that there are no gender differences between how men and women define sexual consent (Graf & Johnson, 2020; Jozkowski et al., 2014a), rather there are differences in their communication (Beres et al., 2004; Hall, 1998; Hickman & Muehlenhard, 1999; Humphreys, 2007; Jozkowski et al., 2014b) and interpretation of sexual consent cues (Jozkowski et al., 2014a; Newstrom et al., 2021). Largely, results seem to suggest that men may be more likely to communicate verbally, whilst women may rely on non-verbal communication (Jozkowski & Peterson, 2013; Jozkowski et al., 2014b). However, it appears to be the other way round for interpretation of sexual consent communication (Newstrom et al., 2021). These results may reflect traditional sexual scripts where men are expected to be proactive in their sexual pursuit of women and women respond to their actions (Laner & Ventrone, 2000; Rose & Frieze, 1993).

Sexual scripts

Sexual scripts provide a culturally and socially constructed set of guidelines for understanding sexual interactions (Simon & Gagnon, 1986). There is no explicit manual for these scripts nor is it clear when individuals learn them (Frith & Kitzinger, 2001), but they do appear to be predominantly hetero-normative and outline how men and women should act in sexual situations involving the opposite sex (Power et al., 2009; Seidman, 2005; Starks et al., 2018). There is a growing body of research that suggests there are differences between same-sex and opposite-sex sexual scripts (Griner et al., 2021; Sternin et al., 2021), but it is still in its infancy. The most well-known sexual script positions women as sexual gatekeepers and men as sexual initiators (Marcantonio et al., 2018; Wiederman, 2005; Willis et al., 2019). This departs from the idea that sexual activity involves a mutual agreement between individuals. Rather, it reflects a dominant sexual consent discourse that views consent as something that is given by one (women) and received by another (men; Hirsch et al., 2019; Ólafsdottir & Kjaran, 2019). Further, it implies that men are constantly seeking sex and women are both passively experiencing it and also in charge of determining how far a given sexual encounter may go (Humphreys, 2007; Jackson & Cram, 2003; Murray, 2018).

The interaction between sexual scripts and consent may be limited because the implication is that the sexual script outlines consensual sex; as such, an individual following the script has engaged in consensual sex by default. There is little research including (or focusing exclusively on) genders outside of the binary, but a recent study found that non-binary participants more often used verbal consent communication during recent penetrative sexual encounters (McKenna et al., 2021). It was hypothesized that this may be because there are no clear sexual scripts for non-binary people resulting in them relying on clear communication to reduce the risk of miscommunication.

Students' sexual consent conceptualization

A consistent theme concerning sexual consent is, firstly, the assumption that everyone understands sexual consent in the same way, and, secondly, their sexual consent understanding fuels their actions and/or motivations for sexual behaviour. Unsurprisingly, at least in HE student populations, these assumptions appear to be false (Hirsch et al., 2019; Marg, 2020; Natzler & Evans, 2021; Wignall et al., 2020). This section will discuss research focusing on university students and their understanding of sexual consent and opinions regarding sexual misconduct policies and campaigns.

General understanding of consent

In 2014, Beres examined how young people in Canada and New Zealand defined sexual consent. The results indicated that participants defined sexual consent in three different ways: as the minimum requirement for acceptable sexual activity; a discrete event; and a feature separate from a relationship. The participants' sexual consent understanding was identified separately from how they understood communicating willingness to have sex; she concluded that these findings demonstrated the necessity of using explicit language in sexual violence prevention education and research.

Sexual consent as a discrete event and irrelevant to pre-established relationships has been previously identified in research (e.g., Beres, 2007; Humphreys, 2000; Humphreys, 2004) and forms part of some sexual consent measurements. Sexual agreement and/or refusal may exist as a more continuous process (Holmström et al., 2020; Schobert et al., 2021; Singleton et al., 2021) and sexual consent negotiations may occur well before the act itself. Considering sexual consent as a discrete event rather than a continuous exchange is associated with stereotyped attitudes and beliefs relating to sexual consent and may refer to rape myths related to marital rape[5] (Ferro et al., 2008).

Rape myth acceptance

Rape myth acceptance (RMA) refers to the extent to which an individual accepts stereotypes related to sexual victimization and/or perpetration (Burt,

1980). Individuals with higher RMA are more likely to believe in these stereo-types. Higher RMA has been linked to men and individuals who hold more traditional attitudes towards gender and sexual behaviour (Burt, 1980; Lonsway & Fitzgerald, 1995; Schewe, 2002). A subset of RMA is token resistance; this refers to the belief that individuals (the perpetrator) perceive refusal or resis-tance to a sexual advance as merely tokenistic (i.e., for show or politeness) and an individual should persist because the person will eventually consent once a socially acceptable amount of "give and take" has occurred (Muehlenhard & Hollabaugh, 1988; Muehlenhard & Rodgers, 1998; Osman, 1998).

The hypothesized relationship between RMA and consent can be under-stood on at least three levels – higher RMA may relate to a lower sexual consent comprehension, decreased likelihood in engaging in sexual consent negotia-tions, and/or decreased understanding of sexual consent cues. Logically, it seems likely that RMA is related to sexual consent (both conceptually and practically), yet this area has been underresearched. During the development of their dual measures of sexual consent, Jozkowski et al. (2014b) found that men who used pressure to engage in sexual consent negotiations had higher RMA and higher token resistance beliefs. This might indicate a potential relationship between rape myths (or RMA) and a decreased understanding of sexual consent cues and lower sexual consent comprehension.

Sexual consent and the law

It should come as no surprise that research suggests that students do not con-ceptualize sexual consent as it is defined in legislation – that is, their under-standing of sexual consent is not consistently in line with how the law defines sexual consent (Beres, 2014; Hirsch et al., 2019; King et al., 2020; Marg, 2020). There are two competing issues here: students' complete ignorance of the law (i.e., their understanding of sexual consent does not match the law) and students' lack of motivation to operationalize the law (i.e., their legal understanding is correct, but their actual sexual behaviour does not appear to reflect their understanding). However, claims about students and their under-standing of consent are difficult to make – there is a paucity of research that has explicitly examined students' sexual consent understanding beyond the use of implicit attitudinal measures (e.g., Humphreys & Brousseau, 2010) and communication measures (e.g., Jozkowski et al., 2014b). Even less research (Bonistall Postel, 2020) has examined international students' knowledge of consent, but they may require specifically designed initiatives.

Communicating sexual consent

Consistently, research has found that students do not verbally express sexual consent (Beres, 2010; Beres et al., 2004; Humphreys, 2007; Jozkowski et al., 2014b; Wignall et al., 2020), also known as explicit sexual communica-tion. In contrast, non-verbal sexual consent expression is often referred to as implicit sexual communication; however, it is also possible for verbal sexual consent communication to be implicit (Beres, 2007, 2010; Curtis & Burnett, 2017). Findings from Curtis and Burnett (2017) suggested that students regarded explicit sexual communication (or, affirmative consent) as awkward and explicitly saying yes or no to sex was not normalized – students model their behaviours on their peers' actions and media depictions of explicit sexual communication is less common.

Interestingly, some researchers have suggested that students understand that it is better to utilize verbal behaviours and appreciate that this is considered best practice, yet continue to rely on implicit non-verbal behaviours to communicate sexual consent (or negotiate the occurrence of sexual activity; Beres, 2010; Curtis & Burnett, 2017). Some researchers have examined whether there are differences in students' use of verbal sexual consent communication. For example, there is a positive relationship between explicit sexual consent communication as the sexual behaviour becomes more intimate (Humphreys, 2007; Marcantonio et al., 2018; Willis et al., 2019) and it appears that sexual consent communication is gendered (Jozkowski & Peterson, 2013; Wiederman, 2005; Willis et al., 2019). Though it might be considered hopeful that students understand the importance of verbally negotiating sexual consent, it speaks to a failure somewhere in the system that they may not feel confident in expressing themselves (Shumlich & Fisher, 2020).

Idealized versus realized sexual consent practices

Several studies have demonstrated that students' understanding of sexual consent (as measured in the study) differs from their sexual consent practices. Results from Beres' (2014) work suggested that consent was distinct from how young people describe their experiences of negotiating sex – "communicating a willingness to participate in sex [was] not the same thing as consenting to sex" (Beres, 2014, p. 385). In short, sexual consent has become so loaded that one person's definition of sexual consent may vastly differ from another's. This has implications for how campaigns and programmes to reduce or prevent sexual violence are designed. This differentiation is also reflected in Marg's (2020) research where some male students struggled to align their understanding of their partner's consent with their partner's willingness. As such, Marg (2020) suggested that educators should discuss willingness or agreement rather than consent; Wignall et al. (2020) had similar recommendations for designing student-focused campaigns.

Substances

Students appear to understand that alcohol and other substances complicate sexual consent negotiations (Beres, 2014; Hirsch et al., 2019; Humphreys, 2004; Marg, 2020); however, this understanding is juxtaposed with confusion about how to give and receive consent under these conditions (Hirsch et al.,

2019; Jozkowski et al., 2019; Marg, 2020). As with much of this research, there are gender differences to consider. Men and women, generally, differ on their substance tolerance for a variety of reasons (e.g., physical differences in alcohol metabolism) and, similarly, their behaviour under the influence may also differ making it difficult to determine someone's capacity.

Consent within university policy

It seems clear that there is some evidence to suggest, albeit varied and not always representative, that students understand sexual consent to some extent. For example, only 9% of students responding to the Brook and the Higher Education Policy Institute's (Natzler & Evans, 2021) survey in 2020 reported that they received any education about sex and relationships whilst at university. Over 50% of students completing this survey wanted sex and relationships education to be compulsory during "Fresher's week", the week where new students arrive at the university, and 67% indicated that they wanted this education to extend beyond the opening weeks of university. Students were confident they understood that consent was important irrespective of an ongoing relationship (92%) but became less confident when asked about the legal definition of consent (74%) and consent in the context of alcohol consumption (70%). Interestingly, 49% of students felt that their school provided them with comprehensive education on sexual consent, but only 27% felt prepared for sex and relationships that might occur at university.

These findings may not be entirely demographically representative of the UK HE student population, but they suggest that students feel confident in their sexual consent knowledge but, knowing that they may experience different types of sexual relationships at university, they feel ill-prepared.

To that point, it is necessary to understand where sexual consent sits within HEIs' framework, how sexual consent is defined within their policies, and what responsibilities they have to ensure students understand sexual consent. Staff (academic and administrative) play a crucial role in the development and implementation of policy, but the focus of this chapter will primarily be on HEI infrastructures[6] as a whole.

Sexual misconduct policies

From the perspective of HEIs, sexual consent exists within the framework of sexual misconduct offences where it should be clearly defined. It is not the intent of this chapter to outline sexual misconduct offences in great detail, rather to highlight how sexual consent might be considered. Each HEI may choose how they define consent – they may define consent strictly in line with the law, or they may choose to define it more (or less) specifically (Cowan & Munro, 2021). They may choose whether it is necessary to establish whether the perpetrator knew (or should have known) that the victim-survivor was not consenting but, equally, they may also choose whether it is only necessary for the reporting party to demonstrate their lack of consent. There is, however, sector guidance available to HEIs produced by Universities UK (UUK) and Pinsent Masons (2016). This guidance encourages HEIs to define unacceptable behaviour, define terms (including consent) that have the propensity to be mis-interpreted, and indicate the relevant disciplinary action afforded each type of behaviour. However, this guidance is not compulsory and there is no mandated structure that HEIs must follow regarding their policies.

The goal of a sexual misconduct (or similar) policy is to outline what is considered (in)appropriate behaviour by the university as an institution and community. It is often mandatory for students to sign a code of conduct that represents their commitment to adhering to these behavioural standards (UUK, 2016). If non-consensual sexual behaviour falls under sexual misconduct (or, similar) as defined by an institution's policy, then any student perpetrating such behaviour has violated the code of conduct.

There is a historic lack of action by university communities to involve themselves in sexual misconduct complaints (Cowan & Munro, 2021). This reluctance may, traditionally, be heavily influenced by recommendations made by the Zellick Review in 1994 (Zellick, 1994). These recommendations sug-gested that universities should avoid investigating serious crimes and should only consider investigating once a criminal investigation had concluded. This practice may have continued, but for a catalytic moment when the National Union of Students (NUS) reported the scale of sexual violence to which female students attending UK universities were subjected (Smith, 2010). Following their publication, an increasing number of reports have documented students' experiences of sexual violence at university (e.g., Brook and Absolute Research, 2019; Phipps & Young, 2015; Revolt Sexual Assault and the Student Room, 2018). Five years later, UUK's dedicated taskforce was set up (Smail, 2019) with the remit to create safer environments for students attending university.

In 2016, UUK published their "Changing the Culture" report where they outlined the impact of violence against women, harassment, and hate crime affecting university students. Their recommendations included setting clear behavioural expectations enforced by disciplinary regulations that should address unacceptable behaviour. They also recommended instituting consent classes to educate students on consent. Choosing to centre consent would still suggest that it is necessary that the university's consent definition is well-understood and known to the student body (DeMatteo et al., 2015).

Consent workshops or classes are considered one of the most popular forms of prevention initiatives (UUK, 2018). Prior to 2020, sexual consent was not a compulsory component of sexual education at UK secondary schools (Hum-phreys & Towl, 2020). As such, consent classes seek to educate students on both the legal definition of consent and the university's definition; behaviours classed as sexual misconduct may also be outlined and defined. These classes also try to educate students about rape myths, sexist behaviour, rape culture, and lad culture. Further, they attempt to reduce the risk of perpetration by decreas-ing beliefs and attitudes known to increase perpetration (e.g., hostile attitudes towards women, hypermasculinity, etc.). They may also provide students with the knowledge, confidence, and tools to recognize unacceptable behaviour and challenge it (Edwards et al., 2018; Humphreys & Towl, 2020). On a community level, improving knowledge about consent may shift campus norms to normal-ize consent conversations and transition away from rape culture and towards a culture of consent (Crocker & Sibley, 2020; Hill & Crofts, 2021). There is a distinct lack of research on the implementation of consent workshops in the UK, but Irish researchers have implemented a series of consent workshops that appear to have improved students' attitudes towards consent and increased their knowledge about alcohol and consent (MacNeela et al., 2018).

UUK reviewed the progress of 95-member organizations' attempts to tackle sexual misconduct and gender-based violence two years later in their report (Smail, 2019). The results indicated that their member universities had updated policies and created initiatives designed to change attitudes and behaviours that might result in sexual misconduct. For example, 89% had created sexual misconduct policies that raise awareness of (un)acceptable behaviour, 65% were delivering student consent training, and 59% had adopted a zero-tolerance culture across institutional activities. Their results also highlighted that 88% of surveyed universities had sought to change institutional culture by embedding changes into university governance structures and institutional policies. How-ever, their report does not provide much detail regarding the specific changes made or the content of sexual misconduct policies. Further, findings from Natzler and Evans (2021) would suggest that some of these changes were not so apparent to students.

Similarly, in 2021, the student-led group Reclaim the Campus (2021) published the Reclaim Report outlining their analysis of 41 HEIs' sexual mis-conduct policies. The universities chosen for their analysis were, at the time of analysis, ranked in the top 40 UK universities by enrolment (Higher Edu-cation Statistics Authority, 2021). Compared to the results mentioned earlier, only 13 universities had a dedicated sexual misconduct policy and only 32% (13 universities) had referenced UUK and Pinsent Masons' guidelines (UUK & Pinsent Masons, 2016); as such, it was no surprise that one of Reclaim the Campus' recommendations was that universities should define consent within the context of sexual misconduct. Though there is a lack of research on students and their understanding of consent (particularly as it pertains to law), there is an implicit acknowledgement by policymakers that it is not well-understood by students (or, staff); thus, a clear definition is necessary. This would also align with findings from Revolt Sexual Assault and the Student Room (2018) who found that 49% of their sample did not completely understand sexual consent.

UUK lists 140 HEIs as member organizations (UUK, n.d.) and all 41 HEIs included in the Reclaim Report are on their list of members. If UUK mem-bers cannot create appropriate sexual misconduct policies, it is no surprise that non-members might have sexual misconduct policies that are not fit for pur-pose. The lack of consistency across policies evidenced by the Reclaim Report that appears to be contradicted by UUK's (Smail, 2019) own report would suggest that further research is required. Additionally, the implementation of mandatory guidelines might ensure that students (and staff) are equally aware of how their institution defines (un)acceptable behaviour. By implementing community-level policies, universities may start to create the "zero-tolerance" culture that is often emphasized as a method for promoting positive behaviour and reducing sexual misconduct and/or misogynistic behaviour (Atkinson & Standing, 2019; Cowan & Munro, 2021; UUK, 2016). HEIs should be clear to students that zero-tolerance is relative (Humphreys & Towl, 2020) – sanctions may include expulsion for some students, but they may also be allowed to remain on campus.

Duty of care and legal responsibilities

In 2015, the End Violence Against Women Coalition (Whitfield & Dustin, 2015) sent a legal briefing to the UK government and UUK members highlighting that, under the Equality Act 2010 (public sector equality duty) and the Human Rights Act 1998, universities were obliged to ensure the safety of students by preventing abuse and addressing violence against female students. This opinion was subsequently affirmed by UUK's (2016) report the following year. According to UUK, "universities have a responsibility to ensure a safe environment for students" (UUK, 2016, p. 14). As such, it is expected that HEIs have clear and comprehensible policies in place that allow for the creation of these environments. In 2018, the Women and Equalities' Parliamentary Committee recommended that the UK government establish and enforce financial sanctions for universities who were not actively prohibiting sexual discrimination and harassment on campus; this system would be similar to the American Title IX requirements (Women and Equalities Committee, 2018) – the government declined the recommendation.

Research is clear that institutional responses to sexual violence influence both how the present and future incidents are handled but also how students make sense of past incidents (Richardson & Taylor, 2009; Smith & Freyd, 2013). Thus, a failure of an institution to clearly define sexual consent may prevent students from reporting but also accessing support services (D'Enbeau, 2017).

Prior to UUK's report and the 2015 briefing, HEIs' responsibility towards their students was unclear; particularly as the management of HEIs is a devolved matter (i.e., it falls to each individual nation). The closest to national guidance (i.e., covering all four UK nations) is the Quality Code for Higher Education which is produced and maintained by the Quality Assurance Agency for Higher Education (2018). The Code outlines what is expected of HEIs and what students can expect of their university; meeting the requirements of the Code is mandatory and appropriate enactment of the Code should protect the interests of students, yet it is clear that the mandatory aspects are not fit for purpose and further action is required.

HEIs have a moral, and now legal (Equality Act, 2010; Human Rights Act, 1998), duty of care to ensure that their students are healthy and safe whilst they are attached to the institution (Cowan & Munro, 2021). UUK (2016) have also stressed this duty of care is not limited to physical presence on campus – it applies to placement and study abroad students. It is equally apparent that universities have a duty to care for their students and should act by educating them, but it is unlikely that consent education alone will end university (and beyond) sexual violence.

Summary of key points

This chapter summarized current knowledge about sexual consent in the context of HE – as a construct, as a topic of communication, and as a core component of sexual education. It seems clear that students do lack consent knowledge and would like it to be supplemented by their university. HE students' reports of unwanted and non-consensual sexual experiences have gone unheard for long enough; it is time for universities to take the next step and prevent further experiences from occurring – on campus and beyond. Though there are examples of institutions seeking to improve campus culture and reduce problematic attitudes, the lack of UK-based research makes it difficult to assess the current state of play. Lasting cultural change is required. Admittedly, policies help provide a baseline marker for acceptability, but if there is no action taken nor attempts to change the behaviour, change may last as long as their degree.

Sexual consent under UK law

- *Capacity:* ability to agree; heavily intoxicated individuals may be unconscious or unable to make decisions due to their judgement being impaired by substance use and therefore cannot consent to sexual activity. There is no legal limit quantified in law making it difficult for individuals to determine at what point a person is too incapacitated to consent.
- *Expressed agreement:* communication of consent; individuals have to communicate their consent (or non-consent) to one another. Explicit verbal consent communication (e.g., saying yes/no) is considered the most effective method of communication because it reduces the likelihood of miscommunication.
- *Free choice:* voluntarily deciding without fear of threat, force, or coercion; consenting to sexual activity should mean that an individual has the choice to say yes (verbally or otherwise) or no – consent is not the default option.

Students and their consent conceptualizations

- Students' legal understanding of sexual consent varies, but the law does not typically feature in their conceptualizations.
- Students are less likely to verbally communicate sexual consent, more often they communicate non-verbally.
- There are differences between students' cognitive sexual consent understanding and their actual sexual consent practices.
- Sexual consent and its relationship to alcohol is poorly understood by students.

Consent within university policy

- Universities may choose how they define sexual consent and there is no mandatory framework to follow.
- UUK and Pinsent Masons produced guidance on sexual misconduct policies and related disciplinary procedures.
- Consent workshops are considered a popular prevention initiative because students receive education on topics that they may not have heard about whilst at school.
- Universities have a legal responsibility to ensure campuses are safe for all – Equality Act 2010 and Human Rights Act 1998.
- There is no national regulatory body ensuring that universities have adhered to their legal duty.

Further Reading

Hill, K. M., & Crofts, M. (2021). Creating conversations about consent through an on-campus, curriculum embedded week of action. *Journal of Further and Higher Education*, **45** (1), 137–147.

This article concerns the case study of a week-long consent-focused initiative piloted at a UK university; this event was then reviewed by student and staff on their experience of the event, experiences of sexual victimization, bystander opportunities, reporting practices, knowledge of support services and their consent understanding. The aim of the initiative was to promote sexual violence prevention to change campus culture and provide traditionally oppressed groups with an opportunity to voice their opinion. The organizers prioritized consent because it has found to be an effective topic in sexual violence prevention and because young people appear to struggle with sexual consent negotiation. Students defined consent most often as "giving permission" and students typically saw it as binary. Consent appeared to be the responsibility of one individual, and it could be given or taken away. There was also some confusion about what consent was. This event allowed staff members to talk about sensitive issues without explicitly referencing sexual violence, but lack of centralized university support is likely to impact up-take. Involving staff members in these initiatives is key as they can help develop and support a change in campus culture. Consent-focused initiatives should exist in the wider campus culture as consent is multi-layered and complex – beyond the 'yes means yes, no means no' often featured in campaigns. It was acknowledged how much signposting towards support services this event provided students, and this is important factor given how many students had experience unwanted sexual advances. Given the number of students deciding not to report their experiences, aside from support, it is clear that a stigma exists on campus, in society or both that is limiting students' confidence in reporting their experience. Universities must ensure that appropriate and accessible reporting mechanisms are in place, first, but also seek to address the stigma associated with sexual victimization.

Muehlenhard, C. L., Humphreys, T. P., Jozkowski, K. N., & Peterson, Z. D. (2016). The complexities of sexual consent among college students: A conceptual and empirical review. *The Journal of Sex Research, 53* **(4–5), 457–487.**

This review by Muehlenhard and colleagues provides one of the most extensive reviews about sexual consent research in the context of university students' non-consensual sexual experiences to date. In its opening sections, it highlights a consistent inconsistency in this field of research – how non-consensual sexual experiences (in this case, sexual assault) are ill-defined or used interchangeably with little clarity about what is being defined. This article positions itself from an American perspective, but this does little to limit the value of research collated. With legalities and political context aside, Muehlenhard et al. turn their focus to the prevalence of sexual assault. They summarize the current literature, a necessity because sex research has been referring to the '1 in 5' statistic since it was first presented in 2007. They discuss factors that might affect the likelihood of being subjected to sexual assault – highlighting that women, transgender and first year students are thought to be most at risk. They discuss the role of alcohol and highlighting the risk factors preceding university entry. Following this, they present university life characteristics that might increase the risk of experiencing sexual assault and/or complicate sexual consent. They highlight the lack of comprehensive sexual education received prior to university entry and the lack of formal education about consent. Further, they discuss the impact of different cultural messages targeting men and women that might impact the choices they make (or feel able to make). In the context of alcohol, they acknowledge that it may create false perceptions in how individuals perceive an individual's willingness. Their section on sexual consent conceptualization covers a wide range of areas for consideration. The research section is equally vast and the section following (integrating results, conceptual issues, and policy implications) only further stresses the complexities associated with consent such that it cannot be a limited discussion. A final point that proves useful for all is their 'five principles to consider when thinking about consent' which includes understanding that consent behaviours occur concurrently, and consent cues indicate likelihood rather than agreement. They conclude with limitations (e.g., lack of sample variation, more qualitative research) and that policy should be informed by research.

Notes

1 Unless specified otherwise, 'HEI' refers to UK HEIs.
2 The age of consent is 18 years old if one person in the relationship is in a position of power or authority over the person in the relationship. Additionally, in England, Wales, and Northern Ireland, it is an offence to share intimate ages with individuals under the age of 18. This is similar in Scotland (18 years) except between 16 and 17 year olds in committed relationships.
3 'Cisgender' refers to individuals whose gender identity is the same as the sex they were assigned at birth.
4 In the UK, for example, marriage created conjugal rights between spouses and as marriage could only be annulled by a private Act of Parliament, it was determined that a husband could not (by definition) rape his wife. In 1991, the marital rape exemption was considered illegal, and this decision has been made more explicit in the Sexual Offences Act 2003.
5 An example of a marital rape myth would be "Wives become the property of their husband and therefore could be raped without a regard for punishment" (Ferro, 2008, p. 765).
6 Staff members' understanding of sexual consent is not considered in this chapter.

References

Atkinson, K., & Standing, K. E. (2019). Changing the culture? A feminist academic activist critique. *Violence against women*, *25*(11), 1331–1351.

Banister, E., & Piacentini, M. (2006). Binge drinking – do they mean us? Living life to the full in students' own words. *ACR North American Advances*, *33*, 390–398.

Beres, M. (2010). Sexual miscommunication? Untangling assumptions about sexual communication between casual sex partners. *Culture, Health & Sexuality*, *12*.

Beres, M. A. (2007). 'Spontaneous' sexual consent: An analysis of sexual consent literature. *Feminism & Psychology*, *17*(1), 93–108.

Beres, M. A. (2014). Rethinking the concept of consent for anti-sexual violence activism and education. *Feminism & Psychology*, *24*(3).

Beres, M. A., Herold, E., & Maitland, S. B. (2004). Sexual consent behaviors in same-sex relationships. *Archives of Sexual Behavior*, *33*, 475–486.

Bonistall Postel, E. J. (2020). Violence against international students: A critical gap in the literature. *Trauma, Violence, & Abuse*, *21*(1), 71–82.

Brook and Absolute Research. (2019). *Sexual violence and harassment at UK Universities*. http://legacy.brook.org.uk/data/Brook_DigIN_summary_report2.pdf

Burt, M. R. (1980). Cultural myths and supports for rape. *Journal of Personality and Social Psychology*, *38*(2), 217.

Clough, A. (2019). Finding the balance: Intoxication and consent. *Liverpool Law Review*, *40*(1), 49–64.

Cowan, S., & Munro, V. E. (2021). Seeking campus justice: Challenging the 'criminal justice drift' in United Kingdom university responses to student sexual violence and misconduct. *Journal of Law and Society*, *48*(3), 308–333.

Crocker, D., & Sibley, M. A. (2020). Transforming campus rape culture. In S. B. Marine & R. L. Lewis (Eds.), *Collaborating for change* (pp. 23–46). Oxford University Press. doi:10.1093/oso/9780190071820.003.0002

Crown Prosecution Service. (2021a, May). *Rape and sexual offences – Annex A: Tackling rape myth stereotype*. www.cps.gov.uk/legal-guidance/rape-and-sexual-offences-annex-tackling-rape-myths-and-stereotypes

Crown Prosecution Service. (2021b). *Rape and sexual offences – Chapter 6: Consent.* Legal Guidance, Sexual Offences. www.cps.gov.uk/legal-guidance/rape-and-sexual-offences-chapter-6-consent

Curtis, J. N., & Burnett, S. (2017). Affirmative consent: What do college student leaders think about "yes means yes" as the standard for sexual behavior? *American Journal of Sexuality Education, 12*(3), 201–214.

D'Enbeau, S. (2017). Unpacking the dimensions of organizational tension: The case of sexual violence response and prevention among college students. *Journal of Applied Communication Research, 45*(3), 237–255.

Dawson, K., Nic Gabhainn, S., & MacNeela, P. (2019). Dissatisfaction with school sex education is not associated with using pornography for sexual information. *Porn Studies, 6*(2), 245–257.

DeMatteo, D., Galloway, M., Arnold, S., & Patel, U. (2015). Sexual assault on college campuses: A 50-state survey of criminal sexual assault statutes and their relevance to campus sexual assault. *Psychology, Public Policy, and Law, 21*(3), 227.

Edwards, K. E., Shea, H. D., & Barboza Barela, A. R. (2018). Comprehensive sexual violence prevention education. *New Directions for Student Services, 2018*(161), 47–58.

Fenner, L. (2017). Sexual consent as a scientific subject: A literature review. *American Journal of Sexuality Education, 12*(4), 451–471.

Ferro, C., Cermele, J., & Saltzman, A. (2008). Current perceptions of marital rape: Some good and not-so-good news. *Journal of Interpersonal Violence, 23.*

Frith, H., & Kitzinger, C. (2001). Reformulating sexual script theory: Developing a discursive psychology of sexual negotiation. *Theory & Psychology, 11*(2), 209–232.

Graf, A. S., & Johnson, V. (2021). Describing the "gray" area of consent: A comparison of sexual consent understanding across the adult lifespan. *The Journal of Sex Research, 58*, 448–461. doi:10.1080/00224499.2020.1765953

Griner, S. B., Kline, N., Monroy, E., & Thompson, E. L. (2021). Sexual consent communication among sexual and gender minority college students. *The Journal of Sex Research, 58*, 462–468. doi:10.1080/00224499.2021.1882929

Hall, D. S. (1998). Consent for sexual behavior in a college student population. *Electronic Journal of Human Sexuality, 1*(10), 1–16.

Hardesty, M., Young, S. R., McKinnon, A. M., Merriwether, A., Mattson, R. E., & Massey, S. G. (2021). Indiscrete: How typical college student sexual behavior troubles affirmative consent's demand for clear communication. *Sexuality Research and Social Policy, 113*, 1–16. https://doi.org/10.1007/s13178-021-00611-9

Hickman, S. E., & Muehlenhard, C. L. (1999). "By the semi-mystical appearance of a condom": How young women and men communicate sexual consent in heterosexual situations. *Journal of Sex Research, 36*(3), 258–272.

Higher Education Statistics Authority. (2021, February 9). *Where do students study?* www.hesa.ac.uk/data-and-analysis/students/where-study

Hill, K. M., & Crofts, M. (2021). Creating conversations about consent through an on-campus, curriculum embedded week of action. *Journal of Further and Higher Education, 45*(1), 137–147.

Hirsch, J. S., Khan, S. R., Wamboldt, A., & Mellins, C. A. (2019). Social dimensions of sexual consent among cisgender heterosexual college students: Insights from ethnographic research. *Journal of Adolescent Health, 64*(1), 26–35.

Holmström, C., Plantin, L., & Elmerstig, E. (2020). Complexities of sexual consent: Young people's reasoning in a Swedish context. *Psychology & Sexuality, 11*(4), 342–357. doi:10.1080/19419899.2020.1769163

Humphreys, C. J., & Towl, G. J. (2020). *Addressing student sexual violence in higher education: A good practice guide.* Emerald Publishing Limited.

Humphreys, T. (2007). Perceptions of sexual consent: The impact of relationship history and gender. *Journal of Sex Research, 44*(4), 307–315.

Humphreys, T. P., & Brousseau, M. M. (2010). The sexual consent scale – revised: Development, reliability, and preliminary validity. *Journal of Sex Research, 47*(5), 420–428. https://doi.org/10.1080/00224490903151358

Humphreys, T. P. (2000). *Sexual consent in heterosexual dating relationships: Attitudes and behaviours of university students. Journal of Sexuality Education, 12*(4), 451–471.

Humphreys, T. P. (2004). Understanding sexual consent: An empirical investigation of the normative script for young heterosexual adults. In M. Cowling & P. Reynolds' (Eds.), *Making sense of sexual consent* (pp. 209–225). Ashgate Publishing.

Jackson, S. M., & Cram, F. (2003). Disrupting the sexual double standard: Young women's talk about heterosexuality. *British Journal of Social Psychology, 42*(1), 113–127.

Jozkowski, K. N., & Hunt, M. (2013, November). *Beyond the "dyad": When does consent to sex begin?* [Paper presentation], Annual Meeting of the Society for the Scientific Study of Sexuality.

Jozkowski, K. N., & Peterson, Z. D. (2013). College students and sexual consent: Unique insights. *Journal of Sex Research, 50*(6), 517–523.

Jozkowski, K. N., & Wiersma, J. D. (2015). Does drinking alcohol prior to sexual activity influence college students' consent? *International Journal of Sexual Health, 27*(2), 156–174.

Jozkowski, K. N., & Willis, M. (2020). People perceive transitioning from a social to a private setting as an indicator of sexual consent. *Psychology & Sexuality, 11*(4), 359–372.

Jozkowski, K. N., Manning, J., & Hunt, M. (2018). Sexual consent in and out of the bedroom: Disjunctive views of heterosexual college students. *Women's Studies in Communication, 41*(2), 117–139.

Jozkowski, K. N., Peterson, Z. D., Sanders, S. A., Dennis, B., & Reece, M. (2014a). Gender differences in heterosexual college students' conceptualizations and indicators of sexual consent: Implications for contemporary sexual assault prevention education. *The Journal of Sex Research, 51*(8), 904–916.

Jozkowski, K. N., Sanders, S., Peterson, Z. D., Dennis, B., & Reece, M. (2014b). Consenting to sexual activity: The development and psychometric assessment of dual measures of consent. *Archives of Sexual Behavior, 43*(3), 437–450.

Jozkowski, K., Drouin, M., Davis, J., & Newsham, G. (2019, November). Effects of acute alcohol intoxication on perceived ability to consent to sex and intervene as a bystander. In *APHA's 2019 annual meeting and expo (Nov. 2-Nov. 6).* APHA.

King, B. M., Fallon, M. R., Reynolds, E. P., Williamson, K. L., Barber, A., & Giovinazzo, A. R. (2020). College students' perceptions of concurrent/successive nonverbal behaviors as sexual consent. *Journal of Interpersonal Violence,* 1–15.

Laner, M. R., & Ventrone, N. A. (2000). Dating scripts revisited. *Journal of Family Issues, 21*(4), 488–500.

Levand, M. A., & Zapien, N. (2019). Sexual consent as transcendence: A phenomenological understanding. *International Journal of Transpersonal Studies,* 1–12.

Lonsway, K. A., & Fitzgerald, L. F. (1995). Attitudinal antecedents of rape myth acceptance: A theoretical and empirical reexamination. *Journal of Personality and Social Psychology, 68*(4), 704.

MacDougall, A., Craig, S., Goldsmith, K., & Byers, E. S. (2020). #Consent: University students' perceptions of their sexual consent education. *The Canadian Journal of Human Sexuality, 29*(2), 154–166.

MacNeela, P., O'Higgins, S., McIvor, C., Seery, C., Dawson, K., & Delaney, N. (2018). *Are consent workshops sustainable and feasible in third level institutions?* www.nuigalway.ie/media/smartconsent/SMART-Consent-Report-2018-web-.pdf

Marcantonio, T., Jozkowski, K. N., & Wiersma-Mosley, J. (2018). The influence of partner status and sexual behavior on college women's consent communication and feelings. *Journal of Sex & Marital Therapy, 44*(8), 776–786.

Marg, L. Z. (2020). College men's conceptualization of sexual consent at a large, racially/ethnically diverse southern California university. *American Journal of Sexuality Education*, 1–38.

McKenna, J. L., Roemer, L., & Orsillo, S. M. (2021). Predictors of sexual consent communication among sexual minority cisgender and nonbinary young adults during a penetrative sexual encounter with a new partner. *Sexuality & Culture, 25*, 1490–1508. https://doi.org/10.1007/s12119-021-09831-y

Muehlenhard, C. L., & Hollabaugh, L. C. (1988). Do women sometimes say no when they mean yes? The prevalence and correlates of women's token resistance to sex. *Journal of Personality and Social Psychology, 54*(5), 872.

Muehlenhard, C. L., & Rodgers, C. S. (1998). Token resistance to sex: New perspectives on an old stereotype. *Psychology of Women Quarterly, 22*(3), 443–463.

Muehlenhard, C. L., Humphreys, T. P., Jozkowski, K. N., & Peterson, Z. D. (2016). The complexities of sexual consent among college students: A conceptual and empirical review. *The Journal of Sex Research, 53*(4–5), 457–487.

Munro, V. E. (2010). An unholy trinity? Non-consent, coercion and exploitation in contemporary legal responses to sexual violence in England and Wales. *Current Legal Problems, 63*(1), 45–71.

Murray, S. H. (2018). Heterosexual men's sexual desire: Supported by, or deviating from, traditional masculinity norms and sexual scripts? *Sex Roles, 78*(1), 130–141.

Natzler, M., & Evans, D. T. (2021). *Student relationships, sex and sexual health.* Higher Education Policy Institute Report 139. www.hepi.ac.uk/wp-content/uploads/2021/07/Student-Relationships-Sex-and-Sexual-Health-Survey_Report-139_FINAL.pdf

Newstrom, N. P., Harris, S. M., & Miner, M. H. (2021). Sexual consent: How relationships, gender, and sexual self-disclosure affect signaling and interpreting cues for sexual consent in a hypothetical heterosexual sexual situation. *Sex Roles, 84*(7), 454–464.

Ólafsdottir, K., & Kjaran, J. I. (2019). "Boys in Power": Consent and gendered power dynamics in sex. *Boyhood Studies, 12*(1), 38–56.

Osman, S. L. (1998). The token resistance to sex scale relationships. *Archives of Sexual Behavior, 33*(5), 475–486.

Phipps, A., & Young, I. (2015). 'Lad culture' in higher education: Agency in the sexualization debates. *Sexualities, 18*(4), 459–479.

Power, J., McNair, R., & Carr, S. (2009). Absent sexual scripts: Lesbian and bisexual women's knowledge, attitudes and action regarding safer sex and sexual health information. *Culture, Health & Sexuality, 11*(1), 67–81. https://doi.org/10.1080/13691050802541674

Pugh, B., & Becker, P. (2018). Exploring definitions and prevalence of verbal sexual coercion and its relationship to consent to unwanted sex: Implications for affirmative consent standards on college campuses. *Behavioral Sciences, 8*(8), 69.

The Quality Assurance Agency for Higher Education. (2018, May 3). *The revised UK quality code for higher education.* www.qaa.ac.uk/docs/qaa/quality-code/revised-uk-quality-code-for-higher-education.pdf?sfvrsn=4c19f781_8

Reclaim the Campus. (2021). *The reclaim report – an analysis of UK universities' sexual misconduct policies.* www.reclaimthecampus.com/the-reclaim-report

Revolt Sexual Assault and The Student Room. (2018). *National consultation into the sexual assault and harassment experienced and witnessed by students and graduates from universities across the UK.* https://revoltsexualassault.com/wp-content/uploads/2018/03/Report-Sexual-Violence-at-University-Revolt-Sexual-Assault-The-Student-Room-March-2018.pdf

Richardson, B. K., & Taylor, J. (2009). Sexual harassment at the intersection of race and gender: A theoretical model of the sexual harassment experiences of women of color. *Western Journal of Communication, 73*(3), 248–272.

Rose, S., & Frieze, I. H. (1993). Young singles' contemporary dating scripts. *Sex Roles, 28*(9), 499–509.

Salazar, L. F., Vivolo-Kantor, A., Hardin, J., & Berkowitz, A. (2014). A web-based sexual violence bystander intervention for male college students: Randomized controlled trial. *Journal of Medical Internet Research, 16*(9), e203.

Salazar, L. F., Vivolo-Kantor, A., & Schipani-McLaughlin, A. M. (2019). Theoretical mediators of RealConsent: A web-based sexual violence prevention and bystander education program. *Health Education & Behavior, 46*(1), 79–88.

Schewe, P. A. (2002). Guidelines for developing rape prevention and risk reduction interventions. In P. A. Schewe (Ed.), *Preventing violence in relationships: Interventions across the life span* (pp. 107–136). American Psychological Association. https://doi.org/10.1037/10455-005

Schobert, K., Cooper, S., Fries, N., & Sonia Chervillil, M. (2021). I thought we were vibin': A qualitative exploration of sexual agency and consent in young people. *Sexualities.* doi:10.1177/13634607211026457.

Seidman, S. (2005). From the polluted homosexual to the normal gay: Changing patterns of sexual regulation in America. In C. Ingraham (Eds.), *Thinking straight: The power, the promise, and the paradox of heterosexuality* (pp. 39–61). Routledge.

Shotland, R. L., & Goodstein, L. (1992). Sexual precedence reduces the perceived legitimacy of sexual refusal: An examination of attributions concerning date rape and consensual sex. *Personality and Social Psychology Bulletin, 18*(6), 756–764.

Shumlich, E. J., & Fisher, W. A. (2018). Affirmative sexual consent? Direct and unambiguous consent is rarely included in discussions of recent sexual interactions. *The Canadian Journal of Human Sexuality, 27*(3), 248–260.

Shumlich, E. J., & Fisher, W. A. (2020). An exploration of factors that influence enactment of affirmative consent behaviors. *The Journal of Sex Research, 57*(9), 1108–1121.

Simon, W., & Gagnon, J. H. (1986). Sexual scripts: Permanence and change. *Archives of Sexual Behavior, 15*(2), 97–120.

Singleton, R., Obong'o, C., Mbakwem, B. C., Sabben, G., & Winskell, K. (2021). Conceptualizing consent: Cross-national and temporal representations of sexual consent in young Africans' creative narratives on HIV. *The Journal of Sex Research, 58*, 1161–1172. doi:10.1080/00224499.2021.1952399

Smail, A. (2019). *Changing the culture: Tackling gender-based violence, harassment and hate crime: Two years on.* https://dera.ioe.ac.uk/34600/1/uuk-changing-the-culture-two-years-on.pdf

Smith, C. P., & Freyd, J. J. (2013). Dangerous safe havens: Institutional betrayal exacerbates sexual trauma. *Journal of Traumatic Stress, 26*, 119–124. http://dx.doi.org/10.1002/jts.21778

Smith, G. (2010). *Hidden marks: A study of women students' experiences of harassment, stalking, violence and sexual assault.* www.nus.org.uk/Global/NUS_hidden_marks_report_2nd_edition_web.pdf

Starks, T. J., Pawson, M., Stephenson, R., Sullivan, P., & Parsons, J. T. (2018). Dyadic qualitative analysis of condom use scripts among emerging adult gay male couples. *Journal of Sex & Marital Therapy, 44*(3), 269–280. https://doi.org/10.1080/0092623X.2017.1359713

Sternin, S., McKie, R. M., Winberg, C., Travers, R. N., Humphreys, T. P., & Reissing, E. D. (2021). Sexual consent: Exploring the perceptions of heterosexual and non-heterosexual men. *Psychology & Sexuality*, 1–23.

Thompson, M. P., Zinzow, H. M., Kingree, J. B., Pollard, L. E., Goree, J., Hudson-Flege, M., & Honnen, N. G. (2021). Pilot trial of an online sexual violence prevention program for college athletes. *Psychology of Violence*, *11*(1), 92.

Thomson, R. (2004). 'An adult thing'? Young people's perspectives on the heterosexual age of consent. *Sexualities*, *7*(2), 133–149.

Universities UK. (2016, October 21). *Changing the culture: Report of the Universities UK Taskforce examining violence against women, harassment and hate crime affecting university students*. www.universitiesuk.ac.uk/sites/default/files/field/downloads/2021-07/changing-the-culture.pdf

Universities UK. (2018, March 28). *Changing the culture: One Year On – an assessment of strategies*. www.universitiesuk.ac.uk/sites/default/files/field/downloads/2021-07/changing-the-culture-one-year-on.pdf

Universities UK. (n.d.). *About us – our members*. www.universitiesuk.ac.uk/about-us/our-members

Universities UK and Pinsent Masons. (2016, October 21). *Guidance for higher education institutions: How to handle alleged student misconduct*. www.universitiesuk.ac.uk/sites/default/files/field/downloads/2021-07/guidance-for-higher-education-institutions.pdf

Whitfield, L., & Dustin, H. (2015). *End violence against women coalition spotted: Obligations to protect women students' safety & equality using the public sector equality duty & the human rights act in higher and further education institutions to improve policies and practices on violence against women and girls available*. www.endviolenceagainstwomen.org.uk/wp-content/uploads/Spotted-Obligations-to-Protect-Women-StudentsEy-Safety-Equality.pdf

Wiederman, M. W. (2005). The gendered nature of sexual scripts. *The Family Journal*, *13*(4), 496–502. https://doi.org/10.1177/1066480705278729

Wignall, L., Stirling, J., & Scoats, R. (2020). UK university students' perceptions and negotiations of sexual consent. *Psychology & Sexuality*. doi:10.1080/19419899.2020.1859601

Willis, M., Hunt, M., Wodika, A., Rhones, D., Goodman, J., & Jozkowski, K. (2019). Explicit verbal sexual consent communication: Effects of gender, relationship status, and type of sexual behaviour. *International Journal of Sexual Health*, *31*(1), 60–70. https://doi.org/10.1080/19317611.2019.1565793

Willis, M., & Jozkowski, K. N. (2019). Sexual precedent's effect on sexual consent communication. *Archives of Sexual Behavior*, *48*(6), 1723–1734.

Women and Equalities Committee. (2018, July 25). *Sexual harassment in the workplace*. https://publications.parliament.uk/pa/cm201719/cmselect/cmwomeq/725/725.pdf

Wood, E. F., Rikkonen, K. J., & Davis, D. (2019). Definition, communication, and interpretation of sexual consent. In W. T. O'Donohue & P. A. Schewe (Eds.), *Handbook of sexual assault and sexual assault prevention* (pp. 399–421). Springer Nature Switzerland AG.

Zellick, G. (1994). *Student disciplinary procedures*. Committee of Vice-Chancellors and Principals (CVCP) of the Universities of the United Kingdom.

7 Sexual violence in Higher Education

Prevalence and characteristics of perpetrators

Samuel T. Hales

High rates of sexual violence on university campuses signal to a public health issue that has plagued the Higher Education (HE) sector for decades. Regular incidents of sexual harassment, sexual assault, and rape have rendered universities as "Petri dishes" where cultures that normalise and encourage sexual aggression proliferate. Nowadays, plans to tackle university-based sexual violence form a key part of official conversations on gender-based violence (GBV) prevention across the world (see Muehlenhard et al., 2016).

In the academic community, there has been a growing body of research since the late 1950s examining sexual violence perpetration within HE. This has been rejuvenated in recent years, thanks to increased media and political attention directed at universities and their (mis)handling of sexual misconduct cases. In this chapter, I aim to help facilitate the development of more effective harm prevention interventions for university-based sexual violence by reviewing current academic understanding regarding perpetration. This includes published findings on the prevalence of sexual aggression on university campuses, as well as the typical characteristics of perpetrators and the risk and protective factors associated with their harmful sexual behaviours. I hope to further contribute to academic knowledge by describing emerging research evidence relevant to staff sexual misconduct, an underreported, yet pervasive, form of university-based sexual violence.

It is worth noting that this chapter will predominantly focus on heterosexual male students as perpetrators, given that they commit the majority of sexual crimes on campuses (Breiding, 2015). However, due to recent advances in social scientific research, contemporary literature pertaining to sexual violence perpetration by female and gender minority students will also be described. To this end, uniquely, this chapter offers a holistic overview of extant literature relevant to the perpetration of sexual harm within the HE system, as well as current gaps in our knowledge.

Prevalence of University-Based Sexual Violence

University-based sexual violence occurs at alarming rates on campuses internationally. Recent reviews of prevalence studies suggest that approximately

DOI: 10.4324/9781003252474-8

20–25% of women students in the United States will be the target of sexual aggression whilst enrolled at university, with up to 8.4% being subjected to rape (Fedina et al., 2018). These findings emulate the worrying prevalence estimates from climate surveys conducted in other countries (e.g., Australian Human Rights Commission [AHRC], 2017; National Union of Students [NUS], 2011; Statistics Canada, 2020), though they are likely to represent conservative estimates of prevalence given high rates of underreporting by victim-survivors (Fedina et al., 2018).

Distressingly, research has shown that rates of sexual victimisation drastically increase amongst marginalised groups, including members of the LGBTQ+ community, disabled students, and those from minority ethnic backgrounds (Bonomi et al., 2018; Coulter et al., 2017). Rates of victimisation are comparatively low (<10%) amongst male university students, though their risk of being subjected to sexual aggression is still notably higher than their non-student counterparts in the wider community (Fedina et al., 2018). Across victim-survivor groups, university-based sexual violence is associated with multiple negative long-term health and academic outcomes (Kaufman et al., 2019), as well as a 60% increase in risk of being subjected to a repeat assault (Walsh et al., 2021).

Compared to sexual violence victimisation, there have been relatively few assessments of the prevalence of university-based sexual violence perpetration (Martin et al., 2020). Of those that exist, prevalence estimates vary drastically as a result of differences in methodological approaches to measuring sexual violence (Jouriles et al., 2020), as well as high rates of underreporting amongst perpetrators (Strang & Peterson, 2017). Perhaps the most reliable assessment to date is Anderson et al.'s (2021) systematic review of prevalence studies published between 2000 and 2017, which reported that 29.3% of university males in the United States and Canada have engaged in sexually violent behaviours, with 6.5% having committed rape. These rates were similar to earlier estimates reported by Spitzberg (1999) who found an overall prevalence of sexual violence perpetration of approximately 25% amongst community males (4.7% for rape perpetration) between 1957 and 1997. As with victimisation, high prevalence estimates of male-perpetrated university-based sexual violence have been reported in other countries (e.g., Hales & Gannon, 2021; Martín et al., 2005; Schuster & Krahé, 2019) and highlight a tragic reality of HE: that university campuses are breeding grounds for harmful sexual behaviours.

Similar to the general sexual offending literature, there is a dearth of empirical research examining the prevalence of university-based sexual violence perpetrated by individuals who do not identify as (cisgender or heterosexual) males. Of the studies that do exist, many are limited by their methodological approaches (see Bouffard & Goodson, 2017). For example, a recent prevalence assessment by Martin et al. (2020) estimated that 6–28% of cisgender female students and 0.2–0.7% of gender minority students were identified as perpetrators in reported acts of university-based sexual violence. However, these estimates were based on the offence-related testimonies of victim-survivors and may not accurately reflect prevalence rates; for example, due to the regular underreporting of offences and the possibility of serial offending patterns amongst perpetrators. To this end, it would be valuable to conduct a large-scale assessment of sexual violence perpetration by female and gender-minority students to provide more context to the harmful sexual behaviours and offence-related risk of understudied university groups.

Typical Characteristics of Perpetrators

Over the past two decades, there has been a notable increase in research on university-based sexual violence perpetration (see Moylan & Javorka, 2020). Indeed, recent government policy attention in Europe and North America, as well as the emergence of feminist grassroots movements worldwide (e.g., #MeToo), have intensified the focus on universities to better tackle sexual violence and deliver justice for victim-survivors (Muehlenhard et al., 2016). A beneficial consequence of this is that there is now a broad evidence base pertaining to the characteristics and motivations of the individuals who engage in sexually violent behaviours at university. This section will review the typical demographic characteristics of perpetrators, as well as the micro- through macro-level risk and protective factors associated with their harmful sexual behaviours.

Demographic Characteristics

Whilst those who engage in university-based sexual violence span a broad offender spectrum, research has demonstrated that perpetrators often possess similar demographic traits. For example, perpetrators are typically heterosexual male students (Cantor et al., 2020). In the majority of cases, they are between the ages of 18 and 21 (Hales & Gannon, 2021; Porta et al., 2017; Walsh et al., 2021) and enrolled on an undergraduate course at university (Campbell et al., 2021). Commensurate with their age and level of study, most perpetrators report their highest level of educational achievement as a high school diploma or Further Education qualification (Hales & Gannon, 2021), with relatively few graduate students perpetrating offences (Campbell et al., 2021). There is also emerging evidence to suggest that ethnic background may be associated with risk of engaging in university-based sexual violence, in that white male students typically report a greater proclivity towards, or more recent examples of, non-consensual sexual behaviours than students from minority ethnic backgrounds (e.g., McQuiller Williams et al., 2016; Palmer et al., 2021). Whilst further research is required to substantiate this claim, it is likely that these findings are ascribable to differences in cultural norms and drinking behaviours between ethnic groups, which bear a strong influence on an individual's sexually aggressive behaviours (McQuiller Williams et al., 2016).

In terms of interpersonal relationships, perpetrators tend to have had significantly more intimate and dating partners than their non-offending peers (Abbey & McAuslan, 2004), as well as earlier sexual experiences and a greater number of one-time hook-ups (Abbey & McAuslan, 2004; Walsh et al., 2021). Focusing specifically on victim–offender relationships, perpetrators typically attend the same university as their victim(s) (AHRC, 2017; NUS, 2011) and are known to their victim at the time of their offending (Campbell et al., 2021). Indeed, several victim-survivors report having had prior sexual relations with those who assaulted them (Cantor et al., 2020; NUS, 2011). This highlights that, contrary to popular opinion, rates of stranger-perpetrated sexual violence are low on university campuses.

The Socio-Ecological Model of Sexual Violence

University-based sexual violence is the product of several levels of influence on behaviour (Centers for Disease Control and Prevention [CDC], 2014). Whilst demographic information helps us to understand more about the personal characteristics of the individuals who commit offences, it does not offer adequate insight into the key factors associated with their risk of perpetration. Subsequently, demographic information alone does not allow us to develop effective sexual harm prevention interventions for those likely to offend.

The socio-ecological model (Dahlberg & Krug, 2002) provides a useful holistic framework by which to understand the complex interplay between the micro- and macro-level risk factors associated with sexual violence perpetration (see Figure 7.1). Though typically used to identify prevention strategies for sexual violence victimisation (see Moylan & Javorka, 2020), the model also offers a useful means by which to help researchers investigate why members of the community engage in harmful sexual behaviours. The following section reviews the key risk factors associated with university-based sexual violence perpetration based on the four levels of the socio-ecological model.

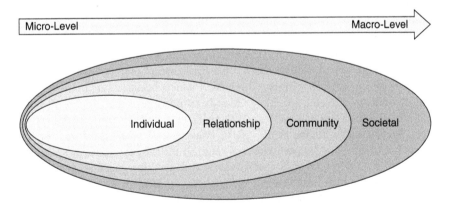

Figure 7.1 A nested illustration of the socio-ecological model of sexual violence. (Adapted from Dahlberg & Krug, 2002.)

Individual Risk Factors

Most research into university-based sexual violence perpetration has examined the influence of psychological, biological, and personal historic factors on a students' risk of engaging in harmful sexual behaviours (see Moylan & Javorka, 2020). These individual-level factors are considered as strong motivators of students' sexually violent behaviours and significantly increase their risk of perpetrating an offence (Teten Tharp et al., 2013). Key risk factors can be classified into four key groups, described subsequently.

The first, and arguably the most validated, category of individual-level risk factors relate to gender-based cognitions. In the context of university-based sexual violence, these typically refer to male students' negative, derogatory, and sexist thoughts about women (see Ray & Parkhill, 2021). For example, researchers have found that male students who self-report adversarial sexist beliefs or hostile attitudes towards women are significantly more likely to have perpetrated a sexually violent act against a female victim at university compared to those with less prejudiced views (e.g., Hales & Gannon, 2021; Kingree & Thompson, 2015; Testa & Cleveland, 2017). Likewise, it has been reported that traditional gender role adherence is highly predictive of sexual aggression amongst male university students (Teten Tharp et al., 2013). Students who score high on measures of rape myth acceptance – a reliable index of sexist attitudes amongst men – are also more likely to report past harmful sexual behaviour (for a review, see Yapp & Quayle, 2018), as well as a proclivity towards future sexual assault perpetration (Palmer et al., 2021).

The second category of individual-level risk factors pertains to a student's sexual behaviours and sex-related cognitions. For example, several research studies have shown that having multiple sexual or dating partners increases a male student's risk of engaging in sexually violent behaviours, as they have access to more opportunities to offend (e.g., Teten Tharp et al., 2013; M. P. Thompson & Morrison, 2013). Likewise, students who have casual or impersonal attitudes towards sex (e.g., a propensity towards uncommitted sexual relationships) typically display more harmful sexual behaviours than those who do not (Abbey et al., 2007; Testa & Cleveland, 2017), as do students with high rates of pornography consumption (Vega & Malamuth, 2007). Interestingly, both of these risk factors are more pronounced in male students with hypermasculine attitudes (Vega & Malamuth, 2007), evidencing the strong link between gender-based cognitions and sexual behaviours. Perhaps the most potent risk factor in this category, though, is past sexual violence perpetration, which a recent meta-analysis has suggested increases a male students' risk of engaging in harmful sexual behaviours by approximately 300% (Steele et al., 2020). This is concerning given that a significant proportion of male students self-report having perpetrated sexual violence before starting university (Salazar et al., 2018).

The third category describes psychosocial and interpersonal factors associated with sexual violence perpetration. A key risk factor here is prior delinquency (i.e., previous non-sexual criminal behaviour), which Steele et al.

(2020) suggested doubles a male student's risk of engaging in sexual aggression at university. Adjustment difficulties and certain aspects of psychopathology (e.g., depression symptoms) comprise another strong predictor of past sexual violence amongst male university students (Nguyen & Parkhill, 2014; Teten Tharp et al., 2013; Walsh et al., 2021), as do impulsivity and attention issues, such as poor self-control (Testa & Cleveland, 2017). Unsurprisingly, students with a tendency towards non-sexual aggression or anger are also more likely to have engaged in harmful sexual behaviours compared to their non-aggressive counterparts (Hales & Gannon, 2021; Kingree & Thompson, 2015). In terms of interpersonal factors, both sexual cue misinterpretation – the miscomprehension of another person's willingness to engage in sexual activity – and empathic deficits have been associated with either past sexual aggression amongst male students (e.g., Martín et al., 2005; Teten Tharp et al., 2013) or other established risk factors for university-based sexual violence (e.g., sexual dominance; Abbey et al., 2006).

The final category relates to substance use and its links with university-based sexual violence. Given the toxic drinking culture that is prevalent across the HE sector, it is unsurprising that several studies have examined the link between alcohol consumption and harmful sexual behaviours amongst students (for a review, see Abbey et al., 2014). For example, many researchers have discovered strong associations between male students' drinking habits or attitudes towards alcohol and their perpetration of sexual violence (e.g., Swartout et al., 2015; M. P. Thompson et al., 2013). Similarly, findings have shown that male students who engage in heavy episodic drinking – a dangerous form of alcohol consumption characterised by excessive intake of alcohol in a short time-period – are significantly more likely to demonstrate sexual aggression than their peers with healthier drinking habits (see Abbey et al., 2014). Given that researchers have discovered that many university students surpass the clinical cut-off for problematic drinking behaviours (e.g., Cooke et al., 2019), these are worrying findings.

Relationship Risk Factors

Research has shown that over one-third of male students would commit sexual assault if assured they would face no negative consequences (see Casey & Lindhorst, 2009). This highlights that conditions promoting university-based sexual violence exist at the relationship and broader community and societal levels; thus, assessing the psychological and personal characteristics of perpetrators alone is not sufficient for understanding their harmful sexual behaviours.

The second level of the socio-ecological model moves beyond individual-level risk factors to examine how proximal social relationships – including those with friends, family members, and intimate or dating partners – influence individual behaviour. In terms of university-based sexual violence, arguably the most compelling relationship-level risk factor is students' perceptions of their peers' attitudes towards harmful sexual behaviours. Several studies have shown that male university students who report having friends that would approve of sexual aggression, or friends that have themselves acted in a sexually aggressive manner, are significantly more likely to report past sexual violence than those without such associations (e.g., Goodson et al., 2021; M. P. Thompson & Morrison, 2013; M. P. Thompson et al., 2013). This perception of peer acceptance of sexual violence establishes a damaging norm that sexual aggression is socially acceptable, which serves as a heuristic that biases perpetrators' ability to make correct decisions in sexual situations (Burkhart & Fromuth, 1991; Hackman et al., 2017).

Sports participation – or rather, participation in certain hypermasculine sports – is another key risk factor for sexual aggression amongst university students (Murnen & Kohlman, 2007). For example, in the United States, students who are members of a "high risk" sports team – that is, a team associated with heavy drinking and a party culture conducive to sexual violence – or who play high-profile team sports (e.g., football) typically report higher rates of past sexual violence than students who are either members of a "low risk" sports team (e.g., athletics or tennis) or non-athletes (Gage, 2008; Young et al., 2017). Similarly, in the UK, involvement in "laddish" sports (e.g., rugby and football), which typically centre around homosocial bonding via inappropriate "banter" and alcohol consumption, has been shown to increase individual risk of committing sexual harassment and assault (e.g., Phipps & Young, 2013). Linked to sports participation, research has also shown that fraternity membership is linked to university-based sexual violence perpetration, particularly amongst US students (Murnen & Kohlman, 2007; M. P. Thompson & Morrison, 2013; Goodson et al., 2021). However, this relationship is arguably likely to be attributable to the drinking and party climates associated with certain fraternities versus membership per se (Kingree & Thompson, 2013).

Relationship-level factors related to childhood upbringing have also been implicated with risk of sexual aggression amongst university students. For example, being subjected to emotional, sexual, and physical abuse (including corporal punishment) in early life have all been demonstrated as strong predictors of university-based sexual violence amongst male students (Porta et al., 2017; Swartout et al., 2015; Walsh et al., 2021). Regular childhood exposure to parental or wider family conflict – particularly physical conflict – has also been linked to expressions of sexual aggression at university by numerous authors (e.g., Swartout et al., 2015; M. P. Thompson & Morrison, 2013). However, Forbes and Adams Curtis (2001) showed that this relationship was weaker for students who reported that their parents used reasoning techniques to end arguments, suggesting that certain parenting styles may be protective factors for university-based sexual violence.

Community Risk Factors

This third level of the socio-ecological model examines how the social environments in which interpersonal relationships occur influence individual behaviour.

For example, research has shown that universities that promote hypermasculine student lifestyles that centre on alcohol consumption, sports participation, and fraternity membership demonstrate increased rates of sexual violence (Moylan & Javorka, 2020; Stotzer & MacCartney, 2016). It has been proposed that this is because these lifestyles reflect a damaging sector-wide *lad culture* – defined as "a group or 'pack' mentality residing in activities such as sport and heavy alcohol consumption, and 'banter' which [is] often sexist, misogynist and homophobic" (p. 28) – that normalises and encourages male students to engage in harmful sexual behaviours (Phipps & Young, 2013). Unsurprisingly then, Higher Education Institutions (HEIs) where levels of alcohol consumption and "frat culture" are less pronounced (e.g., historically Black colleges and universities in the United States) tend to report comparatively lower levels of sexual violence victimisation (see Krebs et al., 2011).

Passive university approaches to sexual harm prevention – such as the non-enforcement of sexual harassment policies, poor campus policing, or lenient outcomes in sexual misconduct cases – are also key community-level risk factors, as they demonstrate to (would-be) perpetrators an institutional acceptance of sexual violence (e.g., Cass, 2007; Stotzer & MacCartney, 2016). These inactions link to the notion of *institutional betrayal* – the deliberate failings of an institution to protect its members' trust and safety – which normalises students' aggressive sexual behaviours and exacerbate sexual trauma amongst victim-survivors (see Smith & Freyd, 2013).

Given that most acts of university-based sexual violence are perpetrated within university-managed accommodation (US Department of Education, 2021), researchers have further proposed various community-level risk factors associated with students' living arrangements and their associations with their community. For example, high levels of residential mobility (where students frequently change accommodation throughout their studies), increased feelings of social isolation, and low levels of social connectedness have all been linked to students' harmful sexual behaviours (Banyard et al., 2021; Dahlberg & Krug, 2002). Similarly, given vast campus-level variations in rates of sexual harassment and assault, geo-economic factors such as university location, funding status, and campus size have also been explored as predictors of sexually violent behaviours. Specifically, US studies have found that rates of sexual violence are typically higher at universities that are rurally located, privately (not federally) funded, and campus-based (Cantor et al., 2020; Cass, 2007; Mohler-Kuo et al., 2004), suggesting that these institutional characteristics constitute key community-level risk factors for harmful sexual behaviours.

Societal Risk Factors

These macro-level risk factors help create a climate in which sexual violence perpetration is considered permissible. As shown in Figure 7.1, societal risk factors encompass individual, relationship, and community-level factors;

thus, they transcend individual HEIs, reflecting instead broader social challenges. Arguably, the most pertinent societal risk factors for sexual violence
are the normative sexual objectification of women and society's nonchalant
attitudes towards sexual harassment and assault (see Szymanski et al., 2011).
With regard to university-based sexual violence, these norms serve two
functions. For male students, they teach that non-consensual sexual behaviours are acceptable forms of interpersonal conduct and reflect a strength of
character. For female students, they teach that individual worth is linked to
sexual promiscuity and underline that sexual violence is an integral part of
one's university experience (see Berkowitz, 2010). These norms are evident
particularly within the milieu of highly sexualised and misogynistically tolerant drinking environments, such as campus bars and nightclubs (E. Thompson
& Cracco, 2008).

It is undoubtable that these social norms link to wider cultural issues with
hypermasculinity (see E. Thompson & Cracco, 2008), patriarchal social structures (Vogel, 2000), and misogynistic religious and cultural belief systems (see
Mikołajczak & Pietrzak, 2014) and may help explain why some university
males do not engage with university sexual harm prevention efforts (e.g.,
Carline et al., 2018).

Federal policies relevant to both sexual violence and wider GBV are also
considered key societal risk factors, particularly if they create or compound
social or educational inequalities between groups (Dahlberg & Krug, 2002).
A noteworthy example from the United States would be the retraction by
the Trump administration of the progressive Obama-era Title IX guidance
on tackling university-based sexual violence. These repeals were believed
by many researchers to increase the risk of sexual harm perpetration on
US campuses, as the amended legislation afforded greater protection to
responding parties in sexual misconduct cases (see Butler et al., 2019).
Given the strong influence that societal risk factors have across other socio-
ecological strata, the influence of policy amendments such as these cannot
be understated.

Staff Sexual Misconduct

Though it receives comparatively little academic attention, various climate
surveys have shown that staff sexual misconduct is worryingly prevalent across
many university campuses.[1] A recent assessment of sexual misconduct amongst
US university students showed that female victim-survivors named members
of staff as perpetrators of sexual assault in roughly 2.3% of cases (Cantor et
al., 2020). These figures were notably higher for both male students and non-
binary students, who named staff as perpetrators in 7.4% and 18.6% of cases,
respectively. In cases of sexual harassment, staff were named as perpetrators in
19.8% of cases overall. Again, high rates of underreporting mean that these are
likely conservative estimates of prevalence (see NUS, 2018); however, similar
reports from Australia (AHRC, 2017), Canada (Statistics Canada, 2020), and

the UK (NUS, 2018) suggest that staff sexual misconduct constitutes a pervasive issue.

Research pertaining to the characteristics of staff perpetrators of university sexual misconduct is scant and, to date, there have been no published studies with those who have committed an offence. However, thanks to work with victim-survivors, researchers do possess some understanding of the demographic characteristics of perpetrators. For example, it is known that most university staff who engage in sexual misconduct against students are employed on academic or research contracts (Cantor et al., 2020; Statistics Canada, 2020) and typically have frequent contact with the individuals they victimise (NUS, 2018). Concurrent with student offending patterns, most perpetrators (>60%) are men, with female members of staff being identified as perpetrators in less than 14% of cases (NUS, 2018). Regarding incident characteristics, evidence suggests that staff are more likely to perpetrate offences against postgraduate than undergraduate students (e.g., AHRC, 2017; Cantor et al., 2020). Similarly, it is known that most staff who perpetrate offences are serial offenders who either offend against multiple individuals or one individual on multiple occasions (Cantalupo & Kidder, 2018). In terms of offence locations, the most common settings for perpetration are within teaching spaces and private staff offices, on public university transport, and on professional placements (AHRC, 2017). In terms of offence types, inappropriate verbal or non-verbal communication (e.g., sexual jokes or unprovoked sexual comments) comprises the most common form of staff sexual misconduct (Statistics Canada, 2020).

Several interesting conclusions can be drawn from the earlier findings. First, that male members of university staff appear to perpetrate the majority of offences underlines that staff sexual misconduct should be considered as part of the wider social issue of gendered and patriarchal violence against women (see NUS, 2018). The aforementioned prevalence estimates suggest that university staff appear not to be immune to the risk factors associated with sexual offending behaviours; therefore, they are likely to be as susceptible towards sexual violence perpetration as male students and should thus receive similar empirical attention. Second, that academic and research staff were the most frequently identified perpetrators in staff sexual misconduct cases suggests that universities need to focus more on the sexualisation of academic learning environments, as well as the influence of power structures on staff offending behaviours. This latter point is evidenced by the disparity in rates of staff sexual misconduct victimisation between undergraduate and postgraduate students, who occupy different levels of authority within university settings. Finally, serial offending patterns appear to be common amongst university staff who perpetrate sexual misconduct. This suggests that university responses to staff who engage in harmful sexual behaviours are too lenient and do not adequately reduce recidivism potential. To this end, universities need to develop more stringent disciplinary processes for staff who have been found guilty of perpetrating offences and appropriately enforce these in sexual misconduct proceedings.

Summary of Key Points

Decades of international research has demonstrated that university students perpetrate sexual violence at higher rates than non-student members of the community. Whilst the prevalence of university-based sexual violence differs between HEIs, recent research has shown that upwards of 29.3% of male students report engaging in at least one harmful sexual behaviour during their university studies, with 6.5% perpetrating rape. Unfortunately, reliable self-report data are not available on the rates of sexual violence perpetrated by female and gender minority students or members of university staff, but research conducted with victim-survivors signals to worrying rates also.

Due in part to recent media and policy attention, academic understanding of the individuals who engage in university-based sexual violence is now well-developed and research findings relevant to the characteristics of perpetrators have been validated across several large-scale studies. The socio-ecological model of sexual violence offers perhaps the most valid framework by which to understand the various micro- through macro-level risk factors associated with perpetrators' past sexual offending behaviours, as well as their proclivity towards future harmful sexual activity. According to the model, risk factors can be divided into four overarching categories that span the various levels of the social ecology; individual-, relationship-, community-, and societal-level risk factors. These risk factors are proposed to interact synergistically to either encourage or discourage sexual violence perpetration.

In terms of sexual harm prevention, effective interventions for individuals at risk of engaging in sexual aggression are likely to be those that adopt a socio-ecological approach to both combat the known risk factors for sexual violence and promote more pro-social behaviours amongst members of the university community. However, robust and comprehensive university policy and procedures for tackling sexual violence – including conscious efforts by university policymakers, administrators, and student groups to promote healthy campus cultures – are also necessary to stop universities being breeding grounds for sexually harmful behaviours. These strategies further demonstrate a university's commitment to tackling the broader issue of GBV and creating safe environments in which students can live and learn.

Ongoing work by social justice campaigns and grassroots feminist movements are likely to catalyse research into university-based sexual violence, thus further increasing our understanding of the risk and protective factors associated with perpetration, as well the efficacy of current campus harm prevention interventions. More academic attention of the time-varying risk factors associated with sexual aggression, harmful sexual behaviours amongst marginalised groups (e.g., female and gender non-conforming students), and staff sexual misconduct will help to fill gaps in current understanding of university-based sexual violence and accelerate positive change.

Further Reading

O'Connor, J., McMahon, S., Cusano, J., Seabrook, R., & Gracey, L. (2021). Predictors of campus sexual violence perpetration: A systematic review of research, sampling, and study design. *Aggression and Violent Behavior,* **58,** **Article E101607. https://doi.org/10.1016/j.avb.2021.101607**

In their recent paper, O'Connor et al. (2021) systematically reviewed 28 empirical articles published between 2000 and 2019 that examined predictors of campus sexual assault amongst US male students. These were appraised against three research questions (RQs): (1) What predictors of campus sexual violence perpetration have been investigated empirically? (2) What sampling methods are used in campus perpetration research studies? And (3) What is the design of these studies?

Regarding RQ1, the authors discovered that a range of variables determined to predict campus sexual assault perpetration had been assessed across the papers included in their review. These could be divided into eight categories: personality factors (the most frequently assessed), attitudinal factors, life experiences, peer influences, alcohol or drug use, sexual behaviour, past perpetration, and other types of factors. Key predictors reflect those described in this chapter and included rape supportive beliefs, derogatory attitudes about women, negative peer associations, adverse childhood experiences, and alcohol consumption. Despite the common knowledge that harmful sexual behaviours are the product of various levels of influence on behaviour, O'Connor and colleagues found that only 11 of the 28 studies included in their systematic review assessed predictor variables beyond the individual level.

In relation to RQ2, the authors discovered large variations in sampling procedures across all reviewed studies. Sample sizes ranged from small ($N = 75$) to large ($N = 6,548$), though the majority of studies (61%) contained fewer than 500 participants. Most studies used convenience sampling techniques to recruit participants, who were predominantly studying at large public universities in the United States. Across all studies, there was a preponderance towards younger White or Caucasian undergraduate participants.

In terms of RQ3, O'Connor and colleagues found vast disparities in the design and measurement approaches across studies. The majority (68%) of the papers they reviewed reported on cross-sectional research that was either observational or experimental in nature. Nine studies were longitudinal, but they used data derived from the same dataset. In all but three studies, the *Sexual Experiences Survey* (Koss & Oros, 1982) was used to probe participants' perpetration of campus sexual assault. Approximately half of the studies (54%) asked participants to report sexual violence perpetrated against a female victim or within the context of a heterosexual relationship.

Based on their findings, the authors proposed several recommendations to guide future campus sexual assault work. First, that more research needs conducting to identify the drivers of perpetration. This includes more targeted assessments of understudied individual-level predictors of sexual violence, as well as broader macro-level factors. Second, that a greater number of longitudinal assessments are needed to assess sexual violence perpetration over time. Third, that researchers should recruit more diverse samples to assess differences in harmful sexual behaviours across student groups. Finally, that studies should adopt valid contemporary instruments to assess sexual violence perpetration, rather than relying on established measures. The authors proposed that their suggestions would improve academic understanding of the aetiology of campus sexual assault, as well as assist in the development of more effective university-based sexual harm prevention strategies.

DeGue, S., Valle, L. A., Holt, M. K., Massetti, G. M., Matjasko, J. L., & Teten Tharp, A. (2014). A systematic review of primary prevention strategies for sexual violence perpetration. *Aggression and Violent Behavior,* **19** (4), 346–362. https://doi.org/10.1016/j.avb.2014.05.004

This CDC-funded review article built on the broad sexual harm prevention knowledge base by systematically examining the effectiveness of pre-existing primary prevention strategies for sexual violence perpetration. Overall, the authors reviewed 140 outcome evaluation reports published between 1985 and 2012 that described the efficacy of a sexual harm reduction intervention. These reports were critically appraised to assess the breadth, quality, and evolution of relevant evaluation research, and to determine "what works" in terms of primary prevention strategies for sexual violence.

Using an empirically-informed criteria, DeGue and colleagues classified each outcome evaluation study as either "rigorous" or "non-rigorous" according to its research design. Based on these criteria, interventions could be evaluated as either effective (i.e., they positively influenced sexual violence perpetration), not effective (i.e., they delivered null effects), potentially harmful (i.e., they negatively influenced sexually violent behaviours in at least one way), requiring further study (i.e., they positively influenced sexually violent behaviours, risk factors, or related outcomes but conclusions were tentative), or providing insufficient evidence.

Having reviewed the interventions, the authors found that 60.0% of studies evaluated one-session programs with university students. The majority of interventions (58.6%) comprised mixed-sex groups and included content on attitudes towards sexual violence (83.6%), knowledge of sexual violence (80.7%), or skills training (44.3%). Despite their established links to sexual violence perpetration, less than 20 interventions included information on sexually harmful behaviours, peer attitudes, social norms, culture, or sexual consent. Very few interventions (<5.0%) were targeted at "high risk" groups (e.g., fraternities, sports teams). Most interventions (33.8%) used single-sex facilitators – typically professionals from allied fields (25.0%) or trained peers (19.3%) – who typically relied on interactive presentations, didactic lectures, or film/media presentations to deliver program content.

In terms of study characteristics, DeGue and colleagues discovered a preponderance towards young White participants. Whilst most studies comprised over 300 participants, sample sizes varied between 22 and 2,643. Most non-rigorous evaluation studies assessed outcomes immediately post-intervention, whilst most rigorous evaluations assessed outcomes at 5-months or longer. Evaluation outcomes published pre-1999 ($n = 73$) were more likely than those published post-2000 ($n = 67$) to adopt a randomised controlled trial or quasi-experimental design. However, more recent evaluations were more likely to assess outcomes immediately post-intervention and include a longitudinal arm.

Regarding outcomes, the authors found that most studies (41.4%) reported mixed effects across outcome types and follow-up periods. Findings showed that pre-post studies were more likely to report positive effects than more rigorously designed studies, including those with a longitudinal arm. Despite the majority of interventions positively influencing participants' knowledge of sexual violence, bystander behaviours, and skills, only three reduced actual perpetration rates. Overall, longer interventions were more effective at influencing outcomes than shorter ones.

Overall, DeGue and colleagues suggested that their findings could help practitioners to develop more effective, rigorously-designed primary prevention interventions for sexual aggression. The authors encouraged more targeted research assessing the long-term outcomes of pre-existing programs, as well as increased funding for research in the area, to help ameliorate the risk of sexual violence victimisation across the community.

Note

1 The term *sexual misconduct* is used to refer to a continuum of sexualised behaviours that incorporate sexual harassment, unwanted sexual contact, and assault (including rape), as well as seemingly 'lower level' non-consensual and predatory sexual behaviours that reflect a power imbalance between members of university staff and students (see NUS, 2018).

References

Abbey, A., & McAuslan, P. (2004). A longitudinal examination of male college students' perpetration of sexual assault. *Journal of Consulting and Clinical Psychology*, 72(5), 747–756. https://doi.org/10.1037/0022-006X.72.5.747

Abbey, A., Parkhill, M. R., BeShears, R., Clinton-Sherrod, A. M., & Zawacki, T. (2006). Cross-sectional predictors of sexual assault perpetration in a community sample of single African American and Caucasian men. *Aggressive Behavior: Official Journal of the International Society for Research on Aggression*, 32(1), 54–67. https://doi.org/10.1002/ab.20107

Abbey, A., Parkhill, M. R., Clinton-Sherrod, A. M., & Zawacki, T. (2007). A comparison of men who committed different types of sexual assault in a community sample. *Journal of Interpersonal Violence*, 22(12), 1567–1580. https://doi.org/10.1177/0886260507306489

Abbey, A., Wegner, R., Woerner, J., Pegram, S. E., & Pierce, J. (2014). Review of survey and experimental research that examines the relationship between alcohol consumption and men's sexual aggression perpetration. *Trauma, Violence, & Abuse*, 15(4), 265–282. https://doi.org/10.1177/1524838014521031

Anderson, R. E., Silver, K. E., Ciampaglia, A. M., Vitale, A. M., & Delahanty, D. L. (2021). The frequency of sexual perpetration in college men: A systematic review of reported prevalence rates from 2000 to 2017. *Trauma, Violence, & Abuse*, 22(3), 481–495. https://doi.org/10.1177/1524838019860619

Australian Human Rights Commission. (2017). *Change the course: National report on sexual assault and sexual harassment at Australian universities*. https://humanrights.gov.au/our-work/sex-discrimination/publications/change-course-national-report-sexual-assault-and-sexual

Banyard, V. L., Rizzo, A. J., Bencosme, Y., Cares, A. C., & Moynihan, M. M. (2021). How community and peer perceptions promote college students' pro-social bystander actions to prevent sexual violence. *Journal of Interpersonal Violence*, 36(7–8), 3855–3879. https://doi.org/10.1177/0886260518777557

Berkowitz, A. D. (2010). Fostering healthy norms to prevent violence and abuse: The social norms approach. In K. L. Kaufman (Ed.), *The prevention of sexual violence: A practitioner's sourcebook* (pp. 147–171). NEARI Press.

Bonomi, A., Nichols, E., Kammes, R., & Green, T. (2018). Sexual violence and intimate partner violence in college women with a mental health and/or behavior disability. *Journal of Women's Health*, 27(3), 359–368. https://doi.org/10.1089/jwh.2016.6279

Bouffard, L., & Goodson, A. (2017). Sexual coercion, sexual aggression, or sexual assault: How measurement impacts our understanding of sexual violence. *Journal of Aggression, Conflict and Peace Research*, 9(4), 269–278. https://doi.org/10.1108/JACPR-05-2017-0292

Breiding, M. J. (2015). Prevalence and characteristics of sexual violence, stalking, and intimate partner violence victimization – National intimate partner and sexual violence survey, United States, 2011. *American Journal of Public Health*, 105(4), 11–12. https://doi.org/10.2105/ajph.2015.302634

Burkhart, B. R., & Fromuth, M. E. (1991). Individual and social psychological understandings of sexual coercion. In E. Grauerholz & M. A. Koralewski (Eds.), *Sexual coercion: A sourcebook on its nature, causes, and prevention* (pp. 75–89). Lexington Books.

Butler, L. C., Lee, H., & Fisher, B. S. (2019). Less safe in the ivory tower: Campus sexual assault policy in the Trump administration. *Victims & Offenders*, 14(8), 979–996. https://doi.org/10.1080/15564886.2019.1671289

Campbell, J. C., Sabri, B., Budhathoki, C., Kaufman, M. R., Alhusen, J., & Decker, M. R. (2021). Unwanted sexual acts among university students: Correlates of victimization and perpetration. *Journal of Interpersonal Violence, 36*(1–2), 504–526. https://doi.org/10.1177/0886260517734221

Cantalupo, N. C., & Kidder, W. C. (2018). A systematic look at a serial problem: Sexual harassment of students by university faculty. *Utah Law Review, 3*, 671–786. https://dc.law.utah.edu/ulr/vol2018/iss3/4

Cantor, D., Fisher, B., Chibnall, S., Harps, S., Townsend, R., Thomas, G., Lee, H., Kranz, V., Herbison, R., & Madden, K. (2020). *Report on the AAU campus climate survey on sexual assault and misconduct.* www.aau.edu/key-issues/campus-climate-and-safety/aau-campus-climate-survey-2019

Carline, A., Gunby, C., & Taylor, S. (2018). Too drunk to consent? Exploring the contestations and disruptions in male-focused sexual violence prevention interventions. *Social & Legal Studies, 27*(3), 299–322. https://doi.org/10.1177/0964663917713346

Casey, E. A., & Lindhorst, T. P. (2009). Toward a multi-level, ecological approach to the primary prevention of sexual assault: Prevention in peer and community contexts. *Trauma, Violence, & Abuse, 10*(2), 91–114. https://doi.org/10.1177/1524838009334129

Cass, A. I. (2007). Routine activities and sexual assault: An analysis of individual-and school-level factors. *Violence and Victims, 22*(3), 350–366. https://doi.org/10.1891/088667007780842810

Centers for Disease Control and Prevention. (2014). *Preventing sexual violence on college campuses: Lessons from research and practice.* www.notalone.gov/assets/preventing-sexual-violence-on-college-campuses-lessons-from-research-and-practice.pdf

Cooke, R., Beccaria, F., Demant, J., Fernandes-Jesus, M., Fleig, L., Negreiros, J., Scholz, U., & de Visser, R. (2019). Patterns of alcohol consumption and alcohol-related harm among European university students. *European Journal of Public Health, 29*(6), 1125–1129. https://doi.org/10.1093/eurpub/ckz067

Coulter, R. W., Mair, C., Miller, E., Blosnich, J. R., Matthews, D. D., & McCauley, H. L. (2017). Prevalence of past-year sexual assault victimization among undergraduate students: Exploring differences by and intersections of gender identity, sexual identity, and race/ethnicity. *Prevention Science, 18*(6), 726–736. https://doi.org/10.1007/s11121-017-0762-8

Dahlberg, L. L., & Krug, E. G. (2002). Violence – a global public health problem. In E. G. Krug, L. L. Dahlberg, J. A. Mercy, A. B. Zwi, & R. Lozano (Eds.), *World report on violence and health* (pp. 1–21). World Health Organization. https://apps.who.int/iris/bitstream/handle/10665/42495/9241545615_eng.pdf

Fedina, L., Holmes, J. L., & Backes, B. L. (2018). Campus sexual assault: A systematic review of prevalence research from 2000 to 2015. *Trauma, Violence, & Abuse, 19*(1), 76–93. https://doi.org/10.1177/1524838016631129

Forbes, G. B., & Adams-Curtis, L. E. (2001). Experiences with sexual coercion in college males and females: Role of family conflict, sexist attitudes, acceptance of rape myths, self-esteem, and the Big-Five personality factors. *Journal of Interpersonal Violence, 16*(9), 865–889. https://doi.org/10.1177/088626001016009002

Gage, E. A. (2008). Gender attitudes and sexual behaviors: Comparing center and marginal athletes and nonathletes in a collegiate setting. *Violence Against Women, 14*(9), 1014–1032. https://doi.org/10.1177/1077801208321987

Goodson, A., Franklin, C. A., & Bouffard, L. A. (2021). Male peer support and sexual assault: The relation between high-profile, high school sports participation and sexually predatory behaviour. *Journal of Sexual Aggression, 27*(1), 64–80. https://doi.org/10.1080/13552600.2020.1733111

Hackman, C. L., Witte, T., & Greenband, M. (2017). Social norms for sexual violence perpetration in college. *Journal of Aggression, Conflict and Peace Research*, *9*(4), 305–313. https://doi.org/10.1108/JACPR-12-2016-0266

Hales, S. T., & Gannon, T. A. (2021). Understanding sexual aggression in UK male university students: An empirical assessment of prevalence and psychological risk factors. *Sexual Abuse*. Advance online publication. https://doi.org/10.1177/10790632211051682

Jouriles, E. N., Nguyen, J., Krauss, A., Stokes, S. L., & McDonald, R. (2020). Prevalence of sexual victimization among female and male college students: A methodological note with data. *Journal of Interpersonal Violence*. Advance online publication. https://doi.org/10.1177/0886260520978198

Kaufman, M. R., Tsang, S. W., Sabri, B., Budhathoki, C., & Campbell, J. (2019). Health and academic consequences of sexual victimisation experiences among students in a university setting. *Psychology & Sexuality*, *10*(1), 56–68. https://doi.org/10.1080/19419899.2018.1552184

Kingree, J. B., & Thompson, M. P. (2013). Fraternity membership and sexual aggression: An examination of mediators of the association. *Journal of American College Health*, *61*(4), 213–221. https://doi.org/10.1080/07448481.2013.781026

Kingree, J. B., & Thompson, M. P. (2015). A comparison of risk factors for alcohol-involved and alcohol-uninvolved sexual aggression perpetration. *Journal of Interpersonal Violence*, *30*(9), 1478–1492. https://doi.org/10.1177/0886260514540806

Krebs, C. P., Barrick, K., Lindquist, C. H., Crosby, C. M., Boyd, C., & Bogan, Y. (2011). The sexual assault of undergraduate women at historically black colleges and universities (HBCUs). *Journal of Interpersonal Violence*, *26*(18), 3640–3666. https://doi.org/10.1177/0886260511403759

Martín, A. F., Vergeles, M. R., Acevedo, V. D. L. O., Sánchez, A. D. C., & Visa, S. L. (2005). The involvement in sexual coercive behaviors of Spanish college men: Prevalence and risk factors. *Journal of Interpersonal Violence*, *20*(7), 872–891. https://doi.org/10.1177/0886260505276834

Martin, S. L., Fisher, B. S., Stoner, M. C., Rizo, C. F., & Wojcik, M. L. (2020). Sexual assault of college students: Victimization and perpetration prevalence involving cisgender men, cisgender women and gender minorities. *Journal of American College Health*. Advance online publication. https://doi.org/10.1080/07448481.2020.1751644

McQuiller Williams, L., Porter, J. L., & Smith, T. R. (2016). Understanding date rape attitudes and behaviors: Exploring the influence of race, gender, and prior sexual victimization. *Victims & Offenders*, *11*(2), 173–198. https://doi.org/10.1080/15564886.2014.960025

Mikołajczak, M., & Pietrzak, J. (2014). Ambivalent sexism and religion: Connected through values. *Sex Roles*, *70*(9–10), 387–399. https://doi.org/10.1007/s11199-014-0379-3

Mohler-Kuo, M., Dowdall, G. W., Koss, M. P., & Wechsler, H. (2004). Correlates of rape while intoxicated in a national sample of college women. *Journal of Studies on Alcohol*, *65*(1), 37–45. https://doi.org/10.15288/jsa.2004.65.37

Moylan, C. A., & Javorka, M. (2020). Widening the lens: An ecological review of campus sexual assault. *Trauma, Violence, & Abuse*, *21*(1), 179–192. https://doi.org/10.1177/1524838018756121

Muehlenhard, C. L., Humphreys, T. P., Jozkowski, K. N., & Peterson, Z. D. (2016). The complexities of sexual consent among college students: A conceptual and empirical review. *The Journal of Sex Research*, *53*(4–5), 457–487. https://doi.org/10.1080/00224499.2016.1146651

Murnen, S. K., & Kohlman, M. H. (2007). Athletic participation, fraternity membership, and sexual aggression among college men: A meta-analytic review. *Sex Roles*, *57*(1–2), 145–157. https://doi.org/10.1007/s11199-007-9225-1

National Union of Students. (2011). *Hidden marks: A study of women students' experiences of harassment, stalking, violence and sexual assault.* www.nusconnect.org.uk/resources/hidden-marks-a-study-of-women-students-experiences-of-harassment-stalking-violence-and-sexual-assault

National Union of Students. (2018). *Power in the academy: Staff sexual misconduct in UK higher education.* www.nusconnect.org.uk/resources/nus-staff-student-sexual-misconduct-report

Nguyen, D., & Parkhill, M. R. (2014). Integrating attachment and depression in the confluence model of sexual assault perpetration. *Violence Against Women, 20*(8), 994–1011. https://doi.org/10.1177/1077801214546233

O'Connor, J., McMahon, S., Cusano, J., Seabrook, R., & Gracey, L. (2021). Predictors of campus sexual violence perpetration: A systematic review of research, sampling, and study design. *Aggression and Violent Behavior, 58*, E101607. https://doi.org/10.1016/j.avb.2021.101607

Palmer, J. E., McMahon, S., & Fissel, E. (2021). Correlates of incoming male college students' proclivity to perpetrate sexual assault. *Violence Against Women, 27*(3–4), 507–528. https://doi.org/10.1177/1077801220905663

Phipps, A., & Young, I. (2013). *That's what she said: Women students' experiences of 'lad culture' in higher education.* www.nusconnect.org.uk/resources/thats-what-she-said-full-report

Porta, C. M., Mathiason, M. A., Lust, K., & Eisenberg, M. E. (2017). Sexual violence among college students: An examination of individual and institutional level factors associated with perpetration. *Journal of Forensic Nursing, 13*(3), 109–117. https://doi.org/10.1097/JFN.0000000000000161

Ray, T. N., & Parkhill, M. R. (2021). Components of hostile masculinity and their associations with male-perpetrated sexual aggression toward women: A systematic review. *Trauma, Violence, & Abuse.* Advance online publication. https://doi.org/10.1177/15248380211030224

Salazar, L. F., Swartout, K. M., Swahn, M. H., Bellis, A. L., Carney, J., Vagi, K. J., & Lokey, C. (2018). Precollege sexual violence perpetration and associated risk and protective factors among male college freshmen in Georgia. *Journal of Adolescent Health, 62*(3), 51–57. https://doi.org/10.1016/j.jadohealth.2017.09.028

Schuster, I., & Krahé, B. (2019). Predictors of sexual aggression perpetration among male and female college students: Cross-cultural evidence from Chile and Turkey. *Sexual Abuse, 31*(3), 318–343. https://doi.org/10.1177/1079063218793632

Smith, C. P., & Freyd, J. J. (2013). Dangerous safe havens: Institutional betrayal exacerbates sexual trauma. *Journal of Traumatic Stress, 26*(1), 119–124. https://doi.org/10.1002/jts.21778

Spitzberg, B. H. (1999). An analysis of empirical estimates of sexual aggression victimization and perpetration. *Violence and Victims, 14*(3), 241–260. https://doi.org/10.1891/0886-6708.14.3.241

Statistics Canada. (2020). *Students' experiences of unwanted sexualized behaviours and sexual assault at postsecondary schools in the Canadian provinces, 2019.* https://www150.statcan.gc.ca/n1/pub/85-002-x/2020001/article/00005-eng.htm

Steele, B., Martin, M., Yakubovich, A., Humphreys, D. K., & Nye, E. (2020). Risk and protective factors for men's sexual violence against women at higher education institutions: A systematic and meta-analytic review of the longitudinal evidence. *Trauma, Violence, & Abuse.* Advance online publication. https://doi.org/10.1177/1524838020970900

Stotzer, R. L., & MacCartney, D. (2016). The role of institutional factors on on-campus reported rape prevalence. *Journal of Interpersonal Violence, 31*(16), 2687–2707. https://doi.org/10.1177/0886260515580367

Strang, E., & Peterson, Z. D. (2017). Unintentional misreporting on self-report measures of sexually aggressive behavior: An interview study. *The Journal of Sex Research, 54*(8), 971–983. https://doi.org/10.1080/00224499.2017.1304519

Swartout, K. M., Koss, M. P., White, J. W., Thompson, M. P., Abbey, A., & Bellis, A. L. (2015). Trajectory analysis of the campus serial rapist assumption. *JAMA Pediatrics, 169*(12), 1148–1154. https://doi.org/10.1001/jamapediatrics.2015.0707

Szymanski, D. M., Moffitt, L. B., & Carr, E. R. (2011). Sexual objectification of women: Advances to theory and research. *The Counseling Psychologist, 39*(1), 6–38. https://doi.org/10.1177/0011000010378402

Testa, M., & Cleveland, M. J. (2017). Does alcohol contribute to college men's sexual assault perpetration? Between-and within-person effects over five semesters. *Journal of Studies on Alcohol and Drugs, 78*(1), 5–13. https://doi.org/10.15288/jsad.2017.78.5

Teten Tharp, A., DeGue, S., Valle, L. A., Brookmeyer, K. A., Massetti, G. M., & Matjasko, J. L. (2013). A systematic qualitative review of risk and protective factors for sexual violence perpetration. *Trauma, Violence, & Abuse, 14*(2), 133–167. https://doi.org/10.1177/1524838012470031

Thompson Jr., E. H., & Cracco, E. J. (2008). Sexual aggression in bars: What college men can normalize. *The Journal of Men's Studies, 16*(1), 82–96. https://doi.org/10.3149/jms.1601.82

Thompson, M. P., & Morrison, D. J. (2013). Prospective predictors of technology-based sexual coercion by college males. *Psychology of Violence, 3*(3), 233–246. https://doi.org/10.1037/a0030904

Thompson, M. P., Swartout, K. M., & Koss, M. P. (2013). Trajectories and predictors of sexually aggressive behaviors during emerging adulthood. *Psychology of Violence, 3*(3), 247–259. https://doi.org/10.1037/a0030624

US Department of Education. (2021). *The campus safety and security data analysis cutting tool.* https://ope.ed.gov/campussafety/

Vega, V., & Malamuth, N. M. (2007). Predicting sexual aggression: The role of pornography in the context of general and specific risk factors. *Aggressive Behavior: Official Journal of the International Society for Research on Aggression, 33*(2), 104–117. https://doi.org/10.1002/ab.20172

Vogel, B. L. (2000). Correlates of pre-college males' sexual aggression: Attitudes, beliefs and behavior. *Women & Criminal Justice, 11*(3), 25–47. https://doi.org/10.1300/J012v11n03_02

Walsh, K., Sarvet, A. L., Wall, M., Gilbert, L., Santelli, J., Khan, S., Thompson, M. P., Reardon, L., Hirsch, J. S., & Mellins, C. A. (2021). Prevalence and correlates of sexual assault perpetration and ambiguous consent in a representative sample of college students. *Journal of Interpersonal Violence, 36*(13–14), 7005–7026. https://doi.org/10.1177/0886260518823293

Yapp, E. J., & Quayle, E. (2018). A systematic review of the association between rape myth acceptance and male-on-female sexual violence. *Aggression and Violent Behavior, 41*, 1–19. https://doi.org/10.1016/j.avb.2018.05.002

Young, B. R., Desmarais, S. L., Baldwin, J. A., & Chandler, R. (2017). Sexual coercion practices among undergraduate male recreational athletes, intercollegiate athletes, and non-athletes. *Violence Against Women, 23*(7), 795–812. https://doi.org/10.1177/1077801216651339

8 The legal framework

Limitations and opportunities

Rachel Fenton and Janet Keliher

There has been a lack of ownership regarding who is accountable for the safety of women at university, with the House of Commons Women and Equalities Committee commenting in its 2018 Report, "Sexual Harassment of Women and Girls in Public Places" that "[b]etween the Government, regulators and institutions, we have been left with a strong impression of passing the buck on who is responsible for women's safety at university" (para 160). Since the NUS (2011) Hidden Marks report of 2010 which first documented the extent of violence against women in university settings, the last decade has seen an incremental but slow and limited change at a policy level to tackle the problem. One of the main issues has been that policy change for universities has come in the form of guidance and recommendations enabling a piecemeal and inconsistent response, rather than requiring any form of actual compliance. Using the law is one mechanism by which change might be achieved and law may operate in different ways. One way is in terms of individual victim-survivors using litigation to get a form of legal redress against their institution – which may in turn lead to institutional policy and process change. Another way is the imposition of overarching regulation or legal obligations on universities to prevent and respond to gender-based violence (GBV) for which compliance may be regulated and sanctions applied. The legal context over the last decade has shifted almost imperceptibly, but what has become increasingly evident is the willingness of individuals to use legal processes to take action against universities for failure to act and ensure their safety, and the recognition by universities that litigation – and ensuant negative publicity – is a real threat.

This chapter will examine the legal regime as it applies to universities at the present time. It is divided into two parts. The first part examines how individuals can, and have, used the law to provide redress and the second part explores the overarching regulatory regime for the Higher Education sector.

Part 1: actions by individuals

Overview

The most important point to note is that the current legal regime is dependent upon individuals bringing an action and that there are a multitude of barriers

DOI: 10.4324/9781003252474-9

facing that individual. The Women and Equalities Committee Report, "Enforcing the Equality Act" (2019), notes how litigation places "a significant burden on individuals" (p. 8). This individual will be a victim-survivor of GBV with all its attendant consequences for mental and physical health, and academic performance, which are well-documented in the literature. This victim-survivor must be willing to bring a complaint to the university (and possibly to invoke the criminal justice process) and submit to its processes. Where the complaints processes are poor or unfair (and recognised as such by the victim-survivor), the individual must recognise their rights and the possibility of legal redress and have the commitment and financial resource to take legal advice, find a lawyer with the requisite expertise, and be tenacious enough to fight potentially all the way to trial. Some legal processes have very strict time limits. Given the imbalance of power in that the object of litigation will be the very institution (with all its lawyers and resource) who is responsible for awarding their degree, it is an invidious position to be in and thus clear that litigation is likely to be the exception rather than the norm. Unsurprisingly, there is consequently a dearth of case law upon which an analysis can be made. However, it is suggested that whilst the threat of litigation has not been a particular catalyst for change on the part of the Higher Education sector, this landscape appears to be changing. The first legal challenge to a university's policy for dealing with sexual misconduct complaints was brought by Elizabeth Ramey in 2015. Although the case failed, it is suggested that the bringing of the case in itself – and the high-profile media coverage it engendered – represents a watershed moment in indicating the willingness of students to hold universities to account for and of legal professionals to represent them as well as the potential for oversight from the Equalities and Human Rights Commission (EHRC) that funded the application. Since then, other students have followed suit and the newspapers report numerous cases pending. There is an inevitability of litigation as the sector seeks to grapple with the issue of GBV and some of this will be brought by responding parties. This litigation will, to some extent, determine the boundaries, remit, and obligations of universities in this area. Whilst in this sense litigation is to be welcomed, the burden is placed on the shoulders of individuals, who are perhaps the least able to bear it.

The complaints process

A complaint may be made to a university by a student of sexual misconduct by another student or a member of staff. Equally, a member of staff may bring a complaint against another member of staff or a student. Where the responding party is a student, the student disciplinary process will apply, and where the responding party is a member of staff, the disciplinary procedures in the relevant contract of employment will apply. Any victim-survivor of GBV may report to the police to initiate the criminal justice process at any time, where the behaviour constitutes a criminal offence.

The student disciplinary process is quasi-legal, in that it is a mechanism for the enforcement of the contractual relationship between student and university. The recent case of *AB v. University of XYZ* (2020a) is interesting in this regard. In this civil case, the claimant had been expelled from the university following an allegation of sexual misconduct proven in a disciplinary process. He applied for an interim injunction permitting him to finish his degree, but the relief was denied in the High Court. Although the judgement is interim and therefore provisional, it is suggested that as the first case of its kind brought by an alleged wrongdoer, it is a useful barometer of judicial thinking. The judge found that "as an enrolled student of the University", the claimant was bound by the standards of behaviour in the contract and that the university had jurisdiction irrespective of his being on a year abroad, in a private apartment, and that the complainant was from another university. Thus, his claim that the university had no jurisdiction could not succeed because on the construction of this contract, the terms were clear. Further, the judge suggested that, "[i]f there was sufficient evidence that he had failed to [adhere to appropriate standards of behaviour], the University was duty bound to investigate the matter in accordance with its disciplinary procedures" – and so a victim-survivor could equally bring a claim in contract law against their university should it fail to act. Thus, universities should take care that the relevant code of conduct and behavioural expectations clearly include sexual misconduct/GBV, the jurisdiction to investigate and bring disciplinary proceedings, apply precautionary measure and sanctions, and that these are incorporated into the contract. It will be an implied (if not express) term of the contract that the principles of natural justice and fair exercise of decision-making power will apply (AB, 2020a, para 98), and universities must follow their processes exactly, in order to avoid claims based on procedural irregularity. The usual contractual rules relating to incorporation of terms, bringing items clearly to notice, publishing policies, making the terms and the policies clear and understandable will apply. The same principles will apply to the disciplinary process under the employment contract where the responding party is a member of staff.

There is good reason to suspect that many universities still do not have good policies and disciplinary processes in place, or if they do, they are exercised badly. There have been a number of recommendations in place for universities to have institutional policies and processes in place, including by Universities UK (UUK) in 2016 and accompanying legal guidance on how to handle alleged student misconduct that may also constitute a criminal offence by Pinsent Masons (2016). Practicing lawyers have also produced legal guidance outlining the obligations on universities to act (Whitfield & Dustin, 2015; Whitfield, 2018), and guidance for investigating staff misconduct (McAlister Olivarius & The 1752 Group, 2018). Despite this, reports reveal differential, fragmented, and unequal progress across the sector (e.g., UUK, 2018; Chantler et al., 2019, 2022). A plethora of media reports illustrate victim-survivors' experiences of not being believed, of being humiliated and re-victimised, being discouraged from reporting, and of poor and traumatic investigative, disciplinary, and appeal practices (Batty, 2019; Busby, 2018; Oppenheim, 2019; Weale & Batty, 2017) and qualitative responses from victim-survivors of staff sexual miscon-duct, who were blocked or dissuaded from reporting (Bull & Rye, 2018). An independent review of the Warwick University disciplinary process following significant media coverage of the failures of the university in the "rape chat" case (e.g., Batty, 2019) was commissioned (Persaud, 2019), with another pend-ing at Oxford Brookes following failures to protect a victim-survivor of stalking (Jeffries, 2021). At present, legal proceedings are being reportedly brought by victim-survivors against the Universities of Warwick (Batty, 2019), Cambridge (Oppenheim, 2019), and the Royal Welsh College of Music and Drama (Dea-con, 2020) for their unsatisfactory handling of complaints.

The Pinsent Masons legal guidance (2016), although certainly open to criti-cism (e.g., Fenton, 2016), was nonetheless a significant step forward, because it clarified a number of important points for universities. These include that the previous Zellick guidance (which advocated that conduct which was a criminal matter should be dealt with by the police and not the university) is no longer appropriate and universities can investigate under their disciplinary processes; that the correct standard of proof for disciplinary proceedings is the civil stan-dard of balance of probabilities because it pertains to a breach of discipline and not a criminal offence; that the duty of care owed by the university is to both to the reporting party and responding (accused) party; that precautionary mea-sures should be put in place (such as suspension of the responding party) whilst investigation (by the university or the police) is underway; and that staff should be properly trained. One aspect of the guidance is that it recommends that disciplinary action should not take place if a criminal investigation is underway, due to "a substantial risk" that the criminal process would suffer interference or evidence be "rehearsed" (2016, p. 9). However, Perry and Hardcastle (2018) in their legal opinion for the Parliamentary Independent Complaints and Griev-ance Policy point out that not only are there are no legal principles prohibiting the same facts being subject to both internal and criminal processes as they are "wholly distinct", but also that they commonly run contemporaneously in an employment context (p. 99). Thus, they conclude that the risks are "not to be overestimated, and should not inhibit an investigator" (p. 108), and so post-ponement of the disciplinary process should be the exception rather than the rule. The recent case at Oxford Brookes University illustrates that universities are following the Pinsent Masons (2016) guidance, to the detriment of victim-survivors (Jeffries, 2021).

It is unfortunate that the Pinsent Masons guidance is generic and not tailored specifically to sexual misconduct: whilst it does mention specially trained staff, it is not clear about what this might mean for this very specific context. For example, in many cases of sexual violence, the issue will be consent and thus the credibility of varying accounts must be assessed. Research has long indicated that many people have beliefs in "rape myths", such as precipitation myths about the victim's behaviour (she brought it on herself through dress, alcohol consumption, lack of personal safety measures) and myths which suggest that the perpetrator "didn't mean to" (things got out of control, it was an accident) and that women lie about sexual violence (e.g., Bohner et al., 2009). A similar set of myths exist around sexual harassment (Lonsway et al., 2008). The myths function to shift responsibility onto the victim and exonerate the perpetrator. Given that such myths are pervasive in society, are held by women as well as men, and permeate the criminal justice process, there is no reason to think that university staff will not hold them. Being actually able to "hear" and assess the credibility of the evidence in a sexual violence/misconduct case in an informed and fair way is something that will take a great deal of training. It is not clear what level of training is being received by university casework staff, nor who is providing it: there is no sector-wide accredited training which staff must undertake to be allowed to investigate or hear these cases: even bodies like ACAS who provide lengthy accredited training for HR internal investigators do not specifically cover sexual harassment.

Concerns have also been raised recently by Cowan and Munro (2021) about what they term a "criminal justice drift" – that universities are turning to the criminal justice paradigm of adversarial proceedings which are well-documented for their failure of victim-survivors. This is echoed, they suggest, by the increasing use of independent investigators coming from criminal justice/ former police background, with the attendant skills in building a prosecutable case. These skills, however, may result in the "risk that criminal justice practices and norms will become embedded through 'muscle memory', or considered 'better', by those initiated in them" (p. 325).

A further issue that lacks clarity is the reference to the duty of care owed to the responding party. Whilst it is correct – and fair – that this is the case in terms of access to support and right to give submissions in evidence, it is suggested that this duty has not been fully explained or explored as to what exactly is required, and how this sits alongside the need to have a victim-centric trauma-informed response. It does not equate to absolute equality of treatment where the survivor's needs and safety should be prioritised, such as in the imposition of precautionary measures. The failure of Oxford Brookes to protect a victim-survivor during months of severe stalking is a case in point (Jeffries, 2021). The case of *AB* likely initiates what will likely become a body of case law brought by accused students – which is likely to increase the threat of litigation and the unease around the extent of the duty of care to the responding party.

One issue pertaining to the disciplinary process and fairness between the parties is the question of whether the responding party has the right to legal representation in the disciplinary hearing. Whilst the exact institutional process is a matter of autonomy for each university, the question was raised in *AB v. University of XYZ* (2020b), and the outcome will affect the disciplinary process for sexual misconduct for all universities. In its disciplinary hearing, the University of XYZ permitted "an accompanying individual in a support capacity but not as an advocate" and the responder was expected to speak "on his own behalf". The High Court found that these rules needed to be "read in light of the overriding duty to ensure 'natural justice'" and thus when fairness in a particular fact situation dictated it, legal representation could be required (para 87). The judge applied the criteria in *Ex p. Tarrant* (1985) and noted that another university's disciplinary process contained these criteria, again illustrative of the differential and varied processes in place across the sector. The *Tarrant* criteria require an assessment of (i) the seriousness of the charge; (ii) whether any points of law are likely to arise; (iii) the capacity of the responder to understand the case against him; (iv) procedural difficulties; (v) the need to avoid delay; and (vi) the need for fairness between the responder and those making allegations. Thus, universities will need to amend their processes to allow for legal representation when the criteria are met – and will need to document carefully their application of the criteria and reasoning – which may also mean, suggested the judge, that, "fairness may even require the complainant to be legally represented" (AB, 2020b, para 90). This may also apply to the university disciplinary committee who will also need representation. On the facts, AB had wrongly been denied legal representation which was a breach of contract and thus a further disciplinary hearing was ordered as specific performance. The judge did recognise the importance of safeguarding the reporting party's well-being and found that the filtering of questions through the Chair would fulfil the aims of natural justice. For reasons of space and remit, a detailed critique of this judgement cannot be undertaken here but it is likely to fuel further academic discussion about what fairness in this process looks like (see, for example, Cowan & Munro, 2021).

It is important to note that perceptions about the likelihood of the university taking action, and having a fair, trauma-informed process will be hugely influential on the victim-survivor's decision to report in the first place. Of further concern is that perceptions of impunity through the non-enforcement, or lack, of institutional sanctions will influence perpetration (Towl & Walker, 2019, p. 29). The Pinsent Masons (2016) guidance requires revisiting.

Law of tort

An individual may resort to the law of tort in bringing an action in negligence against a university for breach of its duty of care. A university may also be vicariously liable for the actions of their members of staff if they cause injury to another. The duty in tort exists where the institution owes a duty of care to a victim-survivor or responding party and the institution is negligent in the discharge of that duty causing the individual to suffer loss or damage capable of being compensated monetarily (by damages). The standard of care is that of an ordinarily competent institution.

Judicial review proceedings

The judicial review process can be used by individuals to challenge procedural irregularity.

Judicial review will be explored more subsequently in terms of the Public Sector Equality Duty (PSED) and the *Human Rights Act* 1998, but it is suggested that one area of potential interest which has not been explored in the literature to date is decisions made by University Ethics Committees which prohibit research into their students' experiences of victimisation and perpetration or related research, ostensibly under the grounds of ethics but in fact to seek to limit any potential perceived reputational damage. Chantler et al. (2019, 2022) found several (seven) examples of this occurring at universities. Judicial review might also be used to challenge decision-making where, for example (as is well-known anecdotally), universities decide not to make public any prevalence research data they have collected, for reputational fears. Whilst the judicial review process could involve the PSED or anti-discrimination provisions of the *Equality Act* 2010, it is suggested that where there is no appeal from an Ethics Committee decision or where it is exceeding its powers/remit (e.g., assessing an application on reputational fear and not ethical grounds) or there is procedural irregularity (such as bias), irrationality (unreasonableness) in the decision, or/and the principles of natural justice have not been applied, then researchers could use judicial review to hold the university to account.

The Equality Act 2010 and the Human Rights Act 1998

(a) **The Public Sector Equality Duty (PSED):** The legal duties of universities under the Public Sector Equality Duty (PSED) and anti-discrimination provisions of the *Equality Act* 2010, and the *Human Rights Act* 1998 have been outlined clearly in the literature since the End Violence Against Women Coalition commissioned a legal briefing in 2015 (Whitfield & Dustin, 2015; Whitfield, 2018; Long & Hubble, 2021).

Universities are public authorities for the purposes of the *Equality Act* 2010 under Part 1 of Schedule 19 and are therefore under a legal obligation to show due regard to the need to (a) eliminate unlawful discrimination, harassment, and victimisation, (b) advance equality of opportunity for those with protected characteristics (including sex), and (c) foster good relations between different groups (i.e., men and women) under the Public Sector Equality Duty (PSED, s.149). This would apply to university decision-making processes such as investigatory/disciplinary policies and practices, both with students and with staff, and resourcing support for survivors (see Whitfield & Dustin, 2015 for a more comprehensive list and examples). Under s.149(3), having due regard to the need to advance equality of opportunity between persons who share a protected characteristic (e.g., sex) and those who do not means in particular to "take steps to meet the needs of persons who share a relevant protected characteristic that are different from the needs of persons who do not share it" (s.149(3)9b). It will be interesting to see how this may play out both in terms of its application and litigation and in terms of decision-making relating to the duty of care to both responding and reporting parties and the right to representation. Failure to consider the equality duty properly could render any policy around GBV unlawful. As a procedural duty, it is enforceable by judicial review proceedings and an individual cannot sue in private law (s.156 *Equality Act* 2010). The formal regulator is the EHRC which has investigatory and legal powers relating to enforcement of the Equality Act. It may itself initiate, support, or give expert evidence in legal proceedings such as judicial review. The Women and Equalities Committee's (2019) Report found that the EHRC, despite its significant powers, rarely uses its enforcement powers and where it has done so, has not publicised outcomes as a deterrent (p. 13). This weak approach to enforcement and compliance fuels the perception that the EHRC will not enforce and so organisations can act with impunity and consequently wider policy change is not achieved (p. 8).

(b) **The anti-discrimination provisions:** A civil claim can be brought by an individual who suffers direct discrimination, indirect discrimination, harassment, sexual harassment, and victimisation on the basis of a protected characteristic (e.g., sex) in employment, the provision of services, and the provision of education under the *Equality Act* 2010. Further examples of the types of claims are set out by Whitfield (2018). Judicial review proceedings could also be brought to challenge both a policy and a specific incident of discrimination (Whitfield, p. 155) as in *Ramey* (2015), discussed subsequently.

(c) **The Human Rights Act 1998 (HRA):** Under the *Human Rights Act* 1998 (HRA), universities are public authorities, and it is therefore unlawful for them to act in a way which is incompatible with Convention rights. Relevant rights and potential for breach encompass Article 2, the right to life; Article 3, the right to freedom from inhuman and degrading treatment; Article 8, the right to respect for private and family life; and Article 14, protection from discrimination. The context under which these may be breached regard protecting the individual through policies and practices (Whitfield & Dustin, 2015 – see p. 13 for examples of possible breaches). Perhaps of most interest is Article 2 Protocol 1 which states that "no person shall be denied a right to education". Whitfield and Dustin (2015) argue that for human rights purposes, "the concept of 'education' . . . covers the whole social process whereby beliefs, culture and other values are transmitted" and is therefore sufficiently broad to "include the internal administration of education institutions" (p. 12): Whilst there is no case-law to date, failure to ensure the safety – and perception of safety – of women accessing education and education-related activities might constitute a breach. However, as with the PSED, enforceability rests with individuals and the EHRC.

The first test case in this context, *Ramey* (2015), was funded by the EHRC in 2015, and was an application for judicial review brought against Oxford University who had, several years previously, failed to investigate Ramey's allegation of rape by another student. Oxford had relied on the 1994 Zellick report, which stated that only very exceptionally should a university proceed internally. The police had decided not to prosecute. Subsequently, the university changed their policy and the judicial review focused on whether the new policy was lawful in stating that the procedure may not be applied for behaviours attracting criminal sanction and – the key sentence – that, "in the first instance, such allegations will normally be a matter for police investigation and action" (para 11). The claim was brought on the basis of breach of the PSED, indirect discrimination, and harassment under the *Equality Act*, Articles 3 and 14 of the European Convention on Human Rights, and irrationality. The judge found that the key sentence did contain a discretion to take action and therefore was not in itself unlawful, but if it was applied inflexibly regardless of circumstance, then it might be unlawful and thus "it is certainly capable of being unlawfully applied in an individual case" (para 19). The correct time to challenge it would be when the policy had been applied arguably unlawfully, and therefore Ramey as an ex-student did not have standing to bring the case as it had not been applied to her, and the application for judicial review was denied. The case is important because it demonstrated that judicial review may well be appropriate and that policies could be unlawful, thus putting universities on notice to review their policies and it is unsurprising that the following year the new Pinsent Masons guidance was published.

(d) **Role of lawyers:** One of the issues Ramey faced was finding a solicitor with the specific expertise to represent her – Whitfield reports that it took Ramey almost three years (Whitfield, 2018, p. 163). It is suggested that the visibility of lawyers with the relevant expertise at national conferences, in the media, and in drafting legal guidelines together with lobby groups (e.g., Whitfield & Dustin, 2015; McAlister Olivarius & The 1752 Group, 2018) has been really important in policy change and in changing the expectations of victim-survivors, and for academics working in the sector who may be approached by victim-survivors, to be able to refer the individual to the right legal professionals for advice.

In summary, the barriers to individuals bringing legal action are considerable and the burden placed upon them unfair, and thus regulatory frameworks may be more efficient and satisfactory in terms of holding universities to account.

Part 2: the regulatory level

Overview

Universities UK (UUK) is the collective voice of 140 universities across the UK and its members are Vice-Chancellors or Principals of the member universities. UUK published its report on tackling violence against women, hate crime, and harassment in UK universities in 2016 (UUK, 2016), which identified seven key components for change (p. 59) and was accompanied by the Pinsent Mason's

(2016) legal guidance. The components include commitment from senior leadership; ensuring an institution-wide approach; effective prevention and response; managing situations where students have committed an offence, and the sharing of good practice. Although a very welcome step, the guidance has no "teeth" – the recommendations are couched in the ambivalent language of "universities should" and "universities should consider". Research carried out by Chantler et al. (2019, 2022), with 134 university staff working specifically in the area, into the barriers and facilitators to implementing the recommendations of the UUK Report (2016) found that some institutions did not have a sexual violence policy, that some policies were deemed inappropriate, and 14% respondents reported that they were right at the start of developing the UUK agenda. The study also found that 49% of respondents reported their institutions were worried about reputational risks of pursuing the UUK agenda or that students might be disproportionately worried, and 35% reported their institutions either had ignored the agenda, refused to believe it was a problem, or did not see it as a priority agenda, with 16 respondents indicating problems getting senior leadership buy-in (Chantler et al., 2019, 2022). The "carrot" approach has clearly been unsatisfactory and has led to efforts being piecemeal, "highly uneven" across the sector, with a fifth making "very limited progress" (UUK, 2018, p. 8), although there are pockets of good practice. The issue is the lack of obligations on universities to implement the guidance and absence of sanctions for non-implementation. Interestingly, 94% of respondents in Chantler et al.'s (2019, 2022) study representing 53 universities across the sector thought it definitely or probably important that universities be accountable for their delivery of the 2016 UUK report. Specifically, 88% of respondents thought it was definitely (41%) and probably (47%) important that the Office for Students be accountable to government for the delivery of the UUK agenda (Chantler et al., 2019, 2022)

The Office for Students (OfS)

The Department of Education has overall responsibility for the regulation of universities. The OfS is the independent regulator for Higher Education and protector of university student interests in England. It was established under the *Higher Education and Research Act* 2017 (HERA), which sets out the broad mechanisms through which the OfS is to regulate universities. It is suggested here that within its mandate for governance, the OfS has the power to effectively enforce legal obligations upon English universities in the context of GBV.

It is important to remember that the OfS, as a public authority itself, is of course subject to the PSED and the provisions of the *Human Rights Act* 1998. These statutory obligations on the OfS were confirmed by the Women and Equalities Committee (2018) which questioned the OfS about its regulatory role on sexual harassment and other issues of safety (para 154). The OfS stated in response that although it would be " active . . . on promoting innovation, galvanising a culture change", it did not have legal duties. These, the OfS claimed, lie with the EHRC (Yvonne Hawkins, para 154). However, the Committee responded with the following strong and definitive statement:

> We do not agree that the Office for Students does not have legal duties in respect of women's safety at university. It is a public body with obligations under the Public Sector Equality Duty as well as the Human Rights Act 1998 and taking action on the safety and equality of women students should be a priority.
>
> (para 155)

In addition to ensuring that the OfS itself is compliant with these laws, the Select Committee reported that the Minister for Women had written to it stating that the OfS "plays a 'pivotal' role in addressing sexual harassment in higher education at the sector level" and that it should work with providers to support them in meeting their obligations under the *Equality Act* 2010 (para 157).

Furthermore, the OfS has specific legislative obligations of its own under HERA. S2 (1) states that in performing its functions, the OfS must have regard to, *inter alia*, "the need to promote *equality of opportunity* in connection with *access to and participation in* higher education provided by English Higher Education providers" (italics added). Two interrelated questions arise as to what is meant by "equality of opportunity" and "access to and participation in". The discourse around equality of opportunity in Higher Education appears to focus largely on access, an area where women are not underrepresented and on the basis of the data, there does not appear to be gender inequality (HEPI, 2020). Thus, on the face of it, women have equality of opportunity. However, experiences of GBV at universities arise because of endemic gender inequality, and those experiences may also create disadvantage and inequality of opportunity for individual victim–survivors, not at the stage of entry but in terms of their actual ability to "participate" fully. This is a key concept in considering why universities need to be legally accountable in the area of GBV. The legal meaning of "participation" remains obscure. Participation in education is traditionally seen almost exclusively in the context of "widening participation", a central policy theme concerned with "redressing historical exclusions and inequalities", notably the underrepresentation of certain groups and which relates back to "access" (Burke, 2012). The latest APP guidance (OfS, 2021a) focuses on key performance measures which are broadly all about the "attainment gap". Burke suggests that "we must move beyond current hegemonic discourses and practices of Higher Education to reconceptualise widening participation as a project of transformation for social justice" (2012, p. 189). In other words, "participation" is not just about "entry" or "access", but about the student experience *in its entirety*, akin to the definition of education for human rights purposes proposed by Whitfield and Dustin (2015) (mentioned earlier). This construction of education is substantiated by evidence of the impacts of sexual harassment in the classroom. For example, evidence provided to the Women and Equalities Committee inquiry into sexual harassment and sexual violence in schools (2016) illustrates that sexual harassment impacts girls' participation in class: "25% of 11 to 16 year old girls say that concerns over potential sexual harassment make them consider whether or not to speak out in class", being "even more unwilling to take risks even in academic areas"; "less likely to participate in activities and 'do anything that will make them stand out and attract attention'" (Women and Equalities Committee, 2016, paras 33 and 34) There is no reason whatsoever to think that this does not continue into university classrooms.

This wider construction of "participation" is supported by the Department for Education's Consultation Guidance (2017) for registration conditions for universities where it is stated that Access and Participation Plans (APPs) will be expected to cover the "whole student lifecycle". Despite this and as stated earlier, OfS targets on inequality still focus on "under-represented groups", and attainment and continuation gaps between them.

However, the increasingly recognised prevalence and harm of GBV and the inequality inherent within that makes it both essential and possible to find space and means within the regulatory framework mandated to the OfS for the imposition and enforcement of obligations upon universities to prevent and respond to GBV.

The four primary regulatory objectives of the OfS under HERA are that all students, from all backgrounds, and with the ability and desire to undertake higher education:

- Are supported to access, succeed in, and progress from, higher education;
- Receive a high-quality academic experience, and their interests are protected while they study or in the event of provider, campus, or course closure;
- Are able to progress into employment or further study, and their qualifications hold their value over time;
- Receive value for money.

(OfS, 2018)

The question should be asked: What steps have the OfS has taken to achieve these primary regulatory objectives in the context of GBV? How, for example, does it enable victim-survivors to "succeed in" Higher Education or to have a "high quality academic experience", and how are their interests protected?

Under S75 HERA, the OfS has an obligation to publish a regulatory framework from "time to time". The latest framework states that "the OfS will regulate at provider level to ensure a baseline of protection for all students and the taxpayer. Beyond that threshold the OfS will encourage and enable autonomy, diversity and innovation" (OfS, 2018, para 15). It is suggested that protection against GBV should be a part of that "minimum baseline". Unfortunately, the remit envisaged by HERA for the OfS does not directly acknowledge the wider issue of "welfare" and the OfS appear resistant to the imposition of baseline duties in relation to GBV as this is perceived as a "welfare" issue. Yet GBV at universities is understood as something which prohibits equal participation in every aspect of education and the negative effect of that on the "student experience" as experienced predominantly by women is clearly something that could – and arguably should – fall under the umbrella terms used in the four primary regulatory objectives as set out earlier.

There was some movement by the OfS on this issue in 2020. As a result of a decade of inquiries and reports on harassment and sexual misconduct (including UUK, 2018; NUS, 2011; WEC, 2018), a consultation specifically addressing the regulation by the OfS of harassment and sexual misconduct affecting students in Higher Education providers was launched (OfS, 2020). It particularly related to the OfS's powers under HERA to impose conditions of registration (S5), but its aim was only ever to "propose a set of expectations of providers, and to require clear, accessible and effective complaints procedures" (p. 4). Following disruption caused by the pandemic, an updated Statement of Expectations was published in April 2021. This provides a "standard", but it very much endorses university autonomy, leaving it to universities to put their own policies and principles in place – an approach which thus far has demonstrably failed to achieve consistency or the desired outcomes. There is some semblance of "teeth", although little real "bite": On release of the Statement of Expectations, the OfS stated that it will "examine how universities and colleges have responded" and will "consider options for connecting the statement directly to [their] conditions of registration" (OfS, 2021c). The Statement of Expectations is in itself disappointing because it is just another set of light-touch recommendations, of which there has already been a plethora, and does not add anything to the UUK (2016) recommendations. It is suggested that the Persaud review (2019) is far more illustrative of the detailed types of requirements for the disciplinary process. There are many omissions from the Statement of Expectations, such as a requirement for proper and effective prevention, for specially trained investigators, and for systematic data collection about student experiences of misconduct, perpetration, and experience of the processes (see Page et al., 2020). As with all the recommendations thus far, the language is vague and open to interpretation and the view of the university in constructing it. For example, it includes "an investigatory process that is demonstrably fair, independent, and free from any reasonable perception of bias" (rec 6(c) and similar for panels rec 6(d)). There is no reference to the factors such as rape myth beliefs which may compromise these principles (discussed earlier) and only very light suggestion that this "*may include* consideration of and consultation with *appropriate* expertise" (italics added). It is suggested that specialist training is in fact essential and should be mandatory: and the minimum requirements or accreditation of training provision, which is agreed by experts as the appropriate training, should be set out. The Persaud review (2019), for example, suggests additional training should include "understanding consent, trauma-informed investigatory practices, and in assessing credibility" (p. 2). The Statement of Expectations also references the Pinsent Masons (2016) legal guidance which, as argued earlier, is subject to criticism and does not include reference to the *Tarrant* criteria for legal representation.

However, it is clear that the OfS now acknowledges the power of conditions of registration in the context of GBV and it should be noted that under S15 HERA, the OfS has the power to impose monetary penalties or, under S16, to suspend registration if a university is in breach of ongoing registration conditions. It is not necessarily clear at what point measures might be taken by the OfS under ss15 and 16. Prior to the publication of the Statement of Expectations, the OfS indicated that the test would be that "harm" has been caused. This could be evidenced by, for example, increasing dropout rates, cuts in investment in services, or complaints from a large number of students. The evidence would have to be, it seems, "so awful" for them to step in and claim that there has been a breach of the registration conditions, because the OfS see their role as supporting practice and innovation with no clear articulation of what a "minimum" standard might be.

Future directions

Of interest is the sentiment of those working "on the ground" in the sector. Interestingly, Chantler et al. (2019, 2022) asked participants working in the sector if they would like to see a mandatory legal duty on universities to prevent and respond effectively to sexual violence. Fifty-six per cent responded "yes" with another 29% responding "maybe". The overwhelming theme from the qualitative responses of those who favoured a legal duty related to the disparity across the sector in the treatment of women. The majority thought that a mandatory duty could help overcome barriers to implementation of the UUK agenda (2016) that they had faced. Participants commented on how they thought a mandatory duty would be a "key driver", forcing their university "to actually reach a baseline"; "to ensure that Universities record data and make some workshops/courses mandatory"; "make institutions more responsive e.g., in relation to reporting mechanisms, prevention work etc."; "create a better case for getting the appropriate resourcing"; and "enforce the duty of care to students". Of note is that even one respondent who was sceptical about a duty felt that this might be the only way to prioritise this agenda as they were unable to think of another way of making this a priority (Chantler et al., 2019, 2022). Thus, there is a sense of disillusionment with the current arrangements and support for examining further legal approaches which carry obligations rather than recommendations.

What then is the way forward? The aim must be intervention at a structural level with a view to achieving both formal and substantive gender equality through strong laws requiring universities to prevent and respond to GBV. To ensure enforcement of these laws, we need to see a shift, from ad hoc and inconsistent institutional responses at the level of the relationship between an individual and the relevant institution and between institution and OfS to regulation of institutions themselves by the state. One way of doing this is through the existing regulatory powers of the OfS under HERA. It is suggested that a further legislative mandate may be necessary for the OfS to take on this responsibility, perhaps to obviate fear of judicial review for exceeding its powers and to clarify exactly when the powers under ss15 and 16 should and must be used to impose penalties for breach of registration conditions.

The Women and Equalities Committee (2018) suggested that regulations to link the state funding of universities to a "requirement to prohibit sex discrimination and sexual harassment and to collect and publish data on the effectiveness of institutional policies" could be introduced under S153 *Equality Act* 2010 (2018, para 161). S153 gives ministers the right to impose regulations on a public authority "for the purpose of enabling the better performance by the authority of the duty imposed by S149" (the PSED). Such regulations under S153 are rare and the EHRC is in any case a poor enforcer (mentioned earlier). It is suggested that such measures are not necessary because the framework for the OfS to impose legal obligations on universities to respond to and prevent GBV already exists within HERA.

It is also suggested that a specific statutory framework of direct accountability for universities to government could be developed. Mandatory duties are used in other jurisdictions such as the United States to hold universities to account for serious sanctions for non-compliance. Although mandatory duties can only be one part of a comprehensive strategy for combatting GBV in universities, their imposition could ensure accountability at scale – the issue would be taken seriously across the sector and a baseline consistency established – which is currently absent and likely to remain so. It would also guarantee that GBV would be in the senior management portfolio. Mandatory duties would force those uncommitted universities to act and would not deter already committed universities from continuing to develop best practice and best research (Fenton, 2018).

One example of a statutory framework is the US *Clery Act* 1990 as amended in 2013 by the *Campus SaVE Act*, which requires Institutions of Higher Educations (IHEs) to collect and report data on (all) reported criminal offences, including sexual offences, domestic violence, dating violence, and stalking to the Department of Education. Of specific interest is that IHEs must include a statement of policies regarding their programmes *to prevent* and *procedures following reporting* of the issues of domestic violence, dating violence, sexual assault, and stalking (McCallion & Feder, 2014). These policies must address education programmes which must include "primary prevention and awareness programs for *all incoming students and new employees*" (italics added) – and these *must include* bystander intervention – and "ongoing prevention and awareness campaigns for students and faculty" regarding domestic violence, dating violence, sexual assault, and stalking. The difference in wording between this and the OfS Statement of Expectations is notable: The Expectations are simply that training must be "*made available* for all staff and students to raise awareness" and this "*may include* covering areas *such as* bystander initiatives" (OfS, 2021b, rec 4(b), italics added). In addition to setting out the procedural requirements for institutional disciplinary action, the *Clery Act* requires that officials who investigate a complaint or hear proceedings must undergo *annual training* on the issues related to domestic violence, dating violence, sexual assault, and stalking in comparison with the OfS Expectation that "panel members should be appropriately trained" (OfS, 2021b, rec 6(d)).

Conclusions

Legal regulation and social reality are therefore at a disjuncture in terms of responding to GBV at universities. Whilst current legal responses are part of the armoury for holding universities to account, the commonality of legal responses is that law can only be enforced ad hoc by individuals or the EHRC after breach. Placing the enforceability burden on individuals is deeply unsatisfactory as it does not enforce consistent institutional responses or actually regulate universities in any way. The barriers are significant. With tenacity and significant resource, an individual may achieve some form of justice – and the spectre of legal proceedings may be a tool to enforce individual institutional policy changes to avoid reputational damage. However, what is required is a shift from ad hoc individually initiated complaints to regulation of universities themselves at state level. It is no surprise that the Women and Equalities Committee (2018) concludes that the current voluntary approach of universities to sexual harassment and other violence against women "has not proven to ensure that women's safety is prioritised consistently and it is now time for the Government to consider legislation" (para 31). We echo that sentiment.

Acknowledgements

This work was funded by the GW4 Building Communities Programme Accelerator Fund project, "Investigating GBV Intersectional (Dis)Advantages and Legal Duties – A Scoping Study of UK Universities".

Further Reading

Cowan, S., & Munro, V. (2021). Seeking campus justice: Challenging the 'criminal justice drift' in United Kingdom university responses to student sexual violence and misconduct. *Journal of Law and Society*, *48* (3), 308–333. https://doi.org/10.1111/jols.12306

In this article, Cowan and Munro consider Higher Education Institutions' legal, ethical and civic responsibilities in relation to addressing student-to-student sexual violence highlighting, in particular, the legal duties in equality, human rights, and consumer law. They provide a brief overview of the current state taken by many UK universities. They present a concern that universities are attempting to recreate the criminal justice system through adversarial approaches rather than addressing sexual violence response through civil justice models which can be tailored, transformative and trauma-informed and provide more opportunity to match what 'justice' might mean to victim-survivors.

Whitfield, L. (2018). Using the law to challenge gender-based violence in university communities. In R. Lewis & S. Anitha (Eds.), *Gender based violence in university communities* **(pp. 149–169). Policy Press.**

In this chapter which is part of a larger volume of work looking at gender-based violence within universities, Whitfield considers existing laws and how survivors of gender-based violence, advocates and activists can navigate this framework to hold universities accountable in upholding women's rights. The Public Sector Equality Duty under the Equality Act 2010, the Human Rights Act, the Istanbul Convention, EU Victims' Directive, and the Committee on the Elimination of Discrimination against Women are each explored.

Whitfield, L., & Dustin, H. (2015). *Spotted: Obligations to protect women students' safety and equality* **. www.endviolenceagainstwomen. org.uk/wp-content/uploads/Spotted-Obligations-to-Protect-Women-StudentsEy-Safety-Equality.pdf**

This legal briefing has been formative in shifting the understanding of UK universities' legal obligations to students and staff, published almost two years before the Universities UK and Pinsent Mason guidance which replaced the 1994 Zellick guidelines. The aim of this briefing is to demonstrate how the Public Sector Equality Duty (PSED) & the Human Rights Act can be used to improve policies and practices on addressing violence against women and girls in Higher and Further Education Institutions. It provides practical examples of how to show compliance with the legal obligations and potential breaches to be aware of and mitigate for, as well as practical advice for students in holding universities to account.

References

AB v University of XYZ. (2020a) [2020] EWHC 206 (QB).

AB v University of XYZ. (2020b) [2020] EWHC 2978.

Batty, D. (2019, July 14). Warwick University not safe, says woman targeted by 'rape chat' *The Guardian*. www.theguardian.com/education/2019/jul/14/warwick-university-not-safe-says-woman-targeted-by-chat

Bohner, G., Eyssel, F., Pina, A., Siebler, F., & Viki, G. T. (2009). Rape myth acceptance: Cognitive, affective and behavioural effects of beliefs that blame the victim and exonerate the perpetrator. In M. Horvath & J. Brown (Eds.), *Rape: Challenging contemporary thinking* (pp. 17–45). Willan.

Bull, A., Chapman, E., Page, T., & Calvert-Lee, G. (2018). *Recommendations for disciplinary processes into staff sexual misconduct in UK higher education.* The 1752 Group and McAllister Olivarius.

Bull, A., & Rye, R. (2018). *Silencing students: Institutional responses to staff sexual misconduct in UK higher education.* University of Portsmouth and The 1752 Group. https://1752group. files.wordpress.com/2018/09/silencing-students_the-1752-group.pdf

Burke, P. (2012). *The right to higher education: Beyond widening participation.* Routledge.

Busby, E. (2018, March 1). Three in five students sexually assaulted or harassed at university, survey finds *The Independent.* www.independent.co.uk/news/education/education-news/ university-students-sexual-assault-harassment-experiences-revolt-student-room-survey-a8234741.html

Chantler, K., Donovan, C., Fenton, R., & Bracewell, K. (2019). *Findings from a national study to investigate how British universities are challenging sexual violence and harassment on campus.* Briefing Paper. https://socialsciences.exeter.ac.uk/law/research/projects/project/?id=652

Chantler, K., Donovan, C., Fenton, R., & Bracewell, K. (2022). *Findings from a national study to investigate how British universities are challenging sexual violence and harassment on campus.* Full report on file with the authors.

Cowan, S., & Munro, V. (2021). Seeking campus justice: Challenging the 'criminal justice drift' in United Kingdom university responses to student sexual violence and misconduct. *Journal of Law and Society, 48*(3), 308–333. https://doi.org/10.1111/jols.12306

Deacon, T. (2020, August 28). Women considering legal action against Royal Welsh College of Music and Drama over sexual assault claims. *Wales Online.* www.walesonline.co.uk/ news/wales-news/royal-college-music-drama-cardiff-18829145

Department for Education. (2017). *Securing student success: Risk-based regulation for teaching excellence, social mobility and informed choice in higher education. Government consultation on behalf of the Office for Students – Guidance on registration conditions.* B Regulatory Framework consultation guidance FINAL 18 October.pdf (education.gov.uk).

Fenton, R. (2016, November 1). Universities need clearer guidelines on how to deal with rape cases. *The Guardian.* www.theguardian.com/higher-education-network/2016/ nov/01/universities-need-clearer-guidelines-on-how-deal-with-cases

Fenton, R. (2018). *Published written evidence to house of commons women and equalities committee: Sexual harassment of women and girls in public places (SPP0109).* http://data.parliament.uk/ WrittenEvidence/CommitteeEvidence.svc/EvidenceDocument/Women%20and%20 Equalities/Sexual%20harassment%20of%20women%20and%20girls%20in%20public%20 places/written/86149.html

Higher Education Policy Institute. (2020). *Mind the gap: Gender differences in higher education.* www.hepi.ac.uk/2020/03/07/mind-the-gap-gender-differences-in-higer-education/

House of Commons Women and Equalities Select Committee. (2016). *Sexual harassment and sexual violence in schools.* Third Report of Session 2016–2017 HC 91. https://publications. parliament.uk/pa/cm201617/cmselect/cmwomeq/91/9102.htm

House of Commons Women and Equalities Select Committee. (2018). *Sexual harassment of women and girls in public places.* Sixth Report of Session 2017–2019 HC 701. https:// publications.parliament.uk/pa/cm201719/cmselect/cmwomeq/701/70102.htm

House of Commons Women and Equalities Select Committee. (2019). *Enforcing the equality act: The law and role of equality and human rights commission.* Tenth Report of Sixth Session 2017–2019 HC 1470. https://publications.parliament.uk/pa/cm201919/cmselect/ cmwomeq/96/9602.htm

Jeffries, B. (2021, December 10). Student stalked at university calls for change *BBC News*. www.bbc.co.uk/news/education-59587275

Long, R., & Hubble, S. (2021). *Sexual harassment in education*. House of Commons Library Briefing Paper 0817. https://commonslibrary.parliament.uk/research-briefings/cbp-8117/

Lonsway, C., & Magley, J. (2008). Sexual harassment mythology: Definition, conceptualization and measurement. *Sex Roles, 58*, 599–615. doi:10.1007/s11199-007-9367-1

McCallion, G., & Feder, J. (2014). *Sexual violence at institutions of higher education*. Report number: R43764. Congressional Research Service.

National Union of Students (NUS). (2011). *Hidden marks: A study of women students' experiences of harassment, stalking, violence and sexual assault*. www.nusconnect.org.uk/resources/hidden-marks-a-study-of-women-students-experiences-of-harassment-stalking-violence-and-sexual-assault

Office for Students. (2018). *Securing student success: Regulatory framework for higher education in England*. www.officeforstudents.org.uk/media/1406/ofs2018_01.pdf

Office for Students. (2020). *Consultation on harassment and sexual misconduct in higher education*. www.officeforstudents.org.uk/publications/consultation-on-harassment-and-sexual-misconduct/

Office for Students. (2021a). *Regulatory notice 1: Guidance for access and participation plans*. www.officeforstudents.org.uk/publications/regulatory-notice-1-access-and-participation-plan-guidance/

Office for Students. (2021b). *Prevent and address harassment and sexual misconduct: Statement of expectations*. www.officeforstudents.org.uk/advice-and-guidance/student-wellbeing-and-protection/prevent-and-address-harassment-and-sexual-misconduct/statement-of-expectations/

Office for Students. (2021c). *How we expect universities and colleges to tackle harassment and sexual misconduct*. www.officeforstudents.org.uk/news-blog-and-events/blog/how-we-expect-universities-and-colleges-to-tackle-harassment-and-sexual-misconduct/

Oppenheim, M. (2019, August 15) Cambridge University graduate sues over handling of sexual harassment complaint Cambridge University graduate sues over handling of sexual harassment complaint. *The Independent*.

Page, T., Fenton, R., & Keliher, J. (2020, January 9). Universities fail sexual violence survivors. Will new rules change the culture? *The Guardian*.

Perry, D., & Hardcastle, K. (2018). *Legal opinion on criminal cases*. In Independent Complaints and Grievance Scheme Delivery Report. UK Parliament. www.parliament.uk/globalassets/documents/news/2018/1-ICGP-Delivery-Report.pdf p.99-

Persaud, S. (2019). *Independent review of student disciplinary and appeals processes*. https://warwick.ac.uk/newsandevents/independent_external_review/review/independent_external_review_10_july_2019.pdf

Pinsent Masons. (2016). *Guidance for higher education institutions*. www.universitiesuk.ac.uk/policy-and-analysis/reports/Pages/guidance-for-higher-education-institutions.aspx

R v Secretary of State for the Home Department Ex p Tarrant [1985] Q.B. 251.

R (on the application of Ramey) v Governing Body of University of Oxford [2015] EWHC 4847 (Admin).

Towl, G., & Walker, T. (2019). *Tackling sexual violence at universities: An international perspective*. Routledge.

Universities UK. (2016). *Changing the culture*. www.universitiesuk.ac.uk/policy-and-analysis/reports/Documents/2016/changing-the-culture.pdf

Universities UK. (2018). *Changing the culture: One year on*. www.universitiesuk.ac.uk/policy-and-analysis/reports/Documents/2018/changing-the-culture-one-year-on.pdf

Weale, S., & Batty, D. (2017, March 6). New sexual harassment claims at Goldsmiths spark calls for inquiry. *The Guardian*. www.theguardian.com/education/2017/mar/06/

new-sexual-harassment-claims-goldsmiths-university-of-london-calls-inquirye-assault-harassment-university-social-media-a8927201.htm

Whitfield, L. (2018). Using the law to challenge gender-based violence in university communities. In R. Lewis & S. Anitha (Eds.), *Gender based violence in university communities* (pp. 149–169). Policy Press.

Whitfield, L., & Dustin, H. (2015). *Spotted: Obligations to protect women students' safety and equality*. www.endviolenceagainstwomen.org.uk/wp-content/uploads/Spotted-Obligations-to-Protect-Women-StudentsEy-Safety-Equality.pdf

Women and Equalities Committee (WEC). (2018). *Sexual harassment of women and girls in public places*. https://publications.parliament.uk/pa/cm201719/cmselect/cmwomeq/701/70102.htm

Part II
Practice

9 Emily Test

From tragedy to change

Fiona Drouet and Poppy Gerrard-Abbott

Part 1: Emily's case

Fiona Drouet MBE

Thursday, March 17, 2016, 9.17 pm

> Mum (text): *Are you out yet? Xxx*
> Emily (text): **Just getting ready. Xxx**

As I read Emily's text, I felt an inexplicable, maternal urge to call her to tell her I loved her. I pressed her number but ended the call before it rang and put my mobile phone back on the table, saying out loud "Oh give her peace, Fiona". My daughter and I had already talked a couple of times that day and I didn't want to be "that mum" who got in the way right at the point the fun was about to start! I couldn't have known the difference that call might have made and will spend the rest of my life torturing myself as to why I didn't just let it ring.

As I put the phone down, Angus Milligan, a fellow student at Emily's university and also in his first year of undergraduate study although a few years older, barged into her bedroom unannounced, for the fourth time that week. He left four minutes later. At the time, my husband and I had no idea any of this was happening. Emily ran out of her room screaming hysterically: "**He's done it again, he's slapped me around, put his hands around my throat again, I can't go on**". Her neighbour tried desperately to calm her, but she was inconsolable and went back to her room, alone. She messaged the friend she was going to go out with: "**I don't think I can go out. Angus just visited and he's angry**." Her friend replied: "I'll be there in 10". Her friend arrived 10 minutes after Emily's last text was sent – she knocked on the bedroom door which was, unusually, locked so she called Emily's mobile phone but there was no answer.

Scared, broken, and all alone, our darling little girl had taken her own life.

Emily Drouet, our wonderful, kind, fun-loving, intelligent, and beautiful daughter, was stolen from us all. The light of all of our lives was taken from us, just months after she enrolled at university.

DOI: 10.4324/9781003252474-11

The prior September, at only 17 years of age, Emily achieved her long-held dream of studying Law and French Law at degree level, receiving an unconditional offer to study at a university a few hours away from our home where my husband and I, Emily, and her younger sister and brother lived. Try as we might to encourage her to stay closer, the adventure for Emily had already begun with Facebook chats and party planning. She was brimming with excitement. As loving parents, we supported Emily and preparations started – we embarked on the all-important trip to purchase pots and pans, knives, and forks, all the things that never get used as a student! We went to John Lewis to get her an extra high tog quilt; Emily always felt the cold. Every detail was thought of, right down to the fairy lights and a photo frame with a collection of family photos. We wanted to make sure Emily's bedroom in student halls was a home from home – a cosy, peaceful, and safe space. Like all parents and guardians, we were emotional as we left Emily to settle in but felt such happiness seeing her excitement about the adventures that lay ahead. At first, freshers' life seemed to be everything she'd hoped for, she was flourishing.

A month into her journey at university she met Angus, a young man studying business and psychology and residing in the same dormitories. When we visited one time, Emily introduced him to us as a "friend" at university. We instantly felt uncomfortable in his presence. Emily's little brother and sister, in particular, found there was no warmth to him. I can only describe a strong sense of arrogance. However, I dismissed it as me being an overprotective mother. After all, he was only a friend and if it was anything more, would I ever think anyone would be good enough for my little girl?

However, my instincts were not as irrational as I thought.

In the weeks and months that followed, Angus subjected Emily to a relentless campaign of physical, emotional, psychological, sexual, and digital abuse. Tragically, we were not to find this out until it was too late. During the Christmas holidays, while Emily was falling head over heels for him, Milligan was sleeping with other women in his hometown. When they both returned to university in January 2016, he made Emily aware of this and it broke her heart. She ended the relationship, but they got back together with his term and condition: "no-one wants a relationship when they are at university, we should sleep with other people like everyone else does." Emily reluctantly agreed to this, in the hope that his feelings for her might grow.

With Emily's 18th birthday celebrations approaching at the end of January, Angus told her he had already bought her a birthday present. She was excited and hoped for something that showed how much he cared for her. When it came, his "gift" was a box containing £200 worth of Ann Summers sex toys, outfits, and restraints. Milligan had introduced Emily to sexual practices that were violent and potentially dangerous but when Emily raised concerns with her friends, they dismissed it as "perhaps this is the way it is".

Throughout the "relationship", Milligan hounded Emily to sleep with the male students in the rugby squad, at one point detailing the flats she should go to, saying what size of penis each boy had – Emily showed clear anguish in response. He repeatedly asked Emily to engage in a threesome with a particular friend, but Emily said no, telling her friendship circle that she found the suggestion creepy. On one occasion when she visited Angus, she was ordered to go away and only come back when she had slept with a particular boy. On an evening out with mutual friends, he poured a pint of beer over Emily's head, later saying it was just a bit of fun and that Emily "only cried after it happened, not when he did it".

Friends report that Emily would jump when he messaged. We later found he would set timers on his phone giving Emily two minutes to get to his flat, and if she didn't get there within that time, he would take the key card back in from his window ledge. When Emily said she was trying her best to get there in time, he replied, "Just hurry the fuck up Emily, I don't make the rules". Angus drafted an email detailing Emily's "bad behaviour" (drinking, partying, relationships – all habitual behaviour of a student) and threatened her that if she did not "change", he would send it to me.

In February, Emily was out in a nightclub with Angus when she was introduced to the friend he had been repeatedly encouraging the threesome with. She was drunk in a way that she was never drunk before, in and out of consciousness with periods of memory loss. Her mobile phone shows a long trace of texts from the friend, "Where are you??" "Is this happening?" "Where are you, Emily?", "Come on!" – ten messages in total. The next thing Emily remembered was being in a taxi with Angus' friend and sister – Angus later claimed he had a long-running dysfunctional relationship with her. Events took place that night which we are not able to elaborate on for legal reasons, however, suffice to say Emily was in no state to consent and there remains many unanswered questions surrounding the circumstances. The following day Emily downloaded information about rape on her computer.

Although Angus orchestrated this, he later stood in the courtyard of the student halls and screamed: "Emily Drouet from flat 86B is a fucking slag!" He also shouted details about their sex life, what she had done to him, and what he had done to her. Emily stayed in her room with the lights out, crouched beneath the window crying. He bombarded her with abusive texts. She tried to calm him down, her efforts were in vain. She became fearful of leaving her flat, scared of confrontation with him or anyone who knew him.

Angus sent messages to friends saying, "I'm going to do something that I might regret for the rest of my life, but it will mean she can't hurt anyone else!" He then said: "I'll wait until tomorrow when I'm sober." He also told friends of how he planned to get "answers" and intended to record himself "questioning" Emily. True to his word, the next day on 10th March, sober, Milligan barged into Emily's flat unannounced, using a key card a female student friend of his had willingly lent him.

He then assaulted Emily so viciously that she was left fearing for her life. He slapped her repeatedly, threw her head down on her desk, and strangled her until she came to the point of passing out. He then left Emily on the floor on her knees pulling her hair rocking back and forward, highly distressed and visibly injured, and returned to his friends laughing about how he would slap Emily every time she dared to look away from him or "lie" to him. Disturbingly, he found assaulting and abusing our daughter highly entertaining. He recorded assaults and played the videos to fellow students – both male and female – including the young woman who had given him her key card to access Emily's room. Not one of them went to check Emily was ok.

Emily told friends she thought she was going to die at the hands of Angus. She also disclosed that she felt so scared that she actually *wanted* to die. Scared for Emily, her friend suggested she talk to the resident assistants (RAs) in the dorms. Crying and with visible facial injuries, marks on her neck, chest, and ear, Emily sought support from them. One RA from the team chatted with Emily, taking her for a walk outside around the residence grounds.

They wrote their report as follows: *Emily came to us concerned about her angry and aggressive boyfriend. We asked Emily if he had hit her and she said* "**No, I don't want to get him into trouble** ", *Emily said:* "**I think I'm hitting the self-destruct button** ". *Emily knows she needs to change her behaviour. No follow-up required.*

That night, Emily returned to her bedroom all alone. This room looked on to his, with her having to pass his window to exit or enter the halls. Too terrified to leave her flat, she became increasingly isolated. Struggling to cope alone, her drinking increased, and her behaviour became erratic. Her friend witnessed what has now been recognised as Emily having a psychiatric breakdown. Silent and distant, in the presence of her friend, Emily ripped her study planner and notes from her walls. She tried to pull the light pendant out of the ceiling. Her friend described this event: "she wasn't there, it wasn't her".

Despite all of this pain, all of her suffering, Emily re-applied herself to her studies and submitted an essay assessment on public law. She received excellent feedback for the paper, but sadly did not live long enough to see her result. In the week that followed the March 10th assault, Angus turned up and assaulted Emily a further three times. The final assault was on the evening of March 17th. It was St Patrick's Day and Emily was preparing to celebrate with friends. On my end, everything seemed normal as Emily, and I had been chatting throughout the day. We had started looking for a flat for her and her friend Sophie to share in their second year. She was in good spirits as she told me her little brother had been messaging her after finding his long-lost iPod. She adored her brother and sister; family has always been everything to Emily. It was around 8.30 pm I said to my son "It's time to go to bed now", and he replied, "Aw Mum, I'm messaging Emily", and I replied, "It's bedtime now son, you can message Emily tomorrow".

Hours later, at 1.30 am on March 18th, Emily's Dad and I awoke to a loud knock at our front door. We jumped out of bed and went downstairs unaware in the moments that were to follow. Our world was about to implode. We opened the door to two police officers who asked if they could come in. I still have no words to describe the depth of the pain we were plunged into at that moment.

How could our little girl be gone? *There must be a mistake, I can fix this.* These were the words that I kept repeating to the police, reassuring them somehow that this would be ok. There was obviously a huge error. . . not Emily, this isn't possible. After the police left, I called one of Emily's friends, sure that she would tell me there had been a terrible mistake, that she could explain the confusion. All I could hear was crying and chaos in the background "Fiona, oh my God Fiona. . . She couldn't tell you, but it's been awful, Angus has been treating her really badly".

We lay awake, my husband, my sister, and I, all on our bed shaking in disbelief. It could not be real – how could we wake her little brother and sister and tell them their big sister was gone? At 6.30 am we woke them and brought them together. We said there had been a terrible accident with Emily that she did not survive. The subsequent wails of agony will never leave us, our beautiful children broken, hearts shattered, and there was nothing we could do to make it better, we couldn't take the pain away. All of this agony because of one person – how could we not have known what had been happening?

Looking back – the benefit of hindsight – it should have been clear to us. When I had last seen Emily a few weeks before, I said "Emy, I feel your eyes have lost their sparkle, are you OK?" Her eyes were tired, her zest for life and infectious energy and spirit were not there. "**Mummy I'm shattered, I was out last night. I am just really tired**". I accepted that. Why wouldn't she be – isn't that what university life is like? I relive such conversations every day and torture myself – what mother does not know when their child is in agony? She was dying in front of me.

In the weeks and months that followed, the horrific details and extent of the abuse unfolded. We received messages, screenshots, various accounts from witnesses of what they had seen Milligan do – accounts of staff intervening when he was verbally abusing Emily, although staff would later deny any such involvement.

At Emily's "goodnight", we invited all of her friends to join us as we needed to have them close to keep us feeling connected to the life Emily had in Aberdeen. One after another they told us of Milligan's assaults, threats, coercive control, and what experts later explained to us was grooming. It was on that day – after we laid our baby girl to rest – that we found out the awful truth that Milligan's violence was so extreme that Emily almost lost her life at his hands in March.

We didn't know where to turn. The attending police had dismissed Emily as "another student suicide" but we knew, for Emily's sake, we had to find out what had been going on. After a long and horrific court case, Milligan was convicted of assault to injury, breach of the communications act, and stalking. He received just a 180-hours community payback order and a one-year supervision order. We received a life sentence.

We couldn't let that happen to anyone else, we had to do something, we had to act. We had so many questions and no answers, as well as no experience or expertise. Could *we* really make a difference? The questions just kept coming and we knew this couldn't happen again. We could not help Emily, but we could help another girl or another family. If nothing else, we had a burning desire to stop this happening again and an eagerness to learn why Emily and so many others were being failed.

We started on working out how this could happen in the first place: how could staff suspect abuse and not act? Why were we not informed when staff suspected abuse and when there was a clear decline in her mental health? Various reports emerged of Emily drinking herself to unconsciousness in the last week and staff taking her to bed, yet we weren't informed, nothing was flagged, no further action was taken. How could Emily be left at such risk, abandoned to a state of such extreme fear, anxiety, and self-blame.

Our victimisation continued – answers weren't forthcoming from the university. Sadly, all we received were standard legal emails and letters. It was as if they were closing ranks. We then approached the Scottish Government desperately seeking answers:

Why were the university departments working in isolation and not holistically? Why were policies not fit for purpose, indeed lacking? Why was there no adequate risk assessment of Emily's case? Why were perpetrators like Angus allowed to remain on campus? Why is there no specialist support for victims/survivors? Why is help not signposted, why is there a lack of clear reporting mechanisms? Why are staff not trained to recognise and respond to the signs of gender-based violence (GBV)?

It was simply incomprehensible that despite some attempts to have GBV and mental health provisions, it seemed institutions were generally failing their students and indeed leaving their staff in a vulnerable position without the necessary skills. We had uncovered numerous opportunities for intervention in Emily's trajectory, all missed. Information held by one department but not shared with others.

We took all these questions to the then Scottish Minister for Further Education, Higher Education and Science, Shirley-Anne Somerville. I was sure that someone would say "Mrs Drouet you have this wrong." But she said: "Mrs Drouet, you have not got this wrong. It's not good enough and it has to change".

Her words overwhelmed us – shocked us that we were right but filled us with hope and confidence that maybe someone did care about our young people, especially young women. Until then we had met repeatedly with "Emily was 18, she was an adult". . . "We had to respect her right to privacy". . . "We did everything we could with the *limited* information we had". What was their definition of *limited*?

We approached the National Union of Students (NUS) and later, Universities Scotland (US), to develop support cards for university staff to signpost students to specialised, local, and national support services. We then worked to extend this project to stickers for halls of residence, inside wardrobe doors, changing rooms, toilets, to direct students to support for GBV and their mental health. Resources that we believe, if they had existed when Emily was alive, may have saved her life.

Working determinedly, the Minister wrote her expectations of the sector in GBV prevention, intervention, and support into her letter of guidance to the Scottish Funding Council, stipulating that if institutions could not evidence sufficient activity and progress in the area, funding would be cut. She announced a further £398k of funding for the Equally Safe in Colleges and Universities (ESCU) project so that they could continue their research and development of an evidence-based "toolkit" for the sector. We then worked closely with Professor Anni Donaldson and her academic team at the University of Strathclyde in the development and roll out of this resource for the sector.

Our campaigning extended to other areas: to end the destructive and immoral practice of non-disclosure agreements (NDAs) in cases of abuse in universities. We came across new failures – the Universities and Colleges Admissions Service (UCAS) removed the question relating to criminal convictions from application forms. We found this extremely alarming – how can you manage risks on campus if institutions do not monitor what risks are there in the first place? We uncovered numerous other areas lacking data collection; case management processes; timely misconduct hearings; GBV training endorsed by violence against women (VAW) experts; clear pathways to support; awareness-raising at open days and throughout the university journey; intersectional, inclusive, and diverse approaches that leave no-one behind; and the fear of reputational damage clouding decision-making. The list goes on and on.

Our vision became crystalised: we want to see universities working together rather than independently guarding successes and failures for fear of reputational damage. We hear about lack of funding and resources, so is it not time to spend more wisely and stop reinventing the wheel? The formation of regional cohorts of institutions, working together for the greater good, has to be one of the best ways to bring down those barriers.

Although progress across the sector has been promising, it is clear to us that it needs to be monitored more closely and that sustainability remains a key concern. The position and longevity of GBV work often appears fragile as it is highly reliant on strong Ministerial leadership, placing progress in jeopardy if there are changes in government and spending priorities. We could not leave this to chance – our campaign was resolute that we needed to do something decisive to ensure this work would be embedded into the DNA of universities and colleges.

That's where the idea for the GBV "Charter" was born. A national, cross-institutional mark of minimum standards and excellence in GBV prevention, intervention of support, and serving as both an internal and external marker incentivising, celebrating, and signifying a responsible institution as well as empowering prospective students and their parents, guardians, and carers, to make informed decisions when choosing where to study. Obviously, we recognise that the core focus and specialism of educational institutions needs to remain on academic achievement but that is only of worth if our children survive their time as a student.

Once the idea for the Charter was conceived, we were overwhelmed with where to start. It was clear we needed a lot of help as there is only so much one person or a set of parents can do. A chance meeting with my now Principal Researcher and Policy Manager, Poppy, at a local conference we were both speaking at, and I knew I had met the person to help me to take the newly formed EmilyTest charity to the next level. We seemed to be on the same wavelength, to appreciate how much had to be done. We shared the same frustrations and the belief that solutions could be achieved. From simple things such as young women like Emily and her friends not relating to services like "Women's Aid" – at what age do girls consider themselves women? What image is conjured up, what stereotypes, is this a space for them? Terms like "domestic abuse" – what was domestic about Emily's situation? She did not live with Angus, they were not married, and their relationship status was in flux; they were young students living independently from each other.

We took all of our thinking, all of our concerns, frustrations, and beliefs and gradually developed the GBV charter, the first in the UK, indeed the world, asking one fundamental question: "Would your institution have saved Emily's life?"

Part 2

Poppy Gerrard-Abbott

In this section, I am going to discuss the findings of the research conducted to create the GBV Charter for universities and colleges (EmilyTest, 2021a), which involved focus groups, interviews, co-creation sessions, consultation, and surveys with hundreds of student and graduate victim-survivors and professionals who work with them across Scotland and the UK. I will be writing to three areas: firstly, the rationale for why we should focus on GBV in education as a narrowed context over focusing on GBV "in general"; secondly, explaining the GBV Charter as a framework; and thirdly, examining what challenges remain for us to contend with in this specialist field, which shape the future success of the rollout of such frameworks.

Thus far, UK research on GBV in education has been disproportionately quantitative. This has served an important utility in creating succinct understandings about the problem at hand and subsequently stimulating strong political and institutional responses, including policy change and awareness campaigns at nearly every UK university and in many colleges. The key headline to take from quantitative understandings that answers this question of 'why the education context?' is that data are building a picture that GBV prevalence rates are higher and reporting rates are lower among student populations "clear indication" (Revolt Sexual Assault and the Student Room, 2018) than the general population (ONS, 2017). Compounding this is that after ten years of interventions, the most recent evidence is revealing that prevalence rates are as high, if not higher (Brook, 2019; NUS Women's Campaign & 1752 Group, 2018; NUS, 2019), than when research and subsequent interventions began a decade ago following on from the publication of the groundbreaking Hidden Marks report (NUS, 2010).

As our Charter research shifted to a mixed methods and qualitative-leaning strategy of inquiry, the limitations in terms of the dominance of quantitative methods in our specialist field revealed themselves. Our research report (EmilyTest, 2021b) found that GBV is *endemic* in our educational institutions and that numbers like "1 in 3" and percentage-based representations, which constitute mainstream understandings, are important but limited understandings. We found that GBV is interwoven and normalised into everyday university and college life – nightlife, the classroom, social life, societies, domestic life, teacher--student relationships – assuming a status as mundane and being of a scale methodologically impossible to capture numerically.

Further bolstering a case for a specialist focus, our research found there are specific characteristics to GBV in the education context, furthering understandings that GBV in education presents unique manifestations and challenges (Humphreys & Towl, 2020). Firstly, certain types of GBV are prevalent in education – in particular, digital mediations, stalking, and sites of resource-exchange such as rent and transport and sites of lone working and power differentials. There are specific characteristics to the education environment that shape the manifestations of GBV *and* its secondary impacts – this being that the social networks and structures of education environments are distinct in that they are tight-knit and multiplex, hosting students' academic, economic, occupational, social, and political life. GBV is global, pancultural, and endemic but social orders shape its localised manifestations. The structures of Further Education (FE) and Higher Education (HE) institutions make surveillance, targeting, and bullying behaviours particularly possible and make disclosure often a high-risk, low-reward calculation, where confidentiality management is highly demanding and victim-survivors are forced to make multipronged considerations relating to housing, finances, studies, friendship circles, and employment when deciding to report and/or seek out advice and safety measures.

The first qualitative study on GBV in HE (Phipps & Young, 2013) details the fundamentally social dimensions to the performance, iteration, and cultural endorsement of lad and rape cultures. Our research uncovered how the close-knit, claustrophobic social climate of education supports enablement towards perpetration whereby the student community overlook and reinforce perpetration in order to keep community membership. Therefore, violence following on from, or running parallel to, the "primary" violence often comes from the student community itself – people orbiting the perpetrator, both in and outside of their social networks. Our work came to understand the "phenomenology" of the student victim-survivor as one of intense community-mediated discrimination, including sequences and hybrids of street harassment, verbal abuse, digital violence, "slut-shaming", and social gatekeeping. This conveys widespread "secondary victimisation" (Williams, 1984) – a term inferring processes and attitudes (originally referring to professionals and systems in the Criminal Justice System [CJS] specifically) that stereotype, degrade, and alienate victim-survivors, leading to further trauma known as "re-traumatisation" (1984, p. 67). Secondary victimisation is used interchangeably with terms like "judicial rape" (Lees, 1997), the "second assault", "second rape" (Williams & Holmes, 1981) of which lived experience of is described as being "raped again" (Temkin, 2002). This concept, born from criminology and socio-legal studies, has expanded out to theorise negative responses to victim-survivors across a range of cultural and institutional sites that all play intersecting parts in reinforcing an entire cultural scaffolding of victim-blaming, with the legal system acting as both a mirror-image of and a baseline-setting mechanism. Recently, GBV in education studies has bridged the term, referring to "institutional betrayal" (Lorenz et al., 2021; NUS & 1752 Group, 2018) in universities.

Our research found that the impacts of secondary victimisation towards student victim-survivors work to inhibit disclosure, significantly increase emotional and psychological suffering, and ex-communicate or sever victim-survivors from their communities. Unsurprising to some, abuse towards victim-survivors following on from "primary" incidences of GBV are both highly *gendered* and *genderless*, where the abuse is of a discriminatory nature (e.g., sexist) but propagated by students of all genders and within "intra-gendered" (Lizzio-Wilson et al., 2020) sexist manifestations pertaining to the gender *order*. Akin to Emily's story, participants spoke about women and girls reinforcing and protecting perpetrators and being active in both primary violence and secondary targeting in order to maintain their membership in the community. Violence as a tool enacted to maintain social orders and police boundaries of social hierarchies is a long-theorised element of intersectional feminist scholarship – when we map this onto the education space, we can observe the iterative, historical nature of GBV in education, mechanised to preserve continuation of class and gender exclusion and privilege in the academy (Phipps et al., 2018; Phipps, 2018, 2015, 2017, 2020a; Phipps & Young, 2015) particularly as contemporary backlash to the advancements of women and feminist principles in education.

Following on from interviews with GBV professionals in rural Scotland, we found that there are many intriguing similarities between GBV in educational environments and GBV in remote and island communities, where disclosures can "split" entire communities. Confidentiality and safety are difficult to manage due to the fast transmission of information – one frontline worker described "stalking-by-proxy" occurring in an environment where the community all intimately inhabit the same spaces. Subsequently, uprooting altogether is common as a victimisation response such as dropping out, moving house, switching course, changing friendship circles, changing appearance, and changing schedule and movements.

Introducing the Charter

The GBV Charter for universities and colleges (EmilyTest, 2021b) has been created as a national, cross-institutional award on the basis that the sector is still not meeting minimum standards of change. Testament to this is Emily's death but also when situating her story in the broader tapestry of data, the testimonies of thousands of students shed light on the non-establishment of minimum standards and on the lack of instruments to measure progress and inform effective strategic and investment efforts.

In the lead up to Emily's death, she was subjected to a non-linear hybrid of physical, digital, verbal, psychological, and sexual abuse, which evidences the importance of employing the GBV umbrella spectrum concept that conceived of systemic violence and abuse as having pluralities and multiple manifestations, perpetrated by people across the "private" and "public" spheres, including the family, the community, and the workplace; as well as cutting across the boundaries of time, space, and cultural sites (United Nations, 1993) embedded and experienced in "all levels of society" (Public Health Scotland, 2021). Subsequently, Emily's story also points to the need for taking multi-solution, multipronged approaches, which is why we talk about the Charter instilling an infrastructure of GBV *prevention*, *intervention*, and *support*.

The Charter award asks universities and colleges to take the "EmilyTest" by answering two questions to instil minimum standards and innovate to excellence zones:

> *'Would you have saved Emily's life?'*
>
> *'How would you have ensured Emily would thrive?'*

These pivotal questions take GBV prevention and intervention beyond the bare minimums of rights and access for (gender-marginalised) students, to consider more ambitious and full dimensions of liberation and justice in educational life and to move institutions beyond "firefighting" risk-mitigation zones to that of adaptation and sustainability. By formatting the two Charter tiers of minimum standards and excellence as flat and as questions, the Charter aims to pioneer new approaches in (equality) charter practices, focusing on standards that ask for continuing, evolving development and that allow institutions to meet the same calibre of universalised standards whilst ensuring sustainability through cross-institutional adaptability by allowing institutions to adapt in ways flexible to their resourcing levels and student body demographics.

From data to principles

When institutions take the "Emily Test", they are examined against five principles, which are a translation of the core findings of the research we conducted to create the Charter. The principles work together and build on one another to represent an "infrastructure" of GBV prevention, intervention, and support.

1   *Foundational principle:* Having an **Open and Learning** institutional culture
    The first principle is born from the findings grouping "foundational needs", which refers to the core, overarching needs that must be considered in order to make GBV provisions possible and robust in universities and colleges. This entails institutions openly admitting GBV

happens "on their watch", prioritising dealing with cases over reputation, banning NDAs, being enthusiastic and transparent collectors and publishers of internal data, and being dual learners and contributors to the GBV in education field of data-driven understandings and subsequent best practice, pro-actively shaping the evolving, niche role of educational institutions in an era of emergent, corporate responsibilities.

2   Educational principle: having **Knowledgeable and Empowered** students and staff

The second principle, from the "educational needs" data grouping, asserts that knowledge and training on GBV for both students and staff needs to be embedded into institutions. Education and prevention work needs to challenge the attitudes and beliefs underpinning GBV, tackle myth-based understandings of victimisation – "rape myths" and "ideal victim tropes" (Brownmiller, 1975) – as well as empowering victim-survivors to know where to turn and equipping staff to offer informed responses.

3   Systems principle: having **Comprehensive and Connected** systems in place

The third principle arose from data which identified inadequacies in university and college reporting and support provisions, primarily disparities between policy and practice. It asks for pathways to be connected and seamless, spanning every corner of educational life "whole-systems approaches" and spanning the whole GBV spectrum – in essence, comprehensive of *space* and *type*.

4   Access: having **Equal and Inclusive** access to those systems

Our focus groups and interviews with students and graduates were identity and experience-specific, grouped by variables such as location, gender, race, study stage, occupation, and sexuality. Experiences of both violence and help-seeking are fundamentally shaped by identity and social characteristics (Beijing Platform for Action, 1995; Hill-Collins, 1990) which needs to be reflected in education and preventative provisions, and in help mechanisms, to ensure equal access to reporting and support and to have an evidence-based understanding of how GBV, and events that ripple out from it, are diversely experienced.

5   Approaches: having **Safe and Effective** institutional approaches to GBV interventions

The fifth and final principle relates to the maintenance of an overall safe community and the installation of risk assessment-driven approaches coming *out* of the GBV prevention, intervention, and support system, complementing the fourth principle which relates to being able to gain access *into* systems. The safety of victim-survivors and the student community should always be a priority in GBV interventions, whether formal reporting has been sought or not.

Remaining challenges

The empirical basis underpinning the Charter creation provided acute insights not just into the experiences of student victim-survivors but also the inhibitors and barriers in the field that are slowing and disrupting change, as well as lowering the efficacy of interventions.

Establishing minimum standards

Emily's death occurred after more than half of the policy and practice developments that have occurred in the UK were in place. Her death was tragic and preventable, as well as compelling a nation-wide realisation that education sectors are still not "getting the basics right" and still not meeting "minimum safeguarding standards" (Towl & Humphreys, 2021). A policy scoping exercise undertook as part of my PhD fieldwork found that 77% of colleges and 67% of universities in Scotland in 2020 do not have a distinct GBV policy, even when taking into account methodological considerations such as conceptual and semantic differences with policy titles like "sexual violence/harassment" or "domestic violence". For institutions that do possess a policy, 37% of colleges and 56% of universities cover the different forms of GBV "comprehensively". Overall, 59% of colleges and 28% of universities do not cover LGBTQIA★ services in any respect in their GBV signposting and 75% of colleges and 39% of universities do not cover ethnic minority or "BAME"[1] contacts and services. There is no GBV or equivalent policy ("zero tolerance" policies are common) in 67% of college and 50% of university student "Unions" or "Associations" – these are legally separate bodies covering functions such as extracurricular, social, sporting, pastoral, and representative student services and are bigger employers of students over colleges and universities themselves, employing three times as many students as non-student staff (NUS, 2017).

Turning to lived experience, the Charter research then found that serious inadequacies exist across institutions in both "intra" and "inter" senses. Student victim-survivors struggle to access basic systems, including locating policies online and navigating reporting procedures, with it being common to be "sent round the houses" and widespread staff responses of not knowing where to direct students. The inadequacies of administrative procedures mean that victim-survivors can "turn inwards" into isolation or disclose only to trusted, untrained people who then bear burdens of knowing criminal information about community members and feel disempowered to come forward. This also means that many stories of GBV never make it to the surface, reinforcing the well-known inhibitor of underreporting due to factors like embarrassment, shame, cultural stereotypes, and fear of disbelief and backlash. In universities, evidence is revealing figures as low as 3% of victim-survivors choose to escalate complaints (Brook, 2019) – one poll conducted by Revolt Sexual Assault and the Student Room (2018) of 4,500 students across 135 universities found that just 2% felt both able to report *and* satisfied with the reporting process.

Furthermore, the Charter report finds that GBV policies and procedures remain geared towards sexual misconduct with a disproportionate focus on *sexual violence* occurring on *university property*, meaning the full spectrum of GBV and of educational life are often not reflected in policy. Not all institutions employ a GBV framework in line with the Equally Safe Strategy (Scottish Government, 2016) and there are many "blind spots" in policy and practice coverage of institutional life. Areas such as transport, digital life, study abroad and exchange programmes, sports away days, study and extracurricular trips, student societies, and local student venues remain areas in need of attention in GBV policy and practice and are areas where victim-survivors experience anxiety and confusion over not knowing where institutional remit ends and where they can turn. Intersectional understandings, such as how racism, ableism, and economic status intersects with sexism as well as more modern legal GBV concepts in the UK such as image-based abuse and Female Genital Mutilation (FGM), are often not covered in policy and lack staff training to develop process and knowledge that fully grasps the GBV umbrella concept.

Casualised employment

Casualised roles in education involve high levels of lone working and lone decision-making for staff, which puts both workers and student victim-survivors in unsafe situations. Participants also reported widespread GBV among pastoral and welfare teams themselves, and from non-student staff towards student staff.

"Casualisation" is a labour union concept (Megoran & Mason, 2020; Universities & Colleges Union [UCU], 2016), often conceptualised to refer to staff on "casual" contracts, including zero-hours and fixed-term, of which two-thirds of researchers and nearly half of teaching staff are employed on. This is underestimated as some workers are hard-to-reach in data collection due to not being officially considered as employees, such as part-time elected officers and Resident Assistants (RAs).

GBV interventions in education rest on entire, hidden ecosystems of informal labour – namely student victim-survivors who feel ostracised from policies and procedures turning to staff that resonate with them rather than appropriately trained staff. This often tends to be young and/or female staff members, staff of colour, and disabled and LGBTQIA* staff who do not necessarily have GBV intervention and support within their roles. These staff members subsequently experience scope creep and unpaid emotional labour supporting victim-survivors. Whilst it is positive that institutions are gradually building infrastructures of GBV prevention, intervention, and support, whose job descriptions this work is being integrated into is a different reality, and concern remains over how GBV work may end up compounding the sexism, racism, and classism that feminist projects are intended to tackle.

Casualisation can be broadened out to include manifestations of "informalisation" across GBV reporting and support mechanisms, where the collecting and referring of information rests on incongruous, leaky, "manual" processes that leave space for human error and results in inconsistent and/or delayed responses. Student employees and ex-employees in our research shared how GBV report statistics can be suppressed by line managers, in particular accommodation managers, to sanitise certain areas of the institution, revealing perspectives among staff that low complaint levels reflect better on them than high. This could point to fear and low confidence among staff about adequately dealing with issues they view as sticky and interpersonally complex, partially due to not feeling adequately knowledgeable and institutionally supported as an employee to be the "proactive" agent of action in a GBV case.

Additionally, there is a psycho-occupational dimension to "passing the buck" and not wanting to be the "sacrificial lamb" concerning high-risk, ethically complex situations, where staff feel interpersonally and professionally safer in not "getting involved" than to be implicated and be wrong in professional judgements and practice. This is compounded by first responder roles being more likely to be lone workers and/or part of marginalised groups, where workers can become targets of abuse from perpetrators and (associated) community members.

Strategic planning and investment

A lack of consensus in the field around "what works?", in addition to patchy university and college datasets on GBV, presents a multifaceted challenge intersecting economic, governance, and policy progress. Evidence-based understandings of what approaches should be promoted in education, and what methods should be employed to measure the effectiveness of prevention and intervention mechanisms, are missing. Empirical work is emerging in the UK context (Miller, 2020), but there is not yet: firstly, field consensus, secondly, consensus reflected in and trickled downwards/outwards to practice, and thirdly, expert focus on education as a specialism within such a consensus.

GBV in education as a field is still in its infancy, learning to walk – educational institutions are in transitional phases concerning adapting to their new corporate responsibilities, figuring out how to carve their role out in contrast to the CJS and professional GBV services. Universities and colleges also have rudimentary and variant datasets on GBV in their individual institutions, with absent insights specifically on GBV case journeys and outcomes. Many do not have specific categories for gathering GBV data. This circles back to the "lacking basics" – having a GBV policy and collecting data are still not widespread, hence why the Charter aims to instil and benchmark minimum standards. The Charter framework will be complemented with an Impact and Evaluation (I&E) framework for the education sectors to start practising the measuring of efficacy, as one of the research outputs from our March–November 2021 pilot of the Charter in two universities and two colleges.

Defining aims and roles

UK Mainstream media and GBV campaigning regularly promotes messaging that universities and colleges are "failing to tackle rape culture on campus" (Murray, 2021) and need to do more to "crack down" (Turner et al., 2021) on GBV. When this sentiment was interrogated in the Charter research, specifically what action is seen as adequate and how this should be measured – for example, by levels of expulsions – dramatically varied across different victim-survivor populations, particularly concerning political relationships with so-called carceral feminist responses (Phipps, 2020b). What is defined as taking adequate action against perpetrators remains vague in the field, a challenge growing larger in an era of increasing corporate responsibility where educational institutions are constructed to have an ever-increasing array of distinct sociopolitical roles in combating global challenges such as climate change and systemic inequalities. In the marketised education era, the scope expansion of duties of care towards victim-survivors as paying customers of educational institutions proves a complex dynamic, where "positive" leveraging of complaints trigger swift changes whilst simultaneously worsening casualisation. Contemporary business-model education possesses investment and financial management agendas where recruitment caps have been removed but staffing infrastructures have not necessarily mirrored student population increases, meaning the *labour of change* (demanded by victim-survivors) trickles down to, and is undertaken by, already overstretched teams experiencing high levels of "burnout", many of which are women, people of colour, and are on the lowest salary bands (UCU, 2019). It is common for universities and colleges, with student bodies of (tens of) thousands to have one "in-house" GBV liaison officer overseeing cases and acting as the main point of contact. Universities annually experience classroom timetabling and accommodation crises due to the influx of overrecruited students. When university-owned properties are full, they are directed to housing organisations working with the private rental sector – during my employment in student housing, an office team of one full-time staff member and two part-time hypothetically served 13,000, managing a portfolio hundreds of properties full weeks before each semester commenced with hundreds more unhoused students flatly directed to our office to find accommodation.

The UK (in particular, England) corporate-business education model came into being during PM Tony Blair's administration (Lunt, 2008) and accelerated under the Conservative-Liberal Democrat coalition (Holmwood, 2014). This shift reconfigured student social justice narratives in ways that pin duty on the institution – the neoliberal education landscape presents an era of complex characteristics of customer care delivery, mixed in with sociopolitical progress goals, sitting alongside commercial consciousness. The results are ever-expanding "on-paper" responsibilities as more customer demands are placed on the institution, hand-in-hand with an increasingly "clipped" relationship with these widening and diversifying responsibilities defined by conservative investment and a risk-averse outlook to safeguard financial and league-table health. The importance of the national policy arena is highlighted here. Where activism anchors the responsibility for change as being with individual institutions and/ or the sector as a whole, this is in danger of missing a bigger, more dominant macro-picture and systems approach whereby the models institutions are assuming are shaped by the parameters of "policy above". This is compounded by the first of numerous ontological issues, where defining what universities and colleges are and, therefore, who they answer to and what laws and policies they are subject to, proves a complex task as they commonly straddle public, private, industry, and charity sectors.

Challenges: concluding remarks

These challenges are challenges in nature because they are systemic and systems-related. They are complex and multifaceted, intersecting numerous disjointed and interconnected spheres outside and inside of institutions, shaped by factors "set above them" like national government policies as well as domestic and institutional economies. Before I undertook my PhD, I believed that sociocultural matters – instiutionalised misogyny, sexual violence myths – would be the most formidable barriers to progress. This remains partially true, due to patriarchy's embedded nature and infusion with power. However, the Charter has to contend with issues of a philosophical and/or macro-scale that go to the heart of FE's and HE's structures – the Charter must be clear about its capabilities, remit, and sphere of influence, and linked to that, have clear, precise, and measurable goals. However, many of the challenges aforementioned relate to the existential processes of carving out of educational institutions as new, valid parts of a societal mosaic of tackling GBV. This emerging role is currently being born and crafted.

At the moments we have felt lost authoring the Charter, we circled back to Emily. When EmilyTest began delivering talks on the Charter in connection with Emily's story, we called them "From Tragedy to Change" – this arose naturally when we established the mission of "no student ending up in Emily's shoes", which is where our minimum standards agenda came in. We intend for the Charter to continue allowing Emily to recentre us in the evolutionary journey of education's special role, answering to the challenges. The role of FE and HE is still in evolution, and this may be its permanent state – the Charter is structured by questions, and the answers to questions are always subject to change. The Charter is in process, as is the carving out of education's role. When the Charter research branched out from its genesis of Emily's story, harmonising hundreds of voices across student victim-survivors and professionals, we observed that the will exists.

Summary of key points

- As detailed by Fiona Drouet MBE, the first half of this chapter focuses on the "tragedy" theme of the title.
- Fiona outlines the timeline of events leading up to and after the death of her daughter, Emily Drouet, in 2016, who took her own life after she was subjected to a campaign of gender-based violence (GBV) from a fellow university student.
- Fiona details a chronology of the abuse and violence Emily was subjected to.
- Fiona concludes the chapter with the story of the formation of the EmilyTest charity and the campaigning tasks and successes that have emerged, bridging to the "change" theme of the chapter.
- The second half narrows focus to the "change" theme.
- Poppy Gerrard-Abbott, PhD researcher on GBV in UK universities and co-author of the GBV Charter for universities and colleges, situates Emily's story in data.

- This broadens out to communicate the UK evidence that exists on GBV in Further Education (FE) and Higher Education (HE), making a case for a specialist focus on education.
- Poppy links the existing data to the novel findings of the 2020–2021 Charter research.
- EmilyTest's GBV Charter framework is introduced and explained.
- Poppy concludes with the various sector challenges that the Charter research identified, which provide barriers and questions for the field as a whole and concerning Charter implementation.

Further Reading

EmilyTest. (2021). *Gender-based violence (GBV) Charter research report*. http://emilytest.co.uk/

The principal researcher and policy manager for the Scottish gender-based violence (GBV) in education charity EmilyTest, Poppy Gerrard-Abbott, presents the findings from Scottish Government-funded national, digital, mixed methods research 2020–2021 during the COVID-19 pandemic with hundreds of further education (FE) and higher education (HE) student and graduate victims/survivors in Scotland and the UK. The peer-reviewed report explains the existing literature, the methods and methodology of the project, and the key findings, making a case for why researchers, campaigners and policy-makers need to have a specialist focus on GBV in the education context, and offering new knowledge on endemic GBV in universities and colleges, covering topics such as intersectional data, disparities between policy and professional practice, and the characteristic manifestations of GBV across the education spaces.

EmilyTest. (2021). *Gender-based violence charter (GBV) for universities and colleges*. http://emilytest.co.uk/

This peer-reviewed report, authored by the Scottish GBV in education charity EmilyTest, explains the timeline of creation for the world's first GBV Charter for further education (HE) and higher education (HE), an evidence-based, Scottish-Government funded project aiming to instil minimum standards and excellence in GBV prevention, intervention and support in universities and colleges. It communicates the data foundation, the co-created design process and the Charter framework itself.

Note

1 Black Asian and Minority Ethnic – a commonly used acronym in the UK Higher Education sector to refer to students and staff who belong to ethnic minorities and students and staff of colour. However, note this is a contentious and widely debated term.

References

Brook Charity. (2019). *Press release: Our new research on sexual harassment and violence at UK universities*. www.brook.org.uk/press-releases/sexual-violence-and-harassment-remains-rife-in-universities-according-to-ne

Brownmiller, S. (1975). Against our will: Men. *Women and Rape, 15*, 105.

Declaration, B. Platform for Action. (1995). United Nations.

EmilyTest. (2021a). *Gender-based violence (GBV) charter research report.* http://emilytest.co.uk/

EmilyTest. (2021b). *Gender-based violence (GBV) Charter for universities and colleges.* http://emilytest.co.uk/

Collins, P. H. (1990). Black feminist thought in the matrix of domination. *Black Feminist Thought: Knowledge, Consciousness, and the Politics of Empowerment, 138*(1990), 221–238.

Holmwood, J. (2014). From social rights to the market: Neoliberalism and the knowledge economy. *International Journal of Lifelong Education, 33*(1), 62–76.

Humphreys, C. J., & Towl, G. J. (2020). *Addressing student sexual violence in higher education: A good practice guide.* Emerald Group Publishing.

Lees, S. (1997). *Ruling passions. Sexual violence, reputation and the law.* Open University Press.

Lizzio-Wilson, M., Masser, B. M., Hornsey, M. J., & Iyer, A. (2020). You're making us all look bad: Sexism moderates women's experience of collective threat and intra-gender hostility toward traditional and non-traditional female subtypes. *Group Processes & Intergroup Relations.* doi:10.1177/1368430220913610.

Lorenz, K., Hayes, R., & Jacobsen, C. (2021). "Title IX isn't for you, it's for the university": Sexual violence survivors' experiences of institutional betrayal in Title IX investigations. *CrimRxiv.* https://doi.org/10.21428/cb6ab371.1959e20b

Lunt, I. (2008). Beyond tuition fees? The legacy of Blair's government to higher education. *Oxford Review of Education, 34*(6), 741–752.

Megoran, N., & Mason, O. (2020). *Second class academic citizens: The dehumanising effects of casualisation in higher education.* UCU.

Miller, R. (2020). *What works to prevent violence against women and girls: A summary of the evidence.* Social Research: The Scottish Government.

Murray, J. (2021, May 17). Universities are failing to tackle rape culture on campus, students say. *The Guardian.* www.theguardian.com/world/2021/may/16/universities-rape-culture-on-campus-students-protest

National Union of Students. (2010). *Hidden Marks: A study of women students' experiences of harassment, stalking, violence and sexual assault.* www.nusconnect.org

National Union of Students. (2017). *Introducing careers in students' unions.* www.nusconnect.org.uk/articles/introducing-careers-in-students-unions

National Union of Students & 1752 Group. (2018). *Power in the academy: Staff sexual misconduct in UK High education.* www.nusco'nnect.org.uk/resources/nus-staff-student-sexual-misconduct-report

National Union of Students Women's Campaign. (2019). *Sexual violence in further education.* www.nusconnect.org.uk/resources/sexual-violence-in-further-education-report

Office for National Statistics. (2017). *Sexual offences in England and Wales: Year ending March 2017.* www.ons.gov.uk/peoplepopulationandcommunity/crimeandjustice/articles/sexualoffencesinenglandandwales/yearendingmarch2017

Phipps, A. (2015). *Sexism and violence in the neoliberal university.* http://sro.sussex.ac.uk/id/eprint/60329/1/Phipps_Gold_keynote.pdf?msclkid=88e32264c0e511ec8ea25323d21781c5

Phipps, A. (2017). (Re) theorising laddish masculinities in higher education. *Gender and Education, 29*(7), 815–830.

Phipps, A. (2018). 'Lad culture' and sexual violence against students. In *The Routledge handbook of gender and violence* (pp. 171–182). Routledge.

Phipps, A. (2020a). Reckoning up: Sexual harassment and violence in the neoliberal university. *Gender and Education, 32*(2), 227–243.

Phipps, A. (2020b). *Me, not you: The trouble with mainstream feminism.* Manchester University Press.

Phipps, A., Ringrose, J., Renold, E., & Jackson, C. (2018). Rape culture, lad culture and everyday sexism: Researching, conceptualizing and politicizing new mediations of gender and sexual violence. *Journal of Gender Studies, 27*(1), 1–8.

Phipps, A., & Young, I. (2013). *That's what she said: Women students' experiences of "lad culture" in higher education.* National Union of Students.

Phipps, A., & Young, I. (2015). Neoliberalisation and 'lad cultures' in higher education. *Sociology, 49*(2), 305–322.

Public Health Scotland. (2021, January 1). *Gender based violence.* Health Topics – Public Health Scotland. www.healthscotland.scot/health-topics/gender-based-violence

Revolt Sexual Assault and the Student Room. (2018). *National consultation into the sexual assault and harassment experienced or witnessed by students and graduates from universities across the UK.* The Student Room & Revolt Sexual Assault.

Scottish Government. (2016). *Equally Safe: Scotland's strategy for preventing and eradicating violence against women and girls: Edinburgh, Scottish Government.* www.gov.scot/Resource/0045/00454152.pdf

Temkin, J. (2002). *Rape and the legal process.* Sweet and Maxwell.

Towl, G. J., & Humphreys, C.J. (2021). *How to do more than the bare minimum on sexual harassment and sexual misconduct.* https://wonkhe.com/blogs/how-to-do-more-than-the-bare-minimum-on-harassment-and-sexual-misconuct/

Turner, B. C., Tegel, B. S., Furness, B. H., Donnelly, B. L., Fisher, B. L., Hymas, B. C., & Donnelly, B. L. (2021, April 19). Universities could face fines if they fail to crack down on sexual harassment. *The Telegraph.* www.telegraph.co.uk/news/2021/04/19/universities-could-face-fines-fail-crack-sexual-harassment/

University and College Union (UCU). (2016). *Precarious work in higher education: A snapshot of insecure contracts and institutional attitudes.* UCU.

University and College Union (UCU). (2019). *Counting the costs of casualization in higher education.* UCU.

United Nations. (1993). *Declaration on the elimination of violence against women.* UN General Assembly.

Williams, J. E. (1984). Secondary victimization: Confronting public attitudes about rape. *Victimology, 9*(1), 66–68.

Williams, J. E., & Holmes, K. A. (1981). The second assault: Rape and public attitudes. In *Social Forces* (Vol. 61, Issue 3, March 1983, pp. 948–950). Greenwood Press.

10 Comprehensive institution-wide approach

What it means to be comprehensive

Clarissa J. Humphreys and Graham J. Towl

Comprehensive: including or dealing with all or nearly all elements or aspects of something.
— Oxford Dictionary of English

In previous work, we have presented a comprehensive institution-wide approach to address student sexual violence. We recommended the use of bespoke sexual violence policies and procedures, creating comprehensive institution-wide education through student and staff training, building partnerships with students and external organisations, breaking down barriers and responding appropriately to disclosures, conducting trauma-informed investigations, and tailoring the disciplinary process that was originally created for academic misconduct to more effectively address student sexual violence (see Humphreys & Towl, 2020). In this chapter, we expand the conversation we outlined in our practical guide to consider more fully what it means to be comprehensive. We begin by describing how the comprehensive institution-wide approach can be used to address gender-based violence (GBV). Then, we present examples of potential gaps or blind spots that Higher Education Institutions (HEIs) may have not yet included in prevention and response initiatives, including specific types of GBV, groups of individuals who may benefit from tailored initiatives, and off-site situations where prevention and response initiatives are needed. We also consider what comprehensive means in relation to consistency and fair practice and consider gaps where prevention and response initiatives may be approached in very different ways depending on who is involved. The aim of this chapter is to demonstrate HEIs can progress beyond saying that they address GBV, for example, when only having a policy or training in place, but to really embed the approach into all or nearly all aspects of the institution. We hope this will help HEIs identify gaps in their prevention and response initiatives and better apply a comprehensive approach to the full institution to ensure safety for all.

What is a comprehensive institution-wide approach?

A comprehensive institution-wide approach, defined as "as an ethical approach that is trauma-informed, survivor-centred, human rights-based and social

DOI: 10.4324/9781003252474-12

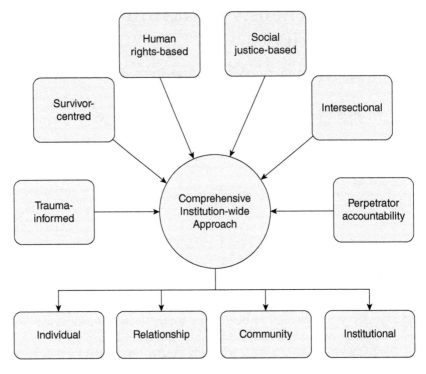

Figure 10.1 Model of the comprehensive institution-wide approach (Humphreys & Towl, 2020, p. 43).

justice-based whilst being intersectional and requiring perpetrator account-ability" (Humphreys & Towl, 2020, p. 43), is used to create a foundation to sustain prevention and response initiatives to address GBV applied at the individual, relationship, community, and institutional levels of a HEI, as shown in Figure 10.1.

These six key elements are purposely included to ensure ethical and safe practices to prevent and respond to GBV. Being trauma-informed in short means, the HEI's GBV prevention and response initiatives will (1) recognise trauma and the impact of trauma on victim-survivors, (2) promote safety, (3) endeavour not to re-traumatise victim-survivors through appropriate internal investigation and disciplinary procedures, and (4) respect victim-survivors' autonomy. By being survivor-centred, the HEI will empower victim-survivors to choose how to take forward a disclosure, for example, choosing to make a formal report or seek support only. The HEI will treat victim-survivors with dignity and respect and challenge victim-blaming attitudes. The HEI will recognise that GBV is a human rights violation and endeavour to prioritise protecting the human rights of all students and employees through a human rights-based approach. Embedding the element of social justice into the approach means the HEI will commit to naming and dismantling the systems which support perpetrators and their misconduct and have institutional ownership of this work rather than allowing the work to be shouldered by one or two individuals. Recognising that we all have different parts of our identity that shape our experiences of privilege or oppression, the HEI that applies an intersectional approach will also identify that victim-survivors may be targeted due to different elements of their identities. Therefore, their prevention and response approach will be tailored to effectively support diverse student and staff populations and identify the different forms of discrimination that intersect and perpetuate GBV. Embedding perpetrator accountability means the HEI will hold perpetrators of GBV accountable for their behaviour and communicate how they do this to those who were harmed and the wider university community.

Underpinning this approach is a commitment in Higher Education (HE) to addressing GBV in an all-inclusive way; no department, individual, or process is left out. Standards for conduct and responses to misconduct are applied consistently to students and staff, contractors, and, where feasible, visitors too. The aim is to promote physical and emotional safety for students and staff to engage in learning and work without being subjected to any form of GBV. Such an approach, we argue, needs to be embedded within the strategic plans of institutions and embodied by staff throughout the university community from leaders, managers, and employees across academic, operational, and professional staff groups. To do this requires appropriate resourcing, training for students and staff, and for most universities, a commitment to challenging and changing the institution's culture that has tolerated, and for all intents and purposes, been protective of perpetrators of GBV within institutions historically.

Finding gaps

Along with resourcing this work and getting engagement from staff at all levels to recognise and begin to engage with culture change, it is also important to consider what it means to be comprehensive. Are all departments engaged? Is the scope of the policy appropriate? Are there any groups being left out? In this section, we present some areas that may be overlooked or placed in the "too hard" box and ignored. This is by no means an exhaustive list. So, as a brief disclaimer, this section is meant as a prompt to help practitioners and university leaders think more thoughtfully about what it means to be comprehensive and to look for gaps within their own institution's GBV prevention and response initiatives.

Types of GBV

Firstly, there is a mixed approach across the UK to addressing GBV. Some HEIs are focused on sexual violence, sexual harassment, and other forms of sexual misconduct. Whilst others have a broader definition to encompass all forms of GBV more fully, for example, domestic abuse/intimate partner violence, rape, sexual assault, sexual harassment, indecent exposure, voyeurism, "upskirting", stalking, cyberstalking, technology-facilitated/online abuse, image-based sexual abuse, or so-called "revenge porn", "honour-based" abuse, "grooming" and exploitation, to name but a few. These forms of gender-based violence *are* impacting university communities, so a starting place to apply a comprehensive institution-wide approach would be to ensure policy definitions of GBV are inclusive of the behaviours happening in the community and explicitly name them.

There are three examples of GBV we would like to specifically highlight as in the past few years disclosures and reports of these appear to have increased. This may be an indicator of an increase in prevalence rates of these kinds of GBV or a sign that some barriers to reporting are successfully being removed. Alternatively, it could be a combination of the two. The three examples which we will address sequentially are non-fatal strangulation, technology-facilitated gender-based violence, and "spiking".

Non-fatal strangulation (NFS)

In our view, this may be one of the most dangerous individual acts of gender-based violence occurring in university communities due to the perilous line between non-fatal and fatal outcomes. Strangulation is the obstruction of blood vessels and/or airway by external pressure to the neck causing decreased oxygen supply to the brain and when this does not cause death, it is referred to as non-fatal (White et al., 2020). Strangulation can result in severe injury or even death as the victim can lose consciousness within 10 seconds and death can occur within 1–3 minutes (Carter et al., 2017). NFS can result in physical injuries, psychological impacts, and neurological and cognitive impairments. The victim-survivor may, for example, experience amnesia, suffer potential long-term damage to the anatomical structures within the neck, and have significant mental health consequences, including post-traumatic stress disorder (White et al., 2020). Examples of non-visible injuries which may occur include difficulty focusing, difficulty breathing or swallowing, confusion, headaches, dizziness, memory loss, vomiting, ear pain, and restlessness; whereas visible injuries may include, for example, bruising on the neck or chest, red marks, scratches, and neck or face swelling (NYC Mayor's Office, 2020). However, unlike other forms of physical assault, NFS does not always leave observable injury. Because of this, NFS risks being minimised by responders when they cannot see physical injuries (Glass et al., 2008).

Victim-survivors may refer to strangulation as "choking". Formally, choking refers to the mechanical obstruction of the trachea, but colloquially it is often used to refer to strangulation. However, choking can also be used in sexual violence too. Victim-survivors may also refer to NFS by describing the action but not naming or labelling it, for example, a victim-survivor may say, "he held me by my throat", "he started to squeeze my throat", "he put his arm across my neck and held me down", or "he put me in a headlock." Strangulation is a gendered act, almost always perpetrated by men against women (Bichard et al.,

2021; White et al., 2021). On domestic abuse risk assessments, strangulation is a lethality marker, meaning it indicates there is a risk of homicide because if a perpetrator applies strangulation to a woman, her risk of being killed increases by a factor of 8 (Glass et al., 2008). Between 2009 and 2018 in the UK, men killed 299 women through strangulation, making it the second most frequent method used for femicide (Long et al., 2020).

In a recent study that considered sexual violence cases at one Sexual Assault Referral Centre (SARC) in the UK over a three-year period, 1 in 11 attendees reported NFS and this increased to 1 in 5 when the perpetrator was a current or ex-partner and 98% of the perpetrators of NFS were men ($n = 2196$; White et al., 2021). In the same study, 11.8% of those who listed their employment status as "in education", that is, student ($n = 208$), reported NFS. Some research indicates that the use of strangulation during sexual acts is becoming normalised for young people as it is portrayed or referenced in various forms of media, including pornography, magazines, mainstream television and movies, social media, and popular erotica (Herbenick et al., 2021; Moore & Khan, 2019).

Perpetrators can use strangulation and the threat of strangulation during sexual violence, physical acts of domestic abuse, and intimidation tactics as a form of coercion and control. Perpetrators often defend their use of strangulation by saying it was consensual, for example, it was "erotic asphyxiation" or "rough sex". In the last few years, activists, survivors, victims' families, and organisations like *We Can't Consent to This* have campaigned against the "rough sex defence" calling on the government to highlight in law that one cannot consent to being strangled (see wecantconsenttothis.uk). In England and Wales, the law was changed through the Domestic Abuse Act 2021, which now confirms non-fatal strangulation is a criminal offence and an individual cannot consent to the infliction of a serious level of harm for sexual gratification (Domestic Abuse Act 2021, s. 70–71).

NFS is illustrative of one reason why universities need to invest in specialist GBV case managers, specialist support and build sustainable partnerships with external organisations. This is a very specialist area benefitting from a particular set of expertise. And this is expertise that we could not reasonably assume that a Head of Department, student services, or Human Resources (HR) would have. Specialist case managers or supporters can respond appropriately to disclosures, conduct risk assessments, and ensure appropriate precautionary measures are used (see Chapter 12). It is not recommended that a non-specialist deals with disclosures of NFS. The specialist would signpost to the SARC for healthcare attention, help the victim-survivor risk assess their own safety, and engage in safety planning whilst providing them with information on their reporting options, including support options for specialist services. In the same way, other behaviours that constitute criminal offences can be framed in policy as a form of misconduct, strangulation, or any other form of physical assault, can be included as a category which constitutes a breach of policy within the HEI's bespoke GBV policy. Consent education programmes for students can address the law, including what individuals can and cannot consent to considering the increase place with organisations such as SARCs, Rape Crisis, Women's Aid, and Police would support multi-agency working which may be required to appropriately assess risk and address this type of GBV.

Technology-facilitated gender-based violence (TFGBV)

It is not surprising to recognise that much abuse happens online (see Chapter 20). GBV, likewise, does not just happen in-person. TFGBV is an umbrella term representing a range of different forms of GBV, including, but not limited to, online sexual harassment, cyberbullying, image-based sexual abuse, so-called 'revenge porn', 'upskirting', 'fakeporn', voyeurism, cyberflashing, cyberstalking, and monitoring, to name but a few (Dunn, 2020).

TFGBV is not new. However, in the move to communicate remotely through technology due to precautions taken during the COVID-19 pandemic, there appears to have been a notable increase in the rates of TFGBV in society and within university communities (UN Women, 2020a; Humphreys, 2021; Universities UK, 2020). For example, during 2020, after the first lockdown in the UK, reports to the Revenge Porn Helpline doubled and cases of sextortion tripled (Ward, n.d.). Zoombombing, or posting pornographic or offensive content during lectures, was reported at multiple universities and at academic conferences during lockdown (Batty, 2020).

In the past, TFGBV may not have been addressed by HEIs because it was overlooked or possibly seen as not part of the HEI's remit. The scope of some HEIs' policies may not include online or technology-facilitated harassment or GBV, especially if this does not occur within a university's virtual learning environment (VLE), as it is seen as not occurring "on" campus. In addition, TFGBV can often be minimised by responders or university officials who deem it as less serious or harmful because it does not occur in person. However, Universities UK produced sector guidance on tackling online harassment noting that the consequences of this behaviour can result in "severe and long-term repercussions for physical, emotional and mental wellbeing and affect academic achievement and future career prospects" (2019, p. 6).

HEIs must continue to adapt and respond to the different ways perpetrators use GBV in order to create learning and work environments safe for students and staff (Humphreys, 2021). In the same way that HEIs are expected to address GBV that may happen off-site outside of university business involving students and/or staff (Office for Student, 2021; CIPD, 2020), HEIs can also address abuse which occurs through technology. It is important that the scope of the policies do not limit online behaviour to university-business only, that is, within online lectures or VLEs, but to cover interactions between members of the university community regardless of location, in-person, or through technology. Bystander intervention courses can address TFGBV too by helping students identify TFGBV, recognise it as a problem through understanding the harms it causes, helping students build empathy and feel responsibility for taking action, and developing skills to intervene safely.

Along with responding to TFGBV, universities can use technology to facilitate support for victim-survivors. Prevention campaigns can be run using technology to raise awareness, communicate reporting and support options, debunk myths, and promote active bystander behaviours (Humphreys, 2021). Online reporting tools, for example, Culture Shift's Report + Support, can reduce barriers to disclosures by providing access to clear reporting options, including anonymous reporting, and support information. Internal university trauma-informed investigations can even be run remotely through virtual meeting rooms. Technology itself can be used as part of a response to address TFGBV.

Spiking

We have included this last example as there appears to be some disconnect in the sector of understanding the connection between spiking and sexual violence. It is a sexual offence to intentionally administer a substance to, or cause a substance to be taken by, another person with the intention of stupefying or overpowering them to enable any person to subject the victim to a sexual act whether the sexual act occurs (Sexual Offences Act 2003, s. 61; Sexual Offences (Northern Ireland) Order 2008, s. 65; Sexual Offences (Scotland) Act 2009, s. 9). Putting aside alcohol (the number one "date rape" drug in HE), the next most common "date-rape" drugs are Rohypnol and Gamma Hydroxybutyrate (GHB) (Humphreys & Towl, 2020). These drugs are odourless, tasteless, can cause retrograde amnesia, and they metabolise rapidly making detection difficult (Colyer & Weiss, 2018; Drink Aware, n.d.). However, these are not the only substances used. Additional alcohol can be added to a person's drink without the victim-survivor's knowledge. Ketamine, Ecstasy, and Lysergic Acid Diethylamide (LSD) may also be used (Drink Aware, n.d.).

In 2021, there was a reported rise of drink spiking impacting university students and communities outside of Higher Education and a new concern of spiking by injection was reported across the UK (UK Parliament, 2021). The Home Affairs Committee launched an inquiry into spiking following a poll by YouGov that found 1 in 9 women and 1 in 17 men in the UK reported they were subjected to drink spiking in 2021 (UK Parliament, 2021).

Drink spiking is often used to perpetrate sexual violence. There can be other motivations for spiking, for example, theft or some form of humiliation. Spiking does not always result in sexual assault, if, for example, the intended target has a group of friends who recognise the signs of spiking and then get that person to safety (home/hospital as appropriate). However, because a sexual assault did not occur does not mean that the motivation was not there. Even if spiking does not result in sexual violence, it is still traumatic resulting in physical and mental health consequences. Those who are subjected to spiking may not know if a sexual assault occurred due to having been drugged.

HEIs can provide information to students to raise awareness of spiking and provide prevention messages. These messages are framed to highlight that only the perpetrator is responsible or to blame for spiking, that is, messages are not victim-blaming. These communications can include messages targeted at would be perpetrators, information for active bystanders (e.g., what signs to look out for, how to get someone to safety, how to intervene if they suspect someone plans to spike someone), information on where to get support and how to make a report, and as appropriate safety messages to mitigate risk. The last type of communication is the one that may be most difficult to present in a way that is not victim-blaming, as many safety messages fail to represent the issues appropriately, placing all the burden on (often) women to protect themselves. From experience working directly with students in training environments and in responding to disclosures, we have had many students say statements like, "I wish I had known not to leave my drink at the table while I went out to smoke", or "I didn't even think about being worried when a guy I had just met gave me a drink". Some students, particularly international students, have asked directly for information on what they can do to mitigate their risk recognising that it is not their fault if they are spiked, but wanting more knowledge on things they can do to make it harder for a perpetrator to target them.

Spiking is another good example for the need for partnership working. HEIs can partner with their local police forces, local councils, public health, and representatives from the nighttime economy to run targeted campaigns for the community and training for staff in bars, pubs, and clubs. Nightclubs have the opportunity to reduce their maximum numbers of customers at any one time to aid surveillance, detection, and as a deterrent (due to the great chance of getting caught) (Hill & Towl, 2021). Partnership working may also help provide testing strips for individuals to test their drinks, or for post-incident urine tests for individuals to confirm if they have been spiked. Training for staff responding to disclosures can include information on signposting to support following a spiking incident.

Specific groups

The aim of embedding a comprehensive institution-wide approach is to ensure that all six elements are embodied in all prevention and response initiatives, but this does not mean it is a one-size-fits-all approach. Training, campaigns, and procedures may need to be tailored to their target audience. We recommend auditing each department and assessing whether all students and employees are protected in all aspects of how they engage with the institution. Consider key groups and what groups may need targeted training or additional support. Are there groups that are more likely to be targeted than others and what is being done to mitigate for that additional risk? Part of a comprehensive institution-wide approach includes being survivor-centred. This means speaking to survivors and representatives of different groups in the HEI to get their input in policy development, training, prevention, and response initiatives. Here we will look at three different groups of individuals. Again, this is only an example of how to sharpen the focus of a comprehensive institution-wide approach, rather than offering an exhaustive list. We consider individuals with disabilities and international students. (See also Chapter 5 focused on the LGBTQ+ community.)

Individuals with disabilities

We start with this group, because it captures a growing, and substantial, minority of students and staff and provides a very good example of why a one-size-fits-all approach does not work. Individuals with disabilities are not all the same. This broad category or label represents individuals with a wide variety of physical or mental impairments that have a substantial and long-term negative effect on the individual's ability to do normal daily activities (Equality Act, 2010). This, of course, intersects with genders, races, ethnicities, sexual orientations, ages, beliefs, cultures, and more. As of 2018, more than one in eight students in England declared at least one disability (OfS, 2020). According to the Office for Students (2020), in 2018, 5% of students studying in England declared a cognitive or learning difficulty, 3.9% of students declared a mental health condition, 2.6% declared multiple impairments, 2.2% declared a sensory, medical, or physical impairment, and 0.6% of student declared a social or communication impairment. It is important to consider the shift towards mental health conditions being reported as the second most frequent reported disabilities. We note, also, these numbers do not include disabled students who have chosen not to declare a disability to their HEI.

We know that women with disabilities are disproportionately subjected to GBV; we see this specifically in HE too (UN Women, 2020b) and reflected in studies of hate crimes and incidents at universities (see, for example, Siddiqui et al., 2019). And this data is against a backdrop of a reticence about reporting GBV (Ghani & Towl, 2017). In England and Wales, women with disabilities are more than twice as likely to be subjected to domestic abuse than women without disabilities and almost twice as likely than disabled men (ONS, 2019). This same study found disabled women were almost twice as likely to be subjected to sexual assault than women without disabilities. One survey with 4,491 respondents across 153 UK universities found 73% of students and recent graduates who had a disability were subjected to sexual violence at university (Revolt Sexual Assault and The Student Room, 2018).

HEIs will already have processes in place to ensure reasonable adjustments or accommodations are available for individuals with disabilities in relation to their studies. These need to be considered for students engaging in internal investigation processes as additional or different accommodations may be needed. HEIs should include information relevant to individuals with disabilities in campaigning and prevention materials. HEIs can consider whether the GBV prevention and response initiatives within the institution are fully accessible for students and staff with disabilities. Are captions and alternative text used for videos and images in online trainings and campaigns? Is information on report and support options within the HEI presented in fully accessible ways? Are spaces physically accessible? Hopefully yes, but in some older institutions, this may be an issue. Are staff who develop training trained in disability accommodation or do they have access to a consultant within or external to the university that can check that training, campaigns, and communications are accessible? In training for responding to disclosures, is information on supporting individuals with disabilities included? Most importantly, we recommend that HEIs work with individuals with disabilities to better understand what is needed, where there are gaps, and what would be helpful.

International students

This is another example of a large and diverse group of students who would greatly benefit from tailored programmes. According to UNESCO Institute for Statistics (2019), approximately 489,000 international students are hosted in the UK in Higher Education annually. Around 122,140 are students from China; 27,300 are from India; 19,418 are from the United States; 19,278 are from Hong Kong; 14,412 are from Italy; 14,094 are from Malaysia, followed by France, Germany, Nigeria, Spain, Greece, and so on.

International students may be targeted due to the vulnerabilities they present in being physically separated from their support network, in a country with a different culture to their own, and language barriers either because English is their second (or third/fourth) language or because the English they speak differs culturally from British English in meaning. International students may also be targeted due to their nationality, race, ethnicity, and other aspects of their identity, for example, sexual orientation, gender, or beliefs. International students may not be aware of the laws within the UK related to GBV. Based on their home country's criminal justice system, they may face additional barriers to reporting. For example, in practice, we have seen international students from Central and South American countries worry they needed to pay for a lawyer before making a report to the police. Others have not wanted to report to the police for distrust in law enforcement that stemmed from their experience or knowledge of police in their home country.

Communication with international students can occur during recruitment and before they arrive to the university. Information on the university's policy and support options may be more accessible if offered in multiple languages. Students may be fluent in English to meet the standards of studying their discipline but may not have the language skills to discuss gender-based violence, and/or in times of crisis may be better able to communicate in their first language. Access to interpreters is crucial. HEIs may wish to modify prevention and response initiatives for different groups of international students.

Recognition for differences in culture may impact how to deliver a course, for example, offering gender-specific rather than mixed sessions. This is another example where partnership working is key. HEIs may already have partnerships to support international studies or may be involved in networks to share good practice globally, so they do not need to spend resource developing new networks. They can utilise existing networks to consider best practice and cultural competence. They can also work with international students through, for example, focus groups to better understand what is needed, where there are gaps, and what would be helpful.

Off-site university business

When we think about university life, we usually focus on life on campus. However, many university-related activities happen off-site, for example, conferences, sporting events, performances, field trips, internships, or work placements, and international study placements at partner universities. In this section, we highlight two examples of university business that happen off-site but that are noted to be high-risk for GBV: study abroad and fieldwork.

Study abroad

This is an example of a possibly overlooked group of students. According to UNESCO Institute for Statistics (2019), approximately 39,500 students go on study abroad from the UK annually. There are a great deal of commonalities across the international student community in terms of the challenges of having a placement or simply being an international student in a country different to one's own (Towl & Walker, 2019). In the same way that international students hosted at UK universities may present with particular vulnerabilities that perpetrators will target, students who go on study abroad from UK HEIs will have similar vulnerabilities in their host country.

There is limited data on GBV and students on study abroad from the UK. However, it may be reasonable to look to studies from the United States where risk of sexual violence, specifically, on study abroad has been documented. In one study of American students on study abroad during a two- to five-month period ($n = 2,630$), 21% of students were subjected to sexual assault (418 women and 61 men), 1.2% were subjected to sexual coercion, 0.8% were subjected to rape, 1.2% were subjected to alcohol or drug-facilitated rape, and 2.4% were subjected to attempted rape (Pedersen et al., 2020). Kimble et al. (2013) found that women students' risk of sexual violence was three to five times higher whilst on study abroad than when they were on campus at their home institution.

Sometimes it is not clear what the shared expectations are about student safety when students are on study abroad. Where HEIs have partnerships supporting study abroad activities, they can help address the safety of students by explicitly capturing safety concerns regarding GBV within the ambit of any such international agreements.

HEIs can equip staff who are responsible for supporting students on study abroad (at the home institution) to be able to respond to disclosures of GBV appropriately, which may include signposting to a specialist GBV case manager or other relevant specialist support available. Specialist GBV case managers can navigate report and support options for victim-survivors with support of the relevant embassy or consulate, including pushing for legal support and interpreters as needed. In addition, case managers can help support victim-survivors in accessing support through the HEI's travel insurance which may offer some additional support for those subjected to crime (e.g., medical or emergency travel coverage and access to counselling). A student subjected to GBV on study abroad may want to return home, but this is not necessarily the case. The victim-survivor may want to continue their studies abroad and access support to do so. And if a police investigation is ongoing, remaining in the country is often paramount to any prospect of a successful conviction as many countries will close an investigation if the injured party leaves the country.

HEIs can provide students who plan to go on study abroad with training to prepare them to recognise the risks and how to access support and reporting options if they are subjected to a crime. This type of training is sometimes met with resistance by staff who worry this could "scare" students into not wanting to go on study abroad. The alternative – not to alert them to such potential dangers – seems to us to be a far worse option. Students need to be able to weigh up the pros and cons of any such placements and personal safety and well-being seem to us to be uncontroversial, important considerations.

We argue this can be done safely to equip students with information to better prepare for their time abroad, for example, on where they can get help in an emergency that hopefully they will not have to use. Students should know how to contact the relevant embassy or consulate as these have local contacts for supporting them if subjected to sexual violence. Students may be required to conduct a risk assessment before leaving and this can be added to the risk assessment, so that they can demonstrate they know what to do if this were to happen. Beyond making sure students know what their support and reporting options are before they leave, the use of training and including this on a risk assessment helps raise awareness for students. It can also help them feel more supported to know their department has supported them to begin their study abroad with support in place with information and knowing the staff supporting them in their home country are trained to provide information to them too.

Fieldwork

Sexual harassment and violence, specifically, have been identified as issues on fieldwork across disciplines, such as Anthropology (Schneider, 2020),

Archaeology (Voss, 2021a, 2021b), and Geography (Ross, 2015), to name but a few. It must be noted that these issues do not occur only in fieldwork and these three disciplines, like the rest of academia, have issues on campus, at conferences, and other related areas of work too (Cardwell & Hitchen, 2022; Voss, 2021a; Schneider, 2020). These issues span across these fields in HE and in professional settings. For the purposes of our sharpening of the lens though, we will focus on fieldwork here as an often "overlooked" area for prevention and response initiatives.

Many staff and students go on fieldwork within the UK and abroad. Off-site activities, like fieldwork, are very different environments and culture from everyday life on campus. On fieldwork in archaeology, for example, participants and staff may live in close quarters, work long hours away from home, and the use of alcohol is often permitted in downtime in the evenings or on days off. Fraternisation is often common and there can be a blurring of boundaries between staff and students' positions. Abuse of power on archaeology digs is well-documented (Voss, 2021a). Individuals are often isolated from their support networks, by physical location and sometimes by communication too if the area is too remote to be able to contact individuals back home. Fieldwork which occurs in another country adds a complication where individuals may not know their options for accessing support and/or reporting or seeking healthcare help. Fieldwork is often a necessary part of training in these disciplines and victim-survivors may feel they have to endure adverse conditions rather than make a report and risk retaliation or loss of access to training (Voss, 2021b). It can be a balance of choosing between collecting data or personal safety (Ross, 2015). Perpetrators can include colleagues, students, or staff on a project from the same or different HEI, research subjects, key informants for the local community, partners on the project, volunteers who support the work, and locals from the community.

There are many similarities between the risk, challenges, and potential responses highlighted in the study abroad section for staff and students on fieldwork. Victim-survivors subjected to GBV on fieldwork may not wish to leave the project and this should not be the HEI's automatic response. If the perpetrator is on the project, HEIs that are responsible for the fieldwork need to be prepared to address GBV on the project with appropriate precautionary measures, including, when necessary, removing the Responding Party from the fieldwork to conduct an investigation. Some funding bodies such as the Wellcome Trust (n.d.) require all involved in activities they fund to "be able to work in an environment where everyone is treated, and treats others, fairly and with respect" (para 1) and require the organisation that is responsible for the funded project to have a bullying and harassment policy in place and to investigate any allegations in a fair and timely manner (among other requirements).

Voss (2021b) presents recommendations for disrupting cultures of harassment in archaeology that are trauma-informed and are applied at the socioenvironmental levels of the discipline which may be helpful in similar disciplines.

Procedures, risk assessments, and contracts for fieldwork should protect staff and students, not just the HEI as some have experienced (see Schneider, 2020). Fieldwork needs to be investigated as an arena that has high potential for GBV and cannot be overlooked when applying a compressive institution-wide approach.

Need for consistent and fair practice

As we can see, there are quite a few targeted areas we may want to consider within our comprehensive institution-wide approach. Beyond these potential gaps, we want to also consider consistency and fair practice. If we were to audit our work thoroughly, we would likely find many gaps in our provision which is expected at this point given the limit in guidance available to universities, lack of regulation, and variable and often inadequate level of resource currently allocated to this work. However, when we have gaps, this means that there will be varied experiences for students and staff in the training they receive, response they receive if disclosing or reporting GBV, and possibly the knowledge they have about what is available within the university. For example, if one department prepares their students to go on study abroad by providing them with training about GBV, conducts risk assessments that include consideration of GBV, and trains their staff on how to respond to disclosures made from students whilst they are studying abroad and we compare that to the department next door that does none of those things for their students preparing for study abroad, then these groups of students received a very different level of input. So, although we have said that we don't subscribe to a one-size-fits-all approach, we do need a basic level of service that all students and staff receive in this challenging area. In this section, we will highlight the importance of consistent and fair practice by considering how staff and students are treated very differently when it comes to responding to GBV in many universities to highlight that comprehensive also speaks to consistency in quality.

Comparing responses to staff and student GBV

To date in the UK, the majority focus from organisations that develop sector guidance (e.g., Universities UK, Office for Students) has been on addressing sexual misconduct and GBV perpetrated by students against fellow students. And this most probably accounts for the overwhelming majority of cases of sexual violence within the university community. There has, however, been a large gap in addressing GBV perpetrated by employees of HEIs. There has been some acknowledgement of staff misconduct to students from these organisations, but this has been limited. Other organisations such as ACAS,[1] CIPD,[2] and EHRC[3] that sit outside of the HE sector have produced guidance on dealing with GBV involving employees, that is, staff-to-staff (ACAS, 2021; CIPD and EHRC, 2020). No sector-leading bodies or UK university leaders appear to have fully addressed staff-to-student or staff-to-staff GBV in HE.

The 1752 Group, a research, consultancy, and campaign organisation, has led the conversation on, and much of the research into, staff sexual misconduct towards students. They have worked in partnership with the National Union of Students to raise awareness of the prevalence of staff sexual misconduct in UK HE. And this has built upon previous research (e.g., Carter & Jeffs, 1995) on what used to be called simply "sexual exploitation" in HE. The 1752 Group have analysed the lack of policies and procedures in place to deal with staff sexual misconduct (Bull & Rye, 2018) and in partnership with the law firm McAllister Olivarius have published sector guidance from their findings (The 1752 Group and McAllister Olivarius, 2020).

Given the dearth of detailed guidance from the relevant sector bodies such as UUK, we have a challenge in HEIs to look at our policies and procedures related to staff and student GBV and consider whether the approaches are consistent. Does a student Reporting Party receive a better, worse, or same service from the university if they are assaulted by a member of staff or fellow student? We view this as very much a rhetorical question, the level of service for staff victim-survivors seems to us to be typically worse than for students, and it needs fixing. Does a Reporting Party have more, less, or the same precautionary measures used to keep them safe during an investigation if the Responding Party is a student or an employee? Does this change if the Reporting Party is a student or an employee? In other words, is the quality of approaches and standards applied consistent and are safety measures used appropriately? We think most probably not, but readers can come to your own conclusions.

To help assess this, we have produced a Standards Check in Table 10.1. This is a template that can be amended to include additional questions. The purpose of the standards check is to see if there are any gaps, inconsistencies, or even forms of unfair or unlawful discrimination embedded in internal processes. If we compare staff-to-staff and student-to-student procedures, there will likely be some appropriately different procedures because employment law covers staff and students are covered by consumer law, broadly speaking. However, the Public Sector Equality Duty of the Equality Act 2010 and the Human Rights Act 1998 apply to both (EVAW, 2015). We would expect that staff and students would be held to the same standard of conduct within the organisation, or arguably that, if anything, staff should surely be held to a higher standard than students given their positions of power and the fact that they represent their employer. We argue that there should not be major differences in the approaches used with students and staff as all six elements of the comprehensive institution-wide approach should be embedded in staff and student procedures and this will lend itself to delivering the same protections and fair practice regardless of staff or student status of either party.

Using the Standards Check shown in Table 10.1, we offer some suggestions on the standards we would hope to see after embedding a comprehensive

Table 10.1 Standards check

Questions to help assess consistent standards for the university community in a comprehensive institution-wide response to gender-based violence	Staff Responding Party★ v. Staff Reporting Party	Staff Responding Party v. Student Reporting Party	Student Responding Party v. Staff Reporting Party	Student Responding Party v. Student Reporting Party
1. Is there a specific policy to address GBV?				
2. Does the Reporting Party have access to specialist support for GBV within the institution?				
3. Who is the case manager?				
4. What training or expertise is required of the case manager? Note any specific requirements related to GBV				
5. What specific precautionary measures can be used to mitigate risk whilst an investigation is conducted?				
6. Who investigates the formal report of GBV?				
7. What training or expertise is required of the investigator(s)? Note any specific requirements related to GBV				
8. What rights does the Reporting Party have within the process from investigation to final discipline outcome?				
9. What rights does the Responding Party have within the process from investigation to final discipline outcome?				
10. What training is required of staff involved in a discipline hearing? Note specific requirements related to GBV				
11. Does the Reporting Party receive the outcome of the investigation?				
12. Does the Reporting Party receive the outcome of the discipline process, including information on sanctions imposed if applicable?				
13. On average how long does the investigation and disciple process take?				

Questions to help assess consistent standards for the university community in a comprehensive institution-wide response to gender-based violence	Staff Responding Party* v. Staff Reporting Party	Staff Responding Party v. Student Reporting Party	Student Responding Party v. Staff Reporting Party	Student Responding Party v. Student Reporting Party
14. Is data recorded on disclosures and formal reports of GBV for trend monitoring purposes?				
15. Does training for students and staff address staff and student perpetration of all forms of GBV in Higher Education?				

*Responding Party refers to the person accused of perpetrating GBV.

Reporting Party refers to the person who reported they were subjected to GBV.

institution-wide approach. Unless noted otherwise, the answers apply to all four categories shown in the table.

1 Is there a specific policy to address GBV?
   Yes, there is a specific policy which addresses all four of these types of perpetration of GBV.

2 Does the Reporting Party have access to specialist support for GBV within the institution?
   Yes, students and employees who disclose they have been subjected to any form of GBV can access specialist support for GBV within the institution.

3 Who is the case manager?
   For cases involving Responding Parties who are staff, a specialist GBV case manager based in HR manages the case. For cases involving Responding Parties who are students, a specialist GBV case manager based in student services manages the case. When cases involve both students and staff, the case manager leading the case liaises with the specialist case manager in the opposite department, for example, HR liaises with student services and vice versa.

4 What training or expertise is required of the case manager? Note any specific requirements related to GBV.
   The GBV case manager is trained or has expertise in understanding gender-based violence, risk management of GBV, and working knowledge of the HEI's policies and procedures related to GBV.

5 What specific precautionary measures can be used to mitigate risk whilst an investigation is conducted?
   In cases involving Responding Parties who are staff, non-judgemental precautionary measures which may be used include, for example, no contact arrangements, change in duties, temporary bans from certain locations on campus, and/or suspension with pay.[4] In cases involving Responding Parties who are students, non-judgemental precautionary

measures which may be used included, for example, no contact arrangements, temporary bans from certain locations on campus, and/or a partial or full suspension. Normally precautionary measures are applied to the Responding Party only with the exception of the no contact arrangement that can also be applied to the Reporting Party.

6   Who investigates the formal report of GBV?
Trauma-informed GBV specialist investigators investigate formal reports made to the university. This may be internal or external investigators.

7   What training or expertise is required of the investigator(s)? Note any specific requirements related to GBV.
The investigators are trained or have expertise to conduct investigations to a civil standard using trauma-informed investigation techniques, have an understanding of GBV and a working knowledge of the HEI's policies and procedures related to GBV.

8   What rights does the Reporting Party have within the process from investigation to final discipline outcome?
The Reporting Party can view and respond to any relevant information submitted as evidence by any party, including the Responding Party and witnesses, can identify witnesses, and can be accompanied to all meetings throughout the process. The Reporting Party is kept updated on the progress of the investigation and is informed of the outcome of the investigation process, discipline process, and any sanctions imposed. The Reporting Party can request a review of the investigation if grounds for review are met.

9   What rights does the Responding Party have within the process from investigation to final discipline outcome?
The Responding Party can view and respond to any relevant information submitted as evidence by any party including the Reporting Party and witnesses, can identify witnesses, and can be accompanied to all meetings throughout the process. The Responding Party is kept updated on the progress of the investigation and is informed of the outcome of the investigation process, discipline process, and any sanctions imposed. The Responding Party can request a review of the investigation or appeal the sanctions if grounds for review/appeal are met.

10   What training is required of staff involved in a discipline hearing? Note specific requirements related to GBV.
Members of the discipline panel will be trained in trauma-informed adjudication and sanctioning training specific to gender-based violence and the relevant policy and procedure being followed, if it differs between staff and student misconduct.

11   Does the Reporting Party receive the outcome of the investigation?
Yes, the Reporting Party receives the outcome of the investigation regardless of the status of the Responding Party or Reporting Party.

12   Does the Reporting Party receive the outcome of the discipline process, including information on sanctions imposed if applicable?
Yes, the Reporting Party receives the outcome of the discipline process, including being informed of sanctions imposed, regardless of the status of the Responding Party or Reporting Party.

13 On average how long does the investigation and disciple process take?
    The investigation and discipline process take no more than 90 days, unless there are reasonable explanations for delays, for example, exceptional circumstance like illness. Any delays are communicated to both parties.

14 Is data recorded on disclosures and formal reports of GBV for trend monitoring purposes?
    Yes, data for all forms of GBV are recorded regardless of the status of the Responding Party or Reporting Party.

15 Does training for students and staff address staff and student perpetration of all forms of GBV in Higher Education?
    Yes, prevention and response training for students and staff includes information on staff and student perpetration.

We anticipate that many HEIs will not have matching answers across all four categories, far from it. There may well also be gaps or specific differences between staff and student procedures.

Choosing what, or who, to protect

The final example we will use to highlight the importance of consistency and fair practice is one that some readers may have been surprised to see in our answers mentioned earlier. We argue that the Reporting Party should receive the outcome of the investigation, discipline process, and be informed of any sanctions imposed on the Responding Party regardless of their status as staff or student. In investigations and discipline processes related to GBV, the entire process is in response to the harm the Responding Party has caused the Reporting Party and decisions are made based on personal private information about the Reporting Party and Responding Party. This information is intertwined and cannot be disentangled.

For example, if a Reporting Party makes a report (complaint) to the HEI that the Responding Party sexually penetrated her vagina with his penis without her consent, this information will be shared with the Responding Party and the investigator(s). It may also be shared with the case manager, note-taker, any decision-makers who put in place precautionary measures for the investigation to be undertaken. Those support contacts for both parties may also know the details of the report. If either of these individuals are staff, then their line manager or head of department may also be informed to some level. Trade union representatives may also be involved and aware. If the investigation finds on a balance of probabilities that a breach of policy occurred, then they would likely refer this to a discipline hearing. Discipline panels may have three to five members and in cases involving students, this may include student representatives. Generally speaking, most UK HEIs at this stage will shift the position of the Reporting Party (if they haven't done so already) from a main party in the process to a witness. In a discipline process, the Reporting Party is often a witness at best, or does not participate at all. The discipline panel, the investigator, the Responding Party, and any other additional witnesses called will discuss the Reporting Party, her personal information including the report.

Currently, a common practice, is that after all of this, the Reporting Party will not be informed of the outcome of the discipline process and the sanctions imposed on the Responding Party. Some universities may share the outcome of the discipline process only, without revealing the sanctions. Others will share the sanctions that are directly related to the Reporting Party, for example, if a No Contact Order is issued because she will be responsible for policing this by informing the university if he breaches it. Very few universities, it seems, will tell the Reporting Party the outcome of the investigation, discipline process, and all sanctions imposed in student cases; Durham University does as it is written into policy. We are not aware of universities that inform Reporting Parties of the investigation outcome, discipline outcome, and details of all sanctions imposed in staff-to-staff and staff-to-student cases.

It is surely not unreasonable for someone raising a complaint to receive the outcome and be informed of what action has been taken. What could be fairer than that? Oft-reported concerns about the privacy of Responding Parties is used to block communication to Reporting Parties, particularly in cases of staff misconduct. However, as you can see in the aforementioned example, the Reporting Party's information is being shared and used and the decisions are being made in response to what happened to the Reporting Party. The discipline panel, note-taker, Responding Party's support contact, and others within the HEI managing the case will know the outcome, but often the Reporting Party – again, the person harmed – will not. We argue that this is placing undue weight on General Data Protection Regulation (GDPR). HEIs need to balance the privacy, equality, and human rights of the Reporting and Responding Party in these cases in line with UK GDPR, Human Rights Act 1998, and the Public Sector Equality Duty (PSED) under the Equality Act 2010. There is no legislation that strictly prohibits sharing this information with the Reporting Party and sector guidance is beginning to recognise the impacts of not doing so.

It is well-established that GBV has many serious consequences for victim-survivors, including physical, psychological, emotional, behavioural, and practical impacts (Humphreys & Towl, 2020). The Equality and Human Rights Commission has highlighted this inconsistency in approaches to sharing outcomes and sanctions, noting the impact this has on trust in the HEI and willingness to report incidents (EHRC, 2019).

ACAS guidance on handling complaints of sexual harassment was updated in 2021 and now states:

> You should consider on a case-by-case basis whether to tell the person who made the complaint about what disciplinary action, if any, has been taken. You should tell them if you can.
>
> You'll need to check your policies and General Data Protection Regulation (GDPR) privacy notices. This is to make sure they allow the person who made the complaint to be told about any disciplinary action taken against the person who harassed them.
>
> (ACAS, 2021)

If the HEI has a rationale and lawful basis for sharing the outcome and sanctions of the investigation and discipline process with the Reporting Party, this can satisfy requirements under GDPR. As noted in the guidance by ACAS, as this view is shifting, it is necessary to ensure privacy notices are updated. It may be useful to conduct data protection impact assessments to make this change in policy.

Refusing to inform reporting parties of outcomes and sanctions may amount to the institutional collusion with perpetrators, hidden by appeasement resistance tactics (see Chapter 16 for a fuller discussion of this aspect of "resistance"), and it may very well be that this is further amplified if the perpetrator is in a position of power or authority whether through their academic prowess, for example, through large grant capture or high citation rates, or their managerial seniority.

Conclusion and summary of key points

As we can see, comprehensive means including all students and staff and dealing with all forms of GBV across all aspects of the institution. It means dealing with the "too hard" box and searching out gaps in services to ensure all are protected and have access to prevention and response initiatives. This requires delving deep into the structures of our HEI communities, searching for gaps in practice and checking that consistent, but tailored, prevention and response initiatives are used to support the safety of all students and staff. What could be more important than that?

- Comprehensive, meaning dealing with gaps, looking for "overlooked" areas, dealing with the "too hard" box, and monitoring for and responding to emerging trends.
- Examples of GBV that may currently be overlooked in HEIs include non-fatal strangulation, technology-facilitated gender-based violence, and spiking.
- There are some groups who are at a greater risk of being subjected to GBV than others and HEIs need to consider their community in full, sharpen the lens, and look for groups within groups who may have particular risks and need tailored prevention and response initiatives.
- To truly embed a comprehensive institution-wide approach means offering consistent and fair practices and providing the same standard to students and staff in expectations of conduct, specialist support available, procedures to address GBV, and communication of outcomes and sanctions.

Further Reading

Towl, G., & Humphreys, C. J. (2021, April 22). *How do to more than the bare minimum on harassment and sexual misconduct.* Wonkhe. https://wonkhe.com/blogs/how-to-do-more-than-the-bare-minimum-on-harassment-and-sexual-misconuct/

In this brief article, we respond to the Office for Students (OfS) Statement of Expectations on harassment and sexual misconduct urging senior management teams and governing bodies to go beyond the minimum expectations. We present ten key recommendations to help HEIs progress this work.

Culture Shift. (2022). *Exceeding expectations revised: Guidance on tackling harassment and sexual misconduct.* **https://insight.culture-shift.co.uk/higher-education/exceeding-expectations-2.0**

This is an interactive handbook created by Culture Shift, the developers of the online reporting platform Report + Support. The handbook provides practical guidance to Higher Education Institutions (HEIs) on how to exceed the OfS Statement of Expectations on harassment and sexual misconduct. The report provides recommendation for HEIs to tackle racial harassment and sexual misconduct using a survivor-centred approach. This handbook builds on the work from the EHRC, NUS, UUK and the 1752 Group. It is full of practical advice to help universities create positive change. The interactive element of the document includes links to video interviews with individuals from various organisations (including us). The interviews cover a range of topics including how to break down barriers to reporting, how to support students through the reporting and investigation process, how to create change from the bottom up, how to use data to prioritise planning, how to build prevention into the strategy and budget and case studies too. It is an accessible and useful handbook.

Notes

1 ACAS, the Advisory, Conciliation and Arbitration Service, is an independent body funded by the government that provides guidance to employers and helps resolve disputes between employers and employees in England, Scotland, and Wales. www.acas.org.uk/
2 CIPD, the Chartered Institute of Personnel and Development, is a professional body that sets standards for HR and people development in the UK, Ireland, Middle East, and Asia. www.cipd.co.uk/
3 Equality and Human Rights Commission is a statutory non-departmental public body established by the Equality Act 2006 that challenges discrimination, promotes equality of opportunity, and protects human rights by working with organisations and individuals to achieve these aims in England, Scotland, and Wales. www.equalityhumanrights.com/en
4 See The 1752 Group & McAlister Olivarius (2021), for additional explanations of precautionary measures that can be used in staff sexual misconduct.

References

ACAS. (2021). *Handling a sexual harassment complaint.* www.acas.org.uk/sexual-harassment/handling-a-sexual-harassment-complaint
Batty, D. (2020, April 22). Harassment fears as students post extreme pornography in online lectures. *The Guardian.* Retrieved January 2022, from www.theguardian.com/education/2020/apr/22/students-zoombomb-online-lectures-with-extreme-pornography
Bichard, H., Byrne, C., Saville, C. W. N., & Coetzer, R. (2021). The neuropsychological outcomes of non-fatal strangulation in domestic and sexual violence: A systematic review. *Neuropsychological Rehabilitation.* doi:10.1080/09602011.2020.1868537

Bull, A., & Rye, R. (2018). Silencing students: Institutional responses to staff sexual misconduct in UK Higher Education. https://1752group.com/sexual-misconduct-research-silencing-students/

Cardwell, E., & Hitchen, E. (2022). *Intervention – "precarity, transactions, insecure attachments: Reflections on participating in degrees of abuse" Antipode Online.* https://antipodeonline.org/2022/01/06/precarity-transactions-insecure-attachments/

Carter, P., & Jeffs, T. (1995). *A very private affair: Sexual exploitation in higher education.* Education Now Books, Publishing Cooperative.

Carter, R., Smock, B., Strack, G., Aceves, Y., Martinez, M., & Peck, A. (2017). *Physiological consequences of strangulation: Occlusion of arterial blood flow: Seconds to minutes timeline.* Training Institute on Strangulation Prevention.

CIPD and Equality and Human Rights Commission. (2020). *Managing and supporting employees experiencing domestic abuse: A guide for Employers.* CIPD and EHRC. www.cipd.co.uk/Images/managing-supporting-employees-experiencing-domestic-abuse-guide_tcm18-84538.pdf

Colyer, C. J., & Weiss, K. G. (2018). Contextualizing the drink-spiking narrative that "everyone knows." *Criminal Justice Review, 43*(1), 10–22. https://doi.org/10.1177/0734016817747011

Domestic Abuse Act. (2021). www.legislation.gov.uk/ukpga/2021/17/contents/enacted

Drink Aware. (n.d.). *Drink spiking and date rape drugs.* www.drinkaware.co.uk/advice/staying-safe-while-drinking/drink-spiking-and-date-rape-drugs/#whataredaterapedrugs

Dunn, S. (2020). *Supporting a safer internet paper No. 1. Technology-facilitated gender-based violence: An Overview.* Centre for International Governance Innovation. www.cigionline.org/publications/technology-facilitated-gender-based-violence-overview

Equality and Human Rights Commission (EHRC). (2019). *Tackling racial harassment: Universities challenged.* www.equalityhumanrights.com/sites/default/files/tackling-racial-harassment-universities-challenged.pdf

EVAW. (2015). *Spotted: Obligations to protect women students' safety and equality. Using the public sector equality & the human rights act in higher and further education institutions to improve policies and practices on violence against women and girls.* End Violence Against Women Coalition. www.endviolenceagainstwomen.org.uk/wp-content/uploads/Spotted-Obligations-to-Protect-Women-StudentsEy-Safety-Equality.pdf

Ghani, H., & Towl, G. (2017, August 7). Students are still afraid to report sexual assault. *Times Higher Education.*

Glass, N., Laughon, K., Campbell, J., Block, C. R., Hanson, G., Sharps, P. W., & Taliaferro, E. (2008). Non-fatal strangulation is an important risk factor for homicide of women. *The Journal of Emergency Medicine, 35*(3), 329–335. https://doi.org/10.1016/j.jemermed.2007.02.065

The 1752 Group & McAlister Olivarius. (2020). *Sector guidance to address staff sexual misconduct in UK higher education.* https://1752group.files.wordpress.com/2021/09/5ed32-the-1752-group-and-mcallister-olivarius-sector-guidance-to-address-staff-sexual-misconduct-in-uk-he.pdf

The 1752 Group & McAlister Olivarius. (2021). *Briefing note no. 3: Precautionary measures on receiving a report on staff sexual misconduct, bullying or discrimination.* Retrieved January 2022, from https://1752group.com/briefing-notes/

Herbenick, D., Guerra-Reyes, L., Patterson, C., Rosenstock Gonzalez, Y. R., Wagner, C., & Zounlome, N. O. O. (2021). "If their face starts turning purple, you are probably doing something wrong": Young men's experiences with choking during sex. *Journal of Sex & Marital Therapy.* doi:10.1080/0092623X.2021.2009607

Hill, K., & Towl, G. J. (2021). Creating safer night-time economies. *The Psychologist.* https://thepsychologist.bps.org.uk/creating-safer-night-time-economies

Humphreys, C. J. (2021). Technology-facilitated sexual violence in Higher Education: Impact on victim-survivors and recommendations for universities. In N. Akdemir, C. J. Lawless, & U. Türkşen (Eds.), *Cybercrime in action: An international approach to cybercrime*. Nobel.

Humphreys, C. J., & Towl, G. J. (2020). *Addressing student sexual violence in Higher Education: A good practice guide*. Emerald Publishing Group.

Kimble, M., Flack, W. F., Jr., & Burbridge, E. (2013). Study abroad increases risk for sexual assault in female undergraduates: A preliminary report. *Psychological Trauma: Theory, Research, Practice, and Policy, 5*(5), 426–430. https://doi.org/10.1037/a0029608

Long, J., Wertans, E., Harper, K., Brennan, D., Harvey, H., Allen, R., & Elliott, K. (2020). *UK femicides 2009–2018: "If I'm not in Friday, I might be dead."* Femicide Census.

Moore, A., & Khan, C. (2019, July 25). The fatal, hateful rise of choking during sex. *The Guardian*. Retrieved January 2022, from www.theguardian.com/society/2019/jul/25/fatal-hateful-rise-of-choking-during-sex.

NYC Mayor's Office to End Domestic and Gender-Based Violence. (2020). *"My partner choked me": Non-fatal strangulation: A pocket guide to best practices when working with survivors of strangulation*. Retrieved January 2022, from www.familyjusticecenter.org/wp-content/uploads/2020/02/Strangulation-Pocket-Guide.pdf

Office of National Statistics. (2019). *Disability and crime, UK: 2019*. www.ons.gov.uk/peoplepopulationandcommunity/healthandsocialcare/disability/bulletins/disabilityandcrimeuk/2019#domestic-abuse

Office for Students. (2020). *Coronavirus briefing note: Disabled students*. www.officeforstudents.org.uk/media/8f61cef7-4cf7-480a-8f73-3e6c51b05e54/coronavirus-briefing-note-disabled-students.pdf

Office for Students. (2021). *Prevent and address harassment and sexual misconduct: Statement of expectations*. www.officeforstudents.org.uk/advice-and-guidance/student-wellbeing-and-protection/prevent-and-address-harassment-and-sexual-misconduct/statement-of-expectations/

Pedersen, E. R., D'Amico, E. J., LaBrie, J. W., Klein, D. J., Farris, C., & Griffin, B. A. (2020). Alcohol and sexual risk among American college students studying abroad. *Prevention Science, 21*, 926–936. https://doi.org/10.1007/s11121-020-01149-9

Revolt Sexual Assault & The Student Room. (2018). *Students' experience of sexual violence*. https://revoltsexualassault.com/wp-content/uploads/2018/03/Report-Sexual-Violence-at-University-Revolt-Sexual-Assault-The-Student-Room-March-2018.pdf

Ross, R. (2015). "No sir, she was not a fool in the field": Gendered risks and sexual violence in immersed cross-cultural fieldwork. *The Professional Geographer, 67*(2), 180–186. doi:10.1080/00330124.2014.907705

Schneider, L. T. (2020). Sexual violence during research: How the unpredictability of fieldwork and the right to risk collide with academic bureaucracy and expectations. *Critique of Anthropology, 40*(2), 173–193. https://doi.org/10.1177/0308275X20917272

Sexual Offences Act. (2003). www.legislation.gov.uk/ukpga/2003/42/contents

Sexual Offences (Northern Ireland) Order. (2008). www.legislation.gov.uk/nisi/2008/1769/contents

Sexual Offences (Scotland) Act. (2009). www.legislation.gov.uk/asp/2009/9/contents

Siddiqui, N., Towl, G., Matthewson, J., Stretesky, C., & Earnshaw, M. (2019). *Religious and race hate experience survey: Report findings*. Durham University Office for Students.

Towl, G. J., & Walker, T. (2019). *Tackling sexual violence at universities: An international perspective*. Routledge.

UK Parliament. (2021). *Home affairs committee launches inquiry into spiking.* https://committees. parliament.uk/committee/83/home-affairs-committee/news/159582/home-affairs-committee-launches-inquiry-into-spiking/

UN Women. (2020a). *Online and ICT facilitated violence against women and girls during COVID-19.* www.unwomen.org/-/media/headquarters/attachments/sections/library/ publications/2020/brief-online-and-ict-facilitated-violence-against-women-and-girls-during-covid-19-en.pdf?la=en&vs=2519

UN Women. (2020b). *Sexual harassment against women with disabilities in the world of work and on campus.* UN Women.

UNESCO Institute for Statistics. (2019). *Global flow of tertiary -level students.* http://uis. unesco.org/en/uis-student-flow

Universities UK. (2019). *Changing the culture: Tackling online harassment and promoting online welfare.* www.universitiesuk.ac.uk/what-we-do/policy-andresearch/publications/ tackling-online-harassment-and-promoting

Universities UK. (2020). *Continuing the conversation: Responding to domestic violence and technology mediated abuse in higher education communities during the Covid-19 pandemic.* www.universitiesuk. ac.uk/sites/default/files/field/downloads/2021-08/continuing-the-conversation.pdf

Voss, B. (2021a). Disrupting cultures of harassment in archaeology: Social-environmental and trauma-informed approaches to disciplinary transformation. *American Antiquity, 86*(3), 447–464. doi:10.1017/aaq.2021.19

Voss, B. (2021b). Documenting cultures of harassment in archaeology: A review and analysis of quantitative and qualitative research studies. *American Antiquity, 86*(2), 244–260. doi:10.1017/aaq.2020.118

Ward, Z. (n.d.). *Intimate image abuse, an evolving landscape.* Revenge Porn Helpline. https:// revengepornhelpline.org.uk/resources/helpline-research-and-reports/

Wellcome Trust. (n.d.). *Bullying and harassment policy.* https://wellcome.org/grant-funding/ guidance/bullying-and-harassment-policy#what-we-expect-from-the-organisations-we-fund-ef38

White, C., Martin, G., Schofield, A. M., Majeed-Ariss, R. (2021). 'I thought he was going to kill me': Analysis of 204 case files of adults reporting non-fatal strangulation as part of a sexual assault over a 3 year period. *Journal of Forensic and Legal Medicine, 79.* https://doi. org/10.1016/j.jflm.2021.102128

White, C., Stark, M., & Butler, B. (2020). *Non-fatal strangulation: In physical and sexual assault.* Faculty of Forensic & Legal Medicine of the Royal College of Physicians.

11 Staff sexual misconduct in Higher Education

Impacts, responses, and challenges

Anna Bull

Sexual misconduct towards students by academic staff[1] in Higher Education (HE) is both a cause and a consequence of gender inequality. Not only that, it also reflects and exacerbates other inequalities: female, queer, trans and non-binary students, and students of colour are more at risk of experiencing sexual misconduct from staff, and experience greater harms when it occurs (Australian Human Rights Commission, 2017; Cantor et al., 2015; Kalof et al., 2001; National Union of Students, 2018). Existing research, policy, and practical interventions into sexual violence in HE have focused on violence or harassment perpetrated by students on other students (see for example Phipps & Young, 2014; Universities UK, 2016). As a result, staff sexual misconduct has only recently been formulated as a policy problem at the national level in the UK. Outside the UK, there has also been recent attention to staff sexual misconduct, for example, in the United States and Australia, where large-scale studies have found a relatively high incidence of staff sexual misconduct towards students (Australian Human Rights Commission, 2017; Cantor et al., 2015; National Academies of Sciences, 2018). In a US study of 150,000 students, out of the 47.7% of students who indicated that they have been the victims of sexual harassment since enrolled, 9.3% of these indicated they had experienced sexual harassment from a member of faculty; a figure which rose to 22.4% among women graduate students (Cantor et al., 2015, pp. 29–31). While no comparable prevalence study exists in the UK, if the proportion is similar, 105,755 students out of the 2018–2019 UK student population would have experienced sexual harassment from HE staff, out of which 36,639 would be women postgraduate students (Higher Education Statistics Agency, 2018). Tackling this issue will therefore affect the lives and careers of many students, predominantly women.

While there are many similarities between student and staff sexual misconduct in terms of how institutions should respond, there are also some differences, relating to the different status of students and staff within HE institutions as well as the different rights and protections for staff under employment law compared to students. In addition, the very fact that students are dependent on staff for their teaching and learning creates a relationship of trust that is also a power imbalance. This chapter draws on data from two research projects to

DOI: 10.4324/9781003252474-13

outline what this power imbalance means for students who are subjected to sexual misconduct from staff: a qualitative study of interviews with 16 students and Early Career Researchers (ECRs), first published as the report 'Silencing Students' (Bull & Rye, 2018) as well as data from the collaborative research with the Women's Campaign of the National Union of Students published in 2018 as the report 'Power in the Academy'. The chapter explores what forms staff sexual misconduct takes; how the context of HE enables misconduct to occur; how survivors respond to misconduct and the impacts it has on them; and how they experience the reporting process, if they report to their institution. Throughout, the chapter draws on a case study from a student survivor, Gemma,[2] and the chapter begins by introducing her experience.

Gemma's experience

I interviewed Gemma in early 2018 about her reporting process that took place in 2016–2017 (Bull & Rye, 2018). While I could have drawn on a more recent account from interviews carried out in 2020–2021, my ongoing research shows that Gemma's experience of reporting – while distressing and life-changing for her – followed standard practice for such reports. It therefore shows how an institutional response that is, on paper, following good practice can still have very poor outcomes for the complainant, and reveals changes that need to be made to such standard practice. There are also other reasons for drawing on Gemma's account here: her experience shows how verbal sexual harassment, stalking, and boundary-blurring behaviours from staff can have a profound impact on students, even while such behaviours can sometimes be minimised as 'not serious' (Jackson & Sundaram, 2020). In addition, it shows how the intersection of class and gender affected her experience; as she describes subsequently, her working-class background made this experience even more difficult and confusing for her. Finally, Gemma wanted her account to be used for educational purposes; she has given permission for it to be used in training (and readers are therefore welcome to use this case study in their own institutional training).

Her experience is atypical in various ways – she is an undergraduate, whereas it is more common for postgraduate students to be targeted. She had written evidence of sexual harassment through messages from the perpetrator to her university email account, as opposed to many cases where there is no written evidence, as a result of which survivors find it difficult to get through a complaints process. And her experience is less complicated than that of many other interviewees, who found the process could drag on for years and fail to come to resolution. However, Gemma herself finds the idea that her case was 'straightforward' laughable, as it felt anything but that to her. Her experience should therefore not be taken as typical, but as one illustration of the types of issues that can come up in institutional responses to this issue.

Gemma was first in her family to go to university, progressing directly from school to an elite university to study a subject she was passionate about. In her first term, she and a friend were having trouble with the department's provision for disabilities as well as finding that their seminars were dominated by male students who made it difficult for the women to contribute. In order to raise these concerns, they met with the member of staff in their department who was responsible for teaching. Following this meeting, this lecturer started sending emails to Gemma and following her on social media. In her own words:

> *I got a follow request off him on Instagram, so did my friend, and then I remember one night, he'd liked a picture from the very bottom of my profile, it was from two years before I'd even started uni – from ages ago, it took a lot of scrolling to get down. So I got a notification that that had been liked, and I was like, 'You're sat there on my profile', and it was, I don't know, 4:00am. It was a bit weird. And then, every time I'd put something on Instagram I'd get a comment or a like from him almost immediately, almost like he'd had my notifications turned on or something. So I very quickly stopped using Instagram, I was like, 'I don't want anything to do with that'. Stuff kept happening, there was an email when he was on holiday, he was in an airport and he called me a 'bad girl' over email. Again over the university email system.*

The lecturer invited Gemma and her friend for coffee off-campus on a weekend. He then persuaded them all to go for dinner together, but her friend left very soon.

> *During that evening. . . I learned all about his ex-wife and his divorce – I didn't ask any of this. He asked me at one point if I had a boyfriend, and I said no. I don't know why I just didn't say yes. Then I got invited to his flat, and I made a face, because I was like, 'Oh my God, no', and he said, 'Oh, was that a bit inappropriate?' And I said, 'Yes'. That was the only time I really ever said anything to him, face to face, about his behaviour. He wouldn't let me pay for the dinner, even though I was like, 'It's not expensive, I really can pay for my own half, it's fine'.*

> *At this point I started blocking him on social media. I was realising this was weird. I didn't tell my mum, because I knew she would be like, 'What the hell are you doing?' So, towards the end of the first semester was when I left university. I withdrew from my course, mainly because of all of the stuff that had been happening with this professor. I wasn't going into uni anyway. I'd stopped going to his lectures a long time before, because he used to watch me. I didn't sit at the front, I used to sit towards the back, near the door, and I used to get emails like, 'I saw you yawning today, are you tired?' And it was, 'This lecture has got at least 100 people in, why are you watching me, constantly?' And it happened on multiple occasions.*

As the next section explores, while Gemma initially thought that these behaviours from the lecturer were just 'weird', in fact they clearly constitute sexual harassment.

What forms does staff/faculty sexual misconduct take?

Sexual misconduct from staff takes a range of forms. Perhaps most well-documented is sexual harassment, which under the UK's Equality Act 2010 is defined as unwanted conduct of a sexual nature which has the purpose or effect of violating the recipient's dignity or creating an intimidating, hostile, degrading, humiliating, or offensive environment. Harassment can also relate to other 'protected characteristics' under the Equality Act, that is, harassment relating to sex, race, age, disability, and others (although notably, class or socio-economic disadvantage is not a protected characteristic). In the United States, harassment on the basis of sex is termed 'gender harassment', defined as 'verbal and nonverbal behaviors that convey hostility, objectification, exclusion, or second-class status about members of one gender' (National Academies, 2018, p. 2). In Gemma's account, the lecturer's behaviour primarily constituted sexual harassment. As outlined earlier, he was trying to draw her into sexualised discussions by talking about what type of women he is attracted to and asking her about her relationship status. He was also engaging in stalking and surveillance behaviours from the lecturer, primarily on social media, but also by letting her know that he was singling her out to watch her in a class of 100 students.

Other forms of sexual misconduct include sexual violence or assault. In the study 'Power in the Academy', out of 1,528 responses from current students, there were 35 respondents who had been subjected to non-consensual sexual contact by a staff member (2.3%), and 9 who had been subjected to sexual assault or rape (National Union of Students, 2018, p. 24). These behaviours could occur alongside bullying, and/or within the context of an intimate relationship with a member of staff, sometimes alongside other coercive and controlling behaviours.

Sexual harassment, assault, or rape can also occur as part of a pattern of boundary-blurring and grooming behaviours. In Bull and Page (2021a, p. 12), we define boundary-blurring as behaviours 'that transgress (often tacit) professional boundaries, and grooming as a pattern of these behaviours over time between people in positions of unequal power that may lead to an abuse of power'. While grooming, under the law, only refers to behaviours by an adults towards a child, this term was used by interviewees in Bull and Rye (2018) to make sense of their experiences of staff sexual misconduct. Indeed, since then, University College London has formally recognised 'grooming' in its Prevention of Bullying, Harassment and Sexual Misconduct Policy (2020, section 3.6):

> Grooming can be defined as a gradual process that someone in a position of power uses to manipulate someone to do things they may not be comfortable with and to make them less likely to reject or report abusive behaviour. Grooming will initially start as befriending someone and making them feel special and may result in sexual abuse and/or exploitation.

Definitions such as these in policy, publicly visible, are important not only to be drawn on in complaints processes, but also to help students and staff make sense of their experiences. A common theme for interviewees in Bull and Rye (2018) was that even if they knew they were uncomfortable about something, they didn't recognise what was happening for some time. Indeed, this was precisely Gemma's experience. She described how, when she was writing up an account of what had happened in order to report it, she took the advice of the Students' Union to write it in a timeline:

> *[S]o that they could really see the escalation and progression of things, because rather than one solo incident, it was like a build-up of stuff over time, and lots and lots of small things that alone would have been just a bit strange, but put together was a serious issue, which again, I only realised when it was at the end of it, and when someone said, 'This is bad', because I was like, 'Oh, that's just a bit weird. He's just a bit weird'. But then when you added it all together, it was strange. It was sexual harassment. That's what it was.*

Gemma's account illustrates a point that comes up time and time again in interviewees' accounts: although she had dropped out of university primarily because of this experience, it wasn't until she wrote it up in a timeline and looked at all the behaviours together that she realised the weight of it. A lot of 'small things' that were about the lecturer 'being a bit weird', when added up together could be seen for what they were: sexual harassment.

How does HE create the context for staff sexual misconduct to occur?

Higher Education is saturated with power hierarchies, whether of age, gender, gender identity, sexuality, knowledge/expertise, class, race, level of seniority or level of study, contract and funding status, visa status, or temporary/permanent membership of the institution. An extensive research literature has documented these inequalities and the various ways that they affect students' and staff members' ability to engage with their work and study (see, for example, Arday & Mirza, 2018; Bhopal, 2015; Clancy et al., 2017).

Inequalities create what Liz Kelly calls a 'conducive context' that allows harassment and abuse to occur (2016). While anyone, anywhere can be subjected to sexual and gender-based violence or harassment, it is much more likely to happen within a relationship of unequal power. Here I focus on one aspect of inequality that has been well-documented in UK Higher Education: class. Working-class students' experiences of Higher Education varied across different types of institutions, but at so-called elite institutions, they had to do considerable 'identity work' to manage to 'fit in' (Reay, 2010, p. 120). However, one aspect of this experience that has been less documented is the way it affects relationships with academic staff. Gemma found that her lack of family history of Higher Education – often used as one indicator of class in the UK – meant she was unfamiliar with how to interact with lecturers:

> *I'm the eldest in my family, I've got no older siblings, no one in my family at all has ever been to uni, so I was the first of my immediate and then also wider family to have ever gone to uni. No one has ever been. So I had no idea what to expect. I didn't have any friends who were older than me or anything, so it was completely new, and it was a similar situation for the friends that I made as well. So we were all very new to the whole university experience. They don't tell you what normal interaction with the lecturers is like. This is the problem. I had no idea what was normal. I thought his behaviour was like, 'Oh, he's just being really friendly, it's fine'. It was only when I sat down at the end and added up everything that I thought, 'No, that's not right', but it took me a long time to realise.*

Class status can also affect help-seeking behaviour as students may not want to disclose that something is wrong if they have already taken a risk by going to university. These issues can be compounded by racial inequalities and/or visa status or international student status, where students may be unwilling to disclose to family or unable to report due to time restrictions on their visa. It's also important to highlight the interactions of disability and sexual misconduct. Perpetrators can target those who are vulnerable in some way – including those who are disabled or have mental ill-health – but also sexual violence or harassment can cause disability in the form of post-traumatic stress disorder. This can then have a long-term impact on the survivor's studies and career.

How do people respond to harassment?

There are numerous ways in which people respond to harassment, but common responses include trying to avoid the perpetrator, trying to appease them, putting up with it, minimizing the behavior or ignoring it, and/or seeking social support from friends and family in order to be able to deal with it (National Academies, 2018, p. 79). In addition, it is important to remember that the vast majority of people who are subjected to staff sexual misconduct do not report to their institution, or to the police, and may not even tell anyone about this. In our report 'Power in the Academy' (National Union of Students, 2018), we found that fewer than 10% of those who had been subjected to any of the behaviours we asked about had reported this to their institution. The reasons given for not reporting are outlined in Figure 11.1.

Free text responses to this question showed that, as well as the points outlined previously, there was a certain amount of low-level boundary-blurring behavior that respondents didn't feel any need to report, for example, *'the odd sexual joke in class [which] wasn't anything untoward'*, or *'I didn't feel*

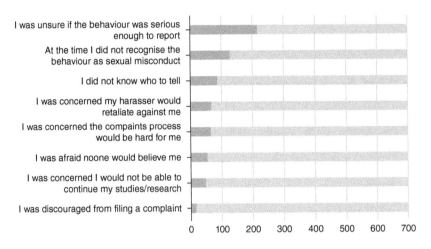

Figure 11.1 The most common barriers to reporting (National Union of Students, 2018).

threatened, just awkward, so didn't feel it necessary'. Other responses pointed to more complex experiences, with one respondent stating that 'I liked the attention and frankly wanted more' and others not reporting due to concerns over ***'retaliation/judgement from everyone else'*** and being ***'concerned it would exacerbate untrue rumours being spread'.*** A number of responses noted that they didn't report misconduct because the experience was something they witnessed rather than experienced themselves; it's important to remember, however, that sexual harassment affects those who witness it, as well as those who are directly targeted (National Academies, 2018, p. 78).

Overall, these responses – unsurprisingly – point towards a wide range of interpersonal experiences between staff and students, some of which may blur boundaries but in a consensual way, and others of which suggest that there are unclear boundaries in staff–student – and perhaps also in staff–staff – relationships. Indeed, not all Higher Education Institutions in the UK have a staff code of conduct and only a few have policies prohibiting staff–student sexual and romantic relationships. This means that the behaviour that Gemma experienced from her lecturer is even more difficult to label as inappropriate, as there is a lack of consensus as to what is acceptable or normal in this relationship. Indeed, one issue that she found very confusing was moving from school, where there are very clear boundaries between teachers and students, to university just a few months later, ***'where anything goes and everyone is supposed to be a consenting adult'*** as she described it.

While prohibiting staff–student sexual relationships is a blunt tool to address unclear boundaries, it does at least send a clear signal that the teaching and learning relationship between staff and students should take priority over romantic or sexual relationships in the higher education space.

Why do people report sexual misconduct?

Deciding to report is sometimes discussed as though it is a straightforward step. However, this is seldom the case. In the accounts from interviewees for the Silencing Students report:

> Multiple, overlapping reasons for disclosure and/or reporting were discussed over the course of what were sometimes very complex accounts. The decision to report could rarely be narrowed down to a single point in time. Initial disclosures could prove ineffective, leading to the decision-making process having to happen all over again in light of this response, or previous decisions *not* to report were later revisited by interviewees in light of changed circumstances.
>
> (Bull, forthcoming)

In Gemma's case, she did not initially intend to report her experiences as she was, effectively, solving the problem – even if in a very drastic way – by dropping out of university. However, before she left, she and her friend met with the Students' Union about the university's failure to support them with their disability support, and her friend mentioned this lecturer's behavior. As Gemma explained,

> *As soon as that was mentioned, the Student Union advisor immediately was like, 'What's this? Tell me everything'. So I did, and she was like, 'This is the problem here. I mean, sure, the department have been rubbish, but this is a really, really massive issue'. I remember leaving that meeting like, 'Oh dear'. So I wrote my complaint with the help of the Students' Union.*

In Gemma's account, it is the Students' Union advice worker who first labels and calls out this behaviour, helping Gemma shift from seeing it as 'a bit weird' to something that was having a powerful impact on her engagement at university. Indeed, a study of 40 academic staff in the United States who were sexually harassed by other staff found that some respondents noted that they had not immediately recognised those experiences as such (National Academies, 2018, p. 236). As a result, it is crucial for others – particularly staff in student-facing roles – to recognise, and avoid minimising, sexual harassment and grooming behaviours.

The most common reasons for reporting staff sexual misconduct given by interviewees were to protect oneself from further harm and get the harassment to stop; to protect other women; to continue ones' career or studies; and because reporting is seen as the 'right thing to do' (Bull, forthcoming; this is in line with the findings from National Academies study (2018, p. 241)). However, besides these rationales for reporting, there were also specific catalysts or triggers that affected the timing of reporting. These could include a change in circumstances, perhaps due to graduating or leaving the institution; finding out new information, for example, realising that others had also been targeted; or being validated by someone within the institution that what they had experienced was not ok. The catalyst for Gemma's report was being validated by the Students' Union advisor that this behaviour was not acceptable. For Gemma, the rationale for reporting came later, during the reporting process, where she found the strength to fight to 'do the right thing'. It is helpful to think about these two different aspects of the decision to report, as it means that institutions can deliberately create catalysts to reporting. This could include explicitly asking students/staff if they want to disclose issues at 'trigger' points such as when they are dropping out of or leaving the institution (as already happens for staff if they have exit interviews), and by making sure staff give clear and consistent messages about what behaviours are acceptable.

How do students experience the reporting process?

Once the initial disclosure or report has been made, the process can be immensely difficult. Gemma moved back in with her mother, away from her university, and dealt with the complaint from there. After just over a month, her report was passed from the student complaints department to Human Resources (HR). Someone from the HR department arranged a phone call with her, which proved to be distressing:

> *I spoke to [the HR representative] on the phone, during which he told me that I should be very careful about what I was doing because I could ruin someone's career, and that things like this were often found to be a misunderstanding. Then I asked, 'How does the process work? What happens from now?' And he told me that at one point I'd be interviewed or questioned by the lecturer that I submitted a complaint against, in front of a large audience, and that I'd be questioned by him and his union representative.*

> *I sat there in my bedroom, on my own, because my mum was at work and my sister was out all day at school, and I vividly remember being in an absolute state after this phone call, because he was really quite intimidating, and made it sound like such a scary thing that I literally wrote out an email to HR and said, 'No, I'm not doing this' which is obviously what they wanted; they wanted me to not go forward with it. But instead, I emailed the Students' Union, and I said, 'I'm having some issues, what on earth does all of this mean? This dude has really scared me, help'. So they rang me back really quickly, and they said, 'That's not okay, he should not have said those things to you. This is not going to happen, there's no way you're going to be questioned by the lecturer and you're not going to do it in front of a large audience'.*

This conversation marked the start of Gemma's fight to make the complaints process safe for her. Together with the students' union, she had to fight to ask for a woman to be included as a member of the disciplinary panel, and to give her evidence at a different time from the lecturer rather than to face him directly. Some issues that she was concerned about were not addressed, for example, she was unhappy that the head of her department was leading the investigation, who was the line manager of the lecturer who had harassed her. While this is standard practice, it felt to her that this was a conflict of interest.

Overall, Gemma felt like they were making it up the process they went along, as the university didn't have policies that explicitly addressed this situation. She found it hugely stressful as she was a long way out of her depth. She also found it made her very angry and frustrated. Throughout the process there was a lack of parity between her and the lecturer. For example, they sent him all the notes from meetings with her, but failed to send her the notes and material from meetings with him until she pushed for this. When she was finally allowed to read notes from meetings and submissions to the tribunal from the lecturer, she found that he was maligning her and calling her a liar, saying that she was only doing this to get her tuition fees back, even though she had never asked for this. This was also distressing to experience. Overall, she felt like the university were protecting the member of staff, and that she was just an inconvenience.

Gemma's experience is sadly not an isolated one. Indeed, the lack of parity between herself and the lecturer in the disciplinary process is not an aberration, but is standard practice for workplace or Higher Education complaints and disciplinary processes. This is because complaints – whether in student–student cases, staff–student cases, or staff–staff cases – are dealt with in a separate process to the disciplinary case that the university takes against the reported party. This means that when a complaint is passed onto a disciplinary process, the complainant becomes a witness to the university's process against the reported party. As a witness, the complainant does not have the right to see evidence presented to the disciplinary panel by the reported party, does not have the right to call witnesses, does not have the right to union or legal advocacy, and does not even have the right to know the outcome of the case.

As myself, Georgina Calvert-Lee and Tiffany Page have outlined (2020), this amounts to a discriminatory process. This is because

> [i]n a society where vastly more sexual misconduct complaints are made by women against men than vice versa, a process for investigating sexual misconduct complaints which gives those responding more rights than those complaining might well be thought to place women as a group at a particular disadvantage and so to amount to indirect discrimination, in breach of the Equality Act 2010.
>
> (The 1752 Group, & McAllister Olivarius, 2020b, pp. 4–5)

Such discrimination is exacerbated in staff–student complaints processes due to the power imbalance between staff and students, whereby staff are usually older, in a position of expertise and authority over the student, and may have permanent contracts at the institution, whereas students are only temporary members.

These inequalities are often compounded by a gender power imbalance as well as fear or trauma stemming from the sexual misconduct.

This discrimination in the complaints process is one of the main problems with institutional complaints processes. However, other problems also arise. These include a lack of knowledge among investigators or disciplinary panel members as to what constitutes sexual harassment or consent; retaliation or victimisation from the perpetrator and his allies during the process; lack of support from the institution during the process; lack of communication from the institution to the complainant; inadequate policies for dealing with staff–student complaints; lack of joined-up working within the institution; or complaints handlers simply failing to follow institutional policies.

In addition, it is common for staff sexual misconduct complaints to take a very long time. Indeed, this was the case for Gemma, who spent nine months pursuing her case. Finally, after the disciplinary panel meeting, she received a short email from HR saying that the sexual harassment complaint had been upheld and 'appropriate disciplinary action would be taken'. This was, apparently, the end of the process.

What impacts do staff sexual misconduct and the reporting process have on complainants?

It is crucial for anyone working or studying in Higher Education to understand the many and varied ways in which sexual misconduct impacts on those who are targeted. This can help to better understand the types of support and remedy that are needed, as well as to build empathy for victim-survivors. As Bongiorno et al. (2019) show, victim blaming for sexual harassment can be explained in a large part through male-perpetrator empathy (or 'himpathy' as it is colloquially known). Therefore, increasing understanding and empathy for victim-survivors may help redress this imbalance of empathy favouring male perpetrators.

Impacts of staff sexual misconduct can be both academic and non-academic. In academic impacts, a survey of 28,270 students enrolled at the University of Texas found 'significant differences in reports of missing class, being late for class, [and] making excuses to get out of class' between students who had been subjected to staff/faculty sexual harassment, compared with those who had not (National Academies, 2018, p. 284; see also Lorenz et al., 2019). Those subjected to staff sexual harassment often report feeling less safe on campus (National Academies, 2018, p. 281; Rosenthal et al., 2016, p. 374; Bull & Rye, 2018, p. 17). Other academic impacts documented include loss of access to teaching; difficulty in getting references; changing research area or subdiscipline; dropping out of degree programme or career; effects on grades and degree results; loss of confidence, affecting ability to work; and loss of networks, or ability to network (Bull & Rye, 2018, p. 17; see National Academies (2018, pp. 245–246) for similar impacts on staff who are targeted by other staff).

Non-academic impacts, including emotional and physical impacts, can also be very severe. In a study of graduate students who were subjected to sexual harassment, Rosenthal et al. found an 'association of sexual harassment with post-traumatic symptoms, even when statistically controlling for other forms of trauma' (Rosenthal et al., 2016, p. 374). There is evidence that being victimised within a trusted institution exacerbates post-traumatic symptoms (Rosenthal et al., 2016, p. 374). Other mental health impacts include depression, anxiety, and suicide attempts, while emotional impacts can include fear, anger, and a sense of powerlessness (Bull & Rye, 2018, p. 17). Not only this, but financial impacts can also occur through loss of earnings, loss of tuition/living costs, and needing to pay legal and counselling fees.

In students' own words, some of the impacts described by respondents to the 'Power in the Academy' survey included:

- *'Avoided staff members associated with the academic who assaulted me'.*
- *'Felt frustrated and helpless. Lost confidence in my institution and their ability to help'.*
- *'Avoided choosing a project I was interested in'.*
- *'Lost a job opportunity'.*
- *'Avoided student support services as they made me feel very insecure with comments about being trans'.*

As the final comment shows, the impacts of staff sexual misconduct can be compounded by those who also hold other marginalised identities. In this case, the 'comments about being trans' meant the student was unable to seek support from the usual channels. This is particularly concerning as LGBTQ+ students are even more likely to be targeted for sexual harassment by staff than other groups (National Union of Students, 2018).

Many of these impacts were experienced by Gemma. She decided to return to the same university the following year, but to do a different degree course on a different campus. This meant she was able to avoid being in any spaces where the lecturer who had targeted her might be. Before she got back to university she checked online, and he was still in post, and as a result she was unable to stomach doing any modules in his department, even though that was a possibility on her new degree course, and the subject she had been studying was her passion.

On returning to the university, there appeared to have been no effects for the lecturer as a result of her complaint. She still felt angry and didn't make friends on her new degree course as she found it difficult to explain to them what happened – a further impact on her was therefore isolation from her fellow students. She did enjoy her new degree but felt nothing like the passion she had for her previous subject, and she remained suspicious of male lecturers, avoiding attending office hours with them. She also avoided any spaces where the lecturer who targeted her might be on campus. Her friends from her old degree course also avoided taking any modules with the lecturer for fear that he would retaliate towards them due to being friends with her. The impacts of his actions therefore continued to be felt both by Gemma and by other students even after the complaint was closed.

Remedy and safeguarding

One of the things that kept Gemma going with her complaint was the knowledge that the lecturer had a reputation for being 'creepy' among other students. She told me that her housemates were aware of the lecturer stalking others on social media, including sending them private messages on Facebook. This points to one area where HE institutions still have some way to go in improving practice: safeguarding both complainants and other staff/students from harm. Indeed, risk assessments have been highlighted as one area that UK universities need to improve on (Universities UK, 2019). Gemma's experience highlights this clearly: despite being the victim, she was the one who had to change her plans and avoid the lecturer on campus, rather than any efforts being made to make the department safe for her. But not only that, other students in the department were also aware of the lecturer's 'creepy' reputation and were warning each other and avoiding his modules. While the university had treated the complaint as an individualised case, such an approach fails to recognise that it is common for multiple students – and sometimes other staff as well – to be targeted by a staff perpetrator (Bull & Rye, 2018).

When institutions receive a report or disclosure of staff sexual misconduct, they should therefore assume that other students have been or will be targeted, and should implement safeguarding actions accordingly (The 1752 Group, & McAllister Olivarius, 2020a). This may include suspending a staff member during an investigation, as well as asking any other students/staff in the department who have been affected to come forward (without naming the staff member) as outlined in The 1752 Group, & McAllister Olivarius (2020b). They can also implement no-contact agreements (during an investigation) or orders (after an upheld complaint) that prioritise the complainant's access to their teaching and learning spaces. In addition, disciplinary panels should consider safeguarding actions as well as disciplinary sanctions after an upheld complaint.

A second area in which HE institutions need to improve their practice is around 'remedy'. Remedy can be defined in the UK HE context, for students, as follows:

> An apology, an explanation of any actions the provider has taken as a result of learning from the complaint, or an academic or financial remedy, depending on the nature of the concern, the impact on the student, and what the student is seeking.
>
> (Office of the Independent Adjudicator for Higher Education, 2018)

Out of 15 student complainants interviewed in 2018 for Bull and Rye (2018), only 4 managed to obtain any form of remedy after making a complaint. For the other complainants, either the institution took no action or inadequate, informal action only on their complaint or disclosure; or the complainant was a witness or third party to a complaint (even if they had been subject to misconduct themselves) and so they did not receive any remedy or information about the outcome; or they were unable to finish the internal complaints process within their institution because it was too convoluted, lengthy, and traumatising. For those who did obtain remedy, as described in Bull and Page (2021b):

> None of [them] thought that the remedy they had obtained succeeded in 'putting things right'.. . . The remedies obtained, in being primarily financial, were in keeping with a private or consumerist model of complaints, and did not safeguard complainants or others from further harm from the staff member, nor address the harms they had suffered during the complaints process.

Remedy is therefore linked in with safeguarding; for many complainants, safeguarding other students/staff was the remedy they were looking for. However, not only was it very difficult for complainants to obtain remedy, but also to obtain information about what had happened during their complaint was very difficult. As already noted, at the end of Gemma's complaint:

> *All I received was this email saying, 'Appropriate disciplinary action will be taken'. So that's the end of that.. . . The head of department could have just sat down with [the lecturer] with a coffee and been like, 'Mate, don't do that again. Don't be an idiot,'. . . I could have spent 10 months of my life stressed to high heaven about this bloody procedure and this stupid man, and it's literally done nothing.*

This is in line with some current interpretations of data protection legislation in some UK universities. However, as the Equality and Human Rights Commission have outlined, it is possible to provide information on disciplinary sanctions to the complainant as long as policies and employment contracts state that this information might be shared (2020, section 5.66–5.68). Other institutions go further; UN Women (2018, p. 5) argue that in order to create a 'new normal' around sexual harassment across society, 'prompt, appropriate, and *publicly disseminated* sanctions against perpetrators, regardless of their status or seniority' are needed (my emphasis). Ongoing discussions on how to balance the Equality Act, Human Rights Act and GDPR are discussed in Chapter 10. Here, it can be seen that failure to provide complainants with any information at the end of a complaint has the effect of alienating them and causing them to lose trust in the institution. Indeed, Gemma felt that it was hypocritical that the leader of her university was talking about 'zero tolerance' for sexual harassment at a time when she was having an awful time in the complaints process, and there were no visible sanctions for the perpetrator.

Unusually, Gemma did indeed receive some remedy at the end of her complaint, in the form of a fees refund for her first year. For her, however, this did not go very far at all towards 'putting things right' by returning the student 'to the position they were in before the circumstances of the complaint', as the Office of the Independent Adjudicator for Higher Education describe it (2019,

p. 4). She lost the chance to study the subject she was passionate about, and she lost trust in male lecturers, and indeed in the institution itself.

Conclusion

I asked Gemma if there was anything her university did well in handling her report. Her response was clear:

Gemma: *The Students' Union were helpful, they were good, but they're not affiliated with the uni. I mean, my harassment advisor that I had, she was really nice and she was helpful, and she did help me, but as an employee of the university [she] was very much, 'They've tried their best'. I mean, she is angry about it as well, I'm sure, but when I was expressing real anger about not finding out what had happened, she was just like [. . .] 'That's just how it is, you're just going to have to accept it'. And I'm, 'I don't want to accept it, that's not the point. I'm angry about it'. I say to people I'm going to die bitter. I'm so fed up.*

Anna: So you're still angry?

Gemma: *Yes, yes. I don't think they did anything right.*

Ultimately, Gemma's anger was due to the lack of accountability by the staff member for his actions, and the extremely stressful complaints process she had had to go through, to obtain no adequate outcome. Her experience points to sector-wide issues in the ways in how HEIs respond to staff sexual misconduct. It suggests – as is confirmed by our findings in Power in the Academy (2018) – that there are still parts of Higher Education where sexual harassment by students from staff is normalised, and that students may be aware of such issues when the institution is not. It suggests that the standard process followed by institutions is not a 'fair' one as required from the Office for Students' (2021), as there is a lack of parity between complainant and responding party. It shows that HR departments urgently need training in dealing with sexual harassment and violence. It points to ongoing questions around what safeguarding and risk assessments should look like in Higher Education, to ensure that not only the reporting party is protected but also other students/staff who may be targeted. And it suggests that current interpretations of 'remedy' for sexual harassment complaints fail to live up to OIA guidance of 'putting things right' and fail to take into account the many and varied impacts of sexual harassment for those who are subjected to it.

In a post-#MeToo world, the extent of the shift that is required for institutions to play their part in tackling sexual and gender-based violence is perhaps only now becoming clear. It requires a seismic shift – even a historic shift – that parallels some of the changes made to tackle violence against women by second-wave feminists in the 1970s and 1980s. Society has finally woken up to the fact that sexual and gender-based violence are endemic, and that it is not only the criminal justice system that has to deal with this issue, but *all* institutions in society – from education institutions to workplaces to community groups. This is a huge task. In HE, such a shift requires universities to *prioritise* tackling sexual and gender-based violence. It also requires a level of care for students and staff that is not incentivised in a marketised system; in the UK, market incentives form part of a wider regulatory system for HE (McCaig, 2018, p. 18), but at the time of writing there existed no statutory requirements for addressing sexual misconduct, and even if these were introduced, it seems likely that the imperative to maximise student numbers would still take priority. Nevertheless, if HEIs were to take this seriously, they would need to engage with specialist sexual and gender-based violence organisations such as Rape Crisis in order to implement survivor-centred approaches to tackling this issue (Bull et al., 2019). More broadly, at a government level, tackling this issue requires specific, careful regulation, for example, around requirements for data collection and publication, and it requires courage and ingenuity from non-governmental organisations that work in related areas such as data protection or complaints adjudication. And from all of us, it requires no longer being complicit with everyday words and actions that minimise or normalise sexual and gender-based violence and harassment, but instead stepping up to challenge these.

Summary

Sexual misconduct perpetrated by academic staff has only recently been formulated as a policy problem at national level in the UK, despite evidence that this issue affects tens of thousands of students, particularly women, LGBTQ+ students, and postgraduate students. Staff sexual misconduct can take a variety of forms: sexual or gender harassment such as sexualised comments or interactions, and/or sexual assault or rape. These behaviours may occur alongside bullying or within an intimate partner relationship. The chapter also introduces the terms 'boundary-blurring behaviours' – those that transgress (often tacit) professional boundaries – and 'grooming': a pattern of these behaviours over time between people in positions of unequal power that may lead to an abuse of power. It can be difficult for those targeted to recognise sexual harassment and grooming while it is occurring, in part due to a lack of clear professional boundaries between staff and students in Higher Education.

This chapter introduces the case study of Gemma, a student who was subjected to sexual harassment in the first year of her degree course from a lecturer and subsequently dropped out of university, and going through a formal complaints process at her university. For Gemma, the impact of sexual harassment was to drop out of university, and then when she eventually returned, to be unable to study the subject that she loved. Sexual misconduct can therefore have both academic and non-academic impacts. These impacts can include day-to-day problems such as being unable to access spaces on campus, or life-changing outcomes such as losing a career, as well as physical impacts such as

PTSD. Most people do not report sexual misconduct and rely on family and friends for support; however, for those who do report, they tend to do so in order to protect themselves from further harm, to protect other students or staff from being targeted by the same perpetrator, or to be able to continue their studies/career. Unfortunately, current practice for handling sexual misconduct complaints in UK HE institutions fails to offer a fair process, as the complainant is relegated to the status of 'witness' in disciplinary proceedings taken by the institution against the perpetrator. This means the complainant has fewer rights in the process than the perpetrator, which compounds other difficulties of going through a complaints process.

Besides addressing this discrimination in the complaints process, the chapter highlights safeguarding issues in relation to staff sexual misconduct, arguing that when institutions receive a report or disclosure of staff sexual misconduct, they should therefore assume that other students have been or will be targeted, and should implement safeguarding actions accordingly. This is also linked with another area that institutions need to improve in: remedy, that is, putting things right for complainants. For some complainants, safeguarding other students/staff was the remedy they were looking for. However this remedy – and any sense of justice or accountability – is difficult to obtain when no information is given to complainants at the end of their complaint. There are therefore urgent sector-wide issues to address in order to move towards justice for staff sexual misconduct complainants.

Further Reading

Bull, A., & Page, T. (2021). Students' accounts of grooming and boundary-blurring behaviours by academic staff in UK higher education. *Gender and Education,* **1–16. https://doi.org/10.1080/09540253.2021.1884199**

This article introduces and defines the terms 'grooming' and 'boundary-blurring' behaviours in HE. It draws on interviews with 15 students and one early career academic in UK Higher Education who had reported or attempted to report sexual harassment/violence from a member of academic staff to their university or the police. Interviews were carried out in early 2018. The article defines **boundary-blurring**: behaviours as behaviours that 'transgress (often tacit) professional boundaries' and **grooming** as 'a pattern of these behaviours over time between people in positions of unequal power that may lead to an abuse of power'. In UK law, 'grooming' as a criminal offence can only occur between an adult and a child. However, some interviewees used the term 'grooming' to describe their experiences and therefore the authors argue that this term is helpful to understand how power relations work in higher education.

One student who used the term 'grooming' to describe her experiences was 'Andrea' (all names have been changed). In her words:

> *From an outsider['s perspective], I was saying 'yes' to doing certain things with him, which, for all intents and purposes, would have counted as consent, but what you don't see is the internal conflict and the invisible power structure where he could make me say 'yes'. [. . .] He knew the right thing to ask and how to ask it in the right way in which it was pretty much impossible. . . I felt it was impossible for me to say 'no'.*
>
> – Andrea, Master's student

The article analyses the power imbalances interviewees described that created the context for these behaviours. These were constituted by social inequalities including gender, class, and age, as well as stemming from students' position within their institutions. The article also explores how heterosexualised normativity allows such behaviours to be minimised and invisibilised.

The 1752 Group, & McAllister Olivarius. (2020). *Sector guidance to address staff sexual misconduct in UK higher education: Recommendations for reporting, investigation and decision-making procedures relating to student complaints of staff sexual misconduct.* **https://1752group. files.wordpress.com/2020/03/the-1752-group-and-mcallister-olivarius-sector-guidance-to-address-staff-sexual-misconduct-in-uk-he-1.pdf**

One of the key actions that needs to be taken in order to encourage students to report sexual misconduct is to make the reporting and complaints process more manageable and fairer to all parties. It is to this end that we have written 'Sector Guidance to Address Staff Sexual Misconduct in UK Higher Education'. The central problem that the guidance seeks to address is that existing student complaints and staff disciplinary procedures are separate processes which fail to offer similar protections and privileges to the student complainant and the responding staff member and, as a result, students are often excluded from the process purporting to resolve their complaint. We suggest that this exclusion arises because current disciplinary processes are modelled on the criminal justice system. In order to address this issue, we suggest that changes could be made to staff disciplinary processes to follow a process more akin to civil justice, thus ensuring that the process accords equal rights to complainants and respondents. This will allow HEIs to move towards a fairer process that is not open to legal challenges under the Equality Act.

We have suggested that HEIs modify their existing disciplinary processes to provide similar protections and privileges in the process to the complainant and the responding staff member. The two key principles that the guidance puts forward are:

1　Where staff disciplinary procedures are used to address student complaints, HEIs must modify these to ensure a fair process for student complainants
2　Student complainants and responding staff members must be accorded equal rights in the complaints process

What this means in practice is that the complaints process must provide both the student complainant and responding staff member equal access to evidence (including relevant sections of the investigation report), equal opportunity to put their case (including submission of evidence and attendance in person or via video link at any formal hearings), equal opportunity to challenge the evidence of the other, and to request an appeal or review, which should have full autonomy to strengthen or overturn previous findings. This is what OIA requires of HEIs handling student complaints of student sexual misconduct (OIA, 2018, p. 24) and there is no legitimate reason for HEIs to treat complaints of staff sexual misconduct differently, especially as they are more often liable for the unlawful actions of their staff. In addition, if the HEI decides to resolve the complaint by way of a settlement, this must be agreed by all parties rather than being solely between the institution and the staff member.

Notes

1　In the United States, the term 'faculty' is used to refer to academic staff, and 'staff' refers to those in administrative or professional services roles. Here, we use the term 'staff' to reflect the UK context.
2　All names have been changed.

References

Arday, J., & Mirza, H. S. (Eds.). (2018). *Dismantling race in higher education: Racism, whiteness and decolonising the academy*. Palgrave Macmillan.

Australian Human Rights Commission. (2017). *Change the course: National report on sexual assault and sexual harassment at Australian universities*. Australian Human Rights Commission. www.humanrights.gov.au/our-work/sex-discrimination/publications/change-course-national-report-sexual-assault-and-sexual

Bongiorno, R., Langbroek, C., Bain, P. G., Ting, M., & Ryan, M. K. (2019). Why women are blamed for being sexually harassed: The effects of empathy for female victims and male perpetrators. *Psychology of Women Quarterly*. https://doi.org/10.1177/0361684319868730

Bhopal, K. (2015). *The experiences of black and minority ethnic academics: A comparative study of the unequal academy*. Routledge.

Bull, A. (Forthcoming). Catalysts and rationales for reporting staff sexual misconduct to UK higher education institutions. *Journal of Gender-Based Violence*.

Bull, A., Calvert-Lee, G., & Page, T. (2020). Discrimination in the complaints process: Introducing the sector guidance to address staff sexual misconduct in UK higher education. *Perspectives: Policy and Practice in Higher Education*, 1–6. https://doi.org/10.1080/13603108.2020.1823512

Bull, A., & Page, T. (2021a). Students' accounts of grooming and boundary-blurring behaviours by academic staff in UK higher education. *Gender and Education*, 1–16. https://doi.org/10.1080/09540253.2021.1884199

Bull, A., & Page, T. (2021b). The governance of complaints in UK higher education: Critically examining 'remedies' for staff sexual misconduct. *Social & Legal Studies*, 09646639211002243. https://doi.org/10.1177/09646639211002243

Bull, A., Page, T., & Bullough, J. (2019). What would a survivor-centred higher education sector look like? In S. Gamsu (Ed.), *A new vision for further and higher education* (pp. 73–82). Centre for Labour and Social Studies. http://classonline.org.uk/docs/A_New_Vision_For_Further_and_Higher_Education_220519_1647_forwebv1.pdf

Bull, A., & Rye, R. (2018). *Silencing students: Institutional responses to staff sexual misconduct in higher education*. The 1752 Group/University of Portsmouth. https://1752group.files.wordpress.com/2018/09/silencing-students_the-1752-group.pdf

Cantor, D., Fisher, B., Chibnall, S., Townsend, R., Lee, H., Bruce, C., & Thomas, G. (2015). *Report on the AAU campus climate survey on sexual assault and sexual misconduct*. Association of American Universities. www.aau.edu/uploadedFiles/AAU_Publications/AAU_Reports/Sexual_Assault_Campus_Survey/AAU_Campus_Climate_Survey_12_14_15.pdf

Clancy, K. B. H., Lee, K. M. N., Rodgers, E. M., & Richey, C. (2017). Double jeopardy in astronomy and planetary science: Women of color face greater risks of gendered and racial harassment. *Journal of Geophysical Research: Planets*, *122*(7), 1610–1623. https://doi.org/10.1002/2017JE005256Equality and Human Rights Commission. (2020). *Sexual harassment and harassment at work: technical guidance*. Equality and Human Rights Commission.

Higher Education Statistics Agency. (2018). *Who's studying in HE?* www.hesa.ac.uk/data-and-analysis/students/whos-in-he

Jackson, C., & Sundaram, V. (2020). *Lad culture in higher education: Sexism, sexual harassment and violence*. Routledge.

Kalof, L., Eby, K. K., Mathieson, J. L., & Kroska, R. J. (2001). The influence of race and gender on student self-reports of sexual harassment by college professors. *Gender & Society*, *15*(2), 282–302. https://doi.org/10.1177/089124301015002007

Kelly, L. (2016, March 1). The conducive context of violence against women and girls. *Discover Society*, *30*. https://discoversociety.org/2016/03/01/theorising-violence-against-women-and-girls/

Lorenz, K., Kirkner, A., & Mazar, L. (2019). Graduate student experiences with sexual harassment and academic and social (Dis)engagement in higher education. *Journal of Women and Gender in Higher Education*, *12*(2), 205–223. https://doi.org/10.1080/19407882.2018.1540994

McCaig, C. (2018). *The marketisation of English higher education*. Emerald Publishing Limited.

National Academies of Sciences. (2018). Sexual harassment of women: Climate, culture, and consequences in academic sciences, engineering, and medicine. *The National Academies of Sciences, Engineering, and Medicine*. https://doi.org/10.17226/24994

National Union of Students. (2018, April 4). *Power in the academy: Staff sexual misconduct in UK higher education*. www.nusconnect.org.uk/resources/nus-staff-student-sexual-misconduct-report

Office of the Independent Adjudicator for Higher Education. (2018). *The good practice framework: Handling student complaints and academic appeals*. www.oiahe.org.uk/media/1859/oia-good-practice-framework.pdf

Office of the Independent Adjudicator for Higher Education. (2019). *Putting things right*. www.oiahe.org.uk/media/2275/putting-things-right-february-2019.pdf

Office for Students. (2021). *Statement of expectations*. www.officeforstudents.org.uk/advice-and-guidance/student-wellbeing-and-protection/prevent-and-address-harassment-and-sexual-misconduct/statement-of-expectations/

Phipps, A., & Young, I. (2014). Neoliberalisation and 'lad cultures' in higher education. *Sociology*. https://doi.org/10.1177/0038038514542120

Reay, D., Crozier, G., & Clayton, J. (2010). 'Fitting in' or 'standing out': Working-class students in UK higher education. *British Educational Research Journal*, *36*(1), 107–124. https://doi.org/10.1080/01411920902878925

Rosenthal, M. N., Smidt, A. M., & Freyd, J. J. (2016). Still second class: Sexual harassment of graduate students. *Psychology of Women Quarterly*, *40*(3), 364–377. https://doi.org/10.1177/0361684316644838

The 1752 Group, & McAllister Olivarius. (2020a). *Briefing no. 1: In cases of suspected sexual misconduct can a university pro-actively investigate and speak to potential witnesses in the absence of any formal complaint or complainant?* https://1752group.files.wordpress.com/2020/03/the-1752-group-and-mcallister-olivarius_briefing-note-1.pdf

The 1752 Group, & McAllister Olivarius. (2020b). *Sector guidance to address staff sexual misconduct in UK higher education: Recommendations for reporting, investigation and decision-making procedures relating to student complaints of staff sexual misconduct*. https://1752group.files.wordpress.com/2020/03/the-1752-group-and-mcallister-olivarius-sector-guidance-to-address-staff-sexual-misconduct-in-uk-he-1.pdf

UN Women. (2018). *Towards an end to sexual harassment: The nature of change in the era of #MeToo*. United Nations. www.unwomen.org/-/media/headquarters/attachments/sections/library/publications/2018/towards-an-end-to-sexual-harassment-en.pdf?la=en&vs=4236

Universities UK. (2016). Changing the culture: Report of the Universities UK Taskforce examining violence against women, harassment and hate crime affecting university students.

Universities UK. (2019). *Changing the culture – tackling gender-based violence, harassment and hate crime: Two years on* (p. 92). www.universitiesuk.ac.uk/policy-and-analysis/reports/Pages/changing-the-culture-two-years-on.aspx

University College London. (2020). *Prevention of bullying, harassment and sexual misconduct policy*. www.ucl.ac.uk/equality-diversity-inclusion/dignity-ucl/prevention-bullying-harassment-and-sexual-misconduct-policy

12 Case management as a dedicated role responding to gender-based violence in Higher Education

Kelly Prince and Peta Franklin-Corben

Since the change in direction in the role and responsibility of Higher Education Institutes (HEIs) in the UK in preventing and responding to Sexual Misconduct and Violence (SMV) in university communities,[1] there has been a welcome increase in attention on the issue, leading to some (though not enough) sector guidance (see OfS, 2020), as well as academic analysis. In line with the updated Scottish strategy *Equally Safe: Scotland's Strategy to Eradicate Violence against Women* (Scottish Government et al., 2018), informed by work done by the United Nations,[2] in 2019 Universities UK[3] moved to consider gender-based violence (GBV) more broadly. However, little has been written on the role of case management in HEI responses to GBV, including SMV. In this chapter, we seek to address this paucity, and demonstrate the benefits of in-house specialist case managers in coordinating university responses to GBV on campus.

A number of sector stakeholders have recognised the need for case management in relation to SMV and harassment more broadly. In 2018, Universities UK (UUK) wrote that 'As an effective response to a case is likely to involve many functions within and across the institution' there is a need for 'a case management system which will support the whole process end to end' (UUK, 2018, p. 2). Others, such as Humphreys and Towl (2020, p. 59), have recognised the central importance of a case manager role in university responses to SMV, while the Office for Students (OfS) has published a report from Coventry University on case management of harassment reports which states that the case manager will

> act as the first point of contact for reporters and would signpost and manage the process as reporters went to other departments/external sources of support. As such, the case manager role was to ensure all reports were responded to and dealt with in a timely manner and that reporters were supported in whatever action they wish to take.
>
> (Osmond, 2019, p. 7)

Nonetheless, detail is limited as to the role of a case manager, how it can be defined, developed, and implemented, as well as the strategic and operational value. In light of this, we seek to address those key aspects in this chapter. After

DOI: 10.4324/9781003252474-14

considering the definition of case management, we divide the chapter into two sections exploring the '*why*' and the '*how*'. We aim to offer both a rationale for including this specialist role and a detailed description of the vital contribution a case manager can make in this field.

What is case management?

The phrase 'case management' has been defined and deployed in a variety of ways by different sectors. In the context of responses to GBV, the definition can be seen to draw on a long history within social and healthcare provision:

> Case management is an approach that originated in the social service and healthcare disciplines in the United States over a century ago. It evolved from the recognition that people seeking health and mental health care often have a range of other social service needs, and that a function was needed to coordinate these often-fragmented services. Thus, the 'case management' function became a specialized role within health and social services, providing information and coordination of care and services to individuals and families, while advocating for the quality of care and services.
>
> (UNICEF et al., 2017, p. 8, notes at point 8)

The core functions of case management in the context of GBV emerge then as follows:

1   The provision of information on health and support options, as well as other services;
2   Coordinating access to and engagement with multiple services;
3   Advocacy, which we define as informing and upskilling relevant stakeholders on the science of GBV and trauma-informed practice, with the aim of improving the quality of responses.

To further understand the role of the case manager in HE responses, consider the case study in Example 1.

Case Study   Example 1

Carmen, a second year student, is seeking help from Student Services because she is struggling to keep up with her studies. In the course of the meeting, Carmen discloses she was subjected to SMV two months earlier. She reports that she lives in the same accommodation block as the perpetrator and studies the same subject. As a result, Carmen has been finding it difficult to leave her room. Carmen has missed two assessment deadlines and has had multiple warnings for non-attendance; she is worried about getting through her exams as they will be in the same room as the perpetrator. She has thought about making a report to the police and university but is scared the perpetrator will retaliate violently.

What started as a meeting about study support has now become much more complex and sensitive; at this point, colleagues can refer the case to the SMV case manager. It is likely to benefit from input from multiple staff from both inside and outside of the university, including a risk assessment panel, student accommodation team, the student's academic department, the records and exams team, counselling and mental health team, a Sexual Assault Referral Centre (SARC), the local Rape Crisis service, and the student's General Practitioner. Carmen will need clear information about why the departments and organisations listed above might be relevant and how they could potentially help, so she can make an informed choice about whether or not to use such services. Clear and knowledgeable guidance on reporting options is also required, highlighting the advantages and limits of both reporting to the police and reporting to the university, so that Carmen can make a truly informed decision about what she wants to happen next.

Without a case manager with relevant expertise on options both internal and external to the university, the student may have to navigate each of these departments and services on their own, having to disclose the SMV time and time again to those who may have a limited understanding. This is likely to negatively impact both their health and their ability to continue with their studies.

Within UK HEI responses to SMV, it is also possible to see the influence of the Independent Sexual Violence Advisor (ISVA) role on the development of the case management function. According to the Home Office, an ISVA will

- tailor support to the individual needs of the victim or survivor
- provide accurate and impartial information to victims and survivors of sexual violence
- provide emotional and practical support to meet the needs of the victim or survivor
- provide support before, during and after court
- act as a single point of contact
- ensure the safety of victims and survivors and their dependants
- provide a professional service.

(Home Office, 2017, p. 1)

Alongside the core functions highlighted earlier, from this definition of the ISVA role, it is possible to identify additional and essential functions of the case manager role, including the provision of information before, during and after a complaints and/or disciplinary procedure (court for an ISVA), and working to ensure the safety of victim-survivors through providing expertise on risk identification and mitigation strategies to relevant decision-makers. Similarly, HEIs can look to the role of the Independent Domestic Violence Advocate (IDVA) to inform case management responses to GBV more broadly.[4]

Some HEIs use Sexual Abuse and Harassment Advisors (SAHAs) or Sexual Violence Liaison Officers (SVLOs) to provide specialist guidance to victim-survivors, coordinating their access to multiple services within and outside of the university, advising on reporting options, and facilitating academic adjustments. They sometimes work on GBV education and training packages for staff and students too. Staff involved are usually highly committed and skilled, but often have to do this role on top of their 'day job'. HEIs must ensure this high-risk area of work is fully resourced, enabling staff to access regular and external supervision, Continuing Professional Development opportunities, as well as workload adjustments to accommodate the complex and highly sensitive nature of this work. Even in a structure which includes SAHAs or SVLOs, we argue a case manager role with oversight of all disclosures and reports of GBV is still required; we go on to highlight the risk attached to structures which exclude the following case management.

In our example, case managers also play a crucial role in the coordination and management of investigations, acting as a conduit between the parties and their support providers, and the investigator. In addition, they may input into the development of GBV training packages for staff and students to ensure it is informed by casework and current research, though this work should be led by experienced trainers/educators who have the capacity to give it the professional attention required; budget controllers must avoid overloading the case manager role, recognising that highly sensitive work takes more time than might be expected.

The work of a case manager is likely to span the four pillars of a response to GBV in HE: prevention, safeguarding, support, and perpetrator accountability. In this chapter, we focus on the pillars of safeguarding, support, and perpetrator accountability; prevention work is considered in detail in Chapter 14 and therefore a full analysis is beyond the scope of this chapter. However, one example of prevention work which is particularly relevant to the case manager is the collection and analysis of data relating to disclosures and reports. Data analysis can highlight trends or patterns which can then be targeted with additional resources with the aim of preventing or reducing the risk of further violence. Where multiple disclosures emanate from a particular department, club, or society, for example, an environmental investigation may be initiated (see Chapter 14), followed by targeted training. At a strategic level, data can evidence the impact of GBV on the university community, informing governance as to local dynamics and highlighting priorities, thereby ensuring that progress and development is informed and effective.

Threading through both definitions of case management in responses to GBV is the key principle of a person-centred approach; the nature of SMV is such that the victim's power and autonomy is taken away from them and in response, the case manager will need to re-centre the victim-survivor so that they are in control of what happens next, in terms of both their support and reporting options. It will very rarely be appropriate to act against the wishes of the victim-survivor, and even when safeguarding legislation imposes a legal obligation to act with or without consent, the victim-survivor should be at the heart of this conversation and consent should be sought in the first instance wherever circumstances allow. In the overwhelmingly majority of circumstances, the normative practice would be for the victim-survivor to be given both the information and the time they need to make informed decisions about what they want to happen next.

If a victim-survivor decides to make a formal report, either to the university or to the police, a second key principle will be impartiality. The case manager will be responsible for ensuring that both the Reporting *and* Responding Parties are informed, updated, and able to access appropriate support and therapeutic options, as well as academic and non-academic adjustments, during the course of an investigation and associated proceedings. They will also be responsible for risk assessment and for overseeing the investigation process, ensuring it is procedurally robust and free from bias. HEIs have a duty of care to both parties, as well as to any witnesses and the wider university community; it is vital that both/all parties are treated equitably. Humphreys and Towl (2020) maintain that as the case manager will be providing equitable information and guidance to both the Reporting and Responding Party through the investigation, the role needs to be neutral in the process. As such, they should not be responsible for providing direct support to any one party in the process, but rather should coordinate access to support options provided elsewhere. In structures which include SAHAs or SVLOs, we would suggest those colleagues lead at pre-formal report stages, with the case manager taking the lead after a formal report is made to either the university or the police.

Impartiality is critical to providing a fair and robust system for responding to formal reports. It reduces the risk of appeals and complaints, with all the further delay and distress this can cause for the parties involved, as well as the institutional cost and risk incurred. In cases where the case manager has worked closely or for an extended period with the Reporting Party prior to them submitting a formal report, it is strongly recommended that structures allow for two case managers so that any actual or perceivable conflict of interest can be avoided. The potential for this conflict should be managed through boundaried roles where the case manager provides specialist information but the Disclosing Party[5] is then supported by another colleague (a SAHA or SVLO or other welfare support provider) until they are ready to make a decision about reporting. This protects the case manager's independence; however, each case of GBV is different and in some cases, it will be impossible for the case manager to avoid multiple meetings with a Disclosing Party as they work through their decision. This can amount to a conflict of interest and it is unlikely to be appropriate for that case manager to continue with the case through the investigation. A degree of flexibility is necessary to ensure a balance between the needs of the Disclosing Party and the need to ensure impartiality if they choose to make a report.

All staff working in this field must be trauma-informed; this means they must understand the multiple and varying ways in which GBV can impact the victim-survivor, and use that understanding 'to develop practices that minimize further harm, foster healing and honor strength and resiliency' (CCLISAR, 2021, p. 4). Where, for example, a case needs to be passed to a colleague, care should be taken to minimise the number of times a victim-survivor has to disclose by seeking consent to share the details of the case with the new colleague.

To sum up this section, we argue case management in relation to university reports of GBV includes the following core components:

- Following a disclosure:
  - Provide information on support and reporting options;
  - Facilitate access to support, negotiating with relevant teams and service providers;
  - Identify risk and escalate to relevant decision-makers, providing specialist knowledge on risk and appropriate mitigation measures.
- Following a formal report:
  - Ongoing risk identification, providing specialist knowledge to decision-makers;
  - Bridge communication between the investigator and the Reporting, Responding and Witness Parties, keeping parties updated throughout the process;
  - Co-ordinate and support the investigation process;
  - Ensure all parties have access to ongoing support, negotiating with relevant teams and service providers;
  - Liaise with the police where the Reporting Party has chosen to make a report to police.
- Additional responsibilities:
  - Data analysis;
  - Input to the development of training packages.

The *why*?: making the argument for a case management role in HE responses to GBV

In the following section, we argue that a case manager role is both an operational and strategic necessity by highlighting both the value of the role, and the risks posed by a response to GBV which relies exclusively on a support function and/or investigative function. We conclude the section by giving an overview of key skills, experience and knowledge a GBV case manager will require.

Why is a case manager needed?

There is a danger, particularly where resources are limited or even scarce, that budget controllers will focus on support provision and disciplinary responses in relation to GBV, while deeming a case manager role as something which would be 'nice to have' rather than essential. However, as Humphreys and Towl (2020, p. 59) persuasively point out: 'A specialist case manager with relevant expertise around sexual violence and related gender-based violence to coordinate responses to reports made to the institution and/or police *is required*' (emphasis added).

In the absence of a case manager, HEIs may be tempted to allocate additional roles and responsibilities around the GBV agenda to the investigator; this may include, for example, policy development, staff training, or prevention campaigns. Based on our experience, we argue that even in relatively small HEIs, investigating allegations of GBV is a full-time job. By allocating additional roles to the investigator, there is a risk that crucial work around prevention activities or evidence-based policy development, community engagement, or culture change will be inevitably limited as investigators are fully occupied by the volume of work related to multiple concurrent investigations. As Humphreys and Towl (2020, p. 59) point out, 'without proper resourcing, there is a high risk of burnout and failure to deliver a comprehensive institution-wide approach'.

Division of roles

The need to separate support and disciplinary functions is commonly understood and accepted in UK HE. Where these are not separate, each function has the potential to undermine the other, so the support relationship is tainted or undermined by investigatory demands and the investigation is subject to allegations or perceptions of bias if the investigator is also supporting one or both parties. In the absence of the conduit of the case manager, there is a risk that roles and responsibilities related to investigators may inappropriately impact upon the support function and vice versa.

Where, for example, an investigator has to deliver difficult or unwelcome news to either party, there can sometimes be an assumption that involving the student's support provider in that conversation will shield the student to some extent. By offering the option to discuss the news in more detail with the supporter after the investigator has left the meeting, the assumption is this will mitigate the risk of emotional distress or a negative impact on mental health. However, disappointment or frustration with the investigation and associated processes can feel like disappointment and frustration with the university as a whole, or what Freyd (2014) describes as institutional betrayal. This is especially true if support providers are left trying to defend or explain what can be felt as a profound injustice. When students feel their support provider is a part of, rather than separate from, that betrayal, they may very well disengage; the relationship of trust, which can often take months to build, can be damaged or break down completely. This can affect the student's immediate well-being, their recovery process, and their confidence in accessing alternative support provision; the consequences can therefore be profound.

Another example would be where the role of the investigator becomes blurred in the eyes of the Responding Party. There are multiple options in terms of campus support, from student welfare teams, chaplaincy and faith teams, to counselling and mental health provision. However, when Responding Parties are sharing detailed and personal information with an investigator who is required to respond impartially, there is a danger they consider the impartial response as supportive, as 'someone who is on my side'. While every investigator must be alert to welfare risks and cause for concern, their primary function is a robust investigation; it is a fundamental part of their role to question the Responding Party's account, ask them, for example, to explain how they established consent, and challenge any rape myths or victim-blaming explanations. If the investigatory and support functions have become blurred, the Responding Party may feel betrayed, respond defensively, and reconstruct the investigator as someone who is 'biased against me'. If the outcome of the complaints and/or disciplinary procedures go against the Responding Party, claims of investigator bias have the potential to open routes to appeal.

The presence of a case manager significantly reduces the risks highlighted earlier. The case manager can discuss and explain unwelcome news and information in a way which is trauma-informed and alive to the dynamics of gender-based violence, while preserving and protecting the separate support relationship as untainted by the frustrations and difficulties of the investigative process. This leaves the investigator to focus on delivering the investigation, where questioning and challenging (though not confrontation) are understood as prerequisites of a rigorous process, unimpeded by conflicting roles and responsibilities.

A good case manager

Case managers will need to have specialist skills and knowledge to be effective in the role. Whilst procedurally, a case manager will have a typical order of action through an investigation process, no two situations will present the same, and often case managers will find themselves as the central point of contact for complex queries and high-risk cases across the university. Student survivors are likely to disclose to a familiar and trusted member of staff in the first instance, such as a tutor or lecturer. Even when disclosure training is offered to staff across the HEI, the practicalities of taking a disclosure can be daunting and staff will frequently seek guidance from the GBV case manager. A knowledgeable case manager will be able to advise on specialist services that are available and appropriate to the circumstances of the case; it is neither fair nor realistic to expect staff without expertise in GBV to know what would be needed in a non-consensual sexual touching case, as compared with a case involving image-based sexual abuse, stalking, or domestic abuse. Matters are complicated further if a student or staff member is abroad[6] when they are subjected to GBV; a specialist case manager will understand the importance of country-specific responses to GBV, working with the relevant embassy where required. This is time-consuming and difficult work, and again, it is neither fair nor realistic to expect either non-specialist staff or volunteer SVLOs to coordinate an international response.

Case Study   Example 2

Zarah is a third-year student who provides peer-led mentoring in her academic department. She approaches a staff member to report that communication with a student she has been tutoring has become increasingly inappropriate. Zarah reported that a friend encouraged them to seek staff guidance after flowers were left outside of her room with no card or information. Zarah shows the staff member parts of the conversation between the pair, noting that it includes repeat sexual advances towards her. The staff member is unsure of what to do; Zarah is visibly distressed and says she does not feel safe in her own room. The staff member contacts the GBV case manager to evaluate risk and to determine what options are available to the Zarah. Alongside formal reporting options (police and/or the university), the case manager can also connect Zarah with the accommodation team to arrange a temporary change of room if this would help her to feel safer. The case manager can highlight support options and make appropriate referrals.

Where a survivor discloses to their tutor, see Example 2, but does not feel ready to disclose or report to anyone else, the tutor may seek advice around any safeguarding risks that need to be addressed. The tutor may be concerned that the victim-survivor is in immediate danger, or that the information disclosed suggests a risk to the wider university community. The case manager is able to talk through concerns with the tutor, advise on what aspects of the disclosure indicate a need for immediate action, and seek additional input from the HEI's safeguarding lead where necessary, so that a route forward can be agreed. Case managers must have the skillset to understand risk, and coordinate an appropriate and often rapid response with others who may not have experience of trauma-informed practice or knowledge of the science of GBV.

A background in social work, criminology, justice, advocacy, or gender-based violence services will provide a solid base on which to build skills around responding to GBV in a HE setting. A strong understanding of all manifestations of GBV is essential, including a comprehensive knowledge of intersectionality. Rape myths and victim-blaming are pervasive throughout society, and a case manager needs to be able to speak knowledgably and persuasively, to engage and upskill others within and sometimes outside of the institution. Experience managing complex caseloads and work with safeguarding legislation will be vital, while experience of designing impactful training is highly desirable.

It is important to note that while case managers will bring skills with them from previous roles, navigation within a Higher Education setting can be challenging. Each academic department, each student college, each professional services directorate can be seen as an organisation in itself, with its own organisational culture, history, values, and expectations. As such, a case manager covering a whole HEI needs to feel confident providing advice and support across the university, to a variety of people from students to senior staff.

The how?: describing the work of a case manager from disclosure to disciplinary outcome

The following section will outline the practical application of a case management role. We hope to demonstrate how, working alongside but separate to an investigator, a case manager can support a case from first disclosure through to disciplinary outcome.

The university has received a disclosure of sexual violence – the pre-investigation stage

Often substantial work takes place before a victim-survivor can arrive at a point where they feel ready to make a decision about whether or not to report, either to the police or university. This decision is rarely an easy one; victim-survivors must weigh-up multiple factors and do so while often experiencing the impact of trauma, such as difficulty sleeping and eating, flashbacks, depression, and anxiety. In our experience, they often refer to a fear that the perpetrator could target someone else as a key motivation in deciding to report (see also Bull, 2021). Besides ensuring that appropriate and specialist support options are provided during this crucial decision-making time, the case manager will need to sensitively navigate a fine line between providing detailed and accurate information about what each reporting process will entail so that the Disclosing Party is able to make an informed choice, while at the same time neither encouraging nor discouraging either option, or giving the impression they are in favour of one option over the other. In other words, signposting should be non-directive as the Disclosing Party must be free to make their own independent decision in the knowledge they are fully informed as to what each process will entail.

As highlighted earlier, university staff across an institution may find themselves the first point of contact for a student making a disclosure. It is important that all staff are aware that a GBV case manager exists, they know how to contact them, and how to refer a case. Some outreach and engagement activities may be beneficial to ensure widespread awareness and buy-in. The case manager should also be available to the staff member who took the disclosure; it is often too easy to overlook the impact that receiving a disclosure can have on staff, especially if the staff member is also a victim-survivor. The case manager will need to be ready to provide information on self-care as well as longer-term support and therapeutic options.

The case manager may need to meet with a Disclosing Party multiple times while they work through their decision about what happens next. It would be inappropriate for an investigator to act in this capacity. A potential decision-maker in a case should not be involved in the informal stages of an investigation, or have any contact that may raise questions during an investigation about perceived or actual bias. A case manager, as an impartial party, has an opportunity in this space to ensure that a number of questions are being considered prior to any formal investigation beginning:

- Is there any immediate risk to the Disclosing Party, or are there any dependents or vulnerable people involved?
- What risk does the Responding Party pose to the wider University, for example, are they staff or in a position of power or responsibility? Have similar disclosures or reports been made by others that would indicate a pattern of behaviour?
- Has the victim-survivor been informed of their right to access support from time-sensitive services such as the SARC? If the incident was recent, have they been advised about forensic evidence preservation where appropriate?
- Does the Disclosing Party have any medical needs? for example, injuries[7] or sexual health support?
- Do they understand what support options are available to them, at the university, in the local community and online?
- Do they have any academic commitments that may be impacted? Do they have assessment deadlines coming up, for example, or are they on a placement?
- Do they have detailed information on the reporting processes and the option to discuss these, possibly at length and multiple times?

Many of these questions will help to inform the formal stages of the investigation (see risk assessment discussed subsequently) should the student choose this route; however, it also ensures that the institution has a good understanding of the risks being held prior to a decision taking place. This is particularly important as we know that reaching a decision to move forward with a formal report (to the police or otherwise) can take weeks, months, or even years (Hester & Lilley, 2018). For the majority, their decision will be choosing to access support only, and unless there are exceptional circumstances and safeguarding concerns, this decision must be respected and supported, while also being clear that there are options if they change their mind and wish to report in the future.

The university receives a formal report to be investigated under the relevant university policy – the investigation stage

A note on time frames

When a report of GBV is received by a university, the time frame from receiving the report to completing all procedures can be far lengthier than for other types of misconduct, largely due to the ultrasensitive nature of what is being investigated. Investigators are acutely aware of the time factor in their work;

they need to strike a fine balance between a comprehensive investigation which pursues all lines of enquiry on one hand, and completing the process and delivering the report expeditiously so as to avoid any unnecessary delays on the other. There are multiple factors beyond an investigator's control which could lead to a delay; for example, one of the parties may experience a decline in their mental health such that they're unable to attend an interview or respond to evidence. An HEI may pause an investigation during assessment periods, or be limited in the extent to which they can progress the investigation during vacation periods. If a party takes a leave of absence, it may impact their ability to take part in the investigation, or if the Reporting Party makes a report to the police, the university investigation may need to be suspended. In addition, there is an inherent complexity in the sensitivity of GBV cases, particularly those with a sexual element; in terms of police investigations, for example, while it takes on average four days to investigate a theft, it takes on average 66 days to investigate a sexual offence (Home Office, 2020).[8] While the Office for the Independent Adjudicator in HE (2019, pp. 6–8) recommends a timely process that will normally be completed from investigation to appeal in 90 calendar days, they also acknowledge that delays are likely when cases are complex.[9] It is important that the parties have a realistic understanding of time frames and are kept updated as to any unexpected delays.

In recognising that the investigation will take time, most HEIs have accepted the need to address risk while any investigation is ongoing and have implemented a process whereby risk mitigation measures, or non-judgemental precautionary measures, can be put in place. These may also be referred to as interim measures or temporary restrictions, with the primary aim of managing risk to the Reporting Party, the Responding Party, and the wider university community. Once a report is confirmed, a case manager will need to work swiftly to assess risk and advise on any necessary precautionary measures.

Risk mitigation and non-judgemental precautionary measures

Non-judgemental precautionary measures[10] may seek to address a number of factors while an investigation is ongoing, but the function of the measures must focus on risk mitigation and safeguarding following a thorough risk assessment. HEIs will often seek to share access to spaces, enabling both parties (where appropriate) to continue to access their education and student experience by keeping them apart. Commonly used interim measures include a no-contact requirement; limiting the days when the Responding Party can access the library, students' union, or other campus building; alternate week access to shared sports clubs or societies; accommodation changes for the Responding Party; and/or tutorial group changes or other academic adjustments.

In cases where shared access cannot be managed, and one student needs to be asked to disengage from activities or spaces for the duration of the investigation, these should, we would argue, be imposed on the Responding Party unless specifically requested by the Reporting Party. Measures must not be punitive;

at this stage, no finding has been made against the Responding Party, so applying punitive measures would be unfair, undermine due process, and open any
subsequent findings to appeal on the grounds of bias. Responding Parties must
be given a right to reply; this should include the opportunity to communicate
with decision-makers if they think the precautionary measures are unduly onerous. The Responding Party may feel aggrieved that the precautionary measures
have been put in place at all and the case manager is able to reassure them the
measures are non-judgemental, based on a risk assessment for the purpose of
safeguarding, and that this is a standard practice.

Feeling aggrieved that the measures are in place is not the same as the measures being 'unduly onerous' and decision-makers may need to stand firm when
challenged in the knowledge that the appropriate policy has been followed and
they are used to mitigate risk presented in the case. An illustrative example of
an unduly onerous measure will be one where the unintended consequences are
disproportionately negative; if the Responding Party is restricted from accessing
the Students' Union on Mondays, Wednesdays, and Saturdays but they have paid
employment there on Mondays and Saturdays, the decision-makers may want
to change the days on which the restrictions apply to allow the Responding
Party to continue with their employment. Decision-makers must not remove
the restriction entirely, as it has been applied in response to a risk which still
exists, but adaptations where there is a disproportionate impact are appropriate.
Risk assessments and precautionary measures should be reviewed on a regular
basis, but particularly when there is a material change in circumstances (e.g., one
party takes a leave of absence) or if there is a breach of precautionary measures,
in which case decision-makers should be ready to take any additional action
required to manage the risk attached to non-compliance.

In some circumstances, a risk assessment will require the HEI to take the most
impactful action. HEIs will have different thresholds for this, but *at a minimum*,
we argue a temporary suspension of the Responding Party from part of, or
the whole of, campus and/or studies should be considered in the following
circumstances, though note this is not an exhaustive list:

- When multiple reports of SMV are received about the same student or staff
  member;
- When the police charge a student with a sexual offence, or an offence connected to domestic violence or stalking;
- Where physical violence is an aggravating factor (including strangulation/
  choking, use of weapons, or repeated abuse);
- Where there are two or more breaches of the precautionary measures
  and an escalation in measures has been ineffective in preventing further
  breaches.

Given the seriousness of the risk assessment process, decisions are often made by
a small panel (with at least three members) of senior staff based in student services and student conduct teams. They will often require executive agreement

for temporary exclusions from studies or campus. Good practice requires that those deciding the risk-based measures are not involved in decision-making regarding the investigation of the report, the findings, or sanctioning.

The case manager's role in the risk assessment process is to first meet with the Reporting Party following a formal report to determine the current risk based on the Reporting Party's account. The case manager must gather enough information to fully assess risk while not asking for so much detail that it becomes investigatory. The case manager will need expertise on the topic of risk as it relates to GBV; victim-survivors are often well-placed to assess the risk they are subjected to. However, they may not be familiar with the disciplines of a systematic approach to the assessment and management of risk in relation to GBV, or they may minimise the risk because of what they have been through and their relationship with the Responding Party. In a case involving domestic abuse, for example, a Reporting Party may have spent a long time justifying the actions of the Responding Party to friends and family, such that it becomes difficult to assess the level of threat posed. They may not be aware that the risk posed by a perpetrator increases when the victim attempts to end the relationship, or that the start or escalation of stalking behaviours also represents a serious increase in risk. It is therefore crucial that the case manager is able to identify those red flags in a Reporting Party's narrative.

The case manager may seek information from a variety of sources to help with the risk assessment, including the parties' colleges or academic departments, welfare or mental health support providers, or the police, where relevant. They will also need to ascertain if the Responding Party is in a position of trust or authority, including whether they are studying on a course which brings them into contact with the general public, especially if they are working with vulnerable people including children. A case manager is responsible for bringing these elements together to determine if a case presents as low, moderate, or high risk. The case manager will then bring this information to the decision-makers; it is not the role of the case manager to be part of the final decision-making on precautionary measures, but they should be available to answer any questions from the panel so that decision-making is robust and informed, and agreed measures are fair, proportionate, and effective.

As part of the internal risk assessment, the case manager is also responsible for determining if any case presented to the HEI meets the threshold for any external referrals. If a student reports that the incident involved a weapon, for example, or that the Responding Party has previously threatened to hurt themselves or others, this may indicate the need for a referral to MARAC.[11]

The mental health and well-being of the parties is a central concern for the risk assessment; where, for example, a student is known to have self-harmed in the past, they are likely to require intensive and coordinated support from multiple providers throughout the investigation, but especially in the early stages. Similarly, if an HEI knows that either party has a diagnosed learning difficulty, the student may need to be informed of and supported through the investigation process in a way which accommodates their needs. The risk here is ensuring that all parties understand the process and are able to engage in the investigation in an equitable and meaningful way.

Once risk mitigation measures are agreed, it is the case manager's responsibility to coordinate any actions that need to take place in order to put the measures in place. This may include arranging an urgent accommodation move, liaising with academic departments (especially where fitness to practice is an issue), and informing relevant stakeholders (such as university security coordinators) on a need-to-know basis which is compliant with policies on confidentiality and data protection.

Handover and investigation

A full consideration of the investigation process is provided in Chapter 13; however, here we highlight the factors which will impact the case manager's role.

After the risk mitigation measures have been agreed, there are a number of actions which need to be completed before the investigation can begin in full. These should be done promptly to make sure risks are mitigated as soon as possible, and to avoid any unnecessary delays between the Reporting Party confirming their report and their first meeting with the investigator. These actions will include the following:

- **Meeting with the allocated investigators**: The case manager can provide an overview of the case and share any evidence which has already been submitted. Any disability or health needs and relevant risk factors should also be discussed to assist in planning the investigation. The meeting also allows for the investigator and case manager to agree next steps; the investigator will decide which parties will be interviewed and when, and the case manager will coordinate those meetings.[12]
- **Notifying the Responding Party**: The Responding Party will need to be informed of the report that has been made against them and any non-judgemental precautionary measures which they will be expected to follow. The policy and procedure and next steps should be explained and the meeting should include the staff member allocated to support the Responding Party to ensure their welfare is centred and they are supported when receiving this information.
- **Communication with the Reporting Party**: The case manager will also need to update the Reporting Party, providing them with information on the non-judgemental precautionary measures and the investigation timeline.

The case manager's role during the investigation

When a case is allocated to an investigator, a case manager's role during the investigation can be categorised into three key responsibilities: (1) providing regular updates to the parties, responding to their needs, and managing any potential impact on the investigation; (2) identifying any changes in the risk profile of the case, including any breaches of the risk mitigation measures, and updating the risk assessment panel accordingly; (3) ensuring that the investigation is progressing in line with the HEI's policy and procedure and that the evidence submitted is relevant, appropriate, and compliant with data protection regulations. Practically, much of this comes in the form of regular communication with the investigators, the Reporting and Responding Parties, and their key support persons.

Communication with the investigator: The case manager should be in regular contact with the investigator, to receive and provide updates on progress and support the investigation into each new phase. We would recommend that fortnightly updates are provided to the Reporting and Responding Parties, as well as the staff allocated to supporting them.[13] Consequently, updates between the investigator and case manager should occur fortnightly too. Typically, this discussion will include instruction from the investigator on what submissions (statements or other evidence) should be shared and with whom, any outstanding questions they have for any party, and updated timelines on the next stage of the investigation. We would also recommend that the investigator updates the case manager following any formal meeting with a Reporting or Responding Party or witnesses to ensure they remain fully informed of developments in the case.

Communication with the Reporting and Responding Parties: The case manager acts as a conduit between the key parties and the investigator. Predominantly, this is to ensure that the parties benefit from a barrier between their questions and concerns on one side and their formal submissions to the investigation on the other. There are often scenarios where a student may be unsure about what information is appropriate for submission to an investigation; being able to discuss this with a case manager can act as a reminder about who will have access to the information, while protecting the investigation from information which could be seen as prejudicial. Where a Responding Party submits a statement which includes sensitive information about a medical condition, for example, the case manager might email them to confirm that they are happy for both the investigator and Reporting Party to access this before it is submitted formally. A case manager will also redact confidential information, such as contact details or third-party information contained in statements.

In all their communication with the Reporting and Responding Parties, the case manager will be alert to any indicators that the risk profile has changed so that this can be managed effectively by the appropriate decision-makers. Alongside any breaches of the risk mitigation measures, other indicators that should be raised with the risk assessment panel include, but are not limited to, a decline in the mental health and well-being of either party, any acts of retaliation, and any additional reports of GBV in relation to the Responding Party. The case manager will need to raise these with the risk assessment panel so that they can assess whether current measures need adapting or additional measures put in place.

Communication with other parties: The case manager will make contact with other key parties in an investigation. Commonly, this would include contacting witnesses to request a statement, or to gain consent for any third-party submission to be used (screenshots of private conversations, for example). Where a witness submits a statement including details about what they have been told about the Responding Party by a third party, the witness will be asked to delete any hearsay before it is formally submitted, to protect the investigation against any perceptions of bias which could prejudice the case and open routes to appeal.

The case manager may also need to liaise with the staff supporting the Reporting and Responding Parties, their departments, counselling, student well-being teams, and any external services as appropriate. They will feedback any relevant information to the investigator, such as any change in circumstances which might affect either party's ability to continue taking part in the case.

Investigation outcome and disciplinary

Following the investigation conclusion, it is the role of the case manager to communicate the outcome with the parties and discuss with them any final stages. For findings of misconduct against a university's policy, this may be either discussing with them the sanctions that have been imposed or outlining the next stages of the disciplinary process, depending on the procedure of the HEI. All discussions will include information on the appeal and/or review process, and any ongoing support that the university can offer.

Additional functions and final considerations

In this chapter, we have focused on the role of the case manager in relation to student disclosures of GBV, student reports to the university, as well as the resulting risk assessment and investigation under relevant complaints and/or disciplinary policies. In this section, we signpost other functions which may sit within the remit of a case manager.

When a student chooses to report to the police

Much of the initial stage work can be applied to cases in which the Reporting Party chooses a formal report to the police. Regardless of the path chosen by the Reporting Party, a case manager will support at the front end – providing information, advice, and coordinating university responses, including risk assessment. At times, cases can come via the police to the university when they are seeking information on named parties. On those occasions, case managers may be making contact with a Reporting Party who has not yet had any support offered by the university.

Links with the university community

In addition to advising on staff and student training,[14] the case manager will need to build relationships and develop a visible presence across the university so that staff and students know where they can seek specialist advice and support on GBV.

HR and staff investigations

In cases where either the Reporting or Responding Party is a member of staff, a case manager may be called on to offer advice and support an HR investigation. However, it should be stressed that investigations into staff misconduct should be conducted by individuals with the appropriate level of seniority, relevant expertise in trauma, and aspects of GBV which include 'grooming' and abuses of power, as well as knowledge of employment law. Crucially, this work needs to be properly resourced.

Institutional responsibilities

The ultrasensitive nature of work in this area cannot be understated. While we have welcomed cross-sector guidance, getting the detail right is important; from large-scale questions around how data rights can be balanced against safeguarding duties, human rights, and rights under the Equality Act to multiple specific questions around what evidence should and should not be included in a disciplinary process, many complex questions about how best to deliver HE responses in this field remain unanswered.

Staff working in this area understand that their work can be profoundly impactful, even life-changing for some, and they must carry the weight of this work in the context of a policy landscape that is far from settled, where practice varies considerably across the UK. It is vital that HEIs recognise their duty of care to staff working in this field; the impact of vicarious trauma or burnout can be significant for staff, those closest to them, the HEI, and the university community. Investing adequately will support conditions where more substantial costs may be avoided later down the line. Adequate investment means staff have time to ensure their service is fully informed and compliant with latest guidance, while inadequate investment means staff have little time for anything other than daily crises management. Resourcing which recognises these dynamics can also protect the HEI against appeals and complaints that carry institutional costs in terms of staff time, financial compensation, and reputational risk, the latter being particularly acute given media interest in this field. HEIs should provide staff with external supervision and access to Continuing Professional Development, as well as adequate resources, particularly in terms of staffing and supportive line management, to ensure the risk and emotional labour inherent in this work is carried out by a team rather than one or two individuals. This will help staff to deliver their best and most effective work while also supporting their health and well-being.

Summary of key points and conclusion

We started the chapter with an overview of how case management is defined, including the key components in the context of HE responses to SMV and gender-based violence more widely. A key point here is that case managers will need a broad but specialist knowledge, on support options both internal and external to the HEI, as well as reporting options and procedures in relation to both the university and the police. They will need skills in trauma-informed practice and a thorough understanding of the science of GBV, including intersectionality, as well as a comprehensive grasp of the risk indicators and mitigation measures. When working with both Reporting and Responding Parties, they will need to understand the value and uphold the principle of impartiality.

In the second section, we highlighted the value of a case manager role as being separate from and in addition to both specialist support *and* investigation/disciplinary functions. In the final section, we offered a detailed description of a case manager's role in assessing risk, supporting the investigation, and advising the parties through the process following a formal report by one student against another.

Finally, we offer this chapter in the hope it will inspire others to think critically and creatively about the role of case management and more broadly, work being done to address GBV and SMV in Higher Education. This work is high risk, first to the victim-survivors, but also to responding parties and the wider university community; we must keep moving forward, keep questioning, evaluating, and listening to students, staff, and experts both within and outside of our own institutions, debating answers to those stubbornly difficult questions. We cannot afford to become complacent, nor allow our progress to stagnate.

Further Reading

UNICEF et al. (2017). *Interagency gender-based violence case management guidelines* **(1st ed.). https://gbvresponders.org/wp-content/uploads/2017/04/Interagency-GBV-Case-Management-Guidelines_Final_2017_Low-Res.pdf**

This resource provides detailed guidance on the development of case management in response to GBV; the resource is aimed at those working in a humanitarian setting but much of the information is equally useful to those looking to develop or evaluate a case management response to GBV in HE settings. It includes valuable insight into core concepts, such as defining and implementing a survivor-centred approach, drawing on research, theory and practice.

Recognising the "tremendous responsibility to create a safe, compassionate and supportive climate for people receiving services" (p. 29), the guidance covers the qualities, knowledge and skills needed by a case manager. It takes the reader through an iterative, step-by-step process of case management, from introduction and engagement, to closing a case and evaluation. The guidance looks at case management in relation to specific examples of GBV (intimate partner violence and sexual violence), as well as taking an intersectional approach by considering how case management can be adapted for more marginalised groups including the

LGBTQI+ community, male victim-survivors and victim-survivors with disabilities. Further, it covers the often overlooked topic of staff support and supervision.

Humphreys, C. J., & Towl, G. J. (2020). *Addressing student sexual violence in higher education.* **United Kingdom, Emerald Publishing.**

In 225 pages, this book is densely packed with evidence-based guidance which will prove invaluable to practitioners, student activists, sector policymakers, senior leadership teams, and researchers alike, indeed anyone who is working to prevent and respond to sexual violence and misconduct in higher and further education, in the UK and beyond. In essence, if your work seeks to challenge and disrupt the harmful norms and beliefs which foster sexual violence in our communities, if you want to see meaningful improvements in how we as an education sector respond to incidents so that victim-survivors are effectively supported and granted equal access to a safe learning environment, while perpetrators are held to account through transformative sanctioning, this book is the place to start. Whether your work is just beginning, or years down the line, you will find content which is thought-provoking, enlightening and even game-changing.

Drawing on national and international guidance and academic research, the authors deftly weave together a solid rationale for pursuing progress that is informed by experts in GBV, local knowledge such as campus climate surveys, as well as ongoing reflection and evaluation. Humphreys and Towl highlight not just the legal and ethical imperatives to act, held predominantly by senior leadership teams who hold the power and resource, but the civic driver for action which asks; if we play a substantive role in preparing (mostly) young people not just for the world of work, but the world more widely, ". . . when we think about the ability to influence society on a macro-level, it begs the key question, why *wouldn't* we address sexual violence in higher education?" (p. 38)

Notes

1 Marked by the *Changing the Culture* report (UUK, 2016) and guidance from Pinsent Masons and Universities UK (2016).
2 See unwomen.org.
3 *Changing the Culture: Tackling Gender-Based Violence, Harassment and Hate Crime; Two Years On.* (UUK, 2019).
4 See Refuge's (2021) website for further information on IDVAs – www.refuge.org.uk/our-work/our-services/independent-advocates/.
5 In this chapter, we refer to someone who discloses and seeks support as the 'Disclosing Party.' If they choose to move forward with a report to the police or the HEI, they are referred to as the 'Reporting Party.'
6 See AMMOSHE (2020) guidance on *Support for students studying abroad: Guidelines for Higher Education Student Services.*

7 Injuries following sexual violence are relatively rare and the absence of injuries does not undermine the credibility of the disclosing party.

8 It should be noted that the 66 days do not run consecutively and police investigations often take 18 months or more before an outcome is reached, an outcome which all-too-often fails to result in a prosecution (Hohl & Stanko, 2015).

9 See OIA (2019) *Good Practice Framework: Disciplinary Procedures.*

10 Note we use the terms non-judgemental precautionary measures and risk mitigation measures interchangeably.

11 MARAC (multi-agency risk assessment conference) is a meeting of relevant services (police, child protection, IDVAs) where information is shared on the highest risk domestic abuse cases.

12 It is good practice for the investigator to meet with the Reporting Party first, however the order of witnesses and or the Responding Party meetings can be at the investigator's discretion (Humphreys & Towl, 2020).

13 This is of course unless alternative arrangements have been agreed; some students will find frequent updates triggering, while others will find them invaluable. Preferences should be discussed at the beginning of the investigation.

14 For an evaluated package on SMV disclosure training aimed at HE professionals, see https://usvreact.eu/

References

AMMOSHE. (2020). *Support for students studying abroad: Guidelines for higher education Student Services.* www.amosshe.org.uk/resources/Documents/Support-for-students-studying-abroad-2020.pdf

Bull, A. (2021). Catalysts and rationales for reporting staff sexual misconduct in UK higher education institutions. *Journal of Gender-Based Violence.* https://doi.org/10.1332/239868021X16270572218631

Canadian Centre for Legal Innovation in Sexual Assault Response. (2021). *Mount Allison University: Independent review of sexual violence response.* Retrieved September 9, 2021, from https://mta.ca/sites/default/files/2021-07/CCLISAR-IRP-Report-on-Mount-Allison-University-June-30–2021.pdf

Freyd, J. J. (2014, July 14). *Official campus statistics for sexual violence mislead.* Retrieved from http://america.aljazeera.com/opinions/2014/7/college-campus-sexualassaultsafetydatawhitehousegender.html

Hohl, K., & Stanko, E. A. (2015). Complaints of rape and the criminal justice system: Fresh evidence on the attrition problem in England and Wales. *European Journal of Criminology, 12*(3), 324–341.

Home Office. (2017). *The role of the independent sexual violence adviser.* Retrieved October 21, 2021, from www.gov.uk/government/publications/the-role-of-the-independent-sexual-violence-adviser-isva

Home Office. (2020). *Crime outcomes in England and Wales 2019–2020.* Retrieved October 14, 2021, from https://assets.publishing.service.gov.uk/government/uploads/system/uploads/attachment_data/file/901028/crime-outcomes-1920-hosb1720.pdf

Humphreys, C. J., & Towl, G. J. (2020). *Addressing student sexual violence in higher education.* Emerald Publishing.

Office of the Independent Adjudicator. (2019). *The good practice framework: Disciplinary procedures.* Retrieved October 12, 2021, from www.oiahe.org.uk/media/2045/good-practice-framework-disciplinary-procedures-section.pdf

Office for Students (OfS). (2020). *Office for students consultation on harassment and sexual misconduct in higher education.* Retrieved December 14, 2021, from www.officeforstudents.org.uk/media/ebff4577-6ada-42af-ba98-07250db97c2f/consultation-on-harassment- and-sexual- misconduct- in- higher- education- 18032020.pdf

Osmond, J. (2019). *Recording harassment/hate incidents: The journey towards an online case management system.* Published by OfS. Retrieved October 27, 2021, from www.office-forstudents.org.uk/media/ceb8c4a8-91fa-47fd-ab5b-d1ba8e1499f9/coventry-university-a-journey-to-a-case-management-system.pdf

Pinsent Masons & Universities UK. (2016). *Guidance for higher education institutions: How to handle alleged student misconduct which may also constitute a criminal offence.* Retrieved December 9, 2021, www.universitiesuk.ac.uk/sites/default/files/field/downloads/2021-07/guidance-for-higher-education-institutions.pdf

Refuge. (2021). *Independent Advocacy.* Retrieved September 10, 2021, from www.refuge.org.uk/our-work/our-services/independent-advocates/

Scottish Government et al. (2018). *Equally Safe: Scotland's strategy to eradicate violence against women.* Retrieved September 12, 2021, from www.gov.scot/publications/equally-safe-scotlands-strategy-prevent-eradicate-violence-against-women-girls/pages/1/

UN Women, Ending Violence Against Women. Retrieved December 9, 2021, from www.unwomen.org/en/what-we-do/ending-violence-against-women

UNICEF et al. (2017). *Interagency gender-based violence case management guidelines* (1st ed.). https://gbvresponders.org/wp-content/uploads/2017/04/Interagency-GBV-Case-Management-Guidelines_Final_2017_Low-Res.pdf

Universities UK (UUK). (2016). *Changing the culture.* Retrieved December 9, 2021, www.universitiesuk.ac.uk/policy-and-analysis/reports/Documents/2016/changing-the-culture.pdf

Universities UK (UUK). (2018). *Guidance for allegations of student misconduct briefing note.* Retrieved October 15, 2021, from www.universitiesuk.ac.uk/sites/default/files/field/downloads/2021-07/uuk-cu-first-disclosures-briefing-note.pdf

Universities UK (UUK). (2019). *Changing the culture: Tackling gender-based violence, harassment and hate crime; Two years on.* Retrieved December 9, 2021, from www.universitiesuk.ac.uk/sites/default/files/field/downloads/2021-07/uuk-changing-the-culture-two-years-on.pdf

13 Investigation and interviewing

Responding to formal reports of sexual violence in Higher Education

Carl Norcliffe and Andrea Pescod

The field of non-academic misconduct investigations in Higher Education (HE) is evolving, with the role of the investigator a significant part of this evolution. There is currently a broad spectrum of views relating to who is best placed to carry out an investigation, as well as how it should be conducted. There are some resources HE investigators can look to when considering how to investigate cases of non-academic misconduct in HE (e.g., Univerities UK & Pinsent Masons, 2016; Office for Students, 2021; Government Equalities Office, 2021).[1] But what there is agreement on is the need for high-quality investigations.

In this chapter, we highlight some of the qualities necessary to equip investigators to undertake this role, whilst highlighting some best practice and suggested guidance to enable an effective trauma-informed investigation to be conducted. We achieve this by writing from a practitioners perspective and using an approach that draws largely from our combined and extensive experience of conducting investigations across sectors, including Law Enforcement and HE. Throughout the chapter, we have used the policy and process currently utilised at Durham University for sexual misconduct as a basis for outlining some of the procedures followed within an investigation. However, we acknowledge that this may differ in other Higher Education Institutions, but the underlying principles of good practice in conducting investigations are much the same both within and across sectors. We highlight the chronology and decision-making process of an investigation and provide practical guidance for an effective interview process, culminating in an overview of a structure for reports produced at the conclusion of investigations.

Introduction to the role of the investigator

There is little evidence that experienced investigators within law enforcement could spot a deception any easier than the general public (O'Sullivan & Ekman, 2004; Vrij & Mann, 2001). Trauma can dramatically affect the way a person behaves, reacts, and recalls an incident. Investigators need to rely upon gathering evidence, deciphering it and assessing its value and weight to be sure of making

DOI: 10.4324/9781003252474-15

a sound decision. It is also important to scrutinise each decision to ensure that all evidence is fully justifiable.

Cognitive bias influences judgement, and if not recognised and carefully managed, this can also lead to an unfair outcome. As bias is something we consciously or unconsciously hold, we need to better understand this, and question whether we are being influenced unjustly by our own heuristics.[2]

Bias and rape-myth acceptance

Bias, rape-myth acceptance, and failure to recognise the effects of trauma should be considered within any sexual misconduct investigation, making it necessary for the investigator to consider additional steps to ensure ethical decision-making. Rape myth acceptance and bias was recently explored amongst jury members within the UK (Thomas, 2020).[3] It was found that 43% of jurors would expect a complainant to be very emotional when giving evidence about a rape, 22% would not expect this, and 35% were uncertain about this issue. It should be noted that when interviewing witnesses who have received disclosures from an unemotional Reporting Party, a different reaction may then be misinterpreted.

One bias in human decision-making is known as 'confirmation bias' whereby we look for evidence in support of what we already think. This may lead the investigator to seek out information, which follows a preferred narrative or belief, causing information that does not fit to be discarded. This is particularly unhelpful at the start of an investigation as a fixed narrative blinkers any ability to be open-minded and undermines the goal of the investigation. In order to counteract this, it is useful to spend time acknowledging the thought process which signposted this early narrative and acknowledge that this is only one hypothesis. At the early stages of an investigation, a range of hypotheses may be helpfully put forward and each of them should be subject to rigorous testing. The investigator should be wary of an overreliance upon similarities with previous cases where a conclusion has already been reached. Using a previous investigation as a point of reference may lead towards the same conclusion, either consciously or subconsciously. By acknowledging and understanding that every case is different and must be viewed as such, this allows for the introduction of a range of hypotheses, which are necessary to avoid any unduly biased pre-judgement.

Another cognitive bias in human decision-making is sometimes referred to as 'affinity bias', which may lead the investigator to favour an individual who is similar to ourselves, or displays something especially relatable. In Malcolm Gladwell's book *Blink* (2006), he talked about illogical decision-making within US recruitment and having polled a list of CEOs found they were overwhelmingly white males and that 58% were 6 ft or above in height. This was in comparison to the general US population where only 14.5% of males were 6 ft or taller. This suggested that bias was present during recruitment of senior staff. This type of bias is particularly problematic during an interview situation as this could naturally lead to unconscious body language. Whilst the investigator may smile more and appear reassuring towards an interviewee who shared their affinity, they may display colder behaviour towards one who didn't. This in turn could reflect upon the interviewee and result in the investigator forming a more or less favourable view of that person. In order to minimise this, it may be helpful for the investigator to have only essential personal contact with the parties. This may include limiting contact to interview appointments only, with any additional contact directed to the case manager. This is explored further in the interview section.

Other forms of bias may also be present throughout an investigation, causing the investigator to be influenced by particular characteristics, behaviours, or reactions from an individual. This can lead to pre-judging a version of events or applying more or less weight to evidence than would be otherwise logical. It is important to realise that forms of bias will be present within any investigation, and steps to recognise and overcome it should always be taken. The investigator should also reflect that the biases outlined earlier also affect the parties involved in the investigation, all of whom may try to express an opinion that may not be justified or based wholly on truth.

Evidence

The ultimate aim within an investigation is to establish a fair, evidenced and accurate account of events based on the balance of probabilities. Equal effort should be made to prove or disprove each investigative hypothesis and all relevant leads should be sought. Having identified relevant leads, it is also important to document what was done to pursue them or justify they were not pursued, for example, why some witnesses were interviewed and others were not following receipt of their statements.

A scenario could be that the Responding Party mentioned in interview that they received a text from the Reporting Party admitting that they had fabricated their account. It would be important to ask for this due to its relevance and because it could assist the Responding Party's case. If the Responding Party explained that they no longer had the text, the investigator should seek other ways to confirm its existence, asking if anybody had witnessed the text or asking the Responding Party if they were able to retrieve it via their phone company, before also exploring this with the Reporting Party. This may also include whether or not either party had taken a screenshot or forwarded the message on to others or discussed the content. They may also explore with the Responding Party why they would dispose of something of this nature. This should not only be mentioned in the final report but should be documented within the meeting notes as it is a potentially strong lead which they were unable to corroborate using this method. Following up enquiries in this format ensures that information that may have been overlooked has, at the very least, been considered, therefore making the investigation as thorough and transparent as possible.

Although some evidence can be harder to gather or corroborate within an HE setting, students generally want to help and are willing to be witnesses. As the Responding Party does not benefit from abstaining from the process,[4] most investigations result in an account from each individual. It is necessary to test each account using the relevant leads that have been identified whilst covering the following potential sources:

- *Digital Data: texts, e-mails, social media, videos, University CCTV* – Digital data may sometimes be submitted highly selectively. If telephone or digital messages are submitted by one party, it is worth ensuring that they are checked with the other so that it can be established that all relevant data has been received. Although there may be access to University CCTV, it is rare that the investigator would be able to obtain CCTV from other public facilities, as they would not have the same level of access to this material as a law enforcement investigator. If this may demonstrate an important factor, the Reporting or Responding Party could be asked to try to obtain this to assist their case. As there is a strong possibility that individuals gathering their own evidence in this way may be unsuccessful through no fault of their own, this should not have an impact upon the investigation outcome. It is evidence that cannot be accessed which can therefore not be weighted so much, although it may be relevant to mention the attempts to obtain it within the report.

- *Witness Statements:* Witnesses can assist in providing direct or indirect evidence. It is rare that there will be a direct witness within a sexual misconduct case; however, witnesses before and after the event can help to establish credibility and consistency within the following areas.

- *Capacity during intoxication/alcohol effect:* Witnesses who may have been present just before or after the event may provide valuable information surrounding how much alcohol was consumed, how tolerant the party was to alcohol, how it affected the party, and whether they were able to function properly at the time. They could also be asked to share an opinion as to how this may have affected the party's capacity which can assist the investigator when considering issues around consent. When discussing alcohol or substance use, it is useful to provide a descriptive benchmark which can be utilised throughout the investigation by the parties involved. Although the effects of alcohol are subjective, this can be achieved by using an increasing scale of 1 = not intoxicated up to 10 = highest level of intoxication. To ensure continuity, this same scale should be provided to all parties within the investigation and identified within the final report. The scale can be supplemented by asking the individual to describe the effects of alcohol which led them to choose the specific number on the scale.

- *Change of behaviour:* Witnesses may be able to describe changes of behaviour relating to either party prior to or after an event, which may include avoidance, isolation, impact upon university work and life, or requirement for emotional support (Herts Rape Crisis, 2020).

- *Disclosure of the event by the Reporting Party:* Witnesses may be able to provide details of the circumstances surrounding the disclosure of the event. They may also be able to cover any reaction during disclosure, which may range from hysteria to numbness and apathy. It is accepted that reactions are individual to people and circumstances and this may not be recognised by the witness. Investigators should maintain a trauma-informed view and consider that the witness's opinion may be unfairly swayed if the Reporting Party's reaction does not sit within their expectations. Within law enforcement, this witness may be referred to as first complainant and often forms a significant part of the law enforcement investigation.
- *Disclosure of the event by the Responding Party:* Witnesses may be able to provide evidence, including any response by the Responding Party upon learning of the accusation, their account which may include admissions or denials, and their reaction.
- *Photographs of injuries/voice recordings/diaries:* An absence of injuries is not an indication that sexual violence did not occur. This may only be relevant if higher levels of force were described as part of the incident. When sharing photographs of injuries or recorded disclosures, it is important to consider how to do this whilst providing a level of privacy to the injured party. It may be enough for the investigator to retain the photograph or voice recording, but to only allow the Responding Party to view or listen to it (but not retain it). This can be done beforehand or during the interview, to minimise the risk of the Responding Party having control over a sensitive personal document. Internal policies regarding General Data Protection Regulations (GDPR) should be complied with and advice sought if necessary from the Information Governance Unit responsible for this within the organisation.
- *Interviews:* The interview can be a significant source of evidence and this will be discussed in greater depth later. For example, a witness who has submitted a four-line statement may have additional information that can only be gathered during an interview process.

The investigation process

An investigation can be broken down into three stages: scope–structure–goal. Without a scope, structure, and goal, a complex investigation quickly becomes convoluted and it is easy to become overwhelmed and lost before being able to reach a decision. To prevent this, we hope the following paragraphs are helpful; they are simplistic in nature looking at only three stages which can be repeated if a scope changes due to additional information.

Scope

The scope of the investigation (also referred to as alleged sexual misconduct) will likely be highlighted by the case manager or the individual who has commissioned the investigation based on the report submitted by the Reporting Party. In some universities, there may be a risk assessment meeting that is conducted before the investigation begins which confirms what support is required for both parties involved, what risk is presented in the case, how this can be mitigated through precautionary measures, and what potential breach of policy (alleged sexual misconduct) will be investigated. If the scope is unclear to the investigator on receipt of the investigation, it should be established in the initial stages, to allow sufficient planning and preparation to take place prior to interview. Such terms of reference are essential.

By comparing the initial concerns raised with the potential breach(es) within the institution's policies, the investigator can establish which breach(es) may have taken place. Consideration should be given to the fact that there may be more than one breach and that this may change throughout the investigation as other information comes to light. The investigation may also fall under other policies which are not specific to sexual misconduct and violence, for example, if there is an allegation of property damage or theft included with other allegations of sexual misconduct.

Once the scope has been established, the investigation should then focus on identifying whether the potential policy breach(es) took place under that policy or policies.

Structure

The structure of the investigation is the process or route-map from scope to goal, which includes the identification, gathering, and consideration of evidence. This in turn allows an informed decision to be made when considering the necessary elements within the investigation. These elements are also referred to in law enforcement as *points to prove*. Once all of the necessary points have been proven, on the balance of probabilities, it should not be difficult to reach the goal.

When looking at a university policy (taken from Durham University's Sexual Misconduct and Violence Policy), the points to prove may follow this example:
Sexually touching another person without consent.

The points to prove within this policy breach could be broken down as follows:

- There was touching.
- It was sexual.
- It was another person.
- It was without consent.

The preceding points to prove would provide the focus of the investigation, and whether all of the points were proven or not, would ultimately lead to a finding.

In proving or disproving each point, on the balance of probabilities, it is important to test evidence to determine how reliable it is. Some of the following comparison methods and insights can support this. Please be aware that trauma and alcohol (or other substance use) may have some impact upon consistency and ability to recall detail, and may result in significant memory gaps.[5] In such cases, remember that these factors could also explain discrepancies within accounts.

- *Corroboration:* This can be achieved by gathering similar accounts from other witnesses or obtaining supporting documentation, which verifies what a party has described.
- *Consistency:* By comparing what the party has told others, or comparing the content of their statements with their account in interview, it is possible to look at discrepancies or lack of discrepancies. This can help to measure consistency.
- *Recollection:* It is necessary to explore levels of recollection with the parties involved and to establish whether it is their own recollection or potentially influenced by another. Some relevant questions could be as follows: (1) Do they have a good recollection? (2) Was it impaired? (3) Have they any memory gaps?[6] (4) Can this be explained? (5) Are they unsure about anything? 6) Has their memory been influenced by speaking to others. Not only is it necessary to establish this in order to weigh their own evidence, but it can prevent the investigator from identifying a wrongful inconsistency with another's account. An example may be that a witness described events in a different order to the Reporting Party. In checking their recollection and asking questions 1 and 5, the witness is afforded the opportunity to allow them to explain that they did not remember the order the Reporting Party told them. Without offering this opportunity, this could have wrongly resulted in a potential credibility issue with either the witness or Reporting Party. This is further explored within the interview section.
- *Motive:* Establishing whether there was any motive to falsely report or exaggerate an incident can be important to both parties as a lack, or presence, of such motives may strengthen evidence in favour of either the Reporting or Responding Party, respectively. False reporting is rare, and is statistically thought to make up 2–10% of reports made to the police in the United Kingdom and in the United States (Ferguson & Malouff, 2016; Kelly et al., 2005; Lisak et al., 2010). The investigator should identify any background or subsequent issues between the parties which could suggest a motive. The motive of the Responding Party is equally important and can be explored by discussing their knowledge and views around consent, their perceived relationship with the Reporting Party, perception of sexual cues, and their mindset. Establishing whether they were influenced by alcohol or substance is important, although it is not a defence for sexual misconduct.

When seeking additional evidence, this should seek to help to prove or disprove the policy breach. Evidence which is not relevant should be discounted. For instance, if it became apparent that the Responding Party cheated at their exams, this would have no relevance to the investigation and therefore should not affect the decision or be mentioned within the final report.

When investigating a potential policy breach from Durham University's Sexual Misconduct and Violence Policy, for example:

Repeatedly following another person without good reason;

The investigator would look at the following points to prove and the steps would be broken down as follows:

* Repeatedly
* Following another person
* Without good reason

It would not matter which of the steps (points to prove) were considered first, as in order to prove this breach, evidence should be gathered to support all steps until attaining the civil standard of proof. Only when the three steps are evidentially sound can it be determined that a breach occurred. In this case, if it was determined that there was strong evidence that the Reporting Party was followed and strong evidence that they were followed repeatedly, it would still be necessary to show that this was without good reason. A possible explanation that the Responding Party had been concerned for the Reporting Party's welfare and had good reason to follow them would need to be carefully considered. If this was found to be a valid reason, this last step would not be evidentially sound and there would be no breach.

The goal is reached when all three points have been proven in the case of this breach or when at least one of the points is not proven in the case of a breach not being found.

Goal

The goal or purpose of the investigation is to establish on the balance of probabilities, whether there has been a breach of university policy, identify those breaches if so, and ascertain whether further discipline action is recommended. In some universities, the investigator may make a finding and in others, they may refer the case to another committee who decides following review of the investigation.

The burden of proof remains on the University to prove the outcome using the civil standard of proof. There is a notable difference between the 51% civil standard of proof required in HE investigations, compared to the criminal standard when proof required is *beyond a reasonable doubt*. The internal investigation within HE is not intended to mimic a criminal process and is unable to access the same level of evidence. It is therefore unlikely that a *beyond reasonable doubt* burden of proof could be achieved within a HE setting and 51% (*more likely than not*) is sufficient to make an internal judgement and considered best practice (Universities UK & Pinsent Masons, 2016).

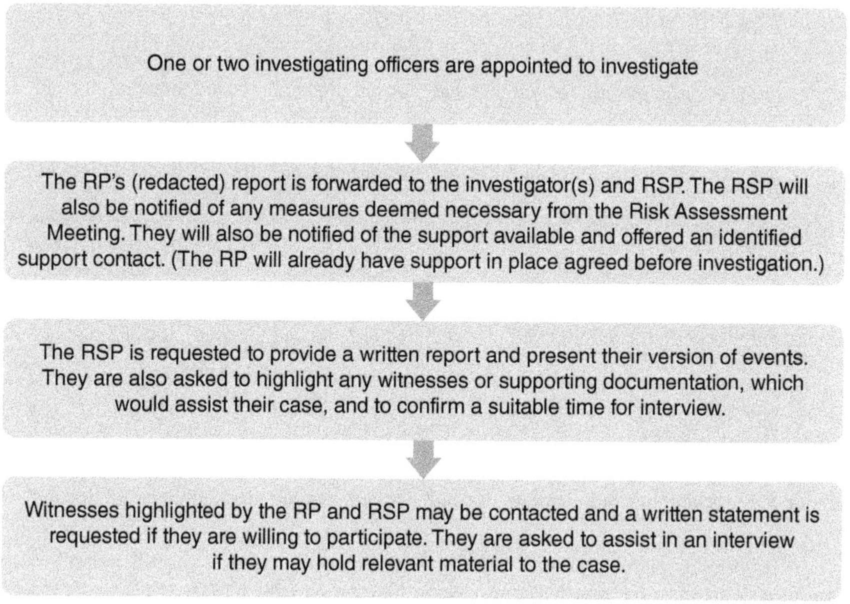

One or two investigating officers are appointed to investigate

The RP's (redacted) report is forwarded to the investigator(s) and RSP. The RSP will also be notified of any measures deemed necessary from the Risk Assessment Meeting. They will also be notified of the support available and offered an identified support contact. (The RP will already have support in place agreed before investigation.)

The RSP is requested to provide a written report and present their version of events. They are also asked to highlight any witnesses or supporting documentation, which would assist their case, and to confirm a suitable time for interview.

Witnesses highlighted by the RP and RSP may be contacted and a written statement is requested if they are willing to participate. They are asked to assist in an interview if they may hold relevant material to the case.

Figure 13.1 Initial investigation process example. (Based on Durham University, 2020.)

Figure 13.1 is a summary of the initial stages of the investigation process, which will lead to the interview stage. Please note that the Reporting Party is referred to as RP and Responding Party as RSP within this flowchart.

Once the investigator or investigators are assigned, they meet with the case manager who provides a summary of the case. The Reporting Party's report is usually the first document considered. This can vary in detail, may not follow a chronological order, and it may be difficult to interpret the sequence of events. An interview plan can be commenced detailing any gaps or topics to cover in interview and the potential to strengthen the evidence of both parties should be considered at an early stage. If the Reporting Party highlights social media/text messages, the case manager should be asked to request these prior to interview if possible. If there are social media messages, it may be prudent to recover them prior to notifying the Responding Party who may cause them to be deleted from their account. The Reporting Party's report will also document witnesses to assist in the case, the investigator and case manager will generally decide if it is appropriate for the investigator to contact the witnesses to arrange a report and consider a later interview.

The Responding Party is requested to provide a written report and present their version of events. They are also asked to highlight any witnesses or supporting documentation, which would assist their case, and to confirm a suitable time for interview (shown in Figure 13.2).

It is important to allow the Responding Party time to consider their response and highlight their case. It is worth noting that some parties may choose to seek external advice for this purpose.

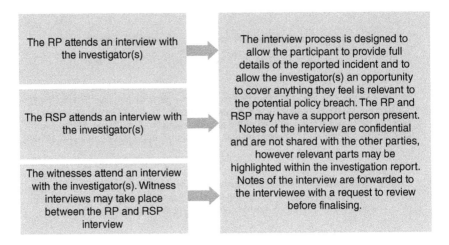

Figure 13.2 Initial interview process example. (Based on Durham University, 2020.)

Witnesses highlighted by the Reporting Party and Responding Party are contacted and a written statement is requested if they are willing to participate. They are asked to assist in an interview if they may hold relevant material to the case (shown in Figure 13.2).

Witnesses may not realise their worth in an investigation into a sexual misconduct case as they are unlikely to have witnessed the incident itself. They may return their statement highlighting that they only saw the aftermath, witnessed the impact, or had some disclosure. All of this evidence may be relevant to an investigation and go some way to assist in assessing the credibility of the Reporting Party or Responding Party and establishing the facts.

Introduction to investigative interviewing

The investigative interview has been established as a tool for eliciting the most appropriate and relevant information from an interviewee. It can direct an investigation and inform decisions for gathering additional material. It can also serve to increase or generate confidence in an investigative process, especially when properly utilised in trauma-informed cases. In turn, this has the potential to create rapport between an interviewer and interviewee, which may become a factor in the quality and volume of information subsequently disclosed.

As documented earlier in this chapter, the interview forms a significant part of the investigation process. Thorough planning and preparation, complete with solid rationale throughout the whole investigation process will lead to the most effective interview, with the following pertinent elements:

From our perspective, the investigative interview:

- Allows for more complete, accurate, and reliable information to be gathered – this is of the utmost importance throughout the entire investigation, with the interview consistently proving to be an invaluable opportunity to obtain this.

- Provides greater consistency across the organisation – by utilising a uniform approach to gathering information, this improves the credibility, confidence, and trust of investigators. It additionally reduces potential duplication during the course of an investigation.
- Creates the opportunity for transparent and ethical decision-making – it is much better to gather information and discard what subsequently becomes unnecessary, rather than being placed in a position whereby not enough information has been obtained to make the most effective and/or safe decision.

The investigative interview builds rapport between the interviewer and interviewee as well as enhancing cognitive recall of events. It is used as standard within UK law enforcement under the umbrella of the PEACE model and the Achieving Best Evidence guidance (Ministry of Justice, 2011).

The PEACE model is a non-confrontational method that relies on a conversational approach to interviewing (Shepherd & Griffiths, 2021; College of Policing APP, 2020). It is the accepted and expected norm within UK law enforcement and was developed specifically for this purpose in 1992. As a result of the structure, this method is almost wholly transferrable from a law enforcement environment into a HE/workplace environment. It is also widely accepted that this type of interview is not simply a tool to establish guilt, rather it is concerned with information gathering. The model itself is explained in detail later in this chapter.

It is important to highlight that within the UK legal system, deceit from the investigator/interviewer may render an interview inadmissible (Police and Criminal Evidence Act 1984, s. 76 and 78), which is highly likely to be a major setback to the overall case in terms of integrity and ethics. It must be acknowledged that whilst investigations in a HE setting do not seek to replicate those of criminal proceedings (as outlined earlier in the chapter), the principles of ethics and transparency remain directly applicable. Figure 13.3 highlights some primary comparisons between an interview and an interrogation.

A conversational approach

When preparing for and approaching an interview, the use of language is important from the start. Before even speaking to an interviewee, it can set the tone and damage rapport if used incorrectly (for example, if the interview has been framed more an interrogation – see Figure 13.3). This is a fundamental difference between an interview and fully conversational approach to any party being interviewed transfers into a HE setting. Once the differences between an interview and an interrogation are understood, the necessary set of skills required by an interviewer become clearer and slot into place under the PEACE model (College of Policing APP, 2020). These skills are explained next.

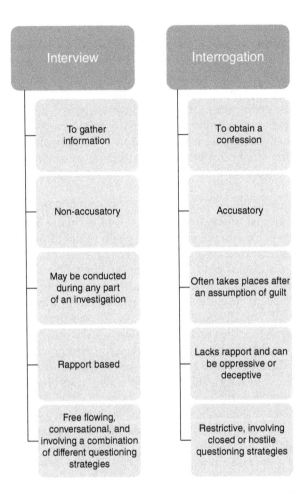

Figure 13.3 Interview versus interrogation. (Adapted from Inbau et al., 2013.)

Knowledge and understanding

As highlighted earlier, it is essential that the investigator has a full grasp of the detail involved in the investigation and understands how this will feed into the interview. It is also crucial to be aware of the intended direction (structure and goal) of the investigation in order for this to translate into the questions asked and subsequently, the information obtained from the interview.

Planning and preparation

It cannot be overstated how critical proper planning is to the interview and investigation overall. Without a disciplined and logical plan, it is likely that the interview itself will suffer from an indiscriminate approach. This may mean that subjects that are vital to the investigation are not fully covered or are even completely missed, leading inevitably to gaps that could reduce the credibility of the eventual conclusion.

Rapport

Building rapport is not something that has a 'one size fits all' approach due to the individuality of each party involved. Within Authorised Professional Practice from the College of Policing APP (2020), this is partially described as establishing a professional relationship that builds trust, including the necessity to refrain from '*allowing personal opinions or beliefs to have an effect*' on how the interview is being conducted. It goes on to state that '*Establishing a rapport means being genuinely open, interested and approachable, as well as being interested in the interviewee's feelings or welfare*'. Within a HE investigation, the desired outcome for the interview is the same (to gather relevant information); therefore, the approach should also be the same for all interviewees.

Active listening

This is a skill that is absolutely invaluable within an interview environment. Actively listening to an interviewee can often lead to the exploration of information that may have gone otherwise unnoticed. It may also highlight nuances from conversation that can change the direction of questioning. Furthermore, an engaged listener will generate confidence in an interviewee, potentially leading to multiple benefits such as further disclosure and a feeling of being taken seriously (this is also directly linked to the continuing building of rapport). From an interviewers perspective, it can also provide valuable time to absorb the conversation and mentally plan for how the interview will continue to progress.

Questioning

This skill is vital to the process, not least as it forms the fundamental part of an interview. It is directly linked to all four of the aforementioned points and can assist if used well, or detract if used inappropriately. It is worth noting that a badly timed or phrased question can immediately and irreparably damage rapport, with the likely result being that the overall quality of the interview is reduced

Open questions. These are best utilised at the beginning of an interview or topic area as they allow the interviewee to provide an uninterrupted account and one that has not been influenced or directed by the interviewer. It is important with this type of question that the interviewer allows the interviewee to complete their answer without interruption. This maintains rapport but also ensures that the interviewer is able to adapt to points raised in this open response. These types of questions are often referred to as TED questions as they usually begin with 'Tell. . ., Explain. . ., Describe. . .' (College of Policing APP, 2020). This provides instruction within the question but does not lead the interviewee. For example '*Tell me what happened. . .*', '*Explain what happened. . .*', '*Describe what happened. . .*'. Some interviewees are inclined to give a vast quantity of detail, especially if being asked for an answer that has a chronological aspect to it. This can be minimised by the interviewer simply adding some parameters to the open TED question. For example, the same question can be phrased as *'Tell me in as much detail as you can what happened on 1st June between 10pm and 11pm at the pub'.* This is still an open question, but by adding boundaries, this becomes a specific instruction to the interviewee that that the investigator only wishes to hear about a certain aspect of events at this point.

Specific closed questions. This type of question narrows down the response from the open question and is a useful tool for clarifying or adding to the information provided. It is vital that this type of question is used in the right way as it is really designed to provide shorter, more succinct answers to whittle down and strengthen the information already provided. These questions are often referred to as 5WH (Who, What, Where, When, Why, How).

Avoiding leading questions. This type of question creates an element of suggestion within it. It is the responsibility of the interviewer to allow the interviewee to provide their own answer without having to consider information that they were unaware of, or may not be relevant. For example, if asking whether a specific item or person was seen, the question *'Did you see X?'* will plant the suggestion that X was there, when in fact they may not have seen X at all. Rephrasing this to an open question *'Tell me who/what you saw?'* gives the interviewee the opportunity to explain exactly what or who they saw without having to consider that they may be incorrect or may have missed something that the interviewer is aware of. This suggestibility is a key factor in the gathering of unreliable information in an investigation, and there is a long history of criminal cases that have been adversely affected by the integrity of information gathered this way. As per Achieving Best Evidence in Criminal Proceedings, *'it will be extremely difficult to counter the argument that the interviewer put the idea into the witness's head'* (Ministry of Justice, 2011, s. 3.64).

The PEACE model

This section will cover the PEACE model (shown in Figure 13.4) in more detail and highlight each part separately, outlining some of the important areas

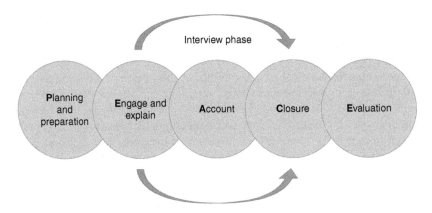

Figure 13.4 PEACE model. (Adapted from College of Policing APP, 2020, section 4 PEACE Framework.)

to consider when following this plan. The structure has been developed to provide a spine for the interview process as a whole, but there are opportunities for adaptation as and when required.

P – Planning and preparation

This area covers the precursor to the interview itself.

- *Interviewers/investigators* – Understanding who is to be involved in the interview process may be overlooked on occasion. If options are available, the needs/requirements of the interviewee can be considered here, covering aspects such as the preferred gender of the interviewer. Considering who will be interviewing is also critical when establishing whether there are any conflicts of interest or personal relationships between interviewer and interviewee. By understanding this, it will maintain the integrity of the process.
- *Location/timing* – Working arrangements during the COVID-19 pandemic have altered the way in which interviews have been conducted, meaning they have taken place via video call. In our experience, there has been a positive reaction to this from those being interviewed, especially in the sense that this method can provide a more comfortable environment for the interviewee. This in turn lends itself to the principles behind Achieving Best Evidence. Additionally, when it comes to welfare, confidence, and fears around this process, there is an allowance for support persons to be present. There is also a reduction in the multiple barriers that may come from a student being invited to attend a face-to-face meeting in an unfamiliar and formal space with potentially three to four other people present. When holding interview in person, it is important that the most appropriate space is used. For instance, utilising a meeting room on a busy corridor, or in a 'goldfish bowl' style is likely to add to anxiety rather than alleviate it. Similarly, the layout inside the room can be equally important, with consideration needing to be given to proximity between parties present, sound, temperature, and lighting. Each of these, if not considered correctly, can have a negative impact on the interviewee.
- *How the interview is to be recorded* – Video interviewing has made this a simple step; however, consideration must be given to whether there is a necessity to record an interview (other than in note format). It is helpful for an investigation as an interview can be reviewed for the purposes of clarification (either for a summary or for pertinent speech). However, if recording, there must be a prior agreement from all parties to engage, as well as an understanding of how the material generated will be used and stored. This may also subsequently become important from a legal perspective in occasional scenarios. An example of how this can be used is to have the video interview recorded for the

purposes of producing the written notes of the meeting and then deleting the recording once the notes have been confirmed by all relevant parties who attended the meeting.

Cultural and/or welfare issues – This is partially covered when thinking about the choice of interviewer; however, it is critical to ensure that support is available (and present) if required. Understanding whether this will be a necessity is likely to have been established in the early stages of the investigation (or beforehand when meeting with Case Managers, see Chapter 12); however, it must remain a dynamic assessment as interviewees may require additional support once an interview has begun. This can include elements such as mental health and domestic circumstances. Additionally, given the diversity across HE environments, it is essential that there is an understanding of any cultural sensitivities that may have a negative impact on whether the interviewee is able to provide the best possible information, including language and religion or belief.

Post-interview support – This is explored in Chapter 12 and is something that can be reiterated throughout the whole interview and investigation process.

Interview plan – As highlighted earlier, solid preparation is absolutely vital to the success of an interview. Understanding the direction of the investigation along with establishing what the required goals are from the interview is helpful. However, early assumptions about information received can potentially misdirect the focus of an investigation or interview and cause relevant information to be overlooked. This is often referred to as personal bias or verification/confirmatory bias, with there being a very real danger that further material and information is then only gathered to support this view (as documented earlier).

An effective interview plan should not consist solely of a list of questions. Whilst this may elicit some information, it is highly likely to also lead to a lack of rapport, minimal adaptation within an interview, or at worst, simply not responding to an answer before moving on to the next question. Not only does this approach stifle a conversation, it also damages the chances of obtaining the best information. As already noted, this may unduly restrict the direction of the investigation, ending with a conclusion that is drawn on less information. From the perspective of a potential appeal post-investigation, this is something that is easily strengthened by the simple act of planning well.

E – Engage and explain

This area covers the beginning of the interview itself.

Introduction (role and reason for interview) – This is important to ensure that all parties understand who is present, why they are there, and what the purpose of the interview is.

Explain the interview procedure – Outlining the structure at the start will be beneficial so the interviewee knows what to expect. This may also alleviate fear and concern, and will also include the necessity for breaks as and when required.

Establish ground rules – This is an important part of the interview procedure explanation as it is imperative that each party present (interviewee/support/ admin) is aware of the responsibility of each role. It creates an environment where this is defined at the start, assisting in the smooth running of the process.

Create a rapport – Despite the formalities of the aforementioned three points, these play a huge part in the subtle creation of rapport when delivered in an appropriate manner. Equally, if delivered in an unapproachable or rigid manner, it is likely that this will be reciprocated, again leading to a potentially stunted conversation. Body language and non-verbal communication are also significant aspects of creating rapport, especially when conducting interviews in person. This includes the choice of location for face-to-face interviews and the layout within a meeting room, when care must be taken to ensure that the interviewee is comfortable and is not placed in a position that will hinder the ability to provide the best evidence. For instance, if the seating arrangement is too close (under 2 m), not close enough, or has a barrier (such as across a large desk), this is likely to inhibit the conversation.

A – Account

This covers the most effective way to gain information in a conversational manner and outlines questioning techniques.

An effective interview plan encompasses the different question types outlined earlier. It also takes into consideration the expectation and direction of the interview, from which subject areas for exploration should have been identified. Figure 13.5 shows how this translates into a conversation using the analogy of a funnel to explain how conversation is narrowed. It is something that should be followed for each subject area, for example, if there are multiple subjects that the interviewer has chosen to speak about (such as background, location, persons present, physical act, conversation, aftermath, witnesses, effect, etc.), Figure 13.5 represents how each is approached before moving onto the next. If illustrating the interview, it should contain multiple duplications of this diagram under each subject heading, allowing for more complete and relevant gathering of information.

Procedure:

TED questions – 'Tell', 'Explain', 'Describe'.

5WH questions – Who? What? Where? When? Why? How?

Use open TED style questions to begin a subject area, until this is no longer productive.

Use specific choice/probing 5WH questions when and where necessary to expand and adapt *to the responses given.*

Use appropriately closed questions, primarily aimed at clarification and confirmation.

Summarise each area, seeking clarification of accuracy, before moving on to the next subject.

C – Closure

This area is the last part of the interview itself.

It gives the opportunity for summary and clarification, led by the interviewer, whom at this point, should be asking whether the interviewee has disclosed all the information they wish to. It provides an opportunity for any additions to be made, or any questions to be asked in the opposite direction. Furthermore, the interviewer should use this as a chance to provide the interviewee with information about what happens next, which may include procedural issues, timescale, and welfare (inclusive of immediate feelings/concerns). This links in with the role of the Case Manager and as such, it will often be the case that the interviewer/investigator can highlight this as part of the closure section.

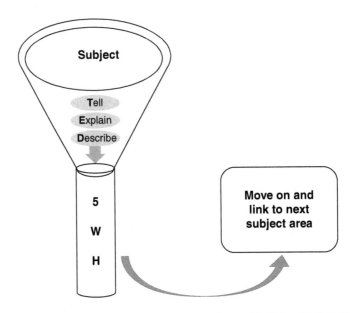

Figure 13.5 Questioning funnel. (Adapted from College of Policing APP, 2020, section 4.3.1 Questions.)

Figure 13.6 Gap analysis. (Adapted from ACPO, 2005.)

E – Evaluate

This is an opportunity for the interviewer/investigator to reflect on the interview.

This will include the quality of the information received and how this will impact the investigation as a whole, which may end up generating multiple new areas of exploration. Using a gap analysis method which seeks to identify four key areas, Figure 13.6 is an effective strategy to understand how the investigation will progress (ACPO, 2005). Besides being useful at this stage of the PEACE process, it is also something that can and should be used at multiple stages throughout the investigation.

Report structure

At the conclusion of the overall investigation, it is important to summarise findings within a formal report that documents all the information received that has led the investigator to reach the conclusion. This conclusion will have been drawn in a balanced, fair, and transparent manner and as such will include evidence that points both towards and away from any breach of policy. It will also be necessary to include and describe the rationale behind the decision made as and where appropriate. A generic template, currently utilised by Durham University, is outlined in Figure 13.7, adapted from Humphreys and Towl (2020).

Conclusions

The key to an effective overall investigation is for the investigator to be aware of potential biases in decision-making and to be open-minded, with a willingness for adaptation when required. It is imperative that the investigator has prepared and has been able to gather as much relevant information as possible in order to reach the safest and most transparent decision at the conclusion. The fundamental aspects of a thorough and effective investigation translate well and easily across all types. However, this it is especially important within trauma-informed investigations. These types of investigation are often not straightforward, nor are they insignificant when considering the impact on the parties involved, and especially reporting parties. By following the basic principles of a well-planned and well-run investigation, exploration of all relevant aspects can be completed. Even if a chosen investigative action is subsequently deemed irrelevant or does not yield a result, the consideration and documentation of the processes followed (referred to within the criminal justice system as 'all reasonable lines of enquiry') ensures that there is justification for each decision made, and importantly, the conclusion reached. It must be understood by the investigator that the sole purpose of an investigation is not simply to establish whether or not there is guilt, it is to reach an understanding of what has occurred (as much as is possible) in an independent, safe, and justifiable manner, based on the information obtained from the investigation. There will be occasions when the final

Procedural History

This section will contain the relevant dates within the investigation process (e.g., date RP reported, date investigator assigned, date RSP informed, date investigation concluded).

Involved Participants

This section will contain the details of all parties involved and their role (e.g., RP /RSP /Witnesses).

Investigation timeline

This section will contain all the information submitted, including the type (video interview/text messages/CCTV) by whom, and the date (e.g., 'Statement submitted by X on DD/MM/VY').

Alleged Misconduct & Policy Definitions

This section will contain an overview of the alleged misconduct and will highlight the relevant policy and sections that the investigation has been conducted under.

Commentary

This section will outline the evidence as presented by each party involved. This will cover the details of all the evidence (e.g., a statement and interview) and can be written in summary format rather than verbatim. It may (if preferred) refer to submitted written documents (such as a statement) as appendices to avoid duplication of content.

Credibility Assessment

This section will outline the credibility of each party involved, with consideration being given to the plausibility of the evidence provided within the overall accounts of each party as well as verifiable facts and information. A separate assessment is necessary for each party with a conclusion drawn highlighting the rationale behind deciding whether they are credible or not (including mixed credibility).

Findings of Fact and Analysis

This section will contain an overview of the pertinent areas of the case (eg - any agreement on facts 'X & Y have both agreed that X had consumed a high level of alcohol'), along with a rationale for the decisions made. It will also contain any areas of policy that have been relied upon to reach the decision (e.g., ' ... consent cannot be given if the individual does not have the capacity ... ' Section A.A of Policy B).

Conclusion

This section will simply contain the overall finding (e.g., 'on the balance of probabilities, Y breached Policy B by engaging in ----------, thereby breaching section C.C of Policy B).

Sanction and Recommendation

This section will contain the sanctions or recommendations decided on by the investigator, or will suggest a referral to a disciplinary panel for a hearing if deemed a serious enough breach.

Figure 13.7 Report structure example. (Currently used by Durham University; adapted from Humphreys & Towl, 2020.)

conclusions may not be universally popular, however, by ensuring that processes have been followed, decisions have been justified, and relevant information has been gathered ethically and with transparency, it is highly likely that this final decision is able to withstand scrutiny.

Summary of key points

- Identify and understand the objective of the investigation from the outset.
- Prepare thoroughly, keeping the objective at the fore but understanding the necessity for adaptation.
- Maintain a professional, trauma-informed approach without bias – applicable when dealing with all parties involved.
- Build rapport with parties involved in the investigation through open and honest conversations or updates.
- Plan and implement effective interviews, utilising applicable questioning techniques and maintaining a conversational approach.
- Ensure relevant and reasonable enquiries are made, gathering as much information as is necessary to support the investigation.
- Regularly review the investigation and the material gathered.
- Be confident in making decisions that are justifiable, disclosing the rationale for these in the appropriate manner (through the final report).

Further Reading

Shepherd, E., & Griffiths, A. (2021). *Investigative interviewing: The conversation management approach* **(3rd ed.). Oxford University Press**.

When undertaking a trauma-informed investigation within a HE setting, this book will assist in leading the investigator/interviewer towards a suitable questioning strategy that takes into account how people recall and disclose their experiences. It covers the importance of building and maintaining rapport within an interview using conversation management as a basis, something that is transferrable between a variety of investigations and a fundamental part of the PEACE process. The book provides invaluable guidance on how to achieve the most effective outcome from this method, making it an appropriate resource for both HE and workplace investigations.

Humphreys, C. J., & Towl, G. J. (2020). *Addressing student sexual violence in higher education: A good practice guide.* **Emerald Publishing**.

This book contains good practise and guidance on how to address sexual violence within an HE setting. It discusses current UK sector guidance alongside international practise and provides a useful insight into this developing field. The subjects range from advice about how to develop a sexual violence policy and procedure, how to respond to disclosures of sexual misconduct, how to conduct trauma-informed investigations and the disciplinary process. Throughout the book there is a clear understanding of good and bad practise, covered within case examples. We found the key resources for the survivor and professional and the consent investigation flowchart invaluable.

Notes

1 This chapter focuses on student sexual misconduct. However, it is worth noting that The Equality Act 2010 is the current legislation used within the UK for workplace sexual harassment cases which states that employers are legally responsible if an employee is sexually harassed at work, if the employer did not take all steps to prevent it from happening.
2 Heuristic thinking drives the use of developed cognitive shortcuts which can inform conscious or unconscious decision making; see e.g., Chery, 2021.
3 See also Chalmer et al., 2021.
4 Abstaining from the process would not assist in an HE setting as the investigation would continue without the Responding Party's account. In that scenario, evidence to either deny or mitigate the policy breach would be absent and a decision would be made without their input.
5 See Chapter 8 in Humphreys & Towl, 2020.
6 Memory gaps can occur with voluntary or forced alcohol or substance misuse, and trauma can affect memory production and retrieval (Humphreys & Towl, 2020).

References

Association of Chief Police Officers (ACPO). (2005). *Extract from core investigative doctrine.* https://library.college.police.uk/docs/APPref/core-investigative-doctrine.pdf

Chalmers, J., Leverick, F., & Munro, V. E. (2021). Why the jury is, and should still be, out on rape deliberation. *Criminal Law Review, 2021*(9), 753–771.

Chery, K. (2021, April 11). *Heuristics and cognitive biases.* www.verywellmind.com/what-is-a-heuristic-2795235

College of Policing APP. (2020). *Investigative interviewing.* www.app.college.police.uk/app-content/investigations/investigative-interviewing/

Durham University. (2020). *Sexual misconduct and violence policy: Procedure for students.* www.dur.ac.uk/sexualviolence/policies/

Equality Act. (2010). www.legislation.gov.uk/ukpga/2010/15/contents

Ferguson, C. E., & Malouff, J. M. (2016). Assessing police classifications of sexual assault reports: A meta-analysis of false reporting rates. *Archives of Sexual Behavior, 45*, 1185–1193. https://doi.org/10.1007/s10508-015-0666-2

Gladwell, M. (2006). *Blink: The power of thinking without thinking.* Penguin Books.

Government Equalities Office. (2021). *Consultation outcome: Consultation on sexual harassment in the workplace: Government response.* www.gov.uk/government/consultations/consultation-on-sexual-harassment-in-the-workplace/outcome/consultation-on-sexual-harassment-in-the-workplace-government-response#executive-summary

Herts Rape Crisis. (2020). *Trauma responses – behaviour.* https://dev.hertsrapecrisis.org.uk/for-survivors/trauma-responses-behaviour/

Humphreys, C. J., & Towl, G. J. (2020). *Addressing student sexual violence in higher education: A good practice guide.* Emerald Publishing.

Inbau, F., Reid, J., Buckley, J., & Jayne, B. (2013). *Criminal interrogation and confessions* (5th ed.). Jones and Bartlett Publishers Inc.

Kelly, L., Lovett, J., & Regan, L. (2005). *A gap or a chasm? Attrition in reported rape cases. Home office research study No. 293.* Home Office Research, Development and Statistics Directorate.

Lisak, D., Gardinier, L., Nicksa, S. C., & Cote, A. M. (2010). False allegations of sexual assault: An analysis of ten years of reported cases. *Violence Against Women, 16,* 1318–1334. https://doi.org/10.1177/1077801210387747

Ministry of Justice. (2011). *Achieving best evidence in criminal proceedings guidance on interviewing victims and witnesses, and guidance on using special measures.* www.cps.gov.uk/sites/default/files/documents/legal_guidance/best_evidence_in_criminal_proceedings.pdf

Office for Students. (2021). *Statement of expectations.* www.officeforstudents.org.uk/advice-and-guidance/student-wellbeing-and-protection/prevent-and-address-harassment-and-sexual-misconduct/statement-of-expectations/

O'Sullivan, M., & Ekman, P. (2004). The wizards of deception detection. In P. A. Granhag & L. A. Strömwall (Eds.), *The detection of deception in forensic contexts* (pp. 269–286). Cambridge University Press. https://doi.org/10.1017/CBO9780511490071.012

Police and Criminal Evidence Act 1984, s. 76 and s. 78. www.legislation.gov.uk/ukpga/1984/60/contents

Shepherd, E., & Griffiths, A. (2021). *Investigative interviewing: The conversation management approach* (3rd ed.). Oxford University Press.

Thomas, C. (2020). The 21st century jury: Contempt, bias and the impact of jury service. *Criminal Law Review, 2020*(11), 987–1011.

Universities UK and Pinsent Masons. (2016). *Guidance for higher education institutions: How to handle alleged student misconduct which may also constitute a criminal offence.* Universities UK.

Vrij, A., & Mann, S. (2001). Who killed my relative? police officers' ability to detect real-life high-stake lies. *Psychology, Crime & Law, 7,* 119–132. https://doi.org/10.1080/10683160108401791

14 Primary prevention in Higher Education

Progress and opportunity

Kelsey Paske

What does prevention look like in practice? In this chapter, I will highlight some of the good practice interventions from a public health–based prevention perspective, including tertiary, secondary, and primary prevention.

- Tertiary prevention or response focuses on supporting survivors and holding perpetrators to account, with the aim of preventing the reoccurrence of violence.
- Secondary prevention aims to change the trajectory for individuals higher-than average risk of perpetrating or experiencing violence.
- Primary prevention includes whole-of-population initiatives that address the primary ('first' or underlying) drivers of violence, which include gender inequality and intersecting forms of structural inequality.

(Our Watch, 2021, p. 58)

I will highlight both gaps and opportunities to share knowledge and resources to strengthen the existing efforts to combat gender-based violence, encourage reflection, challenge the status quo, and spark ideas for our future practice.

Prevention

To prevent violence is to stop it before it starts – this requires examining the continuum of violence and addressing the unacceptable behaviour that leads to significant forms of violence and abuse. The continuum of violence and abuse acknowledges various types of behaviour that can contribute to extreme forms of abuse.

Figure 14.1 highlights some, but not all the behaviours that exist within the continuum. The base of the continuum includes everyday attitudes and behaviours, each of which create or support the conditions needed to normalise gender-based violence. This is crucial in understanding the spectrum of behaviours that exists and contributes to extreme forms of gender-based violence. The pyramid also demonstrates that violence is preventable, if we can challenge and change the behaviours and norms that condone violence.

DOI: 10.4324/9781003252474-16

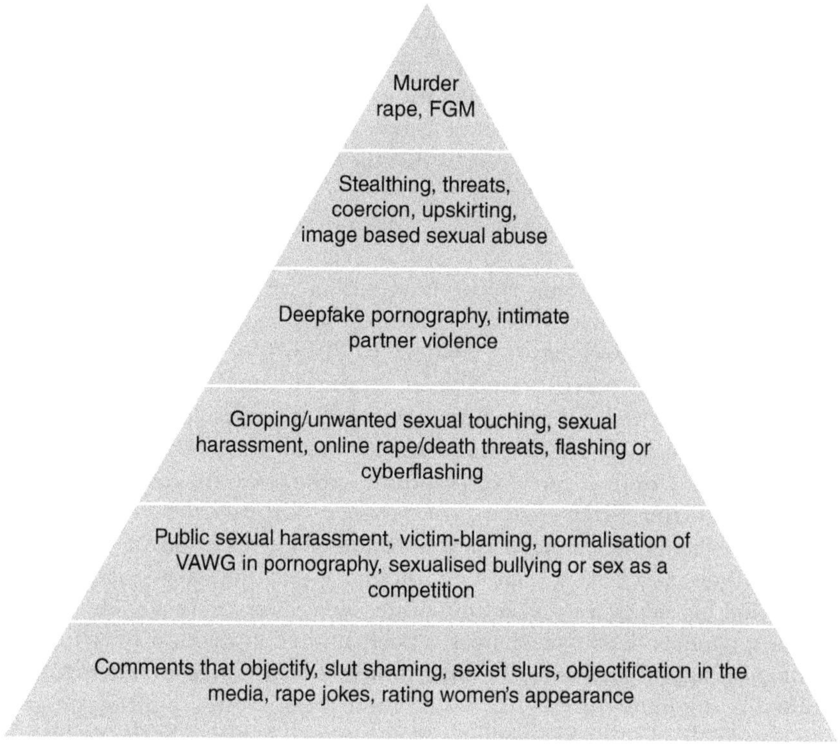

Figure 14.1 Gender-based violence continuum. (Image based on Bold Voices, 2021.)

Frameworks and guidance that have been produced in Higher Education in the UK, and globally, often refer to the need to take a whole-of-institution approach, but that it must be one that advocates for 'zero tolerance' (Universities UK, 2016, p. 34). As a practitioner, I've always struggled to understand what this means in practice. Zero tolerance suggests that this behaviour will not be tolerated, but how is that enforced? Does it mean that formal action will be taken when a disclosure is made, and that any form of unacceptable behaviour will be dealt with in an efficient manner? Or does it mean that the university leaders condemn unacceptable behaviour, and will respond to formal reports when raised?

Language is critical when discussing experiences of, and responses to, all forms of gender-based violence. The language of zero tolerance, in my experience, has caused confusion and mismanaged expectations, particularly for victim-survivors. This is demonstrated clearly in The Hunting Ground documentary (Dick, 2015), where universities in the United States, which had purportedly adopted a zero-tolerance approach and whose Presidents and Vice-Chancellors had issued statements saying they 'take the issue very seriously', had also failed to provide appropriate sanctions when findings of sexual violence were upheld. The language of zero-tolerance sets institutions up to fail, leaving victim-survivors caught between rhetoric and reality. It creates unrealistic and unachievable expectations and creates a confusion that cannot be afforded when there are a range of barriers that exist to disclosing and high rates of underreporting. This is why my preference and practice is dedicated to advancing a preventative and proactive approach: this includes primary, secondary, and tertiary prevention. While the language of prevention may not be as marketable as zero tolerance, primary, secondary, and tertiary prevention address the heart of the issue and set clear parameters for taking a whole-of-institution approach.

Primary prevention stems from public health frameworks and in the last decade has been adopted both internationally and nationally to inform strategy to address violence against women. In 2015, Our Watch, the national organisation for the prevention of violence against women and their children, introduced the first global prevention framework (Our Watch, 2015), followed by UN Women (2015). The image from *Change the Story* (Our Watch, 2021) provides a clear outline for what constitutes primary, secondary, and tertiary prevention (Figure 14.2).

There is a significant need to re-examine the evaluation of prevention interventions and ensure that longitudinal evaluation takes place. Often evaluation has centred on examining individual interventions such as training programmes; however, there has been limited evaluation of whole-of-institution approaches and the effectiveness of the range of interventions utilised. Consequently, this has a significant impact: often limiting progress and potentially wasting already limited resources. However, of the evaluation

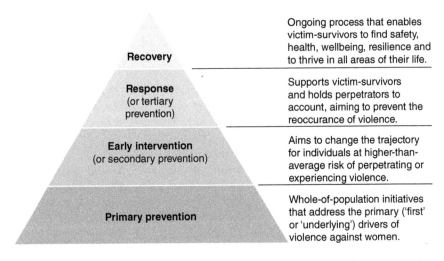

Figure 14.2 The relationship between primary prevention and other work to address violence against women. (Our Watch, 2021, p. 58; used with permission.)

conducted, broader themes from prevention work have demonstrated the following:

- Active bystander training has a positive impact on increasing people's reported confidence to intervene and decreases myth acceptance; however, there is limited evidence to confirm this leads to effective and sustained intervention (Gainsbury et al., 2020, pp. 8–9). Further research is required to measure the longitudinal impact.
- Unconscious bias training has been implemented within the context of conducting investigations, and to address racialised experiences of gendered violence. However, as evaluations of unconscious bias training have shown, there can be limited transference to consciously tackling both unconscious and conscious biases and considering how they manifest with respect to disclosures of gender-based violence, the provision of support, implementation of policies, and investigation of cases.
- Consent training has been widely adopted through online e-learning such as Epigeum's Consent Matters (Epigeum, n.d.) or advocated as a part of the National Union of Students I Heart Consent campaign (NUS, n.d.). Some consent programmes have explored the broader context of respectful relationships, themes of entitlement, and gendered expectations and discussed how consent manifests daily, rather than focusing on consent within intimate contexts. While consent education does play a role, it is not the end goal. Consent is an important component of a much broader prevention framework.
- *Policies and procedures:* A significant focus has been to revise policies and procedures to ensure they clearly outline the process for reporting or seeking support if someone is subjected to gender-based violence. However, little attention across the sector has been provided to effective and consistent implementation and evaluation to ensure the policy is meeting its intended purpose.

Intersectional experiences of gender-based violence

To date, there has been limited prevention work on intersectional experiences: 'intersectionality considers different systems of oppression, and specifically how they overlap and are compounded to shape the student or employee experiences.. . . Intersectionality means we view the whole person, not their characteristics separately' (Culture Amp, 2019, p. 8). While there has been increasing discussion on 'taking an intersectional approach', truly intersectional practice is a significant step change from current equality, diversity, and inclusion practice. In recognising the whole person, we must move away from focusing solely on particular protected characteristics in silos. There are different barriers and opportunities for marginalised identities, and this becomes increasingly complex when these are compounded by multiple points of disadvantage. Where we can understand the needs of those subjected to gender-based violence that have multiple and intersecting characteristics, then our practice can adapt to meet these needs. Much of the practice that has developed in this space is centred on addressing gender inequality or sexism, and then considering the impact of racism, ableism, homophobia, or transphobia. A more meaningful approach would be to understand experiences where there are intersecting and overlapping points of disadvantage and designing programmes based on this. If we don't frame this from the beginning, we risk privileging some experiences over others, and ignoring the social marginalisation that will increase a person's likelihood of experiencing violence. As Kimberlé Crenshaw (2016) has highlighted, we need to begin to bear witness to these experiences so that we can move from mourning and grief to action and transformation. The design of strategies is key here, the challenge remains centring multiple and intersecting forms of discrimination when designing systems, processes, and support. While gender equality programmes like Athena SWAN have traditionally focused and are perceived to focus on women's experiences and improving representation, initiatives introduced have significantly benefited men too, including flexible work arrangements, parental leave provisions, and improved workplace culture (Ortus & Loughborough, 2019), demonstrating the potential for targeted interventions to benefit larger populations. As practitioners, policymakers, and professionals, we need to change the way we design interventions to ensure direct impact for marginalised and intersecting groups, and as a consequence indirectly improve the lives and experiences of all (Figure 14.3).

I will explore each form of prevention in turn and highlight innovative practice and opportunities to advance existing preventative work within universities in the UK and abroad. Where possible, I will highlight the potential to expand intersectional practice and offer comments on considerations in light of COVID-19 and the resources available.

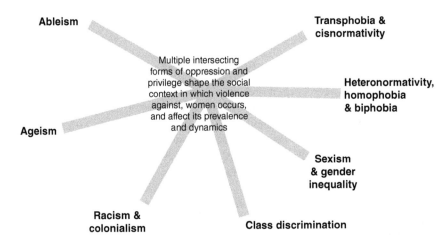

Figure 14.3 Violence against women and intersectionality. (Our Watch, 2021, p. 46; used with permission.)

Tertiary prevention and response practice

Tertiary prevention focuses on victim (or target) support and perpetrator accountability. Hence, it includes key interventions such as specialist support services, investigation processes, policies, and procedures, all with the aim of reducing the escalation of this abuse and reducing the likelihood of it happening again. The majority of the work undertaken across UK universities relates to tertiary prevention and responding to gender-based violence. While this is a key component of overall prevention, tertiary prevention initiatives need to be accompanied by secondary and primary prevention practices to have the desired impact of reducing violence.

Support provision

UK practice has seen a number of institutions focus their prevention efforts initially on ensuring the appropriate specialist support is in place, particularly with respect to sexual violence services. This support provision may include dedicated sexual violence and response managers with a particular focus on student casework, responding to disclosures and overseeing the investigation in addition to Independent Sexual Violence Advocates (ISVAs) or sexual violence liaison officers. This support has required financial resources, and due to limited or consistent provision across the sector, it has left gaps for some institutions.

When reviewing the support provision in place, university leaders may wish to consider the following aspects:

1   The specialist nature of support and where there may be gaps for those receiving support, for example, connections to trauma counselling or criminal justice processes. How does the specialist support link in with university policy and process? Where they are independent, how can this be managed to reduce the number of times a victim-survivor must disclose their experience in order to receive appropriate and wrap-around support?
2   The diversity of staff providing support, including cultural background and language. A lack of diversity in staffing may act as a barrier to accessing support for fear of people not understanding their context, additional challenges, or marginalisation, including those with English as their second language. If support provision ignores intersectional experiences and fails to recognise the additional discrimination that some are living with, it can silence their experiences. The need for a diverse staff needs to be considered within the procurement and recruitment process, and positive action under the *Equality Act 2010* should be utilised when vacancies arise.
3   Accessibility of the support: Is the support available in person only or remotely? What time of day and year is the support available? Is the support available in multiple languages, and if not are interpreters

available? In addition to diversity, accessibility must be considered as part of the procurement process and for future recruitment.

Community-based partnerships have proven effective where universities work closely with regional or local services providers to ensure effective and timely support to those subjected to gender-based violence. However, in order to be respectful of the expertise and experience of community sector organisations providing support, such relationships must be ethical, mutually beneficial, and the support remunerated. Due to the increased demand for such services, there is a need to explore more sustainable partnerships. An opportunity, and arguably a necessity, for the sector, would be to call for a coordinated and regional approach to ensure all universities have appropriate, timely, and consistent support. This would also reduce the burden on charities such as Rape Crisis, who are often stretched for resources nationally, and consequently are working with a number of universities with limited continuity. There is scope to examine the support provided in a regional location and identify what is necessary and appropriate for universities based on region and size. One example of this approach is Fearless Glasgow (Glasgow Caledonian University, 2019), a consortium of university partners working strategically to tackle gender-based violence.

Policy drafting and implementation

The objective of an effective policy is to outline behavioural expectations, clearly and consistently communicate the responsibility for individuals and the university for upholding these behavioural standards, outline the process for reporting if there is a suspected or alleged breach, the consequences for any breaches, and to be clear on the internal and external support available for students and staff. This process should be trauma-informed and person-centred and reduce the number of times someone discloses. It must include information about the wrap-around support that may be required to enable the victim-survivor to continue to access their work or studies, and also ensure appropriate support is provided to both the reporting and responding parties. One area of contention has been the use of non-disclosure agreements following an investigation and disciplinary matter. In 2018, UCL adopted an approach to no longer use NDAs as a matter of course in sexual misconduct and harassment cases, recognising that they may still be used at the request of the complainant, but that they have been implemented often as a tool to silence survivors and protect the accused.

Language in policy drafting is critical, which is why I've found the language of fair treatment or human rights to be simple and accessible. It encompasses the principles of natural justice and due process; however, it still provides safeguards within its framing for the reporting individual, as well as the responding. As a practitioner with a legal background, I understand the importance of natural justice and due process. There is an argument that the understanding of what constitutes due process has been skewed in the direction of the reported individual (this is also arguably present in the application of privacy and data protection laws), with victim-survivors being treated as witnesses to a process, and therefore not privy to the same access to information, ability to respond, and protections. As universities are not courts of law, and therefore under an obligation to investigate breaches of policy, the language and practice of fair treatment enable universities to uphold their responsibilities whilst ensuring necessary fairness to both parties.

University leaders need a focus on both the drafting and implementation of policies. Professor Nicole Westmarland highlighted the importance of giving equal weight to both the policy drafting and its operationalisation, in the University of Sussex report following a high-profile domestic abuse case (Westmarland, 2017). It is critical for effective tertiary prevention, and integrity of the university community, to ensure that policies are implemented in accordance with their intention. Effective implementation requires adequate support, training, and evaluation over time. Without this, ineffective or inconsistent implementation of policies can lead to further distrust in the organisation, including "nothing will be done if I make a complaint", which is one of the key barriers for people reporting, or reasons why people choose to report anonymously (Culture Shift, 2020, p. 15).

Another opportunity (or gap) in the sector relates to sanctions. Some excellent work has been enacted at an institutional level which makes clear the sanctions for associated behaviours, for example, Durham University's Sexual Misconduct and Violence Policy (Durham University, 2019). However, this is inconsistent across the sector and highlights the need to have more standardised sanctions. The message must be clear and consistent across all education bodies: gender-based violence has no place in our community, and should it occur, these are the sanctions, which include dismissal and exclusion where appropriate. Part of the need for clear and consistent sanctions across the sector is to address the risk that students and staff move institutions following an allegation and there is a need to safeguard against repeat behaviour. This recommendation is in line with The 1752 Group and McAllister Olivarius guidance for managing staff misconduct which calls for a requirement that investigations be completed, and that upheld complaints should be stated in staff reference letters (2020, pp. 19, 24).

Data protection

Critical to all policies is secure data protection and clarification of what information will be shared with who and when; this is also vital for trauma-informed practice. However, data protection has acted as a barrier to clear and consistent university practice regarding sharing outcomes. It is unconscionable that someone who has been subjected to gender-based violence, who relives their experience and is exposed to a challenging, often lengthy and draining process of an investigation, grievance, and disciplinary process, and is not informed of the outcomes, including sanctions. However, the way that data protection and privacy laws are constructed is not conducive to this. Sharing outcomes provides a sense of closure, allows for healing, even if the outcome is not what was expected.

When drafting the Prevention of Bullying, Harassment and Sexual Misconduct Policy for students and staff (University College London, 2020), it was important to ensure clarity for all about what information would be shared and when. This transparency was key to building trust. We sought internal and external legal counsel and agreed to focus on the following aspects:

- Clarifying whether the complaint was upheld or not upheld and whether or not the responding party had been dismissed or expelled;
- If not upheld, focusing on sharing information with the reporting party, which may include the sanction so as to minimise any adverse effects in accessing their work or study environment.
- Finally, that any information shared is done so confidentially (UCL, s. 7.1–7.3).

During my tenure at Culture Shift as the Head of Success, we developed sector-first guidance on data sharing agreements (Culture Shift, 2021); providing examples of what information could be shared and when; both during an investigation and/or after it had been completed. This guidance also involved calling for a legal requirement to be introduced for universities to complete investigations even if the student or staff member had left the organisation. Such a requirement would allow an outcome based on the evidence available to be determined, providing closure for the reporting party. Furthermore, it may enable factual references to be provided to address the risk of perpetration for the accused at another institution.

Secondary prevention

Secondary prevention or early intervention involves changing the trajectory for those at high risk of being subjected to or perpetrating gender-based violence. This involves practice around safeguarding and risk assessments, dedicated and specialist support, addressing cultural barriers, and promoting effective active bystanders and allies.

Safeguarding and risk assessments

Safeguarding policies must prioritise early intervention and clarify processes for at-risk adults, including a risk assessment framework. As many individuals may be involved in a risk assessment, the practice and principles applied can vary. At University College London (UCL), I designed a risk assessment to assess people and behaviour risk informed by HR, legal services, planning, student support and equality, diversity, and inclusion. This resulted in a robust process that would be undertaken following a disclosure to ensure associated risks were identified and addressed at the earliest opportunity. Professor Westmarland highlighted the need for such a process in the report for the University of Sussex following a high-profile domestic abuse case. Professor Westmarland noted that inappropriate consideration was given to the academic teaching and promotion of the Senior Lecturer (SL), and undue consideration was given to the fact that no other complaints of violence and abuse had been made. As violence, abuse, and harassment are vastly underreported crimes, there are significant barriers to those subjected to such crimes to come forward. Professor Westmarland rightly highlights that the 'school managers failed to recognise that the way the SL acted towards them as male managers, were not necessarily the way that he interacted with those with less power, including students, early-career academics, and some administrators' (Westmarland, 2017, p. 8). Any risk assessment must involve a thorough examination of the broader context in which the alleged incidents have taken place, including any power imbalances. The framework should account for human rights frameworks, but also workplace safety according to the recommendations from the Respect at Work report from the Australian Human Rights Commission (AHRC, 2020, p. 25). It is critical that those charged with the responsibility of undertaking a risk assessment have been provided with appropriate training, including awareness of the prevalence, barriers, and impact of particular behaviours.

Such a risk assessment framework needs to be incorporated into case management processes. Reporting platforms such as Culture Shift's Report + Support system has provided universities with a user-friendly case management system and the ability to analyse trends and risks in real time. This technology, coupled with a risk assessment process, allows universities to engage more deeply in early intervention. Risk assessments must indicate what early intervention or long-term strategy will be required to change the trajectory for those at risk of being subjected to, or of perpetrating gender-based violence.

The language of safeguarding students can be confusing in practice. The UUK guidance recognises the importance of safeguarding students. Additionally, the *Safeguarding Vulnerable Groups Act 2006* also places legal obligations on universities to safeguard those under 18 years of age and adults deemed at risk. The attitude towards students shifts at university, with the assumption that everyone is an adult and therefore safeguarding risks are reduced: failing to account for contextual vulnerabilities at university. In 2020, there were 1.35 million, or 56.7% of students under the age of 21 (Advance HE, 2020) and many universities offer summer schools and language courses to prepare those under 18 for tertiary study. Another perspective is that the relaxing of social norms between students and university academic staff that occurs can lend itself to productive and successful working relationships and friendships but can also lead to abuse of power. However, the lack of clarity and professional conduct requirements can also increase the potential for abuse. Two examples of this include the relationship between PhD students and their supervisors, and that between post-doctoral researchers and principal investigators. In such contexts, the student or junior researcher is dependent on one individual to shape their career, their future in academia, and beyond. While there are healthy relationships in this context, there have been high rates of abuse, including bullying, harassment, and sexual misconduct reported across the sector. Thus universities must provide safeguards to both students and staff in their policies to uphold research integrity; this includes having clear staff–student relationship policies. In 2020, UCL prohibited close personal or intimate relationships between students and staff where there was direct supervision, to safeguard both students and staff. The policy was modelled on practice in US universities where relationships are banned with undergraduate students. It also recognised the professional practice requirements of many industries where those in power are prohibited from having a relationship with a person in their care, for example, a doctor and patient, or lawyer and client. Historically, successful and productive relationships have existed in this context; introducing safeguards such as this is not a criticism of those relationships, but an intervention that reflects the current need and context.

Environmental investigations

The process of environmental investigation was developed at UCL following the emergence of concerning themes or anonymous reports received through Culture Shift's Report + Support. Trend analysis reports were conducted on a quarterly basis and incorporate the number and nature of reports, including anonymous reports, training uptake data, and a recommended action plan shared with the Dean, Heads of Department, and the HR Business Partner. At the time, there were a limited number of actions that could be taken from anonymous reports, which resulted in the development of environmental investigations. The purpose of these was to understand problematic behaviour in detail and to identify risks and possible solutions to prevent the re-occurrence or escalation of such behaviours. The process was designed by myself with the support of HR colleagues and included clear terms of reference for the investigation and the appointment of an independent investigator to conduct the process. As the nature of an environmental investigation is to uncover, the focus may shift during the investigation; therefore, we ensured the terms of reference highlighted the need for a preliminary report and recommendations to be presented to the department and HR for review.

The process itself could be triggered from a series of anonymous reports if the nature of the behaviour or the volume of reports was concerning, or if there was a risk to student or staff safety and well-being. The process helps to overcome a significant barrier that limited or no action could be taken from reports made anonymously and instead provides an opportunity for the university to take informed action where there is an identified risk. The initial process was managed by HR and with my support, we identified key people to be involved in the process, given their roles and responsibility. In addition, a department or team communication was shared with details about the process, its purpose, and why it had been initiated, inviting anyone who wanted to participate to notify the HR lead. Participants were then connected with the independent investigator to set up a time to be interviewed. Initially, participants would only be identifiable to the investigator and process manager. However, to ensure principles of natural justice, those participating in the process could be identified if the recommendation was for disciplinary action against an individual. The key recommendations from an investigation may include professional development, support interventions, changes in management structures, or disciplinary action where named reports have emerged as part of the process.

Environmental investigations, while time-consuming, are an effective form of secondary prevention or early intervention. This process has since been adopted in other institutions with effect. Due to significant barriers that exist through named and formal reporting, this intervention can have a tangible impact on the workplace and learning culture.

Training programmes

Training has become a key intervention for secondary and primary prevention, including but not limited to raising awareness of the issue and its impact on those directly and indirectly subjected to gender-based violence, consent, unconscious bias, or bystander intervention. However, such programmes are often limited to instilling general principles; few have embedded skill development or been evaluated long term.

At UCL, I partnered with the UCL Centre for Behaviour Change to apply behavioural science, particularly the Behaviour Change Wheel, to reduce bullying, harassment, and sexual misconduct. The Behavioural Change Wheel framework synthesises 19 behaviour change frameworks that draw on a wide range of disciplines and approaches, including the Capability-Opportunity-Motivation-Behaviour (COM-B) model which outlines the necessary conditions for expression of a behaviour (Michie et al., 2014). Applying the behaviour change wheel to existing bullying and harassment training demonstrated the importance of being specific about the pro-social or anti-social behaviours that need to be influenced, and ensuring the content was specifically targeted to change those behaviours. The application was also helpful to both Human Resources (HR) and Equality Diversity Inclusion (EDI) professionals present to address the assumptions made about what the most appropriate intervention may be.

> Of the nine behaviour change interventions, education was relied on heavily in current practice. Through applied research, Dr. Paul Chadwick and I found that whilst education and persuasion are powerful techniques for tackling some aspects of capability and motivation, they may not be particularly effective at changing other influences on behaviours relating to bullying and harassment. They would not, for example, help staff acquire the interpersonal skills needed to give feedback constructively or intervene to stop an episode of bullying in a tactful way.
>
> (Chadwick & Paske, 2021, s.3)

Through applying the COM-B model: capability, opportunity, motivation = behaviour, colleagues and I were challenged to focus on the specificity of the behaviours that we wanted to shift. This included encouraging and discouraging behaviours, and asking what necessary environmental conditions and drivers enable positive behaviours and discourage unacceptable forms. The take-home message was clear though when designing training programmes: general principles will not change behaviour. While there are impactful programmes, both existing and emerging, for allyship and active bystanders, there is an opportunity to explore how behavioural science may be applied to strengthen such programmes by utilising the full range of interventions and maximise their impact.

Primary prevention

Primary prevention focuses on addressing the drivers of gender-based violence, which can include gender inequality, homophobia, and transphobia. When examining intersectional experiences, this also includes systems of oppression, including racism and white supremacy, ableism, and heteronormativity. This is why primary prevention is often placed in the 'too hard basket', and the focus remains solely on tertiary prevention. However, we need all three forms to effectively tackle and prevent all forms of gender-based violence, including those with intersecting identities or experiences.

Primary prevention requires institution-wide initiatives to address the drivers, threaded throughout all relevant strategies and strategic plans. Charter Marks, Athena SWAN, the Race Equality Charter, Stonewall, and Disability Confident all provide necessary frameworks to examine and redress structural barriers and inequities related to protected characteristics. Work to address the awarding gap, increase the representation of marginalised groups within leadership positions, and improve organisational culture are all critical levers in addressing drivers of inequity that contribute to intersectional experiences of gender-based violence. Whole-of-population initiatives must examine both student and staff life cycles and identify key opportunities for intervention, as well as the reach of the university: research, alumni, policy, and community reach. In practice, there is a need and opportunity to ensure this work is connected. The complex nature of universities results in siloed work that may be unknown or duplicated across departments or divisions. A key action moving forward is to ensure efforts are aligned. This is challenging, but it's possible.

Legal frameworks and responsibilities

A positive duty to prevent sexual harassment is increasingly being called for, particularly within the workplace context. This approach has been adopted by the Equality Human Rights Commission (EHRC) in the recent technical guidance on workplace harassment (EHRC, 2020). Furthermore, it is a key recommendation from the Respect at Work enquiry by the Australia Human Rights Commission. This enquiry also highlighted the need for occupational health and safety frameworks to acknowledge the issue of harassment, its impact, and the need for this to be considered and prioritised within organisational safety strategies. I would argue that should such a positive duty exist for workplaces, it should be extended to educational settings. As universities fall within category of being a workplace, education provider, and research institution, they can fall through the gaps between safeguarding, employment, and human rights law, despite having unique vulnerabilities and power dynamics.

In the UK, employers can be held vicariously liable under the *Equality Act 2010* for incidents of harassment committed by employees. The defence to this is if employers take all reasonable steps to prevent incidents of harassment from being perpetrated by employees. This test is difficult to meet, and requires a step-change in thinking: moving away from the entrenched practice of managers only taking action once a formal complaint has been made. Case law has highlighted that any knowledge or suspicion of employee predilections would require a higher threshold to be met.

Legal frameworks that require workplaces and education providers to have a positive duty to prevent, and not just respond, will be essential for the future and sustainability of this work. Such a duty encourages shared ownership and will shift current practice to being proactive about prevention.

Power, privilege, and entitlement

As primary prevention centres on the drivers of a particular behaviour, there are key gendered drivers that underpin the continuum of gender-based violence. However, examining these drivers' intersectional experiences means that the drivers will vary, for example, they may include the impact of colonisation for experiences of racialised gender-based violence. There are common themes that underpin structural inequalities that relate to how violence is perpetrated and experienced. The three I wish to highlight are power, privilege, and entitlement. Power structures relating to racism, sexism, ableism, homophobia, and transphobia must be considered, and while there may be some overlaps, assumptions should not be made about how they manifest.

> Men don't abuse women because society tells them it's okay. Men abuse women because society tells them they are entitled to be in control.
>
> (Hill, 2019, pp. 7–8)

It is not the violence itself that is deemed acceptable, it's the entitlement behind it that has been rationalised. Entitlement is a tool in the belt of systems of oppression: it is the thread running through rigid societal norms about who holds power. Striving for equity and inclusion in our learning environments, workplaces, and broader society is seen as an 'imbalancing act' as taking power away from the status quo. Those with a sense of entitlement will use this to belittle, to assert dominance, and to 'rebalance' the environment to their sense of comfort.

It is power, privilege, and entitlement that fuel different forms of violence and abuse. The example from the quote focuses on men's violence. This reference does not mean that men cannot be subjected to violence; however, it recognises that men's violence against women, and indeed towards other men, is disproportionately perpetrated by men (this may be referred to as the triad of men's violence). The resistance of 'not all men' and 'all lives matter' are examples of extreme discomfort centred on the understanding that achieving equality is a zero-sum game and that their rights, their entitlements, and privileges are being eroded. This thinking is highly dangerous and must be addressed. These conversations also seek to delegitimize the issue by refocusing attention elsewhere. For conversations about 'not all men', the focus shifts to issues of male mental health rates and male suicide. All of these issues are concerning and must be addressed; however, they are not mutually exclusive. In fact, the drivers of men's violence and poor mental health include harmful gender stereotypes and pressures to perform dominant forms of masculinity. The same argument could be made for resistance to anti-racist work and the argument regarding the white working class. While classism is evident, addressing structural racism and classism is not one or the other, what is required is challenging dominant forms of who holds power based on particular characteristics. We need to move away from polarising rhetoric and focus on shifting attitudes and behaviours along the continuum. Recognising and accepting that structural barriers exist for marginalised people is the starting point; for example, accepted that structural racism exists. This is not easy, but it's necessary. Prevention work that does not recognise structural inequalities will not effectively tackle the drivers. This is why examining the whole system, the whole structure, and the institution is critical.

Behavioural systems mapping

One approach to this analysis is through behavioural systems mapping which Dr. Paul Chadwick and I applied to examine the issue of staff to student sexual misconduct at UCL. This research was a proof of concept and is believed to be the first application of its kind. Behavioural systems mapping lends itself to systems-level change, focusing on points of intervention and design through the creation of a causal loop diagram, identifying both individual- and systems-level interventions. The process involved inviting key stakeholders to participate in a series of interviews and focus groups to identify the actors, influences, and behaviours operating in the UCL system that enabled sexual misconduct. These actors, behaviours, and influences were further refined over the consultation period: identifying the positive and negative reinforcement factors, and identifying key themes or priority areas to intervene with maximum impact. Once the themes had been refined, we tested these with the initial stakeholders consulted to determine if the map reflected an accurate picture of what they had described. The themes identified included addressing the organisational measure of success; reducing the power-differential and providing safeguards in PhD student and supervisor relationships; people management and providing effective feedback; judicious and investigative processes that are burdensome. This exploratory study provided a rich description of the complex nature of sexual misconduct and allowed for a shared understanding between stakeholders. Recommendations were then developed in conjunction with HR and EDI and have since been revised in light of COVID-19.

The whole-of-institution approach

In 2020, Our Watch Australia, Universities Australia, and the Victorian Government produced the Educating for Equality framework to support Australian universities to address the norms, practices, and structures to effectively prevent violence against women. The framework outlines a whole-of-institution approach and names the key areas for engaging when devising a prevention strategy, including student life, teaching and learning, workplace, research, and business and operations (Universities Australia, 2020, p. 15, 16).

Universities have undertaken a range of different approaches, including training, campaigns, and practice, to engage in primary prevention. The following is a range of examples of emerging primary prevention practices, a key opportunity for future practice will be to evaluate the range of interventions utilised as part of an organisational strategy:

- A national campaign that increases knowledge and changes behaviours that drive gender-based violence (AHRC, 2020, p. 24), as well as continuing important campaigns to combat racism, ableism, classism, homophobia, and transphobia.
- Social media movements that have harnessed important discussions, including #Black Lives Matter and #Me Too. However, it is important that these movements promote ongoing engagement; for example, through the use of educational and behaviour change campaigns. Some examples of national and organisational campaigns include No Excuse for Abuse by Our Watch on addressing the minimisation of violence, Dear Daddy by CARE in Norway, Let's Talk about Race at UCL, It Gets Better to uplift, empower and connect LGBTQ+ youth around the globe, White House campaign It's On Us for universities to tackle sexual assault, and Race to Equality led by UNISON to address racism in the NHS and many others.
- A clear overview of all educational and workplace rights, responsibilities, and support available. The Respect at Monash online course is an excellent example of how e-learning can be utilised to set clear expectations and define behaviours. It also introduces frameworks of active bystander, respectful relationships, and consent education, whilst signposting to support. Such programmes must be mandatory and followed up with in-person training that allows for further awareness and skill development.
- It is imperative that the prevention of gender-based violence is not considered wholly in isolation in a dedicated strategy. Having a dedicating strategy is important, but this must be threaded through key organisational strategies to ensure that the work is not siloed and remains business-critical.

- Universities can set the tone for culture and behaviour within their procurement processes. This is key for all third-party contracted staff, but also in service contracts, including residential services, security, health and wellbeing contracts, as well as making clear to all university partners the values and commitment of the organisation.
- Sharing practice with delivery partners, for example, NHS Trusts, third parties, and alumni. The dedication to prevention cannot exist within the walls of the university; taking a whole-of-institution approach within higher education is also about examining the reach of the university.
- Communication campaigns co-designed with students, staff, researchers, and support services, to promote awareness of an issue, signpost to support, and set clear expectations on what is acceptable and unacceptable in the community. The messaging can be designed to challenge attitudes and encourage or discourage particular behaviours.

Preventing gender-based violence before it starts will not be achieved by a tick box approach or treating the work as 'nice to do'. While gender equality needs to remain at the centre of efforts to prevent gender-based violence, it must be addressed concurrently with other forms of discrimination and disadvantage such as racism, colonisation, ableism, homophobia, and religious discrimination (Universities Australia, 2020, p. 8). There must be a sustained strategy to address the drivers of these behaviours if we are to prevent them.

What's next?

It's important to take stock of the processes and support that exists and prevent duplication where possible. Following COVID-19, the key challenge to continuing this important work will be resourcing. With uncertain times, and diverted attention, it is important that this work is considered essential, and resourcing decisions reflect this. In fact COVID-19, remote working, and living have presented new challenges for the way that gender-based violence is perpetrated and experienced, and this must be considered remote living and working, and within hybrid models of working.

While the issue of gender-based violence does not exist solely in higher education, the way it is perpetrated and experienced poses unique challenges for higher education. However, prevention work cannot exist in a vacuum, but rather it needs to align with work in schools, professional practice, and regulators. There is significant scope to pilot programmes within procurement practices, through NHS Trusts, through alumni communities, and with industry bodies, and expand if interventions prove impactful. Universities are uniquely placed to undertake prevention work on a large scale given their close ties to schools, innovative research, and links with broader sectors. As university education and research continue to innovate and explore interdisciplinary models for tackling global issues, so too must prevention practice. The opportunity is significant, but the political will must also be there to undertake this work long term, and to do this requires strategic planning and resources. What we have seen in the UK is pockets of funding provided through HEFCE or institutions following high-profile incidents, rather than sustainable models. Reactive responses do not and will not work long term. This work must be considered within organisational planning, institutional risk registers, and as such appropriately resourced and evaluated over time.

I want to end with a thank you to all those who have shaped the current prevention practice; we are so grateful for the opportunity to learn from you. Thank you to those who are slogging it day-in and day-out to make sure this work stays on the agenda and to those to come; whose experiences, whose passion, and dedication for meaningful change will move us forward.

Summary of key points

- There are many examples of good practices in the UK relating to effective and trauma-informed support for those subjected to gender-based violence. However, this lacks consistency across the sector. For example, there are inconsistencies in policies balancing fair treatment to both reporting and responding parties, effective specialist support services working with universities to provide 'wrap-around' support and reduce the number of times someone must disclose.
- Intersectional experiences are not an add on. When addressing the drivers of particular behaviours, we must examine all drivers and not just one form of inequality. This will perpetuate different privileges within our universities. To be intersectional, is to consider these experiences from the outset.
- To ensure the sustainability of this work, feedback loops must be created to allow people who have engaged in consultations or campaigns to feel heard, and to increase transparency in decision-making and action taken.
- Equal weight must be given to policy drafting and implementation. When drafting new policies, be mindful about who needs to be supported to implement the policy in accordance with the intention and identity key evaluation metrics to measure success.
- To build the business case for increased support services or role, evaluation should be considered for both reporting and responding parties. The evaluation of support should include all-inclusive support, including therapeutic responses, but practical considerations such as accommodation, coursework, and/or work environment.
- Ensuring a robust risk assessment framework that links to the institutional risk register and is evaluated over time is critical to effective early intervention. Those undertaking such risk assessments need to be appropriately trained and regularly undertake refresher courses.
- There are a range of interventions, including training; however, consider whether training is the most appropriate intervention and if the content of the training is meeting the intended outcome.

- Relationship policies may be controversial, but they can provide appropriate safeguards and set clear expectations for what constitutes professional conduct. Such policies are consistent with other professional sectors and practice codes.
- There are a range of legal frameworks that are applicable for preventing gender-based violence, including positive duties that support proactive intervention measures.
- While there will be common threads across the sector where interventions may be similar, the context and history of each university are important to consider. Behavioural systems mapping is just one tool for assessing the whole university approach, but it is necessary to examine and not rely on assumptions.
- Primary prevention is very difficult to achieve without long-term resourcing and buy-in from senior leadership, and collaboration – the sharing of knowledge, research, and practice is key to enabling meaningful change.

Further Reading

Chadwick, P., & Paske, K. (2021). *Applying behavioural science to reduce bullying, harassment and sexual misconduct within academia.* UCL.

There has been increasing reference for behavioural, or attitudinal change when preventing gender-based violence, however, limited application of behavioural science to prevention-based initiatives in universities. This blog explores the first of two projects between the UCL Centre for Behaviour Change, and UCL Equality, Diversity and Inclusion, specifically with my role the Behaviour and Culture Change manager. It provides the reader with considerations for applying the behaviour change wheel when designing, or to existing training programmes to ensure that the full range of behavioural interventions can be utilised. During the application, colleagues who participate in the training from Human Resource and Equality, Diversity and Inclusion were challenged to name the specific behaviour that needed to be addressed, this was quite a challenge, moving away from behavioural themes, to providing the specificity required for tailored interventions. It was here where colleagues and I reflected on the trainings we had in place and conducted a rapid assessment and application of the COM-B framework to existing training and soon identified that we were only harnessing one of the possible nine interventions to change behaviour. As a result of this assessment, we identified a further four interventions through minor tweaks to the content and delivery that would maximise the opportunity to shift behaviour – in this case, developing the skills of an active bystander. This blog provides clear examples of specific behaviour relating to bullying and highlights how the Behaviour Change Wheel may be applied to improve a range of interventions, including as a prompt to ask if training is the most appropriate intervention required in that context.

Our Watch. (2021). *Change the story: A shared framework for the primary prevention of violence against women in Australia* **(2nd ed.). Our Watch.**

Our Watch was established as Australia's national organisation for primary prevention of violence against women and their children. The key framework that underpins Our Watch's work is *Change the story*, first published in 2015 by Our Watch, Vic Health and ANROWs was the first primary prevention framework to address violence against women and their children. The framework provides the basis for all primary prevention work undertaken by Our Watch nationally in workplaces, universities, schools, TAFEs, local government, sporting associations and media engagement. The first edition of *Change the story* was adopted as Australia's national policy framework for prevention by all Australian Governments under the *Third Action Plan 2016–19 to Reduce Violence Against Women and their Children*. The second edition of Change the story was published on November 24th, 2021, drawing from international and national evidence base in Australia, and provides a detailed framework for effective intersectional primary prevention practice. *Change the story* draws on key publications from Our Watch, including *Changing the Picture: A national resource to support the prevention of violence against Aboriginal and Torres Strait Islander women and their children*; *Men in Focus: unpacking masculinities and engaging men in the prevention of violence against women*; *Tracking progress in prevention: a national monitoring report on progress towards the primary prevention of violence against women and their children in Australia* and upcoming publication, *Changing the Landscape: A national resource to prevent violence against women and girls with disabilities*. *Change the story* has been recognised in many international contexts as a world-leading contribution to the field of prevention and has inspired work towards similar approaches in other countries. This second edition aims to continue and strengthen Australia's leadership on this issue and is an essential framework for those working to prevent intersecting forms of gender-based violence.

References

Advance HE. (2020). *Students statistical report 2020*. Self-Published.

Australian Human Rights Commission. (2020). *Respect @ work: National inquiry into sexual harassment in Australian workplaces, community guide*. Self-Published.

Bold Voices. (2021). *Gender-based violence continuum image*, as seen in www.sec-ed.co.uk/best-practice/sexual-harassment-and-violence-what-can-schools-do-me-too-pshe-rse-bold-voices/

Chadwick, P., & Paske, K. (2021). *Applying Behavioural Science to reduce bullying, harassment and sexual misconduct within academia*. Retrieved January 2022, from www.ucl.

ac.uk/behaviour-change/news/2021/jan/applying-behavioural-science-reduce-bullying-harassment-and-sexual-misconduct-within

Crenshaw, K. (2016). *The urgency of intersectionality*. TED Women.

Culture Amp. (2019). *Diversity, inclusion and intersectionality report*. Self-Published.

Culture Shift. (2020). *Exceeding expectations: Guidance on tackling sexual misconduct and harassment by culture shift*. Self-Published.

Culture Shift. (2021). *Data sharing guidance for case management*. Self-Published.

Dick, K. (2015). *The hunting ground*. RADiUS-TWC.

Durham University. (2019). *Sexual misconduct and violence policy*. Self-Published.

Epigeum. (n.d.). *Consent matters: Boundaries, respect and positive intervention 2.0*. Oxford University Press. Retrieved January 2022, from www.epigeum.com/courses/support-wellbeing/consent-matters-second-edition/

Equality Human Rights Commission. (2020). *Sexual harassment and harassment at work: Technical guidance*. Self-Published.

Gainsbury, A. N., Fenton, R. A., & Jones, C. A. (2020). *From campus to communities: Evaluation of the first UK-based bystander programme for the prevention of domestic violence and abuse in general communities*. (20, 674). BMC Public Health.

Glasgow Caledonian University. (2019). *GGU hosts launch of Fearless Glasgow*. Self-Published.

The 1752 Group & McAllister Olivarius. (2020). *Sector guidance to address staff sexual misconduct in UK higher education: Recommendations for reporting, investigation and decision-making procedures relating to student complaints of staff sexual misconduct*. Retrieved January 2022, from https://1752group.files.wordpress.com/2020/03/the-1752-group-and-mcallister-olivarius-sector-guidance-to-address-staff-sexual-misconduct-in-uk-he-1.pdf

Hill, J. (2019). *See what you made me do: Power, control and domestic abuse*. Black Inc.

Michie, S., Atkins, L., & West, R. (2014). *The behaviour change wheel: A guide to designing interventions*. Silverback Publishing.

National Union of Students. (n.d.). *I heart consent campaign*. Retrieved January 2022, from www.nusconnect.org.uk/liberation/women-students/lad-culture/i-heart-consent

Ortus Economic Research Ltd & Loughborough University. (2019). *An impact evaluation of the Athena SWAN Charter*. Advance HE.

Our Watch. (2021). *Change the story: A shared framework for the primary prevention of violence against women in Australia* (2nd ed.). Our Watch.

Our Watch, Australia's National Research Organisation for Women's Safety (ANROWS) & VicHealth. (2015). *Change the story: A shared framework for the primary prevention of violence against women and their children in Australia*. Self-Published.

UN Women. (2015). *A framework to underpin action to prevent violence against women*. Retrieved January 2022, from www.unwomen.org/en/digital-library/publications/2015/11/prevention-framework

Universities Australia, Victoria State Government & Our Watch. (2020). *Education for equality: A model to address gender-based violence at, and through, Australian universities, A whole of university approach*. Our Watch.

Universities UK. (2016). *Changing the culture: Report of the universities UK taskforce examining violence against women, harassment and hate crime affecting university students*. Universities UK. www.universitiesuk.ac.uk/policy-and-analysis/reports/Documents/2016/changing-the-culture.pdf. (Last access January 2022).

University College London. (2020). *Prevention of bullying, harassment and sexual misconduct policy*. Self-Published.

Westmarland, N. (2017). *Independent review into the university of Sussex's response to domestic violence*. Self-Published.

15 Reflections on accessing and reporting on employee well-being data

Implications for hybrid-working and gender-based violence

Rosanna Bellini

Disasters, such as the global pandemic of COVID-19, can disrupt the nature of work, creating cultures of ambiguity that constitute shifting priorities for individuals, organisations, and their wider communities. For many Higher Education employees, the sudden transition to pandemic-induced working from home state required a significant renegotiation around space and time, with boundaries between work and home dramatically blurred. While operating in subsequent uncertain environments can promote a positive reassessment of labour and well-being in general through promoting new ways of working, there has been a strongly positive association with disasters and the rise of patterns of gender-based violence (United Nations Women, 2021). The literature is clear that the pandemic has affected the time and conditions of academic and professional labour, with women, on average, more negatively affected than men (Jung, 2020; Myers et al., 2020). Indeed, existing studies cite anecdotal evidence around a reduction in productivity such as academic paper publishing by women, an uptake in the proportion of working hours dedicated to care work, and an increase in job loss (Viglione, 2020). Such data can highlight the stark disparities in Higher Education experience, yet there remains a lack of scrutiny into the role of gender-based inequalities in policy and social decisions around combating this in the workplace. This is in the face of evidence that the pandemic has been identified to be a direct driver of gender-based violence for higher education staff, leading to increased exposure to environments that include domestic violence (John et al., 2020) and sexual harassment (Rights of Women, 2021).

In times of information overload, it is essential to pay critical and explicit attention to what data are being used to inform the working experience of the future for women's well-being and safety. As such, this work acts on the advice kindly offered by feminist sociologist Maria do Mar Pereira (2021) that by highlighting the emergence of gendered inequalities *inside* universities, not just the division of work *outside* of them (i.e., caring responsibilities), we might make universities more accountable for pandemic-cultivated gender inequalities. To challenge criticisms of '*historical and conceptual amnesia*' that such studies of technological change have had levelled (Ackers & Wilkinson, 2003: p. 200),

DOI: 10.4324/9781003252474-17

I put forward that such a crisis presents an ample opportunity to re-examine existing research on data in the workplace and how they might help or hinder combatting gender-based violence in practice. Applying a reflective and retrospective approach to understanding issues central to prior technology and working practice may be just as important as novel research on our current crisis (Hodder, 2020).

In this chapter, I offer a critical re-analysis of the role of employee-generated data around the topic of gender-based violence, focusing on sexual harassment, bullying, and gendered thermal discomfort. I do this through examining two cases of prior, pre-pandemic, academic studies in Higher Education contexts around how we might define the scope of employee accounts, how we might elicit this from the employees themselves, and then put this knowledge into practice. In this works' first study, I introduce a critical analysis of a design and deployment of a discursive artefact titled *Harassment Bingo* that introduced a novel data collection approach that focused on gendered accounts of bullying and harassment in the workplace. I follow this with the second study of this chapter that describes how occupants of a Higher Education building related to quantitative metrics of thermal discomfort as sourced by another novel data collection approach named *ThermoKiosk*. Through following this critical analysis, I contribute pointers to how subtle indicators of gender-based violence in the workplace can be leveraged as means to improve equality in hybrid-working cultures for Higher Education employees. I conclude with a discussion for how we might position the relative safety of disclosure through the positionality of researchers may provide survivors, and how novel data collection approaches can highlight normalised harms in the workplace.

Background literature

Due to the threat posed by COVID-19, many colleges and universities around the world opted to switch to remote working and online teaching to keep their students, professors, and staff safe during the pandemic emergency. Many managers in Higher Education have indicated that some of the impacts from the global pandemic on workplaces might be lasting, where flexible working hours and digital meetings are expected to increasingly replace corporate culture. Indeed, the overarching approach to this transformation is experimenting with a '*new digital work culture as effective and productive*' as working in physical offices (Kim, 2020). As Jenkins (2020) argues, universities have '*[requisitioned] the home as a condition of continuing to work*', with Manokha (2020) arguing that the domestic rhythms, routines, and characteristics of home life are now subject to a considerable degree of greater scrutiny than before. Importantly the '*eradication of leisure*' that may be experienced by home workers can increase the pressure of being always available and ready to report one's work for approval (Boggis, 2001). As the power dynamics of labour and surveillance shift, it is important to scrutinise what new modes of data collection on employees have emerged, and how they relate to women's well-being and safety. In laying out the existing problems of Higher Education workplaces, I focus on how occupational gender-based violence have become embedded in the very digital systems used for work, and how data-driven reporting processes obscures workplace harms, prioritising efficiency over well-being.

The changing face of occupational gender-based violence

Sexual harassment in Higher Education can happen to anyone; however, women are disproportionately affected, impeding their safety, comfort, and equal access to career progression and education (Bondestam & Lundqvist, 2020)s. An area that has seen relatively little analysis with the turn to pandemic-enforced ways of working is that of the rates of occupational bullying and harassment and gender-based violence in Higher Education. While many accounts theorise that women's well-being could improve due to a reduction in exposure to the physical workplace environments where toxic behaviours may be manifest (Hu et al., 2021), these are largely speculative in nature and do not respond to the growing number of reports that show women have experienced an upsurge in sexual harassment from working from home (Strenio & Chowdhury, 2021). *Rights of Women*, a women's rights charity, reported that the 15% of women responding to their survey reported an increase in online harassment while working from home, and one in two women who had experienced sexual harassment related some to all of it taking place online (Rights of Women, 2021). Some reports have offered preliminary findings that indicate the relatively 'informal' nature of working from home may elicit different types of sexual harassment, such as cyberflashing, targeted private messaging, inappropriate work attire during video calls, and calling out of work hours (D'Souza et al., 2020; Ahuja & Padhy, 2021). Researchers have theorised that this could be due to harassers taking advantage of new work channels for communication (e.g., Slack and Asana) and blurring the boundaries between work and social media communication between colleagues (Ahuja & Padhy, 2021).

Escaping occupational bullying and harassment may be particularly acute in remote working contexts due to an underlying expectation of an employee being always present on their digital devices and continuous virtual group meetings may continuously expose one to their harasser. In particular, enforced work from home policies rarely take into consideration that such working environments can be actively unsafe for women, such as those at risk of intimate partner violence (Roy, 2021). As such, in line with Karami et al.'s (2021) recent review of occupational sexual harassment studies, it is important to expand the understanding of sexual harassment '*beyond the conventional physical workplace*' when millions of people have transitioned to home working. This is particularly important as many Higher Education Institutions may not include off-campus sexual harassment within the scope of their policies related to staff. I now turn our attention to how we might elicit novel understandings to familiar environments as they pertain to information about Higher Education employee data regarding their well-being.

The challenges with data-driven reporting processes

When it comes to designing Higher Education policy around sensitive issues such as gender-based violence, including sexual harassment and domestic violence, the sector has been repeatedly criticised at the lack of transparency on the role of what data is being used to guide organisational decisions (Taylor, 2020). When such data do exist regarding complaints around gender-based violence, this data is often abstracted from the complex situations that produced them, such as the normalisation of toxic workplace behaviours (Bellini et al., 2018). Such data can provide an insight into the inner workings of academic systems, through making apparent some of the factors that contribute to gendered inequalities, such as a normalization of gender-based violence, a culture of silence, and a lack of active leadership (Karami et al., 2021). Importantly, in recent years, there have also been several turns to critically examine the politics of data, and the judgements made on behalf of data-driven approaches in the workplace to both organisational and social goals (Taylor et al., 2015). For instance, the term *data-driven* has seen a rapid uptake in Higher Education contexts, has been carefully challenged by several scholars for the distinctive loss of vital contextual information, cultural norms, and interpersonal interaction between employees. For instance, being driven by data can result in an institution see metric data surrounding publication counts, research output, and grant funding that may be seen as being inherently more valuable than how an individual may treat their colleagues (Pereira, 2021). When such data do exist regarding complaints around gender-based violence, it is often abstracted from the complex situations that produced them, such as the normalisation of toxic workplace behaviours (Bellini et al., 2018).

Reducing the gap between employees and their accounts must go beyond merely amending existing reporting processes as such efforts can fail to consider the existing problems of disclosure of gender-based violence (Anitha et al., 2020). In her in-depth composite ethnography of university culture, Alison Phipps (2020) identified disclosures of sexual harassment and violence were met with '*institutional airbrushing*', protecting the institution and (frequently) privileged male members bound up with its success. Women and their accounts are processed through long, arduous processes that are bound by confidentiality that may individualise complex toxic workplace cultures and make it difficult to address as a problem for multiple individuals. However, how accounts of occupational bullying and harassment are currently processed through bureaucratic systems entail that aggressors can hide behind non-disclosure agreements and right to confidentiality, despite the existence of patterns of violence (Prasad, 2018). When women make a complaint about the culture in Higher Education, reports indicate that the overwhelming majority of respondents state management is not doing enough to respond to concerns (Rights of Women, 2021). As such, it is important to restructure thoughts on how to bridge this gap between women, their accounts of gender-based violence, and how such accounts can be gathered without losing the nuance of office cultures and norms, through formal or informal reporting processes.

A method for re-analysis of engagements

My approach takes two examples of prior, self-*contained* research studies that share the common qualities of having explored issues on employee well-being and safety in Higher Education contexts and sought to challenge standardised data collection practices. From the original outset of both studies, the research teams were motived to understand the '*data worlds*' from the people *inside* these environments and how they related to such data in such a context (Riley, 2013). As I have mentioned earlier, working with only abstracted or 'de-contextualised' data often includes little to no discussion about the social context, ethics, values, or politics of data (D'Ignazio & Klein, 2020), all of which conveniently may touch on the holistic experiences of harm. When I observed that important information about individual or collective discomfort is at best unintentionally obscured by the Higher Education contexts that both studies took place within, or, at worst, deliberately excluded, the research teams sought to identify ways that people relate to representations of their relative safety from harm through data practices *first-hand*.

I scrutinise the design rationales behind each study to unpick design decisions and examine the reported reflections upon the benefits, limitations, and general application of designing for and with data that represents gender-based violence. To ensure consistency in this approach, and based upon the insights from the aforementioned literature, I pay particular attention to the conceptual *orientation* to employee-generated data in respect to how each study sought to collect, analyse, and feed this data back into practice. To do this, I pay particular attention to the *scope* (how are data selected), the method of *elicitation* (how are data collected), and the *practice* (how are data utilised) of using such accounts to bring about change in working environments inspired by other critical lenses as applied in this space. Focusing on these three facets will ideally provide a consistent analytical lens to establish commonalities across these research projects, upon which I then theorize how such commonalities may have implications for novel data-informed 'work from home' cultures.

Research study 1: De-normalising toxic workplace cultures

Across the summer of 2017, Bellini et al. (2018) sought to investigate how accounts of bullying and harassment within academia could be used to design bespoke training sessions for the workplace. This was in response to the lack of bullying and harassment training for academic contexts, a workplace that maintains organisation and work features that may increase the likelihood of hostile interpersonal behaviours (Skinner & Aziz, 2021). Over the space of three months, accounts of occupational bullying and harassment from Higher Education employees were gathered to inform the design of a novel data collection artefact and environment. *Harassment Bingo* was one such artefact that permitted survivors of occupational bullying and harassment to be in control of how they could identify, define, and quantify negative workplace behaviours through pressing one of 16 self-labelled buttons that could be edited or wiped clean using its whiteboard feature. Such buttons included descriptions

 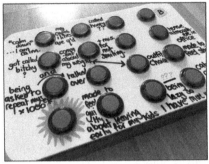

Figure 15.1 Harassment Bingo data collection. *Left:* Incomplete data collection artefact Harassment Bingo consisting of a raspberry pi, circuit board, 16 physical buttons encased in a wipe clean white board for annotation. *Right:* A complete Harassment Bingo artefact with a range of self-described bullying and harassing behaviours experienced in the workplace.

of emotions ('*felt uncomfortable*'), actions ('*being talked over*'), and events ('*tense atmosphere*'), but also some participants also used symbols to indicate instances of occupational violence that were hard to describe. Five participants shared accounts of explicit gender-based violence in the workplace, including sexual harassment by a male colleague, gendered insults shared via a work call and being directed to work overtime with disregard for their caring responsibilities.

The data from the accounts and *Harassment Bingo* were then used to inform the design, content, and delivery of specialised seminars that encouraged prosocial discussion and reflection on negative workplace behaviour between employees. Bellini et al. (2018) reported that there were interesting responses to the visibility of such data as evidence; that, if such data would continue to be kept confidential would reinforce the 'insidiousness' of negative workplace behaviours, while exposure of data only on bullying and harassment could skew the impression of a workplace. This delicate balancing act reinforces the challenges in how data related to gender-based violence might be captured, and how concealment or exposure of such accounts can disrupt behaviours in Higher Education contexts.

Research study 2: Negotiating thermal comfort

In the summer of 2016, Clear et al. (2018) undertook a four-week deployment of a technology probe *ThermoKiosk* to explore the collective experience and understanding of occupant comfort levels in a modern university building. Through the introduction of a range of different interfaces, *ThermoKiosk* was designed to elicit experiences of workplace comfort through five pre-established, yet subjectively framed, options. Similarly, the data elicited from *ThermoKiosk* was then used to draw out accounts from office staff members

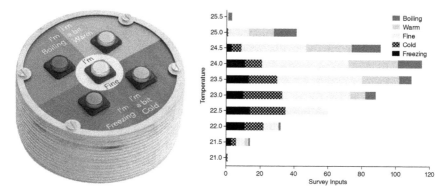

Figure 15.2 ThermoKiosk survey and data. *Left:* ThermoKiosk survey device that offered five Likert-type scale of thermal comfort in the workplace. *Right:* Survey device inputs mapped against the quantitative records of thermal temperature in the office space. (Graph credit to Samantha Mitchell Finnigan.)

on their perspectives on thermal comfort management, what the expectation of such data would show, before being presented with the actual quantitative data. While this work did not explicitly target the collection of gender-based violence, nevertheless, many accounts around thermal comfort indicated gendered experiences of the workplace, and provide commentary for how such data could be used to shape better experiences for its occupants. Women in this work were identified as potentially being more sensitive to temperature changes, and having their concerns more frequently spoken over or disregarded by the building management. As such, this work was included in my analysis as it represents an interesting mirror of how gendered dynamics and expressions of power can manifest in topics as seemingly 'neutral' as interior temperature.

Clear et al. (2018) identified that the quantitative data, such as the optimal interior temperature, that *ThermoKiosk* managed to elicit may illustrate the conditions of a Higher Education context, but is of little utility to the occupants without their accounts to better contextualise such findings. The qualitative accounts alone however may mask some more specific time-sensitive patterns (Figure 15.2) that would be challenging to determine on their own, indicating a variety of different types of workplace account could be valuable to appropriately represent the 'culture' of a workplace.

Thinking on the scope, elicitation, and practice of employee-generated data

Through examination of these two research studies, I identified commonalities in respect to how they define, collect, and utilise different digital and technological approaches to first-hand engagement with employee-generated data on harms and discomfort for women. Despite the variation in topic between occupational bullying and harassment and thermal comfort, both works attempt to capture so-called hard to represent topics by offering participants first-hand the ability to contribute aspects of this experience that may fly 'under the radar' in normal workplace environments. While a subjective feeling of discomfort or exposure to a micro-aggression may not meet the threshold of being severe enough to warrant making a formalised complaint, both works highlight these experiences as important to still draw attention to and challenge, matching other calls in literature around violence and abuse (Anitha et al., 2020; Phipps, 2020). In both research studies, decisions by the research team have been made to *scope* data that, in their opinion, may challenge what is or what is not captured through existing reporting mechanisms around employees. In addition, the research teams aim to pair tried and tested approaches of the *elicitation* of data, such as interviews, alongside novel and creative approaches to elicitation of accounts, such as button presses. Finally, both studies presume that the visualisation and engagement of such data may result in a change in occupational policy, *practice*, and a critical reflection on norms that may produce negative workplace behaviours. For clarity, I now break down these components.

Scope: what data are selected?

Choosing *what* is worthy of measurement and *how* it is defined (i.e., language) about topics that are hard to contextualise such as violence is an implicit expression of political power (D'Ignazio & Klein, 2020). I take pause to examine what data are being selected for scrutiny and why around employee-generated data that include implicit and explicit accounts of gender-based violence, including thermal discomfort, sexual harassment, and bullying.

In the first research study, Bellini et al. (2018) capture discrete instances of bullying and harassment in Higher Education, potentially smaller than those captured through other approaches, that are importantly self-defined by the participants using the artefact. This suggests an approach to gathering data on harms that is open-ended in nature and demonstrated the flexibility for data to be defined specific to workplaces with a few common characteristics. Presenting participants with an artefact that records button presses does also indicate the research team were interested in collecting frequency of the presses and the time; potentially to draw patterns in the data of negative workplace behaviours and when participants sought to engage with data collection on this topic. This can also be seen in the design decisions surrounding ThermoKiosk that prioritise personal perspectives ('*I'm boiling*') over 'ground truth' reporting processes such as actualised temperature recordings in the office. Positioning workplace occupants as the primary producers of these accounts help to resist the decontextualization that takes place when data are abstracted from a workplace, particularly around accounts of occupational gender-based violence.

First-hand accounts of workplace experiences through a direct interaction are also selected as being more valuable to explore here than looking over historic data, indicating there is value in the contemporary and situated nature of this data. Such artefacts are unusual in their elicitation of accounts of the workplace in the same environment and even in the same instance that it occurs: from a feeling of being too hot in that moment to feeling uncomfortable after a conversation with a colleague. In both artefacts case, this may work to its advantage, capturing data as it happens 'in situ' before it is subsumed into workplace culture, capturing data that is hyper-specific to that space, moment, and feeling (Skinner & Aziz, 2021). In the case of *Harassment Bingo*, while the types of data such as the number of button presses remained fixed, participants could write down on a whiteboard what they would like to record as what they personally found important to record in relation to gendered harms, including subtle cases of bullying and harassment such as being continuously talked over or ridiculed publicly for a contribution. Such an approach is especially valuable for gender-based violence as permitting a participant to be in control over what *feels* like harassment to them may significantly be more valuable than presenting them with a list of predefined (and frequently legalised), formal definitions such as 'assault' or 'harassment' that may not resonate with their experiences (Hurren, 2018). Nevertheless, caution should be taken here that too greater flexibility in approaches to data collection can run the risk of *blank canvas paralysis* where participants may be too intimated to contribute their experiences due to lack of boundaries in reporting negative workplace behaviours. A reflection could be made here that the research team engage directly with this understanding, that the value of understanding that specific environment by people in their own terms is more valuable than a generalisable format that can be expanded out to other Higher Education contexts as reflected in the design of both research artefacts.

Upon greater reflection, *Harassment Bingo* is a somewhat naive interpretation of how bullying and harassment happens, harms that frequently build into the texture of workplace interactions, thereby being hard to solidify as an 'instance' to be recorded. The same issue would apply for sexual harassment, 'grooming' or boundary blurring, and creation of an uncomfortable sexualised workplace where these are normally not one-off incidents but rather behaviours that occur over time which are hard to pinpoint or define (Kelly, 1988). Quantifying the level of bullying and sexual harassment can also mask important qualities such as severity and patterns by the same aggressor that may be left outside of these reporting processes. Simultaneously in *ThermoKiosk*, it appears that it is not possible to establish which office occupant was performing the acts of contributing their perspectives, or even if such occupants voted at all in the study. Perhaps unintentionally, this does potentially obscure the role of individual office occupants in aiding shape decision-making as connected to their data, once more indicating the political and ethical dimensions to employee-driven data on uncomfortable or harmful experiences.

Elicitation: how are data collected?

The term 'how' is interventionalist in nature, questioning by what means that something happens or comes about, and, most frequently in academic research, in what way can it be changed (Muller, 2011). Having now established what aspects of employee experience both studies sought to capture, I now turn my attention to the processes to which this was done, what characteristics were considered, and how were data collected.

In both research studies, the research teams evidently saw value in creatively exploring alternative approaches to data collection around sensitive topics, resisting the urge to encourage participants down a reporting route for complaints. Indeed, the newness or originality of such approaches are imbued with novelty effect on ways to interact with this mode of data collection, in both positive and negative ways. In *Harassment Bingo* (Figure 15.1), the process of identifying frequently gender-based micro-aggressions (e.g., 'being talked over') to write down and then record as it happened incited interest by affected participants, potentially in a way that reporting such events at a later stage may not. The same can be demonstrated in *ThermoKiosk* where the survey device (Figure 15.2) was disproportionately preferred over the other data input approaches in the study. In many ways, these discoveries indicate that there is inherent value to distilling the complexity of subjective discomfort down to an interaction as simple as a (self-)labelled button press.

Despite being rarely mentioned in other studies on sensitive disclosures of occupational harms, research artefacts are explicit in both where they were located physically around the workplace to elicit these accounts and the nature of their public or private visibility to other office occupants. For *ThermoKiosk*, designed for the collective sharing of accounts, it is perhaps unsurprising that all survey devices were placed in public locations, appealing to a subjective experience of a shared space around individual experience of comfort. Conversely, participants who were provided *Harassment Bingo* took it upon themselves to decide how, when, and where such information could be offered through concealing the artefact within their workplace, such as in a desk drawer, or on display on their desk. In cases where participants recorded instances of harm, this appeal to privacy is a form of self-censor when we may consider that participants may report harms caused by other colleagues. A commonality across both works however is the acknowledgement of performativity that button pressing provides that may impact the behaviours of others in the office. For instance, a public display of the unacceptability of a social harm or thermal discomfort can provoke others into a response or action, both positively and negatively. In such a way, this could provide more methods to bias experiences in offices towards those who may be more comfortable voicing their discomfort on the harms they are subjected to than others.

When the 'how' of such data collection processes around workplace harms are questioned, it also appears inevitable that such approaches elicit accounts on how existing processes for data collection are insufficient or fail to capture matters of importance to workers. The novelty effect certainly had an impact on the types of interactions participants made with interfaces on their well-being and safety, but this may be because existing processes do not take the granularity of experience into account through deliberate abstraction and cleaning of relevant information (Zhang et al., 2020). As both research teams reflected on, the artefacts were deployed over a relatively short time frame as part of a research study, with *Harassment Bingo* deployed to five participants over one week each, against ThermoKiosk over the space of four weeks. In such a way, this may be just a window into not only a specific environment, but a specific time and a specific configuration of people in that moment. While cases of harassment, bullying, and ongoing exposure to uncomfortable workplace environments may require more investigation, such artefacts may provide meaningful insights into the emergence of negative workplace behaviours that may prompt further, formal investigations.

Practice: what does it change?

Data are useful to inform understanding of the relationships between different agents, entities, and environments, to diagnose the source of problems and improve processes that work towards ensuring employee well-being. For this final stage of my analysis, I reflect on the practice of the data, or how the data was used or positioned critically to achieve (or at least inspire) change or improve women's safety and well-being when working in Higher Education.

Both works we have discussed so far sought to leverage the collated data to explore the participant experience of interacting with produced data from theirs and their colleagues accounts. Approaching the higher educational context in this way indicates a subtle interventionalist approach (that I have drawn attention to in my prior section) that both studies change something inherent to this workplace practice. For instance, this could be around what data are included for consideration in measuring and intervening in toxic workplace cultures for female staff where continuous reports of bullying and harassment emerge (Pereira, 2021). Regarding the second study in my comparison, hints are made to the potential for passing over control of interior thermal temperature from building managers who may merely extract thermal data information from Higher Education environments but not engage with changing them in the interest of employee well-being. Both studies, although never explicitly stated, indicate there is a significant lack of a role of participatory activities in co-designing more comfortable and safe workplaces for all that may be rectified through collective sense-making around complex social issues. In this way, both works pose that the power of the collective should challenge top-down approaches to decision-making; whether through passing direct control to office workers or prioritising individual accounts of harm that would normally go unnoticed.

For *Harassment Bingo*, the research study sought to directly feed such findings into the content for bespoke bullying and harassment training specific to the Higher Education context that holds unique characteristics that make such behaviour more likely (Skinner & Aziz, 2021). For instance, through extracting labels from the whiteboard and recording mechanism, discursive seminars directly leveraged these descriptions of negative workplace behaviours to facilitate critical discussion on attendees' own behaviour and potential contribution to these experiences. Following these seminars, it was the intention of the research team to use these findings to inform the policies for managing incidents in the Higher Education context for Higher Education members. In this way, data collected here are treated as *evidence* of the existence of these behaviours, elevating individual accounts that may normally fall outside of formal reporting processes such as a complaint. The practice of data for the study that contained *ThermoKiosk* was similar, where engagement with the probe '*raised the voices*' of members of the office that may normally be excluded. Importantly, the visibility of such accounts in both studies is notably rare for Higher Education contexts where complaints around workplace behaviour are kept strictly confidential (Prasad, 2018), making it harder for members of a workplace to critically reflect on their own potential contribution to a toxic workplace environment. What appears a common theme across these research projects is crafting novel approaches to provide a portfolio of mechanisms for reporting and highlighting concerns.

A final theme that has been identified during this critical reflection is leveraging data as a practice to consider workplace challenges that may be treated in isolation as a collective and shared experience. In this way, while each method of data collection could only be used by one individual at one time, the practice of the data brought about a sense of solidarity and unity around tackling complex workplace harms together. Nevertheless, the elevation in understanding the experiences of others that may be hard to contextualise still runs into the wider problem of where this data fits in larger Higher Education systems. For instance, while data may be a welcome representation of a workplace for its occupants, Higher Education management may be reluctant to adopt this as an accurate representation of a wider institution, leaving such approaches vulnerable to *institutional airbrushing* (Phipps, 2020).

Thinking temporally: the pandemic and beyond

Now that I have conducted a critical retrospective review of interventionist technologies that sought to disrupt the still of workplace harms, I turn my attention to the present where 'the workplace' for Higher Education no longer holds such fixed boundaries as it once did. In contextualising my analysis in the here and now for Higher Education, I consider how the potential benefits and challenges might be to handing over control of participant-authored accounts of gender-based violence and discomfort. This permits this work to contribute the notion of feminist data generation as a productive method for empowering and promoting design enquiry into workforces that prioritise an employee's safety, well-being, and ability to thrive (D'Ignazio & Klein, 2020). I do this as an effort to support approaches that seek to be disruptive to and destabilise toxic workplace cultures that disproportionately impact women (Karami et al., 2021). This is done through five design recommendations for how those in Higher Education can engage directly in working towards challenging cultures of gender-based violence through novel data collection methods and beyond.

In pandemic-induced work contexts, many problems around gender-based violence in the workplace have both intensified, increased, and changed in nature (United Nations Women, 2021). In respect of the changing landscape of work, many aggressors may seek to take advantage of this rapid upheaval of protocol and procedure, such as aggressors using novel tools for communication and harm, and taking advantage of the blurring of boundaries between home and work (Strenio & Chowdhury, 2021). If bullying and harassment accounts are known to de-contextualise complex experiences, this analysis points out to the value of positioning participants as experts of their own personal experiences. In respect to these changing contexts, providing participants who may be unsure of what constitutes gender-based violence or a matter of concern with the tools and channels to self-describe discomfort I find to be extremely promising. As such a recommendation for how data collection processes can be designed with this in mind is to (1) *provide a flexible process for participants to self-determine what they find important to capture about their experiences of harm and discomfort.* This can help to mitigate the concerns around labelling patterns and incidents with legalised terms such as harassment, bullying, or assault that may not resonate with the individual(s) who have experienced gender-based violence. Yet future tools that seek to investigate the hybrid-working environments need to take care in mitigating from the *blank canvas paralysis* and individuals truly interested in exploring accounts of gender-based violence must take care to not deliberately exclude matters of concern, thereby making a political choice on what is valuable to record (D'Ignazio & Klein, 2020). A basic structure around defining experience could be useful here, such as requesting information around the channel of abuse or discomfort, intensity, frequency, and its intersection with other aspects of a workplace. Alternatively, beginning reporting processes with so-called softer and more accessible language through the sentence-completion method such as 'I feel uncomfortable when. . .', instead of the emphasis placed on chronology and history in existing reporting procedures (Karami et al., 2021). For instance, with the awareness that now many Higher Education employees deploy a hybrid approach to moving between home and work, there is greater potential to map how negative workplace behaviours and environments may manifest differently for workers.

Following directly on from this suggestion, consider back to how both studies identified participants who appreciated being able to voice their discomforts *without* having to proceed with the long arduous reporting processes in their institutions. I highlight this not as a means to disparage attempts by those within Higher Education that seek to improve reporting processes so that they are both trauma-informed and survivor-driven, but rather to reinforce the need for alternative and diverse interventions for negative workplace behaviours. As such, the second recommendation for this work is to (2) *provide a range of different measurement mechanisms for gender-based violence from casual disclosure to formal reporting processes.* In particular, the role that signalling something about current working arrangements may be awry, yet without escalating this to the role of a complaint may be of specific value. Such a wider variety of ways of signalling potential gender-based violence are also of significance when we consider particularly that such systems may still be managing the pause created by a pandemic backlog. There is a caution to this recommendation on the discovery that the newness or novelty effect of each reporting process may occur where interesting interaction mechanisms may be prioritised over tried and trusted approaches, such as interviews or focus groups. As mentioned in my analysis, a button-press on *Harassment Bingo* imposed a somewhat naive interpretation as to how micro-aggressions and bullying and harassment may manifest in workplaces. Such novel approaches should thus be introduced with caution, and may be supplemented with richer approaches to reporting, such as interviews or observations, where appropriate.

My third recommendation for this work, that if reporting processes are deemed to be the most suitable avenue to address a concern, (3) *emphasise the collective experience and solidarity that may support the individual making a complaint.* For instance, both studies sought to form an impression of a shared environment through individual accounts, rather than bestowing the responsibility on a single individual to recount their experiences. As my analysis indicated, when participants witnessed each other using *Harassment Bingo* or *ThermoKiosk*, this prompted a form of solidarity and encouragement through shared experience. As reporting processes rely on an individual sharing their account, rarely are these processes designed with solidarity or support from others in mind. While individuals who wish to elicit accounts should be careful to not breach confidentiality of those involved, matters in relation to negative workplace behaviours need to be conceptualised as the product of cultural and social norms and not as individual transgressions alone (Kelly, 1988). In this way, we realise that the request for employee-generated data has distinctive power dynamics baked into it (Taylor, 2020): Is the data asked for, demanded, or freely offered?

Providing a range of portfolio of data collection methods has always been discussed as being valuable by researchers, yet it can be challenging to manifest these within institutional structures. Nevertheless, consider how (4) *research artefacts and projects can be valuable testing grounds for designs to alternative processes for highlighting employee discomfort and harm before they may be built into institutional processes.* While tests or trials can inadvertently give off the impression that such approaches are less important or temporary, consider that a test permits different data collection approaches to capture how workplace behaviour may be both positively and negatively changed as a result of the intervention. The two research studies in this analysis were able to stand outside of the traditional hierarchical structure by their position as researchers, rather than senior management, and the conduct of research. However, the same power dynamics and positionality does not hold for the design of Higher Education workplace and may have to be navigated more carefully. Questions remain about the role of context in both these analytical findings; how might employees '*weave their experience within their whole environment*' as they may move between work and home? (Bolchini et al., 2009)

Finally, the hybrid way of working will simultaneously expand potential places for work for some occupations and constrain some others, such as workers who cannot return to their workplaces due to closure or health reasons. For matters such as employee bullying and harassment and thermal discomfort, there may be attempts from Higher Education management to roll back the coverage of their scope due to the lack of guidance around behaviour off-campus or outside of traditional communication channels (Ahuja & Padhy, 2021). Nevertheless, it is not enough for workplaces to wash their hands of the issue, specifically now when a small number of assertive (and potentially vocal) individuals may have more authority over the workplace experience due to a smaller number of people returning to work. As such, the final recommendation for work in this space is to (5) *consider the temporal and spatial nature of how such gender-based data may be collected and seek to reduce the impact of re-traumatisation through different approaches.* For instance, if sexual harassment has taken place through video-conferencing mechanisms, it may be sensible to trial an approach that does not rely on this data collection method. Additionally, as Higher Education staff may experience different privacy considerations at home than in the workplace – such as cohabiting with an abusive partner – consider how such reporting mechanisms may harm or hinder attempts to reach out for help.

In hybrid-working contexts, many of the core characteristics that I have considered in my critical analysis can be translated simply by critically analysing what aspects of employee experience are being considered, where does gender-based violence fit with this; what data are being looked at and by whom, and how flexible the ability to deviate from the reporting apparatus is provided. Such challenges resist easy fixes, but rather continuously point to how we continuously innovate to scope, elicit, and use employee well-being data in practice to combat the insidiousness of gender-based violence.

Summary

As Higher Education workplaces have dramatically changed in the past few years, it is vital for greater scrutiny to take place around how employee data is being leveraged to exacerbate or combat occupational gender-based violence. In this chapter, I presented a novel retroactive analysis of two research studies as conducted in Higher Education, suggesting the potential for novel data collection methods for capturing subtle, hard to speak about harms, in the context of research. Through discursive approaches that encouraged collective action around individual discomfort and placing the survivor of targeted bullying and harassment directly in the author seat of their experience, I highlight how much more we should be leveraging participatory practices in the design of the workplace of the future. Following this analysis, I offer five design recommendations for working directly with capturing employee accounts with respect to their own well-being that look at reporting alternatives, the role of research, and the value of flexibility around interaction and language.

I anticipate that further research is required into how data on negative workplace behaviours may manifest in the hybrid workplace of now, particularly as they pertain to video-conferencing software and asynchronous communication. I also see great potential in exploring how top-down decision-making around workplace practice may take place as Higher Education employees are further decentralised and distributed.

Further reading

Bellini, R., Olivier, P., & Comber, R. (2018). That really pushes my buttons: Designing bullying and harassment training for the workplace. In *Proceedings of the 2018 CHI conference on human factors in computing systems* (pp. 1–14). Association for Computing Machinery. https://doi.org/10.1145/3173574.3173809

This work could be of interest to readers of this chapter whom found the descriptions of *Harassment Bingo* to pique their curiosity. In my work, I narrate how identifying key qualities of occupational bullying and harassment directly went into the design of a novel data collection method, such as interviewees describing micro-aggressions, struggling to find the language for their discomforts and using humour as a vehicle for expressing accounts that may be otherwise challenging to share. This work is also joined by a second discursive artefact referred to as *Lifting the Lid*, a data collection tool styled as a music box that would replay the last message that was spoken into it. Participants who used both *Harassment Bingo* and *Lifting the Lid* were asked to share their experience of Higher Education with particular focus on micro-aggressions and negative workplace behaviours. This data were then used to design bespoke bullying and harassment data that used accounts from each artefact, with permission from participants, on the delivery of discursive seminars where such data could be invested in more detail. Such data were used as *evidence* of such behaviours, as a means to *discredit* someone's representation of their workplace and as a way to reinforce the same power inequalities that could inadvertently contribute to environments of harm. Following an analysis of these interactions with the data, a point is made around the role that novel data collection processes can have in identifying and challenging harms that are normalised and rarely represented through other reporting processes.

Finnigan, S. M., Clear, A. K., Farr-Wharton, G., Ladha, K., & Rob Comber. (2017). Augmenting audits: Exploring the role of sensor toolkits in sustainable buildings management. *ACM J. PACM Interact. Mob. Wearable Ubiquitous Technol. 1*, 2, Article 10. doi:10.1145/3090075

Although not directly on the topic of gender-based violence, the following work explores how digital technologies can be used to creatively explore both quantitative and qualitative approaches to thermal temperature control in Higher Education environments. In this work, Samantha Mitchell Finnigan et al. highlight that relying too heavily on supposed 'smart' buildings impose restrictions on what information is worth measuring, normally at the detriment to the building occupants. For the future of building design, many characteristics such as sustainable materials, heat efficiency and space utilisation are prioritised to promote a workplace that extracts the optimum level of labour from its employees while keeping overhead costs low. This work challenges this overarching narrative through leveraging participatory activities to deploy flexible sensor toolkits that playfully place the participants in the shoes of the building auditors that elicits important tensions around what is important to occupants and building managers. In doing so, the work raises fascinating questions around who are the building's 'end users' so to speak, who is the building actually designed for and how might its existing occupants rally for change if this answer is different for building managers. Shared standards and practices that directly involve occupants in how buildings should be considered is of significant value for the future, particularly in creating comfortable work environments for all. As hardware has become substantially cheaper than previously for sensor kits, democratising access to the creation of digital tools can provide exciting opportunities to thinking about their intersection with environments that generate gender-based violence.

References

Ackers, P., & Wilkinson, A. (Eds.). (2003). *Understanding work and employment: Industrial relations in transition* (1st ed.). Oxford University Press.

Ahuja, K. K., & Padhy, P. (2021). The cyber avatar of sexual harassment at the workplace: Media analysis of reports during COVID-19. *Journal of Psychosexual Health, 3*(4), 322–331. doi:10.1177/26318318211047832

Anitha, S., Marine, S., & Lewis, R. (2020). Feminist responses to sexual harassment in academia: Voice, solidarity and resistance through online activism. *Journal of Gender-Based Violence, 4*(1), 9–23. doi:10.1332/239868019X15764492460286

Bellini, R., Olivier, P., & Comber, R. (2018). That really pushes my buttons: Designing bullying and harassment training for the workplace. In *Proceedings of the 2018 CHI conference on human factors in computing systems* (pp. 1–14). Association for Computing Machinery. https://doi.org/10.1145/3173574.3173809. Retrieved November 2, 2021.

Boggis, J. J. (2001). The eradication of leisure. *New Technology, Work and Employment, 16*(2), 118–129. doi:10.1111/1468-005X.00081

Bolchini, C. et al. (2009). And what can context do for data? *Communications of the ACM, 52*(11), 136–140. doi:10.1145/1592761.1592793

Bondestam, F., & Lundqvist, M. (2020). Sexual harassment in higher education – a systematic review. *European Journal of Higher Education, 10*(4), 397–419. doi:10.1080/21568235. 2020.1729833

Clear, A. K. et al. (2018). ThermoKiosk: Investigating roles for digital surveys of thermal experience in workplace comfort management. In *Proceedings of the 2018 CHI conference on human factors in computing systems* (pp. 1–12). Association for Computing Machinery. Retrieved November 2, 2021, from https://doi.org/10.1145/3173574.3173956

D'Ignazio, C., & Klein, L. F. (2020). *Data feminism*. MIT Press (Strong Ideas).

D'Souza, N., Forsyth, D., & Blackwood, K. (2021). Workplace cyber abuse: Challenges and implications for management. Personnel Review, 50(7/8), 1774–1793. https://doi. org/10.1108/PR-03-2020-0210

Hodder, A. (2020). New technology, work and employment in the era of COVID-19: Reflecting on legacies of research. *New Technology, Work and Employment, 35*(3), 262–275. https://doi.org/10.1111/ntwe.12173

Hu, X. et al. (2021). Time to disentangle the information and communication technology (ICT) constructs: Developing a taxonomy around ICT use for occupational health research. *Occupational Health Science, 5*(1), 217–245. doi:10.1007/s41542-021-00085-6

Hurren, W. (2018). Call it by its name: A partial glossary about sexual harassment for faculty members. *McGill Journal of Education/Revue des sciences de l'éducation de McGill, 53*(3). doi:10.7202/1058421ar

Jenkins, F. (2020). Did our employers just requisition our homes? *The Canberra Times.* Retrieved October 26, 2021, from www.canberratimes.com.au/story/6701054/did-our-employers-just-requisition-our-homes/

John, N. et al. (2020). Lessons never learned: Crisis and gender-based violence. *Developing World Bioethics.* doi:10.1111/dewb.12261

Jung, H. (2020). *COVID-19 stay-at-home orders worsen academic scientists' home-life: Women experience more difficulties.* SSRN Scholarly Paper ID 3642732. Social Science Research Network. doi:10.2139/ssrn.3642732

Karami, A. et al. (2021). A systematic literature review of sexual harassment studies with text mining. *Sustainability, 13*(12), 6589. doi:10.3390/su13126589

Kelly, L. (1988). *Surviving sexual violence* (1st ed.). Polity Press.

Kim, R. Y. (2020). The impact of COVID-19 on consumers: Preparing for digital sales. *IEEE Engineering Management Review, 48*(3), 212–218. doi:10.1109/EMR.2020.2990115

Manokha, I. (2020). Covid-19: Teleworking, surveillance and 24/7 work. Some reflexions on the expected growth of remote work after the pandemic. *Political Anthropological Research on International Social Sciences (PARISS), 1*(2), 273–287. doi:10.1163/25903276-BJA10009

Muller, M. (2011). Feminism asks the "who" questions in HCI. *Interacting with Computers, 23*(5), 447–449. doi:10.1016/j.intcom.2011.02.001

Myers, K. R. et al. (2020). Unequal effects of the COVID-19 pandemic on scientists. *Nature Human Behaviour, 4*(9), 880–883. doi:10.1038/s41562-020-0921-y

Pereira, M. do M. (2021). Researching gender inequalities in academic labor during the COVID-19 pandemic: Avoiding common problems and asking different questions. *Gender, Work & Organization, 28*, 498–509. doi:10.1111/gwao.12618

Phipps, A. (2020). Reckoning up: Sexual harassment and violence in the neoliberal university. *Gender and Education, 32*(2), 227–243. doi:10.1080/09540253.2018.1482413

Prasad, V. (2018). If anyone is listening, #MeToo: Breaking the culture of silence around sexual abuse through regulating non-disclosure agreements and secret settlements. *Boston College Law Review, 59*, 2507.

Rights of Women. (2021). *Rights of Women survey reveals online sexual harassment has increased, as women continue to suffer sexual harassment whilst working through the Covid-19 pandemic.* Retrieved December 11, 2021, from https://rightsofwomen.org.uk/news/rights-of-women-survey-reveals-online-harassment-has-increased-as-women-continue-to-suffer-sexual-harassment-whilst-working-through-the-covid-19-pandemic/

Riley, R. (2013). Dataveillance and countervailance. In *'Raw data' is an oxymoron* (pp. 121–145). MIT Press.

Roy, A. (2021). *The COVID-19 shadow pandemic: Domestic violence in the world of work-private sector.* SSRN Scholarly Paper ID 3953287. Social Science Research Network. Retrieved November 9, 2021, from https://papers.ssrn.com/abstract=3953287

Skinner, T., & Aziz, S. (2021). The relationship between occupational category and workplace aggression: Workaholism as a potential moderator. *River Cities Industrial and Organizational Psychology Conference.* https://scholar.utc.edu/rcio/2021/posters/6

Strenio, J., & Chowdhury, J. R. (2021). Remote work, sexual harassment, and worker wellbeing: A study of the United States and India. In *Handbook of research on remote work and worker well-being in the post-COVID-19 era* (pp. 32–52). IGI Global. doi:10.4018/978-1-7998-6754-8.ch003

Taylor, A. S. et al. (2015). Data-in-place: Thinking through the relations between data and community. In *Proceedings of the 33rd annual ACM conference on human factors in computing systems* (pp. 2863–2872). ACM (CHI'15). doi:10.1145/2702123.2702558

Taylor, L. D., Jr. (2020). Neoliberal consequence: Data-driven decision making and the subversion of student success efforts. *The Review of Higher Education, 43*(4), 1069–1097. doi:10.1353/rhe.2020.0031

United Nations Women. (2021). *The shadow pandemic: Violence against women during COVID-19.* United Nations. Retrieved November 9, 2021, from www.unwomen.org/en/news/in-focus/in-focus-gender-equality-in-covid-19-response/violence-against-women-during-covid-19

Viglione, G. (2020). Are women publishing less during the pandemic? Here's what the data say. *Nature, 581*(7809), 365–366. doi:10.1038/d41586-020-01294-9

Zhang, A. X., Muller, M., & Wang, D. (2020). How do data science workers collaborate? Roles, workflows, and tools. *Proceedings of the ACM on Human-Computer Interaction, 4*(CSCW1), 022:1–022:23. doi:10.1145/3392826

16 We should do something (someday)

Identifying and working through resistance to gender-based violence prevention

Clarissa J. Humphreys and Graham J. Towl

Since Universities UK published guidance on addressing sexual misconduct in 2016,[1] we are often asked, "How do you get started?"; "How do you get senior leader buy-in?"; "How do you get Human Resources on board?"; and the most common question we hear is "How do you get anyone to resource this?". On the surface, these questions appear to be focused on beginning this work, but at their core, are asking the same thing: "How do you work through resistance?" And there seems to us to be some significant resistance to change in the sector.

Should students and employees be able to study and work in environments free from harassment, violence, and the fear of harassment and violence? Will senior leaders prioritise and allocate resources to ensure the health and safety of staff and students? Do Human Resources staff agree employees should be kept safe? The answer to each of these questions should surely be an emphatic "yes". It is hopefully uncontroversial to expect that when students attend university, live in residence halls, participate in extracurricular activities, or interact with fellow students or staff, they do so without being subjected to harassment or violence. Likewise, we all expect that when we go to work, we also will not be subjected to harassment or violence too. In other words, we expect the health and safety of students and employees to be prioritised and preserved and, to put it in its legal context, that we are not prevented from accessing education or employment.

When we sharpen the focus of student and staff health and safety issues to look solely at gender-based violence, health and safety often becomes controversial and an array of resistance responses are used. Gender-based violence (GBV) is pervasive in Higher Education (HE) and society globally (Towl & Walker, 2019; UN Women, 2018). It is happening every day impacting, most commonly, women who attend universities or work for them; it is the status quo. The reality is HEIs' structures and cultures support perpetration of GBV. Thus, the sector has a problem which is largely institutionalised. Therefore, addressing GBV within HEIs means changing the status quo, and this is often met with resistance. If there was not resistance, then the necessary changes would already have been made.

DOI: 10.4324/9781003252474-18

Not only does resistance prevent structural change within an organisation to effectively address GBV impacting the university community as a whole, but it also can exacerbate the impact of trauma experienced by victim-survivors. When resistance impacts victim-survivors directly or rather when victim-survivors are subjected to resistance, this may frequently be experienced as what may be termed "institutional betrayal". Institutional betrayal is defined as "institutional action and inaction that exacerbates the impact of traumatic experiences" (National Union of Students (NUS), 2018, p. 33). Making it difficult to report the experience, denying the victim-survivor's experience in some way, creating an environment where GBV is seen as normal are just some examples of resistance directed at victim-survivors (NUS, 2018).

We recognise that most change in this area is led by individuals who are activists, practitioners, and/or academics and it can be incredibly tedious and disheartening to face resistance in its many forms when trying to work towards the greater good for students and staff at an institution. Burnout is a very real risk. In this chapter, we present different forms of resistance that appear to be commonly used to block change. Hopefully, this will be helpful to those working in this area to identify what type of resistance is being faced, to better employ strategies to challenge, and work through such resistance. We provide examples of the different forms of resistance we have heard of or seen used in HE. We will present strategies on how to push through the resistance and highlight ways to mitigate the risk of burn out. This chapter is not only focused on individuals though, and at an organisational level, we implore senior leaders to assess whether they have fallen into any of these forms of resistance and to monitor this work to assess for resistance blocking positive change. Recognising this and creating a plan for working through resistance can help progress GBV prevention and response initiatives.

Identifying resistance

Resistance is a term that is used in different ways, including in social justice movements, for example, "resisting the patriarchy". For illustrative purposes, we have adopted "Our Watch's" definitions of resistance to addressing GBV as defined as "any active or passive action, behaviour or attitude which seeks to block change, uphold the status quo of gender relations, or re-establish male privilege and power" (2021, p. 52). Resistance is a factor that reinforces GBV and perpetuates the problem. It can be used to discredit victim-survivors, can be victim-blaming, and used to deny, justify, or otherwise excuse GBV.

There are many reasons why organisations and individuals engage in resistance tactics. Organisations (led by individuals) may resist this work because they have concerns for (1) reputational risk (equating prevention work as acknowledging a problem on campus), (2) financial implications for implementing change, (3) financial implications for dismissing perpetrators (e.g., losing staff can mean losing research leaders), (4) being seen to take political "sides", and (5) alienating donors who disagree with such change initiatives. Organisational or "collective" resistance can be formal or informal and can occur following a response to specific incidents or be coordinated by specific groups (e.g., senior management teams, men's rights activist groups). Individual resistance may be motivated by (1) personal behaviour or experiences, (2) concerns about being "responsible" for ending the perpetrator's career, rather than say attribute such culpability to the perpetrator themselves, (3) not agreeing that HEIs should be involved in this type of issue, (4) protecting colleagues or self, and (5) understanding GBV through a lens of myths that distort the issue. This, of course, is not an exhaustive list but we hope illustrates a range of motivations. Ultimately, it may be that resistance is used to maintain the status quo as this is "easier" than engaging in culture change. Individuals who benefit from the status quo are, it has been argued, more likely to display resistance tactics (Flood et al., 2018, 2020, 2021).

Being able to identify resistance tactics can help individuals who are working to implement change initiatives to plan for resistance, call out resistance when appropriate and effective, mitigate its impact, and work through, or around, it to progress GBV prevention and response initiatives.

In this chapter, we draw upon the model of resistance to violence against women prevention and gender equality initiatives used by Our Watch (2021) and the Victorian Health Promotion Foundation (VicHealth, 2018) in Australia, to help practitioners, activists, and university officials identify tactics used to prevent, stall, or stop work to address GBV. The model, shown in Figure 16.1, demonstrates different forms of passive and active resistance which may be used by organisations and individuals. Next, we provide examples of resistance used at an institutional level, individual level, and tactics used against victim-survivors directly.

Denial

Gender-based violence doesn't happen here.

In this model, denial is defined as denying the problem or the credibility of the case for change. This form of passive resistance essentially says there is no problem within the institution; therefore, there is no reason to make changes, or in the more extreme, denies that GBV is a problem at all. Individuals and organisations can use denial to block change. For example, denial may be defended in terms of evidence such as very low reporting rates (if any). The idea is that such low reporting levels are taken as evidence of either there not being a problem, or at least not a problem, of any substance in terms of frequency rates which would require the university to do anything. This, even though low reporting rates seem far more plausibly to reflect significant under reporting. And such underreporting may very well be a product of a lack of trust from students and staff in the institution to address GBV-related problems.

It is tempting, but fallacious, to think that with the global #MeToo movement, few institutions would be able to use denial. Despite decades of international research demonstrating that sexual violence, specifically, is pervasive

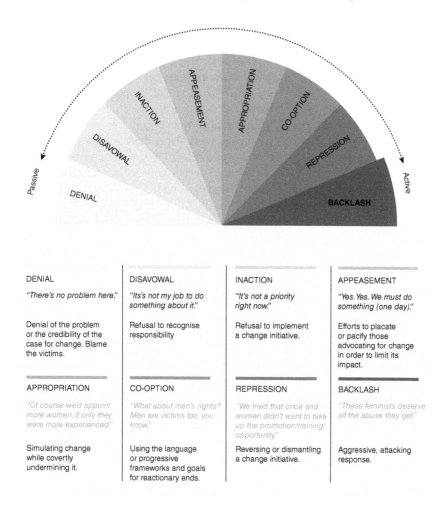

Figure 16.1 Forms of resistance. (VicHealth, 2018, p. 4, used with permission.)

in HE (Towl & Walker, 2019), there still appears to be denial by some HEI leaders that GBV is an issue that impacts their institution, perhaps citing the uniqueness of their institution implying they are an exception, for example, too rural, too small, too selective, or related. Thanks to changes to sector guidance by Universities UK (2016) and the Office for Students (2021), it is becoming more difficult for HEIs to use this form of resistance. The genie is out of the bottle. Institutional leadership teams and governing bodies would, in the current environment, struggle to be in complete denial that HEIs have a problem and a substantive one with GBV at universities.

However, it is still common to see denial used internally in institutions even when the organisation has publicly recognised issues with GBV. Such duplicity, of course, is by no means exclusive to the HE sector. Just because university leaders and governing bodies have identified the issue does not mean that all departments and staff will. Nor does it mean that all members of governing bodies or executive leadership teams will be wholly committed to acknowledging and addressing institutional problems with GBV. Raising awareness and getting institution-wide buy-in is much harder. Leaders of departments may not think it is an issue in their department; hence from their perspective, they do not need to place any focus on prevention or response. Of course, there may be some departments which have bigger problems than others. For example, those departments with more men students and staff than women may have more of a problem with more potential perpetration of sexual violence. We recommend using a comprehensive institution-wide approach (see Chapter 10 in this volume and Humphreys & Towl, 2020).

We also see denial used when we expand the discussion from sexual violence to GBV. There is more acceptance and awareness that certain forms of sexual violence do happen in university communities, for example, an older male student rapes a first-year woman student who is drunk. When we start discussing domestic abuse, boundary blurring and "grooming", staff sexual misconduct, technology-facilitated sexual violence, and stalking, it is easy to see how denial can quickly be raised as a form of resistance. People more readily will agree that a male student raping a female student is an issue facing some universities, long before they will recognise that domestic abuse and stalking are issues in HE settings too. In the past few years, we have seen domestic abuse and stalking cases in universities be mishandled and this has resulted, for some, in tragedy (see, for example, Chapter 9; Jeffreys, 2021; Batty, 2019; Westmarland, 2017).

We also see denial used towards victim-survivors directly when an institution/employee denies the experience of a victim-survivor. In a study conducted by the National Union of Students (2018) and The 1752 Group on students' experiences of staff sexual misconduct, half of respondents reported their institution had denied their experience. This can occur during a disclosure response and/or during a victim-survivor's attempt to report to the institution. This must surely reflect very poorly upon us as a sector. This form of resistance can be, unsurprisingly, experienced as institutional-betrayal; it re-traumatises victim-survivors and entirely and understandably reduces trust in HEIs. Thus, we need to be clear that such institutional responses are in no way neutral, rather they are actively damaging.

Disavowal

> *This is not a university issue; this is a police issue.*

In this model, disavowal is defined as a refusal to recognise responsibility. Disavowal is the traditional "it's not my job" form of resistance. We come across and have heard of this attitude being manifest in the workplace, and we may experience it ourselves from time to time. When it comes to GBV, disavowal is an easy form of resistance because many types of GBV include behaviours which also constitute criminal offences. Therefore, it is simple and feels "right" to say, "It's not our job; this is a job for the police." From 1994 to 2016, universities largely appear to have followed the "Zellick Guidelines" which told universities not to investigate rape and sexual assault through internal disciplinary proceedings. After 22 years of guidance that said, "it's not your job", shifting away from that has, unsurprisingly, been met with resistance. Often disavowal is coupled with genuine concerns university leaders have about not being equipped to do this work, not knowing how to investigate, and feeling uncomfortable or even adamantly against using the civil standard of proof to investigate misconduct when the same behaviour in the criminal justice system would be assessed using the criminal standard of proof.

Understandable concerns do not in and of themselves justify inaction. As a sector, the guidance changed in 2016 following recognition that HEIs' legal duties and obligations under the Public Sector Equality Duty of the Equality Act 2010 and the Human Rights Act 1998 meant that HEIs needed to have internal processes to deal with misconduct, even if this could constitute a criminal offence (Pinsent Masons & UUK, 2016). Therefore, HEIs are now expected to deal with formal reports of sexual violence, and other forms of GBV, through internal disciplinary procedures. This change means progressing to become equipped to do this work, accessing training or hiring qualified staff to conduct trauma-informed investigations, and recognising why the civil standard of proof to determine misconduct is the appropriate standard to use by any organisation that is not part of the criminal justice system.

The criminal justice system has a role to play when those subjected to crimes choose to report them to the police. This is largely independent of the responsibility universities have to address those behaviours internally to ensure the safety of students and employees. When it comes to internal investigations, university staff lack the legal investigatory powers and access to forensic evidence that police can access. For this and other important reasons (see Humphreys & Towl, 2020) HEIs use the civil standard of proof to investigate allegations of GBV as per sector guidance (Pinsent Masons & UUK, 2016; Office of the Independent Adjudicator (OIA), 2018).[2] Such investigations are undertaken (or not) at the request of reporting parties.

Moving from the institution-level of resistance to the individual-level, we see disavowal used by employees who do not think it is part of their job to engage in initiatives to prevent and/or respond to GBV within the institution. Staff may decline to attend training to learn how to respond to disclosures of GBV if well-being or support is not explicitly part of their job description. They may view this work as an "Equality, Diversity and Inclusion" (EDI) issue and expect only that a "department lead" for EDI attend the training or receive disclosures. As GBV is gendered, staff may see it as woman's issue only, and therefore fixing it is women's work. An illustration perhaps of everyday misogyny in the largely insular academic world.

We also see disavowal used towards victim-survivors directly when an institution chooses not to investigate a report of GBV if the incident(s) did not occur on university premises, at university-related event, or was not reported in a timely fashion. GBV perpetrated by employees or students of the HEI can occur in-person, online, and through other forms of communication. A student who is raped by another student in their private accommodation should surely have access to the same reporting and support options offered to a student raped by another student in their university accommodation. Likewise, if an employee is subjected to coercive and controlling behaviour in their accommodation by another employee, they should surely have access to the same reporting and support options if this behaviour occurred on campus. If a student receives harassing messages online from a fellow student or university employee, then their physical location at the time of receipt is not relevant. The responsibility of the HEI is to keep the community safe for staff and students. Behaviours between community members off-site and online may still impact safety and equal access to education and work on-site. This may be even more identifiable following new ways of remote learning and working due to the COVID-19 pandemic. In addition, given the many barriers to reporting, delayed reporting is expected, and it is recommended, in the interests of justice, that no time limits are placed on reporting GBV within the university (Humphreys & Towl, 2020).

Inaction

Our priorities are set for this year, so we won't be making any changes.

In this model, inaction is defined as refusing to implement a change initiative. This form of resistance is simply a refusal to act. This can be shaped by many excuses such as the university has other priorities at this time, the budget has already been agreed, we don't have anyone available to work on that right now, or some similar related platitude. This is a form of passive resistance as it requires only inaction, to have the impact of not addressing the issue.

Resources in any organisation are limited. The way an organisation allocates its resources demonstrates the organisation's values and priorities. HEIs tend to be well-resourced compared to, for example, the third sector organisations that provide specialist support to victim-survivors. HEIs can choose whether to act and allocate resource to GBV prevention and response initiatives accordingly. However, withholding resource is not the only form of organisational inaction. A failure to enforce and monitor the effectiveness of policies is another effective form of resistance which stops prevention and response efforts. An example of this might be if an HEI has a sexual misconduct policy but then refuses to use it and instead filters sexual misconduct complaints into other policy frameworks. This overlaps with what in the model is termed "repression", which we discuss later in this chapter.

Individuals can also use inaction as a form of resistance to stop or prevent change acting as gatekeepers to information and resources. Inaction can be used inconspicuously, hidden behind superficially plausible narratives around demanding workloads, limited resource, and differing priorities. An example of an individual using inaction would be a head of department who fails to advertise training to their staff regarding GBV prevention when, for example, by contrast, another head of department has made it compulsory for all staff to attend. A chair of a committee refusing to add a discussion on GBV prevention to an agenda because the committee's agenda is purportedly "too full" for the next 6–12 months.

We also see inaction used towards victim-survivors directly when an HEI chooses not to investigate a report of GBV because, for example, the victim-survivor chooses not to report to the police, or the issue reported is not seen as warranting investigation because it is not "serious enough". Individuals may choose not to act on disclosures or reports of GBV to protect the individual accused if they know that person, value their contribution to the department or university, or see acting against the individual as an internal political risk. Inaction can also be used at the end of an investigation or disciplinary process when a discipline committee or other staff responsible for decision-making choose not to impose any proportionate sanction for founded misconduct. We are clear that inaction can be yet another form of institutional betrayal. Sometimes those involved in making such "inactions" may have been former perpetrators of GBV themselves and thus they may be conflicted in such cases but are highly unlikely to be open about such potential conflicts of interest.

Appeasement

> *Yes, this is a problem, and we should address it (someday).*

In this model, "appeasement" is defined as placating or pacifying those advocating for change in order to limit its impact. Appeasement is a form of resistance that may be more difficult to identify because the words are often right, but the action and authenticity is not there. This is one reason why we often challenge institutions to demonstrate their commitment to addressing GBV through resource allocation. It is one thing to agree that GBV is an issue, but it is more persuasive to simply allocate appropriate resources and implement change.

This form of resistance may resonate, especially perhaps, with student activists when, for example, university leaders placate student leaders agreeing that there is a problem and change is needed, but then stall action waiting for the inevitable transition of new student leaders who have different goals. We see in Chapter 3 of this volume, that student activism and leadership in this area has been a catalyst for change and it is, thanks predominantly to student leaders and activists for keeping sexual violence and GBV on the agenda in UK HE since 2010. And at one level, this is a very poor reflection upon the sector where the sector has defaulted to students rather than staff to show institutional leadership. Indeed, it is perhaps telling that in a sector as advanced as HE, which focuses on research and education, that 12 years later since NUS's Hidden Marks (2010) we are still grappling with, and, in some cases, even only just beginning to address GBV.

Individuals may use appeasement to agree that change should happen, that they will be part of change, but then use work capacity levels to argue that they are unable to participate in the change at that time. For example, an individual may agree that training is very important, and they would like to attend, but it is not something they can do in the next year. Appeasement can also include saying yes, we should make this change, but let's wait and see what others are doing, that is, other universities within a similar group (e.g., the Russell Group) or what other staff in the university will do. Again, the words are right, but the willingness to take action and/or prioritise the work is not.

We also see "appeasement" used towards victim-survivors directly when an institution indicates that they will respond to a report of GBV and then fails to hold perpetrators accountable for their actions. This has been highlighted as a common reality in universities in response to staff sexual misconduct, particularly in imposing no (or light) sanctions, for example, a verbal warning, on a member of staff who has subjected another member of staff to sexual violence in breach of sexual misconduct policies. These practices were highlighted in the recent Al Jazeera Degrees of Abuse investigation which examined how British universities deal with reports of gender-based violence (2021). Due to limited guidance and highly risk-adverse interpretations of General Data Protection Regulations (GDPR), many universities in the UK choose not to share the outcome and sanctions of any disciplinary process with reporting parties. This is commonly the case in staff misconduct but may also be used by some universities in student misconduct too. When universities fail to inform reporting parties of the outcome of an investigation and/or discipline process and do not share what sanctions are imposed, reporting parties have no way of knowing what, if anything, was done to hold a preparator accountable for the GBV they committed. The reporting party may be left with the impression that the HEI did nothing, and the word will spread, impacting on the level of trust and confidence victim-survivors have in the HEI; after all, why report if we have no evidence that anything has ever been done about such reports? This is in plain view and seems to us to be clearly unjust and will only serve to reduce the likelihood of reporting and may be damaging for those who have been brave enough to have come forward and made a report.

Appropriation

Training is important, but I don't think the trainer is qualified.

Appropriation in this model is defined as simulating change while covertly undermining it. In other words, placing a façade over the issue, but making no substantive change and/or actively compromising the change initiatives in place. For example, an institution may add GBV prevention work to an employee's already full-time role without changing their workload making it near impossible for that individual to make progress. It is resistance when an organisation chooses to under-resource this work, so that progress is stunted. An organisation may put together a good communications plan highlighting how they take GBV very seriously and have a "zero-tolerance" policy, while at the same time victim-survivors are dissuaded from reporting, reporting mechanisms are not available, support is not available, investigations are conducted poorly, and/or no discipline action is taken against perpetrators. If an HEI says it is addressing GBV, check to see if the expulsion rates or dismissal rates for sexual misconduct or gross misconduct have changed at all. That may well be one such indicator of whether or not there has been a positive change in terms of addressing such issues.

Individuals may use the tactic of appropriation through undermining GBV prevention initiatives by, for example, voting against changes, criticising the initiative or staff leading the initiative, refusing to display campaign posters, or challenging the credibility of GBV prevention trainers (Flood et al., 2020). Perpetrators can purposely join groups working towards addressing GBV for the purpose of undermining the work or may be placed there for this purpose. For example, if someone is asked to chair a working group on GBV prevention but they are openly described as "handsy". (This is a euphemistic term for someone who routinely sexually assaults chiefly women through inappropriate and unsolicited touching.) The group is set up to fail, or at the very least trust and credibility will be in question. This is a form of appropriation (as defined by this model) and undermines the chance of contributing to enacting real change in the HEI. And this plays to a more general and challenging point about the extent to which powerful men in particular, within institutions, still seem to be heavily protected which in turn will serve to discourage reporting.

We also see appropriation used towards victim-survivors directly when an institution places staff in roles to support victim-survivors who are not qualified and/or unwilling to do so. The institution may be able to say they have support available, but as the support is inappropriate this is not truly the case.

Co-option

> *What about men? They are victims too and are often falsely accused.*

In this model, co-option is defined as using the language of progressive frameworks and goals for reactionary ends or to maintain the status quo, that is, gender inequality and GBV (VicHealth, 2018; Flood et al., 2020). It is often demonstrated by trying to erase the gendered patterns of perpetration and victimisation using myths about GBV to shift the focus from the evidence that demonstrates the problem.

Co-option can also be used by delegating the change initiative to someone who disagrees with it (Flood et al., 2020). For example, asking an opponent of the change initiative to chair a working group leading on the initiative who can then use appropriation as a resistance tactic as previously discussed.

Co-option is a way to muddy the waters, shift focus, and distract from GBV prevention progress. This may also include watering down the message. For example, shifting a campaign focused on GBV to address all forms of harassment and discrimination or taking an active bystander course focused on GBV and adding in information on all forms of hate, harassment, and discrimination without expanding the length of the course, requiring information and activities related to GBV to be shortened or removed. Intersectionality is essential, but there is a difference between presenting intersectional understandings of these issues to effectively engage in culture change versus ticking a box by saying all students received training on these issues (but it was all done in one hour).

"Co-option" may be used towards victim-survivors (Reporting Parties) directly when perpetrators (Responding Parties) are given the role of "victim" in formal proceedings and the harm caused by the behaviour of the Responding Party is minimised and the impact of the investigation on the Responding Party is prioritised. This may be coupled with ignoring the impact of the investigation on the Reporting Party. This may include allowing for counter-complaints from the Responding Party within the same investigation and if the Reporting Party is restricted through precautionary measures instead of the Responding Party.

Repression

> We paid for specialist counsellors last year, but this year we will use that money to pay for a new wellbeing building.

In this model, repression, is an active form of resistance defined as reversing or dismantling a change initiative. The most obvious form of organisational repression is when funding is cut or rerouted to a different issue, thus reducing resource available for GBV prevention and response initiatives.

In 2016, the Higher Education Funding Council for England (HEFCE; replaced by the Office for Students in 2018), allocated £4.7 million through rounds of Catalyst funding to support the implementation of Universities UK's Changing the Culture framework. A question many asked was would initiatives and staff jobs be sustained once the funding from HEFCE was used or would the programme end at that point. The distribution of the monies was allocated on a principle of matched funding whereby receiving institutions agreed to "match" whatever level of funding distributed from the Catalyst funding with their own. In practice, it seems at least questionable that many chose not to continue with their investment in this work once the Catalyst funding had come to an end (Baird et al., 2019). Yet it was intended to help pump prime such activities (see Chapter 20).

Repression can be used to stop progress, rather than just block it from beginning after doing only just enough – in other words, the bare minimum. We argue that meeting the Office for Students Statement of Expectations is not enough (see, for example, Towl & Humphreys, 2021). We advise the sector to be on the lookout for this form of resistance, particularly once HEIs have successfully done the bare minimum to meet the low bar set by the Office for Students Statement of Expectations. What may happen is a shifting of funding to the next high-profile issue, defunding work to address GBV to focus instead on, for example, racism only, rather than funding both initiatives or taking an intersectional approach to address both.

We also see "repression" used towards victim-survivors directly when an institution removes or reduces funding for specialist support previously available. For example, if a university pays for specialist counsellors from an external organisation, for example, rape crisis, to deliver services to students and staff and then cuts funding for this service. Often organisations like local rape crisis services have very long waiting lists in the local community to offer services to victim-survivors due to limited resources/funding. Paying for that service to be delivered in-house means victim-survivors can access specialist support faster and, often, in spaces that feel safer or more accessible. To cut this funding would be a good example of "repression" as articulated in the model.

Backlash

> *Women deserve it because of how they act.*

Backlash, in some literature, may be used to describe other forms of resistance we have already covered. In this model, backlash is defined as an active form of resistance that is normally an attacking or aggressive response. We can easily find backlash on social media where aggressive responses are becoming the norm. Backlash can include verbal or online attacks or even physical violence (COFEM, 2018).

It may be less common to see backlash demonstrated outright collectively in an HEI or by employees of an institution as the nature of backlash, by this definition, would be outside of professional behaviour and would possibly be a form of misconduct within itself. However, it is still important to consider this form of resistance within the HE lens.

We see backlash used towards victim-survivors directly when victim-survivors are subjected to retaliation and/or victimisation for disclosing or reporting GBV by students or staff. In one study into staff sexual misconduct, multiple reporting parties dealt with retaliation from their perpetrator or someone who supported the perpetrator; this included spreading malicious rumours about the reporting party in the university community, loss of teaching and authorship opportunities, and threats to their physical safety (Bull & Rye, 2018). HEIs need to include protection from retaliation and/or victimisation for those who make disclosures or reports. Without this, perpetrators and those that support perpetrators, can use threats, intimidation, and other behaviours to negatively impact the victim-survivor to either intimidate them not make a report, withdraw a report, and/or punish them for making a report.

Strategies to work through resistance

Resistance will occur, and this is often a sign that work is in progress (VicHealth, 2018). Anticipating the different manifestations of resistance and having strategies in place to address them may help mitigate the impact of resistance on the progress of the change initiative and on those leading the work. In this final section, we provide strategies that may support mitigating for the effectiveness of resistance, either by addressing the resistance directly or moving around the resistance to reach the goal.

Recommendation 1

Monitor, assess, and report on progress towards prevention and response initiative goals, including documenting any evidence of resistance, in order to identify patterns of institutional resistance that can be addressed (Our Watch, 2021; Flood et al., 2021). This recommendation is useful for addressing all forms of resistance because it documents resistance specifically and helps identify what tactic is being used. For example, an evaluation of training may include identifying participant demographics. Analysis of the attendee list may show that say 75% of departments in the HEI have sent staff on training and 25% have sent none. Work can then be done to understand why 25% of departments have not had any staff attend training and determine if this was, for example, an issue with communication that these departments were not informed about the training or if there is wilful resistance such as inaction, denial, or disavowal at play. Evaluating progress, action, and outcomes is also a useful tool in mitigating for appropriation. Having set timescales for the completion of actions and using a RAG (Red, Amber, Green) action plan can help monitor delays. Amber and red actions require explanations for why progress is not being made. This strategy is most impactful when a senior leader, the executive team, or the governing body owns the monitoring of progress or expects to receive updates from this.

Recommendation 2

Articulate the rationale and benefits for doing GBV prevention and response work and connect it to the wider strategic values and goals of the HEI whilst highlighting potential resistance tactics and the strategy to address them. In other words, create a "business case" for why the HEI needs to engage with the GBV prevention work and embed it directly into the strategic framework. A strong business case will demonstrate how this work benefits the HEI, provides compelling accounts of the problem and solutions, and presents the risks for doing nothing or getting it wrong and the potential forms of resistance the change initiative may face and strategies for addressing. Adding this last part into a business case has three aims: (1) to create buy-in, (2) to identify resistance tactics and create a plan from the beginning, and (3) to notify senior leaders of these forms of resistance so that they are harder to use. To strengthen the business case, it may also be helpful to outline a cost-benefit analysis and conduct an equality impact assessment (EIA) to demonstrate how this work is all about not disadvantaging any group.

Recommendation 3

Help people better understand the problem of GBV by dispelling myths and offering compelling accounts of the problem and solution (VicHealth, 2018). Use case studies to present voices of survivors in a safe and appropriate way (with their permission even when anonymised). Part of working through resistance is debunking myths about GBV. We recommend that all prevention and response training includes myth busting using the Fact -> Myth -> Fallacy approach which focuses on the fact and then explains the fallacies that create the myths (VicHealth, 2018). This will ensure that the entire time myths are being discussed they are framed with facts first, compared to approaches where myths are presented first, but little time is spent on the discussion of facts. When preparing for potential resistance responses, having this already prepared to help debunk myths that may be raised in a discussion in a measured and evidence-based way can assist.

Recommendation 4

Build a network of champions and allies. Pushing back against individual and organisational resistance may be political within the organisation. Secure support from senior leaders across different departments. Senior leaders can actively speak out impactfully against resistance. Likewise, consider key influencers in the HEI who may be able to champion the GBV prevention in local areas of the organisation. Engage student activists in this work and provide resources and support for them to engage in this safely. Consider allies in external partnerships who will be willing to promote the change initiative too.

Recommendation 5

Use communication plans that include tailored information for different audiences. How information is presented on the initiatives to academic staff may be different to professional support staff or operational staff. Employee communication may need to be tailored from student-facing messages. Consider the network of allies and champions and consider who is best placed to communicate to the specific audience. Is this a university-branded video message from the vice-chancellor or a student representative message from the students' union, should it come from the coach of the rugby team or the music director? The more diverse group of allies and champions willing to speak on this topic, the better as more community members will be willing to listen.

Recommendation 6

Create opportunities for discussion and debate in moderated spaces, for example, training or round tables. This is a challenging but useful strategy. Staff training sessions provide a great opportunity to, for example, debunk rape myths. Creating opportunities for people to openly question why GBV prevention and response is needed is key in shifting minds and culture. Remember the status quo will shift, and even though that will be positive for the HEI, not everyone will want this even if change is in their best interest. Sometimes having space to talk it out, without judgement, being allowed to ask "silly" questions, and just vent frustrations and confusion can help move people forward.

Recommendation 7

On an institutional-level, senior leaders can make preventing GBV part of everyone's job. GBV is a health and safety issue, an equality, diversity, and inclusion issue, and a safeguarding issue. Elements of all three of these areas are already embedded in all employees' roles within HEIs. During recruitment, applicants may be required to answer an EDI question in their interview, and if successful be expected to engage in training during their induction that covers health and safety, EDI, and safeguarding issues. Likewise, current staff may be expected to complete annual or biennial training in these areas too. Embedding GBV prevention into all employees' training helps staff realise they too have a role to play, shifting the culture of the institution. This is a helpful strategy to address disavowal.

Recommendation 8

Ensure support is available for those working in this area. It is important to ensure that any staff or students working on GBV prevention and response initiatives are appropriately supported and protected, both in their work and in case they are directly impacted by resistance tactics or targets of backlash (Our Watch, 2021, Flood et al., 2021). Senior leaders and managers should ensure that those working in this area maintain work-life balance and are offered support to do this work which may include clinical supervision where practitioners can process their work with the support of a fellow professional. If students are involved in GBV work, for example, projects, campaigns, peer-facilitators for training, working groups, or internships, information on self-care, boundaries, and work-life balance can be explored to help them too. There are others to consider too: note-takers, investigators, discipline-decision-makers, case managers, trainers, and so on. Champions of this work require support. The work is hard, and facing resistance is even harder.

Conclusion: protecting from burnout

Many of the strategies we have discussed are focused on organisational ways to combat resistance. These eight recommendations are a starting point and in the Further Reading section we offer additional resources with more strategies and ideas on responding to resistance. We focus our last thoughts on this subject directly to practitioners and activists (and the university leaders listening).

We know that it is individuals doing this work on behalf of organisations and often it is individuals' passion for social justice and change that motivates this work. Many practitioners and activists will already have ways of coping with discussing GBV in their work and will build this into their practice. From speaking to practitioners in this field, many find that the hardest part of the job is not, as many may anticipate, hearing the stories of abuse and violence we hold. The hardest part instead is often dealing with resistance, whether it is as an institutional level, an individual, or used against victim-survivors directly. Resistance is extremely disheartening, frustrating, and exhausting. It undermines the good work, stalls progress, and can even stop it altogether. It reduces trust in the institution for victim-survivors and those progressing this work. Resistance places practitioners and activists at risk for burnout. And it is a recognised form of institutional betrayal for victim-survivors.

To mitigate for this, we encourage practitioners, activists, and any individuals involved in implementing GBV prevention and response initiatives to first realise that resistance is inevitable, but also a sign that progress is happening. After all, if the threat of successful change wasn't present, resistance wouldn't be necessary. It also helps to focus on what can be changed and recognise limitations. Small goals are more achievable and can build up to large successes. Each step forward should be celebrated and take time to look back at the progress made over time. These reflection points are powerful. Most importantly, practice self-care and prioritise your well-being; this is crucial.

Summary of key points

- Within the outlined framework, there are eight forms of resistance tactics that HEIs and individuals may use to stop or stall GBV prevention and response initiatives.
- When resistance impacts victim-survivors directly or when victim-survivors are subjected to resistance, this can be experienced as institutional betrayal.
- Identifying resistance tactics can help individuals who are working to implement change initiatives to plan for resistance, call out resistance when appropriate and effective, mitigate its impact, and work through or around it to progress GBV prevention and response initiatives.
- We have presented a list of eight recommendations to help prepare for and address resistance tactics.
- Resistance has a negative impact on practitioners and places them at risk for burnout. Formal support and self-care strategies are crucial.

Further Reading

VicHealth. (2018). *(En)countering resistance: Strategies to respond to resistance to gender equality initiatives*. Victorian Health Promotion Foundation.

This publication has been an invaluable resource over the past few years as it has helped frame behaviours that were counterintuitive (like appeasement) into formal tactics of resistance. It provided language to codify resistance to GBV prevention and response work, even though it was focused more broadly on gender equality initiatives. Our chapter builds from that work to set these tactics within the HE setting. However, we highly recommend this resource as there is so much more to gain from it including their 13 steps to manage resistance:

1 Don't be surprised
2 Understand the form
3 Assess who it's from
4 Be willing to listen
5 Focus efforts on those you can influence
6 Get leaders involved
7 Harness the power of your peers
8 Frame, don't shame
9 Make sure to monitor
10 Defend against domination techniques
11 Put guidelines in place
12 Practice self-care
13 Celebrate success

(2018, pp. 14–15)

Our Watch. (2021). *Change the story: A shared framework for the primary prevention of violence against women in Australia* (**2nd ed.**). **Our Watch**.

Change the story is an evidence-based framework for a national approach to preventing violence against women in Australia. It helpfully frames GBV beyond the focus of individual bad actors and considers the broader social, political and economic drivers that perpetuate GBV. It outlines the essential actions needed at all levels of society – including workplaces and higher education. The aim of this is to address the stop GBV before it starts. A main theme of this framework is the action to "Plan for and actively address backlash and resistance", our Watch identify resistance as a reinforcing factor that perpetuates violence against women. In this publication, it is clear, failing to anticipate and take action to mitigate potential backlash and resistance to the message is harmful practice (p. 87).

Notes

1 See Changing the Culture: Report of the Universities UK Taskforce, examining violence against women, harassment, and hate crime affecting university students (Universities UK, 2016), and Guidance for Higher Education Institutions: How to Handle Alleged Student Misconduct (Pinsent Masons & Universities UK, 2016).
2 The Health and Social Care Act 2008 requires the civil standard of proof for fitness to practice procedures too (OIA, 2018).

References

Al Jazeera. (2021). *Degrees of abuse.* https://interactive.aljazeera.com/aje/2021/degrees-of-abuse/index.html

Baird, H., Renfrew, K., Nash-Henry, Z., & Towl, G. (2019). *Evaluation of safeguarding students catalyst fund projects: Summative evaluation report.* Office for Students.

Batty, D. (2019, December 6). Newcastle University faces student backlash over stalker's return. *The Guardian.* Retrieved January 2022, from www.theguardian.com/education/2019/dec/06/newcastle-university-faces-student-backlash-over-stalkers-return

Bull, A., & Rye, R. (2018). *Silencing Students: Institutional responses to staff sexual misconduct in UK higher education.* The 1752 Group and University of Portsmouth.

Coalition of Feminists for Social Change (COFEM). (2018). Backlash: What is it and how do we address it safely? *Feminist Pocketbook Tip Sheet, 9.*

Flood, M., Dragiewicz, M., & Pease, B. (2018). *Resistance and backlash to gender equality: An evidence review.* QUT Crime and Justice Research Centre.

Flood, M., Dragiewicz, M., & Pease, B. (2020). Resistance and backlash to gender equality. *Australian Journal of Social Issues, 56,* 393–408.

Flood, M., O'Donnell, J., Brewin, B., & Myors, B. (2021). *Engaging men: Reducing resistance and building support.* Eastern Health, Eastern Domestic Violence Service (EDVOS), and Queensland University of Technology (QUT).

Humphreys, C. J., & Towl, G. J. (2020). *Addressing student sexual violence in Higher Education: A good practice guide.* Emerald Publishing Group.

Jeffreys, B. (2021, December 10). Student stalked at university calls for change. *BBC News.* Retrieved January 2022, from www.bbc.co.uk/news/education-59587275

National Union of Students. (2010). *Hidden marks: A study of women students' experiences of harassment, stalking, violence and sexual assault.* Retrieved January 2022, from www.nusconnect.org.uk/resources/hidden-marks-a-study-of-women-students-experiences-of-harassment-stalking-violence-and-sexual-assault

National Union of Student. (2018). *Power in the academy: Staff sexual misconduct in UK Higher Education.* National Union of Students.

Office for Students. (2021). *Statement of expectations: Preventing and addressing harassment and sexual misconduct in universities.* Office for Students.

Office of the Independent Adjudicator. (2018). *The good practice framework: Disciplinary procedures.* Retrieved January 2022, www.oiahe.org.uk/media/2045/good-practice-framework-disciplinary-procedures-section.pdf

Our Watch. (2021). *Change the story: A shared framework for the primary prevention of violence against women in Australia* (2nd ed.). Our Watch.

Pinsent Masons & Universities UK. (2016). *Guidance for higher education institutions: How to handle alleged student misconduct which may also constitute a criminal offence.* Retrieved January 2022, www.universitiesuk.ac.uk/sites/default/files/field/downloads/2021-07/guidance-for-higher-education-institutions.pdf

Towl, G. J., & Humphreys, C. J. (2021, April 22). *How to do more than the bare minimum on harassment and sexual misconduct.* Wonk HE. Retrieved January 2022, https://wonkhe.com/blogs/how-to-do-more-than-the-bare-minimum-on-harassment-and-sexual-misconuct/

Towl, G. J., & Walker, T. (2019). *Tackling sexual violence at universities: An international perspective.* Routledge.

UN Women. (2018). *Guidance note on campus violence prevention and response.* Retrieved January 2022, from www.unwomen.org/-/media/headquarters/attachments/sections/library/publications/2019/campusviolence%20note_guiding_principles.pdf?la5en&vs53710

Universities UK. (2016). *Changing the culture.* Retrieved January 2022, www.universitiesuk. ac.uk/policy-and-analysis/reports/Documents/2016/changing-the-culture.pdf

VicHealth. (2018). *(En)countering resistance: Strategies to respond to resistance to gender equality initiatives.* Victorian Health Promotion Foundation.

Westmarland, N. (2017). *Independent review into the university of Sussex's response to domestic violence.* Retrieved January 2022, from www.sussex.ac.uk/webteam/gateway/file. php?name=westmarland-review.pdf&site=303

Part III

Partnerships

17 How to involve students in work on gender-based violence

Sunday Blake and Jim Dickinson

In response to the 2016 report of the Universities UK (UUK) Harassment Task-force, *Changing the Culture*, the Higher Education Funding Council for England and its successor body the Office for Students (OfS) provided matched "catalyst" funding support to English HE providers for 119 projects through three funding calls during the period 2017–2020 (Office for Students, 2019). The aim of the funding was to identify and support good practice in the sector to improve and enhance student safeguarding, specifically to tackle sexual misconduct, hate crime, and online harassment.

An interim evaluation report published in 2019 noted that most project teams sought to involve students in the design and delivery of their initiatives – and that while there were some good examples of where this was achieved on a voluntary basis, many of the project teams reported barriers to engaging students:

> Factors cited included: the timing of projects and the difficulty of being able to design student engagement around the cycle of the academic year; the turnover of Student Union sabbatical officers each year; and more generally low participation rates in student surveys and focus groups, common across the sector.
>
> (Baird, 2019, p. 32)

This is not a new or especially novel conclusion. Funded project rounds on many issues in Higher Education tend to call on providers and project teams to take steps to engage students in the design and delivery of initiatives – and bids tend to describe an in-principle commitment to doing so, if not detail on how that will be achieved. Then when evaluation reports emerge, the same types of "challenges" over doing so in practice tend to appear. What is going on?

Over multiple years observing and supporting students and students' unions with these types of projects, we have identified common misconceptions and mistakes made by those responsible for the delivery of both project work and service design when trying to involve students that unless addressed can depress the volume and quality of participation – particularly in areas which concern students being harmed.

DOI: 10.4324/9781003252474-20

We have identified different ways that Higher Education providers and students talk about and frame the issues that can also depress the volume and quality of participation unless steps are taken to develop a shared understanding. We have also identified the different roles that students and their representatives can play in work on gender-based violence which we argue should be clearer from the outset to avoid confusion. And we explicitly raise the sometimes hidden issue of the extensive "labour" – both financial and emotional – in use from students in multiple projects.

Assumptions and misconceptions

There is a long history of student volunteering in Higher Education in projects, groups, and roles that serve both students and the wider community. The "volunteer assumption" – that students both can and will give up their time to participate and that doing so will be of educational value – is dominant in student clubs and societies, student-led campaigns, and project groups, prominent in employability discourse and even underpins the basis for the remuneration given to full-time student representatives ("sabbatical officers") in students' unions.

But it is clear that increasingly, it is based on a set of assumptions that no longer work. The majority of students engage in part-time (some full-time) employment alongside their studies. Significant proportions of students already have multiple and onerous responsibilities in student clubs, activities, and projects. Others have complex personal and/or caring responsibilities. As such the financial and opportunity costs even of participating in a working group or project team, usually alongside full-time salaried university staff, are too high to bear.

Traditionally, the "simple" way to obtain student involvement in university decision-making has tended towards asking (full time) students' union officers to undertake roles. While not handsomely remunerated, these individuals tend to have enhanced availability and have usually benefitted from both training and other duties that familiarise them with committee work and the language and processes of project and service planning or evaluation.

But in our experience the cumulative expectations of students' union officers generated by these types of roles are often too great – and the necessary turnover of those undertaking the roles can cause frustration, at best because new officers have to be re-familiarised, at worse because new officers may lack the commitment or passion for a project exhibited by their predecessor. There also tend to be diversity concerns depending on the characteristics of those elected, and a concern that while a student officer can bring a student perspective, they may not bring a perspective that is broadly representative, sufficiently victim-survivor or trauma-informed, or sufficiently engaged in cynicism or opposition to any initiatives – something which teams are often trying to combat.

In some cases, Higher Education providers have tended instead to attempt to identify student "survivor" volunteers drawn from those who have been subjected to sexual misconduct, and/or students who have been involved in activism over the issues drawn from student societies or ad hoc campaign groups. Frustration here tends to surround finding willing participants at all, a "drop off" in commitment after initial enthusiasm, and the rhythms of the academic year disrupting students' capacity and willingness to participate. We have seen students "re-traumatised" by their participation and thus withdrawing – at worst such "engagement" can be both exploitative and damaging.

We have also encountered an assumption that survivors will be willing to come forward, when many survivors will not – which can mean a pool of "activist survivors" emerges who are happy to shout/publicly disclose but who are not fully representative of student survivors, and can burn out. There is also an often implicit assumption that anyone else engaging in this work outside of the designated "survivor" role has not personally faced sexual violence. There should be an understanding that student officers asked to participate as student officers may also be survivors – which in turn may impact their willingness to be involved in such work in comparison to predecessors or successors. Some may want to be involved, but not disclose their survivor status.

In all of these cases we take the view that insufficient initial planning and risk assessment has taken place when considering the participation of students. A deeper understanding of the student body and the nature of the participation that is required helps, as does understanding the nature of the problem-solving and leadership frames being used – which we discuss subsequently. But fundamentally, taking simple steps to consider the capacity and long-term commitment of student participants (especially beyond initial enthusiasm) is crucial. Once done, steps to mitigate can include:

- Remunerating their participation and budgeting to do so at the outset;
- Budgeting to compensate the students' union for the participation of any of its officers or staff;
- Taking formal steps to recognise and reward the educational and skills development benefits of participation;
- Ensuring that students' union reps are formally supported in their role by students' union or university staff;
- Ensuring that processes are in place to train and support handover for students who may not last the course of a project or initiative;
- Understanding where pools of student activism and enthusiasm around gender-based violence exist, and taking steps to ensure that relationships are struck with and maintained with these;
- Never taking at face-value enthusiastic commitments from students or SU officers to deliver unbudgeted work outside of meetings (research, communication tasks, etc);
- Considering the emotional labour that may be expended by participants (including but not exclusively by students) when discussing gender-based violence and planning to deliver support from the outset.

Problem frames and cultural understandings

In 1973, Rittel and Webber coined terms to describe problems facing social and urban planners, and Grint added a category in 2008. "Tame" problems were complicated, but contained and easily solved as long as someone prioritised the issue, allocated the resources, and followed the instructions, because someone had solved it before. "Critical" problems were those when there was danger, peril, or harm, requiring faster thinking, taking charge, and not worrying too much about resources or planning. "Wicked problems" were more complex – requiring deeper thinking, contested negotiation over the nature, scope and definition of a problem, the identification of multiple drivers of a problem, the involvement of those a problem impacts, and hypothesis generation and piloting of solutions.

In theory, each type of problem required a different type of leadership. Tame problems required management skills – resource allocation, monitoring and evaluation, delegation, and budgeting. Critical problems needed command and control – someone to stand at the front and shout in order to get people to safety and galvanise action. And wicked problems needed the ability to facilitate definitions, draw in different points of view, engage those affected, develop hypotheses, synthesize data, to coordinate investigation and piloting, and know when to push emergent solutions into tame.

We take the view that students are capable of engaging in all three types of solution over gender-based violence on campus – but frequently come across a mismatch between the frame that they would apply to a problem, and those being applied by university managers, service heads, or project teams.

One heuristic may be to assume that university managers are likely to want to treat issues as "tame"; student activists are likely to want to treat issues as critical; and academics are likely to want to view issues as "wicked".

The design and delivery of projects, services, and initiatives, by definition, tends to be "tame". A Gantt chart tends not to be agonised over when the critical problem of a spate of drink spiking incidents generates demands for "something to be done", or when the problem of the online radicalisation of young male students into an "incel" "manosphere" is poorly understood. We have seen students respond suspiciously to "tame" framing by labelling it as bureaucracy and "wicked" framing as insufficiently conclusive or action-focused.

On the other hand, because the treatment of a problem as "critical" tends to imply a crisis and is often surrounded by a public outcry, we have seen university managers keen to suggest a problem is framed in other ways or minimised as a component of a wider problem, or not as big a problem as is being made out – often in opposition to students who demand rapid action over immediate risk and harms to people they know or have met.

Student activism tends to be "critical" in nature. Groups tend to involve or be led by survivors, and student leaders can become lightning rods for disclosure – which means demands tend to be unsubtle, urgent, and framed around harm and safety. That kind of framing is not immediately compatible with the sort of delivery planning and evaluation processes required when an issue is tame, or the academic curiosity and emotional commitment required when addressing a problem as wicked.

All three types of framing may be required over a particular issue in a university – although there is an open question as to whether university leaders are capable of effectively deploying the skills required over all three framings, let alone student volunteers, representatives, or activists. What is clear is that disagreement over the type of leadership and action required over gender-based violence both in general and in relation to specific meetings, initiatives, or descriptions generates frustration both amongst students and universities.

Academics, activists, practitioners, and key partners should consider the way in which they frame the problem, the way others frame the problem, take steps to reconcile the approaches, and collectively consider the most appropriate leadership at the most appropriate stage of development.

Case study   "Girls Night In" groups and spiking

At the time of writing, there is considerable media interest in a burst of student-led activism over the issue of "spiking" in licensed premises. The movement has established support in almost 50 locations, including London, Essex, Edinburgh, Liverpool, Bristol, Falmouth, Hull, St Andrews and Swansea.

In the two months to November 2021, there have been 200 reports of drink spiking and 24 reports of spiking by injection, according to the National Police Chiefs' Council. Campaigners believe the financial impact on venues – from people not attending – is what is required to generate action, and each local Girls Night In group has issued demands of local licensed premises that would see them improve practices such as training of security staff, better CCTV, and disclosure receipt training for bar staff.

The movement contains all three elements of heuristic used above:

Critical: The framing of the issue as a crisis with the potential for significant harm to come to students unless action is taken; the issuing of "demands" with urgency framing.

Tame: The identification of a solution (licensed premises practice improvement) that can be adapted; the ongoing assessment of practice against defined standards borne out of responsibilities set by the local authority in pursuit of the Licensing Act 2003.

Wicked: A debate over whether the issue of "needle spiking" is in reality a moral panic; wider debates about harms arising from the securitisation of venues; questions being raised as to whether such actions will have an impact; claims that spiking is more likely to happen in (quasi)domestic settings; calls for better prevalence research on sexual misconduct experienced by students to ensure effective targeting of resources.

Roles and responsibilities

Away from the issues of expectations and assumptions and the framing of issues and leadership to address them, we have frequently encountered examples of confusion over the role that students are expected to fulfil when being "engaged" in project or committee work surrounding gender-based violence.

Here we have identified three types of active contribution that students might be expected to play. It is not to suggest that there are no other things that students might contribute, nor is it to suggest that students are not capable of undertaking a mixture of these three roles. We also exclude student contributions to be made through their participation in surveys or research work. It is to say that in our experience, unless the role that we expect students to play is clear, effective participation will be depressed.

It is also to stress that student members of strategic-level committees are never meaningfully in a position to describe, on-demand, "what students think".

Student as strategic partner: In this role, students are engaged in (co-) commissioning, evidence gathering, and developing, prioritising, designing, and choosing solutions at the strategic level.

- This can include students contributing to discussions on research or survey design, helping with decision-making over participation in those types of exercises, and offering a student (or student survivor) perspective on findings.
- For example, a students' union welfare officer may be a member of a university committee, or a students' union women's officer may be a key member of a funded project group or working group on the reform of disciplinary procedures.

Student as facilitator/deliverer: In this role, students are engaged in the design, operation of, running (or supporting other students to run) interventions, and local work to solve a problem.

- This can involve students and their representatives being supported to deliver bespoke interventions that pertain to gender-based violence, or being offered support for existing activity that relates to gender-based violence.
- For example, a students' union feminist society may be funded to deliver a week of talks on the issues for the student body to participate in, a group of volunteers involved in a student listening service (i.e., "nightline") may be trained in handling disclosures of sexual harassment or assault, and a group of student bar staff or those involved in the running of societies may take the lead on bystander training for that group.

Student as evaluator: In this role, students are invited to participate in activity that evaluates existing provision and processes, or critiques ideas for improving them.

This can involve students who have been subjected to gender-based violence, or students who are the target of awareness raising work consent understanding interventions. For example, a group of previous complainants may be invited to participate in a focus group on the way the complaints process worked, or a group of prospective students may be invited to reflect on proposals for consent training.

In each of the roles, consideration should be given to training, recruitment, support, and remuneration of participants. There may be significant opportunity costs associated with participation and while SU officers may be familiar with committee work, other students may not be. Where participation is likely to involve significant emotional labour, appropriate support should be built in from the start.

Case study   Evaluation of Safeguarding Students Catalyst Fund Projects

There are multiple examples among the funded providers of student-centred interventions being developed by the Catalyst funded projects, many of which have involved students in their design and delivery. Successful approaches include students creating content for the project with staff oversight, peer-to-peer interaction e.g. in the facilitation of student focus groups or delivery of in-person training or campaign information.

> Research with the projects showed that students were heavily engaged in the co-creation and design of initiatives, and therefore that there are more student-centred interventions in place tackling sexual misconduct through the Catalyst funding. Student involvement and engagement, particularly in training, is considered most successful when projects are conducted in collaboration with Student Unions, or where they are tied to students' academic interest areas.
>
> (Baird et al., 2019, p. 42)

Students' unions as membership bodies

There is a natural tendency in the Higher Education sector to think of students' unions as representative bodies which are able to encourage, harness, and supply student engagement in work on gender-based violence. But they are also membership organisations in their own right – where leaders, managers, and trustees owe a duty of care in relation to both directly run activities and events, and those carried out by student clubs and societies affiliated to or a component part of the union.

As such although students' unions established within universities are usually legally autonomous, there are likely to be a range of issues that it would be valuable to consider to ensure that students are appropriately protected from harm, and able to raise complaints and concerns.

The kernel of the issue is that while student sexual misconduct may take place in a context unrelated to the local students' union, sexual misconduct that takes place in the context of a students' union event, activity, club, or society is likely always to also be a matter that should be of direct concern to a university and any student code of conduct.

In recent years, in our work with students' unions, we have noticed that they are reporting that students are increasingly raising complaints about other students – and where that concerns the activities or office holders of students' unions or their clubs and societies, that is creating real pressure on students' union staff and officer teams.

There are two ways to interpret the trend. One is to argue that where students involved in activities would previously have collectively self-regulated their own behaviour, now they are unfairly asking authority figures to do that for them in an unsustainable way. As such they lose the ability to "call each other out", and students' union officials end up in endless quasi-legal processes over quarrels that previously would have been settled over a coffee.

The other is to argue that previously, serious cases of harassment and sexual misconduct were left unaddressed – and having better defined what counts as unacceptable behaviour, there is now rightly an onus on bodies like students' unions to tackle it now that students are "calling it out" in complaints.

As such we have identified a range of issues that warrant serious joint attention from students' union and university teams responsible for the prevention and processing of allegations of gender-based violence:

- Multiple processes and policies. If a student is an employee of the students' union, works over the summer for the university at open days, is involved in running a society and a sports club, and lives in halls of residence, in some universities that would mean six different disciplinary procedures – and in some cases six different definitions of misconduct – that we expect students to understand. Gaps, overlaps, and double jeopardy can all be a problem – as can jurisdiction.
- If complaints are handled separately by six separate departments – all respecting data protection principles – there is a danger that an institution will fail to "join the dots" when they should. And why would one part of the campus define harassment differently to another?
- There is the issue of standards. Most students' unions would demand high standards of training of their university when it comes to investigations or panels. But where students' unions investigate complaints, the question is whether they are able to meet those standards themselves.
- It is right that students see their students' union as being led by students. But does that mean that they trust the students' union to handle any complaint they might have fairly – especially if high-profile elected officers are in some way involved in the process?

- Where students' unions are faced with legal threats or actions by students involved in harassment or misconduct cases, are they appropriately resourced and advised to proceed effectively?
- Some students' unions refer cases onto the university on the basis of context – was the issue "about" the students' union or one of its groups, or events or not? Others refer cases onto the university on the basis of severity – but many trustee boards of students' unions, with their own duty of care to their members, may not trust their university to handle cases effectively. And where students' unions find that a student has breached their code of conduct, what if the worst that can happen to that student is they cannot take part in students' union activity? In some cases, they clearly should lose student privileges too.
- Lots of students' unions struggle with group issues and group complaints, which can include "initiations" or other dares and stunts that involve sexual harassment and misconduct. Can or should students' unions "punish" a whole group or club for its culture? Can or should students' unions prevent its clubs and societies from trying to run their own processes? Where is the appropriate balance between "culture change" and "punishment"? When should students' unions refer a case to the Police?
- And if a case comes in through a university "Report + Support" site, is the SU informed? Should it be? In what circumstances?

We raise these issues without a bank of good practice or case studies to draw upon – students' unions and universities have been struggling with the issues we have identified in the absence of national guidance, often in the teeth of difficult cases. We take the view that an approach that reviews serious cases involving students' unions across small groups of universities would be a valuable way to proceed.

Student involvement in disciplinary processes

Finally, we turn our attention to the involvement of students and students' unions in university disciplinary processes.

In its Good Practice Framework – the de facto sector standard on complaints handling in Higher Education in England and Wales – the Office of the Independent Adjudicator (OIAHE) sets out multiple suggested roles:

> Providers should direct students to the support services available, for example the students' union, which can provide independent support and advice. This applies to students who are going through student disciplinary procedures and to students who are providing information about someone else's conduct that is being considered under those procedures. It is good practice to give students access to support and advice and, where it is not practicable to do so internally, providers should consider arranging for students to access support services at neighbouring institutions, partner providers or other local community services.
>
> (OIAHE, 2018, p. 9)

In our experience, most providers have well-established support available (usually through the students' union advice function) in this "support" space, although there have been two common issues in recent years.

The first surrounds small(er) providers where there may not be an active students union, or where it may lack the resource to provide professional staff support, which we believe essential in cases surrounding gender-based violence. We generally take the view that all providers should take steps to work with their local student representative body(ies) to ensure that all students are able to access independent support in the event of complaints of this nature, collaborating with other providers where necessary.

The second surrounds the provision of support for all students involved in a case. In a number of incidents, the local students' union has acted as the representative, advisor, or advocate for the student(s) that first approach them, which in some cases has left students on the other "side" of an allegation unable to access support locally. Again, we take the view that collaborating with other providers and their SUs should be able to address the issue.

In addition to the issue of supporting students making complaints or those accused of misconduct, there is the issue of student involvement in disciplinary panels. Here, OIAHE advises:

> It is good practice to include trained student representatives on disciplinary panels where possible, although there must be appropriate separation between the representative on the panel, and those providing advice and support to students.
>
> (OIAHE, 2018, p. 7)

Notwithstanding the sensible advice on separation, the simplicity of the recommendation does not give justice to the range of practice in this area and concerns raised about the issue of involvement in panels in recent years by both universities and students unions.

Much of the student unrest in the UK in the 1960s and 1970s concerned the struggle for fair disciplinary codes. One of the basic principles – that on non-academic matters, university officials/academics have no (more) special perspective than students' peers – was hard won and is now long established. A National Union of Students pamphlet in 1966 had argued that British justice allowed trial by one's peers, and on these grounds NUS suggested that students be included on any discipline panel or committee.

This slowly became the norm throughout the late 1970s and 1980s, with universities tending to invite the students' union to supply (full time) student officers for any panels that were convened.

However when carrying out reviews, in recent years universities and students' unions have tended to become concerned about the practice:

- Reports of some student representatives misunderstanding their role, who may have thought they were there to support the student being accused;

- Concerns about the "profile" and surrounding "bias" of a student offi-cer, particularly where they may have campaigned on issues surrounding gender-based violence and resultant concerns about bias or perceived bias;
- As standards and expectations on panel members have increased, questions surrounding the capacity of an otherwise busy elected student representa-tive to make effective contributions and judgements;
- The problem of student panel members not turning up despite having confirmed attendance, insofar as that represents something outside of a university's control;
- The need to progress cases during the summer when some student panel members may not be available around;
- The emotional and time burden on student members of panels involved and concern at insufficient support for students engaged in these processes;
- The risks when a student panel member may have used phrases or engaged in conduct which not only placed that particular panel at risk but risked legal proceedings against the university;
- Ambiguity around the extent to which a student would be covered by any insurances in place, and questions over the liability of student members where employees would be able to shelter under vicarious liability in an employment contract;
- Where an unpaid student representative is deployed, a version of the "unpaid person in the room" problem highlighted earlier in the chapters.

We do not take the view that these concerns should automatically involve the removal of student members of disciplinary committees, however complex and onerous the duties, where cases involve gender-based violence. We do take the view that an important point of principle, and a way of strengthening confi-dence in processes amongst the student body is to retain student involvement in them, and that appropriate safeguards can be put in place to address all of the aforementioned concerns.

For example, at one university we have encountered, there is a pooled disciplinary panel volunteers scheme, and all of the volunteers are cur-rent students. The students' union advice centre recruits and manages the volunteers. They undertake training at the beginning of the year with external and university staff, including on the issues surrounding "burden of proof" and gender-based violence, as well as effective and appropriate panel conduct.

At another university, a scheme involving the recruitment by the students' union and university of recent graduates into a pool operates effectively, with recruited students paid on a sessional basis to undertake the duties involved.

In any event, we take the view that any review of disciplinary procedures should take into account the issues identified, seeking to retain the principle of student involvement while ensuring effectiveness, fairness (and the perception of fairness), and a reasonable burden on participants.

Conclusion: comfort in discomfort

We do not anticipate that readers of this book generally or this chapter specifically need to be reminded of the idea of "Nothing About Us Without Us!" – the idea that no policy should be decided by any representative without the full and direct participation of members of any group(s) affected by that policy. It has long been accepted that the principle is of particular importance when it comes to groups that are otherwise marginalized from political, social, and economic opportunities, and/or when we are discussing individuals or groups with little relative power.

But we do believe that it is important to emphasize how important empathy, support, and discomfort are in the processes and activities we discuss in this chapter.

Universities at their best support student leaders, activists, and representatives to undertake the roles we have identified, by doing things like inviting them to attend training available for staff, linking with expert academics, allowing them to audit a course/attend lecture on gender-based violence, and by promoting access to support for how this work may affect them, through training on boundaries or burnout.

But often – to initial dismay – this may generate participation that is deeply uncomfortable and outside of the "norms" of a university's culture. In all types of student engagement – but especially in relation to gender-based violence – from time to time and to shift the culture, the student will raise issues at a time and a pace that the institution would not otherwise have chosen, and have to say things that, given a choice, an institution may not have said out loud. The bravery involved in doing so is valuable to change.

Finding ways – both formal and furtive – to ensure that students in these roles are democratically or culturally supported to raise things out of sync, raise the uncomfortable, and issue challenge is almost always something to celebrate rather than lament.

Further Reading

Day, M., & Dickinson, J. (2018). *David versus Goliath: The past, present and future of students' unions in the UK.* HEPI Report 111 www.hepi.ac.uk/wp-content/uploads/2018/09/HEPI-Students-Unions-Report-111-FINAL-EMBARGOED1-1.pdf

In this pamphlet for the Higher Education Policy Institute, Day and Dickinson interrogate the origins of students' unions and summarise their role and history through the major Higher Education debates of the past century. It covers student rights, in loco parentis, massification, marketisation, freedom of speech and the co-production of educational outcomes. It also reflects on emerging practice in students' unions in relation to innovation in student-led activity.

Lowe, T., & El Hakim, Y. (2020). *A handbook for student engagement in higher education.* **Routledge**.

This book explains the concept of student engagement insofar as it means the practices that surround students being engaged in decision-making about how that education is planned, run, delivered, evaluated or governed. It provides theory, ideas, examples and research-based evidence to offer a useful exploration of how students and staff can work together to transform Higher Education institutions and experiences.

References

Baird, H. (2019). *Evaluation of safeguarding students catalyst fund projects*. Advance HE. www.officeforstudents.org.uk/media/21a55030-ab94-425c-ba68-05997a9fa1d6/catalyst-evaluation-thematic-analysis-report-two.pdf

Baird, H., Renfrew, K., Nash-Henry, Z., & Towl, G. (2019). *Evaluation of safeguarding students catalyst fund projects: Summative Evaluation report*. Advance HE. www.officeforstudents.org.uk/media/e3c0bd5e-7e03-4235-941a-f933da269728/catalyst-evaluation-summative-report.pdf

Day, M., & Dickinson, J. (2018). *David versus Goliath: The past, present and future of students' unions in the UK*. HEPI Report 111 www.hepi.ac.uk/wp-content/uploads/2018/09/HEPI-Students-Unions-Report-111-FINAL-EMBARGOED1-1.pdf

Grint, K. (2008). Wicked problems and clumsy solutions: The role of leadership. *Clinical Leader, I*(II). http://leadershipforchange.org.uk/wp-content/uploads/Keith-Grint-Wicked-Problems-handout.pdf

Lowe, T., & El Hakim, Y. (2020). *A handbook for student engagement in higher education*. Routledge.

National Union of Students. (1966). *Student participation in college government*. NUS.

Office of the Independent Adjudicator for Higher Education. (2018). *Good practice framework: Disciplinary procedures*. www.oiahe.org.uk/resources-and-publications/good-practice-framework/disciplinary-procedures/

Office for Students. (2019). *Catalyst for change: Protecting students from hate crime, sexual violence and online harassment in higher education*. www.officeforstudents.org.uk/publications/catalyst-fund-projects-evaluation/

Rittel, H. W. J., & Webber, M. M. (1973). Dilemmas in a general theory of planning. *Policy Sciences, 4*, 157–169. https://doi.org/10.1007/BF01405730

Universities UK. (2016). *Changing the culture: Report of the Universities UK Taskforce examining violence against women, harassment and hate crime affecting university students*. www.universitiesuk.ac.uk/sites/default/files/field/downloads/2021-07/changing-the-culture.pdf\

18 Gender-based violence and HE partnerships with sexual assault services

Liz Hughes and Tammi Walker

Gender-based violence in UK universities – current policy developments

Sexual and gendered violence in the education sector is a worldwide concern, affecting schools, colleges, and universities in 'developed' and 'developing' nations alike (Phipps & Smith, 2012). However, it was only in the early 1990s that UK Higher Education contexts started to pay attention to the victimisation of women students (Towl & Walker, 2019). This was partly because of the Zellick Guidelines created in 1994 by the Council for Vice-Chancellors and Principals (CVCP, now Universities UK) in a response to a high-profile rape case. The guidelines provided advice to Higher Education Institution's (HEIs) on handling alleged student misconduct which may also constitute a criminal offence. One of the main problematic issues in relation to the Zellick Guidelines was the proposal that rape and sexual assault should never be investigated via internal disciplinary procedures until the complaint is formally reported to the police (NUS, 2015). Although these guidelines were not strictly legislation for many years, after their introduction many universities continued to use them as a basis for internal disciplinary procedures (Universities UK, 2016). However, in 2016, the increased criticism, including a campaign by the National Union of Students (NUS) launched in November 2015 (#StandByMe), called upon HEIs to reject the Zellick Guidelines and for the creation of new robust reporting and disciplinary guidelines and survivor support.

Eventually, in 2016, Universities UK published a report entitled *Changing the Culture*, which was focused on violence against women, harassment, and hate crime affecting university students. Universities UK issued a series of practical recommendations to support the implementation of a strategic framework to tackle these issues. Also in 2016, a steering group drawn from the Universities UK taskforce published new guidance for universities on how to handle alleged student misconduct, in response to concerns about continued reliance on the Zellick guidelines. The new guidance recommended:

- Maintaining a clear distinction between an internal disciplinary process and a criminal process – the criminal process must take priority.

DOI: 10.4324/9781003252474-21

- Universities should consider implementing precautionary measures relating to a student who is alleged to have committed a criminal offence at an early stage, pending the outcome of criminal/disciplinary proceedings. These precautionary steps must be reasonable and proportionate.

(Universities UK, 2016)

In 2017 and 2018, Universities UK conducted a research study to follow up on the 2016 *Changing the Culture* report, and the outcomes of which were published in 2018 suggesting that some, albeit comparatively modest, advancement was being made at individual institutions – particularly in tackling gender-based-violence – with common activities including increased training for staff, preventative campaigns, and development of partnerships with third sector and specialist organisations. However, despite this progress, the research also showed that much more still needed to be done to drive positive change across Higher Education, and in response Universities UK set out six recommendations for universities to consider further:

1 Ensure accountability for tackling harassment and hate crime sits at senior management/executive level – just under half of responding institutions indicated this was currently the case.
2 Involve responding students and reporting students and bystanders to develop and improve response strategies. Only 32% currently involve them in developing an institutional strategic response, although almost all work with students' unions on this.
3 Setting all students, including pre-arrival, with clear behavioural expectations, linked to potential sanctions if these are breached.
4 Make resource allocation for this part of the strategic planning process – 45% identified a lack of resources as a key barrier to enhancing progress.
5 Ensure regular reporting and reviewing to governing bodies or committees.
6 Ensure that the principles and priority status afforded to handling sexual misconduct are also given to other forms of harassment and hate crime.

(Universities UK, 2018)

Sexual violence against university students in the UK

Debates about sexual violence in UK universities began with concerns about 'lad culture' and student-on-student violence; discussions have now widened to include sexual misconduct towards students by staff (Towl & Walker, 2019). Although work on violence against women students dates to the 1980s (Phipps & Young, 2013), the first national research on women students' experiences of harassment and violence in the UK was in 2010 by the NUS. *The Hidden Marks* report found that one in seven women students had experienced a serious physical or sexual assault during their studies, and 68% had been sexually harassed (NUS, 2010).

Following this, Phipps and Young (2013) were commissioned by the NUS to explore the links between sexual violence and 'laddish' masculinities characterised by competitive displays of sexism and misogyny. Using a qualitative interview study with 40 women students at UK universities, they explored the experiences of and feelings about 'lad culture' in their communities. 'Lad culture' was defined as a group mentality residing in behaviours such as sport, heavy alcohol consumption, casual sex, and sexist/discriminatory 'banter'. The report *That's What She Said* found that many of the behaviours collected under this banner encompassed sexual harassment and were normalised within student communities, with 'casual' non-consensual groping being usual at parties and in social settings, and expectations around sexual activity which needed young women to be regularly available yet almost entirely passive. Phipps and Young suggested that this created the conditions in which potentially serious boundary violations, including sexual assault, could happen and created a conducive context for more serious forms of sexual violence.

Today, one in three women students in the UK report being subjected to sexual assault and 71% of men students who are assaulted deal with it (or fail to do so) entirely alone. Over half of all students who have been subjected to sexual assault and/or sexual harassment have indicated that it took place on campus. Of the students who had been sexually harassed, 12% had at least one incident take place in university halls. These recent figures come from the Empowered Campus 2020 report "*A Lot Left to Learn: Student Experiences of Gender-based Violence at University*". Empowered Campus covers over 100 universities' students and is led by 43 student unions. In 2020, an anonymous survey led by Trendence, student market research company, and a consortium of 26 UK students unions encouraged students to disclose instances of gender-based violence. A total of 8,106 Higher Education students from 124 universities completed the online survey: 97% of students disclosed not reporting these incidents to their university, and only 2% of students felt satisfied with their university's reporting system and policies.

The survey explored the impact of identity and gender-based violence and found that Lesbian, Gay and Bisexual students are 15% more likely to experience sexual harassment. White students reported being sexually assaulted in the Student Union at twice the rate of Black and Minority Ethnic (BME) students and BME students were reported as being twice as likely to be sexually assaulted in a classroom, lecture room, lab, or theatre compared to their white peers. Empowered Campus have outlined a threefold policy approach to prevent such incidents happening in the future, and to help victims in any way possible:

- Supporting both survivors and universities to review and identify if there are areas for growth and revisions in official policy.
- Helping to create better access to support.
- Building a national network to target and resolve sexual assault cases more easily and in a sensitive manner.

(Empowered Campus, 2020)

Office for Students standards on harassment and sexual misconduct

In April 2021, the Office for Students (OfS) published "seven expectations" for Higher Education providers to help them prevent and respond to serious harassment and misconduct affecting students. The statement of expectations follows a consultation process that began in 2019 but was halted because of the pandemic but builds on the guidance from Universities UK on changing culture produced in 2016 and 2018, and research by the Higher Education Policy Institute (HEPI) into students' views on the issue. The expectations are in no danger of setting the bar too high. Furthermore, it comes at a time when there is increased focus on harassment and sexual violence within the education system, with 119 universities named in testimonies from survivors of rape and sexual abuse on the *Everyone's Invited* platform (2020).

The statement provides a clear and consistent set of standards for colleges and universities to help them to develop and implement effective systems, policies, and processes to prevent and respond to incidents of harassment and sexual misconduct. The statement covers sexual misconduct as well as harassment connected to a range of protected characteristics – including race, religion, disability, and sexual orientation. Expectations extend beyond the campus to social media and the internet, where harassment is increasingly prevalent. The seven expectations are set out herein:

> Expectation 1: Higher Education providers should clearly communicate, and embed across their whole organisation, their approach to preventing and responding to all forms of harassment and sexual misconduct affecting students.
>
> Expectation 2: Governing bodies should ensure that the provider's approach to harassment and sexual misconduct is adequate and effective.
>
> Expectation 3: Higher Education providers should appropriately engage with students to develop and evaluate systems, policies, and processes to address harassment and sexual misconduct.
>
> Expectation 4: Higher Education providers should implement adequate and effective staff and student training with the purpose of raising awareness of, and preventing, harassment and sexual misconduct.
>
> Expectation 5: Higher Education providers should have adequate and effective policies and processes in place for all students to report and disclose incidents of harassment and sexual misconduct.
>
> Expectation 6: Higher Education providers should have a fair, clear and accessible approach to taking action in response to reports and disclosures.
>
> Expectation 7: Higher Education providers should ensure that students have access to appropriate and effective support.
>
> (Office for Students, 2021)

The OfS Statement of Expectations on harassment and sexual misconduct have been welcomed by senior management teams and governing bodies, however, some have questioned if they go far enough. Firstly, one key area is whether the Expectations will be incorporated into the registration requirements. If it does, there may be scope for some of the OfS sanctions such as enhanced surveillance or specific registration conditions to be imposed on institutions. Secondly, safeguarding in universities may become something which is mandatory to ask, and answer, questions about in references for certain roles just as it is in other regulated sectors. Thirdly, as mentioned earlier, 119 universities were mentioned on *Everyone's Invited* website, and the website includes resources such as template letters to educational settings. It is possible that this movement may increase, and universities should remain vigilant to the risk of disclosures being posted anonymously on it or receiving testimonies from former students about past and present staff behaviour.

Lastly, Towl and Humphrey's (2021) have put forward ten recommendations for teams and governing bodies about building on the Expectations guidance. For example, all prevention and response initiatives for sexual violence being trauma-informed, the sharing by universities of their approach to tackling sexual violence at Open Days, universities explicitly stating whether staff are permitted to have sexual relationships with their students and creating partnerships with the external organisations that work with survivors and perpetrators such as the NHS, whether based at local Sexual Assault Referral Centres (SARCs) or at local General Practitioner practices. This last recommendation by Towl and Humphreys will be the focus for the rest of the chapter and will discuss how SARC's may work in partnership with universities to support university students.

The sexual assault referral centre model

Services specifically for sexual assault have been around for several decades and now are a common model across the world. The Sexual Assault Nurse Examiner (SANE) model (Campbell & Wasco, 2005) is a US model that originated in the 1970s but saw a bigger expansion in the 1990s. The aim of SANE is to offer a comprehensive multisystem service which spans emotional support, healthcare, and a forensic examination. Campbell et al. (Campbell et al., 2005) reviewed evidence for the SANE model and concluded that whilst the evidence was limited by methodology used, there were indications that SANE had a positive impact across medical, emotional, and legal domains. A number of other models now exist in Australia and Europe such as Sexual Assault Centres (SACs) in Nordic countries (Nesvold et al., 2005) and Holland (Bicanic et al., 2014).

In the UK, Sexual Assault Referral Centres (SARCs) have been established over the past three decades to provide a "one stop shop" for people who report a sexual assault (NHS England, 2015). There are approximately 50 SARCs in England and they offer broadly similar services at initial contact (initial assessment and if required, a timely forensic examination (FE)) but then vary in terms of follow-up care. There are broadly three models of aftercare: signpost and refer to other "partner agencies"; inhouse short-term support – usually delivered by counsellors; and more rarely, a co-located psychological therapies service (Hughes et al, in preparation). They bring together healthcare and FE (if requested) and are commissioned via national special commissioning team at NHS England in the Department of Health. SARCs have come about due to the recognition that sexual assault survivors can be re-traumatised by the experience of recounting the assault, and the forensic examination.

Forensic examinations are performed by specially trained and accredited forensic examiners (FE) who are often medical examiners (FME), but increasingly there are also Forensic Nurse Examiners (FNE) who perform these tasks. The aim of the FE is to gather evidence to be used in criminal proceedings, including swabs for DNA, examination, and photographing injuries. Naturally, these procedures involve intimate parts of the body, including penetrative procedures such as swabbing into the vagina or rectum. In addition, they offer a range of health interventions such as post-exposure prophylaxis (to prevent HIV), Sexually Transmitted Infection testing, tests for pregnancy, HIV, and hepatitis. SARCs are staffed with Crisis Workers. They are often the people who make the initial contact with the survivor (either by phone or face to face) and their role is to offer support throughout the contact with SARCs. They often remain with the person whilst they undergo the FE and play a critical role in preparing the person for the procedure by explaining what is likely to happen but also giving the survivor the choice and control about every aspect of what happens. In recognition of the heightened state of emotions that the survivor may well be experiencing, SARCs seek not to overwhelm the reporting party with too much information at the time of attendance and will give an information pack to take away for when they are ready read it. Many SARCs will undertake follow-up calls to see how the person is doing, review if referrals are proceeding as planned, and if any new issue has arisen which they could help with.

The Independent Sexual Assault Advisor (ISVA) service (UK Government, 2017) is in place to support survivors post-assault. They provide physical and psychological space and time to talk through whether the person wishes to pursue criminal proceedings and if they do, they provide support through that process to court. ISVAs aim to offer continuity, advocacy, and impartial advice to survivors, including risk assessment, assessment of need, and a support plan. Whilst they do provide some element of emotional support, it is not in their remit to offer counselling, so if a mental health or other health need is identified, they will refer the person to the right service in the locality. ISVAs are not employed within the SARC but often work alongside the SARC staff and will attend meetings to pick up new referrals or discuss existing people on their case load. People can access SARCs via self-referral, but often attend after first contacting the police or another agency such as a GP or, in the case of university, a member of staff from the counselling or welfare service.

Optimising access to sexual assault services for university students

Despite the availability of SARCs, and the evidence that they can be a relatively positive experience (Stefanidou et al., 2020), they are not accessed by the majority of people who are subjected to a sexual assault. There are several reasons why this might be, such as lack of knowledge about the existence of SARCs, 'rape myths' which are societal attitudes that implicitly and explicitly blame victim behaviour on the experience of sexual assault, which also serves to minimize the severity of sexual violence (Moore & Baker, 2018). Examples of this include blaming the victim's behaviour (including intoxication) and clothing as 'provocative' and indicative of 'sexual availability', misinformation about sexual assault, shame and stigma about sexual assault including fear of 'victim blaming', fear of consequences from the perpetrator, and other more practical barriers such as having money to get to sexual assault services. These attitudes and beliefs may impact on help-seeking, especially in younger people such as university students. Timing of help-seeking can be important in terms of collecting forensic evidence as well as being able to provide immediate emotional support; however, there are some indications that younger people may be less likely to attend sexual assault services immediately after having been subjected to sexual violence.

Nesvold et al. (2005) undertook a study in Norway to explore differences between those who attend Spell outACs immediately in the aftermath of an assault and those who attended later. They found that late presenters tend to be younger, were subjected to a penetrative assault, and that the perpetrator was known to them. They hypothesised that younger people may have been influenced by rape myths which are compounded by a lack of general knowledge about what behaviours and actions constitute sexual assault from both the perpetrator and the survivors perspective. With many people understanding sexual assault as a violent rape by a stranger, there is a risk of people minimising what has happened to them and therefore not seeking help. Nesvold and colleagues recommend that there needs to be extensive public information around what constitutes sexual assault to dispel unhelpful rape myths and encourage reporting. In addition, people need to have prior, and accurate, knowledge of where to get help and support should a sexual assault be disclosed. This is especially pertinent for staff and students in universities given that younger people are often not quick to report.

In addition to the age of the survivor and knowledge about sexual assault and support services, there is a need to consider the needs of underserved groups of students with additional vulnerable characteristics which may very well create additional barriers to accessing SARCs. Sexual assault services are accessed mainly by white, middle-class females (Koss et al., 2017) and a review by Hardenberg-Bach et al. (Bach et al., 2021) identified other groups with vulnerabilities that are less well served. They identified that there were additional barriers for those who had the following characteristics:

- Black and ethnic minority groups including, but not restricted to, those whose first language is not English;

- Those with low financial resources;
- Those with pre-existing mental health and drug and/or alcohol use;
- Sexual and gender minorities.

Some people will belong to more than one of these groups and intersectionality will compound the challenges and barriers. Sexual assault experiences are common amongst trans and non-gender conforming (TNGC) students with studies reporting between 14% and 58% had been subjected to some form of sexual assault (Marine & Nicolazzo, 2020), and 29% in a large study of over 10,000 college campus in the United States (Cantor et al., 2015). However, trans people find additional barriers to accessing help and support due to stigma and transphobia. Some sexual assault services offer 'women only' services which by default, may sometimes, exclude trans women. However, whilst most sexual assault services are trans-inclusive, there is a lack of training and competency in trans issues in the sexual assault workforce (Du Mont et al., 2020). Therefore, there may well be an understandable hesitancy in the trans community to come forward and seek help for fear of rejection and discrimination.

To improve awareness and support for underserved groups, Hardenberg and colleagues recommend that services should ensure they are universally accessible to all minority groups. This means having diversity reflected in the workforce both at the university and in sexual assault services, a culturally competent workforce, and ensuring service information is inclusive, accessible, and welcoming to all. The latter could be addressed by co-producing information with diverse student groups such as LGBTQ+. In fact, despite many services describing themselves as 'inclusive', there is a need to be more overt about how they support diverse populations to use their services. Information should also be available in a range of languages as even if the student has a good level of English as a second language, in times of extreme stress, they are more able to process information in their own language. Staff in the university and in SARCs should be culturally aware of how sexual assault and how distress and trauma may be manifest. In addition, attention should be paid to the practical barriers to accessing specialist sexual assault services such as whether students have the financial resources to access and attend follow-up services.

Post-sexual assault support

Many people who are subjected to sexual assault and attend a SARC have pre-existing mental health problems (Brooker et al., 2018) and in addition, sexual assault is associated with an increased risk of post-traumatic stress disorder and other mental health issues. People who have been subjected to sexual assault will experience a heightened state of emotion at the time and may need some days to process what has happened before more formal mental health screening takes place. In addition, people who support survivors should be aware of how trauma can manifest itself as acute distress and rage or dissociation such as incongruous affect, numb, or feelings of detachment. Some survivors may increase their use of drugs and/or alcohol as a coping mechanism. Most SARCs will undertake follow-up calls to survivors following initial attendance to check in and see if any additional needs have arisen, including progress on any referrals made. Some SARCs offer in-house psychological therapy for trauma, but usually they refer to local NHS psychological services (NICE, 2018). Many survivors will not require such intensive therapy but may find supportive counselling helpful. However, this needs to be able to meet the specific needs of someone who has experienced sexual trauma such as specialist Rape Counselling.

Generic counselling may be useful, but the counsellor should be familiar with trauma informed practices such as believing the victim, placing the blame entirely with the perpetrator, and offering choice and control to the person in all interactions. If counselling is offered within the University services, then it is vital that this must be trauma informed. SARCs can offer advice to external services for best practice in working with survivors of sexual assault. If the sexual assault occurred within the context of an intimate relationship and there are other concerns such as physical and/or emotional violence, then safeguarding processes should be followed by any service involved with the survivor to maintain their safety.

There are other non-talking therapies that can help a survivor regulate their nervous system following a traumatic experience when their "fight/flight/freeze" sympathetic nervous system is hyper-aroused. This can cause problems with focus, anxiety, being startled easily, and being in a state of hypervigilance. Activities that activate the vagus nerve will switch on the 'rest and digest' parasympathetic system, and survivors find they can get a great deal of relief from their symptoms by doing this. Things that activate the vagus nerve include yoga, meditation, deep breathing exercises, cold water immersion (such as wild swimming), hot baths, and weighted blankets.

Recommendations for partnership working between university, SARCs, and other relevant local agencies

All students need to know four things: (1) what constitutes consent and non-consent, (2) actions and behaviours that constitute sexual assault, (3) who and where to ask for compassionate and supportive help, and (4) what sort of help is offered. This is because most students will most likely first disclose to their friends and in a student survey in New Zealand, only 8% of those who disclosed sexual assault reported this to a member of university staff or university welfare or counselling service (Beres et al., 2020). The information regarding local sexual assault services should be accessible and available. University welfare services should consider the needs of underserved groups such as international, BAME, and LGBTQ students and how to reach out to these groups. Equally, the local SARCs should consider how 'student-friendly' their information is and there is the potential to work with local student groups to improve this if need be. There are examples of close working between the SARCs and the local universities. For example, staff from the SARC in Sheffield attend Freshers Week at the local universities to hand out information and are available for students to talk to. This could be applied at other SARCS working with local universities.

Reporting assault and forensic examination

Staff and students alike should understand the implications around the timeliness of the forensic examination following a sexual assault and should be able to offer the right advice such as trying not to go to the toilet, avoiding showering, washing and cleaning teeth until after the examination, putting unwashed clothes from the incident in a clean plastic bag, and having an examination within 72 hours gives the best chance to obtain any DNA evidence which could support a criminal prosecution (Rape Crisis South London, u.d.).

Trauma Informed Care (TIC)

Sexual Assault services are delivered with a trauma-informed approach with a specific focus on the following:

- Believing the survivor.
- Dispelling any self-blame and rape myths that the survivor may have internalized.
- Giving the survivor complete choice and control over every aspect of the process from initial attendance, the forensic examination (if undertaken) and what follow-on care they may wish to access.
- Ensure that the option to report to the police and/or undergo a forensic examination must be their own choice and not use coercive strategies such as, somewhat outrageously, suggesting they protect other potential victims if they report. Ultimately there is a requirement for a frank discussion that engagement in the criminal process will be a difficult and traumatic process, with the potential for retraumatisation.

These aspects of TIC should be universally applied in any setting, including pastoral care at universities, as these strategies really support and empower the person and aid in their recovery processes.

Conclusions

All students and staff need a good understanding of what consent is, and what constitutes sexual assault and/violence. In addition to this, students and staff need to know exactly where to signpost someone if a disclosure is made, as many first disclosures are made to a friend. Timely access to a forensic examination is essential for the collection of evidence, especially if planning to proceed with a prosecution. However, forensic examinations can be traumatic and so prior knowledge of what will occur reduces risk of re-traumatising the person and attendance at a specialist sexual assault service can be a positive experience in terms of accessing help from people who really 'get' sexual trauma. Some people may need specialist trauma therapy, so it is important that people get follow-up monitoring, especially as psychological distress may develop over time after the event. Survivors of sexual assault may benefit from generic counselling, but the counsellor should have a good understanding of impact of sexual violence, and be able to work in a trauma informed way. Survivors should also be signposted to other relevant, local services such as domestic violence, sexual health, and rape-counselling services.

Future directions

Given that sexual assault is common amongst students, there needs to be more emphasis on general awareness of what constitutes sexual assault and where to get help that is easily accessible for all students, including those who are gender diverse, from Black and ethnic minorities and identify as LGBTQ. Support services at the University including the more informal peer support student groups should consider their role in ensuring that disclosures can be made safely and without judgement, and that they are aware of local external support agencies such as police, SARCs, and rape counselling. SARCs should consider how they work with universities in their local area, ensuring that their promotional materials are shared with the student population (e.g., link to website included in university welfare webpages) and that they offer open sessions to explain what they offer and how to refer/access. SARCs should also consider the diverse needs of the local students, including issues of language and cultural barriers as well as being accessible for those with neurodiversity and mental health.

Further Reading

Towl, G., & Walker, T. (2019). *Tackling sexual violence at universities: An international perspective*. **Routledge**.

Sexual violence is a problem well beyond universities; however, universities are uniquely well placed to contribute to reducing sexual violence, encouraging those affected to come forward and speak about their experiences and actively encourage increased reporting. This book is unique, in that it offers an international perspective on the incidence, reporting and impact of sexual violence at universities.

Drawing on evidence from the UK, North America, Australia and Europe, this book explores the psychological and structural challenges to reporting sexual violence. It provides a set of policy and practice guidance recommendations that move beyond awareness campaigns to call for systems to be put in place whereby reports of sexual assault are handled promptly, fairly, and consistently. The authors also discuss how universities can strengthen their approach to prevention, promoting safeguarding and the welfare of victims and survivors, and involving victims and survivors in the development and improvement of services. However, fundamental to their approach is keeping decision making with the victim and survivor and emphasising that their health and recovery is paramount.

Hughes, E., Lucock, M., & Brooker, C. (2019). Sexual violence and mental health services: A call to action. *Epidemiology and Psychiatry Sciences,* **28 (6), 594–597. doi:10.1017/S2045796019000040**

In this guest editorial, Hughes and colleagues highlight the high likelihood that people who use mental health services have been subjected to sexual assault. This is due to increased vulnerability factors such as intimate partner violence, drug and alcohol and sexual abuse histories. There is evidence that sexual violence occurs in mental health inpatient settings and, counter intuitively appears not to be mitigated by single sex sleeping accommodation. Mental health services are not undertaking routine enquiry or fostering the atmosphere that would support disclosure and subsequent actions to safeguard the person or provide additional and appropriate trauma informed care. There is limited evidence that mental health services have policies on sexual violence and pathways to sexual assault services. There is also concern that mental health staff lack awareness of local sexual violence services in the event of a disclosure. The recommendations are for improved approach to facilitating disclosure, believing the person making the disclosure, as well as being aware of what options are available in terms of actions according to the situation.

References

Bach, M. H., Beck Hansen, N., Ahrens, C., Nielsen, C. R., Walshe, C., & Hansen, M. (2021, April 9). Underserved survivors of sexual assault: A systematic scoping review. *European Journal of Psychotraumatology, 12*(1), 1895516. https://doi.org/10.1080/20008198.2021.1895516

Beres, M. A., Stojanov, Z., Graham, K., & Treharne, G. J. (2020, October 9). Sexual assault experiences of university students and disclosure to health professionals and others. *New Zealand Medical Journal, 133*(1523), 55–64.

Bicanic, I., Snetselaar, H., De Jongh, A., & Van de Putte, E. (2014). Victims' use of professional services in a Dutch sexual assault centre. *European Journal of Psychotraumatology, 5.* https://doi.org/10.3402/ejpt.v5.23645

Brooker, C., Tocque, K., & Paul, S. (2018, February). Assessment of the mental health status of a one year cohort attending a two sexual assault referral centres in England. *Journal of Forensic and Legal Medicine, 54*, 44–49. https://doi.org/10.1016/j.jflm.2017.12.018

Campbell, R., Patterson, D., & Lichty, L. F. (2005). The effectiveness of sexual assault nurse examiner (SANE) programs: A review of psychological, medical, legal, and community outcomes. *Trauma, Violence, & Abuse, 6*(4), 313–329. https://doi.org/10.1177/1524838005280328

Campbell, R., & Wasco, S. M. (2005, January). Understanding rape and sexual assault: 20 years of progress and future directions. *Journal of Interpersonal Violence, 20*(1), 127–131. https://doi.org/10.1177/0886260504268604

Cantor, D., Fisher, B., Chibnall, S. H., Townsend, R., Lee, H., Thomas, G., Bruce, C., & Westat, I. (2015). *Report on the AAU campus climate survey on sexual assault and sexual misconduct.* Westat.

Du Mont, J., Saad, M., Kosa, S. D., Kia, H., & Macdonald, S. (2020, 2020/10/01/). Providing trans-affirming care for sexual assault survivors: An evaluation of a novel curriculum for forensic nurses. *Nurse Education Today, 93*, 104541. https://doi.org/https://doi.org/10.1016/j.nedt.2020.104541

Empowered Campus. (2020). *A lot left to learn: Student experiences of gender-based violence at university.* https://uploads.strikinglycdn.com/files/63bf1e36-a5ce-4b18-a314-cf0a067dde70/Empowered-Campus-%202020-%20Report%20%20(1).pdf

Everyone's Invited. (2020). *Everyone's invited: Online sexual abuse campaign.* www.everyonesinvited.uk/

Hughes, E., Brooker, C., Tocque, K., Lloyd-Evans, B., Stefanidou, T., Majeed-Ariss, R., Sleath, E., & O'Doherty, L. (in preperation). *A National Survey of How Sexual Assault Referral Centres Identify and Respond to Mental Health and Drug/Alcohol Needs.* School of Health and Social Care, Edinburgh Napier University UK.

Koss, M. P., White, J. W., & Lopez, E. C. (2017). Victim voice in reenvisioning responses to sexual and physical violence nationally and internationally. *American Psychologist, 72*(9), 1019–1030. https://doi.org/10.1037/amp0000233

Marine, S. B., & Nicolazzo, Z. (2020). Campus sexual violence prevention educators' use of gender in their work: A critical exploration. *Journal of Interpersonal Violence, 35*(21–22), 5005–5027. https://doi.org/10.1177/0886260517718543

Moore, B. M., & Baker, T. (2018). An Exploratory Examination of College Students' Likelihood of Reporting Sexual Assault to Police and University Officials: Results of a Self-Report Survey. *Journal of Interpersonal Violence, 33*(22), 3419–3438. https://doi.org/10.1177/0886260516632357

National Institute for Health and Care Excellence (NICE) (2018). *Post-traumatic stress disorder: NICE guideline.* www.nice.org.uk/guidance/ng116/resources/posttraumatic-stress-disorder-pdf-66141601777861

National Union of Students. (2010). *Hidden marks: A study of women students' experiences of harassment, stalking, violence and sexual assault.* www.nusconnect.org.uk/resources/hidden-marks-a-study-of-women-students-experiences-of-harassment-stalking-violence-and-sexual-assault

National Union of Students. (2015). *How to respond to complaints of sexual violence: The Zellick report.* www.nusconnect.org.uk/resources/how-to-respond-to-complaints-of-sexual-violence-the-zellick-report

Nesvold, H., Worm, A.-M., Vala, U., & Agnarsdóttir, G. R. (2005). Different Nordic facilities for victims of sexual assault: A comparative study. *Acta Obstetricia et Gynecologica Scandinavica, 84*(2), 177–183. https://doi.org/https://doi.org/10.1111/j.0001-6349.2005.00641.x

NHS England. (2015). *Sexual assault services provider service specification and commissioning framework for paediatric sexual assault referral centre (SARC) services.* www.england.nhs.uk/commissioning/wp-content/uploads/sites/12/2013/05/SARCs-service-spec-contract-template-and-paed-framework.pdf

Office for Students. (2021). *Statement of expectations: Preventing and addressing harassment and sexual misconduct in universities.* Office for Students.

Phipps, A. & Smith, G. (2012). Violence against women students in the UK: Time to take action. *Gender and Education, 24*(4), 357–373.

Phipps, A. & Young, I. (2013). *That's what she said: Women students' experiences of 'lad culture' in higher education.* https://www.nusconnect.org.uk/resources/thats-what-she-said-full-report

Rape Crisis South London. (n.d.). *Recent rape and sexual assault.* www.rasasc.org.uk/independent-sexual-violence-advocate-service/recent-rape-and-sexual-assault/

Stefanidou, T., Hughes, E., Kester, K., Edmondson, A., Majeed-Ariss, R., Smith, C., Ariss, S., Brooker, C., Gilchrist, G., Kendal, S., Lucock, M., Maxted, F., Perot, C., Shallcross, R., Trevillion, K., & Lloyd-Evans, B. (2020). The identification and treatment of mental health and substance misuse problems in sexual assault services: A systematic review. *PLoS One, 15*(4), e0231260. https://doi.org/10.1371/journal.pone.0231260

Towl, G., & Humphreys, C. (2021, December 11). *How to do more than the bare minimum on Harassment and sexual misconduct.* https://wonkhe.com/blogs/how-to-do-more-than-the-bare-minimum-on-harassment-and-sexual-misconuct/

Towl, G., & Walker, T. (2019). *Tackling sexual violence at universities: An international perspective.* Routledge.

UK Government (2017). *The role of the independent sexual violence advisor- essential elements.* https://assets.publishing.service.gov.uk/government/uploads/system/uploads/attachment_data/file/647112/The_Role_of_the_Independent_Sexual_Violence_Adviser_-_Essential_Elements_September_2017_Final.pdf

Universities UK. (2016, December 12). *Changing the culture: Report of the universities UK taskforce examining violence against women, harassment and hate crime affecting university students.* www.universitiesuk.ac.uk/policy-and-analysis/reports/Documents/2016/changing-the-culture.pdf.

Universities UK. (2018, December 12). *Changing the culture: Tackling gender based violence, harassment and hate crime: Two years on.* www.universitiesuk.ac.uk/sites/default/files/field/downloads/2021-07/uuk-changing-the-culture-two-years-on.pdf

Zellick Guidelines. (1994). *How to respond to the complaints of sexual violence: The Zellick Report.* https://universityappg.co.uk/sites/default/files/field/attachment/NUS%20Zellick

19 Rape crisis

Taking a partnership approach to addressing gender-based violence with universities and colleges across Scotland

Niamh Kerr and Kathryn Dawson

There is increasing awareness in Scotland and the rest of UK of the prevalence of sexual harassment and violence in Further and Higher Education Institutions (see, for example, Phipps, 2020). On the front line of providing support to those affected, Scotland's Rape Crisis centres have a keen sense of the scale of the problem; in 2019, Rape Crisis Scotland surveyed centres and found that one had 70 student survivors awaiting support, whilst another had supported 85 within the last year. Whilst robust data on the prevalence of gender-based violence (GBV) in Further and Higher Education is limited, it is clear that rates remain high across university and college communities. Universities and colleges have a duty of care to all students, and a specific duty under the Equality Act 2010 to ensure that students with protected characteristics have equal access to education. Yet, we know that women, as well as trans, queer, and non-binary people, are subjected to disproportionate rates of GBV (Bull et al., 2019). Tackling GBV requires Further and Higher Education Institutions to take action to dismantle the culture and structures that allow GBV to thrive, in order to make equal access to education a reality.

The consequences of GBV are far-reaching, and addressing them requires institutions to take a comprehensive approach encompassing policies, preventative measures, reporting procedures, and guidance and training to improve responses to disclosures of GBV. Such measures need to be shaped and informed by the needs of survivors, and specialist organisations can support institutions to take a survivor-centred and trauma-informed approach.

Momentum for change has continued to build and there is a growing acknowledgement that universities and colleges need to take more robust action. Student survivors, activists, and GBV organisations have actively campaigned for change across the Further and Higher Education sectors and institutions have responded, but the scope and scale of change has been limited by underfunding and inconsistent prioritisation (Bull et al., 2019). In order to achieve transformative change, the sector must implement comprehensive, consistent, and collaborative approaches to tackling and responding to violence.

In this chapter, we will argue that strong partnerships between universities, colleges, and specialist organisations should be a central focus of the sectors' approach to addressing GBV. We will present examples of how Rape Crisis

DOI: 10.4324/9781003252474-22

Scotland and local centres have formed partnerships with universities and colleges to provide staff training, student education interventions, and on-campus specialist support services. We will demonstrate how institutions can create meaningful partnerships to provide gendered, intersectional, and survivor-centred interventions to address GBV, sharing the successes and challenges of partnership approaches and offering key recommendations based on our learning. We discuss the work of the Rape Crisis network with schools, colleges, and universities within the context of Scotland's national policy approach to eradicate Violence against Women and Girls (VAWG), before expanding on three key areas of development in which the network is supporting colleges and universities to develop their practice: staff training; student education, and specialist on-campus support. In each area, we present case studies to illustrate practice and share perspectives from Rape Crisis centres and institutions. In this chapter, we include contributions from Rape Crisis Centres as well as perspectives from Higher Education staff and student survivors.

Section 1: The Context

The Rape Crisis network in Scotland comprises 17 autonomous local centres and the national office, Rape Crisis Scotland (RCS). The work of centres is primarily in delivering support to adults and young people affected by sexual violence. Their support model is survivor-centred, trauma-informed, and underpinned by a feminist analysis which locates the causes and consequences of GBV in structural gender inequality. These gendered inequalities intersect with other forms of inequality (relating, for example, to race, social class or caste, age, disability, gender identity, sexual orientation) to shape the differing nature and impacts that violence can have, and mean that steps need to be taken to address barriers and specific needs of different groups. A gendered analysis also recognises that boys and men are affected by GBV, the perpetrators of which are usually male, and the impacts of which are also gendered.

In recent years, there has also been substantial growth and development in prevention work carried out by Rape Crisis centres, which has focused on young people and schools, colleges, and universities. This work was initially led by a number of individual centres and was subsequently expanded through Scottish Government funding to fund The National Prevention Programme coordinated by RCS which is now delivered in every local authority area and reaches approximately half of Scotland's secondary schools. This programme enabled the Rape Crisis network to develop a local–national partnership delivery model which balances consistency and quality assurance on the one hand with local autonomy, leadership, and flexibility on the other.

Whilst the schools-focused programme has been the primary focus of our prevention work, there has been increasing engagement with Further and Higher Education sectors and Centres have been involved in supporting their local institutions through training and education – though without specific resourcing these activities tend to be on an ad hoc basis. RCS was also involved in joint work between the University of Glasgow (UoG) and Glasgow Caledonian University (GCU) (for further details, see Burman et al., 2020) and subsequently took part in the EU-funded *It Stops Now* project led by the National Women's Council of Ireland (NWCI, 2019), which developed a toolkit comprising staff training materials and campaigning and awareness-raising tools, to which UoG and GCU were partners.

While this project was in its early stages, the Scottish Government brought a national strategic focus to the issue of GBV in Higher Education as part of its *Equally Safe* strategy to prevent and eradicate VAWG (Scottish Government and COSLA, 2018). Through this strategy, the University of Strathclyde was funded to develop the *Equally Safe in Higher Education* toolkit, which sought to take a whole campus approach to preventing and responding to GBV (Donaldson et al., 2018). It included guidance on conducting research, policy development, responding to GBV, primary prevention, intervention, curriculum and knowledge exchange. A number of partners including Glasgow and Clyde Rape Crisis Centre were involved in the development and piloting of the toolkit (see Case Study 1). This included a three-tier staff training model, whose delivery was led by Rape Crisis but incorporated content on domestic abuse to be delivered by a specialist service.

The toolkit was published in 2018 and the Scottish Government introduced a further phase of funding to support its implementation and adaption to the college sector, led by the University of Strathclyde. Henceforth the strategic work was referred to as *Equally Safe in Colleges and Universities* (ESCU). A strategic working group was set up with representation from the college and universities sectors as well as violence against women and other equalities agencies.

This phase also included funding for RCS to establish the Training and Education Coordinator for Colleges and Universities post, which would take the Toolkit's staff training model and tackle the logistics of delivering it across Scotland. Rape Crisis Centres were keen in principle to be involved but in most cases had insufficient strategic and delivery capacity to do so at the scale needed. Colleges and universities were not necessarily aware that Rape Crisis Centres could offer training and other support, and there was no readily accessible information about this available to them.

RCS therefore mapped out a programme of work for the new Coordinator to encompass relationship-building with the college and university sector, and capacity-building with Rape Crisis Centres and the Women's Aid groups who would deliver the domestic abuse component of the training. Building on the local–national partnership developed through the prevention programme, RCS planned to develop a menu of options incorporating the core training programme from the Toolkit, along with flexible options for student educational programmes so that local centres and institutions could determine together what best suited their needs. It also undertook to scope options for the delivery of on-campus support, drawing on the successful partnership between Rape Crisis Glasgow and Clyde and the University of Strathclyde established for the toolkit development.

Case Study 1   Glasgow and Clyde Rape Crisis and ESHE Toolkit Partnership

In July of 2016 Glasgow and Clyde Rape Crisis (GCRC) was approached by the University of Strathclyde to work in partnership with the newly-formed project Equally Safe in Higher Education (ESHE). The University undertook a two-year pilot project to implement Equally Safe in a Higher Education setting. Its strategy was informed by an NUS study which found that one in four female students had been subjected to unwanted sexual experiences on campus (NUS, 2011). This reflected the experiences of women across Scotland and highlighted barriers to reporting incidents of sexual violence, harassment and domestic abuse.

The ESHE team approached GCRC to seek its support and expertise in the field of GBV, and its assistance in the development of a Toolkit. The ESHE Project aimed to provide new research into attitudes around GBV and student experiences on campus. The findings would inform the development of new prevention and education training programmes for staff and students. The project ensured its success by recognising a partnership approach was key to good practice, and this approach was encouraged by the Toolkit.

Based on the research undertaken by the ESHE Project, a First Responder training was developed for staff, recognising the impact of GBV and that staff would often be the first point of contact for disclosures. The training would equip staff with the knowledge and tools to support survivors in accessing support and reporting.

With regard to student education programmes, Melanie McCarry from the ESHE team led on the development of The Scottish Intervention Initiative (TSII) bystander training programme for students, which was adapted from the original programme developed by Fenton et al. in 2014. The programme recognises that some students may initially feel more confident in disclosing to a peer. Students were offered the opportunity to participate in an eight-week training course which included information about GBV, how to offer initial support, and how to access reporting and support pathways. Trainees completed evaluations which were overall very positive.

The experience of the partnership project provided information to the Scottish Government to shape its national strategic approach, highlighting key learning and challenges including:

- The partnership between the University of Strathclyde, ESHE and GCRC was successful in reaching hundreds of staff and students.
- Staff and students at the University felt more safe and secure knowing that GBV was being taken seriously

- Training for those providing support to survivors needed to be a key feature of an institution's approach
- The opportunity offered to TSII-trained students to play a role in training their peers strengthened the project in terms of engagement within the student community
- Initial challenges around staff and students understanding the need for the training dispersed when it was clear the overall project aims were to provide a safe and thriving environment for all staff and students
- Ongoing support and training was needed to maintain the confidence of trained staff and students.
- A support service facilitated by GCRC is hosted on campus, and this has played a key role in increasing accessibility of support to students (Glasgow & Clyde Rape Crisis, 2021).

Section 2: Staff Training

The impacts of GBV can be far reaching for survivors. We know that the response a survivor receives when disclosing can have a significant impact on their ability to heal and recover from trauma (Hester & Lilley, 2018). Many student survivors tell no one about their experiences of GBV, and research has identified four key reasons for this: they felt it wasn't serious enough, they felt ashamed or embarrassed, they thought they wouldn't be believed, they thought they would be blamed (NUS, 2011). Thus, disclosure often feels risky (Hester & Lilley, 2018).

It is vitally important that university and college staff provide helpful responses to disclosures and reports of GBV, so that they can identify needs and provide appropriate support and access to services. Crucially, it also helps those reporting to feel that their institution has taken their concerns seriously and prioritises their safety and well-being. RCS has been involved in developing and implementing two staff training programmes which aim to improve these responses: the *Equally Safe in Colleges and Universities (ESCU) GBV First Responder Training* which follows the model developed for the ESHE toolkit; and the *Investigation Training* developed more recently as institutions have sought guidance on how to conduct investigations into staff and student conduct. We will discuss how we have worked to support the implementation of these programmes in partnership with local Rape Crisis Centres and Women's Aid groups.

The role of the Training and Education Coordinator post has been key to the substantial progress made in delivering the ESCU First Responder Training programme at scale in Scotland. The Coordinator works to provide strategic leadership, high-quality materials, and centralised monitoring and evaluation systems. Local capacity has been a significant challenge as Rape Crisis Centres must always prioritise provision of support services and have limited capacity to take on additional pieces of work without sustainable funding. The pricing structure for training developed by the Coordinator allows for local flexibility whilst broadly delivering a consistent approach across the country, and the funds generated through this will in time increase local capacity.

The Coordinator also delivers training and development sessions and co-facilitates training with new workers, with the aim that local GBV organisations can take on leadership of work in their area. Whilst the role of the Coordinator has been crucial in enabling the training to be delivered at scale, the post has been consistently subject to short-term funding cycles, which has significant implications for project planning.

ESCU GBV First Responder Training

Since 2018, the Coordinator has supported 13 Rape Crisis Centres and several Women's Aid groups to deliver First Responder training to staff in 12 universities and 12 colleges (some of which are multi-campus institutions). Several institutions have completed multiple rounds of the training.

The training aims to equip staff at colleges and universities with the skills and confidence to provide a helpful response to disclosures of GBV. We know that survivors are often met with unsupportive responses from friends, family, and professionals (Hester & Lilley, 2018) and the training centres their perspectives, drawing on examples of positive and negative responses to prompt reflection and illustrate good practice. Some of the key issues highlighted by survivors are demonstrated by the following two accounts, which reinforce the need for improvements to practice as well as more joined-up systems for supporting students with the aftermath of GBV:

> *It was like. . . you need to speak to that person, and then they'd be like, no you can't speak to me, you need to speak to that person, and then they didn't know what to do. I remember having to go onto a computer and having to type out what happened.. . . A lot of it is like, just tick this box and do this process that's just devoid of emotion.*
>
> (Anonymous survivor)

> *The university has a much bigger role to play in publicising and normalising [GBV].. . . It gets to the point people wait for so long because they don't know how to get help.*
>
> (Anonymous survivor)

The training has three separate tiers, each building upon the previous one to address issues in greater depth. The structure is detailed in Table 19.1.

Table 19.1 GBV First Responder training structure

Level	Participants	Contents	Time commitment
1 Essential (Delivered by Rape Crisis)	All staff	• What is GBV? • Prevalence and statistics • Legal definitions • The impact of myths and misconceptions about GBV on survivors • The criminal justice system • Introduction to responding to disclosures • Case studies	1 Day
2 Enhanced (Delivered by Rape Crisis)	Staff in frontline, student facing roles, or who have a remit relating to GBV, who have completed Tier 1	• Core listening skills • Defining trauma and traumatic symptoms • Trauma-informed practice • In depth input on responding to disclosures • Impact of vicarious trauma • Boundaries • Self-care for staff	1 Day
3 First Responder (Delivered Women's Aid/ Domestic Abuse service)	Staff in frontline, student facing roles, or who have a remit relating to GBV, who have completed Levels 1 and 2	• Domestic abuse and its impacts • Assessing risk • Responding to disclosures • Input from the institution on internal policies and procedures	1 Day

Staff feedback has highlighted some of the key benefits of the approach and content:

> *I appreciate the depth it went to and the quality of factual information was excellent.*
> *I feel hearing from survivors really helped my understanding of the effects of GBV.*
>
> *[Presenter] was fantastic. It was a very thought-provoking and informative session. . . .. And it was great that the fact survivors might be present was mentioned and people were encouraged to take care of themselves. I also like that you are scheduling in time for us to take a break afterwards. I think on the whole it shows a very trauma-informed way of working.*

Case Study 2   RASASH experience of working with UHI to address GBV

The Rape and Sexual Abuse Service Highland (RASASH) and the University of the Highlands and Islands (UHI) have a positive and productive partnership in working collaboratively to end GBV. RASASH are represented at UHI's Equally Safe Group, and both partners are active in the training subgroup of the Highland Violence Against Women Partnership. UHI and RASASH have also worked together to develop a joint campaign for the global 16 Days of Activism Against GBV.

Most recently, RASASH has supported RCS with the delivery of the ESCU GBV First Responder training programme at UHI. Over 2020–2021 more than 50 members of staff across UHI have undertaken the GBV First Responder training to date, with a further 25 due to undertake the training in autumn 2021.

Before the COVID-19 pandemic each UHI campus would have received training from their local Rape Crisis centre. However, due to Covid-19 restrictions and the geographical spread of UHI's campuses, training during 2020/2021 has been limited to online delivery. On the one hand, this has led to a reduction in the duration and interactivity of the training sessions, but on the other it has enabled staff to attend training from across the UHI campuses and share best practice with one another irrespective of their location. Central and online delivery has also meant that the Rape Crisis Centres covering these campuses have been able to pool their resources thereby increasing its capacity to deliver training.

Indeed, centralised coordination and delivery of the ESCU project has been instrumental to its success. With 12 campuses, represented by seven different Rape Crisis Centres, a central contact point at both UHI and RCS is necessary for efficient communication and planning as well as for monitoring and evaluation. Central delivery also means that all of UHI's campuses can benefit from the training, even if their own campus may not have enough participants to hold the ESCU training locally. However, centralised delivery has meant that campuses do not necessarily benefit from making links with their local Rape Crisis centre.

Overall, RASASH's experience of delivering the ESCU project at UHI has been overwhelmingly positive. Key to this has been the role of the RCS Training and Education Coordinator role. The Coordinator is able to ensure that the training is up-to-date, effective, and consistent as well as build relationships and coordinate across the campuses and Rape

Crisis centres. This role is thereby crucial to maintaining the quality of ESCU and continued engagement by institutions. Without the Coordinator, RASASH would not have had the capacity to coordinate and deliver training of this scale as funding for our prevention work is limited.

Dr Iain Morrison, Dean of Students at UHI commented that:

> *We greatly value the partnership working we have enjoyed with RCS/ RASASH. As the largest post-school educational institution in Scotland, with over 35,000 students, we are able to extend the reach of their specialist advice and training opportunities across our region and we benefit from their support, encouragement and advice. We want our university to be a safe place for all our students and to promote societal change, so that together we can eradicate gender-based violence. We have much to do institutionally and societally to achieve this and sincerely appreciate the support and resources we can call upon from our friends at RCS/RASASH in taking our work forward.*

Investigation Training

Whilst universities and colleges are increasingly engaged in addressing GBV and equipping staff with knowledge and skills to respond to disclosures, there remains much more to do. In particular, underreporting and the lack of transparent, robust, and trauma-informed reporting processes is of great concern across the Further and Higher Education sectors (UUK, 2016).

In recent years, media coverage has revealed how student survivors are being let down by poor reporting processes and investigative practices. Research by the Sunday Herald found that in a three-year period, from 2014/2015–2016/2017, only 134 incidents were reported to colleges and universities in Scotland. Of Scotland's 19 universities, 12 responded to a Freedom of Information request. This identified 105 complaints, the majority of which were against students. In addition, 12 of Scotland's 20 colleges responded to the request, noting 29 complaints. Some institutions had recorded no incidents of sexual misconduct in the same period (Swindon, 2018). Yet we know that low reporting rates do not equate to low prevalence of GBV on campus. In fact, as argued by Humphreys and Towl (2020), we would agree that institutions with low rates of reporting are less likely to have effective reporting and supportive measures in place and are therefore likely to pose higher risks to staff and students.

There has been work undertaken to improve reporting mechanisms and investigation practices within the sector. In 2016, Universities UK commissioned guidance on handling reports of misconduct which may also constitute a criminal offence (Pinsent Masons LLP and UUK, 2016). Universities Scotland is in the process of developing similar guidance for Scotland.

There are also some emerging examples of innovative approaches to improving access to reporting (UUK, 2016), in particular the implementation of online platforms to reduce barriers to reporting and accessing support. This year nine colleges and universities within the *Glasgow Fearless* Partnership (a regional partnership between Further and Higher Education providers across the West of Scotland) were funded by the Scottish Government to pilot and evaluate the implementation of Culture Shift's Report and Support Tool (Culture Shift, 2021). This tool includes the option to make an anonymised report, something survivors often wish to do if they have concerns about making a formal report. This feature also enables institutions to gather better prevalence data. However, without identifying information, institutions are limited in the actions they can take.

Reporting tools must be accompanied by comprehensive guidance and training for staff conducting investigations. *The 1752 Group* found evidence of students attempting to report sexual misconduct to their institution being faced with long, re-traumatising, and ineffective processes (Bull & Rye, 2018). As universities in Scotland have made progress in improving initial responses to disclosures, some are now reviewing their investigative procedures, which in most cases were not developed with GBV in mind and therefore aspects of procedure and practice are not fit for this purpose. RCS therefore undertook to develop an Investigation Training programme with the primary aim of improving the experience of those reporting GBV to their institution. The training drew substantially from the guidance and principles set out in *Addressing Student Sexual Violence in Higher Education* (Humphreys & Towl, 2020) and aims to equip staff with the knowledge, understanding, and skills needed to conduct interviews as part of student and staff misconduct procedures, incorporating principles of natural justice (the right to a fair hearing) with a trauma-informed and survivor-centred approach. The training defines key forms of GBV clearly to provide a clear basis for gathering relevant evidence. It also addresses some of the common myths and misconceptions that can arise during investigations where investigators lack knowledge and understanding about sexual violence, which can lead reporting parties feeling that they are being blamed in some way for violence perpetrated against them – for example, when an investigator asks them about their alcohol consumption without being clear that this is to determine their capacity to consent, rather than to suggest they are to blame for 'putting themselves at risk'.

The training also includes content on trauma, seeking to raise awareness of normal trauma responses such as fight, flight, and freeze responses, and challenging preconceived ideas about how survivors 'should' act after experiencing a traumatic event so that these do not lead to inaccurate assumptions entering into the way that evidence is gathered and interpreted. There is also practical guidance for conducting interviews with reporting parties, responding parties, and any witnesses.

It is important to note that whilst the training seeks to improve investigation procedures and ensure that survivors are treated with compassion and dignity, it is recognised that survivors are nevertheless likely to find the process challenging, and often the outcome feels unjust and fails to protect their right to study and work in safety. Whilst the burden of proof that applies to these investigations is based on the 'balance of probability' and technically a lower burden of proof than required by a criminal justice process, institutions are more limited in terms of the evidence they can gather, and are often unable to uphold a complaint even where they believe the account of the reporting party. To mitigate against these limitations, it is crucial that staff receive specialist training before investigating reports of GBV, so that procedures are as effective as possible in keeping staff and students safe and minimising harm, and in holding perpetrators to account.

The Investigation Training is in earlier stages of implementation than the ESCU First Responder training. As there is a body of technical knowledge entailed in the training, it is likely that a small consortium of trainers from the Rape Crisis network will be identified and trained to deliver the training across the country.

Section 3: Student Education

RCS and local Rape Crisis Centres have also been involved in the delivery of student education interventions in colleges and universities, but delivering such programmes across large student populations raises challenges of scale. This section will focus on two interventions that have sought to address these; the *Let's Talk* peer education programme and an eLearning module.

Let's Talk about Sexual Violence

In 2016, RCS formed a partnership with the Student Representative Council (SRC) at the University of Glasgow and the Student Association (SA) at Glasgow Caledonian University (GCU) to develop a peer-led initiative called *Let's Talk*, which took its name from a campaign run by student groups affiliated with the SRC.

Partners agreed that a feminist analysis of the causes of sexual violence would underpin the programme and that the content would be based on three key themes:

- A survivor-centred perspective, which would encourage students to engage with issues of sexual violence from a perspective of empathy and understanding of the realities survivors face while at university. A survivor worked with RCS to record an interview in which she speaks about how the community responded to her in the aftermath of her assault – what helped and what hindered her recovery.
- Consent, explored through scenario-based activities looking at principles of free agreement (as enshrined within the definition of consent in the Sexual Offences [Scotland] Act 2009), mutuality, and the role of interpersonal and societal power imbalances.
- 'Bystander' approaches to help equip students with options for intervening safely where they have concerns about sexual harassment or violence. In keeping with Rape Crisis's principles, there was an emphasis on sensitivity to the needs and wishes of the person affected.

The Universities had student communities active in human rights, feminism, LGBT equality, and mental health and so there was a pool of students with the skills to take on a peer education role. RCS developed a two-tier programme comprising four-day training for peer trainers, and a 90-minute workshop they would deliver to their peers. The SRC and the SA, with support from GCU, put in place the delivery logistics.

The train-the-trainer programme has to date been delivered in four successive years. Key learning has been as follows:

- The partnership between RCS and the student administrations was a key feature of the successful design and delivery of the programme. Importantly, there were shared aims in terms of key values and principles, and an understanding of the importance of the engagement of student activists and societies in driving cultural change within the student community and wider university.
- There needs to be sufficient staff resourcing to administer the programme, so that workshops can be organised regularly, and student trainers have opportunities to develop and sustain their skills. It is also important to build in regular development sessions to support student trainers and assure consistency.

Let's Talk has since been delivered to other institutions by local centres (see Case Study 3). For further explanation of its development and delivery, see Burman et al., 2020.

Case Study 3 WRASAC Dundee and Angus and University of Dundee Experience of 'Let's Talk' Peer Education Programme

Following the successful delivery of the ESCU GBV First Responder Training Programme to staff at the University of Dundee, the University got in touch with Women's Rape and Sexual Abuse Centre Dundee and Angus (WRASAC) and RCS to request delivery of the Let's Talk about Sexual Violence Peer Education Programme to support students to have informed and confident conversations about sexual violence. A recruitment and induction process was established, and the University initially recruited a small group of 8 volunteers to enable them to test the approaches before rolling the programme out more widely. The main aim of the peer education programme was to prepare the volunteers to facilitate a workshop about sexual violence to their fellow students.

The volunteers involved in the programme spoke of the importance of having peers address these issues and about ensuring that sexual violence prevention messages continue from secondary education into Further and Higher Education. One volunteer spoke about a family member receiving a consent workshop at school from the Rape Crisis National Sexual Violence

Prevention Programme and how this made them reflect on their own understanding of sexual violence and encouraged them to get involved with the Let's Talk programme. The Let's Talk programme had also prompted another student to enquire about volunteering with WRASAC and RCS.

One key factor which enabled Let's Talk to be implemented was the role of Sarah Browne, Support and Prevention Worker at the University of Dundee whose role is focused on GBV, not only encompassing student support and wellbeing, but also sexual violence prevention, her role has enabled continued momentum long after *Let's Talk* was initially delivered.

After completing the training, student-led sessions were advertised for March 2020 – however because of Covid restrictions these were not delivered. As most students were not able to be on campus, Sarah and some of the volunteers organised a student-led prevention network who met regularly throughout 2020–2021 on MS Teams. This was a space for people to discuss, share information and ideas, and to talk about events and activities. It led to a group from this network facilitating an online session for fellow students about dealing with a disclosure of GBV. The feedback from this session was overwhelmingly positive and it is clear that the reason it had been impactful was because it had been led by students.

Strengths

The *Let's Talk* programme has helped the University of Dundee, WRASAC and RCS to build and maintain a strong relationship. It has also provided students at the University of Dundee who are passionate about ending sexual violence with the opportunity to spread awareness and prevention messages to their peers and bring about positive cultural change.

Challenges

The *Let's Talk* programme was delivered in January which, for those who were graduating, did not ensure enough time to advertise and get workshops up and running due to lots of deadlines from March onwards and graduation after this. Considerations around when the *Let's Talk* Programme is delivered – perhaps September would be a better alternative so that volunteers have use of the full academic year.

Sarah Browne, Prevention and Support Worker at University of Dundee commented that:

> I knew that training delivered by Rape Crisis Scotland and WRASAC would be of an extremely high quality. What I had not expected was to

witness how their training not only raised awareness but also contributed to a transformation in attitudes and approaches. It continues to be one of the best prevention activities rolled out by Student Services to date. The benefit of these sessions is that they are non-judgemental and they give participants time and space to reflect and discuss. They also help build community and empower people to feel that they can contribute to making change. The student volunteers used words such as 'engaging', 'inspiring' and 'empowering' to describe their experience of the training and comments focused on the importance of a safe space having been created for open discussion. They also suggested that future programmes of this kind should focus on all forms of GBV.

What we have learned is that working in partnership with specialist organisations like Rape Crisis Scotland and WRASAC are integral to ensure that we don't just raise awareness but we also transform attitudes and approaches.

GBV eLearning Module

To address the challenges of scale involved in reaching student populations with prevention education, RCS developed a short, interactive GBV eLearning module designed to complement face-to-face programmes, though it should not be seen as a substitute for these. It was launched in October 2020 and has been sent to 23 institutions, some of whom have implemented it whilst others are working to identify which students to target and decide whether to make it mandatory. To date feedback from staff and students has been overwhelmingly positive.

The module uses a range of learning tools, such as quizzes, videos, and case studies, to introduce students to a difficult topic in an engaging way. The content draws on the *Let's Talk* programme and includes information about GBV, consent and healthy relationships, how to be a supportive friend, and how to help foster a supportive university community. It signposts to support services and gives self-care reminders throughout. It was developed with input from survivors and other key stakeholders in the GBV, Further Education and Higher Education sectors. The module is specific to the Scottish context as relates to the legislative context, support services, links to ESCU strategic work, and the ESHE Toolkit.

To implement the tool, universities and colleges need to make it accessible to students through their online portals, encourage participation from students, and embed the national survey to allow Rape Crisis to collect monitoring and evaluation data.

What students say they liked about the module:

Providing a link of phone numbers and names of associations where to ask for help in case of a problem.

> *Getting to know more about what GBV is and if it happens and how I can get help if needed.*
>
> *I learned that everyday things can be classed as gender violence.*

Section 4: Access to On–campus Specialist Support

Whilst many universities and colleges across Scotland have committed to working with local GBV organisations to provide staff training and student education programmes, they have been slower to offer comprehensive support options to student survivors. However, in recent years, several universities have resourced their local Rape Crisis Centre to provide specialist support on campus. This section will highlight why increasing access to crucial support services should be considered a priority by all Further and Higher Education Institutions.

GBV has an impact on every area of a survivor's life (Hester & Lilley, 2018). In recent years, several studies have highlighted the significant impact that GBV can have on a survivor's ability to participate in university life. The *Hidden Marks* study of women students' experiences of harassment, stalking, violence, and sexual assault (NUS, 2011) found that all survivors experienced deterioration to their mental health and well-being, with one in four survivors of serious sexual assault reporting difficulties with their studies; one in seven survivors of serious physical assault reporting that their attendance had suffered; and a quarter of survivors of stalking noting that their studies had been impacted. About 13% of survivors of serious sexual assault had considered leaving their course altogether. GBV had negative impacts on students in Further Education, leading 18% of survey respondents to miss classes and 17% lowering their academic performance (NUS, 2019). As already noted, as women are disproportionately affected by GBV, serious concerns are raised about equality of access to Further and Higher Education.

Timely, trauma–informed specialist support on campus can aid recovery and play a key role in protecting students' rights to continue their course of education. Whilst most universities and colleges offer counselling, it is often short–term support which is unlikely to be appropriate for survivors of complex trauma, and could risk re–traumatisation if the service is not equipped to deal with GBV (Henderson, 2012). Staff at universities and colleges recognise the value of specialist GBV services and regularly refer student survivors to their local Rape Crisis centres. However, students can face long waiting times to access this support. GBV services like Rape Crisis and Women's Aid are able to provide survivors with responsive support that meets their unique needs, but they can only do this if they are sustainably resourced to meet the demand for their services. In some cases, universities and colleges have formed partnerships with their local GBV services to provide support on campus, enabling sustainable services to be delivered to student communities with reduced waiting times so that students access timely support that reduces the risk of loss of education and as well as supporting safety, recovery from trauma, and improved mental health.

In 2018, The University of Strathclyde piloted an on–campus specialist support service for students in partnership with Glasgow and Clyde Rape Crisis. Demand for this service has continued to grow, with provision increasing from one day per week to three days by April 2019. Stirling University and Forth Valley College have on-campus support provided by Forth Valley Rape Crisis. The University of St Andrews has recently commissioned Fife Rape and Sexual Abuse Centre to provide on-campus support. Edinburgh Rape Crisis Centre also has a student support project jointly funded by four universities through the *Fearless Edinburgh* partnership. Case Study 4 explores this partnership in more detail. Some colleges have taken a similar approach to providing mental health support, with posts being funded jointly by the college and the mental health service provider, a model which could be explored for GBV support services in the future.

Survivors have explained some of the benefits of an on-campus support service from their perspective:

> *The way it's set up at [university] is that it's just in the counselling base, which again was daunting for me to even go to, but it's just there and nobody knows why you're there or who you're seeing.. . . Because I'll be at uni anyway, it felt like making it a part of my routine was a lot more natural that way because it just slotted in with other things I had at uni that day, other commitments, so it didn't feel as much of a 'I need to go out of my way to do this' when it's already such a difficult thing to be doing anyway.*

> *It made such a massive difference. To me, it was life-changing.. . . The need is humongous, other people won't even know that they've been subjected to sexual violence or know where to turn but it was the best thing that ever, ever happened to me in terms of helping me come along and get better.*

The value and impact of providing on-campus specialist support cannot be underestimated, and may make the most immediate direct difference for survivors at college or university. Sufficient and sustainable funding must be identified to support this, along with a strong working partnership and regular communication between the institution and the service provider, especially during the early stages of the service, to review progress and identity and address any challenges.

Case Study 4   Edinburgh Rape Crisis Student Survivor Project

Fearless Edinburgh is a strategic partnership between Further and Higher Education providers in Edinburgh, Police Scotland, NHS Lothian and Edinburgh Rape Crisis. The Partnership works towards preventing GBV in Further and Higher Education Institutions and improving institutional responses to and support for students and staff who disclose GBV. In 2019, the Higher Education Institutions in Edinburgh pooled their resources to fund a support post through Edinburgh Rape Crisis. The Student Survivor Project is a partnership between Edinburgh Rape Crisis Centre, University of Edinburgh, Edinburgh Napier University, Heriot Watt University and Queen Margaret University. This pooling of resources could provide a model for future funding.

The project is staffed by one full time worker who works with students of all genders who have experienced sexual violence at any time in their lives. The service offers trauma-informed support that takes a person-centred approach in the form of long-term counselling support. Students also have access to other Rape Crisis services such as criminal justice advocacy and group work. The project became operational during the pandemic and is at the time of writing, continuing to offer remote support to survivors. As we emerge from the pandemic, we plan to offer in person support, and we expect that this will be offered on campus.

The collaboration between the universities is a strength of this project and enables students to access sexual violence support which has been designed to meet their needs and acknowledges their experience as survivors on campus. Moreover, the worker is able to support survivors to access additional support that they might need to ensure that their university experience is a positive one. However, it is already evident that the need is far greater than the current capacity of the project and survivors are waiting for support.

Survivors' experiences of the service:

> *Now that I have received support I feel I am in a better mindset to carry on with my studies, and I feel others would probably feel the same benefits.*
>
> *Unfortunately, sexual assault is still quite a taboo topic, so I know not many people know where to turn to; many people I personally know won't even turn to their friends about this sort of thing, so having a healthy outlet in the form of this service, I believe, would really help people.*
>
> *Previously, I would never have wanted to say that I was "survivor" as I didn't deserve the label; I didn't think what I went through was "bad" enough to be justified as sexual violence and domestic abuse but it was. I gained a sense of closure and inner peace.*

Summary

In this chapter, we have highlighted the ways that partnership approaches have been key to Scotland's progress in tackling GBV in Further and Higher Education Institutions. We have discussed the role of the RCS ESCU Coordinator, who has worked to embed a partnership approach between Further and Higher Education Institutions and their local specialist GBV organisations into the implementation of staff training, student education, and provision of support services. The approach taken in Scotland is founded on the *Equally Safe* strategy which provides a coherent theoretical underpinning for tackling GBV as a cause and consequence of gender inequality, recognising that women as well as trans and non-binary students are disproportionately affected, and that intersecting inequalities increase risk for some groups of students whilst increasing barriers to accessing services. Rape Crisis Centres and Women's Aid groups in Scotland hold this analysis at their core and are best placed to support colleges and universities to tackle GBV, and to deliver educational programmes, training, and services that are effective in preventing violence and ensuring that survivors receive the support and responses they deserve.

Our key recommendations are as follows:

Partnerships

- Building and maintaining sustainable partnerships between universities, colleges, and specialist GBV organisations should be core to addressing GBV across the Further and Higher Education sectors.

Staff and Student Education

- Specialist GBV organisations are best equipped to deliver trauma-informed and survivor-centred staff training that equips staff to respond appropriately to disclosures of GBV.
- Universities and colleges should engage with students as agents and leaders of cultural change to address GBV. Campaigns should be student-led, survivor-informed, and should represent intersectional experiences of GBV.

Support

- There should be a clearly identified group of staff within the institution who are equipped to deal with disclosures and reports of GBV and have access to practical and emotional support to help them in this challenging role.
- Universities and colleges should evaluate students' experiences of disclosing, reporting, and investigation procedures, and work to continually make improvements.
- Pathways for students to report and access support (internal and external specialist services) should be clear and accessible, with measures to reduce barriers faced by specific groups.
- There should be sufficient and timely access to support for survivors (students and staff), with an on-campus model delivered in partnership with a specialist GBV service particularly recommended.

Policies and Procedures

- Institutions should work to develop a coherent GBV policy that covers prevention, response, and support that links to suite of other relevant policies, for example, Staff Disciplinary Policy/Code of Student Conduct.

Further Reading

Burman, M., Dawson, K., McDougall, L., Morton, K., & Nokhbatolfoghahai, F. (2020). Building authentic partnerships for responding to gender based violence in universities. In S. B. Marine & R. Lewis (Eds.), *Collaborating for change.* **Oxford University Press.**

This chapter includes coverage of the critical importance of coalition-building in challenging GBV in universities, drawing on the example of a partnership between the University of Glasgow, Glasgow Caledonian University and Rape Crisis Scotland. The chapter details the collaboration undertaken by student organisations, professional and academic staff, local service providers and the police and identifies challenges and achievements in driving forward meaningful change. Rape Crisis Scotland's involvement in this partnership helped to lay the foundations for its subsequent leadership role in developing partnership approaches at a national level, as discussed in this chapter.

Humphreys, C. J., & Towl, G. J. (2020). *Addressing student sexual violence in higher education: A good practice guide.* **Emerald Publishing.**

This book represents the first authoritative work on addressing sexual violence in Higher Education for a UK context and supports the local Rape Crisis centre, the *Rape and Sexual Abuse Counselling Centre.* In common with the approach that Rape Crisis advocates in Scotland, it is trauma-informed and survivor-centred and understands sexual violence in the sociocultural context of gender inequality, recognising that certain groups – in particular women, LGBT people, disabled people and immigrant communities – are disproportionately targeted. It offers detailed practical guidance which was of particular value and application in the development of our Investigation training discussed in the Staff Training section of our chapter.

References

Bull, A., Bullough, J., & Page, T. (2019). What would a survivor centred higher education sector look like. *A New Vision for Further and Higher Education.* Retrieved October 12, 2021, from http://classonline.org.uk/docs/A_New_Vision_For_Further_and_Higher_Education_220519_1647_forwebv1.pdf

Bull, A., & Rye, R. (2018). *Institutional responses to staff sexual misconduct in UK higher education*. The 1752 Group/ University of Portsmouth. Retrieved October 12, 2021, from https://1752group.files.wordpress.com/2018/09/silencing-students_the-1752-group.pdf

Burman, M., Dawson, K., McDougall, L., Morton, K., & Nokhbatolfoghahai, F. (2020). Building authentic partnerships for responding to gender based violence in universities. In S. B. Marine & R. Lewis (Eds.), *Collaborating for change*. Oxford University Press.

Culture Shift. (2021). www.culture-shift.co.uk/

Donaldson, A., McCarry, M., & McGoldrick, R. (2018). *Equally safe in higher education toolkit*. University of Strathclyde.

Fenton, R. A., Mott, H. L., McCartan, K., & Rumney, P. (2014). *The intervention initiative*. UWE and Public Health England.

Glasgow & Clyde Rape Crisis. (2021). *Strathclyde Uni campus support*. Retrieved December 8, 2021, from www.glasgowclyderapecrisis.org.uk/content/strathclyde-uni-support/

Henderson, S. (2012). *The pros and cons of providing dedicated sexual violence services: A literature review*. Rape Crisis Scotland.

Hester, M., & Lilley, S. (2018). More than support to court: Rape victims and specialist sexual violence services. *International Review of Victimology, 24*(3), 313–328.

Humphreys, C. J., & Towl, G. J. (2020). *Addressing student sexual violence in higher education: A good practice guide*. Emerald Publishing.

NUS. (2011). *Hidden marks: A study of women student's experiences of harassment, stalking and sexual assault*. Retrieved October 12, 2021, from https://itstopsnow.org/sites/default/files/2018-02/Hidden%20Marks-A%20study%20of%20women%20students%27%20experiences%20of%20harassment%2C%20stalking%2C%20violence%20%26%20sexual%20assault%20%28NUS%29.pdf

NUS. (2019). *Sexual violence in further education*. Retrieved October 12, 2021, from www.nusconnect.org.uk/resources/sexual-violence-in-further-education-report

NWCI. (2019). *It stops now*. www.itstopsnow.org/en/home

Phipps, A. (2020). Reckoning up: Sexual harassment and violence in the neoliberal university. *Gender and Education, 32*(2), 227–243. ISSN 0954–0253

Pinsent Masons LLP and UUK. (2016). *Guidance for higher education institutions: How to handle alleged student misconduct which may also constitute a criminal offence*. Universities UK.

Scottish Government and COSLA. (2018). *Equally safe: Scotland's strategy to eradicate violence against women*. Retrieved October 29, 2021, from www.gov.scot/publications/equally-safe-scotlands-strategy-prevent-eradicate-violence-against-women-girls/

Swindon, P. (2018, April 15). Students fear 'academic consequences' if they report sex attacks on campus. *The Herald*. Retrieved October 12, 2021, from www.heraldscotland.com/news/16160140.students-fear-academic-consequences-report-sex-attacks-campus/

Universities UK. (2016). *Changing the culture*. Retrieved October 12, 2021, from www.universitiesuk.ac.uk/sites/default/files/field/downloads/2021-07/changing-the-culture.pdf

20 The role of regulation in addressing gender-based violence in Higher Education

Amy Norton and Graham J. Towl

Regulation has a potentially key role to play in ensuring that Higher Education providers address their problem with high levels of sexual violence. Sexual violence is gender based insofar as the vast majority of such cases involve women being subjected to sexual violence. Universities are independent institutions and as such the fundamental responsibility lies with their leaders to address their problem with sexual violence (Humphreys & Towl, 2020).

Regulation takes place on a continuum from light to much heavier regulation. In practice, regulators appear to tend to try to keep regulation as 'light touch' as possible to have the intended impact. This helps preserve the independence of institutions whilst endeavouring to ensure that there is a public benefit – in this case, the safety and well-being of students. So, regulation has a potentially key role, but the accountability for delivery lies squarely with the Vice-Chancellors of individual institutions who, in governance terms, are held to account for by their governing bodies. Governing bodies generally have student representation on them.

In this chapter, we outline some key background material which has been pivotal in influencing the sector – we trace the germane immediate policy research and development antecedents to the setting up of the Office for Students in 2018. We reflect upon some of these developments with a view to informing what a future regulatory framework on addressing sexual violence at universities may look like.

Background to funding and regulation of HE 2016–2018

The Higher Education Funding Council for England (HEFCE) was established by government under the terms of the Further and Higher Education Act 1992 as a Non-departmental Public Body (NPD). The Council's main function was to administer grants provided by the Secretary of State for Education which funded education, research, knowledge exchange, and the associated activities within Higher Education Institutions (HEIs) as well as HE courses in Further Education (FE) colleges. The Council had regulatory roles in assurance of public funding, financial sustainability of HE providers, and was the principal regulator for universities and colleges who were exempt charities.

DOI: 10.4324/9781003252474-23

They also maintained a register of HE providers with delegated powers from the Secretary of State for Education to designate university title and degree awarding powers. It ceased to exist as of 1 April 2018, when its duties were divided between the newly created Office for Students and Research England (operating within United Kingdom Research and Innovation), both of whom were established by the Higher Education and Research Act (2017) (HERA).

Changing the culture report

Universities UK (UUK) is the membership body for universities across the UK representing the voice of vice-chancellors and university leaders. It has 140 member institutions and is funded by subscription from them. In 2015, they were tasked by the Secretary of State for Education to investigate the nature and extent of violence against women, harassment, and hate crime affecting students and make recommendations for urgent change and reform. UUK established a taskforce, conducted research, and heard evidence from a range of stakeholders, including students with lived experience, academic experts, and third sector organisations. When the taskforce's 'Changing the Culture' report was published (Universities UK, 2016), there had been little-to-no publicly funded policy, funding, or regulatory intervention to prevent or respond to gender-based violence in Higher Education. The UUK report and its recommendations was arguably a key turning point for directing political and public pressure towards tackling gender-based violence, sexual misconduct, and all forms of prejudice-based hate crime and harassment affecting students and formed the beginning of an evidence-base on which to build new policy and funding strategies. The report highlighted serious and widespread problems in the Higher Education sector and made recommendations encompassing the need to develop disclosure response involving relevant external agencies, to develop centralised reporting systems for incidents, to conduct a thorough assessment of staff training, to build new relationships with local specialist services and referral pathways to them for students, and to develop partnerships with local police and NHS services to aid both prevention and response activities (Universities UK, 2016).

HEFCE's policy and funding response

Following the publication of the Changing the Culture report, the Minister for Universities, Science, Research and Innovation asked HEFCE to support the implementation of the report's recommendations. The report had been sector-led and therefore its recommendations were voluntary for universities to adopt; and this has been the source of some concerns across the sector in terms of the failure of some institutions to prioritise such work. HEFCE was not given additional legal or regulatory powers, therefore the policy levers focused on incentivising, promoting, and testing the extent to which providers had adopted the recommended practices.

Development of the Catalyst Fund for safeguarding students

HEFCE identified a budget within its 'Catalyst Fund' for a competitive bidding exercise to incentivise innovation and development and support the implementation of the 'Changing the Culture' recommendations. The Catalyst Fund's purpose was to make discretionary investments in support of the Council's (or Government's) strategic priorities and to support developments where fixed-term programme or project-based funding could advance progress. The fund was launched in December 2016 and invited applications for funding for small-scale projects (up to £50,000 per project) to identify and support good practice to improve and enhance student safeguarding on campus (Higher Education Funding Council for England, 2016).

Successful projects were expected to deliver activity and outputs for a full year to 31 March 2018, with the expectation that funding would be matched by the institution and the activity would be sustained beyond the funding period. It is not entirely clear that this was a widely held institutional view with some ceasing activities once the external funding had come to an end. HEFCE encouraged proposals which:

- developed the 'bystander' initiative, which trains staff and students in preventing or reducing violence against women and hate crimes, particularly among students
- developed projects, systems improvements, training packages and partnership working models to drive real change in this area
- delivered key activities and partnerships with students' unions
- developed excellent transferable good practice for the benefit of students and institutions across Higher Education.

The criteria against which bids were assessed were:

- the ability to develop strategic responses and enhancements, which could have a significant positive impact on student safeguarding
- robust project design methodology, considering appropriate and relevant ethical considerations, appropriate to determining 'what works' in improving safeguarding for vulnerable groups of students
- ability and willingness to embed and sustain key activities and enhancements
- meaningful engagement with students in the proposed activities and processes
- evidence of alignment with the institution's own safeguarding and related strategies, and its priorities
- clear commitment to provide matched resources
- a willingness to be involved in HEFCE's evaluation and dissemination of student safeguarding on campus for the benefit of the wider sector, as well as associated work led by Universities UK and other partners

(Higher Education Funding Council for England, 2016)

Following an assessment process and decisions taken by an external advisory panel, HEFCE announced £2.45 million of Catalyst funding for 63 projects (Office for Students, 2021e) which were considered to have most closely matched the assessment criteria. Additional factors informing decision-making were location, provider type (for example, large, campus-based provider, FE college, small or specialist) and ensuring a breadth of activity across the programme's aims. An additional aim was to organise the projects into a 'community of practice' to share emerging lessons, themes, and methodologies. A further round of £1.8 million of Catalyst funding for 45 projects which aimed to tackle hate crime and online harassment was announced in November 2017; and a third round in April 2018 (£480,000 for 11 projects) to address religious-based hate crime.

Evaluation of the catalyst fund

An independent evaluation was commissioned to run alongside the projects over their year of implementation. The appointed team was from the Leadership Foundation for Higher Education (now Advance HE) and their aim was to support and enable learning, exchange, and dissemination of innovative and good practice, and help establish 'what works?' Evidence was collected through a mix of analysis of the projects' documentation, secondary research sources, ongoing discussions with experts, and key stakeholder organisations, such as UUK and the National Union of Students (NUS). In reflecting on the challenges of making change rapidly through the provision of funding rather than regulation, it is notable that the projects were reasonably spread geographically and by provider type but necessarily could only support activity within 63 providers, a small proportion of the eligible institutions funded by HEFCE at the time. The UUK study which followed up on Changing the Culture in 2018 found that providers who were in receipt of Catalyst funding made more progress on tackling gender-based violence than those who did not (Universities UK, 2018). Additionally, the funding was short term as noted previously and it proved difficult for such brief and relatively small-sum projects to be sustained into the long term within providers. Although it is noteworthy that some appeared to have prioritised such work more than others. The independent evaluation findings discussed in the following section (Advance HE, 2018) were instructive and helped to augment the evidence base around providers' practices but it proved difficult to mobilise and translate the learning and resources from the individual projects across the sector. The common problem of applying learning and 'what works?' effective practices across a diverse range of provider types was also noted.

Findings of the formative and summative evaluations of the student safeguarding Catalyst funding

There were two stages of the evaluation for the first round, (most relevant to this chapter) of the Catalyst funding which focused most specifically on gender-based and sexual violence; the first was a formative evaluation (Advance

HE, 2018) published shortly after the projects concluded and the second was a summative evaluation (Baird et al., 2019) which encompassed findings and outcomes from both the first and second rounds of projects (including those covering hate crime and online harassment).

Findings of the summative evaluation of the first two rounds of funding (108 projects) (Baird et al., 2019) focused on the more lasting impacts and outcomes of the projects and found that there was some duplication of effort and little time for providers to be able to learn lessons as to the effectiveness of different approaches. Nevertheless, this work had become embedded as part of 'business as usual' within some, though by no means all, providers. The funding had enabled providers to progress their safeguarding work more quickly and more comprehensively than would otherwise have been the case (and this may well speak loudly to what is sometimes a lack of institutional prioritisation for work addressing the problem of sexual violence at universities). It was also noted that the Catalyst funding was timely in that it helped to maintain the momentum from the 'Changing the Culture' report, particularly in tackling sexual misconduct. The wider media and societal interest in challenging sexual misconduct across multiple sectors has also been a significant part of the context and supported the pressure for change. In particular, the #MeToo movement may well have set the broader context for the impetus for such work which has historically been activist led and driven. The scale of the funding across 108 projects in the HE sector meant that 'there was huge safety in numbers' for providers and their leaders to feel more confident in openly tackling these issues (given concerns over potential reputational risks). Overall, the findings from the evaluation showed that although there are many issues to be resolved, tolerance for sexual misconduct (by both staff and students) had decreased within the HE sector in recent years through awareness-raising, and correspondingly, reporting of incidents by students is now increasing. This is, we would argue, most likely a reflection of students' increased confidence that their provider will respond to their reports and disclosures, and this was an important early outcome and evidence of emergent culture change, although the pace of change was arguably slow and still entirely subject to individual providers' prioritisation of the work and their implementation of their policies.

Changing the culture: one year on

In 2017, the Minister for Universities, Science, Research and Innovation asked Universities UK to follow up on the Changing the Culture report to investigate the progress made by HE providers in reforming their systems, policies, and process in accordance with the report's recommendations.

The evaluation study (Universities UK, 2018) found significant but highly variable progress to have been made across the Higher Education sector in tackling student-to-student sexual misconduct since the Changing the Culture report was published in 2016. It noted that the majority of Higher Education providers had focused predominantly on tackling student sexual misconduct, with similar action towards hate crime/harassment having a lower profile and priority status. The study also found that handling reports of alleged incidents of staff-to-student sexual misconduct tended to be kept within the remit of Human Resources (HR) departments rather than within student service functions. This reflects the organisational structures of HE institutions whereby there is a separation of processes for students and staff. This reflects the different contracts that the organisation has with each party. However, in terms of addressing sexual violence or harassment, such cases can become especially problematic when there is say a student reporting a member of staff, or vice versa. Institutions, students, and staff would benefit from clear policy in terms of the handling of such cases, which is, we understand, likely to be further supported possibly in 2022 from UUK's 'staff to student sexual misconduct' task group. Of course, there is nothing stopping university leaders with executive authority from actively addressing in advance of any such further guidance; it comes down to priorities.

The findings also indicated that the scale of HEFCE's Catalyst safeguarding funding of £2.45 million had accelerated and supported change across the English Higher Education sector. The report concluded that

> despite evidence of significant progress being made in implementing the Taskforce's recommendations across the Higher Education providers participating in the study, it remains highly uneven; perhaps one-fifth of the providers in the sample have made very limited progress in meeting the recommendations and addressing this agenda, with most of the participating providers somewhere between these extremes.
>
> (Universities UK, 2018)

These findings, taken together with the findings from the formative and summative evaluations of the Catalyst Fund, were important in informing the next stage of the regulatory response, which would now be taken forward by the new Office for Students (OfS) from 1 April 2018.

So, the aforementioned text provides the background in terms of work within the sector under the governance arrangements immediately prior to the launch of the Office for Students as the regulator.

The Office for Students (OfS)

The OfS was created by the Higher Education and Research Act (HERA) 2017 to be the independent regulator of Higher Education in England; it also took over the funding responsibilities of HEFCE (except research funding which passed to Research England) and the powers of the Office for Fair Access to require and approve Access and Participation Plans. The OfS also controls access to the register of Higher Education providers through the operation of its regulatory framework (Office for Students, 2018b) and its 24 conditions of initial and ongoing registration. The general duties granted to OfSs by the Act are to have the need to protect the institutional autonomy of English Higher Education providers, to promote quality, and greater choice and opportunities for students, to encourage competition between English Higher Education providers (where that competition is in the interests of students and employers, while also having regard to the benefits for students and employers resulting from collaboration between providers), to promote value for money, to promote equality of opportunity in connection with access to and participation in Higher Education, to use the OfS's resources in an efficient, effective, and economic way and to act under the principles of best regulatory practice, including the principles that regulatory activities should be – (i) transparent, accountable, proportionate and consistent, and (ii) targeted only at cases in which action is needed.

Sector-level and provider-level regulation

The OfS's regulatory framework (Office for Students, 2018b) enables regulation at both a provider level (for example, acting against a provider who is at risk of a breach, or has breached, a condition of registration) and at a whole-sector level. The OfS works to regulate the sector in the interests of all students and secure value for money from higher education for the taxpayer. Regulation is focused on achieving four primary regulatory objectives:

1 **Participation** – All students, from all backgrounds, with the ability and desire to undertake higher education are supported to access, succeed in and progress from higher education.
2 **Experience** – All students, from all backgrounds, receive a high quality academic experience, and their interests are protected while they study or in the event of provider, campus or course closure.
3 **Outcomes** – All students, from all backgrounds, are able to progress into employment, further study and fulfilling lives, and their qualifications hold their value over time.
4 **Value for money** – All students, from all backgrounds, receive value for Money (Office for Students, 2018b).

The framework describes sector-level regulation as 'creating the conditions for informed choice, competition, and continuous improvement' and one of the potential activities highlighted was to 'champion issues and share evidence and examples of effective and innovative practice for students. It will be unafraid to speak out on behalf of students, and in particular will promote value for money for students and taxpayers and will highlight inequalities wherever it sees them' (Office for Students, 2018b). This provided a basis for developing a sector-level regulatory approach to tackling sexual misconduct and harassment affecting students in HE.

Development of sector-level regulatory role in student welfare and safeguarding

The findings from the Catalyst programme evaluations and the Changing the Culture follow-up reports indicated some progress in implementing robust systems, policies, and processes to both prevent and respond to sexual misconduct and harassment affecting students was variable, with many students' HE experiences being adversely affected. In a paper to the OfS Board in September 2018, a new strategy for sector-level regulation for student safeguarding and welfare was proposed, building on the OfS's HERA 2017 functions and regulatory framework. The paper described the proposed approach in the following way:

> In shining a strategic, sector-level spotlight on student welfare and safeguarding OfS can champion change where that is needed to ensure the best possible outcomes for students. However, having regard to the protection of institutional autonomy must remain at the heart of our approach and we will never prescribe how autonomous providers should act or what methods they should use. Instead, when the [OfS] board discussed its sector regulatory role in May, 2018 it agreed would use its position to champion, challenge and shape sector wide debate and focus, including through the identification and dissemination of best practice and 'what works?' activity.
> (Office for Students, 2018a, para 8)

The paper proposed that Section 23(1) of the HERA 2017 allows the OfS to assess, or make arrangements for the assessment of, the quality of, and the standards applied to, Higher Education provided by English Higher Education providers. Here in the paper it was argued that the OfS could consider that the 'quality of higher education' includes the broader experiential aspects that include student welfare and well-being. Concerns around gender-based violence in HE are often captured under the broad rubric of 'student welfare and wellbeing' institutionally. Neither the HERA 2017 nor the OfS's regulatory framework contained duties or conditions which relate specifically to promoting or addressing the safety and well-being of students. This all means that, for all intents and purposes, the OfS is constrained such that it may be viewed as a 'light touch' regulatory body. But is 'light touch' the 'right touch'? We address this later in this chapter.

The paper also examined the regulatory tools that the OfS could operate at a sector level to champion a safe, healthy, and inclusive environment for students. These were described as follows:

- **Funding** – targeting funding to support innovation in the areas of greatest risk or need.
- **'What works?' activity and thematic reviews** – sharing effective practice between providers and encouraging communities of practice.
- **Partnership working** – working together with relevant HE, Government, and third sector partners to develop, commission, and share advice and guidance to providers.
- **Data, evidence, and insight** – identifying and reviewing sources of data, evidence, and insights to spot emerging concerns, risks, or gaps at an early stage.

- **Response to OfS notifications, complaints, and reportable events –** identifying trends or issues emerging at a system level.

The principal actions taken following this paper focused on completing the funding and evaluation of the Catalyst Funding programme and identifying resources and effective practices from the projects which could be published and promoted for the benefit of the whole sector (Office for Students, 2021c).

Women and Equalities Select Committee Inquiry and Report, 2018

The House of Commons Women and Equalities Select Committee published its Sixth Report of Session 2017–2019 (Women and Equalities Select Committee, 2018) on 23 October 2018 following evidence sessions and literature review in summer 2018. The OfS's Director of Teaching Excellence and Student Experience, Yvonne Hawkins, was invited to give evidence and questioning focused on the regulator's role with regard to regulating to protect women and girls from sexual harassment; where the responsibility lies between the regulator and individual HE providers for collecting data about instances of sexual misconduct; and what sanctions the OfS should be taking against providers who do not take adequate steps to safeguard their students. When Yvonne Hawkins was asked about the OfS's role in tackling sexual harassment, she responded:

> In this area [preventing sexual harassment], the Office for Students has been charged with having a duty to have regard to promote equality and diversity across the whole student lifecycle.. . . When the Department for Education consulted on our new regulatory framework, it concluded that the Office for Students could be most effective in relation to student welfare and safeguarding issues if it took a sector regulatory approach. We will be active with the mechanisms I have described to you on promoting innovation, galvanising a culture change, evaluating what works and doesn't et cetera. We haven't got legal duties; they reside with the [Equality and Human Rights Commission].
> (Women and Equalities Select Committee, 2018)

The Committee did not agree with the OfS's assessment of their powers and felt that as a public body with responsibilities under the Public Sector Equality Duty as well as the Human Rights Act 1998, the OfS should be prioritising the safety and equality of women students.

The Minister for Universities subsequently wrote to the Committee to clarify the OfS's role and powers, saying that the responsibility for data collection about incidents of sexual harassment lies with individual universities, but that the OfS has a 'pivotal role' in addressing harassment at a sector level. The Committee's report concluded:

> Between the Government, regulators and institutions we have been left with a strong impression of passing the buck on who is responsible for

women's safety at university. A voluntary approach has not proved to ensure that women's safety is prioritised consistency across the Higher Education sector and it is now time for the Government to consider legislation.

(Women and Equalities Select Committee, 2018)

The Committee recommended that public funding for Higher Education should be linked to a requirement to prohibit sex discrimination and sexual harassment, and to collect and publish data on the effectiveness of institutional policies (which could be achieved by introducing Regulations under s.153 of the Equality Act 2010) (Women and Equalities Select Committee, 2018).

In its response to the Committee's report, the Government pointed to HE providers' own responsibilities under the Equality Act 2010 and the Human Rights Act 1998, and the enforceability of those duties by the Equality and Human Rights Commission. They highlighted the good practice work being led by both the OfS and Universities UK (albeit not a regulatory body) and noted that this approach was in line with the wider risk-based regulatory approach brought in by the HERA 2017 which aimed to foster continuous improvement and create space for innovation. The Government also reaffirmed their commitment to driving effective change in the sector by taking a 'non-legislative approach' to tackling sexual harassment but stated that they would continue to monitor the sector's performance (House of Commons, 2019). So, the government lead appears to remain one of more of a 'light touch' and non-legislative or prescriptive approach to regulation which had been highlighted by the Women and Equalities Select Committee as creating a void where no organisation with powers over the sector (be it the OfS, the Government, the Office of the Independent Adjudicator, or the EHRC) was able to compel individual providers to take action or sanction them when students experienced a poor response.

Development of a provider-level regulatory approach to tackling harassment and sexual misconduct

During 2019, the OfS evaluated the evidence regarding the extent and scale of all forms of harassment and sexual misconduct in HE, as well as evidence of inadequate practice within some HE providers and reflecting on the criticism levelled at the regulator and Government by the Women and Equalities Select Committee (Women and Equalities Select Committee, 2018). The following are the three key areas of evidence which indicated a lack of consistent and effective systems, policies, and processes in place to respond to incidents (Office for Students, 2020c):

1   The notifications received by the OfS in respect of individual providers, together with evidence set out in Changing the Culture follow-up reports published by Universities UK (Universities UK, 2018) (Universities UK, 2019), show that while there has been some progress in tackling these

issues, progress in widespread adoption of recommended practice is slow and not widespread across the sector.

2   The independent evaluations carried out by Advance HE of the OfS's 119 Safeguarding Catalyst projects (Baird et al., 2019) showed that there is still a significant level of variation in the response by providers, including by their executive leadership teams and governing bodies.

3   The EHRC's enquiry into racial harassment in HE (Equality and Human Rights Commission, 2019) which highlighted significant issues in relation to students experiencing racial harassment in HE providers.

In considering their response to the evidence, the OfS started exploring new or expanded regulatory interventions it could make at a provider level and how these could be operated within the existing – or a revised – regulatory framework. The aim of any such work was determined to be that all students registered at a provider, however and wherever they may be studying, should be protected from harassment and sexual misconduct from other students, staff, and visitors.

In developing their approach to regulation, the OfS is required to have regard to its general duties as set out in Section 2 the HERA 2017, its Public Sector Equality Duty and guidance from the Secretary of State (under Section 2(3) of the HERA). The relevant general duties were assessed as being (b), (d), and (e) which relate to quality, value for money, and equality of opportunity. These were balanced against duties (a), (f), and (g) which related to institutional autonomy, efficient use of the OfS's resources, and best regulatory practice. In September 2019, the Secretary of State issued the following guidance:

> I would like the OfS to prioritise work supporting students as empowered consumers.. . . And students must be able to access transparent and effective complaints processes when their consumer rights are not met. Beyond consumer rights, I want every student to be confident their institution stands up for free speech and that they will not experience unacceptable behaviour during their time at university, such as harassment, racial abuse, antisemitism and other forms of intolerance and prejudice.
>
> (Williamson, 2019)

It is interesting to observe the language of students as 'consumers' of education. This perhaps plays into wider notions of the marketisation of HE whereby institutions compete for students. Traditionally, there appears to have been a reluctance to talk about how universities are addressing their problems with sexual violence on 'open days'. The fear appears to have been that admitting there was a problem would put prospective students, especially young women off. With the cessation of student number limits and the opening of the 'market', there may well have been a concern that prospective students may prefer to go to a university that did not talk about its problem with sexual violence. Yet there is no evidence to support the idea that this will put prospective students off going to particular universities and thus damage their 'revenue streams'. On the contrary, when such safety sessions were piloted at a university in the North East, that recruitment cycle included around 1,500 additional applicants – tellingly perhaps, around 1,000 of them were women and around 500 men. Talking about what institutions are doing to address sexual violence does not seem to put prospective applicants off, many welcome the openness and investment in student safety.

The OfS decided not to have a new condition of registration which specifically required providers to address harassment and sexual misconduct, but that they would instead create a 'statement of expectations' for providers to meet and that these would be linked to the initial and ongoing conditions of registration.

HE providers are already subject to regulatory requirements in relation to the way they handle complaints from students. The OfS considered that the existing conditions of registration provided them with the regulatory tools to intervene where they had evidence of a failure of a provider's complaint-handling process to respond to reports of harassment or sexual misconduct, which could constitute a breach, or an increased risk of a future breach, of initial and ongoing conditions B2 (quality) and C1 (guidance on consumer protection law). This new regulatory approach plus the draft statement of expectations was launched as a public consultation in January 2020 (Office for Students, 2020c).

The drawbacks to implementing this approach centred on the narrowness and limited nature of the regulatory force – which would be focused solely on complaint handling and linked to conditions which were intended to be used for consumer or quality-related complaints by students, rather than reports of harassment or sexual misconduct. The OfS was unable to link their expectations around prevention, training, and awareness-raising to a specific condition, so these areas had to remain as 'best practice' but voluntary. A more forceful approach might have been to create a new specific condition of registration that required compliance with the statement of expectations, which would have created clarity for students and given the OfS stronger regulatory tools to use to sanction providers where there was a breach or an increased risk of a breach of the condition. At the time of writing, this does not appear to be considered as the most proportionate way to achieve the outcome they are seeking (wholesale reforms to policies, systems, and processes within providers) and would be in conflict with Section 7 of HERA for proportionate conditions of registration; unless the voluntary approach set out subsequently fails to drive improvements – they will lack the evidence to place a new regulatory requirement on providers.

A further option explored was to create a new public interest governance principle requiring transparency over policies on harassment and sexual misconduct. This would relate to conditions E1 and E2 as mentioned earlier; however, the requirement would be for the provider to publish its commitments and policies in a sufficiently accessible context, which could then be supplemented by the OfS drawing attention to these (e.g., on the OfS Register or the Discover Uni website). The efficacy of this approach would rely on students acting as informed consumers, empowering them to choose providers that made compelling commitments, while consumer protection law would, we understand, mean those commitments had to be delivered in practice. This option was not thought to be effective enough, as it is not clear that this information would be well-understood by applicants or students or would drive the desired changes within providers, although the example cited earlier from the NE where transparency of safeguarding arrangements was made clear on open days, it actually served to enhance awareness and attractiveness of the provider. As awareness amongst students and their representatives grows, this could become another viable and effective regulatory option for the future.

The statement of expectations

The OfS made the decision not to close the consultation as planned in March 2020 due to the COVID-19 pandemic. The consultation remained open – but paused – and over 100 responses were received. In November 2020, the OfS launched the first phase of a consultation about their approach to regulating quality and standards in HE (Office for Students, 2020a) which aimed to take their regulatory approach forward for the longer term, now that their initial focus on assessing providers seeking registration had largely been completed. The consultation was focused on the 'B' conditions of initial and ongoing registration and the responses received led to a second phase of consultation launched in July 2021 that proposed changes to the wording and purpose of condition B2 (Office for Students, 2021a), which would no longer enable linkage, for regulatory purposes, to the statement of expectations to tackle harassment and sexual misconduct. The regulator indicated that they also planned to review and refresh the 'C' conditions at a later stage, which may lead to similar changes in framing and wording.

It was therefore decided to close the consultation, carry out informal engagement with HE stakeholders, student representatives, and students with 'lived experience' of harassment or sexual misconduct, and then publish the statement of expectations, then publicise and promote them with the aim of encouraging HE providers to adopt the recommended practices voluntarily at least by the start of the 2021/2022 academic year.

The expectations (Office for Students, 2021d) were developed by drawing on the principles and recommendations from Universities UK's Changing the Culture report (Universities UK, 2016), their own evaluation reports from the Catalyst Fund programme, and the good practice in handling complaints and academic appeals recommended by the Office of the Independent Adjudicator for Higher Education (Office of the Independent Adjudicator, 2016). The expectations are formed of seven areas and cover the recommended processes, policies, and systems providers should have in place to both prevent and effectively respond to harassment and sexual misconduct. The scope of the expectations set out both the OfS's definitions of 'harassment' and 'sexual misconduct' and the expected coverage of the recommendations. The definition of harassment draws largely from the Equality Act 2010's definition of harassment, but includes criminal acts motivated by prejudice as well as domestic abuse or intimate partner violence (which can also involve control, coercion, and threats) and stalking. They were also clear that their definitions include misconduct perpetrated through any medium, including online.

The seven themes of the statement of expectations cover the following areas:

1   Providers should create and communicate clear policies on their approach to preventing and responding to all forms of harassment and sexual misconduct and the behavioural expectations of students, staff, and visitors.
2   Governing bodies of providers should ensure that their approach to tackling harassment and sexual misconduct is adequate and effective and that risks related to this are identified and effectively mitigated.
3   Providers should sensitively engage with students, including those with lived experience, to develop their systems, policies, and processes to address harassment and sexual misconduct.
4   Providers should implement adequate staff and student training to raise awareness of, and prevent, harassment and sexual misconduct.
5   Providers should have adequate and effective processes in place for all students to be able to report and disclose incidents of harassment and sexual misconduct.
6   Providers should have a fair, clear, and accessible approach to taking investigatory and disciplinary actions in response to reports and disclosures.
7   Providers should ensure that all students involved in an investigatory process have access to appropriate and effective support (Office for Students, 2021d).

Each one of the headline statements then contains some more detailed recommendations on the practices, systems, and processes that providers are expected to put in place.

While the statement of expectations is voluntary for providers to adopt and is not augmented with regulatory enforcement powers, the OfS has strongly encouraged providers to do so – and has indicated they will review their position on provider-level regulation and enforcement if they are slow to put the principles into practice. In her blog to mark the launch of the expectations in April 2021, Nicola Dandridge (OfS Chief Executive) said:

> Publishing this statement of expectations represents a major step in ensuring that all students feel safe during their time in higher education. It is a real opportunity for universities and colleges to make a difference and I would strongly urge them to grasp it. Over the next year we will examine how universities and colleges have responded. We will particularly want to hear from students and Students' Unions that things are changing for the better. As part of this process, we will consider options for connecting the statement directly to our conditions of registration.
>
> (Dandridge, 2021)

Some in the field have sought to build further upon the statement of expectations maintaining that they are minimum, rather than desirable requirements (Towl & Humphreys, 2021). Other useful guidance for universities may be found in the earlier mentioned table of minimum safeguarding practices which includes eight key actions: (1) Annual reports to governing bodies covering numbers and types of reports and outcomes; (2) Communications with prospective students about student safety to include coverage of sexual violence; (3) Campaigns to actively encourage reporting; (4) Student and staff training, for example, consent and how to respond to a disclosure training; (5) A member of the Executive to have clear leadership of work to address sexual violence; (6) Good policy and practices – with clear and accessible documentation; (7) Resources – a recommended minimum of one FTE per 10,000 students to provide expertise and coordinate the work including investigations and prevention; and (8) Partnership work – with local health providers and charities such as 'Rape Crisis' (Baird et al., 2019).

The OfS wrote to the accountable officers (usually the head of an institution) at all registered providers on 10 June 2021 (Office for Students, 2021b) to draw their attention to the statement of expectations and requested they made any necessary changes before the start of the 2021–2022 academic year or inform the OfS if they were unable to do so. At the time of writing, the OfS is drawing up plans to evaluate the impact of the expectations, and providers' progress in implementing the recommendations; cross-validating any evidence they receive from HE providers with the views of students and victim-survivors.

Regulation – limits and possibilities

Regulation may be viewed as one potentially impactful way of contributing to improving outcomes. Regulatory levers for change tend to be comparatively blunt levers for enacting change. This is the case both within HE and well beyond to other sectors such as health and social care. One intuitively appealing starting point for greater regulation of GBV is through the mandatory reporting of GBV to the regulator. As a starting point this would, so the argument goes, create a baseline for what is happening in universities in terms of the numbers of such cases and it may well serve to keep tackling GBV high on the institutional agenda. If it is measured it is monitored; and if it is monitored, it may well be more likely to be actively managed. We see at least three problems with such a comparatively heavy hand of regulation. First, at best, what such reporting would serve to do is simply measure how many reports a university did have. It would not measure how many it did not have. The majority of cases of GBV go unreported (Towl, 2018; Towl & Walker, 2019). One question for proponents of such an approach would be what would we do with such data? Second, and related to the first point, like many such metrics, counting would be open to institutional gaming. For example, suppose an institution simply reported that it had no reports of GBV. Would that really tell us that it was safe for students? Or would it indicate a leadership team not prioritising addressing its problems with

GBV? Conversely, if there were exceptionally high numbers of reports when compared with other universities, would that indicate a particular problem? The truth is we would not know from such limited data. Third, as a general principle, it seems to us that, one characteristic of effective regulation may well be making it as light touch as possible to achieve the desired goal. Such a proposal would fail both such tests. It would not be 'light touch', nor would it achieve the intended goal which presumably would be to effectively address sexual violence through prevention, support, investigations, and robust policies and practices.

Mindful that it is perhaps intellectually easier to criticize than to develop and enact policy, we have alternatives which we don't think falls short in the way that the simple introduction of mandatory reporting on its own would.

We would argue strongly in favour of a national prevalence survey in HE providers. This data would likely give us a much better picture of the actual prevalence rates of sexual violence rather than the more limited 'reporting rates'. If a national prevalence survey was implanted, say every three years, this could also be a potentially powerful evaluation tool of any interventions, policies, and practices that had been introduced over the three-year period. We could measure real impact. The prevalence survey would also indicate whether or not respondents had been subjected to sexual violence. This would help us establish what good looks like. In terms of the patterns in the data that we would be seeking would be decreasing prevalence rates and higher reporting rates. This would be good because we would all surely agree on the need for decreasing prevalence rates. Higher reporting rates would afford institutions with opportunities to better understand any patterns of such behaviour, for example, is it occurring at particular times or places. But crucially it would mean that we could get support to students who need it and undertake appropriate investigations if that is something that the victim-survivor would want.

So, the idea of a prevalence survey is much lighter in regulatory terms than mandatory reporting; however, the regulator would be well-placed to routinely commission such a prevalence survey which we believe would make a more effective and ongoing contribution to influencing the field to move towards a reduction is sexual violence at universities whilst potentially facilitating more effective support too. In regulatory terms, simply ensuring that such a survey is undertaken meets the tests of both light regulation but also effective in terms of having the potential to help us achieve what we would aim for in terms of decreased prevalence and increased reporting and supporting of students.

The results from such a survey also have the potential to build the knowledge base into sexual offending. Much of our purported knowledge of sex offenders has been derived from individuals who have been imprisoned. These may very well not be representative samples of sex offenders. A national prevalence survey would also have the potential to add to our understanding of this field which has challenged policymakers and practitioners. There is the opportunity in terms of the methods adopted to take a far more inclusive approach to collecting the data by way of a larger yet representative stratified sample. Thus, such research within universities has the potential to be of huge influence across health and criminal justice communities and well beyond.

We would however be in favour of university governing bodies receiving detailed data including outcomes on sexual violence cases at individual institutions. This would be on similar lines as outlined by a number of commentators (e.g., Baird et al., 2019; Humphreys & Towl, 2020). In view of the independence of institutions, executive leadership teams have the power to enact changes in a far more nuanced and effective way than a, at least one step removed, regulator would. And such management information could inform the identification of specific problem areas whilst also constantly seeking local improvement in service provision.

We have focused on sexual violence as an illustrative example; however, GBV in all its forms could perhaps best be captured under the broader rubric of say 'safety and well-being'. We know that to thrive both students and staff need to feel safe. If we feel safe, we are surely much more likely to contribute to and get the best from the full range of what universities have to offer, and as a sector, universities have a great deal to offer as we have seen recently with the development of COVID vaccines, but they are also subject to clear legal duties under the Equality Act 2010 and the Human Rights Act 1998.

Future directions

In addition to the aforementioned idea for a prevalence survey, we understand that the OfS will be taking a twin-track approach to determining the future of regulation to tackle harassment and sexual misconduct. Firstly, they need to assess the extent to which providers have adopted the practices recommended in the Statement of Expectations and understand where gaps remain. They will do this via independent evaluation and in-depth engagement with victim-survivor groups, academic experts, service leaders, and student representatives. Understanding the evidence base and closing gaps in evidence will be critical to this and ultimately in determining whether there needs to be more regulatory force connected to the Statement. Hand-in-hand with this work is the need to continue to identify and share effective practices and 'what works?' in preventing and responding effectively to harassment and sexual misconduct; harnessing the expertise of academic experts, policymakers, those on the front line of providing services to and supporting students, and those from the statutory and voluntary sectors. The OfS, sector bodies like UUK, professional associations like the Association of Managers of Student Services in HE (AMOSSHE), and the NUS can all play a part in identifying these practices and mobilising the knowledge. It's important to provide spaces for practitioners, experts (including by lived experience), and policymakers to share learning from complex cases and the impact of wider world events (for example, the pandemic, or the impact of high-profile cases) and how these should inform future practice and regulation. All regulation, prevalence surveying, and 'what works' activity should be to achieve the aim of universities being places where minds and ideas can flourish without the blight of GBV. Together we can make a difference.

Further reading

Towl, G. J., & Walker, T. (2019). Tackling sexual violence at universities; An international perspective. In *New frontiers in forensic psychology*, Series Eds., Walker and Towl. Routledge.

This book includes a brief overview of some of the work happening internationally at universities in terms of work to address sexual violence. The work includes a set of policy recommendations and guidelines drawing from the international evidence. A great starting point for anyone who wishes to explore international developments in tackling sexual violence at universities.

Office for Students. (2018b). *Securing Student Success: Regulatory framework for higher education in England.*

This is the regulatory framework operated by the OfS for all registered HE providers in England. It sets out the risk-based approach to regulating the sector and describes each one of the initial and ongoing conditions of registration in detail, as well as the nature of the regulator's relationship with individual providers and information about our functions and duties. This is a foundational publication for anyone wanting to understand the regulatory system for HE in England.

Office for Students. (2020b). Insight event recording, '*Regulator and Regulated – what's the right relationship?*'

This event (the recordings of which can be found following the citation) explored the role of principles-based regulation in higher education, why it matters and what's in it for students. It explored the relationship between HE providers as the 'regulated' and the OfS as the regulator, as well as discussing the differences between principles and rules-based regulation. The event also featured student perspectives about their priorities for regulation from the NUS president. This is a useful source for anyone wanting to delve deeper into the different types of regulation and the realities of operating the English HE regulatory framework.

The views expressed in this chapter are that of the contributors and may or may not represent the views of their employers.

References

Advance HE. (2018). *Evaluation of safeguarding students catalyst fund projects: Thematic analysis Report 1.* Advance-HE.

Baird, H., Renfrew, K., Nash-Henry, Z., & Towl, G. (2019). *Evaluation of safeguarding students catalyst fund projects: Summative evaluation report.* Office for Students.

Dandridge, N. (2021, April 19). *How we expect universities and colleges to tackle harassment and sexual misconduct.* Office for Students. www.officeforstudents.org.uk/news-blog-and-events/blog/how-we-expect-universities-and-colleges-to-tackle-harassment-and-sexual-misconduct/

Equality and Human Rights Commission. (2019). *Tackling racial harassment: Universities challenged*. Equality and Human Rights Commission.

Higher Education Funding Council for England. (2016, December 22). *Catalyst fund: Student safeguarding on campus*. Higher Education Funding Council for England (accessed through the National Archive). https://webarchive.nationalarchives.gov.uk/ukgwa/20170110131439/http:/www.hefce.ac.uk/pubs/Year/2016/CL,362016/

House of Commons. (2019). *Sexual harassment of women and girls in public places: Government response to the committee's sixth report of session 2017–19* (HC 2148). House of Commons.

Humphreys, C., & Towl, G. (2020). *Addressing sexual violence in higher education: A good practice guide*. Emerald Publishing Limited.

Office of the Independent Adjudicator. (2016). *The good practice framework: Handling student complaints and academic appeals*. Office of the Independent Adjudicator.

Office for Students. (2018a, September 26). *5th meeting of the OfS Board*. Office for Students. www.officeforstudents.org.uk/about/board-papers/ofs-board-meeting-26-september-2018/

Office for Students. (2018b). *Securing Student Success: Regulatory framework for higher education in England*. Office for Students.

Office for Students. (2020a). *Consultation on regulating quality and standards in higher education* (OfS 2020.50). Office for Students.

Office for Students. (2020b, December 3). *Insight event: Regulator and regulated: What's the right relationship?* Office for Students. www.officeforstudents.org.uk/news-blog-and-events/events/insight-event-regulator-and-regulated-what-s-the-right-relationship/

Office for Students. (2020c). *OfS consultation on harassment and sexual misconduct in higher education*. OfS.

Office for Students. (2021a). *Consultation on quality and standards conditions*. Office for Students.

Office for Students. (2021b, June 10). *Letter about the statement of expectations for preventing and tackling harassment and sexual misconduct affecting students in higher education*. Office for Students. www.officeforstudents.org.uk/publications/letter-about-the-statement-of-expectations-for-preventing-and-addressing-harassment-and-sexual-misconduct/

Office for Students. (2021c, August 27). *Resources for student safety and wellbeing*. Office for Students. www.officeforstudents.org.uk/advice-and-guidance/student-wellbeing-and-protection/resources-for-student-safety-and-wellbeing/

Office for Students. (2021d, April 19). *Statement of expectations*. Office for Students. www.officeforstudents.org.uk/advice-and-guidance/student-wellbeing-and-protection/prevent-and-address-harassment-and-sexual-misconduct/statement-of-expectations/

Office for Students. (2021e, September 1). *Student safeguarding evaluation and resources*. Office for Students. www.officeforstudents.org.uk/advice-and-guidance/student-wellbeing-and-protection/student-safeguarding-evaluation-and-resources/projects/

Towl, G. J. (2018, January). Tackling sexual violence at universities. *The Psychologist, 31*, 36–39, Leicester, BPS.

Towl, G. J., & Humphreys, C. J. (2021, April 22). *How to do more than the bare minimum on harassment and sexual misconduct*. Wonk HE. https://wonkhe.com/blogs/how-to-do-more-than-the-bare-minimum-on-harassment-and-sexual-misconuct/

Towl, G. J., & Walker, T. (2019). *Tackling sexual violence at universities: An international perspective*. Routledge.

Universities UK. (2016). *Changing the culture: Report of the Universities UK taskforce examining violence against women, harassment and hate crime affecting university students*. Universities UK.

Universities UK. (2018). *Changing the culture: One year on (an assessment of strategies to tackle sexual misconduct, hate crime and harassment affecting university students)*. Universities UK.

Universities UK. (2019). *Changing the Culture, tackling gender-based violence, harassment and hate crime: Two years on*. Universities UK.

Williamson, G. (2019, September 16). *Guidance from Government*. Office for Students. www. officeforstudents.org.uk/media/1a105d7c-e6ef-4e3d-ab23-bd3e93e01257/letter-from-the-education-secretary-sept19.pdf

Women and Equalities Select Committee. (2018). *Sexual harassment of women and girls in public places (HC 701)*. House of Commons.

21 Working with schools to tackle online harms and gender-based violence

Andy Phippen and Emma Bond

At the time of writing, the media landscape in the UK is once again reporting on the harms associated with social media, the hate distributed on online platforms, and how as a society we might tackle this. The current media narrative, underpinned by calls for greater regulation of digital platforms and a "strengthening" of the proposed Online Safety Bill legislation, currently at pre-scrutiny committee phase in Parliament, draws heavily on examples of gender-based violence online. Specifically, the gender-based abuse to which women MPs are subjected,[1] (Merrick, 2021) and the impact of online content on (predominantly female) young people's mental health (Gayle, 2019).

The prevailing media, and political narrative, is one of responsibility for social media platforms themselves – if the abuse happens on these platforms, it should be the platforms responsibility to deal with them (Milmo, 2021). An approach which places the focus of tackling online harms solely with the domain of a single stakeholder – the platform itself.

However, whilst an in-depth exploration of this discussion falls outside of the scope of this chapter, it is an important starting point for an exploration of the relationship between schools and universities in understanding online abuse and gender-based violence. We need to move away from the perspective that "someone" needs to do something about these issues and instead, reflect upon what we, as key stakeholders in student welfare, might do to better support reporting parties. And, more specifically to this chapter, how institutions might better work together to support students who might become subjected to this form of abuse or, preferably, working towards an environment that adopts preventative and harm reduction approaches to what is sometimes broadly referred to as "online safety".

Both of us started to work in this area at the turn of the century, when online abuse was, in general, limited to messaging platforms and mobile text messages. Before the mainstreaming of social media, and the growth on smartphone technology, there were certainly fewer opportunities for online abuse. Nevertheless, it still existed and institutions struggled to understand how they might respond to or support victim-survivors. Indeed, in many instances, educational institutions would feel this was not their concern, given that the abuse happened outside of their physical institutional perimeters, that is, 'off campus'. Over the last 20 years, much has changed in the statutory education sector, with both

DOI: 10.4324/9781003252474-24

the regulator, Ofsted and the Department for Education, making demands on schools to address online abuse in all of its forms, through a mix of policy, education, and safeguarding (discussed later in this chapter). However, we have seen little regulation in the University sector that mirrors this.

Therefore, it might initially seem strange that this chapter explores the potential partnership between universities and schools in how they might support each other in developing responses to online gender-based violence and, more broadly, all forms of online abuse. Surely, given the statutory expectations placed upon schools, this is something they are on top of, and universities, with a lack of clear steer from regulators, have little to offer?

Sadly, in our experience this is not the case. Schools, regardless of the demands of the regulator and governments, still struggle in this area, because statutory responsibilities tend to be imposed without effective support. And universities, in an unregulated space, are just waking up to student welfare as a core function of the academy, sadly as a result of high-profile media stories where they have been found seriously lacking.[2]

Therefore, within this chapter, we explore the nature of online safeguarding, approaches that do not work, and how each partner can best work to their strengths in tackling issues of online abuse, rather than resort to knee-jerk reactions to whichever incident they face in any given week. We will explore the nature of online safeguarding in schools and how university expectations on student preparedness to address online abuse, once they transition into the Higher Education sector, are not borne out in reality and how these expectations reflect a more deep-rooted view that besets this whole area of online safeguarding – "surely someone should do something about this, but I don't think it should be me". We will, throughout this discussion, define a number of "directives", which we see as good practice for both school and university partners in tackling gender-based violence online. This is not intended to be a step-by-step guide to working in partnership to eliminate online abuse. However, it is drawing upon our expertise and we do advocate approaching online safeguarding from a new, evidence-informed approach. We know, as a result of working in this area for a long time, what is and is not effective, and we believe a harm reduction and risk mitigation, rather than a prohibitive approach to supporting victim-survivors can be most productive in terms of outcomes.

Directive 1 – you do not know best

Working in partnership – some common errors

In our experience working across the sectors, both schools and universities suffer from the infamous "do something, anything" approach that is sometimes encapsulated in the mythical politician's syllogism[3]:

> Something must be done.
> This is something.
> Therefore, we must do it.

In the case of schools, they are "doing something" because they have been told to, regardless of whether staff are sufficiently trained to understand the issues in depth. And university leaders seem to be retrofitting policies and practices in knee-jerk reactions to students going to the press to disclose abuse as a result of unsatisfactory responses from their Higher Education Institutions.

We have directly experienced "do something" from both types of institutions. As part of our work over the years, we often deliver talks, training, and workshops around online behaviours, tech law, online safeguarding practices, and similar. We have, as a result of this, certainly seen from both sides of the educational partnership how not to collaborate in this area.

From the schools' perspective, with pressures with a looming inspection or a need to demonstrate online abuse is being considered in the annual safeguarding return, we have been frequently asked: "Can you come in and do an assembly about online safety?" or "Could you do a half hour training session with our staff in a twilight session?[4]" While we have often accommodated these requests historically, we have, in more recent times, done them far less. The main reason for our resistance being that there is little evidence they do anything to actually change practice in the setting, they simply tick a box over doing "something" about issues of online abuse.

The core finding that emerges repeatedly from our work is that victim-survivors of online abuse are rarely willing to disclose in school settings (Phippen, 2016). The predominant reason given is that they do not believe the staff will do anything, and that staff do not understand the issues sufficiently to understand what the victim-survivor is experiencing or that they actually fear they will get into trouble. Short assemblies and ad hoc training sessions do little to tackle this fundamental issue. Young people want knowledgeable staff to whom they can disclose and expect support. They do not need an assembly from a stranger who, while potentially delivering an entertaining talk based on expert knowledge about online issues, will do little to reassure them that the school is capable of supporting them if they become subjected to online abuse.

When considering the flipside of our experiences, within Higher Education settings, there is a similar view that a "quick talk" might solve all of the potential issues that come with new students on campus, potentially living away from home for the first time, and unfiltered online access. "You know about this stuff, can you do an induction talk for our students to tell them how to protect themselves online", or similar, is something we have been frequently asked to do. And then introduced as "This is Professor Phippen, he's going to talk to you about online safety", followed by groans from the students who have been subject to endless assemblies, videos, and PowerPoints about "staying safe online" at their schools, and, when they finally think they are free of this, the receive a similar sticking plaster during university induction. From the institutional perspective, they have ticked a box – an "expert" has done a talk.[5] We need not worry about this anymore.

The fundamental problem with tackling issues of online abuse lies with the term, and as fall out from that, the approaches used. The term "online safety" means we start from a prohibitive position that is doomed to fail. If we are happy with the term "safety" related to online abuse, is this actually achievable? Safety implies free from harm or risk of harm. A lot of online safeguarding discourse draws analogies from road safety – we frequently hear comments about how "we teach them how to cross the road safely, and we should do the same for being online". Interestingly, if we compare terminology in relation to abuse, misrepresentation is start and the 'victim blaming' tone is apparent. Physical abuse, sexual abuse, domestic abuse, and financial abuse are frequently used in professional, educational, and public discourses, yet we have traditionally referred to "online safety" and "keeping yourself safe online".

Furthermore, if we consider road safety, there are few threats but the main one is serious and can cause an individual serious harm – if they are struck by a car while crossing the road. Therefore, we can put simple rules in place to mitigate this risk. We can tell individuals to look both ways before crossing, make sure they have clear view up and down the road, listen out for traffic, and make use of the tool available within the road environment (such as pedestrian crossing systems) to further mitigate that risk. The focus is entirely upon the prevention of an accident between individual and motor vehicle. And we can have rules about which side of the road to drive upon, speeding restrictions, traffic calming measures, and also, for example, have drink driving rules.

If we compare this with the online world – firstly what are the threats? These are multiple, and range from exposure to upsetting content, abuse by peers, unsolicited sexual contact by predators, non-consensual sharing of indecent images, being hacked and having identity data from being shared, and so on. And, in contrast to the road environment, which is well-controlled, with established standards (e.g., cars travel on roads, pedestrians travel on pavements) and a stable environment (it would be unusual to wake and discover we had decided that cars should now travel on the opposite side of the road to the day before), whereas new online risks emerge as the digital infrastructure evolves and develops. Unlike roads, digital environments have few boundaries other than the ever-expanding capacity of networks upon which all online services operate, and the imaginations of the developers who put services and platforms in place for billions of citizens to use. This poses the question:

> What practice can we put in place to make sure a person is *safe* online?

Simply, we cannot. Therefore, we argue by using safety analogies, we further risk revictimisation – "you have received instruction on how to be safe online, therefore if you are subject to harm, it must be your fault".

Directive 2 – dispose of the "online safety" rhetoric and adopt a victim-survivor-centric approach

We advocate the provision of a supportive environment where a victim-survivor can confidently disclose and expect support that will help them. We need to move away from a mindset where we are going to eradicate online abuse and, instead, recognise that online abuse is a risk anyone who goes online might have to face, and how we can help them mitigate that risk, and support them in the event of abuse occurring. As a caveat to this, we would also raise the issue of recognising online abuse in the first place.

Universities have, within their DNA, a natural inclination towards critical thinking and the need for evidence to support both educational and life choices. If we are to return to the purpose of the academy, we are reminded of the often (mis)quoted comment from John Stewart Mill in his inauguration speech at St Andrews University in 1867 (Mill, 1867):

> The proper function of an University in national education is tolerably well understood. At least there is a tolerably general agreement about what an University is not. It is not a place of professional education. Universities are not intended to teach the knowledge required to fit men for some special mode of gaining their livelihood. Their object is not to make skilful lawyers, or physicians, or engineers, but capable and cultivated human beings.

The quote is frequently used to illustrate the universities should not merely take the arguably neoliberal perspective of return on investment and the value of the graduate to the economy (Olssen & Peters, 2005). Instead, we should have a focus upon the development of individuals capable of independent thought, critical appraisal, and digital literacy in order to process evidence to make informed decisions. These are, we would suggest, also necessary characteristics for any stakeholder making decisions regarding online abuse.

Directive 3 – introduce critical approaches to understanding the nature of online abuse and support the development of evidence-informed practice

Learning from evidence

Perhaps the most telling example of the failings of learning from evidence around sexual abuse (including online sexual abuse) that has impacted upon the broad education sector recently has been the publication of the Ofsted investigation (Ofsted, 2021) into abuse that was triggered by the Everyone's Invited website.[6] The media coverage of the website resulted in the then Secretary of State for Education, Gavin Williamson, in tasking Ofsted with an investigation into the prevalence of sexual abuse in schools. We herein include a small sample of disclosure from the website:

> *Boys in my school would make explicit comments on particular girls in a sexual manner, asking them how much pubic hair they had etc. and objectifying us as year 7s. I was disgusted but had no way to speak out as teachers would brush it off as jokes, and "boys being boys". Now, older, I realise just how disgusting comments made to me and my peers were, and that I should never be made to feel that way as a young teenage girl, and I certainly would never accept that behaviour as a young adult now. Even small comments not*

being penalised encourages further damaging discourse about women and young girls and it needs to be taken more seriously by teachers.

A guy I considered one of my closest guy friends continuously pressured me to send him pictures and sent me multiple unsolicited nudes. He would use our friendship against me and say if I didn't send pictures we couldn't talk anymore which felt like a horrible ultimatum considering we were such good friends and I was so young i didn't realise that it was wrong.

I know of SO many people who had access to a google drive of all the nudes they'd managed to collect from girls in our year. The guy who started it was only popular for that reason.

I remember on numerous occasions hearing guys proudly talking about how they'd record themselves having sex with/getting head from girls without the girls being aware of it. I hate that I didn't even think to report them or call them out on it. Gross behaviour like that was just so normalised. I think about whether they have the footage to this day, or if this ever happened to me, and I, like those girls, was completely unaware of it.

These quotes are a random sample from the website and extremely typical of the many disclosures. We use these quotes to illustrate a number of factors common throughout the disclosures on the website:

1   The fear that underlies the unwillingness of many victim-survivors to disclose abuse and the belief that there is no point in disclosing.
2   The role of digital technology in the abuse, particularly the use of images to both record abuse and the non-consensual storage and sharing of intimate images.
3   The failures of stakeholders to respond effectively.

Certainly, the website very clearly, once again, raised concerns about the normalisation of sexual violence and harassment in British society. Given the volume of disclosures, and the sadly familiar descriptions disclosed by victim-survivors, it became very difficult for government to ignore this issue, and therefore "something" needed to be done.

The report published by Ofsted (2021) was thorough and produced a good body of evidence regarding the scope of sexual assault among young people, for example:

•   Girls can be harassed via text by many boys in a night for intimate images.
•   64% of girls experience unwanted touching "a lot" or "sometimes".
•   80% of girls have been pressured into sending intimate images.

The report subsequently made a number of excellent recommendations for schools:

•   A carefully sequenced Relationships, Sex and Health Education (RSHE) curriculum, based on the Department for Education's statutory guidance, that specifically includes sexual harassment and sexual violence, including online. This should include time for open discussion of topics that children and young people tell us they find particularly difficult, such as consent and the sending of 'nudes'.

- High-quality training for teachers delivering RSHE.
- Routine record-keeping and analysis of sexual harassment and sexual violence, including online, to identify patterns and intervene early to prevent abuse.
- A behavioural approach, including sanctions when appropriate, to reinforce a culture where sexual harassment and online sexual abuse are not tolerated.
- Working closely with local safeguarding partners in the area where the school or college is located so that they are aware of the range of support available to children and young people who are victims or who perpetrate harmful sexual behaviour.

Perhaps most significantly, and this is advice we feel should be shared across the sector, is that settings should "assume that sexual harassment and online sexual abuse are happening in their setting, even when there are no specific reports, and put in place a whole-school approach to address them" (Ofsted, 2021).

However, whilst the findings of the report were indeed concerning, far more so was the reaction to it by those in senior education positions in the country. Media reporting (Sellgren & Willis, 2021) quoted the Secretary of State and Head of the Ofsted as seeing the findings of the report as "shocking" and "a real moment of realisation".

While we agree that the findings are disturbing reading, they should not come as a shock to anyone who has worked in schools or conducted research around the harassment of young people in these settings. In highlighting the need for us to be always working from evidence, there is nothing in the findings of the Ofsted research that is not already in the literature. There is a considerable body of literature that considers the issues of normalised sexual assault in education settings. For example, in addition to our own work highlighting this issue (Phippen, 2016; Bond, 2010, 2014), there is an excellent report by Ringrose et al. (2012) which was commissioned to explore image-based abuse in schools, drew from a considerable qualitative body of evidence to show casual attitudes towards sexual harassment, and a weariness to the frequency of occurrence. However, we acknowledge that academic literature is sometimes inaccessible to practitioners and policymakers, which can therefore be a challenge in informing practice. For this reason, we would encourage academic research in this area to be more accessible, in both form and language, for practitioners and policymakers.

Directive 4 – make academic research related to online harms and gender-based violence, wherever possible open access, or supported with accessible outputs

However, significantly, a parliamentary enquiry in 2016 by the Women and Equalities Select Committee conducted an enquiry into this "sexual harassment and sexual violence in schools", to which many of us gave evidence, and the published report (Women and Equalities Committee, 2016) at the end of the inquiry made a number of recommendations:

13. The Department for Education should develop, publish and publicise national guidance on adopting a whole school approach to reducing and preventing sexual harassment and sexual violence in all primary and secondary schools. This guidance should be published so schools can implement it in September 2017.

(Paragraph 92)

15. The Government should create a statutory obligation in the forthcoming Education Bill for all schools, primary and secondary, to develop a whole school approach to preventing and tackling sexual harassment and sexual violence. We also recommend that the Department for Education remind all school Governors of their legal obligations to address sexual harassment and sexual violence in school. Guidance and support on how to achieve this most effectively should be provided to Governing Bodies.

(Paragraph 94)

When considering the recommendations of the committee, the crossover with the Ofsted report is telling. Effective training, a curriculum that delivers education related to this area, support for young people and working in partnership are all part of the recommendations. Perhaps most telling, however is the statement:

4. The Government and schools must make tackling sexual harassment and sexual violence an immediate policy priority.

We should bear in mind that this, evidence-based, report was published in 2016. Five years later the regulator conducted "urgent research" as a result of alarm around the disclosures on the Everyone's Invited website. What is of significant concern is that up until now the regulator appears to have been in denial about the problem, even though a parliamentary committee, five years previously, had clearly articulated the issue and the need for a response by the education sector as a whole. And the HE sector still seems to be in denial too with high prevalence levels and low reporting levels.

What do schools have to do? – "they learn about this stuff at school"

So, how can universities work in partnership with schools to better support young people who become subject to online harms and gender-based violence? We are frequently met in the university sector (see the following section) with assumptions that "they learn about this stuff in schools so why should we have to deliver education on this?" It is worthwhile, therefore, to reflect upon the requirements placed upon schools by the regulator and government, and how this is operationalised.

"Online safety" has, arguably, existed as a safeguarding requirement in schools for 15 years, but did not become part of any statutory framework until 2012. The two major changes to this online safety landscape have been the inclusion of online safety as part of the Ofsted, the schools regulator of England, inspection framework in 2012 (Ofsted, 2013), and its inclusion in the Department for Education's Keeping Children Safe in Education statutory guidance since 2015 (Department for Education, 2021). If we consider the latest requirements regarding online safety in school settings from the Department for Education, we can see there are requirements around training:

14. All staff should receive appropriate safeguarding and child protection training (including online safety) at induction. The training should be regularly updated. In addition, all staff should receive safeguarding and child protection (including online safety) updates (for example, via email, e-bulletins and staff meetings), as required, and at least annually, to provide them with relevant skills and knowledge to safeguard children effectively.

89. Governing bodies and proprietors should ensure an appropriate senior member of staff, from the school or college leadership team, is appointed to the role of designated safeguarding lead. The designated safeguarding lead should take lead responsibility for safeguarding and child protection (including online safety).

117. Governing bodies and proprietors should ensure that, as part of the requirement for staff to undergo regular updated safeguarding training, including online safety (paragraph 114) and the requirement to ensure children are taught about safeguarding, including online safety (paragraph 119), that safeguarding training for staff, including online safety training, is integrated, aligned and considered as part of the whole school or college safeguarding approach and wider staff training and curriculum planning.

Management of risk:

128. Whilst considering their responsibility to safeguard and promote the welfare of children and provide them with a safe environment in which to learn, governing bodies and proprietors should be doing all that they reasonably can to limit children's exposure to the above risks from the school's or college's IT system. As part of this process, governing bodies and proprietors should ensure their school or college has appropriate filters and monitoring systems in place. Governing bodies and proprietors should consider the age range of their children, the number of children, how often they access the IT system and the proportionality of costs vs risks.

129. The appropriateness of any filters and monitoring systems are a matter for individual schools and colleges and will be informed in part, by the risk assessment required by the Prevent Duty. The UK Safer Internet Centre

has published guidance as to what "appropriate" filtering and monitoring might look like.

And curriculum:

> 119. Governing bodies and proprietors should ensure that children are taught about safeguarding, including online safety, and recognise that a one size fits all approach may not be appropriate for all children, and a more personalised or contextualised approach for more vulnerable children, victims of abuse and some SEND children might be needed

However, there is nothing in the document that defines *what* online safety training is, who should deliver it, or what curriculum should look like. While the Department for Education recently produced non-statutory guidance on teaching online safety (2019), this was for guidance only. In it the management of risk centres mainly on ensuring appropriate technology is in place to make sure inappropriate content cannot be viewed, and online activity is monitored with appropriate alerts in place should abuse occur. Therefore, to fulfil statutory duties, a school needs to have "appropriate" tools in place to filter and monitor internet access, they require staff and governors to be trained about online safety (with no guidance on who delivers this training), and some form of curriculum needs to be delivered, with little advice on what this curriculum should be. It would seem that the people responsible for ensuring effective curriculum are the governors of the setting, who may well be poorly informed about the topic prior to training, which can be delivered by anyone with whom the school wishes to engage.[7] While this is not specifically an exploration of online safeguarding policy and practice in schools, we feel this brief discussion is worthwhile to debunk some of the myths about consistent delivery of education and practice around online harms, such that any student would arrive at university knowledgeable and confident about the risks they face and how they might best tackle them.

Directive 5 – develop evidence-based training to fulfil statutory requirements that are effective in practice. Do not adopt a tick box approach

While the advent of the new compulsory Relationships curriculum (Department for Education, 2020) has been proposed as a way to tackle this inconsistency, an inspection of the curriculum specification highlights the lack of coverage of both online harms and gender-based violence.

By the end of secondary school, pupils should know the following:

- The concepts of, and laws relating to, sexual consent, sexual exploitation, abuse, grooming, coercion, harassment, rape, domestic abuse, forced marriage, honour-based violence and FGM, and how these can affect current and future relationships.

- How people can actively communicate and recognise consent from others, including sexual consent, and how and when consent can be withdrawn (in all contexts, including online).

Given the age of victim-survivors on Everyone's Invited, we would suggest that the end of secondary school is far too late in a lot of cases. We also note a highly legal focus related to gender-based violence and online abuse. The only other mention of either lies in a section titled "The Law", which states:

It is important to know what the law says about sex, relationships, and young people, as well as broader safeguarding issues. This includes a range of important facts and the rules regarding sharing personal information, pictures, videos and other material using technology. This will help young people to know what is right and wrong in law, but it can also provide a good foundation of knowledge for deeper discussion about all types of relationships.

There is something of an ideological obsession by policymakers to believe articulate law is an effective preventative measure, and it is worrying that it still remains. Legal approaches are widely viewed as problematic in other areas of safeguarding education (for example, drugs and alcohol awareness, as explored in detail by Levinthal [2005]) but seem to persist around online harms in particular. While a detailed exploration of image-based abuse among young people is again outside of the scope of this chapter, our work in the area (Phippen & Brennan, 2020) has highlighted the problematic nature of educational messages such as "don't take and share intimate images, if you do you will be breaking the law", and result in further unwillingness of victim-survivors to disclose abuse. After all, if you have been told that by taking the image you have broken the law, why would you risk arrest when it is subsequently shared non-consensually.

The university context – or "they're digital natives, they know about this stuff"

On the other side of the partnership, it is equally worthwhile to reflect upon the university context around online harms and gender-based violence. While the Ofsted report, of course, focuses upon the schools and colleges sector, there are some clear commonalities with our problem with sexual violence across Higher Education. If we are to consider the role universities can play in working in partnership with schools to support young people in developing knowledge around online harms and gender-based violence, it is useful to understand both the sector's statutory responsibilities and the state of practice. Ultimately, universities have a vested interest in working with school partners to understand the nature of online harms and gender-based violence, because the students they welcome on to their campuses will then be both better equipped to address sexual violence and also have effective knowledge in adopting a zero-tolerance approach.

In order to take stock of the state of the sector around addressing online harms and gender-based violence, a practice we see more and more in the sector perhaps highlights the challenged faced. In the digitally connected world in which we all now live, we see many examples of social media platforms being used to introduce students to each other during the transitional phase between school and university. A typical scenario is students who will reside in the same hall of residence are put together in a social media group so that they can "get to know each other". Again, we have been in meetings where we are told "this is how young people communicate, that's why we have to use social media".[8] While we can see this is done for the best of intentions, we have further been told that sometimes these environments result in online abuse and harassment and they struggle with how to support those being subjected to abuse, or disciplining abusers. Whilst policies may be in place such as Code of Conduct or Anti-Bullying policy (Phippen & Bond, 2020) for enrolled students, these policies arguably do not apply for those applicant students. We have certainly, on more than one occasion, heard the excuse "but they're not our students yet, what can we do", even though the institution has actually placed the abusers and abused into an environment where such attacks can take place, with no support, guidance, or routes for disclosure.

Directive 6 – do not place transitioning students into social media groups without clear risk assessment, policy, transparent sanctions (up to and including withdrawing of offer of a place and reporting to the police), and routes for disclosure

While the school sector has had safeguarding as part of core practice for many years, this is, arguably not the case in Higher Education. Furthermore, we would argue that school practice around online safeguarding only became a management priority when there were regulatory and statutory requirements to make it so. While this might be a slightly cynical perspective, it is no coincident that September 2012 was a tipping point for online safeguarding policy and practice in schools (Phippen, 2016), given this was when Ofsted first announced online safeguarding would be part of the inspection process.

The reality is the Higher Education is far behind schools in understanding the scope of the sexual violence on campus. Work by Baird et al. (2019) evaluated a number of funded projects across the sector related to both physical and online abuse and highlighted a number of good practices but certainly nowhere near consistent practice across the sector, and certainly highlighted that sexual violence and abuse is not limited to students of school age. It further identified a belief that many university governing bodies and executive leaders have implicit assumption that, by the time they reach our institutions, students have a good understanding of the unacceptability of harassment and abuse, regardless of evidence to the contrary. The minimum safeguarding practices advocated by Baird et al. seem to have gained little traction in the sector despite their practical focus at addressing our problem with sexual violence in the sector in its various forms. So, the guidance is out there, but we are actively choosing not to use it as a sector.

Within the Higher Education sector, we see far fewer "regulatory sticks" with which to encourage universities to bring issues of online harms and gender-based violence up the senior management list of priorities. In terms of institutional responses, there may be some merit and shared learning across sectors when we look at, for example, the Office for Students' (2021) Statement of Expectation on preventing and addressing harassment and sexual misconduct,[9] developed in part as a response to research and media reporting around sexual assault and harassment at universities.

Our own research (Phippen & Bond, 2020), which served a Freedom of Information request on the sector to explore policy and practice addressing online abuse and harassment, and which is discussed in more detail at the end of this chapter, would suggest the sector as a whole is not well prepared for the expectations of the Office for Students, with serious concerns around policy, training, and reporting routes. Perhaps more concerning during this research were responses from institutions stating that safeguarding is not their concern because their students "are adults", and further statements such as "this is something that they learn in schools".

One further term we have experienced in many discussions with university senior managers who dismiss any need to address issues of online harm or gender-based violence on campus because it has been dealt with before students arrive on campus is the hardy perennial "They're *digital natives*". It would seem that it is almost impossible to have a strategic discussion around any safeguarding issues with an online element without someone using the term to explain that, given that students are, in general, younger than those in the meeting, they have, as if by osmosis, an ability to navigate and respond to online threats because they happen to have been using digital technology from an early age.

Coined by Prensky (2001), this is as a phrase differentiating between children – *digital natives* – and adults – *digital immigrants* – the concept rapidly found its way into academic and educational discourse and we still encounter it regularly in spite the volume of criticism levied against the term.

Prensky's Digital Native idea comes from an article that proposes a theory where because someone was born in an era where digital technology was ubiquitous, they had some inbuilt ability to engage with it with capabilities that are missing from previous generations generalized as digital immigrants. While this crude generalisation is now widely debunked (for example, Selwyn, 2009; Helsper & Eynon, 2010; Kirschner & De Bruyckere, 2017), its use still unhelpfully pervades in popular discourse.

Brown and Czerniewicz (2010) are also highly critical of the concept as such terminology hides inequalities in digital experiences. Furthermore, given that *Digital Native* ties in with the concept of *Millennials* (born between mid-1980s and early 2000s) and *Generation Z* (late 1990s – approximately 2015), this is not a term that could simply be applied to children and young people now – it is both unproven and now obsolete when we are concerned with the online safeguarding of young people in 2021.

We have attended seminars and workshops around digital literacies and safeguarding where senior speakers from government and regulators have unhelpfully spoken of younger generations being natives capable of navigating the digital world without further support. To paraphrase one professional in a training session:

> They know more than me because they're a digital native, it comes naturally to them.

We would suggest that the term has become adopted as an excuse to not tackle the issues of online abuse and gender-based violence in a particular setting. When someone says "they're a digital native, they know more than me", the implication is

> [t]hey're digital natives, they should know about this sort of thing, and therefore if something bad has happened it's their fault.

Or it is used to deflect responsibility back to the child or young person:

> I'm not a digital native like they are, they know more than me, therefore I can do little to help.

Directive 7 – never use the term "digital natives" again, or use it as an excuse to ignore the responsibilities of the sector to support victim-survivors of online abuse

One thing we frequently observe across all settings related to online safeguarding is the view of the institution, or even an individual in that institution, what we might refer to as the *online hero complex*. A safeguarding approach which prevents any form of harm through a mix of technical tools that prevent exposure to harmful content and monitor every conversation that takes place across the institution's networks, educational messages that make it clear what the risks are and how it's best not to engage in anything risky online, and a disclosure route so terrifying no student will ever make use of it.[10] "We've done all we can", we are told, "and we have no disclosures anymore". The hero complex is one that focuses upon an eradication of harm through prohibitive means and should someone become subject to abuse, it's not the fault of the individual or institution – "I've done all I can".

Directive 8 – break the online hero complex, communities work better

Working in partnership lies at the heart of any effective solution to online safeguarding, regardless of the age of the person being subject to abuse. While, as we have discussed at the start of the chapter, the prevailing narrative from government is "Social media companies need to sort this out", the reality is no one stakeholder has all of the answers and the idea of prevention of harm is a pipe dream. We can best illustrate this with a stakeholder model which is underpinned by the seminal work of Bronfenbrenner and his ecological framework of child development (Bronfenbrenner, 1979).

In Bronfenbrenner's framework, he described different systems that operate around a child that have direct or indirect influence upon them:

- **Microsystem** – The child's immediate environment, such as home, family, and close friends.
- **Exosystem** – People and places that have an indirect impact on the child's life, such as their wider community, formal and informal education settings, social care, healthcare settings, etc.
- **Macrosystem** – Government policies and cultural values, including laws, social values, and economic drivers.
- **Chronosystem** – The influence of change and constancy in a child's environment, acknowledging that the child's environment, and influences, will change over time.
- **Mesosystem** – Different parts of the child's immediate environment interacting together.

This ecosystem of interconnections facilitates the development of the child, and highlights the different, and equally important, roles players in the system have. A critical aspect to note about this ecosystem is that it clearly shows that there is no one independent entity that ensures positive development of the child at the exclusion of others. It is an ecosystem of cooperative individuals and organisations and the interactions between them that results in healthy development. Perhaps most importantly in his model, and is perhaps lacking when we consider online safeguarding, was the importance of mesosystems – the interactions between the different players in child development.

We would argue that this model is equally applicable, with some modification, to the pending university student and we illustrate this in Figure 21.1.

In the model we can show that, as a university student, there are many stakeholders with an influence and they all interact as the student develops. However, the difference with positioning "the student", rather than "the child", is that the student does not enter university from a vacuum but with their prior experiences and thus their development is underpinned by factors related to risk and resilience that have occurred before coming to university.

Risk factors might arise from previous negative experiences related to online harms or gender-based violence and resilience factors, or through the development of informed knowledge regarding engaging in online behaviours which may be perceived as risky by some, but ones that the young person has successfully navigated. If, for example, we consider online gaming – there are some that view this is risky because of the risk of abuse or inappropriate contact as a result of the gaming environment. However, the young person might have navigated

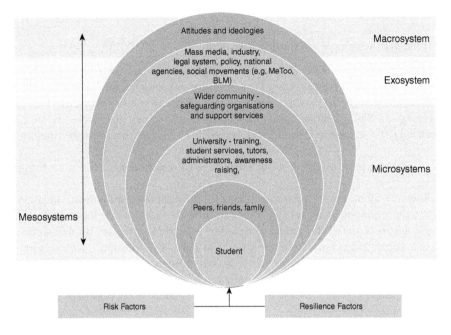

Figure 21.1 Stakeholder model for student development.

that risk and developed strategies, such as muting abuse and reporting abusers, as a result. However, a poorly supported young person who discloses abuse to an adult and receives a negative response would arrive at university with very different risk factors.

Resilience factors are the potential counter to risk factors, and also emerge from prior experiences. They may arise either as a result of developing coping strategies through personal exploration, or with the support of those involved in their support when tackling issues related to online harm. Resilience factors could have evolved through effective education or a supportive safeguarding environment where disclosure had resulted in a positive outcome, whereas those issues a young person has faced on their own might still develop as resilience factors, but perhaps will not be as effective. Nevertheless, all of these factors will be different for each individual, which goes some way to explaining why blanket solutions to tackling online abuse are usually doomed to fail.

What is clear, however, is that if universities can influence the resilience factors and inform risk factors prior to arrival on campus, they can have a positive impact upon the student's development. And by making use of this model, we are also reminded that the development of the child, and subsequently the student, is not something done in isolation.

Directive 9 – assume your institution has a problem, and tackle it

What does working in partnership look like?

At the start of this chapter, we explained that we would be exploring how universities can work in partnership with schools so that students were knowledgeable about issues of gender-based violence and online harms prior to moving to Higher Education. Since then, we have unpicked both the school and university setting related to these issues and found both wanting. This might then pose the question:

> If the partners are equally poor at this, how can a partnership achieve anything?

However, all hope is not lost! We have also, through this exploration, suggested that the problems exist because the way they are being tackled are ineffective and fail to listen to the young people we purport to protect. By working in partnership and acknowledging none of us have "the solution", we can progress together towards a victim-survivor centric approach that is responsive and evidence led, rather than a hero complex that hopes to stamp out online harms.

A comment from the Ofsted report (Ibid.) is particularly pertinent here:

> School and college leaders should create a culture where sexual harassment and online sexual abuse are not tolerated, and where they identify issues and intervene early to better protect children and young people.
>
> In order to do this, they should assume that sexual harassment and online sexual abuse are happening in their setting, even when there are no specific reports, and put in place a whole-school approach to address them.

This advice is clearly relevant to Higher Education Institutions too. As a starting place for more effectively partnership working, it is important that universities get their own houses in order first. Doing surveys to "try to measure the problem" seems like, at best, to be kicking the can down the road and hoping that, as a result of survey result showing small numbers, the institution has some proof that they do not have a problem. We would also question whether a survey is going to collect anything meaningful – "Have you ever received education on sexual violence?" and "Have you ever been sexually assaulted?" hardly seem like an appropriately measured and sensitive way to start a conversation about this subject between student and institution, yet we know of examples where this appears to have happened.

Universities claiming they do not have a problem because they have hardly any students reporting incidents or making complaints relating to gender-based violence or online abuse are ignoring what is staring them in the face – they have a problem in that their students are unwilling to disclose and do not believe they will get support.

Equally, saying "it didn't happen on campus, therefore it's not our problem" would also suggest a complete lack of ownership of the problem on the part of the institution. A student who is being harassed or has been assaulted should be the concern of the institution regardless of where the assault took place. And this is perhaps particularly so if the abuser is also a student or member of staff of the institution.

Directive 10 – listen to those disclosing harm

When we speak to young people about what support they want, they will say a number of things consistently:

> *I want to be listened to.*
>
> *I want to be able to disclose without fear of being told off or not believed.*
>
> *I want to be able to speak to someone who knows how to help and believes me.*

Ironically, these things are all readily tackled without the need to adopt the online hero complex or detailed understanding of the latest technologies or apps. We need, collectively, to refocus our understanding of online safeguarding from agonising over the prevention of a specific type of behaviour online by an individual to one of understanding how we respond to a disclosure. It is true that some online behaviours warrant some level of risk, and it is important that education is delivered that allows young people to understand these risks, and how harm occurs. However, adopting a "and therefore do not do this" achieves little for any party.

We have all too often in our work been asked "How do you stop young people sending nudes?" Our response is generally "You can't, but you can support them more effectively in the event that someone non-consensually shares them further". This is not to say we should give up on education and simply accept young people will do this. But we know, from discussing this particular issue with young people for over 20 years (for example, see Bond, 2010), that education that starts with "You shouldn't do this because it's illegal" is doomed to fail. A more progressive approach of exploring the risks and potential for harm, generally arising from the non-consensual sharing of the images, is far more effective. Even better is the opportunity to ask questions about how to get help and support should this occur.

So, What Can Be Done?

We have, throughout this chapter, presented ten "directives" which hopefully give some pointers around what we might do in partnership with schools to better support young people. They all emerge from a similar place – a refocusing of thinking and practice from prevention to support and response. We repeat them here:

Directive 1: You do not know best

Directive 2: Dispose of the "online safety" rhetoric and adopt a victim-survivor-centric approach

Directive 3: Introduce critical approaches to understanding the nature of online abuse and support the development of evidence-based practice

Directive 4: Make academic research related to online harms and gender-based violence, wherever possible open access, or supported with accessible outputs

Directive 5: Develop evidence-based training to fulfil statutory requirements that are effective in practice. Do not adopt a tick box approach.

Directive 6: Do not place transitioning students into social media groups without clear risk assessment, policy, transparent sanctions (up to and including withdrawing of offer of a place and reporting to the police) and routes for disclosure.

Directive 7: Never use the term "digital natives" again, or use it as an excuse to ignore the responsibilities of the sector to support victim-survivors of online abuse.

Directive 8: Break the online hero complex, communities work better

Directive 9: Assume your institution has a problem, and tackle it.

Directive 10: Listen to those disclosing harm

We need to break the cycle of believing we can prevent online harms, and move towards an evidence led, young person–centric, approach that places the victim survivor at the heart of the institutional response. Perhaps the most powerful thing that can be achieved prior to reaching university is developing a belief by any prospective student that if they are subject to abuse, their first reaction is to disclose this and be confident they will receive effective support. This is not achieved through assemblies or snatched staff training sessions, it is achieved through true collaborative working with all parties focused on the best outcomes for young people, not box ticking prior to an inspection or a hope that "someone" will sort this prior to the student arriving on campus.

And we need to listen to what young people are asking us to do, rather than deciding we know best.

Further Reading

Phippen, A., & Bond, E. (2020). *Online harassment and hate crime in HEIs.* University of Suffolk. www.uos.ac.uk/sites/www.uos.ac.uk/files/FOI-Report-Final-Jan-2020-rgb.pdf

This was the work we undertook that made us realise how poorly prepared the Higher Education sector is to support students who are subject to online abuse, and has been driving our campaigning to change university mindsets since. The motivation for the work were anecdotal experiences across the sector in either tackling online harms poorly, or simply dismissing them as a concern across the sector. The use of Freedom of

Information requests allowed us to collect a lot of data quickly across a range of online safeguarding issues, such as:

- University policies related to online safeguarding
- The scale of reporting of online abuse on campuses
- The nature of training of staff in tackling online abuse
- How universities work with partners to achieve better outcomes for students

What we discovered was a sector that was, at best, slowly reacting to a growing problem and, at worse, responding to say that safeguarding was not their concern because all of their students were adults. We saw many universities provide use with policies that claimed to tackle online abuse, yet upon exploration made no reference to it whatsoever, and many universities who claimed the lack of reporting of online abuse illustrated that it was not an issue (even what a dearth of staff training and no means of recognising online abuse meant that the institution had no way of knowing the prevalence of abuse on campus).

While there were pockets of good practice, the overall picture was a sector that, in general, did not even have effective policy in place to tackle online abuse, and we were reminded of the practices in the school sector prior to the emergence of the regulator. With that in mind, it illustrated how important it is to have a regulator who can focus the intentions of senior management should concern for student welfare fall down the list of priorities for institutions.

Phippen, A., & Bond, E. (2020). *Organisational responses to social media storms: An applied analysis of modern challenges.* **Springer Nature**.

This monograph explores a different growing phenomenon effecting educational settings across the sector – the rise of the social media storm and how organisations respond. This text follows a similar path to that explored above around the need for critical thinking and evidence-based response, rather than knee jerk reaction to moral panics. Drawing upon cases studies in different educational contexts – the Little Teds nursery scandal, the Momo "suicide game" in 2019, how schools tackling knee jerk reactions to teen sexting, and the Warwick University "rape chat" social media storm – the text explores the nature of moral panics and the need to develop practice from an informed position and the implications of failure to do so.

By way of example, one chapter considers the Momo 'suicide game' became both a major press story and subsequent moral panic in early 2019. The panic followed a familiar pattern of online rumour about something that would appear on children's devices and encourage them to self-harm. Clearly this is a cause for concern for both parents and educational settings. Or it would have been if it existed. In exploring the social media storm around Momo, we showed the impact of a broad range of stakeholders (parents, teachers, police and even celebrities) who failed in their responsibilities to fact check prior to sharing and, instead, exacerbated this risk. We prove, through traffic analysis, that poor responses by stakeholders resulted in negative outcomes for the young people they claimed to wish to safeguard.

The underlying theme of the book complements the discussion above around the need for stakeholders to be responsible and victim centric in their reactions to concerns, and not assume they know best.

Notes

1 A study in 2017 by Amnesty International UK at the time of a general election came to the alarming conclusion that the MP for Hackney North and Stoke Newington, Diane Abbott, was subject to, on average, 51 abusive tweets per day over the 158-day study. www.amnesty.org.uk/online-violence-women-mps [Accessed October 2021]

2 There are increasing numbers of high-profile media stories about online abuse in higher education. Warwick (www.theguardian.com/education/2019/jul/14/warwick-university-not-safe-says-woman-targeted-by-chat), Bath (www.theguardian.com/education/2020/apr/20/i-told-my-university-i-was-harassed-online-they-asked-me-what-a-hashtag-was), and Exeter ((www.theguardian.com/world/2018/mar/20/university-of-exeter-claims-of-racist-whatsapp-group-law-society) are all recent examples.

3 The politician's syllogism, or fallacy, has its roots in an Episode of the BBC sit-com and political satire "Yes Minister", to explain the need for politicians to be seen to do something regarding their understanding of the nature of the problem which they face. It has, since broadcast, taken on a life of its own among those who research and critique technology policy. https://devblogs.microsoft.com/oldnewthing/20070226-01/?p=27853

4 For those not familiar with school practices, a "twilight session" is an after-school session where staff will receive training or discuss whole-school issues.

5 We take some creative license in this scenario – we have no doubt our talks are interesting and enjoyable, and not at all boring. However, they do not, on their own, do much to support students who are subjected to online abuse.

6 The website provided a channel for victim-survivors of abuse that occurred either in school settings, or at school age, to anonymously disclose the abuse they were subjected to, its impact, and the response by those to whom they disclosed. At the time of writing, the website hosts over 54,000 disclosures. www.everyonesinvited.uk/ [Accessed October 2021].

7 Furthermore, while we know that Keeping Children Safe in Education makes it clear that online safety should form part of whole-school safeguarding training, we know from other work (Phippen, 2021) that 40% of schools in England (in a sample of 12,000) have no training in place.

8 In reality, what Higher Education practitioners view as the leading edge of social media engagement among young people, we are told by many students in transition that the platforms used – generally Facebook or WhatsApp groups – are not familiar to them and many have to create Facebook accounts or download WhatsApp for the first time in order to engage. As one student once told us: "Only drug dealers and boomers use WhatsApp, why would I have that on my phone?"

9 We should also note that this statement makes scant acknowledgement of online abuse beyond the claim that harassment may take place online.
10 We have heard many times from senior leaders in schools comments such as "Well the DSL (Designated Safeguarding Lead) will give them the hairdryer treatment so they won't do it again". We would suggest, rather than not do it again, the young person will simply not disclose the harm and potentially experience long-term harm as a result.

References

Baird, H., Renfrew, K., Nash-Henry, Z., & Towl, G. (2019). *Evaluation of safeguarding students catalyst fund projects*. Advance HE. Retrieved October 2021, from www.officeforstudents.org.uk/media/e3c0bd5e-7e03-4235-941a-f933da269728/catalyst-evaluation-summative-report.pdf

Bond, E. (2010). The mobile phone = bike shed? Children, sex and mobile phones. *New Media & Society, 13*(4), 587–604.

Bond, E. (2014). *Childhood, mobile technologies and everyday experiences. Changing technologies = changing childhoods?* Palgrave.

Bronfenbrenner, U. (1979). *The ecology of human development*. Harvard University Press.

Brown, C., & Czerniewicz, L. (2010). Debunking the 'digital native': Beyond digital apartheid, towards digital democracy. *Journal of Computer Assisted Learning, 26*(5), 357–369.

Department for Education. (2019). *Teaching online safety in schools*. Retrieved October 2021, from https://assets.publishing.service.gov.uk/government/uploads/system/uploads/attachment_data/file/811796/Teaching_online_safety_in_school.pdf

Department for Education. (2020). *Relationships education, relationships and sex education (RSE) and health education*. Statutory guidance for governing bodies, proprietors, head teachers, principals, senior leadership teams, teachers. Retrieved October 2021, from https://assets.publishing.service.gov.uk/government/uploads/system/uploads/attachment_data/file/1019542/Relationships_Education__Relationships_and_Sex_Education__RSE__and_Health_Education.pdf

Department for Education. (2021). *Keeping children safe in education 2021 – statutory guidance for schools and colleges*. Retrieved October 2021, from https://assets.publishing.service.gov.uk/government/uploads/system/uploads/attachment_data/file/999348/Keeping_children_safe_in_education_2021.pdf

Gayle, D. (2019, September 14). Facebook aware of Instagram's harmful effect on teenage girls, leak reveals. *The Guardian*. Retrieved October 2021, from www.theguardian.com/technology/2021/sep/14/facebook-aware-instagram-harmful-effect-teenage-girls-leak-reveals

Helsper, E. J., & Eynon, R. (2010). Digital natives: Where is the evidence? *British Educational Research Journal, 36*(3), 503–520.

Kirschner, P. A., & De Bruyckere, P. (2017). The myths of the digital native and the multitasker. *Teaching and Teacher Education, 67*, 135–142.

Levinthal, C. F. (2005). *Drugs, behavior, and modern society*. Pearson Education New Zealand.

Merrick, J. (2021, October 19). *Ban anonymous social media accounts under 'David's Law', murdered MP's friend says*. The I. Retrieved October 2021, from https://inews.co.uk/news/politics/ban-anonymous-social-media-accounts-under-davids-law-murdered-mps-friend-says-1255902

Mill, J. S. (1867, February 1). *Inaugural address: Delivered to the university of St. Andrews*. Longmans, Green, Reader, and Dyer.

Milmo, D. (2021, October 13). TechScape: UK online safety bill could set tone for global social media regulation. *The Guardian*. Retrieved October 2021, from www.theguardian.com

com/technology/2021/oct/13/techscape-uk-online-safety-bill-could-set-tone-for-social-media-regulation-worldwide-facebook-google

Office for Students. (2021). *Prevent and address harassment and sexual misconduct.* Retrieved October 2021, from www.officeforstudents.org.uk/advice-and-guidance/student-wellbeing-and-protection/prevent-and-address-harassment-and-sexual-misconduct/statement-of-expectations/

Ofsted. (2013). *Inspecting eSafety.* Retrieved August 2021, from www.eani.org.uk/sites/default/files/2018-10/Ofsted%20-%20Inspecting%20e-safety.pdf

Ofsted. (2021). *Review of sexual abuse in schools and colleges.* Ofsted. Retrieved October 2021, from www.gov.uk/government/publications/review-of-sexual-abuse-in-schools-and-colleges

Olssen, M., & Peters, M. A. (2005). Neoliberalism, higher education and the knowledge economy: From the free market to knowledge capitalism. *Journal of Education Policy, 20*(3), 313–345.

Phippen, A. (2016). *Children's online behaviour and safety: Policy and rights challenges.* Springer.

Phippen, A. (2021). *UK schools online safety policy & practice – assessment 2021.* Retrieved October 2021, from https://swgfl.org.uk/assets/documents/uk-schools-online-safety-policy-and-practice-assessment-2021.pdf

Phippen, A., & Bond, E. (2020). *Online harassment and hate crime in HEIs.* University of Suffolk. Retrieved October 2021, from www.uos.ac.uk/sites/www.uos.ac.uk/files/FOI-Report-Final-Jan-2020-rgb.pdf

Phippen, A., & Brennan, M. (2020). *Sexting and revenge pornography: Legislative and social dimensions of a modern digital phenomenon.* Routledge.

Prensky, M. (2001). Digital natives, digital immigrants part 2: Do they really think differently? *On the Horizon.*

Ringrose, J., Gill, R., Livingstone, S., & Harvey, L. (2012). *A qualitative study of children, young people and 'sexting': A report prepared for the NSPCC.* NSPCC. Retrieved August 2021, from https://letterfromsanta.nspcc.org.uk/globalassets/documents/research-reports/qualitative-study-children-young-people-sexting-report.pdf

Sellgren, K., & Willis, E. (2021, June 10). Girls asked for nudes by up to 11 boys a night, Ofsted finds. *BBC News.* Retrieved October 2021, from www.bbc.co.uk/news/education-57411363

Selwyn, N. (2009). The digital native – myth and reality. In *Aslib proceedings.* Emerald Group Publishing Limited.

Women and Equalities Committee. (2016). *Sexual harassment and sexual violence in schools.* Retrieved October 2021, from https://publications.parliament.uk/pa/cm201617/cmselect/cmwomeq/91/9102.htm

22 Conclusion

Future directions in addressing our problem with gender-based violence in higher education

Graham J. Towl and Clarissa J. Humphreys

In the past decade or so in the UK, there has been growing concern and a recognition of the problem of sexual violence at universities (Towl, 2016). More recently, discussions and debates about our problem with sexual violence have been contextualized and broadened in terms of gender-based violence (GBV). However, recognising the gendered nature of these forms of violence is sometimes met with what has become termed 'whataboutery' calling into question the focus on women. This may serve to deflect from the substantive nature of GBV and distract from implementing prevention initiatives. It is only one example of the many resistance tactics that may be used to stall progress, as discussed in Chapter 16.

The frustration at the lack of progress in GBV prevention in Higher Education (HE) is indeed palpable in several chapters in this book. In one sense, no more research is needed regarding prevalence rates; we know that we have a problem, and we know that it is of substantial proportions. More accurate measurement is not needed for us to make progress. Our focus surely needs to be upon the prevention of GBV and the way to achieve that is through a truly comprehensive institution-wide approach whereby tackling GBV is embedded in strategic policies and all of our practices. As we bring this book to a close, we take this time to note ongoing challenges and consider future directions in addressing our problems, as a sector, with GBV.

A culture of secrecy

Academic prowess has parallels in other sectors, for example, if we look at the revelations in recent years in Hollywood (Towl & Paske, 2017) whereby those with power abused it à la Weinstein. Some may find academia is largely built on competition and individualism, rather than a culture of collaborative and transparent working. Those in power often benefit from one pernicious aspect of academic culture, the oft-cherished culture of secrecy. This may present in many forms. For example, there is the much-vaunted process of reviewers of academic work remaining 'anonymous' through blind peer-reviews. This is in contrast to say a transparent approach of open peer-reviews where reviewers are named. A culture where constructive challenge and support are valued above secrecy is one that speaks loudly to changing the culture of GBV in our communities. Peer

DOI: 10.4324/9781003252474-25

review could be rigorous whilst also being open. It is through open dialogue that we can test and take forward our ideas. Some readers may cherish the notion of both single- and/or double-blind reviews even if it is potentially at the expense of a greater levelling of existing power inequalities in the sector.

This culture of secrecy is reflected elsewhere within the academy too. There are open secrets about which members of academic departments engage in harassing behaviour. These 'secrets' can be kept by management and fellow colleagues to protect perpetrators who are seen as valuable to the institution. After all, there is a 'cost' to the institution for losing say researchers bringing in large grants or academic prestige to the institution. Sadly, some may decide that such contributions outweigh the need to keep students and employees safe.

However, these 'secrets' are known by more people than we might be willing to admit. The work of The 1752 Group and National Union of Students has highlighted that students know too (Bull & Rye, 2018; NUS, 2018). There are also whisper networks that women use to warn others about perpetrators. These networks are not specific to HE and are found in many sectors or industries where gender inequality and GBV fail to be addressed. In other words, if a whisper network is needed, it is because formal methods to address GBV are not working. Women often fear retaliation by the perpetrator or victimisation by the institution itself adding to the many barriers to reporting staff sexual misconduct. In these cases, women may choose not to report and choose to warn others instead. As we saw in Chapter 11, as a sector we often lack a willingness to address staff perpetrators and to communicate outcomes in cases where staff are found to have committed sexual misconduct.

When women report and the institution does nothing, women often still feel a sense of responsibility to keep others safe too. In fact, this is a common motivation for reporting in the first place. The reporting and investigation process can be re-traumatising, but a victim-survivor may feel a duty to report for others despite the expected difficult investigation. The burden should not be placed on the victim-survivor to prevent future perpetration. It is on us as a sector to take responsibility for our problems with GBV. If the institution will not take action, a victim-survivor may act on their own, for example, warning others to avoid being alone with a specific male professor who is known for sexual misconduct. This parallels the culture of secrecy where perpetrators are protected by colleagues or senior management. In both examples, people know about the perpetrator and yet no action is taken against them. At least in the latter example, women and victim-survivors can communicate safety information to potentially mitigate risk of being targeted by the perpetrator. However, this shifts the burden of responsibility onto women and victim-survivors to protect themselves rather than us as a sector taking responsibility by holding perpetrators accountable, protecting all (including those not privy to such secrets), and creating a safe learning and work environment for all students and staff.

To better understand the importance of addressing our culture of secrecy, we need perhaps to also better understand how sexual offenders benefit from this. Secrecy may be viewed as a psychological currency that sexual predators trade in. Victim-survivors may be exhorted not to tell anyone about a particular act of sexual violence by perpetrators. In the academic world characterised by often steep power inequalities, allusions or more direct comments may be made to indicate career damage for victim-survivors, especially if the perpetrator is a senior and high-achieving academic member of staff. We build in dependencies whereby, for example, junior academic staff may feel beholden to senior influential colleagues. It is as if we fixate upon research achievements to such an extent that some remain untouchable. This exposes, amongst other things, a de-prioritisation of ethical values in HE and a lack of leadership willing to keep students and staff safe. We all surely have a role to play in changing our culture in the academic world.

Unless we address our problem with a culture of secrecy in academia, we cannot expect to make the progress that we could in tackling our problems with GBV. We recognise that change will be met with resistance as discussed in Chapter 16. But unless we are willing to address some of the more distinctive and sometimes cherished, issues which further institutionalise our problem with GBV, we risk continuing to maintain the status quo – endemic levels of GBV within our universities.

Unfair practices

A fair criticism of HE is how we choose to address our problem with GBV differently when the responding party is an employee compared to when the responding party is a student as discussed in Chapters 10 and 11. When staff or students make a report against a member of staff, they are often not informed of the progress or outcomes of investigations and disciplinary processes. How can that be right? Students by contrast, at least in some universities, are rightly kept up to date with the processes and outcomes in relation to their cases, including being informed of any sanctions imposed, if applicable.

What do we have to hide? Again, it seems that the culture of secrecy in the academic world is readily acquiescent in such cases. But we question this; we do not think that it is just for victim-survivors of GBV at universities. In this respect, what seems clear to us is that a commitment to addressing GBV cannot be viewed in isolation to other areas of activity at universities which reflect the underpinning culture and values. We would argue that current such cultures of secrecy serve to maintain existing power inequalities which serve victim-survivors of GBV very poorly indeed and create unfair (possibly discriminatory) practices. There is no such thing as a truly neutral response to GBV insofar as not to act is to maintain current inequalities of power.

An elephant in the room

An elephant in the room relates to the demographic of executive teams and governing bodies at universities. In 2018 in universities across the UK, only 40% of governing body members were women, only 27% of governing bodies were chaired by women, similarly only 29% of universities were led by a woman Vice-Chancellor or Principal, and a mere 37% of executive or senior team members were women (Jarboe, 2018). The majority of leaders in UK HEIs in 2018 were men. Statistically speaking, it is likely that some university leaders may have behaved in ways that would not be acceptable by today's standards and may have included forms of GBV. This may lead to a reticence to taking a bold approach for fear of being retrospectively 'exposed' for their inappropriate conduct. For example, we take a view that academics should not have sex with students. Some executive members may have, in their past, had relationships with students themselves. Thus, taking a leadership role in convincing a university academic senate that staff should not have sex with students may feel like an awkward conversation and one with a constant risk of exposure for one's own past.

This has parallels in the sex offender literature. Specifically, there is a common myth that the majority of sex offenders will be strangers to those they target when in fact the opposite is the case. There has historically been too much focus on 'stranger danger' when the evidence demonstrates that perpetrators more often target someone they know. This can be a difficult message to process for each of us. An unpalatable parallel for us in HE is that sometimes our colleagues, or even our friends, may have engaged in varying levels of GBV. This is an important, if often unspoken, consideration for us when trying to negotiate leadership 'buy in' to addressing this pervasive issue. We must be willing to base our decisions on ethics, rather than personal relationships progressing GBV prevention and response initiatives regardless.

Underpinning these key aspects of the academic and broader cultural context of GBV are the structures and institutions that maintain the very behaviours we want to see change. *What we permit is what we promote.* So, currently it could be argued that as university communities, we are in some ways promoting GBV by virtue of a series of our inactions. We find it worrying when we hear university leaders assert words to the effect that 'it is not just a problem for universities but for wider society too'. Whereas there is a fundamental truth to such assertions, making such statements may be seen as conveying a reluctance to own the problem at universities. As if because it is happening elsewhere, we should somehow be less concerned about it. On the contrary, we think that we should be more concerned about it. And this is especially so given that there is evidence that young women full-time students are at the highest risk being subjected to rape, assault by penetration, and sexual assault compared to any other profession (Office of National Statistics, 2021). Thus, the likelihood is that we have a bigger problem in universities than wider society has. And we are uniquely well-placed to address our problems, so why wouldn't we? Maybe if university leaders, politicians, think tanks, regulators, commentators, and media figures started to acknowledge that we have a particular problem with GBV at universities over and above in broader society, this would be a good starting point for us to address GBV more robustly. In short, it is the combination of us having a bigger problem and being uniquely well-positioned to tackle it that speaks to our capacity to make a huge difference in tackling GBV in the first instance at universities, but we think also that this may well have positive knock-on effects elsewhere in society too as a new generation of graduates go out into the wider world.

A failure of accountability

It is not clear to us that university governing bodies have been holding executive teams to account on the lack of progress in this area. Despite some truly awful mishandling of individual cases, including inappropriate communications to students from executive leaders highlighted most recently through the Al Jazeera *Degrees of Abuse* documentary, we do not know of any sanctions having been enacted in such cases on anyone in senior teams or positions of executive power. It could be due to the culture of secrecy that we simply have not heard sanctions that have been implemented. But, for us this underscores part of our problem as a sector – even when we are taking actions against staff no one else, let alone the victim-survivor – is getting to hear about our sometimes good work. Not even in anonymised accounts. Thus, why wouldn't the assumption be in the wider university community that nothing has been done or does get done? Surely, such secrecy serves to undermine assertions about, for example, 'taking sexual violence very seriously'? The message for would-be perpetrators is clear – impunity. The message for victim-survivors is also clear – don't report because nothing will be done – and it pains us to write that.

But it is not just apparent inaction on the part of governing bodies. We would welcome more action and engagement from the trade unions supporting our staff, for example, UCU, UNISON, and Unite representing many university employees. Trade unions have a powerful voice and a role to play in enacting change in Higher Education Institutions (HEIs), especially when that change is expected to be met with resistance.

And trade unions have been by no means silent on these matters. UNISON led a #UsToo campaign to raise awareness of workplace sexual harassment. Unite has urged employers to back the International Labour Organisation convention to stop violence and harassment in the workplace. UCU is affiliated with the End Violence Against Women (EVAW) coalition and has previously provided a model domestic abuse violence policy for employers and guidance on addressing violence against women for branches. In December 2021, UCU published the findings of their sexual violence task group which surveyed approximately 4,000 university and college staff. UCU offered 20 recommendations for employers and UCU branches, regional offices, and head office many of which will require approval through UCU's democratic structures before implementation can begin. Still, trade unions are able to do more. They are uniquely placed outside of HEIs to challenge and lobby for change with employers and governments. In addition to offering recommendations that have yet to be ratified and running awareness campaigns, we welcome action taken by trade unions to engage employers more effectively in implementing GBV prevention and response initiatives through a comprehensive institution-wide approach.

We agree with the UCU recommendations around reducing the numbers and proportions of university academic staff on fixed-term contracts. This could help in reducing risk with sexual misconduct because it is one small, but potentially impactful, step at reducing power inequalities between those more likely to be victim-survivors and those more likely to be perpetrators. However, it is disappointing that the UCU (2021) report does not include a recommendation to ban academics from having sex with their students despite highlighting this concern in the survey findings. A clear position statement on this matter would be most welcome from the UCU. This is another way in which we can make impactful change to reduce problems with power inequalities. It is interesting to note that other professions seem to have no problem with this being a normative expectation. For example, healthcare staff are not to have sexual relationships with patients and schoolteachers aren't to with their pupils (even if aged 18 so adults in law). The university world seems to have been less subject to scrutiny on such matters than elsewhere in the public sector.

Solutions to addressing GBV – a civil justice-based contribution

The UK Criminal Justice System (CJS) does not enjoy a successful track record on the prevention, detection, and prosecution of cases of gender-based violence. Far from it. There are well-rehearsed historic and current challenges for the CJS in making meaningful inroads in addressing GBV.

Now for the good news. As a sector, we are well-positioned to make a real difference. University communities are well-placed to contribute to addressing GBV and our influence has the potential to stretch well beyond the impervious walls of academia. Research and education gift us with some powerful tools for enacting change. We can use research to inform how we may best identify and address patterns of sexual violence and GBV. We can use education to aid prevention within universities and beyond. This latter point is especially impactful if we consider one function of universities is providing future leaders across the public and private sectors. Such future leaders from current cohorts of students have the potential to be very influential in whatever domains they provide their leadership in. They can set the tone and values of their organisations with impacts across their staff groups.

Our overarching goal surely needs to be one of prevention. We have made the case elsewhere for the need for a comprehensive institution-wide approach (see Humphreys & Towl, 2020 and Chapter 10 in this book). In this final chapter, we have further articulated some of the HE-specific challenges that we need to address if we are to substantively contribute to prevention.

Practical solutions to address our problem with GBV have some key underlying themes. In the case of our culture of academic secrecy which creates opportunities for perpetration, we recommend moving to a culture of openness and transparency. To address the problem of the culture of secrecy, there has been at least one helpful change as the use of Non-Disclosure Agreements (NDAs) or confidentiality clauses by universities in sexual violence cases has come under scrutiny and recommendations for banning these in the cases of GBV have been made. Universities Minister, Michelle Donelan MP, and her predecessor Rt Hon Chris Skidmore MP, both raised concerns about the misuse of NDAs by universities in preventing victim-survivors from disclosing sexual violence. In 2019, Chris Skidmore stated:

> But in no circumstances should [NDAs] be used by universities to 'gag' staff after experiencing poor behaviour in the workplace, including bullying, discrimination or sexual misconduct. Let me be clear that any use of this sort of agreement to silence people or hide details of unfair practices is an outrage and risks bringing the reputation of our world-leading higher education system into disrepute.
>
> (BBC, 2019)

In 2021, Michelle Donelan wrote to all Higher Education providers:

> The use of NDAs with regards to sexual harassment cases is wholly inappropriate, and this lack of transparency does not encourage students or staff to come forward. Any misuse of these agreements to hide workplace harassment or withhold details of student complaints is completely unacceptable and cannot only distress individuals but also risk bring the reputation of our world-leading higher education into disrepute. A culture of transparency should be promoted at all times in regards to harassment and sexual harassment.. . . Transparency is key to this and a clear message that the sector rejects NDAs for matters of sexual abuse is absolutely imperative.
>
> (Donelan, 2021, image)

And at the time of writing, around only 12 universities in the UK have signed up to the pledge, invited by government, to not use NDAs in cases of student and staff sexual misconduct (Can't Buy My Silence, 2022).

These are clear messages that confidentiality clauses or NDAs are not suitable for cases involving GBV and this view was supported in the UCU recommendations published in 2021 calling employers to reject the use of NDAs. Likewise, ACAS (2020) issued guidance for the use of NDAs covering when NDAs cannot be used and cautioning how they might be used in sexual harassment cases. The key here is that victim-survivors are not to be silenced. We caution that the resistance to the approach of not using NDAs will be that universities will continue not to share outcomes and sanctions with victim-survivors as a different way to silence them. In some places where they may have informed the victim-survivor of the outcome and sanctions but issued an NDA may see the tactic of 'repression' used to positively withdraw the use of NDAs, but negatively withdraw the sharing of the outcomes and sanctions. Openness and transparency are required for the prevention and response of GBV, not only for victim-survivors but also for the wider HE community.

Communication

Communicating our values and behavioural expectations is key to any GBV prevention strategy. Open days for prospective students afford us with a great opportunity to begin communicating our values. For example, we might say:

> although our research and academic educational offer are very important to us – your safety and wellbeing are more important to us. We know that if we don't address such fundamental issues then you may not be able to give the best of yourselves educationally or indeed in any research roles.

This message for prospective students is perhaps especially powerful in the context of us being rightly very clear about how important education and research are to us.

Communications to existing students and staff are key too. It is one thing to have robust policies in place – one test of them is if they are used. Thus, policies, reporting options, and support options need to be clearly communicated to students and staff.

Earlier we touched upon the importance of conveying outcomes and sanctions to Responding Parties *and* Reporting Parties. HEIs can also communicate outcomes to the wider university community informing the community of outcomes and sanctions in staff and student cases of GBV by anonymising cases. This is important as part of the conveyance of the values of the institution. Too often, we suspect, university leaders seem more concerned about the reputational damage associated with being open that GBV happens at universities as compared with the reputational damage associated with doing nothing, or very little about it. Growing numbers of observers may simply view this in terms of being indicative of lack of leadership.

Universities reporting low levels of sexual violence and other forms of GBV are, quite possibly, those doing the least to address their problem – hardly a recommendation for any prospective students or regulator concerned about equitable access to education. Increasingly, it seems to us that those university leadership teams that are not directly addressing problems with GBV will be seen as 'in denial' and engaging in resistance tactics rather than running universities safely. In short, such leadership teams may well sometimes be part of the problem. But again, a solution can be to move to a culture of transparency. This will assist in building trust in the institution and send clear messages to would-be perpetrators that GBV results in consequences within the university.

Regulation

In other sectors (e.g., healthcare, social care), professionals who are regulated are guided by a clear set of ethical standards and professional expectations. These professional standards guide behaviour and help organisations ensure that staff in professional roles are maintaining safe working environments.

Regulation of us as individual academics also has the potential to help tackle the 'roaming academic' problem whereby an academic engaged in sexual misconduct or GBV can simply move onto a new university environment to continue with such predation without a requirement for the HR department, at least, to be informed of such a past. The culture of academia may well not warm to professional regulation despite it being in place for public protection purposes elsewhere, for example, in health and social care and teaching professions. Such professional regulation also allows for the possibility of academics being 'struck off' in much the same way that teachers and healthcare workers are. Most importantly, issues of 'fitness to practice' could then be dealt with by an independent body with a clear set of ethical standards and professional expectations. Such a body would not be burdened by the conflicts of interest at an individual institutional level which may have been influential when endeavouring to tackle staff sexual misconduct in particular.

It is interesting to note that some funding bodies are taking more serious views on these issues. For example, Wellcome Trust (n.d.) requires that for all grant applications, there is confirmation that the lead applicant (and sponsor or supervisor) have not had a bullying or harassment report upheld against them. If the applicant has been at the organisation for less than a year, then the organisation applying for the grant is expected to check with the applicant's former employer. They may reject the grant application if there is a currently formal disciplinary warning or active sanction in place. We welcome these developments.

There is, of course, also a case for the sector regulator to have more powers to give direction at a sector-wide and institutional level. And the case for such further regulation begins to look more compelling as we continue to perform quite so poorly in addressing our problems with GBV in HE. The powerful message that we are currently sending to the regulator as a sector is that we are not taking addressing GBV sufficiently seriously, so there may well be benefit in some more prescriptive statutory regulation.

Final thoughts

This volume contains 22 chapters of information from 30 contributors (editors included) that can be used as a guide for the HE sector to create positive change in addressing GBV and includes further reading recommendations which build on each contributing authors' work. This is an area that continues to need development to identify effective and meaningful cultural change that truly prevents GBV. If we, within the HE sector, could nationally implement some of the good practice that we already have identified, this would go a considerable way to making some significant improvements nationally and potentially internationally too. Staff and students might increase their trust in our institutions to make reports, would-be perpetrators may be deterred, and communities would be safer for our students and staff to access their learning environment (for some their accommodation), and workplace, without the fear of violence and harassment.

The time to act is *now*. It is not acceptable that students and employees in HE are subjected to sexual harassment, sexual assault, rape, stalking, 'grooming', image-based sexual abuse, technology-facilitated gender-based violence, domestic abuse, and coercive and controlling behaviour. It is not acceptable that we have left the burden of maintaining safety and progressing this agenda chiefly on victim-survivors and, often, student activists or lone under-resourced staff. We expect better, we deserve better, and we should no longer have to wait for change. Finally, we very much hope that this book will be a useful resource for anyone concerned about addressing our problem with gender-based violence at universities.

References

ACAS. (2020). *ACAS publishes new guidance on non-disclosure agreements*. Retrieved January 2022, from www.acas.org.uk/acas-publishes-new-guidance-on-non-disclosure-agreements-ndas

BBC. (2019, 5 May). NDAs: UK universities misusing 'gagging orders' described as 'outrage'. Retrieved January 2022, from www.bbc.co.uk/news/education-48166884

Bull, A. & Rye, R. (2018). *Institutional responses to staff sexual misconduct in UK higher education*. The 1752 Group/ University of Portsmouth.

Can't Buy My Silence. (2022). *Universities pledge list*. Retrieved January 2022, from https://cantbuymysilence.com/universities-pledge-list/

Donelan, Michelle [@michelledonelan]. (2021, 3 July). Victims of sexual harassment must be protected and supported. [Tweet; image of letter]. *Twitter*. Retrieved January 2022, from https://twitter.com/michelledonelan/status/1411442626348339204

Humphreys, C. J., & Towl, G. J. (2020). *Addressing student sexual violence in higher education: A good practice guide*. Emerald Publishing Group.

Jarboe, N. (2018). WomenCount: Leaders in Higher Education 2018. *WomenCount*. Retrieved January 2022, from https://women-count.org/portfolio/womencount-leaders-in-higher-education-2018/

National Union of Students (NUS). (2018). *Power in the academy: Staff sexual misconduct in UK Higher Education*. National Union of Students.

Office of National Statistics. (2021). *Sexual offences victim characteristics, England and Wales: Year ending March 2020*. Retrieved January 2022, from www.ons.gov.uk/peoplepopulationand community/crimeandjustice/articles/sexualoffencesvictimcharacteristicsenglandandwales/march2020#understanding-sexual-offences

Towl, G. J. (2016). Tackling sexual violence at UK universities: A case study. *Contemporary Social Science, 11*(4), 432–437. doi:10.1080/21582041.2016.1260764

Towl, G. J., & Paske, K. (2017, November 7). The Weinsteins of academia can no longer be tolerated. *Times Higher Education*. Retrieved January 2022, from www.timeshighereducation.com/opinion/weinsteins-academia-can-no-longer-be-tolerated

University College Union (UCU). (2021). *Eradicating sexual violence in tertiary education: A report from UCU's sexual violence task group*. Retrieved January 2022, from www.ucu.org.uk/media/12269/UCU-sexual-violence-task-group-report-20211220/pdf/UCU_sexual_violence_task_group_report_20211220.pdf

Wellcome Trust. (n.d.). *Bullying and harassment policy*. Retrieved January 2022, from https://wellcome.org/grant-funding/guidance/bullying-and-harassment-policy#what-we-expect-from-the-organisations-we-fund-ef38

Index

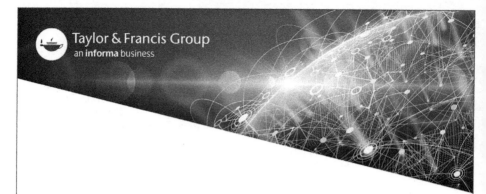

Ingram Content Group UK Ltd.
Milton Keynes UK
UKHW022033290323
419385UK00005B/14